HEROIN
IS KILLING OUR CHILDREN

MISSY H. OWEN

ISBN-9780692581452

DEDICATION

This book is dedicated to the memory of my precious first-born son, Davis Henry Owen. He suffered with the disease of addiction and died of a heroin overdose on March 4, 2014. He is my strength, and his memory gives me the courage to reach out and help others as a way of honoring him. He lost his battle with addiction, but he would have wanted me to continue the fight in an effort to help those who still have a fighting chance to beat this monster we know as Heroin.

Davis Henry Owen
4/27/1993 — 3/4/2014

May He Rest in Peace and Rise in Glory

ACKNOWLEDGEMENTS

There are so many people who had a hand in the creating of this book, but none more so than my beautiful family who stayed by my side every day for a year as I shared my feelings, thoughts, knowledge and dreams in an effort to save others from this horrible epidemic of opioid abuse. They also contributed in so many ways, whether they sent me information, wrote stories of their own, or just read and re-read my posts and offered their humble opinions. To Chelsea, Connor, Spencer, and Shelbea – I love you!

My amazing husband, Michael, supported me in every part of my journey even though he was experiencing a journey of his own. He is the only person on this earth who knows the depth of my pain over losing our son. We wept together and grew together in God's love. Thank you my love.

Thank you to Jason Gribble for the beautiful graphic art and marketing expertise and to Terri Reece for her academic and editing skills. Without them, the book would still be on my computer!

Thank you to everyone who shared a story of personal experience and exposed yourself to others. Thank you to those who paved the way for others to find themselves in recovery. You are truly making a difference.

Thank you to our DDF supporters and Facebook followers. Your comments throughout the journey were so very valuable – I wish I could have included them underneath every Constructive Act. I realized the value of each of your comments as did all of our readers.

For those of you who helped me evolve in my learning and understanding of the disease – THANK YOU… your mentoring was priceless.

For those of you who lifted me and my family up in prayer over the first year of our journey. Thank you all from the bottom of our broken hearts.
Without your love and support, we would have struggled alone in silence.

Thank you to the Amazing DDF Board of Directors for your support.

Finally and most importantly, I thank my Lord and Savior who comforted me, gave me strength and provided that "one set of footprints in the sand" when I could no longer walk alone. Thank you for taking my precious Davis home until we are reunited once again in Heaven. Thank you for knowing what I needed and providing it when I had no clue. Thank you for loving all of us unconditionally and being "enough."

PREFACE

On March 4, 2014, the doorbell rang and two detectives stood at my door asking to come inside to tell me that my precious 20-year-old son, Davis, was found dead in his car from a suspected drug overdose. That night forever changed my life. A senseless death that I was so unprepared for never should have happened. It became a mission and a ministry to make sure that I did everything in my power to prevent this tragic fate from happening to one more family.

This book is filled with "Constructive Acts" that can be carried out to prevent drug addiction, promote awareness of the effects of opioids and heroin, educate about the latest drug therapies, antidotes, and statistics, as well as share emotions and raw feelings that come after losing a child to this monster. I began with a one or two sentence act that would be important in preventing drug addiction in general. As I got further and further into the book and into my journey, my heart began to open up and the walls of grief and desperation to save others came tumbling down.

My yearlong daily writings began just two and a half weeks after the death of my child. I wrote every single day for a year without fail. You can read my book in several ways. As a grieving parent, you can begin on day one and read along throughout the year with me as you experience your own grief. As a parent of an addict, you can read for knowledge and insight on how to save your own child. You can read beginning on the particular date of the year and read one entry per day for the entire year. You will experience each new season, each holiday, and every significant day that was important to me as I endured my journey. You can read the book completely as a story of hope and healing. You can read it page by page or you can pick a day randomly because of the particular content.

The daily writing became a source of strength and healing for me. Sharing my story was a way to help others while helping myself. I met many amazing and wonderful people along the way, people that God placed directly in my path. The book is full of miracles, and the hand of God is so obvious throughout the entire journey.

Reading this book will give the reader a blueprint for making a difference in the community in which he or she lives. It details the events and ceremonies that took place, the fundraisers, and the steps in establishing a 501(c)(3) non-profit foundation that was able to raise awareness, affect change, and hand out life-saving Naloxone kits that would prove to be instrumental in keeping those suffering with opioid/heroin addiction alive until full recovery could take place. The book was written for addicts, families of addicts, grieving families, and families supporting other families going through the pains of addiction. It was written for community members in order to teach them how to make a difference in their own communities.

It is obvious that there were changes made throughout the course of the year in which new and cutting edge information paved the way for new legislation, new treatments, and new understanding about how we perceived the disease and how to treat it. Statistics were updated at alarming rates, and we realized as a nation that we had an epidemic on our hands and a long way to go before we could reverse the effects of many years of people being prescribed into addiction. Blame was placed in many different directions to no avail; the epidemic was and is alive and growing at the publishing of this book. At the time of publishing, all web links throughout the book were operational.

I continue to write "thoughts" of what I consider to be important to the entire population on our website, www.davisdirection.com. Please follow us on Facebook (Davis Direction Foundation) and Twitter (Davis Direction), and continue to educate yourself and others on the most recent and relevant ways to take a stand against opioid/heroin addiction. Recovery is our new focus, and how to help those precious souls in recovery stay in long-term recovery while attaining successful re-entry is our goal. Please understand that if I seem to contradict myself as you progress through the book, it is merely that I have researched and learned new and updated ways of thinking about this epidemic. Please don't hesitate to email me if there is something that you would like to discuss. missy@davisdirection.com

For more information, contact us at info@davisdirection.com or call us at +1-(470)-362-1994. We are here to help in whatever capacity you need.

Missy H. Owen
Co-Founder & CEO
The Davis Direction Foundation, Inc.

DAVIS DIRECTION
FOUNDATION

Moving Onward Through Life... Looking Upward To God

Heroin Is Killing Our Children

3/21/14 – Constructive Act #1 – Clean Out Your Medicine Cabinet Today!

Don't think this couldn't happen in your family. Throw away all medicine that is not actively being consumed in accordance with a doctor's orders.

3/22/14 – Constructive Act #2 – Family Tree

Fill out a Family Tree template and highlight the known addicts. Show your children the predisposition that they have to become an addict. Knowledge is POWER! www.familytreetemplates.net

3/23/14 – Constructive Act #3 – Bear Hug Your Kids Today

Bear hug your kids today. Tell them that there is nothing they could ever do that would keep you from loving them, and there is nothing they have ever done that can't be dealt with and forgiven or forgotten. The last words that Davis and I ever spoke were, "I love you, son," and he replied, "I love you, too." Through until the bitter end, there was no shortage of love shared with Davis and his family. As we gather for his memorial service today, it is comforting to know that his love for Jesus was as strong as his love for his family. Thank you, God, for allowing me to raise my child in a Christian home.

3/24/14 – Constructive Act #4 – Educate Yourself!

Know what we are dealing with! www.isate.memphis.edu/opiate.html

The above link is an excellent website explaining the use of opiates — what they are, how they work, and their addictive properties. The picture is the actual heroin that was found in Davis's car when he was found dead. It is wrapped in a receipt and folded like a piece of trash. The detectives actually mistook it for trash, and Michael found it when he was cleaning out the car when we picked it up from impound. We have since turned it in to the authorities.

3/25/14 – Constructive Act #5 – Tell One Person!

I am convinced that we have to make this disease, issue, problem, epidemic -- whatever you want to call it -- a PUBLIC FORUM!

The shame, embarrassment, guilt, and protection for our child kept us from sharing our experience with others. There is still a great deal of ignorance out there regarding drugs in general, but especially heroin.

We are not blaming ourselves, but realistically, there are things we would have done differently if we had known the things we have learned at this point. A lot of things we have learned due to speaking out. THIS IS A DISEASE!

Davis's dad has the disease of Type 1 Diabetes. I have no problem telling others about it and networking when we run into issues with managing it. We have learned so much from others about to handle it and live with it. Yet we told no one about our son and his struggle with addiction. If you are a young person struggling with addiction, tell a person who will help you – or an adult other than your parent – assuming you have already told your parent. Tell someone who will hold you accountable for managing your disease. If you are a parent or spouse of an addict, tell someone who will support you as you work to find out how to help your loved one! We have to support one another. Don't be afraid to tell someone. The drug dealer who sold Davis his heroin (who is on video) and then went back the next day and found him dead (also on video) called 911 (on tape) and waited for the police, ambulance, and detectives to show up (also on video). He walked away scot-free because they couldn't prove what he handed him across the table on the video! You will not get in trouble with the authorities for telling someone and soliciting help for yourself! TELL ONE PERSON TODAY!

3/26/14 – Constructive Act #6 – Know Your Counselors

As a Professional School Counselor with a degree in School Counseling and having practiced for 26 years, I was shocked at the widely varying requirements in both the educational level and training for a person to become a drug and alcohol counselor. Some states don't require any degree for becoming a "credentialed addiction counselor," and many require just a high school diploma, General Equivalence Diploma (GED), or associate's degree, according to a groundbreaking 2012 National Center on Addiction and Substance Abuse at Columbia (CASA Columbia) report on the state of addiction treatment titled "Addiction Medicine: Closing the Gap Between Medicine and Practice." Although there has been a movement to professionalize treatment, much counseling still is provided by minimally trained addiction survivors-turned-counselors whose own rehabilitation forms much of the basis for their expertise. And sometimes, when standards are raised for newer counselors, old-timers are "grandfathered" in with their existing credentials (or are given a certain amount of time to obtain the new ones), and they may or may not be well qualified (Source: "Inside Rehab" by Anne M. Fletcher).   When you are spending thousands of dollars on a program, DO YOUR RESEARCH!

3/27/14 – Constructive Act #7 – Understand Generation Y

If we are ever going to change anything to help them, we MUST know who they are. Generation-Y Facts:

- It is generally agreed that Generation-Y means anyone born between the early 1980s and the early 2000s. In terms of technology, that means that the oldest members of Generation-Y were born at the same time the Compaq Portable PC was issued, and the youngest members at the same time as the first generation iPod mini.

- Generation-Y adults live with their parents, on average, longer than members of older generations did.

- It is estimated that only 5% of Generation-Y adults do not own a mobile phone, and even fewer do not own a computer. Generation-Y makes up a rapidly increasing proportion of the world-wide workforce. A frequent criticism of Generation-Y is that it is a generation that typically has unrealistic expectations about what can be achieved in the workplace.

- Members of this generation, some social critics say, seek to put in next to no effort and be rewarded for it, leaving them frustrated and unfulfilled when this is not a reality. However, many Gen-Y adults contest the notion, saying that their generation is not lazy, but one inspired by all the possibilities in the world and all the opportunities for job satisfaction within it.

- Generation-Y adults are considered more narcissistic than those of previous generations.

- Of all work-age adults, it is those from Generation-Y who are most averse to working long hours, preferring a more flexible approach to the working day.

- Roughly one-third of Generation-Y adults use the internet as their primary source of news updates.

- Generation-Y can also be referred to as, amongst others, 'Millennials,' 'Generation 9/11' or the 'Global Generation.'

- Over the course of their lifetime, most members of Generation-Y will hold down more jobs than their parents or grandparents did. On average, they only stay in one particular job for around two years before seeking to move on to the next one. Some social critics say that this is because, as children, they were taught that simply by participating in activities, they were entitled to a reward. As such, the concept of 'winning' is almost lost on Generation Y, and they expect reward for relatively little achievement.

- As a general trend of thought, most Generation-Y adults are more interested in job fulfillment and satisfaction than they are large salaries.

- On average, Generation-Y adults are more liberally minded than people from older generations.

- Approximately 65% of Generation-Y says that they support same-sex marriage.

- Generation-Y is considered overall the most ambitious of all the generations.

- The medium of communication that Generation-Y adults favor is the e-mail, whereas most of their parents in Generation X would opt for the telephone.

(Source: www.generationy.com/characteristics)

3/28/14 – Constructive Act #8 – Don't Drive Under the Influence of Drugs

Don't drive or let your loved ones drive if you suspect they are under the influence of drugs. A 2009 study conducted by the National Highway Traffic Safety Administration revealed 18% of drivers killed in traffic accidents had at least one drug present in their system.

See more at: www.unityrehab.com/rehab-corner/kerry-kennedy-drugged-driving

3/29/14 – Constructive Act #9 – DE-STRESS!

As I sat here and looked through my entire folder of collected addiction information this morning, one common theme is on almost every page. STRESS is a major indicator of addiction. Although genetic make-up is approximately 50% of the disease, stress and availability are two of the major indicators that we have to be aware of. Availability should be clear at this point: Heroin in our community is CHEAP and EASY to find. We all know everyone has STRESS – especially our children. Find one way TODAY to remove stress from your life and the lives of your family. The De-Stress Dozen:

- Listen to music
- Call a friend
- Remove unnecessary events and negative people from your life
- Eat right
- Belly breathe
- Laugh out loud
- Drink green tea
- Pray
- Exercise
- Sleep
- Clean and organize your space
- Count your blessings

3/30/14 – Constructive Act # 10 – Connect Spiritually

Go to church, read a devotional book, or get involved in a bible study. Do whatever it takes to allow God to help you. I don't know how my family would have dealt with Davis's death without Him. We attend Marietta First United Methodist Church, and the people there have truly been the Wind Beneath Our Wings. They were there for us, along with our other Christian friends at work and in the community. I have a daily devotional that comes to my email every morning called "God's Minute." I also read the daily devotional book "Jesus Is Calling." Reach out to God; He will never leave you. Read "Footprints in the Sand."

One night I dreamed I was walking along the beach with the Lord.

Many scenes from my life flashed across the sky.

In each scene I noticed footprints in the sand.

Sometimes there were two sets of footprints,

other times there were one set of footprints.

This bothered me because I noticed that during the low periods of my life,

when I was suffering from anguish, sorrow or defeat,

I could see only one set of footprints. So I said to the Lord,

'You promised me Lord, that if I followed you,

you would walk with me always.

But I have noticed that during the most trying periods of my life

there have only been one set of footprints in the sand.

Why, when I needed you most, you have not been there for me?'

The Lord replied,

'The times when you have seen only one set of footprints in the sand,

is when I carried you.'

(Author) Mary Stevenson

God Loves You!

3/31/14 – Constructive Act #11 – Check Your Bank Accounts Daily

When you are living with an addict or an addict has access (whether honestly or dishonestly) to your debit and credit cards, financial status can get out of hand quickly. Toward the end of his addiction, my son was making a habit of taking an extra $20 or $40 every time I would let him use my debit card for gas or other necessities. Because I was not checking regularly, I did not know. There were also times that he was sneaking my cards out of my purse and then sneaking them back into my purse; I never knew. Those kinds of transactions can add up quickly!

4/1/14 – Constructive Act #12 – Make a Bucket List

If you are an addict, it allows you to plan forward and think about life beyond your addiction. If you are a loved one trying to help an addict, you need to take care of yourself as well. It allows you to think about and actually do some of the things you always wanted to do and take a break from one of the most stressful lifestyles you will ever encounter. Here are some ideas to get you started: www.bucketlist.net/lists/all_lists/

4/2/14 – Constructive Act #13 – Know What Is Available in Colleges and Universities for Addicts

With heroin on the rise for the 18–25 age group, it is important to be able to support these students when they are away on a college campus. I have included the link to the Kennesaw State University Collegiate Recovery Program. Know what is available in your area. www.kennesaw.edu/studentsuccessservices/crc/

4/3/14 – Constructive Act #14 – Don't Be Deceived by Perception

Heroin addicts can function on a daily basis, and you may never know they are continuing to use. What you know about their drug use is quite probably only the tip of the iceberg. The weekend before Davis died, he helped me put mulch in the flower beds and made a DVD for me for another person's memorial service. He was my #1 go-to in the house if I needed help because he was willing and able to help me with whatever I needed. I believe that he used drugs at night to deal with the anxiety in order to sleep.

4/4/14 – Constructive Act #15 – Don't Underestimate Heroin Medically Assisted Treatment

Don't underestimate heroin. It's different from other addictions. Looking back, the biggest thing that we believe we missed about what was going on was that we didn't understand that heroin was different from other addictions. Although the rehab facility that Davis was in had an entire family week that I attended every day, not ONCE did they specify heroin to be the most addictive of all drugs. They lumped it in with alcohol and other gateway drugs. If you go back through all the postings on the DDF, you will see that heroin is in a class of its own. If you know your child is taking or has taken heroin, please educate yourself as to what that truly means. Most websites and addicts will tell you there is no turning back. Had we known then what we know now, we would have considered drug therapy. (MAT)

4/5/14 – Constructive Act #16 – Consider a Tracking Device

Consider a tracking device on the vehicle the addict is driving. Perhaps OnStar® or a similar service? The night Davis died, he had turned the location services off on the iPhone. I don't know whether or not it might have made a difference, but I do know that when midnight came around on that Monday night, I knew something was terribly wrong. The authorities did not find him until 5:11 PM on Tuesday afternoon.

If I had OnStar on the car, I could have found out immediately where the car was.

4/6/14 – Constructive Act #17 – Join a Gym with Your Addict

One of the best Stress Relievers, as well as a coping skill for relapse, is to work out physically. You can get a gym membership for as little as $15.00 a month for unlimited workouts (Workout Anytime). For $10.00 more, you can get an unlimited bring-a-friend membership there as well. I'm posting the prices for this particular gym because that's where my membership is and Davis would go with me on occasion. Not as often as we should have, but we were trying. Everyone needs to work out, but especially those with addiction. Workouts release endorphins that make you feel good naturally. Check in to a membership today. Lots of companies have workout space inclusive in the workplace.

4/7/14 – Constructive Act #18 – Drug Test Often

Opiates can be gone from your system within 48 hours. Don't rely on outpatient rehabs to do the testing. Although they advertise that they do random testing, Davis was tested only once in five weeks of IOP (Intensive Out Patient) therapy. There are also over the counter drugs that can show false positives as well. Benadryl can show a false positive for opiates according to information on the internet. Davis had experienced an allergic reaction to anti-freeze and had taken Benadryl as directed by a minute clinic physician. When given a drug test, it showed up positive. Who knows if it was the Benadryl or something else? Just know what you are dealing with and the timeline for the drugs to show up. Addicts can be very savvy with explanations for everything.   www.qtestinc.com/icup.html

4/8/14 – Constructive Act #19 – Count Your Blessings

"Count Your Blessings. You might surprise yourself." This is a tweet from Davis on 8-22-2012. He still had many blessings in his life that I wish he would have stopped and thought about. Knowing that you are loved and that you have people who are willing to help you at all costs is a very powerful tool if you can see through all the smoke and mirrors and use it. Heroin distorts a person's thinking and perceptions. Remind your addict of all that is good and right in their life. Help them to count their blessings today.

4/9/14 – Constructive Act # 20 – Revisit the first 19 Constructive Acts. Watch the Videos and Visit the Website.

A friend of mine lost her son last night to heroin. She had reached out to me after Davis died. Please keep her family in your prayers. This HAS to STOP! There is HOPE! We just have to come together and find it.

How to Fix Rehab: Expert Who Lost Son to Addiction Has a Plan

www.nbcnews.com/storyline/americas-heroin-epidemic/how-fix-rehab-expert-who-lost-son-addiction-has-plan-n67946

4/10/14 – Constructive Act #21 – Understand the HIPAA Law

If your child is under the age of 18 and is in need of addiction help through rehab or other medical care, ACT NOW! When he or she turns 18, your ability to get them help is reduced to what your child agrees to. There are so many websites explaining the law that I have chosen not to post one (they are very in depth and confusing). BUT, in a nutshell, your child has to make the choice to get help after the age of 18, and you cannot force them into rehab or any other medical help. You also are NOT entitled to their records or information at the doctor's office, which means they can go to a doctor without your permission and your knowledge. This includes your family doctor or any health care (doc in a box) facility. Even though you are responsible for them financially, carry them on your insurance, and claim them on your taxes, YOU ARE NOT ENTITLED TO THEIR MEDICAL INFORMATION!

4/11/14 – Constructive Act # 22 – Know What Your Insurance Policy Offers for Rehab

Know what your insurance policy offers in the way of rehab services. Be willing to fight for what your policy says. For instance, mine gives 30 days of rehab for a calendar year. Davis was denied after 21 days. Although they were ready to release him, it would have been a fight for him to get the last week of the year. We need to work on changing that law in Georgia. Pennsylvania has a law on the books that says the doctor has the final say, NOT the insurance company. Come on Georgians, what are we waiting for?

4/12/14 – Constructive Act #23 – Have a Plan

When your child is in crisis, it is too late to come up with a plan. You need to know what you would do if your child was unconscious due to an overdose. Of course you would call 911. But when the immediate threat was over, what is the plan? If you are living with an opiate addict, call your doctor today and ask if he or she is writing prescriptions for the Naloxone nasal spray. If so, get them to write a prescription for you and keep it with you at all times. Also, where would you turn for therapy? Have you researched rehabs in the area, or do you know a private therapist you would turn to? Start doing your research now. Don't wait until it's too late. I have included a link for evaluating rehab and treatment facilities. You need to know the answers to the hard questions. It is extensive but an amazing instrument.

http://www.tresearch.org/wp-content/uploads/2012/08/Questions-to-Ask-Treatment-Providers.pdf

4/13/14 – Constructive Act #24 – Read This Article

I have addressed STRESS before, but this article is exactly right and I couldn't agree more. We cannot let a system define our kids. Our generation did just fine, and I never even took a math class past ALG 2. Nor did I take Physics or AP classes, if there even were any back then. By the way, I'm only 54 years young. My, how school has changed.

www.huffingtonpost.com/entry/teachers-viral-resignation-letter-has-strong-messages-about-education-today_563a10abe4b0411d306ee731

4/14/14 – Constructive Act #25 – Stop Joking About Drugs

Addiction is NO joke. Addiction is a disease just like diabetes or heart disease. So my question is this: Why do we joke about it? Lately I have seen casual jokes on FB about crack and the heroin epidemic. The jokes are in poor taste and cause pain and raise questions. To begin with, families affected by addiction are offended and in pain already. Even more important than this, it gives your kids the indication that you are clueless about the state of emergency this country is in over drugs, making you an easy target for denial. It also raises the question about whether or not you are using the jokes as a defense mechanism, possibly covering up an addiction of your own. It creates shame and embarrassment for the addict, making it less likely that they will seek out help if and when they truly need it. We're trying to help educate and support families, not create more stress and difficulty. Please re-examine your motives when making jokes about drugs!

4/15/14 – Constructive Act #26 – Find a Source of Strength!

Everyone needs an inspirational theme that helps you stay the course or gives you strength. Whether it be a song, a quote, a poem, or a bible verse, find something that is meaningful to you and reinforces the reasons you are doing what you are doing or helps you stay committed to your goals. It's kind of like the "Rocky" theme song; you may think it sounds corny, but there is research that music inspires and soothes the soul. Poetry or meaningful quotes or verses can do the same thing. Find what works for you.

4/16/14 – Constructive Act #27 – Keep a Journal

If you already have a journal, re-read your journal entries today. Keeping a journal gives you a way to get your thoughts out of your head and preserved into history. It also gives you a tangible way to see the struggles you have worked through and how far you've come. It gives you strength and allows you to see your progress as you continue your journey into recovery. A journal can become like a friend that you tell your deepest secrets to and share your most significant success stories with. It can (if you choose to share your thoughts) even become a manual to others who will say that they have no idea how to begin their recovery, that no one has written the manual! It will become your "Book of Life," and may just be the "friend" that saves your life one day.

For family members of addicts, it can provide the therapy to get you through the days, months, and even years of living with an addict. It does not have to be fancy or expensive; it can be a 79 cent composition book from the grocery store. Write your first entry today and begin the documented story of your journey. Who knows, you just may become the "Anne Frank" of recovery.

4/17/14 – Constructive Act #28 – Define Your Light at the End of the Tunnel

As an addict, as a Recovery Resource, or as a family support member, what does the light at the end of the tunnel mean to you? What is it that you are searching for? When is it over, and what does that look like? There is no right or wrong answer, and the answer will be different for everyone. Write the answer in your journal and refer back to it often. Remind yourself where you are trying to go and what you want to look like when you get there.

Be realistic. I know that Davis would tell me that he wanted to go back to a time where he had the opportunity to make that very first decision again and make a different choice. He would never have started the opiates if he had known. But that would not be realistic. One analogy we heard in rehab was that "when a cucumber becomes a pickle, it can never be a cucumber again." In other words, you have to accept what you have become and make that your starting point to move forward. "Moving Onward through Life...Looking Upward to God." You can do this!

4/18/14 – Constructive Act #29 – Live to Fight Another Day

Last night when I got home, I had a private message asking for help for a family member shooting heroin. I gave the family the HelpLines, Free Rehab Resources, Websites for Quitting Cold Turkey, and then I sent a message about turning them in to the Narcotics Unit to have them picked up. Putting your loved one in jail on purpose may seem very harsh, but it just might keep you from burying them. If you feel there is no other way, there is HOPE for recovery if you go this route. Call the unit in your area and ask to speak with an agent to help you with the process. Your loved one will be placed in the infirmary to detox; if they are a first offender, they can have their criminal history cleared after they have served their time. I have included a link explaining the First Offender Act. Many addicts in recovery have used this act to go to work in a professional capacity and have a good life as they continue in their recovery.

http://www.gjp.org/programs/criminal-records/faqs/faqs-first-offender/

4/19/14 – Constructive Act #30 – Fight for Your Insurance Coverage

And here's how! One of the greatest obstacles in the way of recovery for opiate addiction is the fact that insurance companies deny the coverage you are paying for. As you will read in the article, most insurance companies bank on the fact that the majority of people will accept their "NO" without question and just give up. I know personally that with double coverage for my son, he was denied after 21 days of inpatient rehab. We were paying for 30 days of inpatient rehab for both policies. He was moved to outpatient therapy at that time, and we all know how that worked out. Follow this lady's lead and DON'T GIVE UP! Until we can work on getting the law changed in Georgia to allow the doctors to have the final say, you will have to be your child's advocate.

4/20/14 – Constructive Act # 31 – PRAISE THE LORD

Thank God that he allowed his son Jesus to bear your sins on the cross so that you can be forgiven. No matter what you have done in the past (and, YES, that means drugs of any kind,) when you ask for forgiveness, you are washed as white as snow. So simply today – the holiest day of all for Christians – PRAISE THE LORD! If you don't know Jesus, seek him out. He is the only way to become whole again. Thank you, God, and thank you, Jesus, and BLESS the DDF!

4/21/14 – Constructive Act #32 – HIDE YOUR VALUABLES

Pawn shops love addicts! Addicts love pawn shops! Over the course of his addiction, Davis pawned many things; some were his and some were not. When the addiction takes over and the cravings become so strong, the disease makes addicts do things that seem uncontrollable. Davis took things from us that he never would have done if he had not been an addict. The pawn shop does not discriminate. They are in it to make a living. Even though Michael and I went to the pawn shop and got back things and told them what was going on, they continued to take things from Davis, knowing that he was an addict and that he was ruining his life. To this day, we are still finding out things are missing. NOTHING is sacred to an addict in the throes of addiction. HIDE the things that you do not want to lose.

4/22/14 – Constructive Act #33 – GET INVOLVED

Today at Kennesaw Mountain High School in Georgia, there will be an assembly to address drug use in our area. This was put together by one of the teachers and a "Recovery Resource" (former addict) who were willing to get involved. They sought out a forum and got permission to make a difference. If you are a "Recovery Resource," go to your old high school or middle school and ask to speak at an assembly. Ask the police detectives, or chief, or even the medical examiner to accompany you. Ask a doctor to join you. BUT ASK!!! It will help you gain more people in your support system, it will spread the word from a valid perspective, and it will get the words heroin, opiates, addict, and (best of all) RECOVERY out in public where they need to be. If you are able to do this before the summer, where lots of kids have unsupervised free time on their hands, it may save a life or two. GET INVOLVED! Please post on the DDF if you are able to plan and implement this Constructive Act! MAKE A DIFFERENCE!

4/23/14 – Constructive Act #34 – FOCUS ON WORTH

Help your addict focus on his or her strengths. I know as a Counselor for 24 years that it is Best Practice to begin every parent conference with the strengths of a child because it gives a parent HOPE and it gives a child VALUE. Even if there are no academic strengths, you focus on the fact that maybe they have perfect attendance or they get to school on time every day. Find something that gives the addict some worth. I know that I've said before that Davis told me that he felt "worthless," but I know that there were still so many good internal values in spite of his addiction. Davis had a special ability to make people smile and make them feel good about themselves. He was also incredibly smart, but in his eyes, the addiction stripped all those qualities away. Addicts are their own worst enemies and they beat themselves down every day. Then in rehab, they're made to repeat the negative words "I'm an addict" every time they want to speak in a meeting. As a parent of an addict, you have to find a way to help them focus on their worth in order for them to find value. Help your child find a reason to recover by focusing on his or her worth. Remind them EVERY DAY of their WORTH.

4/24/14 – Constructive Act #35 – Talk to Your Pre-Teens

PREVENTION is key in the war on heroin and opiate addiction. NEVER…NOT EVEN ONCE has got to be the golden rule of these dangerous drugs. Yesterday I received a message from a mom with two young girls. She asked for information to talk to her daughters. I found a really good article and I'm posting it for her. One of the points in the article states to keep to the facts and avoid fear. I told her last night that a healthy fear is a good thing and I do believe that. I understand what the article is saying as well. The fact is that drugs are scary! So the fear that comes from the facts is what I refer to as a "healthy fear," and that is a good thing, in my humble opinion.

This is for you, Laura, and others in your stage of life with young children (pre-teens). The Counselor in me especially likes the role-play suggestion.

www.falmouthprevention.org/how-to-prevent-drug-abuse-in-your-preteen.html

4/25/14 – Constructive Act #36 – Stabilize and Manage

I had the distinct pleasure of speaking with Dr. Jeremy Engel yesterday afternoon. He is the doctor in Northern Kentucky who is signing prescriptions for the rescue kits containing the Naloxone. He is PASSIONATE about helping with the cause of opiate addiction, especially heroin. He promised to hook me up with the people who can walk us through the process of passing the legislation to get the rescue kits here in Georgia. It will take a community effort of "movers and shakers," as my husband Michael puts it, but I know we can do it. We will need government officials, doctors, and passionate people willing to work with the Foundation to make this happen. Dr. Engel does have definite views of treatment for opiate addicts, and I ask him for his advice regarding rehabilitation. He believes that medically approved drug therapy is the way to go. He gave me this quote which relates to the constructive act above: "In order to disrupt the destructive cycle of opiate addiction, we need to stabilize the addict in order to gain the opportunity to manage the recovery on our terms. When the addict gets his or her life in order and is ready to make the changes necessary to remain in recovery, then and only then will he/she experience success." He further believes that Vivitrol or Suboxone are individual choices for recovery according to the habits of the addict. He promised to stay connected with the Foundation and exchanged contact information with me. He also promised me that he would get on FB and read the Foundation page to make sure I got his quote right. Thank God for angels like Dr. Engel!

4/26/14 – Constructive Act #37 – Complete Your Funeral Planning Sheet

As a counselor, I have always believed in reality. If I worked in a rehab facility for opiate/heroin addiction, the first thing I would have the addicts do would be to complete the funeral worksheet. As many people have stated in the articles and videos of this site, opiate/heroin addicts are very likely to end up in jail or dead. Here is a worksheet for funeral planning. Have your addict take a look at it and go ahead and make their own plans. It will be a huge dose of reality and possibly a wake-up call to their future. I wonder what my son would have written down?

www.shareyourwishes.org/worksheet.pdf

4/27/14 – Constructive Act – #38 – Write a Tribute/Letter

If you are an addict, why not work on step four of asking forgiveness? I know it's sometimes hard to say face to face what you want to say to those you love and may have hurt. So write your thoughts down and hand deliver them to your family.

If you are a parent or a sibling, write to your addicted sibling or child. Tell them how much you love them and remind them of all the wonderful things that you love about them. Send them encouragement and support with your words, maybe in the form of a poem or short story about a memory you may share. It's something they can read over and over when they need it most. Words are SO powerful. Use them today in a positive way for the ones you love. Here is a tribute I wrote for Davis on what would have been his 21st birthday today.

To Davis…On your 21st Birthday
Welcome to adulthood
My precious first-born son.
Today you would be twenty-one,
But your time on earth is done.
You bore your burden all alone;
You felt you weren't "enough."
I loved you more than life itself;
I begged you to be tough.
Addiction drew its mighty sword,
A prisoner you became.
You fought so hard with all you had.
You couldn't bear the shame.
I loved you then; I love you now.
I wish I could have known
the things to do – The things to say
So you wouldn't have died alone.
What's done is done and can't be changed.
My love won't bring you back.
I would have taken your place, my son,
On that lonely, deadly track.
In the arms of God…You rest my child
I'll hold you again one day.
For now you are free; your body is whole.
There are no more dragons to slay.
The hole in my heart will diminish with time.
Tho' it will never be complete.
Until the day we're together again,
And we sit at Jesus' feet.
You left a void in my "perfect" world

and that I can't explain…
But I promise you now for your birthday gift…
"You did not die in vain."
I love you Davis… Mom 4/27/2014

4/28/14 – Constructive Act #39 – Recommend a Book

Do you have a book that has had special meaning to you as you have journeyed through addiction, supported an addict, or made your way through recovery? Share it with us now. I know for me, as a mother of an addict, and in addition to the Bible, which of course has been my book of choice, I have enjoyed "One Thousand Gifts" by Ann Voskamp. I am actually making a list of 1,000 gifts that I am thankful for. There are pages in the back of this book for making the list. This book has allowed me to keep a positive attitude while I move through the journey of supporting an addict. Please recommend your book of strength or knowledge. We will begin a book list on the website. www.onethousandgifts.com

4/29/14 – Constructive Act #40 – Don't Take Their Phones!

This is purely my opinion. I had a "closet" addict, but I can tell you for sure, it doesn't keep them from getting in touch with dealers! What it did do for my son was keep him from his family – his brothers, his sisters, his girlfriend, his buddies – and everyone who was good and right in his world! That is the first thing parents are encouraged to do that was written on the discharge contract as a consequence for non-compliance. The first time we were lied to, we took the phone; looking back, I think we took his whole support system away when we did that. Generation-Y lives by the phone. It's as natural for them as our network at work or community is for us. I'll never forget driving back from the store one day when Davis was with me. We pulled up behind one of his friends. He rolled down the window, got the boy's attention, and smiled so big. I asked him why he didn't go to lunch or dinner with his friend. He said, "Because I can never get in touch with him." I felt so bad! As I stated before, I think rehab is outdated and overrated, and this is one of the main reasons why! Let them have their phones! It is their whole SUPPORT SYSTEM.

4/30/14 – Constructive Act #41 – Strip, Trash, and Redecorate

This was advice Ellen G. received from her son's rehab facility. Why not take the opportunity to re-do your child's room while they are in rehab? I know I did that for Davis. I didn't throw anything away that wasn't very obviously trash, but I did box up a lot of things and put them away.

He never asked for them when he got home. It felt good for him to come home to a clean room with fresh sheets and everything in its place. It was like a new beginning. His "using" memories were cleaned away and "tools of the trade" were gone forever. Give your child a fresh start and a new beginning. It feels good to them and it shows them how much you care about them.

5/1/14 – Constructive Act #42 – Don't Second Guess Yourself

When living with an addict and things began to go missing, I remember thinking I must be going crazy! I would get cash out and put it in my wallet for a specific reason. Then when I went to get it, it was gone. I would rack my brain trying to remember where I put it or if I spent it. I would look for hours and sometimes even days for things I knew in my heart were either sold, traded, or pawned. After Davis died, I continued to miss things, and to this day, I still look for them. To me, this was just further assurance that my child had been overtaken with this disease. He never would have done these things in his right mind. Addiction is a DISEASE, and OPIATE ADDICTION is like NO OTHER! If a rehab facility or a therapist tries to tell you that it is the same as any other addiction, WALK AWAY! Look for another therapist or another rehab facility, one that actually understands and can help you and your addict.

5/2/14 – Constructive Act #43 – Put It into Perspective

Put your life into perspective and help your addict do the same. I think in our country we all overrate our importance. Whenever I get really stressed out about my life and the things that I need to get done, I think of myself as a grain of sand in a vast beach on a beautiful ocean, because in reality that's about our size in this universe. Nothing is so absolutely important that makes it worth our life and our soul.

We have to help our children realize this. Anxiety is caused by the expectations of society, and it creates great stress and causes people to do things to escape. Help your child to see that even though they are so very important to you, that we are all just "creatures" here on earth and that none of us are so important that when we are gone the earth will cease to exist. Help them to understand that they can only do what they can do; sometimes it will make a difference, and other times it will not.

A test or final at the end of a semester does not define them or make them a better or worse person. It only measures what they have in their head about a subject. It doesn't mean they are incapable of learning more or even becoming an expert in the subject. It just gives a measure of knowledge on any given day. Help them PUT IT INTO PERSPECTIVE!

5/3/14 – Constructive Act #44 – Lift Others Up

Davis had a special gift for always making others feel special. A sweet, precious young lady who went all through school with Davis messaged me today, and this is what she said…

"He was always so kind to me throughout our years of school together. I was always shy in school, and Davis is one of the few people who never made me feel bad about it. Rather than poking fun at me for it, Davis always made a point to be kind to me and say hello. I know that all of his peers have had a difficult time coping with this loss, so I cannot imagine how you must be feeling. I am sorry I didn't get a chance to speak with you at Davis's funeral. It was a beautiful service and it was wonderful to see how loved Davis was. His humor was what would get me through the day sometimes. It was always nice to be uplifted, because most of the time I really needed it. I know that when we all see Davis again, he will put the same smile on our faces that we've always known and loved."

Today, be the person that someone will remember because you made them feel special. You never know who may be in need of a kind word or an encouraging thought. You may be the one who keeps someone from relapsing or, even worse, taking their own life.

My daddy always told me to never let someone be nicer to me than I was to them. Those are good words to live by. They can change a life.

5/4/14 – Constructive Act #45 – Be an Active Observer

This may sound strange, but what I am about to say continues to blow my mind! I have tried my best to be as honest as I can be when writing posts for the DDF. With that being said, what I am about to tell you is going to be very graphic and perhaps very hard for some of you to read. When Davis died, he was in his car in a public parking lot for possibly 22 hours. He was at the Cumberland Hooters, parked behind the restaurant in clear view of anyone driving through the parking lot. From what we have learned, he left the restaurant (where he is on video receiving his drugs) around 7:30 PM.

He went to the parking lot and got in his car around 8:00, shot up heroin, and died sometime between 8:00 PM on Monday night and 5:11 PM on Tuesday afternoon when 911 was called. He was not hidden in any way. It blows my mind that he sat in the parking lot of a strip mall shopping center for 22 hours and not one person became suspicious or passed him by and wondered whether or not he was okay. So for today's Constructive Act, I'm challenging you to be aware of young people or any person who seems to be "asleep" in their cars. Knock on a window and ask if they are okay. Call 911. Blow the horn in your car as you are parked close to them. DON'T JUST WALK OR DRIVE AWAY!!! I wonder every day how many people drove by my son and "wondered" whether or not he was okay. Could it have saved his life? I guess I'll never know! Don't be THAT PERSON!

5/5/14 – Constructive Act #46 – Understand Sibling Loyalty

Siblings often feel a divided loyalty between the addicts and their parents. Although they often are privy to things that the parents are not, they feel a loyal need to

protect their brother or sister. They often believe the addict when they say they are not using anymore or that they are sorry for what happened. Siblings have a HARD time dealing with the situation of living with an addict, especially the younger they are. I know that when Davis started using, his younger brothers and sister were 16, 14, and 12; his older sister was 20. They would second guess themselves when dealing with Davis. They loved him so intensely that they didn't want to see him have to leave or have to be somewhere he didn't want to be. I didn't know the depth of the things they knew and never mentioned until after his death. Talk with your other children and give them some guidelines for keeping conversations and actions to themselves. They don't need to carry the burden of protection with them before, during, or after addiction. Give them a healthy avenue for discussion with you, their parents, and let them know they are not doing their addicted sibling any favors by not reaching out for help. Let them know they didn't cause it, they can't control it, and they can't cure it. They CAN, however, let their parents know what they know about the addicted sibling. They don't need to bear that burden by themselves. ADDICTION affects everyone in the family, and sometimes the siblings suffer silently because they don't know how to get the help they need.

5/6/14 – Constructive Act #47 – Educate Yourselves about Upcoming Elections

These people will be the key people who will change all of the legislation and laws we have been talking about, such as addiction insurance laws, the legislation to get the Naloxone drug rescue kits into the states, and the banning of drugs like Zohydro. You still have time to email your questions to the candidates and to get answers as to where they stand on the opiate addiction epidemic. Let your voices be heard on May 20th, but educate yourselves in the next two weeks so that we have the right people in office to help us make the necessary changes that we have been discussing. BE PREPARED to exercise your right to VOTE! Each of the following states are having general elections in 2 weeks and each have also reported opiate addiction in epidemic proportions.

May 20, 2014:

Arkansas – Primary Election

Georgia – Primary Election

Idaho – Primary Election

Kentucky – Primary Election

North Dakota – Filing Deadline (Primary Write-Ins)

Oregon – Primary Election

Pennsylvania – Primary Election

Look up the election in your state. Here is the link for Georgia.

https://ballotpedia.org/Georgia_elections,_2014

5/7/14 – Constructive Act #48 – Mark Your Calendar and Invite a Friend

The First Opiate Addiction Summit will be held at the Marietta Performing Arts Center at Marietta High School on Tuesday, June 3rd, from 7:00 – 9:00 PM. Experts in every facet of the addiction epidemic will be there to explain and answer questions regarding opiate/heroin addiction. Come and learn the story of the Davis Direction Foundation, why it was established, and how you can get on board to help support and save the youth of Cobb County and across the nation. Learn the statistics, warning signs, and prevention techniques to use with your own children, students and co-workers. Learn why this epidemic is the fastest growing problem in our nation and what you can do to stop it. Hear from the experts in the field and know the help available and how to access it. Receive booklets, bracelets, and door prizes, and participate in the opportunity to speak directly with "Recovery Resources" who will be in attendance. You don't want to miss this awesome opportunity. This event is FREE to anyone interested. You will have an opportunity to make a donation to the Davis Direction Foundation.

5/8/14 – Constructive Act #49 – Plan Ahead

Always have something to look forward to. The old saying, "Idle Time is the Devil's Workshop," is so very true. Especially in the case of recovery, it is so important to have a schedule and stay busy. When Davis got out of rehab, he was not in school and he had quit his job because he didn't want to tell anyone he was going to rehab. He was at home alone all day, every day during the week with nothing to do. He did not have his phone, which I have already addressed (see Constructive Act#40), so he didn't have friends' numbers to make plans with and/or talk to.

Although, we did sit down together and make a schedule and plan his day every day, the plans didn't really have anything in them that he truly looked forward to. Most of his friends were either in school or working and it didn't really matter because he didn't have his car anyway. Remember, I told you before, we were doing the things suggested to us by rehab counselors, so he had no phone, no car, basically no privileges, and his life had nothing in it to look forward to. Of course he was going to relapse! Follow your gut, parents. We are not stupid. They have to live. It's a catch 22, but you can't take everything away and expect your recovering child to be happy! It just doesn't work that way. And the truth is, the reason they started using in the first place was because they were not happy! Help them plan a good and productive schedule that includes things they enjoy.

5/9/14 – Constructive Act #50 – Watch "Saving Mr. Banks"

The plot is the TRUE story of how Disney got the rights to Mary Poppins. BUT the bigger message is the story of what addiction can do to a family. Even when the addict is no longer alive, the addiction does not die; it stays with the rest of the family for a lifetime. It has everything to do with how much the addicted family member is loved. There are aspects of Davis's addiction that I know everyone in my family will take to the grave. Mainly the "What ifs…" It's just a natural human response. We don't blame ourselves or each other; we just always think of the different scenarios that could have been. And Davis's precious child will grow up without her daddy. As awesome as I hope her life will be, and I pray every day for her to have a daddy to love her like Davis did, the fact remains that her biological daddy is forever gone from her life. The movie will break your heart. Take your tissues and understand that this is a movie that is still affecting the "Banks" family. Addiction changes the course of history, and not for the better. I saw this movie during the time that Davis had come home from rehab, but before he died. I thought my heart was going to EXPLODE.

5/10/14 – Constructive Act #51 – Mark Your Stuff

I just did a little research on pawn shops this morning, and this is what I found out: If you can match serial numbers, or if you have identifying marks on jewelry and other things without serial numbers, pawn shops have to give you your stolen merchandise back or, at the very least, sell it back to you for what they paid for it. That's with or without a ticket.

I know Davis pawned things that were not his, things that we did go and get back. Even after his death we were still retrieving things from the pawn shop. We did get to buy them back for the "pawn ticket" price, but that could have been because the time for them to be shelved was not up yet. I'm still searching for one piece of jewelry that I have an appraisal on, but with no identifying marks. That's the one thing we have not been able to locate, and it's because we didn't know about it until I went to put it on recently. An addict will usually find the pawn with the longest "wait time" and "highest prices paid" to deal with. Yes, it can vary significantly. They want the most money, and Davis, at least, had every intention of getting things back, so wait time was important to him as well. Write down serial numbers on power tools, lawn equipment, electronics, and kitchen appliances, and mark jewelry. Have expensive pieces appraised. Make it so that you can leave no doubt that what you came to claim as stolen Merchandise is YOURS!

5/11/14 – Constructive Act #52 – Rest (My First Mother's Day)

On the Seventh Day, He rested. Remember the Sabbath and keep it holy. Tomorrow will be my first Mother's Day without my Sweet Davis. I have no words. I will REST!

5/12/14 – Constructive Act #53 – Don't Work Harder Than They Do

When Davis was in IOP (Intensive Outpatient Therapy), I was corresponding with one of the nurses and she made a comment to me: "This is his recovery. Don't work harder than he does."

As parents, sometimes we want things to work out for our children so badly that we start working harder than they do at recovery. Those parental instincts kick in and we want to take over -- asking all the questions, confirming times, asking for confirmation on drug tests, checking up on answers. The list goes on and on. As a parent, we have to take a step back and make sure the children are the ones doing the work. We don't need to do for them the things they can do for themselves. It is important to stay involved and to know what is going on, but we don't need to speak for our addicts; they need to tell and take responsibility for their own story and recovery.

5/13/14 – Constructive Act #54 – Write Short and Long Term Goals

Sometimes it's hard to see the forest for the trees, which is why it is important to write not only short term goals but long term goals as well. Especially for an addict who tries to live their life by the Serenity Prayer…Just for Today. Making the long term goals is where the DREAMS come in – the future that gives you something to live for and strive for. For the family members of addicts, writing short and long term goals gives you HOPE. It allows you to think about a day when the addiction is under control and you are not living in fear or frustration every day. As an addict when you write a long term goal, it allows you to see yourself as a successful and contributing individual possibly helping others through the worst times of their lives. As a recovering addict, you really can have SO much to offer. It's all up to you! www.wikihow.com/Write-Personal-Goals

5/14/14 – Constructive Act #55 – Ask and Ye Shall Receive…or Not

But what have you got to lose by asking? As a child, I know my parents taught me not to ask for things because it was rude! If people offer, that's a different story. I taught my children the same thing: Don't ASK; if people want to offer you something, it's up to them. Well, I'm changing my mind on this one. Sometimes I wonder how people got things accomplished while minding their manners at the same time. As an addict, you have to ASK for help because no one knows what's going on in your mind. As parents, we need to ask for help because others have been through what we are going through and they have experience with recovery.

One of my goals is to tell everything that I know I dealt with so that people don't have to ask. Because ASKING IS HARD! Some people, myself included, think it is a sign of weakness or a lack of intelligence, even a statement that says, "I'm incapable of doing this alone." So, let me role-model my Constructive Act this morning. I need HELP with the June 3rd Symposium! Who will help me? We need help with refreshments, fundraising efforts, book donations, and giveaways. I will publish a separate list of items and efforts needed before the weekend. Be praying about your part in this because IT NEEDS TO BE A COMMUNITY EFFORT! That's how CHANGE is accomplished.

5/15/14 – Constructive Act #56 – Play Up

I will try to explain this "ACT" by using a sports analogy, and I hope I can make my idea very clear. When tennis players are trying to improve their game, they always seek to play against someone who is better than they are so that they have to work really hard to aspire to be better. It really does not do them any good to play against someone who has nothing to offer their game in order for them to improve. When "Recovery Resources" (former addicts) are in recovery, they are almost always asked to be involved with community service, and some programs even mandate that they do so. However, they often end up working in homeless shelters, soup kitchens, donation centers, or something similar. Now, in and of itself, that is not a bad thing. BUT it does not put the "Recovery Resource" in the presence of people that they aspire to be like.

One of the reasons is that early in their recovery process, they often don't feel worthy of being around people who have their life in order and are moving "Onward and Upward."

We need to help provide opportunities for them to work alongside people who are at a point in their lives where they are making a difference for others. Those people can offer encouragement, act as role-models, offer advice, and share positive stories about life in general, giving the "Recovery Resource" HOPE for a better and more fulfilling life. So, if you are a former addict looking to do community service during your recovery process, look for a positive environment with people you look up to and aspire to be. Ninety-nine % of the time, those people will invest in you and help you in your recovery process. They will be able to see what a wonderful and valuable person you are, which in turn will keep you on the road to active recovery "MOVING ONWARD THROUGH LIFE…LOOKING UPWARD TO GOD."

5/16/14 – Constructive Act #57 – Make a List

Sometimes when you are feeling a little overwhelmed with everything you need to accomplish, it helps to make a list and then to check off the things you have completed! You can even start with the very easy and simple items on the list to build up your momentum. Once you begin to see that you are making progress, you begin to pick up speed and confidence. You can do this in your work life and your personal life as well.

When people become overwhelmed, it causes anxiety; anxiety often leads to panic, and people in recovery often relapse at this point. For people in the education field and for students as well, the end of the semester or the end of another school year has a tendency to bring about these feelings. So let's combine a few of the previous Constructive Acts at this time and *Put things in Perspective, *Ask for Help if you need it, and *Make a List. Good Luck to everyone out there trying to finish up another year/semester of education, students and staff alike. Make your list and stay calm.

5/17/14 – Constructive Act #58 – Sleep!

I believe that often people don't realize how important sleep is. It's very scientific, and I don't pretend to know all of the science behind it. I do know that a lack of sleep alters attitudes and personalities. It alters a person's state of mind. It makes a person less aware and less observant. It makes a person irritable. It's NEVER a good thing. The article posted below suggests that lack of sleep is a reason a young person might turn to drugs and further suggests that sleep patterns in pre-school children may be an early indication of later drug abuse.

Here is one positive and definite way to address the prevention of drug abuse.

Parents, establish a curfew and enforce it. Turn the video games off and require your children to get in bed WITHOUT ELECTRONICS! Davis had terrible issues with sleep and told us that the reason he started opiates in the first place was because of anxiety that caused him not to be able to sleep. He slept with a computer and a phone in bed with him every night. An inability to sleep has long been associated with highly intelligent people; their brains just never turn off.

5/18/14 – Constructive Act #59 – Pass on Compliments

People often talk among themselves, and in their conversations they often say wonderful things about others. The problem is that the "others" in most cases never get to hear the wonderful things being said about them. Davis worked in the same school as I did, and teachers and students alike would tell me nice things he did and how much they thought of him. Davis had a strong connection with kids that others had a hard time dealing with.

His heart was so big and he hated to see kids get in trouble. I always made it a point to tell him the nice things that were said in his absence. Whenever I would do this, he would always say something like, "Really?" Then he would say, "Now tell me that again. She said what?" He wanted to hear it again because it made him feel worthy and it was always nice to hear that someone had noticed his kindness. After his death, one of the teachers at my school who works with children who have behavior and emotional disorders told me that Davis loved her students and they knew it. She went on to say that they loved him, too. Davis would have been so proud to hear that.

Addiction, depression, anxiety — all of these diseases cause self-esteem to plummet. By passing on compliments or saying them directly, you may just give someone the boost they need to continue on a path to recovery or, better yet, to begin a journey to recovery. If you hear or you think something good about someone else, PASS IT ON!

5/19/14 – Constructive Act #60 – Get Involved

Don't sit back and applaud the efforts of others and not involve yourself. Let's abolish the 80/20 rule (the one that says that 20% of all the people do 80% of all the work).

GET INVOLVED, whether it is in your own community or someone else's. Our June 3rd Symposium is going to be awesome. I hope that all of you are planning on coming if you are in the area. If you are not in the area, let's find out how we can live stream it to you.

It is going to be so powerful and informative. Let me know if you have any expertise in this area. One of our goals is to become a page or website that everyone else can emulate to make a difference. What better way to accomplish this than by live-streaming throughout the nation? MAKE A DIFFERENCE! It will take all of us, but somebody has to do it. I had a conversation with some of my friends the other day and told them that people make a difference every day. Why can't it be us? My daughter had it exactly right when our family started this FB page and then the website: God doesn't call the qualified. HE QUALIFIES THE CALLED! Get on board with us and let's do this!!!

5/20/14 – Constructive Act #61 – Respect the Zone

This post is for all of the ones who have lost a loved one and the ones who care about the ones who have lost loved ones. I hesitated to make this post, but I've had the conversation three times this week with family members and a friend who lost her child. Every day when someone who has lost a loved one to addiction walks out the door, they are "in the zone."

They have physically, emotionally, and mentally prepared themselves to be productive and to accomplish whatever the goal for the day is. Even if that goal is to go to the grocery store and buy dinner for the evening or to go to work or to a social gathering, meeting, or even church, we have to "get in the zone." When people who genuinely care about us see us out and about, they naturally want to "check on us" and find out how we are doing. So we often get questions like, "How are you doing?" "How is the family getting along?" "Are you okay?" And while we do understand how very much you care, those questions completely take us "out of the zone" and completely undo all of our physical, mental, and emotional preparation. As a counselor, I often get questions about how to interact with people who have lost a loved one, so I will tell you what I would like to hear if I see you out and about.

"Hey, it's good to see you." "Hey, friend!" "Give me a call sometime." "Let's get together soon." "You're looking GREAT." (my personal favorite, haha)

The point is, we need to be able to stay "in the zone" in order to be productive, and it gives us confidence to keep moving forward. I know I missed a party that I really wanted to go to this weekend because I just didn't have the strength to go and face all the questions that I thought I would hear. I would have been around people I have not seen in a while and, out of courtesy, those people would have felt obligated to acknowledge my loss. It is not necessary. We know your hearts and how much you love us, but the best thing you can do for us is to allow us to "stay in the zone." If we are at a party, we need to be happy; if we are at work, we need to be productive; if we are at the grocery store, we need to focus and not forget what we came in for; if we are at a meeting, we need to pay attention. There will be times when we need to talk about the death and our feelings, but please let us initiate those conversations when we have prepared ourselves for the emotional place that it will take us. It's not easy to come back from that place

5/21/14 – Constructive Act #62 – Pray Specifically

In 14 days we will gather at Marietta High School for our "Taking Aim at Addiction" Symposium. Please begin to pray NOW if you have not already started that we will be able to reach out to our community and make them aware of what a BEAST we are dealing with.

Let's be very specific in our prayers:

Pray for our presenters

Pray for our panel representatives

Pray that the RIGHT people will show up

Pray that we will fill the auditorium to capacity

Pray for our volunteer efforts

Pray for divine intervention for addicts in attendance

Pray for strength for our families dealing with addiction

Pray for the political leadership who will show up

Pray that they will advocate change at a legislative level

Pray for good weather for our event

Pray that all the pieces will fall together in perfect order

Pray that God will show you how to become involved

Pray for God's abundant blessings

"The Prayer of Jabez" was circulating heavily several years ago. It's a little book that people could read in 30 minutes and then pass along to a friend to read. The idea in the book was that there was a Storehouse of Blessings waiting to be bestowed on each of us, and they were there for the asking. There were endless blessings with each of our names on them, just waiting for us to ask God to send them to us.

5/22/14 – Constructive Act #63 – Let It Go

Yes, I did just use the famous line from "FROZEN," but it needed to be said! Crying is a good thing sometimes, and it can be a major stress release. I know it works for me and I know it worked for Davis. There were times in his drug use where he would absolutely break-down and tell us that he needed help. He was tired, exhausted, stressed out, and hopeless. When he would find himself up against a wall with no way out, he would "Let It Go," and he would feel so much relief afterward. It was times like that when he would just absolutely melt into my arms and let me hold him like a baby; I know it must have felt so good to him. He would let us help for a while, and then he would regain his strength and begin doing things behind our back again.

Last night, I "Let It Go." Sometimes, I get completely overwhelmed with my life and all that I have going on right now. Every night when I go to bed, I think about Davis and how much I miss him and I cry. But last night was different.

I completely "Let It Go." It had been building all day as I sat and watched the last day of school and Davis's first group of 3rd graders graduating from 5th grade. He should have been there to watch them and tell them how proud he was of them. I saw children who had filled our home with laughter by being the subject of Davis's stories for the last two and a half years having a great last day of school, and he should have been there to celebrate with them. I was overcome with sadness yesterday, and when I got home I had a lot to do with the Symposium preparation; the thoughts of doubt and fear kept edging into my mind: "Am I qualified to do what I'm doing?" "What if I fail?" "What if I let people down?" and worst of all, "What if I fail to save someone?" My thoughts were completely irrational and I was almost in a panic. People think I am so strong and they tell me that all the time. The truth is I'm a grieving mother doing what I think I am supposed to be doing, and God grants me the strength to do it because HE wants me to do it.

I pray every day for this Constructive Act that I post, and sometimes I get signs that He approves. Yesterday was one of those days, after my post about the Prayer of Jabez.

My online daily devotional was about abundant blessings and even had scripture from Colossians quoted in it. WOW! That was pretty cool to me. It gave me confidence and validation. So – I feel like I am starting to ramble, but my point is this: I am weak but HE is strong, and that is OKAY! I am human! Sometimes you just have to "LET IT GO." Afterward, you pick yourself back up, get "in the zone," and carry on! Thanks to my AMAZING husband and children who are there for me when I fall apart and for my wonderful friends who give me strength and courage to carry on! I love you all (…and I feel much better today!).

5/23/14 – Constructive Act #64 – Just Start

Twenty-three years ago at the beginning of another school year, I had the pleasure of attending an inspirational meeting set up by my principal, Sherri Sallinger. She brought Mamie McCullough in from Texas to speak to our elementary school staff. What an experience that was! One thing that Mamie said has always stuck with me, and that was, "When you don't know what you are doing, just START." That's how this Foundation began. That's how you can begin the next phase of your life as well. JUST START. When you want to make a change or you NEED to make a change, one of the things that keeps us from making the change is that we don't know how to get started. Mamie says, "Sometimes the best work is done by people who don't want to do what they have to do but who are nonetheless courageous enough to get up and get going! Who are the successful people? They are the ones who do the things that unsuccessful people refuse to do." At the time I heard Mamie speak I was about to explode as a severe anemic pregnant woman! I was scared to death, as it was my first pregnancy. I had no idea what I was getting into, but in that situation, I had no alternative but to "just start." Mamie gave me the courage I needed to become confident, and she inspired me to be the best I could be. So, whatever life changes you need to make, or whatever you need to do as the next phase in your life, don't be afraid to JUST START.

Mamie McCullough: About Mamie www.mamie.com

5/24/14 – Constructive Act #65 – Invest in the Unusual

Looking back over the last year of Davis's life, I have to say that there were several "unusual" things that happened. How many of you have ever seen a 20-year-old with thrush? Or how about a 20-year-old who suddenly develops restless leg syndrome? Or a 20-year-old who has worked with cars alongside his dad for the last five years suddenly has an allergic reaction to something from the engine of his car, possibly antifreeze? Or has hallucinations because of prescribed anxiety medication?

You are probably thinking I am pretty stupid right about now, but the last thing a mother ever suspects is that her child is a heroin addict. Looking back, I should have been suspicious of the "UNUSUAL" things that were happening and insisted that he go to the doctor. Instead, he would tell me that he looked up what to do on the internet and that it should be gone in a couple of days, which it usually was.

The allergic reaction to the antifreeze was scary enough to both of us that we did go to a minute clinic after hours. The doctor didn't even raise suspicion, which, looking back, was a little strange to me at this point. Changes in habits – especially bathroom habits, like spending lots of time every day in a locked bathroom -- are a red flag but were explained away by having a "messed up stomach." TRUST YOUR INSTINCTS, parents. If it has feathers like a duck, waddles like a duck, and quacks like a duck, IT'S A DUCK! God gave parents that 6th sense for a reason; rely upon it!

5/25/14 – Constructive Act # 66 – Live in the Present

None of us have any guarantees for tomorrow! Yesterday is History, Tomorrow is a Mystery, Today is a GIFT – That's why they call it the PRESENT! I could go on and on with quotes about living for the moment. It's really TRUE, and no one knows that better than the "OWEN7!" Today we put one of our members on a plane to Peru to go and build water systems for impoverished regions there. Is it hard? YOU BET IT IS! Another of my children asked me last week, did I worry that another member of the family would die? Although as a counselor, I know that is completely normal, I have to tell you that I don't worry about losing another child or spouse. I know that life is and has always been in God's hands.

The night Davis walked out of the door for the last time, I had an uneasy feeling. In fact, he was going to a "meeting." I had a friend over planning a funeral reception for another friend, and I wouldn't even give him a final answer. I told him, "Ask your dad." He was very persistent.

"Mom, Dad isn't answering his phone and I need to go." I just had this feeling and I said, "Well, you better hope he calls back." Something inside me wouldn't let myself make the call the he could go. If I had not had a friend over and had not been trying to "protect his privacy," I would have probably had a lot more to say. I would have made him show me the meeting. I would have asked a million questions. Something just didn't feel right about leaving the house for a meeting at 7:00 PM. But at 7:00 PM, I hugged my precious son for the last time as we exchanged "I love you's." That is a moment in time I will never get out of my mind.

When 10:00 rolled around, I was still waiting up for him, but I wasn't overly concerned; he had been talking to some of his friends in recovery that week, and I thought that he might be hanging out with them catching up. When 11:00 rolled around, I was worrying. Midnight has always been the house curfew on weeknights for even my college kids. Nothing good ever happens after midnight!!! Davis was not home. He had NEVER missed a curfew, and he had never not come home without asking to stay somewhere else for the night. I was terrified. at 1:00 AM. I woke Michael up and told him something was wrong. Michael told me he would come home and to stop worrying. At 1:30 when I went to bed, I prayed to God to protect him and not let him suffer! I knew he was dead or dying! I did not get the "doorbell" until 8:00 that night. When the detective walked in my house, I looked him in the eyes and said, "He's dead, isn't he?" As a mother, I knew my child was gone one hour – maybe even one minute -- past curfew. I just knew!

Now today I will hug another precious son and exchange "I love you's." I can't even see what I am writing right now for the tears filling my eyes and running down my cheeks. BUT I will put him in God's loving hands and continue to live in the present because I know I can't change the course of life unless it is in God's design for me to do so. I can only hope and pray every day that the Davis Direction Foundation is God's design for us to help save others. He keeps sending me affirmations that it is. So, I will keep working to do God's work right here in our own community while I send one child to Peru today and another on Thursday to Miami on choir tour to do what God has planned for them to do.

This was my very long way to say, "Live in the present" and know that God is in control! Please keep the "Owen7" in your prayers this week. Pray for safe travels and for God's abundant blessings to flow freely.

5/26/14 – Constructive Act #67 – Make Your Bed

That's right – just make your bed. First thing in the morning right after you get out of it. Make your bed and make it to perfection. This advice comes from a Navy Seal quoted in the Wall Street Journal.

I remember on Sunday mornings growing up, my daddy would come into our rooms and offer a quarter to the most perfectly made bed. The reason for the quarter was that he would drop it onto the bed, and if it bounced up, you had done a good job (a trick he learned from being a military man himself). Now my daddy, being the softie that he was, usually ended up giving every one of us a quarter because we all tried so hard to make the quarter bounce. We did take pride in receiving that quarter though!

The Seal stated that the wisdom of the simple act had been proven to him over and over again. You will feel a sense of accomplishment with your first task of the day, and it will give you a small sense of pride that will encourage you to do another task and another, etc. At the end of the day you will have completed many tasks, and making your bed will reinforce the fact that little things in life do matter. If you can't do the little things right, you will never do the big things right. And we all know from reading the DDF that being in active recovery is no small task! Even at the end of the day, if your day has been one miserable event after another, you still have a perfectly made bed to come home to.

Advice from the Navy Seal: "If you want to change the world, start off by making your bed." WSJ May 24-24, 2014

5/27/14 – Constructive Act #68 – Believe You Are Enough

This is probably the core of all problems in the world today. I just finished watching a "Ted Talk" by a lady who calls herself a "researcher-storyteller." Her name is Brene Brown, and the name of her talk is, "The Power of Vulnerability." At some point today, you need to find 20 minutes to watch the video I am going to post. Although I will try to hit the high points for you, I cannot begin to do for you what this woman will!

To begin with, realize we are ALL hard-wired for connection. Connection is why we are here – it gives purpose and meaning to our lives. Shame UNRAVELS connection. Shame is the fear of not being connected because we all have something that makes us feel we are NOT ENOUGH! We all have shame; it's universal. The only people who don't have it have no capacity for human empathy and connection. No one wants to talk about it; the less you talk about it, the more you have it!

Connection comes from having a sense of love and belonging. People who are connected have the courage to be IMPERFECT and the compassion to be KIND, to themselves first and then kind to others.

Connection means you are willing to let go of who you think you should be to be who you are. In other words, be AUTHENTIC. What makes you vulnerable makes you beautiful.

Vulnerability is the core of shame, fear and worthiness, but it is the birthplace of joy, creativity, belonging, and love. We all need to live whole-heartedly. Don't numb vulnerability; embrace it and learn to feel ALL of your feelings because if you "numb" the bad feelings through addiction, shopping, overeating, etc., you also "numb" the good feelings. You CANNOT selectively "numb."

Learn to be authentic and real. Say I'm sorry and we'll fix it! Let yourself be deeply seen; love with your whole heart even though there is no guarantee! Practice gratitude and joy. When we start believing and raising our children to believe we are worthy of love and belonging, we WILL see change. We will no longer be the most in debt, obese, addicted, and medicated adult cohort in US history!

PLEASE find the 20 minutes to watch this. Thanks to my 19-year-old son, Connor, for sharing this video with me! I will watch it again and again.

http://www.ted.com/talks/brene_brown_on_vulnerability?language=en

5/28/14 – Constructive Act # 69 – Come Up with One Question

What do you want to know about opiate/heroin addiction? The entire second half of the Symposium next week is going to be a panel discussion. Members of the audience will receive a 3×5 card when they come into the auditorium and will be able to write down a question for the panel to answer. What is that burning question that you want to know?

I know after Davis died I had so many questions, and I could not find out everything that I wanted or needed to know. Before he died, I didn't know what I didn't know, but there will be people there who do know, and you will receive their knowledge. I wish I could have had a panel of experts at my disposal before and after his death. I could have spent hours finding out everything I was curious about.

The Symposium will address issues that are real and happening right here under our noses, maybe even right under your roof. Please take this opportunity to educate yourselves so that you can be prepared to deal with this monster if it ever comes into the path of one of your loved ones.

If you are unable to attend, go ahead and post your questions in the comments section or private message the DDF and I will make sure that we get the answers to your questions. Remember, there is no such thing as a stupid question, and don't let your shame or embarrassment get in the way of helping or treating your loved one like I did. You will be among friends and people searching for the same answers and solutions as you. KNOWLEDGE IS POWER.

5/29/14 – Constructive Act #70 – Talk to Your Loved Ones

I really don't know why I waited so long for this Constructive Act because it seems so simple. Michael and I have said at least a million times. I wish Davis had just told us. We would have moved Heaven and Earth if we had truly known what he was going through. Addicts, if your parents don't know what you are dealing with, take the responsibility to educate them. Find a good article and a good set of stats to show them what you are going through. We truly had NO idea how intense and horrific heroin was. If you can open up to the ones you love and let them into your world, they will have a better chance of helping you. I would have taken him to get the meds he needed to stabilize and maintain in order to have bought time IF I HAD KNOWN! Parents can't help with what they don't know!

Just TALK; nothing ever gets solved by hiding it. Remember it is a disease. Would you not ask for help if you had any other disease in the world? Speak up for yourself and be your own ADVOCATE! I know I speak for parents everywhere when I say we would walk to Hell and back for our kids if they would only let us! TALK TO US AND LET US HELP!!!

5/30/14 – Constructive Act # 71 – Reach Out

Reach out to those loved ones that you have not seen or you have grown out of touch with over addiction issues. Reach out and tell them you have become more educated and that you are understanding more of what they are going through. Bring them to the Symposium with you so that they can be VALIDATED! Not only is heroin addiction a disease, but it IS one of the worst addictions that we know about (and you will learn all that and more on Tuesday night at Marietta High School!). I know for sure that treatment centers all over this state and country are telling us to "kick them out," "turn your back," "don't answer their calls." Would you really do this with any other disease you can name? They only say this because they don't have the right answers and don't know how to "FIX" this problem. I have decided that this problem has to start with validation for the addict.

Yes, we know this world is full of stress, the kind that older adults did not have growing up. Yes, we know that our expectations were so much higher than the expectations that were put on older adults. Yes, we know that you are faced with things through social media and the like that we as older adults never had to deal with. Yes, you are in a world that no one has taught you how to deal with and we don't have the answers. BUT, you did turn to drugs as a choice, and now you are addicted! Now it's my turn to HELP you with the DISEASE, and we can figure out how to do it together...but you have to give us the DATA we need in order to fix the problem. WE have to know what you are experiencing, feeling, taking, getting. We have to know the FACTS in order to find the SOLUTION! YOU are a vital part of the team that finds a solution, and YOU HAVE TO HELP US HELP YOU! We will do WHATEVER it takes to make this happen because WE LOVE YOU!

5/31/14 – Constructive Act #72 – Network

Whenever you are in a group of people who are sharing similar circumstances and working toward the same cause, there's a chance someone knows something that you don't! Seriously, we will be among a group of people who are passionate about the community we live in, the children in it, the people who run it and work in it, and the people who plan to live here until they die. Why not get to know each other? Yesterday, I was a little angry about a story I heard about a parent having to pay $1,200.00 for one shot of Vivitrol, a drug used to help people in withdrawal. This will be a monthly expense to help their child who is trying desperately to come off of heroin. Vivitrol is a new drug that is supposed to be non-addictive, but allows a person to go through withdrawal and stay clean without experiencing the urge to relapse. What a wonderful opportunity for this child, but what a burden for any parent. This needs to be addressed. I mentioned it to another family going through the same thing, anonymously of course, but immediately the other family told me about a $500.00 coupon on the Vivitrol website. Yeah, we were able to cut the family budget for meds almost in half, even though it is still outrageous. (New cause for the DDF!)

I also introduced the new billboard on the website yesterday, and it has been shared 30 times just from the DDF. I also had a dear high school friend tell me to give her a call; she works for an outdoor company and may be able to help! She knows to be expecting a call!

I've met so many wonderful people, and the DDF has had so many things and so many hours of time donated by wonderful people just through simply NETWORKING! So, when you come to the Symposium on Tuesday night, please, please introduce yourselves to others and let's get busy solving the crisis we are experiencing! If we can put a man on the moon, collectively as a nation, certainly we can find a solution for the DISEASE of ADDICTION! Gear UP, folks! WE are on this journey together! WE will make a difference!

6/1/14 – Constructive Act #73 — "Do NO Harm"

This was the message that my pastor spoke on last week. I think often as we go through a painful journey, others try to help us by giving advice that worked for them (or didn't work for them).

Addiction is a personal journey that is different for everyone. Let's face it, if there was a "cure" there would be no need for this book or any other like it.

Some things, drugs included, will work for some while they will not work for others. We have to keep our eye on the goal and the goal is the same for everyone --RECOVERY! Whatever it takes for that one person is what is needed for that one person.

I posted a couple of articles yesterday about a drug called Vivitrol. One was simply a medical discount card and the other was simply explaining how the drug was designed to work. This and other drugs -- as well as rehab and individual therapy and total cold turkey abstinence -- are all OPTIONS. Just like one diet does not work for all people, one solution does not work for all addicts.

So, when commenting on articles, please "DO NO HARM." Remember that addiction is a personal journey, and how you choose to deal with it is a personal choice. The DDF is designed to expose all the latest information available regarding opiate/heroin addiction. Arm yourselves with the knowledge offered, and make personal decisions accordingly. Please feel free to comment on your personal experience with any of these options, but allow others to do what they need to do without feeling judged or scrutinized because of your experience. When the end result of the journey has been death, all other options look pretty good to some of us.

We're all in this together, and we need to support each other and allow each other freedom in this journey to do WHATEVER IT TAKES to find the personal road to recovery!

6/2/14 – Constructive Act #74 – Bare Your Soul

Sometimes it's just necessary to bare your soul and expose your deepest feelings, thoughts, and concerns. It's healing; it's cleansing; and above all it keeps us humble. As I prepare for Tuesday night's Symposium, I am planning to bare my soul to an audience of hundreds, and, yes, that is concerning. But the bigger question is, "Could I possibly help someone else by doing so?" I believe that answer is yes. In the Bible, James 4:17 says, "If anyone, then, knows the good they ought to do and doesn't do it, it is sin for them."

For the past 33 years, I have been called to "teach children." The first eight years I taught them how to "read, write and do arithmetic." The last 25 years, I have "counseled" them in life skills and helped them learn to live in the world they were born into. It cuts me to the core that I couldn't do that for my own child. As a parent who has lost a child, I can tell you that the "what ifs" will haunt me to the grave. I will never stop wondering "what if." So now, as I look toward retirement in the coming year, my goal becomes to help families going through the nightmare my own family has lived through by allowing you to look through the open window of my soul to gain insight into how to help your child, brother, sister, spouse, niece, nephew, or friend.

Every day I pray and ask God to allow me to honor Davis's death so that his life was not lived without reason and his death was not in vain. For the past 74 days, He has given me something to offer others through my own experience. I will continue to pray and I will continue to write and I will continue to bare my soul as long as He wants me to, in an effort to save lives and prevent the ongoing use of opiates and heroin.

Is there something inside your soul that could help others with opiate/heroin addiction? If so, let's begin talking about it and let others know what to expect. I believe with all my heart that this topic NEEDS to become a public forum. We need to stop whispering the word "HEROIN" when we say it. We need for our young kids to know what it is and what it can do to them, and we need to spread the resources and information that are available to those who are already deep in the throes of this addiction.

There is HOPE. There is RECOVERY. There is a return to ABUNDANT LIFE We will find all of these things much more quickly when we put our heads together and begin working collectively for the good of the cause. Moving forward we have to say, NEVER – NOT ONCE; but working in the present we have to say, WE WILL SURVIVE.

6/3/14 – Constructive Act # 75 – Always Say Thank You

As I sit here this morning, I am humbled and blessed beyond belief at the happenings over the last couple of weeks as Leigh Colburn, Principal of Marietta

High School, and I have been planning the Symposium. People in our community and beyond have stepped up to the plate and hit home-run after home-run for the DDF, all in the name of helping those struggling with opiate/heroin addiction. The response has been overwhelming.

I have found out that people are embracing the addicts and their families that are going through this struggle with compassion, respect, and a sense of urgency to help make things better. Churches are talking from the pulpits. Lawmakers and enforcement agencies are taking great strides to get involved and train their folks to help in a time of crisis. Doctors and EMT's are trying to get the proper tools in place to be the most effective. Parents and family members are talking publicly in an effort to gain knowledge and make changes. The list goes on and on, and I want to say to all of you, "THANK YOU FROM THE BOTTOM OF MY HEART!" Because of you, we WILL make changes and lives WILL be saved!!!

People are going out of their way to put things in place, such as the VERY HEAVY medicine drop-off box that will be at the Symposium tonight thanks to the Marietta Police Dept. So do a clean-out sometime today and bring your outdated and leftover meds to the Symposium with you tonight. Dispose of them properly.

I am amazed at what a PROFESSIONAL Symposium we have been able to put together and all WITHOUT A BUDGET! Donations have made the event tonight entirely possible. People have generously handed me blank checks and said, "Get whatever you need for the Symposium, and if there is leftover, put it in the basket for donations to the DDF at the end of the night." WOW – UNBELIEVABLE!

There is a list of businesses and groups of people on the back of the program tonight at the Symposium, and you will see who they are – I won't even begin to attempt to re-create the list. But please say a HUGE THANK YOU to each and every company/individual/group/ and every volunteer you see tonight because they have invested their time and talent into the cause of opiate/heroin awareness and change.

They are the ones on the front lines making a difference for our community. AND, I have been told that word of our Symposium has made its way down to the "BLUFF" (the most heroin accessible place we know of in our area), and the people who volunteer in the "Bluff" on a weekly basis are applauding our efforts! WE ARE MAKING A DIFFERENCE!

6/4/14 – Constructive Act # 76 – Sharpen the Saw

Last night was completely amazing!!! There were over 450 people in attendance, and the night ran as smoothly as any event I have ever attended. Thank you to ALL of the many volunteers who came and stayed for the entire time and absolutely ran the event, while the presenters – including myself – were allowed to concentrate solely on our presentations. We absolutely reached our GOAL, and our Foundation is now "OPEN FOR BUSINESS." Thank you to all of the generous people in attendance who donated to the Davis Direction Foundation. There is continued work to do and it WILL get done!

However, today is "Sharpen the Saw" day. Stephen Covey writes in the "7 Habits of Highly Effective People" that every now and then, you need to take a break to regenerate and renew. If you chop wood with a dull axe, it will take you twice as long to chop a load. So, take a break and sharpen the axe -- and work smarter, not harder. I will renew my spirit today and continue with a more productive fervor.

I know there are things that need to be done, and now is a great time to regroup and chart our path so that we can begin to offer some solutions to the crisis we are dealing with. Last night's goal was that of awareness for not only the drug, but also the changes that need to be made dealing with the drug and the crisis it has created. I believe we accomplished that goal. Now we need to begin finding solutions to address those changes that need to be made.

Thanks to the many organizations that came bringing materials and information to distribute in order to help make a difference. The more people who join our crusade, the more progress we will make. Spread the word – We are going to Make A Difference! Now, off to visit my Mom.

6/5/14 – Constructive Act # 77 – Celebrate Accomplishments

Every day that a former opiate/heroin addict stays in recovery is an accomplishment and deserves celebration. Just like they say at the end of the Serenity Prayer, "Just for Today." Celebrations are often overdone in life, and as a counselor I get that. But as a mother of a child who died of an overdose, I say if your child is in "active" recovery they deserve to be CELEBRATED every day! If they relapse, support them, help them get back on track, and look at the new options available medically in order to help them sustain their recovery. Statistics show that relapse is almost a given for an opiate addict…BUT you only fail when you stop trying! We WILL figure this crisis out and you WILL RECOVER!!! New research is being done every day.

There are a few other celebrations that are in order this week as well, and I would like to list a few. Tuesday night we Made a Difference!

At the Symposium
- We announced 10 digital billboards in operation, donated by CBS Outdoors.
- We raised over $6,500.00 for the DDF.
- We opened eyes throughout the community.
- We had doctors re-examining their pain protocols.
- We networked with other organizations for the cause.

- We gave our first award – Congrats Det. D. Raissi!
- We had over 450 people attend our Symposium.
- We reached more people through the newspaper – MDJ.
- We distributed published information in the community.
- We put Recovery Resources to work in a positive way.
- We announced our 2nd Symposium: Oct. 8, 2014.

As a result of the Symposium

Police Departments in attendance are looking for ways to get Naloxone in patrol cars. Cherokee County PD Chief inquired about our Symposium being brought to his community. Recovery Resources and families of addicts in attendance now have a recovery kit in their hands. Community residents of all ages are asking how to become involved with this crisis. The Davis Direction Foundation became an "operating" foundation according to the criteria of Cobb Community Foundation. Our Facebook page members are growing rapidly.

This Foundation is moving and shaking, and we are EXPECTING great things to happen in the way of solutions for this crisis. Get on board with us and be a part of the growing number of people in our community who are educating themselves and others in order to be a part of the solution.

Continue to read and share the DDF page and website, and don't forget to CELEBRATE the great things that are happening.

6/6/14 – Constructive Act # 78 – Do Your Own Research

Remember that so-called experts are often just "legends in their own minds." I have found that in my 54 years of life that there are "experts" and then there are "experts." What I mean is, do you even know what an expert is? By definition it is someone having comprehensive or authoritative knowledge in a particular area. The true "experts" in this opiate/heroin crisis are the addicts. They are the only ones who know exactly what it means to be addicted to the drugs. I know that on a day when Davis would "bare his soul" to us, we would gain knowledge about what it meant to be an addict. I remember one day him telling us that his soul didn't belong in his body. WOW – that's powerful to be so conflicted. I can't even imagine. And unless you are an addict or have been an addict, you can't imagine either.

My point is that if we are going to try and make a difference and find solutions to this opiate/heroin crisis, then the ones who have experience with these drugs will be our greatest asset. We cannot begin to fix what we have not experienced without their help. They are NOT bad people. They got caught up in a situation, for whatever reason, that spiraled out of control very quickly. Now they have options but no real solutions. To my knowledge, there is NO solution, NO addiction counselor, NO drug, NO therapy of any kind with a 100% success rate in treating opiate/heroin addicts. I know that 100% is very rare in any field, but we are not even close.

If you go onto Erowid.org or Bluelight.org, you will be on websites that are written and maintained by addicts. That is where the real information or the "expert" information is. That is where the majority of the people on the websites will tell you that if they had it to do over again, they would NEVER EVER take the first dose. This is where you will get the best sense of what an addict goes through or what an addict thinks.

If you are living with an addict, or are working closely with those in recovery, LISTEN to them! They will help us with what we need to know. They WANT help. They WANT a cure. They WANT to be "normal" again. The problem is that once you become a "pickle," you can never go back to being a "cucumber."

At least not now! Keep reading and educating yourself. Keep listening and talking with the "experts" to understand how to help. We WILL Make a Difference.

6/7/14 – Constructive Act # 79 – Know the Stats

A heroin addict takes an average of four – six relapses before they will actually stop (if they can live that long). The first time they quit and go back to heroin (and most do), it is called a "lapse." After they quit again, and each time they go back and stop, is called a "relapse." Davis was in the "lapse" phase when he died. It was his fist time to quit and start back. He was in active outpatient therapy nine hours a week and meeting with a counselor and a minister each week. He was surrounded by family and was included in everything that we did together. It was not enough! Heroin is a strong addiction and an even stronger craving when you stop, especially for the first 32 weeks. That's eight months that the cravings don't seem to weaken at all, and it is the most vital part of recovery. It's not an easy journey and everyone involved – the addict and those who are helping him – must realize this.

I think one of the biggest mistakes we made was in the fact that Davis had no job, he was out of school, and he had no one with him during the day when he was home. He must have been lonely, and with his self-worth at an all-time low because of what he was going through, I know he felt worthless and hopeless. He told me so. The images of him with his head in his hands hiding in a place where he thought no one could find him is one of the reasons I move forward with such passion. I cannot bear to think of young people going through that kind of pain. I didn't know how to help him other than to tell him I loved him and hold him and let him cry it out. In a lot of ways, heroin addiction is like being in remission from cancer: You know you are "clean" for the moment, but you live scared to death that at any moment, the monster will rear its ugly head again.

We have to start thinking outside of the box in order to make a difference. We need a paradigm shift in how we think. We have spent years hearing the same story and the ending remains the same.

Try something different if you are going through this. In one rehab article I read, it said that there are as many forms of addiction as there are individuals who are addicted to heroin. Everyone must find their own end to this journey and it won't be easy. Find a way to stabilize and maintain while you are searching for your "ending." Don't give up or let your loved one give up. Understand that the consequences along the way will NOT be pretty, but if you come out on the other end, it will be worth everything you endured to get there. Godspeed on your journey and my prayers are with you.

6/8/14 – Constructive Act # 80 – Revisit Rehab

On October 8th, we will have our second Symposium and the topic will be the "Continuum of Care." Rehab will be a large part of this symposium. You need to come prepared and educated to understand and ask questions because the right people will be in place to answer those questions. There are lots of websites out there reviewing rehab centers and offering new programs outside of the 12-step model.

One of the most interesting books I have seen and plan to read to prepare myself is Anne Fletcher's "Inside Rehab." She puts lots of statistics out there dealing with success, and she also offers options to users and families. Although she deals with rehab in general, she does talk specifically about different kinds of addicts.

Personally, I think rehab has got to deal with the physical, the emotional, and the mental in order to work. I also think that individual therapy should be a large part of treatment, but the addicts need to be around others who are sharing their struggles as well. Many experts in the field are now beginning to realize that drug therapy may be necessary to give opiate addicts the jump-start they need to STAY in recovery. We also need to think about sending our young people in recovery home with a rescue kit of Naloxone because -- let's be real -- statistics show as of right now, most opiate addicts relapse an average of four times.

We need to think outside the box and ask our experts – "addicts" and "Recovery Resources" – what in their opinions would constitute the most successful rehab setting and ongoing groups for them to join. The DDF is putting together a survey for them to respond to, and we have results to share at the Oct. 8th Symposium. Mark your calendars now to attend.

6/9/14 – Constructive Act # 81 – Be Constructive

Constructive is a key word when it comes to rehab. It doesn't take a rocket scientist to figure out that addicts are a defensive breed. They are trying to protect themselves, their habits, and many times their families. If you attack them verbally, or non-verbally, the therapy is over and the defense comes into play. When Davis was in rehab, I attended every meeting that I was allowed to attend, and of course the counselor in me was there to listen and learn. The mother in me was also there to listen and learn, and I listened and learned in both roles. As a mother, I listened as children opened up and tried to help each other. I listened as children gave "in your face" remarks to everybody there as they thought they had beaten and conquered the system. Often times they bragged about how they had "won" battles with parents, friends, schools, and other addicts. On the other hand, I heard remorse, sincere grief, and anxiety about a life that these great kids were unprepared for. I heard that they were "sick and tired" of being "sick and tired." My son never spoke a work during these meetings. I know he listened and I know he heard what others were saying. Often we would talk about the meetings after they were over and he would have distinct opinions about things being said. Why did he never talk? That is easy: He had been shut down by judgmental counselors who forgot they were there to listen and encourage the kids to open up about their feelings. They forgot they were there to allow a kid to ask questions and challenge the status quo. They forgot they were there to look at all angles and walk a mile in someone else's shoes. They forgot they were there to help.

I watched with my own eyes as one night something was said in group and a counselor looked over her shoulder, raising her eyebrows at my son as if to say, "I told you so! Are you listening?" Well, as you can imagine, the therapy for him was over with that one look from her. At that point it became all about her and her shortcomings and faults. Could she not have waited for a private moment to ask about the point she was trying to make? Could she not have waited on him to possibly bring up what he had heard? NO – she had to call him out in front of every peer, parent, and other counselor in the room. How unprofessional. This practice goes against everything I was ever taught. It is an automatic shut-down and it serves no purpose.

The point is, when counseling and/or rehab become less than constructive, you are wasting your time and your money. You MUST find someone your addict connects with and trusts. They need a confidant and a mentor. That's why "sponsors" were started many years ago.

The most important trait of a counselor, sponsor, mentor, whatever, is that that person must be CONSTRUCTIVE. We need to keep our addicts and our Recovery Resources moving in a positive direction. Everything we say and do in working with them has to be CONSTRUCTIVE. These kids have seen enough destruction to last a lifetime; we have to help them grow into the awesome adults they are meant to be and can be. That can only happen by being CONSTRUCTIVE!

6/10/14 – Constructive Act # 82 – Validate

I think one of the biggest problems with opiates/heroin is that once you are hooked on either of them, it is so shameful. Nobody wants to talk about it. Nobody understands what you are going through, and instead of talking about it and trying to figure out how to help and what to do, the lies, deceit, manipulation, and withdrawal begin. That's one of the biggest problems in my opinion. The addict begins to pull away, and I know sometimes when they are not around, you get to be just a little bit normal for a short period of time. This addiction will change everything about the way you live and exist for the entire family.

Since we are looking for solutions, I believe you have to validate the addict and the effects of the drug. Let them know that you understand that it is for the most part out of their control. As long as they continue to use, they will continue with the behaviors listed above. I believe that if we had validated Davis and the effects of the drug, he MIGHT have opened up to us a little more and let us in to his world. He hated being in the "vise grip" of heroin, but he wasn't strong enough to make a change. Although he continued to try many times, the drug always won out in the end.

The lack of money to buy drugs is what creates a lot of the terrible behavior. If the drugs grew out in the backyard and everyone had easy access, many of the problems would go away. So many of the users are in prison for stealing to get the drug as opposed to just using the drug.

If you truly believe that it is a DISEASE, and I believe it is, then you have to validate the addict and learn to help them on their terms until they can work on yours. This part is the hard part and that is why there is still such a disconnect. Many people don't believe that addiction is a disease, and as long as that is true, the addicts will continue to feel shame and disgust for themselves due to societal pressure.

Find a doctor who is willing to work with you and your addict for the physical addiction component and let the medical world in on this disease.

With what other disease is the doctor completely left out of the treatment process? When we begin to validate the addict and treat the disease as we would any other disease, then we might begin to get some answers.

Yes, we do need the psychiatrists in on this as well, but the "physical doctors" have got to be included. It is not an emotional/mental disease only. There are lots of physical components as well. I know that while Davis was using, he got an ear infection. Because we had not let the physical doctor in on our situation, he walked out with opiate pain killers for his earache. That would never have happened if the doctor had known what he was dealing with. Personally, I feel that before prescribing opiates, the doctor should have to do an opiate test on the patient to determine if they already have opiates in their system…but that's another post on another day. For today, VALIDATE your addict and get everyone on the same page with the same belief system. Then, just maybe, conversations will begin that lead to solutions due to the fact that the door has been opened to honesty because of VALIDATION.

6/11/14 – Constructive Act # 83 – Educate and Advocate

As I accompanied my mom to a doctor's appointment yesterday morning to have a very minor surgery on her hand, I was amazed at what I witnessed. To begin with, the surgical center was a very nice, clean, and well-run center. The employees could not have been nicer and the doctor himself was extremely well mannered and as nice as he could be. But what happened at checkout nearly took my breath away.

After the surgery was complete and Mom was ready to leave from recovery, the discharge nurse came over to complete the discharge. She handed Mom her papers for recovery and a prescription for "pain medication." Being the well-intended daughter that I thought I should be, I asked the nurse, "Was the prescription for pain an opiate?" The nurse gave me a somewhat puzzled look and asked, "What's that?" I nearly fell out of the chair I was sitting in. A surgical nurse older than myself just asked me what an opiate was. I told her that I was concerned that Mom might have been prescribed an opiate, which was an addictive drug. She assured me that Norco was very safe and a very low dose of a narcotic. REALLY?

Norco is a form of Hydrocodone. Here is what the first Google pop-up has to say: "Norco contains a combination of acetaminophen and hydrocodone. Hydrocodone is an opioid pain medication. An opioid is sometimes called a narcotic.

Acetaminophen is a less potent pain reliever that increases the effects of hydrocodone.

Norco is used to relieve moderate to severe pain. Norco may also be used for purposes not listed in this medication guide.

Hydrocodone can slow or stop your breathing. Never use Norco in larger amounts, or for longer than prescribed. Narcotic pain medicine may be habit-forming, even at regular doses. Never share Norco with another person, especially someone with a history of drug abuse or addiction. Keep the medication in a place where others cannot get to it.

MISUSE OF NARCOTIC MEDICINE CAN CAUSE ADDICTION, OVERDOSE, OR DEATH, especially in a child or other person using the medicine without a prescription."

Now I ask you, did my mom really need a prescription for an opiate for a one-half inch incision in her hand? I don't know. I'll be honest and be the first to tell you that I don't want my mom to be in pain for any reason. She has never had addiction issues and is probably one of the most anti-medication people you will ever meet. She even told me herself that she did not need those pills. But did she really need to walk away with a prescription for "35" pills for pain? We'll see! Even if she is in pain, should she have been warned about opiates and the fact that they are addictive and that if she does not use them all, she needs to dispose of them properly and then tell her what properly is? NONE of this happened. Did anyone at the clinic warn her that people in epidemic numbers are stealing and selling these pills, and then DYING from overdoses!!! NO – NO ONE MENTIONED A WORD!

My mom is in her eighth decade and is from an era when doctors were trusted friends for the most part and never questioned. Those days are gone, friends! Speak up! Ask questions! Advocate for your parents! Our elders are suffering from addiction needlessly and this is a perfect example why. We have got to change things! Perhaps opiates should be prescribed in lesser amounts. Perhaps contracts should be signed outlining all of the dangers of opiates (as happened in a local doctor's office this week according to one of my friends).

Here is what a well-respected neurosurgeon wrote in an email after attending our first Symposium this past week:

"Personally and professionally, this was an eye-opener. As a neurosurgeon that performs spinal procedures, it has been so matter-in-fact for me to prescribe opioids – the goal being to alleviate as much of my patients' pain as possible. So many in that auditorium are dealing with the downstream destructive effects of the medications, that I as the upstream gatekeeper prescribe. There is no doubt that some (too much) of what I have prescribed has fallen into the wrong hands over the last seven years of my practice. It will definitely make me re-examine how I prescribe and how I guide people through their physical pain."

WOW! I wish more doctors would take this man's lead and just ask themselves, "Is what I have prescribed really necessary, and is the quantity that I prescribed realistic?" That's all! Just stop and think about what you are doing.

Friends, ADVOCATE and EDUCATE your elder parents. Tell them these medications need to be under lock and key and that if the pain continues after several days, they need to re-connect with the doctor and re-evaluate. I'm still VERY upset over the happenings of yesterday. THINGS HAVE GOT TO CHANGE!

6/12/14 – Constructive Act # 84 – Take Every Opportunity

Whenever you have an opportunity to go to bat for the cause, you need to take that opportunity and make the most of it. I have been asked to do an interview with WSB TV again tomorrow. They want to focus on the billboard campaign and the awareness and changes we are trying to bring about. I thought long and hard about this interview because of getting "burned" last time I did an interview. The story was spun into a media frenzy about a "grieving mother on the hunt for a drug dealer." That was such a stretch from what was intended.

Although we don't have control over the media and how a story might come out in final print or preview, if we get through to one person, we have to rest in the fact that what we did made a difference for that one person. I decided when all of this started that I would put it in God's hands and allow Him to use me and the Foundation in whatever way He saw fit. Everyone associated with this foundation and the decision-making processes involved has the same feeling and intention.

We do what we do and then let God do the rest. He has been so good to us so far, and things continue to come our way in the form of opportunities and gifts. Our very young foundation (which is not even three months old) has already been gifted with beautiful artwork from Jason Gribble of Formetco Inc. and billboards

from CBS OUTDOOR to display it. We have not incurred one dime for any of this effort. We have had vendors come forward to donate profits back to the foundation, while at the same time making beautiful items to sell for advertisement. Thanks to GraceGirlBeads for the beautiful signature jewelry and Ogorzaly Originals for donating hats and t-shirts so that when we represent our foundation, we can look official and advertise at the same time. Visual Images Ad

Specialties, Inc. did a huge rush order for us for t-shirts and then did many items that were donated for door prizes and presenter gifts. All of these people have fallen into our lap and made us better and more professional.

We will continue to take every opportunity afforded us by the media, the newspaper, other organizations who are asking us to partner with them on projects, doctors, pharmacists, parents, and addicts in order to make a difference. These opportunities are what will put us in the forefront of the opiate/heroin addiction crisis and allow us the opportunity to make a difference. If you are offered an opportunity to help make a difference in any way, you should embrace that opportunity as well and possibly save a life. We don't need to lose one more life to this deadly epidemic. Always be willing to help. My daddy always told me, "What goes around, comes around." Hopefully our good will bring about good for the foundation and allow us to make a difference on a grander scale than we ever imagined.

Please continue to follow us on our Facebook page or our website, and if an opportunity comes up that you think would allow us to help make a difference in our community, please notify us and expect us to be there to make a difference, even if it is only for one person.

6/13/14 – Constructive Act #85 – Know Your Alternatives

At the Symposium on June 3rd, we had a question and answer session. We did not get around to answering all of the questions, and this was one of them: "What are alternative pain killers that are NOT addictive?" Here are three alternatives: Motrin, Anaprox and Toradol. All of these are prescription strength, anti-inflammatory drugs. If you are having a minor surgery done, ask your doctor to start with one of these pain relievers.

If you find that they are not working and you are in unbearable pain, then request something stronger, BUT always inquire about the drugs you have been prescribed and if they are addictive.

When you are done with the medication, return the leftover drugs to a dropbox and dispose of them properly and safely. REMEMBER, most prescription drug abuse BEGINS IN THE HOME!

6/14/14 – Constructive Act #86 – Don't Sweat the Small Stuff

This morning I know I am late with my post, and I have been worried about it all morning. I went out to breakfast with my husband and I got one of my kiddos off to take the ACT and I needed to pick up a few things while we were out. All morning all I could think of was, I really need to write my CA for today. People are waiting on it and looking for it and it's not there! Maybe the importance of the CA is a little overblown in my head, but I wanted it out there early this morning.

Sometimes I think all of us "over-blow" things in our own heads. We all need to take a step back and ask ourselves, "What's the worst thing that could happen because of what I did or didn't do?" That's a counseling technique that I use with my students a lot and it helps them to put things into perspective. Usually they kind of raise their eyebrows and say, "Well, I guess it's not as bad as I thought." Things that stress us out often have very little significance in the grand scheme of life, but we let them build up and take over our thought processes and our lives until we feel that we need help coping.

There is an "anecdote" that has been around for a very long time that starts off like this…

> One hundred years from now
> It won't matter
> What kind of car I drove
> What kind of house I lived in
> How much money I had in the bank
> Nor what my clothes looked like

Those lines are very true, but what comes next is the part that we all need to write for ourselves. The part that will matter. What matters to me may not matter to you and vice versa, but something should "matter" for all of us and we need to figure out what it is.

We need to focus on what the BIG picture holds for each of us and let the stress of daily life go. Sure, it may inconvenience others or ourselves from time to time, but hopefully people will be understanding about those times. Nothing is so important in this life that we should ever turn to drugs to help us make it through. Learn to share your stresses with a friend or a loved one that can offer help, or put you in touch with a professional who is trained to help you if your stress turns into anxiety or depression, or God forbid, abuse that you can't handle. Even in the darkest situations, there is help if you seek it out, and you can usually find it for free.

DON'T SWEAT THE SMALL STUFF. IT WILL MAKE YOU LOSE SIGHT OF WHAT IS TRULY IMPORTANT.

6/15/14 – Constructive Act #87 – Reconnect

It is a fact that addiction causes separation. People are often afraid and they are tired of the person they used to know not being that person anymore. They are tired of being robbed and taken advantage of, and they turn their backs for many reasons. Whether it is a physical separation or an emotional separation, either way it breaks hearts. So today, on this special "Father's Day," – reconnect. Lay it all out on the table. Try to understand your addict's plight. They are someone they never intended to become and they don't know how to get back.

There is a song called "Dig" that Davis used to play, and here are some of the lyrics:

So when sickness turns my ego up

I know you'll act as a clever medicine.

If I turn into another

Dig me up from under what is covering

The better part of me.

Sing this song!

Remind me that we'll always have each other

When everything else is gone.

Oh each other...

When everything

Else is gone.

One day, I hope we can figure out what that clever medicine is and how to dig our beautiful children and loved ones up from under what is covering the better part of them.

I know my sweet husband will have a bittersweet day today as he is missing one of his best friends, his firstborn son. I know there is a precious little girl who will not have her "Daddy" today to put her arms around and tell him "Happy Father's Day." She will never have him again because of this horrible addiction. It is too late for my family because my precious child is gone. He knew we loved him although we didn't understand what he was going through at the time.

Don't let the separation of the disease destroy the relationship you had or have with your child. Reconnect today and let them know you love them and you will help them in the best way you know how. No one has the answers; if they did, we would not be talking about it. We are still searching and hoping every day for an answer, but until we have one, DON'T turn your back. You may be all that is left for your loved one. RECONNECT and RESOLVE the separation and find a way to help and love the person you used to know. They are still there. WE JUST HAVE TO DIG.

6/16/14 – Constructive Act #88 – Know When to Take Action

This may be one of the hardest decisions to make when working or living with an addict. I know we never knew when to take action, and that was largely due to not knowing what action to take when we knew it was time. The problem with taking action a lot of times is that when a kid turns 18, you can no longer make decisions for them. They have to make them for themselves. Now we both know that when an addict is high, he or she is in no condition to "Take Action."

I remember one morning very vividly when I knew in my heart Davis was on something and could hardly keep his eyes open. I asked him to help me haul some trash off to the recycle place, and a grill was among one of the things we were hauling off. Davis was for the most part a "jack of all trades" due to his daddy teaching him so much of what he knew. He definitely knew how to tie down stuff in the back of a truck, but when we pulled out of the neighborhood, the grill went in about a thousand directions. We were picking it up off of a very busy road and it was a scary thing.

When we got back home, he kept nodding off while he was making a sandwich. I was very scared and I didn't know exactly what to do. I was embarrassed to take him to my personal doctor, and I was embarrassed and ashamed to call around to drug testing places to ask questions and make appointments.

So I called Michael and he made the phone calls. I ended up taking Davis to a drug screen. That was quite an experience. If you try twice and can't give a sample, they send you on your way. Well, what addict knowing that information is not going to fail twice. So I went into "Mama" mode and begged them to let him try until he gave a sample.

Long story short, he gave a sample, but I had no idea that it only checked for illegal drugs and that they would only report to him – not me. Luckily we were with him when the call came into my phone and we put it on speaker phone while they told him the results. It was negative for opiates and they only screened for illegal drugs anyway. He later told us that he had taken Xanax and it all made sense.

We knew it was time to take action, but we obviously took the wrong action. I made him sleep on the sofa in front of me the rest of the day because I wasn't sure how close to an overdose he was. I still don't know, but I kept watching him breathe and even woke him up from time to time to make sure I could.

I guess the point to this very long post is follow your gut! STOP being embarrassed and ashamed and let's stand together for answers. When we decided to go public with all of this information, the whole family agreed we would do it to help others like us who had no experience with drug addiction. On the DDF, people have been SUPER encouraging and we have helped so many people – parents, friends, and addicts included. One day I will post anonymously the comments people have made.

In the mainstream media when we go public with a story, people can be brutal and it's those people who continue to make drug abuse so secretive because they create the feelings causing embarrassment and shame. I have drawn my own conclusions about those people and I will keep them to myself for obvious reasons. But I can tell you this – they are not worth the life of one more child!!! When you are worried about your child, "TAKE ACTION."

6/17/14 – Constructive Act #89 – Follow Your Gut

When you are living with an addict or your loved one is an addict living away from you and you know something in your heart or "GUT", don't let other people who are not living your life call the shots for you! It's so easy to want to believe what you know isn't true when your loved one or your child is an addict.

On the night Davis never came home, I knew something was very wrong. Even the next morning, I knew what I knew in my heart. I continued to let people tell me it would be okay and that he would come home – and it delayed our actions, even though at that point it probably would not have mattered.

Just for the record, you do NOT have to wait a certain period of time before making a missing person's report. There is a belief out there that you have to wait for 24 – 48 hours. NOT TRUE!

Make a plan with your addict when they are thinking logically (and they do from time to time) about when you will touch base throughout the day or week. If you do not hear from them and you cannot find them and you have that feeling in your gut, DON'T WAIT – Take Action! It could save a life.

People want to help you feel better, and that's why they will never go to the deep dark corners of life with you. Make your own decisions when you know there is something wrong. Your friends' intentions are good and well meaning, but they don't have the experience and background that you do with the addict's habits, thoughts, and activities.

If the addict is found, they are encouraged to touch base with you, but that is all the police can do. If you don't hear from the police, that is a good thing – HIPAA at work! (Did I mention that I hate HIPAA?) The police truly want to help find these kids and they work very hard to locate missing persons, especially as soon as they are called in. Make sure when your addict leaves the house – if they are living with you – that you know what they are wearing and anything else about them that could help identify them.

As soon as the location services were turned off on the phone, I should have filed the report or gone looking myself – at least that's what my GUT said.

6/18/14 – Constructive Act #90 – Give of Your Time

This one can be a hard one with an addict. In the beginning, everyone wants to help the person get back on track and include them in everything they do. The problem is that more often than not, the addict – at least in Davis's case – would decline the offers of inclusion. After hearing "no thanks" so many times, you begin to think, "There's no point in asking him to go. He'll only say no." Then you STOP asking! Davis's two brothers spent a weekend at school at which they didn't ask Davis to join them. We are ALL quite sure he would have said NO, but the fact remains that he wasn't invited.

On the other hand, an addict usually asks very little of others – at least in Davis's case. They are used to being alone, and in the beginning, it is still very hard for them to assimilate back into their previous life (meaning before the drugs). They are often full of anxiety and depression. We wanted our Davis from two years ago back!

The day before Davis left the house for the last time, he asked his sister and his dad to go running with him. Looking back, he was probably trying to fight the craving of extreme addiction. His sister was studying, trying to finish her last semester in school, and his dad was busy catching up on chores over the weekend. Both of them declined the offer (which by the way was in the heat of the day) and said maybe later or next time. Both of them wish they had gone running that day, of course. They both have said on more than one occasion, "If I had only gone running." Another "What IF." On the other hand, they had both asked him to go running with them on numerous occasions when he had declined.

His sponsor was also a student and had limited time to help or talk, and although when he told Davis the times he was available, often Davis did not reach out during those times.

The truth is that we ALL second guess our decisions that were made prior to his death on a daily basis, and we wish we could have done more to help him. When you are living with an addict, you live on eggshells, never knowing what to expect from day to day.

I'm certainly NOT saying that you should stop living your life and live for the addict. But what I am saying is that, if at all possible, when an addict reaches out to you, give of your time and attention whenever you can. AND if you are an addict, you MUST advocate for yourself. Remember to "TELL ON IT" if you NEED someone, then tell that person you NEED them as opposed to just WANTing to be with them. It has to work both ways. NEVER stop asking if you are the support person and NEVER stop telling if you are the addict. Either way, it just takes a few minutes of time to ask or tell. What happens next could save a life.

6/19/14 – Constructive Act #91 – Seek First to Understand

I think one of the most important things that anyone can learn to do is "LISTEN." I know as a counselor I have been trained with so many different disciplines to just listen, but my family will probably tell you I am a terrible listener. Why? Because I don't listen to them as a counselor; I listen as a wife and mother. That is way different. I listen with the intent to control, advise, and change. I DON'T seek first to understand and listen with my heart. I am trying to do better.

I think at the end when Davis was finally opening up to me about his disease, I finally began to LISTEN. I learned several things: I learned that he was scared. I learned he was helpless. I learned that he knew what he was doing was high risk. I learned that he was doing everything in his power to try and beat his addiction. I learned that he loved his family more than anything in the world. I learned that he would have given everything to go back to the day he had taken that first pill. I learned all these things because I finally started listening.

If you are lucky enough to still have your addict here on this earth, LEARN TO LISTEN! It really is a skill that has to be worked on. The earlier that you learn to listen to your children, the sooner it will become a habit that you will enjoy for the rest of your life. Learn also NOT to make judgmental comments about others, because if and when those same comments can apply to your own family, you will have already shut down the conversation that you need to have. Kids remember how you feel about situations and people by the comments you make. Guard your words and judgments because you may need to use them constructively one day.

I am posting a link to Stephen Covey, the guru of being a "Highly Effective" person. He explains why it is so hard to listen and how you can become better at it. Learning to listen will be the greatest goal you will ever accomplish.

www.stephencovey.com/7habits/7habits-habit5.php

6/20/14 – Constructive Act #92 – Bring Happiness to the Table

This little anecdote is so true. Living as an addict or a family member supporting an addict is so hard because there is not a lot of happiness to be found. There is heartache and pain for the most part and a complete and eternal yearning for things to be different and better.

When it's possible, and I realize it is NOT always possible, bring happiness to the table. Whether it's in a relationship, a job, or as a parent, try to focus on the positive and try to be the one who brings joy.

Even in the last months of living with Davis, there were moments I will treasure always – laughing at Uncle Si together, silly faces and voices, hugs, smiles, jokes, working together on a project, singing hymns in church, pushing wheelchairs filled with sweet little ladies at the nursing home, shopping at the grocery store, working in the garden, deep conversations about God, but mostly that infectious smile and contagious love. He tried so hard to be the smiling dog when he could, and I believe that is what others remember most. The memories shared and posted are those of my happy, beautiful son, the one who brought joy to others and the one I choose to remember. Maybe if there were more people who brought happiness to others, there wouldn't be so many people looking for a way to stop the stress and pain of daily life through drug use.

Take a second to read this all the way through. Which dog are you?

http://belegendary.org/blog/2014/01/08/the-story-of-2-dogs/

6/21/14 – Constructive Act #93 – Teach Your Kids

I know in this fast paced world we live in, it's sometimes easier to just hire others to "fix" our daily problems (like cars, plumbing, squeaks and jams), but I know for a fact that my husband has saved our family thousands of dollars over the years of our marriage because he had these skills (and we didn't have money). It also seems that kids these days don't have any of the skills that we learned as young adults to help save money. They are too busy studying, doing community service, playing video games, watching TV, adding new apps to the phone, or on the computer.

Instead of making a peanut butter sandwich and pouring a glass of milk for lunch, they feel like they need to run to the nearest fast food restaurant in order to have lunch. They are definitely an entitled generation.

As I was sitting in the barber shop with my husband this morning, he handed me an article to read from Popular Mechanics titled "The 25 Skills You Should Teach Your Kid" by Walker Lamond. It didn't differentiate based on gender either. I do however think that girls of my generation didn't learn most of these skills due to the fact that skills were still very stereotyped "back in the day" as the kids say. Anyway, I would like for my girls and guys to know all 25!

It is my belief that the kids we have raised that fall into the "heroin at-risk age group" (18 – 36) are part of the "Y Generation" who expect immediate gratification. They also have very little patience for anything out of order, thus self-medicating. They can't handle the stress of things being out of order (sadly, this does not include their rooms). They have also not been taught to creatively figure out alternative solutions to problems or to use higher order thinking skills. For goodness sakes, 90% of all the tests kids take are still asking for answers that they can find in 10 seconds or less on Google! I guarantee you that if you gave tests in US schools and let the kids use Google, we would indeed be the leading nation in K-12 once again!

Why is this happening? Because kids don't know how things work!!! I know I'm getting off on my soapbox here, but it's true! We have so much to teach our kids. Why not insist that they help you or even their grandparents – who are also very skilled for the most part! We need more hands on learning!!!

I also think that rehabs should take a good long look at this list. I know Davis and his buddies sat around on the weekends with NOTHING to do! They were so bored that Davis asked us to bring him his Nintendo, which we did. At least they had fun together building relationships as opposed to sleeping because they had nothing else to do! I've said before that "Idle Hands are the Devil's Workshop" and it's true! I know in a community like ours, you could get numerous volunteers to come and teach in rehab settings. Learn some skills that will make you valuable! Hopefully, the next time this article is reprinted, it will be titled "25 Skills Every Dad (OR MOM) Should Teach His Kids." Just Sayin'.

6/22/14 – Constructive Act #94 – Buy a Prescription Lockbox

With the growing number of heroin addicts starting their addiction with prescription drugs, invest in a lockbox for ALL prescription drugs. They are very affordable and very necessary if you have to have prescription pain meds in your home.

I know for a fact that Davis took pain medications from our home, from his Grandmother's home and from his Friends' homes. All of this prescription abuse could have been prevented with a prescription lockbox. I know that you shouldn't have to lock up your personal belongings in your own home to protect them from others, but it is the same as a loaded gun. People are dying from the abuse of prescription opiates, and they are taking them from others who have prescriptions for them whenever possible.

Prescription opiates have become extremely expensive to buy on the streets (anywhere from $40 – $80 per pill), which is causing people to either take them from people's homes or switch to heroin.

Protect your medications FOR yourself and FROM those who maybe be abusing them. It's a good practice and it may save a life!

www.lockmed.com/product_p/asa-950.htm

6/23/14 – Constructive Act # 95 – Check Your Progress

So with that being said, let's check the progress of the DDF. Let's see if we can get all 50 states to reply. If you have liked the DDF Facebook page or you have seen it and read it from time to time, please reply to this post with your city and state. I know we have been overseas at least to Norway and Colombia, but I would love to know how many of the "Fifty Nifty United States" we have been in and how many states are aware of what we are trying to accomplish.

It's important to understand your progress and be able to measure it. Even as an addict, you should be making small steps every day to recovery. How do you measure that? I don't know; I'm asking! This week, I will be meeting with a leading Recovery Director in our area to come up with a survey for addicts and former addicts to take. We are hoping to get some answers to help with making a difference with this epidemic. It is always necessary and useful to do a needs assessment and truly ask the people who need the help exactly what kind of help they need.

When the survey is ready, we will be asking those of you who are in need of help or continued recovery to take the survey. Hopefully it will give us a starting point to be able to address the needs of opiate/heroin users and recovering addicts. From there we will be able to chart our progress and see how we are doing. If we aren't making as big of a difference as we would like, we will back up and shoot from a different angle. Data is a good thing when you need to make a difference. It's your roadmap to guide your journey.

Let's figure out where the DDF journey has taken us so far, then we will be able to tell where we need work. Give us a shout on Facebook with your city and state and let's see where we are making a difference. Thanks for taking part in our data collection! If we need something in your neck of the woods, we may be calling on you! READY, SET, GO!

6/24/14 – Constructive Act #96 – Be Persistent

It took six posts, several texts, and a couple of phone calls yesterday to reach the goal I had set in my head for how many states we had readers and supporters in. I knew from private messages, comments, and "likes" on the DDF that we had readers in at least half of the United States and even in foreign countries as well. I was bound and determined to make sure that the statistics reflected what I knew.

In a lot of ways since Davis died, I don't care about things that I may not have done in the past. I would not have been as persistent about many things, and I would not have asked and then asked again if I had not been answered the first time. I would not have reached out to people I did not know and I certainly would not have launched a campaign or co-founded a foundation that I wanted to have a national and even international voice. I didn't think I had the strength or knowledge to make it happen. I wouldn't have known how to begin, and because I had not been directly affected by the problem, I would have, quite frankly, not chosen to be involved.

Then BOOM – all of a sudden I was involved, like so many others before me. The heartbreak and destruction that opiate/heroin abuse causes left me no choice but to become involved. These kids and young adults need help, and someone has to step up and help them. Through rehab, many of these people became friends with Davis, and he would have expected no less from me. He would have helped them if he had only known how.

So I will do whatever it takes to educate, create awareness, and make changes where they are needed. AND I won't apologize for my persistence. I also won't apologize because I am a white, middle class mom and this seems to be a white, middle class issue from what I have read. I do what I do because my son DIED needlessly and I want to help others…ALL OTHERS!

Everyone has a right to be involved or not be involved, and that is as it should be. But I'm tired of political correctness standing in the way of progress when it comes to saving the life of a child. It could be your child! There are people working around the clock (Harm Reduction Coalition) to change the fact the Naloxone (the drug that brings an opiate addict out of an overdose) is not readily available in every drugstore in every state. Do they all have children that died? NO, they do not. But they are PERSISTENT because it NEEDS to happen – and they are making great progress. Progress that could save your child!

There are law enforcement officers putting their lives on the line every day, being PERSISTENT in order to get this drug off the street and sellers behind bars. Do they all have children that died? No, they do not. But again, they are being PERSISTENT because it NEEDS to happen.

Addicts and their families need to become PERSISTENT in the search for a recovery program that works, whether it is individual counseling, an independent program, a rehab facility, a drug therapy, or something no one has even thought of or heard about yet. PERSISTENCE is what will get us all where we need to be. I will continue to be persistent with this cause and I will do it for others like my son who needed help and couldn't find it. We will find it, there is HOPE, and we WILL BE PERSISTENT.

6/25/14 – Constructive Act #97 – List Your Beliefs

I believe that whenever you are dealing with a problem or an issue either personally or publicly, it is imperative to decide what exactly you believe about the issue and then challenge those beliefs with the truth. I know that with addiction, there are plenty of different schools of thought. Specifically, with opiate/heroin addiction there are lots of beliefs as well, but there are also lots of unknowns!!! One of the main reasons there are so many heroin deaths is that you NEVER know exactly what you are getting when you start dealing with heroin. It is cut in many different ways and the amount of heroin in what you may have purchased and the ingredients that it was cut with can be vastly different. Knowing that information, you still have to decide what you believe about your addiction.

When listing your beliefs, I think the first question you have to answer is, Is opiate/heroin addiction a disease? I personally believe it is and I can support my belief. What do you believe and can you support it?

I further believe that opiate/heroin addiction is a stronger addiction that any other addiction we know of. I can support that belief as well.

Now, I know that I can support my beliefs, but that doesn't make me the authority. It just means that I have researched my beliefs enough to decide what I believe and why. Do I close my mind and ears to further research because I have made my decisions? ABSOLUTELY NOT! There is new research being released every day regarding opiate/heroin abuse and addiction. I would be a fool to be fighting a cause and not keep up with the daily information and findings about that cause.

Why is it important to know your beliefs? To begin with, your beliefs dictate how you will deal with your problem. They provide you with a starting point and a roadmap to work your way to your goal. I believe that if you are an opiate/heroin addict, your roadmap will take you down a different path than an alcoholic or a pot smoker. Just like you would not treat diabetes with radiation or cancer with insulin! You have to know your addiction and treat it individually!

If you are in a rehab facility and your choices do not include a different "roadmap" than that of an alcoholic, then perhaps you need to find one that does. I have found in researching rehab facilities for opiate/heroin addiction, lots of the opiate addicts are lumped in with every other addict regardless of their age, gender, or drug of choice. This is a belief that you will have to come to terms with as well. Personally, I don't believe that,"addiction is addiction." In my belief system, addiction comes in degrees of severity, and as an opiate/heroin addict, you need to find the right rehab for you. You also need to find a rehab that will help you navigate through assimilating back into the mainstream society. Aftercare is vitally important and often overlooked! It is perhaps the most important aspect for an opiate addict because of the continued and acute cravings. There are studies that show that four weeks to six months out of rehab for an opiate addict are the most dangerous times for an overdose and even death. That is the time period in which I lost my son.

Know what your beliefs are and then challenge those beliefs with research and healthcare providers and don't leave all the work up to others. KNOW WHAT YOU BELIEVE AND WHY!

6/26/14 – Constructive Act #98 – SYNERGIZE

Most of you have probably heard of the "Power of One." It is a very inspiring story of determination and the will to succeed. On every level, opiate/heroin addicts need to somehow find the 'Power of One" – that "one" being the addict. However, just as in the "Power of One," there is plenty of help and support along the way.

There are teachers, mentors, advocates, animals, role-models, and surrogates. On the other hand, there are also the bullies, the hard-core, the overbearing, and the non-believers. As an addict, I think you have to embrace ALL of these roles and let them help you reach your goal of RECOVERY.

Let your heart learn from the wonderful people in your life – those who encourage and support you. Let your head learn from the ones who discourage, berate and put you down. Think back to when you were very young; to get you to do something all your parents had to say was, "Don't you take a bite of that broccoli!" "Don't you pick up those dirty clothes!" "Don't you close your eyes and sleep!" That's all it took to get you to try or even pretend to try. Let the nay-sayers become the challengers and PROVE THEM WRONG! Some of the greatest accomplishments of our time have become reality because someone said it couldn't be done.

Let the supporters become your "Go-To's" and your inspiration; let them share in your success. Here again, some of the greatest accomplishments of our time have become reality because someone encouraged and believed in someone else – YOU!

Day to day you will experience different and changing emotions. Don't expect to wake up every day to the same set of feelings and circumstances. You will need a repertoire of strategies and a variety of people to help you combat the daily cravings and physical want to continue to use. SYNERGIZE with your army of people. Let the power of ONE become the power of MANY and gain strength from whomever you need the power from in any given situation. Sometimes you need to get mad and be powerful, and other times you need to get determined and be positive. Know your needs and SYNERGIZE with the right people for the right day and situation.

Speaking of SYNERGIZING, the DDF is putting together a coalition of LEADERS to brainstorm and become the power of MANY to combat the epidemic of opiate/heroin addiction in our community. We are working hard for you. WORK HARD FOR YOURSELF!!!!! LET'S SYNERGIZE!

www.stephencovey.com/7habits/7habits-habit6.php

6/27/14 – Constructive Act #99 – Follow Us On Twitter!

Short and sweet today! Just do it! When you are trying to be a national model for awareness, you need to try and get your message out every way you can! Follow us and retweet when you can. Just another way to try and save lives.

twitter.com/davisdirection

6/28/14 – Constructive Act # 100 – Mark Your Milestones

Why is #100 such a milestone? I avoided writing early this morning and now as I sit to write this CA – I feel nauseous. As a little girl, I thought 100 was a huge number and if somebody lived to be that old, that was older than anything I knew...it was ancient! If I had $100.00, I was the richest little girl in the universe. Now, I think... that's only a little longer that 3 months...but It seems like an eternity, like a hundred years instead of 100 days. I don't even count the first 2 and a half weeks, I just count from when I started writing...I don't really remember the first 2 and a half weeks.

I look back over the past 3 and a half months and I think of all the "firsts." Then I realize everyday was a "first." It was the first date of the first year that I was without Davis. One day was not any harder or easier than any of the others. I may have stayed busier on some of those days than on others, but every free moment and even some of those that weren't so free were consumed with thoughts of my sweet boy.

Davis and I were both "counters," we counted everything and anything, it was part of our "OCD" ways! We loved counting, it gave purpose to things and made them final! So, I guess my rationale here is that if I keep counting days, it will never be final until I am with him again one day. That gives me purpose. I have things to accomplish and people to help. Until that day...... I will keep counting...... until I see him again.

I can "Mark the Milestones" along the way and look back over the accomplishments of the DDF and know that GOD is carrying us every step of the journey. The DDF was established on March 21, 2014. On April 27th, Davis 21st Birthday, we rolled out the website. On May 29th, we had a Logo and artwork for a Billboard thanks to Jason Gribble.

On May 31st, we launched our Signature Jewelry line thanks to Amy Boyle and Grace Girl Beads. On June 3rd, we rolled out 12 Beautiful Digital Billboards thanks to CBS OUTDOORS and Vickie Crenshaw and Doug Penner. On June 3rd as well, we held our first Symposium – "Taking Aim at Addiction" thanks to Leigh Colburn and the efforts of all the DDF Board of Directors and the fundraising committee. On June 4th, The Davis Direction Foundation became a "recognized" foundation with the Cobb Community Foundation due to the amount of money we had raised. On June 13th, "Ogorzaly Originals" asked to partner with us as our embroidered line of apparel. On June 27th, we announced our First DDF Golf Tournament, and offers of help and requests for registration are pouring in from all over! On June 28th, we currently have 3,170 readers and they come from 29 states and 4 different countries that we know of. On July 25th, West Cobb Chiropractic has chosen us as the "Charity to Fund" for their First Annual Women's Night Out. On September 15th, we will host our Golf Tournament. On October 8th, we will host our 2nd Symposium – the "Continuum of Care."

We are growing by leaps and bounds and Davis is with us every step of the way... that's what keeps us moving! God is in control and we will remain obedient to Him in our fight to bring about awareness and change to the epidemic of opiate/heroin addiction. To our "AWESOME PARTNERS" all 3,170 of them...Stick with us, continue to help us in our efforts and...WE WILL MAKE A DIFFERENCE! I wonder what the second 100 days will bring.

6/29/14 – Constructive Act #101 – Love Like There's No Tomorrow

This is so true for families living with addicts. When the addict walks out of the door, they may never come back...how well my family knows this. It's so hard to remember that addiction is a disease sometimes. So many times they do not look sick, or even act sick. They tell you things that you know are not true, like where they are going and when they will be back. It's so hard to remember that the words that come out of your mouth may well be the last words you ever speak to that one you love so much.

You are the one that will have to live with those words. I'm forever thankful that my last words to Davis were "I love you." There were many days before that I could not have said that. I know there are several families I have been in constant contact with this week about addicts who are coming and going and using and trying to stay clean.

They have been trying to stay clean long enough to get a drug called Vivitrol. It's a drug that completely blocks the high of an opiate. The problem is that you have to be completely clean for 7 – 10 days before you get the injection that will last 30 days. Even though some of those people have been clean for the 7 days that it takes, the drug or the doctor to prescribe the drug has not been available.

Please go on to the vivitrol.com website and find a doctor near you if you are interested in this therapy. Educate yourselves about how this drug works.

I know this is all very new and very difficult to get going in our state at least, but we are working on lots of issues and finding doctors who are willing to help get these precious people what they need in order to stay clean. Don't give up... keep trying...... keep calling... and keep telling your addicts "I love you" when they walk out of the door...They may be the last 3 words you ever speak to them.

6/30/14 – Constructive Act #102 – Listen to God's Voice

For those of you who have been reading the DDF for a while, you know that my higher power is God. You also know that I pray for His guidance everyday with this post and with the Foundation. Two days ago on Day #100, I almost stopped writing, thinking that I had pretty much said what I had to say. One of the kids even said that I would probably start repeating myself pretty soon. 100 seemed like a logical number to stop on and so I really considered it.

However, I woke up on Day # 101 and I wrote a post…Go figure! BUT…then I received a comment on that post and for those of you who never saw it, this is what it said:

"I cannot begin to tell you what your writings have come to mean to me, it is like I can't wait each day to read it. This one is full of vital information. My grandson is 23 years old and a heroin addict. When I thought I had no hope and had cut myself out of his life, you came along. Thanks will never be enough to express my gratitude."

I have to tell you that this reader had NEVER commented before on a post and I have really never noticed a post that she even "liked" before. BUT, yesterday, God used her to speak to me and I heard HIM loud and clear. This, coupled with the fact that I was speaking to a friend the day before who was heartbroken that her daughter seemed to be out of her life and didn't want her around anymore because the daughter's son was an addict and the daughter seemed to be shutting everyone out of her life. I explained to her that when a family is dealing with an addict, it takes top priority and everything else seems to fall by the wayside as you try and put your life back together to the pre-drug days, not to mention the shame and embarrassment that goes along for the ride. She was so filled with gratitude that she understood why her daughter seemed to not want her around anymore.

The 2 things that happened on day 100 and day 101 spoke to my heart and kind of sealed the deal for me to continue writing for a while. Not only does it help me in my healing process to know that I am helping others, but I do feel that people are genuinely being helped from time to time with the Constructive Acts, and I truly enjoy writing them.

The point of this Act is that you have to Listen and Watch for the ways that God will speak to you, but it doesn't stop there. You also have to be obedient to HIM when he does guide you and trust that He is in control and that what He is guiding you to do is what you NEED to do. Proverbs 3:6 says…"In all thy ways acknowledge Him and He shall direct thy paths. That was probably one of the first Bible verses that I ever committed to memory and I have tried to live by it. I don't always understand why God is leading me to do the things that He does, and I certainly don't understand the things that have happened to my family over the past year and why we were chosen to be the family that it happened to, but I do trust that God is in control and that He loves my family unconditionally. One day I will write a post – or it may take a book – to tell you all of the ways God has had his hand in the Foundation and everything that has come out of it. It will knock your socks off! I will tell you about all of the wonderful people who have come into our lives because of the tragedy we endured.

LISTEN for that still small voice. You may never have met the person that speaks or writes the words you needed to hear, and they most probably don't know that God is using them to speak those words to you. God does work in MYSTERIOUS ways, but there is NO MYSTERY about what He intends for you to hear or what He intends for you to do when you hear His voice speak to you. LISTEN......just be still and LISTEN.

7/1/14 – Constructive Act #103 – Know When to Keep Silent

This is probably one of the hardest skills to acquire especially for those of us who are parents. I know it was not one of my greatest gifts. Standing on the outside, looking in, and realizing all the possible disastrous outcomes of a situation and keeping your mouth closed is almost impossible. As parents, we want to rescue, we want to prevent and quite frankly...we want to SAVE our children.

One of the major obstacles in the war against opiate/heroin addiction is the age range of the user... 18 – 36 is the average range. Why is this a major obstacle? These children (to us) are adults in the eyes of the law. We don't and can't legally have the last word any longer – even if it can save their lives.

I have a DDF friend who was told by the police that he had to give his son his car keys back last night. The loving father was trying desperately to save his child from using last night so that he could check into a treatment facility tomorrow morning. Unfortunately, the son needed to leave last night and every parent that lives with a user, knows what that means. The Dad would not give the son his keys and the son called the police. The police told the Dad that he HAD to give the keys back... because he had no choice. The law was on the side of the child – turned adult.

The Dad wisely knew that he was defeated and simply said..."I love you son...and I always will." He did not scream and shout and berate and throw verbal daggers which is what you want so badly to do. You think the louder you scream and the worse things you say...you will finally get through to the user. You won't; Words and volume are no match for heroin. The Dad knew that the words he spoke as his son left his house may well be the last words he would ever speak to him. He knew when to keep silent...Such a hard skill to use.

"Silence is Golden" was a term I heard as a little girl growing up. It was often used in a humorous way to keep children quiet for a little while. Now, as I think about that quote – and look up the true origin...It was meant to allow "think time" so that a person might not say something that he or she regretted later. It gave a person time to say something educated and profound in order to make a difference. It allowed time for a situation to de-escalate and not be made worse with continued speech.

I think in dealing with users, we have to ask ourselves…"Is what we are about to say going to make the situation better or worse?" "Is what we are about to say going to help the hopeless user?" If the answer is not "YES" then…I would contend that "Silence is Golden."

A "Recovery Resource" of 25 years told me last night that "LOVE" was what brought her back. Ironically it was not parental love but love from a single stranger and then a group of strangers. Love and Acceptance are what turned her world around for her. Strangers who kept their negative comments and judgmental thoughts SILENT.

If we continue to listen to the "experts" – those who have used and lived to tell about their recovery — we may just figure a few things out that WILL make a difference. Guard your words and judgmental thoughts…"KNOW WHEN TO KEEP SILENT."

7/2/14 – Constructive Act #104 – Share Your Story

There is HOPE friends and I am going to find it! A few days ago, Michael (Hubby) said to me, "Missy – Why don't you write a post that you need to find people who have been in recovery for 20+ years out there? We need to find people who can offer HOPE by sharing their stories of Recovery!" What a GREAT idea! He doesn't say a lot most of the time…but when he does, it's usually very PROFOUND! Long story short – I posted it and I have received some of the most BEAUTIFUL stories of HOPE and RECOVERY you could ever imagine!

Some have written and are proud to share their names and their stories and would love to help others who are working hard in Recovery…or even those who are still using but wish they weren't. Others, for specific reasons, want to remain anonymous, but their stories are so heart-wrenching, yet full of HOPE, that they need to be told. Here is the first of the "Stories of HOPE and RECOVERY" that I will proudly be sharing on the DDF.

Who Am I?

I have been asked to share my story in writing, and I have chosen to write it anonymously. One reason I have decided to remain anonymous is because I want you, the reader, to think about who I am. I could be anyone. I could be a person in the grocery store line behind you, or I could be the person at Starbucks ordering a drink. Either way, judgment is a part of the life of an addict. If I told you who I was, would you judge me? Would you scrutinize me? Let me tell you who I am.

I was born in a large northeastern city to parents that were religious. I knew God as a child and understood the teachings of my religion. My father was a binge drinker, and my mother was a loyal, dedicated wife and mother. When my father was sober, he was a great father and husband. When he drank his binges were short, and my mother sheltered us from any consequences of his drinking. The only memories I have of my father's drinking were good. I always remember him laughing and having fun. I remember thinking I wanted to be like him when I grew up.

In my early teens, my parents decided to move to Georgia. I spent the rest of my childhood growing up in East Cobb. I went to Walton High School; however, I did not graduate. I was kicked out of all Cobb County schools by the time I was 16 years old. I had started smoking marijuana at 8 years old. My older sister smoked with me, and she told me that I was only allowed to do it with her. By the time I was 10 years old I was suspended from school for having a marijuana cigarette in my purse. This was the beginning.

After being kicked out of school, I worked full-time and continued to smoke marijuana, but also added a multitude of drugs to my recreational habit. The drugs that were popular at the time of my teen years were acid, uppers, downers, cocaine, etc. I tried just about anything that came my way. By the time I was 17 years old, I was so high that I left a party walking in the middle of the night and was raped by two men. I "came to" in Ridgeview Institute. There I was told that I was a drug addict and an alcoholic. My blood level was extremely high and I was kept in the detox for months. Valium was my drug of choice at the time. I was then sent through their 28-day program. I relapsed the minute I left Ridgeview. I was then sent to another program. Something very significant happened to me while I was there; one of the psychiatrists told me that one-day I would be a junkie! I told her she was crazy, and I was afraid of needles and would never be an IV user. Many treatment centers later, many consequences later I had become what she said I would become. I was a junkie. In my 9th treatment center, I met someone who introduced me to narcotics and eventually heroin. Broken, ashamed, guilty, fearful, and remorseful, I did not know where to turn.

I had two children that I could not stop for; a dying mother, and I could only pray every day that I would die. With nowhere else to go, I went to church, I asked the priest for help. I told him what I was doing with complete abandon. He told me to come to church every Sunday and sit in the front row. He told me he would pray for me every day. I didn't know what else to do I was desperate. Looking back, I now know that this man helped save my life. Without any judgment or criticism, he prayed for me. I continued to use; however, I went to church and within a few weeks, and I had a major spiritual experience. Granted, I almost died, but I "woke up." I was able to see and hear the truth. My spiritual experience was quite simple,

I knew within my heart that I was addicted, it was no one's fault, it just was my truth. I was powerless over my addiction, and I needed help. I asked for it, and I got it

and all I had to do was reach out for it. It was like a veil of darkness was lifted, I could see. All I had to do was quit fighting and surrender to the truth. I could not do this alone. I immediately moved into a women's shelter with my children where I could be somewhat protected from myself and sought counseling and started attending AA meetings. Again, without judgment, the ladies in this AA group did not criticize me or ask me to leave because I was a junkie. They welcomed me with open arms. They told me to keep coming back. I told them I didn't know if I could stay clean. They told me to keep coming anyway. I told them that I didn't care about myself that I only cared about my dying mother who begged me to get clean and my two sons whom I loved dearly. I didn't want to hurt my loved ones anymore. This AA ladies group loved me until I could love myself. I thank God for them every day!

I haven't had a drink or a drug since that day of my spiritual experience. It has been 25 years. A miracle happened that day. It happened because one person accepted 100% where I was at with just love. That continued to happen with the AA ladies. I am not sure that I would be clean today, spiritual experience or not, if it weren't for that priest and those women back then. I was able to put together 6 months clean before my mother died, and I honor her and my grown son's today by remaining clean. I honor myself by sharing the message of hope, especially to young people.

Who am I? I could be anyone. Today, I am a very grateful clean and sober woman who has had an extraordinary life because of my addiction. I crawled out of hell and have found my way to recovery. I have a beautiful, honest relationship with my sons whom I love with all my heart. I have a precious daughter-in-law that I love like my own daughter. I have been married for 20 years to a wonderful man.

My many hardships through my addiction taught me a work ethic that I still have today. Never give up. I have since gone back to school and obtained my GED, my bachelor's degree, and I am currently working on my masters with every intention to continue onto my doctoral degree.

I honor and respect my life today. I have no shame, guilt, fear or remorse for who I am. I only ask that you consider who you are. How do you treat the addict you meet? Do you meet them with love or judgment? I hope you can meet them with love so that you might be the person who can help save their life.

7/3/14 – Constructive Act #105 – Relocate

I know this is kind of one of those words that you look at and say... "Yah – that's a long shot" ... "Who has money for that?"...... "Where would I go?" It's one of those less likely options...BUT – it does have its place.

For many addicts, their groups of people consists of dealers, other users and people who may not use, but don't care if you do. Are those really the people you need in your life? Sometimes getting away from them is the key to recovery! Anne Fletcher in her "Inside Rehab" book suggests that the people who get in recovery and stay there do it #1 – completely on their own, #2 – with a small support group of people, or #3 – with an individual Counselor. The majority of people NEVER go to rehab and Rehab is not at the top of the list for recovery options. So, maybe you should take the money you would use in rehab and RELOCATE.

I love to work in my yard and gardening is one of my favorite hobbies, so I know this to be true...Some of my plants will NEVER thrive in their current location. Perhaps there's not enough sun or maybe there's too much sun. Maybe it's too dry and the soil is all wrong. The truth is, until I relocate that plant, it will continue to hang on in a sickly state, or it will eventually die. That's a FACT! Now don't misunderstand, there is that rare plant that will make it in spite of all other circumstances...but it is a RARE occasion!

HOWEVER, If I move that plant into a more conducive location based on what I know it needs, more often that not, it will thrive and live up to it's full potential. Blooming plants for the most part need sunshine! Lots of sunshine! Roses need Sunshine...Lots of sunshine. Will they still have thorns? Yes – of course – but they will be healthy thorns and ones that will grow with them and protect them from predators and vulnerability.

This option is NOT for everyone, but for the age group 18 – 36, it seems like a logical solution, especially when you think that successful Generation Y people are changing jobs every 2 – 3 years on average anyway! A new beginning with new surroundings may be just the key to Recovery for some of you and the idea may be worth considering. Can you BLOOM and be BEAUTIFUL where you are currently planted? FOOD FOR THOUGHT...

7/4/14 – Constructive Act #106 – Participate

As I sit here and watch as my husband and two of my children are running in the Peachtree Road Race, I remember how Davis mostly hung around the house and never participated in much.If the whole family was doing something, he would always go with us, but he never ventured out much on his own during his addiction. I know at least for him, he felt like people were judging him. For the most part, no one knew of his addiction, but there was an element of paranoia that kept him from participating in things.

Heroin addiction is horrible on the body – it wreaks irreversible havoc on the body. It's important to find things to participate in that will at least counteract the destruction happening within. Yoga, for instance would be a great activity to get involved in. It helps to reduce stress and provides a time of self-reflection and physical activity. Road races happen every weekend in most cities and towns. There's always a race happening somewhere. Find a running partner and start participating. Colleges and Universities always have community courses available and most cities and towns have activities like garden clubs, book clubs, pet clubs and organizations. There truly is something for everyone. You need to find your niche and get involved.

As you work through Recovery, an activity helps you keep your mind off of addiction and gives you something else to focus on. What are your passions? "Work on your Bucket List." Find something that keeps not only your body healthy, but your mind strong as well. Find a website like "Pinterest" and find a project that you like to do. Find a "Project Partner" and get going! Being productive gives you a sense of accomplishment and completeness. It reminds you that you have talent and you can do something meaningful. If you find something that you enjoy doing, do it over and over again and give the finished product away to someone special. Making others feel good creates a good feeling for yourself in return.

Don't just sit at home with nothing to do…Get involved and PARTICIPATE in something that makes you feel good about yourself. www.pinterest.com/

7/5/14 – Constructive Act #107 – Regain Independence

Maybe this should have been yesterday's post, but it came to me last night as I was sitting in my driveway watching a very impressive fireworks display from a neighboring subdivision. It actually hit me like a brick thinking how hard our forefathers fought to gain our independence and how ironically we have "imprisoned" ourselves through the use of prescription drugs and other addictive products. I'm not talking specifically about the consumers here; I'm talking about the pharmaceutical companies and the doctors who prescribe recklessly, the marketing industry who put out false information regarding products as well as glamorizing their use…… and yes – even the tobacco industry that enhances their product. Did you know the amount of nicotine absorbed in "snuff" can be controlled by different cutting of the tobacco, increasing the nicotine concentration and raising the pH of the tobacco by adding various salts? It's just a little trick to promote addiction!

We did all of this on our own! Oxycodone, hydrocodone, morphine, and even heroin were marketed to be "NON-ADDICTIVE" pain killers. Think back about the marketing campaigns over the years where alcohol and tobacco were made to be so glamorous and of course consumed by the rich and famous! Who doesn't remember the "Marlboro Man" or the "Margarita pitcher draped in Christmas lights?" Numerous attempts at education reform and even warning labels attached to products have counteracted marketing abuse, but are we as consumers doing our part? When is the last time you sat down with your children and discussed these issues? When is the last time you questioned your doctor about the pain prescription that you left his or her office with?

I know as a Counselor, when I was handed a county approved drug/alcohol/tobacco program, there was always a section in there for teaching the children about people you could trust. I was actively teaching young children that Doctors were people you could trust. Although for the most part I would like to think that is true, I go back to the day with my mom when she was given 35 opiate pills from her surgeon for a small incision on her hand. I do think that his intentions were good, but I DID write him a letter asking him to re-think his prescription protocol in light of the present opiate epidemic. Doctors are HUMAN and they are not above being questioned. Our DDF Doctor invites questioning into his practice – in fact he told me once, as his patient, that he takes pride in helping people understand the reasons behind his decisions. If you have a doctor who does not answer your questions, then I would tell you it's time to find a new doctor!

Let's "REGAIN OUR INDEPENDENCE" in the field of addictive substances! Know what your prescriptions are and seek to find a non-narcotic substitute when you can. Especially advocate for our children. Addiction is not always a choice as many people like to think. I have heard countless stories where young children were in accidents or had to have surgeries involving a great deal of pain. They became addicted to opiates not even knowing they were receiving them. Don't misunderstand, there is a place for narcotic pain medication, but the amount and length of time it is used is often abused. If addiction runs in your family, and it does in most families...BE INFORMED! It's your RIGHT and it's your RESPONSIBILITY! Remember...our Forefathers fought and died for it!

7/6/14 – Constructive Act # 108 – Share Your Story Sunday

Today's story of HOPE and RECOVERY comes from Catherine S. – who has a little over 2 years clean. She goes into great depth to help us understand what an addict is and how they think. Congratulation Catherine on your clean time – WE ARE PROUD OF YOU!

To The Davis Direction Foundation,

I am writing this letter to express my understanding, experience, and knowledge of drug addiction. Let me preface this letter with the idea that addiction can be something somewhat difficult to understand, especially for someone that does not have personal experience with it and/or that has not had the opportunity to recover from it. Throughout this letter I will reference the "Big Book" of Alcoholics Anonymous; the book that held the solution to recovery from my "addiction".

Let me start off by explaining, who an addict is. As described in the "Big Book", an addict is simply a man or woman suffering from a seemingly hopeless state of mind and body, who can't stop when they want to stop and who has little to no control over the amount they take. An addict is NOT necessarily the stereotypical homeless person living under a bridge begging for change, or robbing homes just to get their next fix, although some addicts do end up in those situations. An addict can be a "successful" businessman, a doctor, a lawyer, your neighbor, your best friend, your parent, your child, etc. Anyone who has lost the power of choice in whether they use or not may be an addict. Only an addict themselves can make that determination, although others around usually can tell long before an addict readily admits it.

With this being said, I'll talk a little bit about what "causes" an addict to use. Why do they do it? The greatest school of thought that I have come to understand is that no one really knows why. Generally, there is not a life event or trauma directly linked to an addict's using, although many addicts will tell themselves that that is the reason why and often trauma or difficulty does occur in an addicts life; sometimes before using and frequently during active addiction.

The definition which makes the most sense to me and has allowed me to recover is the idea that an addict is suffering from a "spiritual malady" coupled with a mental obsession and a physical allergy. What this means is, my mind would mentally obsess until I put the drug into my body, immediately afterward a physical craving would develop which would cause me to not be able to stop when I wanted to stop. This process was repeated over and over and over again, until recovery.

Speaking of the mental obsession, the "Big Book" states, "these men were not drinking to escape, they were drinking to overcome a craving beyond their mental control". What this means to me is although my mind may tell me, "I want to stop using, I want to stop hurting my family and friends, I want to stop ending up in hospitals and jails, I will NEVER do this again, etc." my mind is not powerful enough to stop me from doing those things. Without fail, every day for the past few years of my using I would wake up and tell myself, "Today, is the day, I am NOT using today". Within hours (sometimes I'd last a few days), I would be intoxicated or on my way to doing so, wondering how I ended up using, AGAIN. This went on for a few years, swearing I'd never use, promising I'd never use again, really meaning I'd NEVER use again, to using, then feelings of guilt, terror, remorse, and shame, with questions of why and how almost immediately after. In the end of my using, I was frequently ending up in emergency rooms due to overdoses, only to gain consciousness, rip the tubes out of my body, and immediately meet my drug dealer in the hospital parking lot. WHY? WHY? WHY? Would I do that? It made no sense to me, and it certainly made no sense to those around me. This answer was best explained in what I'm about to write, "At a certain point in the drinking (using) of every alcoholic(addict), he passes into a state where the most powerful desire to stop drinking (using) is of absolutely no avail. This tragic situation has arrived in practically every case long before it is suspected. The fact is that most alcoholics(addicts), for reasons yet obscure, have lost the power of choice in drink(heroin, etc.). Our so-called will power becomes practically nonexistent. We are unable, at certain times, to bring into our consciousness with sufficient force the memory of the suffering and humiliation of even a week or a month ago. We are without defense against the first drink(drug)."I will do my best to explain what this means to me; In short, this means the memories of the tragic things that happened while using, failed at keeping me from doing it the next time. When I'd get the thought to use after making a resolution to never do it again, I did not remember the resolution, I did not remember the pained looks on the faces around me, I did not remember that several hours before I was laying in a hospital bed almost dead, etc. The obsession was more powerful than the memories. I could rely on my memory for other things, such as getting burned on a hot stove, and using the memory to know never to touch a stove again. If I were to touch it again, I would get burned. I kept getting "burned" in active addiction but, was not able to recall being "burned", therefore not able to stop it.

A spiritual malady; just what do I mean by that? When I was first told I was suffering from a spiritual sickness, I was just as shocked as you probably are reading this. How could that be? What I have found out is that I had been suffering spiritually, that alcohol and drugs were not actually a problem for me, they were a solution for me, although, from the very start they were a problem for those around me. I can best describe this as, when I was using my family would ask me what was wrong with me and I would answer nothing. But, when I was sober I would ask myself what was wrong with me, and if you asked my family, their answer would be nothing. It was backwards. The very first time I ever remember feeling great in my life was when I took my first drink at 13 years old. Prior to my first drink, I was planning it for months, I was planning what lies I was going to tell my parents, where I was going to stay, who was going to be there to make sure no one would find out. My first drink was pretty abnormal; an obsession right off the bat. I remember during my first time drinking planning out all of the drinks for the rest of my life; my sweet 16, college, my 21st birthday party, my wedding, my children's graduations, etc. I WAS 13! I was not okay without drugs, where as a non-addict is okay without drugs. I felt crazy, anxious, restless, insecure, overwhelmed, worthless, apart, different, unloved…the list goes on. As out-of-bounds as this sounds, heroin and God as I know Him today, were seemingly closely related. Heroin did a lot of things for me, it temporarily relieved me of all of the feelings expressed above. I didn't stop using heroin until it no longer worked for me, until it stopped removing those things for me, and started doing them to me, until the consequences outweighed the relief. This is different for everyone, and I don't know what it takes for every addict, I just knew what it took for me, and even during that time I did not know when it would be over. I wanted it to end several years before it finally did. It got to the point where I could not live sober, and I could not live high, I did not want to live and I did not want to die. I was at the point where I was living only to use and I hated every minute of it. What I know now is, through all of that, and through the process of recovery that in the tip of every needle I stuck in my arm, I was searching for what I have now found in the loving arms of God.

Okay, the fun stuff, let's talk about RECOVERY! The short version. My sobriety date is April 23, 2012. Many tragic things happened, some mentioned above, and I ended up in recovery. Upon my final arrival into recovery, I was ready and willing to do whatever it took to stay sober. Whatever was required of me, I was willing to do. I was willing because I did not want to live the life that I was living, and I could not successfully kill myself. Upon entering sobriety, I got a sponsor. A sponsor is someone who takes you through the program (12 Steps) of recovery. Prior to taking the steps, I met with my sponsor and discussed a lot about my drinking/ using, and my history. And, she explained some of the things that I have explained above. She told me that in order to stop using that I was going to need to know what I was suffering from. Once knowing what addiction was, admitting that I was powerless and that my life was unmanageable, I was then able to take the rest of the steps and have a life changing experience. I am trying to keep this short but, for more detail on what taking the steps was like, please feel free to ask.

Talking about life changing experience, all I wanted was to not think about using. I would do anything to not be obsessed. I didn't care if I had food or shelter, I just wanted to be free of my mind. Addiction centers in the mind. And, boy did I get freedom and a WHOLE lot more!

By practicing the program, gaining a relationship with God, and realizing that my mind lies to me on a fairly regular basis, I have been able to accomplish all sorts of things and I have been freed. A relationship with God(the God of my understanding) is freedom. I needed a sufficient substitute, something better than alcohol and drugs and that has been what the program of recovery has given me. In addition to that, I have regained a relationship with my mom, dad, brothers, and friends. I have been afforded the opportunity to marry my soul mate, raise a baby with him, and be a loving wife(most of the time...haha) and a wonderful, caring mother. I am able to be a daughter, a friend, an employee, a student...I am able to be the child I was created to be. These are the main reasons, although difficult at times, I am able to stay sober and live happily. This is what gives me courage on a daily basis to keep growing in my sobriety and my relationship with God. In addition to all of these things, carrying the message of sobriety to other alcoholics and addicts is what brings the most joy into my life. There is nothing better than the feeling I get when I see the lights turn on in the dark world of the addict.

7/7/14 – Constructive Act # 109 – LOG YOUR MEDS

Just like logging your hours for accountability at work, or logging your miles in order to be reimbursed, anyone taking narcotic medication needs to keep a log of when and how many pills were taken at a given time. If you are alone and having to give yourself narcotic medication, it is imperative that you keep a log. Chances are if you are taking pain medication, you are pretty much out of it for the most part. You may not remember when and if you took your last dose of medication. If something were to happen to you as in overdose or just somebody finding you and it being very hard to wake you up, they can look at your log and know what you took and when you took it.

It is also important to know if you are mixing meds with other meds. Keeping a log of prescribed medication mixed with over the counter medication can be very revealing if you are experiencing side effects or discomfort. If you keep a log, there will be no doubt as to how you can be helped if you have accidentally overdosed.

On the other hand, if you are taking your narcotic medication exactly as prescribed and then you are running out of pills before you are allowed a refill, then you might want to take a look around and see who has had access to your medication. Narcotic pain pills sell anywhere from $40.00 — $80.00 on the street and kids are going through them in epidemic proportions. Not only is the practice of logging your medications important when you are at home, it is vitally important to keep a log of your medications while you are in the hospital as well. Many times what you are prescribed and what you are receiving are in direct contradiction. It is a known fact that medical personnel are some of the most addicted groups of people where prescription medications are concerned. Many arrests have been made at hospitals across the country for hospital employees taking the patients' medications.

I know these are hard truths to accept, but until we begin to honestly look at what is really happening and who is taking them and how medications are being abused, we cannot begin to fix the problem. There are good and bad people in every profession, and the good always pay for the sins of the bad. That's life and we have to deal with it. So, in light of what we know to be true, LOG YOUR MEDICATIONS, and take the guess work out of taking narcotics. The numbers don't lie!

7/8/14 – Constructive Act #110 – Choose a Book

Visit the local bookstore and find a book that speaks to you. You can even do a little research before you go. If you are an addict, find a book written by another addict about how they worked recovery; If you are the parent of an addict, there are books for you as well; If you are the spouse or a best friend to the addict, there are book for you too! FIND THE RIGHT BOOK!

I have my personal favorites and I own the "personal favorites" of a lot of people. When you lose a loved one, people often come around bringing books for you to help you go through the grieving process. That is a good thing. I have truly enjoyed looking at every book that I have received. Although I have not read all of them, I have them ready to be the "next book to read.

I guess if I was going to give someone a book to read, I would certainly advocate for Anne Fletcher's "Inside Rehab" book, but I would also consider giving a friend "One Thousand Gifts" by Ann Voskamp . If nothing else, this book makes a person think about their blessings and how they have affected their life.

You can literally spend hours searching through books that have been written about addiction. You can even become very specific and search books about opiate/heroin addiction. I have found several, but I have yet to read all of them. At this point in my grieving process, I pick and choose "snippets" of information that I believe to be valuable. I have not read many books in their entirety since Davis died, but I have read bits and pieces of all of them.

Reading books written by other people allows you to know that other people have gone before you and that you are not on this journey alone. If you have a book that has touched your heart, please post it for others to read and benefit from. Reading occupies the mind and often keeps you from worrying or fixating on the things that have happened that are beyond your control. Every unaccounted minute of my mind is filled with thoughts of Davis and how very much I miss him. Find a book to help you continue living that occupies your mind in a positive way and teaches you how to grow.

And while you are at the bookstore – Be sociable and make friends. Who knows, you might find someone who can be very valuable in your recovery process while you are there. VISIT THE BOOKSTORE AND READ!

7/9/14 – Constructive Act #111 – Keep Moving Onward

For those of you who don't know, the Davis Direction motto is "Moving onward through life…Looking upward to God." Even if it is one baby step at a time or one step a day at first, keep moving onward. Your progress may be slow at first and you may not have the whole picture, but if you are moving onward…You will get there! Where is there? RECOVERY – or at peace if you are the loved one of an addict.

I've always been told that headlights only shine for a limited view, but as you move onward making progress, the view continues to increase. With each increase in the view, the picture becomes more clear and the destination becomes closer. We don't always have to start knowing the entire journey. Just know the goal and then continue to do the things and make the decisions that move you closer to the goal.

So many times when we try to think about the big picture, it becomes very overwhelming and we become defeated. Some days your steps may be giant steps with lofty destinations. Other days your steps may be shuffles that just barely keep you from moving backwards. THAT"S OKAY! Every day doesn't have to be a marathon and its fine to rest and reflect along the way.

Too many addicts think that recovery should come quickly just because they are not using anymore. That's just the FIRST step. And YES – it is a giant step with a lofty destination, but the journey has just begun. As with any disease, the disease does not go away, you just learn how to manage it.

Certainly don't forget the second part of the motto — "Looking upward to God." I always told Davis that God was there for him in EVERY circumstance. Sometimes going to battle is harder than you could ever imagine. It doesn't always work out like we would like. BUT – Jesus suffered and died for OUR sins to be forgiven and to not consider ourselves worthy of the value of that gift is not up to us! Jesus made that decision and he deemed us worthy enough to make the sacrifice. So......Onward, Christian soldiers, marching as to war, with the cross of Jesus going on before.

ONE STEP AT A TIME...

7/10/14 – Constructive Act #112 – Find Your Place

I spent the last five wonderful days at the beach. There is nowhere on earth that I feel closer to God. I feel His power and majesty; I smell the fragrance of heaven; I can touch the softness of God's love; I can see the beauty of awesomeness. I love the ocean!

Everyone needs to know where their place is. For some it may be in the mountains all alone, and for others it may be in a meadow full of wild flowers. Everybody has a place that makes them feel at peace and you need to go there as often as you can.

As a little girl going to the beach, I remember looking for the Spanish moss in the tress. I knew that it meant the beach was close. When we turned down the beach road, I remember looking down the side streets to get a glimpse of the beach before we got to the hotel. The beach spoke to me and it spoke of peace and love and God's grace and mercy.

My heart has been full of emotion all week long. I have laughed until my sides hurt with my family; I have cried because my heart was broken that Davis was not with us; I have shared memories with family members of past trips; I have prayed and asked God to give me peace and forgiveness; I have felt majesty and power; I have hurt and healed all because I am in MY PLACE.

KNOW YOUR PLACE; Go there often; Inhale the power of love and majesty and exhale your doubts and worries. Davis was never more at peace than when he was at the Beach. It was because of him that we began coming to the Beaches of South Walton. He and his best friend Bobby planned our first trip here to Seacrest and we have come back every year. We ride our bikes, walk for hours and drive down 30A like it is the highway to Heaven. Even though we went to the beach before, the Beaches of South Walton have become our vacation home. The beach here is like an old familiar friend that welcomes us year after year.

I have felt a closeness to Davis this week that filled a void that I have not been able to fill since his death. I'm not sure where exactly I did that but I know I did. I'm not sure if it was on the beach during the day or on the beach at night walking and watching the sunset. All I know is that after I melted down with emotion from all the sweet memories of being here as The "Owen7," I felt a peace come over me that we would all be together again. Find Your Place – it will give you the PEACE that you need to carry on. So Long Dear Friend…See you next year!

7/11/14 – Constructive Act #113 – Choose a Side

Okay – so I'm home from vacation and there's lots of work to be done! So, with that being said, I'm just going to jump in headfirst and say what I think needs to be said! GET OFF THE FENCE!

Either you believe addiction is a disease or you don't! I touched on this briefly a few weeks ago as I outlined my own beliefs. But, I think we need to put this issue into perspective. We can't talk out of both sides of our mouths and I feel like that is what is going on.

When you ask people directly whether or not they believe addiction is a disease, most of them will reply with a "yes, of course." Then there next words or sentences will directly contradict what they have just claimed. The number one contradiction to me is the "Secrecy" that surrounds the addiction and believe me…I was bound and determined to help Davis keep his addiction a secret. Name another disease where people go to such lengths to keep a disease a secret. The only one I can even think of is venereal disease and that can be a disease directly caused by addiction in some cases.

The second contradiction is the fact that many, many people NEVER seek professional medical advice or in other words go to the doctor in order to treat this disease. Yes – people even keep it a "secret" from their doctors. Sometimes if you drink or smoke and of course if you take drugs illegally… No one EVER lists that on the medical information sheets. In most cases, it has spiraled out of control before the doctor ever even hears that his or her patient is an "addict."

As I sat on the beach this past week and I looked around at the thousands of people out there every day. I thought to myself, some statistics say that 1 in every 10 people is an addict of some kind and I am completely surrounded by addicts. I don't know who they are: They don't look different or unusual; They don't lose their hair; they don't wear a pump; they don't make noises or have seizures; They don't walk or move in different ways. For the most part, they are hidden among the masses and can function secretly on a daily basis.

WHY are we so embarrassed and ashamed to speak of this disease? I'll tell you why…People believe that it is self-inflicted! Let me ask those of you who know that you are not an addict, did you know before or after you took your first alcoholic drink? Did you know before or after you smoked pot or took a pain pill the first time? The old saying… There but for the grace of God go I…takes on a whole new meaning for some people.

Can any of you name the National Addiction Fundraiser? You know like the "Jump Rope for Heart" for heart disease and the "Relay for Life" for cancer? Both of these events are heavily participated in throughout public schools…BUT, more children's lives are affected by addiction than any other single disease out there. Why are we not fundraising like crazy to figure this out?

I know this is a very long post, and I don't even know exactly what all the reasons are for the secrecy and shame involved with addiction. I found out last week that there is even a "rule" in AA that you cannot use your whole name when you reference anything about AA. WHY? What I do know is that we need to get it into PUBLIC view and conversation in order to gain insight and information in order to help all of the people who suffer with it. It was not an easy decision to put my son's picture on a Public Billboard for everyone to see as the "Heroin Poster Child" but it was a start to what I hope to be a "GREATER MOVEMENT" to educate others and make a difference so that others might live TO EXPERIENCE FULL RECOVERY!

7/12/14 – Constructive Act #114 – Take Your Meds

(Choose a Side Part 2)

I just really didn't feel like I finished yesterday's post. There was another part of it that I wanted to say. If you think about diseases, each of them usually come with medications that keep people from living lives of pain, or simply dying. For instance, My husband is a Type 1 diabetic. If he doesn't take his insulin, plain and simple…he will die. People with cancer are told they usually have two choices: Radiation or chemotherapy – and then pain pills to manage the intense pain that they suffer through. Kidney disease comes with dialysis, ITP with steroids or spleen removal, heart disease with diuretics, ace inhibitors or beta blockers; High blood pressure has its meds; high cholesterol even has its meds. The list goes on and on and thank GOD that it does or I would be a widow right now.

BUT…(bet you knew that was coming) 99% of the time any family member finds out that there is a user in the family, that family member expects the addict to go "COLD TURKEY" and kick the habit. It's really easy…just stop! I remember saying those exact words to Davis. When I did, he very lovingly said to me…trying to help me understand…" Mom, you know that 50 pounds you've wanted to lose for the past 20 years…Why haven't you lost it? Touché! What could I say to that? I finally understood that an addict needs more help than being told to just STOP!

When we found out about his addiction, after we tried cold turkey and really tried to find the cause instead of the solution, we found out how serious his anxiety and depression had become. We did go to the doctor and talk to her about meds to help him relax and sleep. He got 2 prescriptions for anxiety and depression. He did begin to sleep better, but the medication was making him sleep during the day and it was making him nauseous as well. We did try other meds and for Davis, we just really never found anything that worked quite right. Maybe he thought they were supposed to make him "well" instead of making the disease tolerable. I don't really know, but for whatever reason, they didn't work for him according to him. And if the truth were known, he could have still been using on top of the drugs and I'm quite sure that would have made a difference too. But for others, the meds make a huge difference and there is nothing wrong with taking them.

The fact remains. Don't discount medication. All medication is not bad and addicts need to be working with their doctors to help with their Recovery. In fact, I would even advocate for Recovery doctors to become a specialty. Yesterday I mentioned Heart Doctors and Cancer Doctors with their specialties, Recovery Doctors need to form a practice of their own. They need to be overseeing Naloxone and drug therapies for Suboxone and Vivitrol…and that's just for the opiate/heroin addicts. They can also manage anxiety and depression. Then they can refer out to Psychiatrists and Therapists for the mental and emotional confusion addicts experience. Somebody needs to become the experts in treating this disease. Research needs to be done regularly. Like I said yesterday…More children are directly affected by addiction from living with a parent or sibling than are affected by heart disease and cancer (maybe even combined) and yet there is no National fundraising effort done in the schools to fund this disease.

There is no need for addicts to have to go to "Back alley clinics" to get their meds. Let's get this disease out in the open from the ground up and give these precious people…"God's children" a decent place to go and receive help without embarrassment and shame. MEDICATION CAN SAVE LIVES! GET TO THE DOCTOR!

7/13/14 – Constructive Act #115 – Share Your Story

This is a different twist on Share Your Story Sunday! Today I am posting a story from the family of an addict. I received it this week and I think it's important for others to see what families go through or see that you are not the ONLY family going through this.

The HOPE and RECOVERY of this story is that even though he is in prison, he is in RECOVERY. Sometimes Recovery is harder to come by, but the outcome can be the same, when the time is up. Please pray for this sweet family.

Jul 12th, 1:56 am

I wanted to let you know that I thank you for your site… currently my husband is incarcerated for possession of less than 1 gram of heroin. He is a serving a 15 year do 5 for that, as a repeat offender. He did get an assault charge (a fight with his uncle and 2 cousins) 1-2 weeks before his sentencing hearing on the drug charge because he was drinking so bad. Within a few weeks of my husband using heroin, in which he started because his doctor cut off his prescription of hydrocodone for 1 year… and then he resorted to heroin.

He took scrap money, secret money, to purchase from a dealer and he went into Home Depot, shot up in the bathroom and before he made it out of Home Depot, he passed out. Home Depot employees searched his pockets for identification and found a needle, spoon, and baggy.

He has struggled with addiction off and on throughout our marriage-of 12 years. I have known him since I was 13-14 and I married him at 20… I met him in a neighborhood where I grew up. We were just friends for many years. I have not done any drugs since I was 16, when I accepted Christ as my savior but I married an addict. I am 32 now and life has thrown me curves and so many things, it's really unbelievable. My faith in Christ, has lead me to stand by my husband through the binges, violence (not necessarily toward- there have been many, many scary moments-were I were very much afraid of him), adultery, the financial failures, and so much more…

78

My husband prior to this drug charge, had only 1 misdemeanor charge of drugs for a roach/joint when he was a young teen… since then his other charges were not for drugs but behavior as a result of his drug use. In all the years of his drug use going on, his mom and dad, both, were very ashamed and embarrassed of his behavior. They always kept is secret… when they found out he smoked a joint, they sent him away for that… (to me a very strong measure to take)… however, he got passed that and his addiction grew worse.

His parents, both with addicts and siblings on both sides of their family (but not them-they could probably count the times that they actually have drunk alcohol on one or both hands-very straight laced) … on both sides, their brother and or sisters did drugs with my husband while he was growing up. Crank, was his problem… so…long story short, I agree strongly that because his drug use, was embarrassing there was a lot of turning of his parents heads, they did not want people to know and then in a rage he was even kicked out at age 16-17, for not knowing how to handle his problems.

I think that they did the best that they could… I now after 12 years of marriage and our 3 daughters ages 11, 8, and 4… the older 2 in Cobb County public schools… I do not want people to know he is incarcerated, because I do not want to be judged or my children to be treated different or even left out because their father is a criminal… I am private yet… I am not when it comes to feeling strongly that there is a major issue with drug use and abuse in our community, state, and country…

I agree that knowledge is power and I want people to know, to hear, to learn… about what is going on around them. I recently told him that I have a real hard time trying to open up to active addicts, from what I have been through with him and even a few of my dear friends/loved ones. I feel like that in my husbands case, my friends case, they are not reliable, there for me-like I would be there for them. My friends aren't or weren't good friends to me, because during this year of my husband being gone-in prison, I lost a baby in July (and I trust that God knew what I could handle and everything happens for a reason-even still-a lot of anguish and I had never had a miscarriage before)… after all of that, my friend is strung out, she has openly told me that she does not call me when she uses because she's ashamed, she lost her kids to her parents, she lies and is/was actively living in addiction… when I needed a friend, she wasn't there for me (can I even call her my friend anymore)… and I can say… well all I need is God, and that is truth and fact and that's the best person to have.

I love my husband… when and before my husband was sentenced, I did not know if I would stand by him. He was caught in October 2012 with possession, he got out and never touched heroin again but then he started drinking really bad and the court system drug out the charge, calling him to court- 5-6 times, putting off his sentence date (he was sentenced in July 2013), drug court did one drug test- with like a 1 month mailed notice of the date and time he would take it... instead of considering my husband as having a problem... they just threw the book at him.Anyhow, I did not know if I wanted to stay with him through any sentence because... I AM SO SICK OF THE DEVASTATION OF ADDICTION.

I spent the last few months with him going to work and then coming home to get vodka or whiskey just to get through the rest of the night. I had my children go home with a friend instead of home to their father because he might drink and drive with them and he got home from his job at 2:30-3:00 when my kids got home and I could not rely on him to be the man/dad he was supposed to be.

It's been a whirlwind and a lot of emotion, facts, love, and life and I have decided to stay. He has been fortunate enough to be at a Faith Based Prison, Walker State Prison, this is something that I hope that you take a look at/research when you have some free time! It is nothing like you expect to find in prison. I can share a link with you another day and time, to research it... however, what a strain... I do not even think that the judge cared that my husband had a job, was in school as an apprentice, had a wife, and 3 kids... I wish that it did not have to take prison but my husband is sober!

God did what my husband was not going to do for himself... he saved his life and probably someone else's because he would drink and drive often.
I pray that my husbands sobriety last a life time and it's a scary thought to think it won't... I like your question today about being on the fence... I am on the fence... where the young lady that told her story the other day, that she... had a spiritual malady and that is what I really think it is... it is a self-induced problem... yet when they begin obsessing like my husband would-there would be nothing that would stop him from using... when he made up his mind... he would, like they say "white-knuckle it" until he used. I would walk on egg shells and it's so hard to love the addict through their active drug/alcohol use.

I will assure you in the 12 years of our marriage, my children were never subjected to needle drug use, or drugs at all, just the effects of his behavior, my reactions... . In the 12 years of marriage, we have separated several times-months and once almost a year. God only knows... in spite of my anger toward the things I have been through, I do have compassion as well... it's like loving 2 different people. In regards to the disease... I just think once the addict falls and is active, it's hard to come out of it...

Like the 12 steps teach the 12th step as sponsoring-helping other addicts, is so important. When the recovering addict is busy and not taking their sobriety for granted, not 1 day, they have power over their addiction...

I want to get involved and do more to help in the fight against addiction... I want to see people set free... I believe in miracles, the grace of God, and I need hope-others need hope. These our loved ones or someone else's loved one. I do not know if what I type is important or will really matter... I do not know why but I felt compelled to share my story. It's not easy and we need each other... again, I am sorry for your loss of Davis... sometimes it's hard to understand why-but you do have a story that is touching others lives and including mine. I am sharing your page and inviting others, mothers, friends, family... who have been down this path, are on this path, who are sober, who are using... I pray that they will open their eyes and hearts and seek freedom in and from their addiction... by sharing yours and other stories to give them truth and clarity... I feel like I am rambling on. Thank you for listening at the very least. It's a broken road

7/14/14 – Constructive Act #116 – Turn Plans Into Actions

As I sat last night and did research on initiatives and statistics regarding opiate/heroin use, one thing became abundantly clear..."EVERYTHING IS A PLAN"......"WHERE'S THE ACTION?"

I get so frustrated when I read things, especially legislation and statistics which are always so NOT up to date. But, it is clear that the problem is getting worse not better! With major elections coming up in November...it is imperative that we begin holding some feet to the fire regarding this issue. Enough already with plans and initiatives that are NOT being implemented or at least not being implemented correctly...... (Forty-one states have established programs allowing physicians and other authorized users to check a patient's history of receiving controlled-substance prescriptions, but some of these programs are unfunded or nonoperational, and few prescribers have signed up to use them.) New England Journal of Medicine Perspective.

What one state figures out and takes action to solve their problems, other states receive their problems and have no action in place to take care of it! Florida, Texas, and Louisiana recently passed laws (2011) to crack down on "pill mills," imposing state registration and other restrictions on pain clinics. GUESS WHAT? Those pill mills just picked up and moved to adjacent states that have no laws. Alabama is now #1 in the nation in narcotic prescribing. Now people cross the state lines to get what they need. I understand that there are pill mills all up and down Interstate 75 – throughout Georgia.

We have a PROBLEM! We need to stand together as a nation and fix it. It seems simple to me. ACCOUNTABILITY is the answer. Who is prescribing OPIATES (narcotics)?

Who is receiving these Prescriptions? How many pills are being prescribed at a time and with how many refills? What information is being given to the people receiving the prescriptions in order to educate them about what they are receiving? Where are the bring back programs with drug boxes? How are these pills being destroyed? Is it really that hard?

If Michelle Obama can regulate the school lunch program nationally…Why can't someone regulate the abuse of prescription medication? I haven't heard of a school lunch killing anyone!

I'm a little emotional today as I received the full report of Davis' death this weekend and just finished reading it. This could have been so preventable if I had only known what a bottle of Vicodin in my medicine cabinet had the potential of destroying. I took ACTION and I am working hard every day to help with a solution to this problem…but I am one person! Others need to get mad and do something before you have to bury a child or a spouse or any loved one! NO ONE IS IMMUNE!

Ultimately, "we probably need a complicated, multifaceted solution" to the problem of opioid abuse and overdose, said Utah's Rolfs. "I don't think we have the answer." Robert Rolfs is Utah's State epidemiologist. YOU THINK? We need a solution and we need it NOW…before one more child dies! That one more child could be yours!

Quit talking about what needs to be done and DO SOMETHING!!! Tomorrow the CA #117 will be to "CHOOSE SOMETHING" I will compile a list of things you can do to get started in helping with this initiative. Be ready to choose something TOMORROW!

Below I will post the article from the New England Journal of Medicine where I got some of this information for today's post. The article was updated in 2011. I know it's old…but believe it or not, it's one of the most current.
www.nejm.org/doi/full/10.1056/nejmp1011512

7/15/14 – Constructive Act #117 – Choose Something

I told you yesterday that today was going to be a day of action! There's something for everyone no matter where you are in your journey. Even if your journey is to educate yourself in order to help others.

I can tell you that I don't think any of my friends or family ever thought they would be helping support me as I walked through the valley of death. You just never know what tomorrow will bring. Last night alone, we learned of 2 deaths and 2 overdoses. Everyone needs to invest in this problem. Chances are YOU will be affected…if not directly, then indirectly through a friend or family member. I didn't mention that a person wrote me last night telling me that they had a 35 year old friend die last week of a Heroin overdose and that person was also a Cobb County School graduate. This disease knows NO boundaries. Please move into action.

Here are a list of ways:
- Read the DDF daily and do your own research. KNOWLEDGE IS POWER.
- Write a letter to the Governor asking him what is being done.
- Invite your friends to "Like" the DDF page and have them invite their friends.
- Join or "Like" any organization trying to make a difference in opiate awareness.
- Clean out your medicine cabinet and find the nearest drug dropbox.
- Pray that God will continue to make things happen in our fight against opiates.
- Send a donation to the DDF, an organization trying to make a difference. $10.00 helps.
- Share the Constructive Acts on your own FB page.
- Organize a town hall meeting to discuss what your community is doing to help.
- Get the civic, school and church groups on board to fight opiate use and promote awareness.
- Talk to your children about addiction in your family tree.
- If you are living with an addict, find 2 Naloxone kits… 1 at home and 1 with your addict
- Consult with your doctor and let them know what is going on with you or your addict.
- Alert family and close friends of the situation so they can help support the situation.
- Create an Emergency Plan if you are living with an addict.
- Support the events of the DDF – Upcoming Golf Tournament – Oct 8th Symposium.
- Support events dealing with addiction. Shatterproof; Heroes in Recovery Run.
- Come to "Ladies Night Out" posted on DDF – all proceeds to DDF.
- Ask your doctor for a narcotic ALTERNATIVE for pain.
- Go on Political FB pages and ask candidates where they stand on this.
- VOTE on July 22nd! Know who you vote for…Make it COUNT!
- GO TO CHURCH!
- Spend quality time with your children.
- Ask for a specific job with an organization.
- Watch "The ANONYMOUS People DVD.

- Speak PUBLICLY and OPENLY about opiate/heroin addiction. SAVE A LIFE!
- BURY SHAME and let's help our kids!!!

There are many other ways to jump into action and many organizations to support. It doesn't have to be the DDF, although we appreciate any support we receive. The DDF's mission is to focus on OPIATE/HEROIN Awareness and Change. That is a more severe form of addiction according to our beliefs. It is the addiction that is claiming the lives of our kids...

STAND FOR SOMETHING...or you AND YOUR CHILDREN will fall for ANYTHING...including drugs! GET UP and GET BUSY!

7/16/14 – Constructive Act #118 – Keep The Faith

I have been feeling very defeated this week with all of the news of overdoses and death. It's heartbreaking to hear of yet another young adult losing the battle with opiates/heroin. It causes us to temporarily lose hope and to plunge into the depths of despair. Last night I was up late and I went ahead and wrote the Constructive Act (CA) for today, but when I got up this morning, things changed.

I always get an internet devotion called "God's Minute." I have received this devotion for years and sometimes I tell people I feel like God pulls me up to his throne and sits me in his lap and reads it directly to me...JUST ME! I feel sometimes like it was written personally and entirely for ME! There could be millions of "ME's" on the same day that feel the same way I do, but nonetheless, this morning...God spoke to me. So, I have saved my "other CA" for a different day because I am writing what I believe God needs for me to say this morning.

Remember the story of David and Goliath? How amazing was that...I woke up to be reminded of the story of when a young shepherd boy took a single slingshot with a single stone and defeated the Philistine Giant because God had given David strength.

God was telling me that Opiates/Heroin may indeed be the present day "Goliath" but they are still NO match for HIM!

THEN DAVID PUT HIS HAND IN HIS BAG AND TOOK OUT A STONE; AND HE SLUNG IT AND STRUCK THE PHILISTINE IN HIS FOREHEAD, SO THAT THE STONE SANK INTO HIS FOREHEAD, AND HE FELL ON HIS FACE TO THE EARTH. (1 SAMUEL 17:49 NKJV)

Sometimes, we are no match for things of this earth and we have to live by FAITH and not sight! God so blatantly reminded me this morning that He is on our side and He is going to help us defeat this GIANT that is killing our children. We are growing in numbers to become the ARMY of God and He will provide us with the "SINGLE STONE" when the time is right.

> "FEAR NOT, FOR I AM WITH YOU; BE NOT DISMAYED, FOR I AM YOUR GOD. I WILL STRENGTHEN YOU, YES, I WILL HELP YOU, I WILL UPHOLD YOU WITH MY RIGHTEOUS RIGHT HAND." (ISAIAH 41:10)

Sometimes God's timing is not our timing, but we have to trust that in His infinite wisdom, He will take care of us. I have questioned God's timing on many occasions in taking Davis home. We were not ready to give him back to God. However, I have to trust that God in His infinite wisdom, rescued Davis from what could have been so much worse if he had stayed on earth and continued his drug use. His demons are gone and he is in the arms of God. For that I praise God every day.

> FOR ASSUREDLY, I SAY TO YOU, IF YOU HAVE FAITH AS A MUSTARD SEED, YOU WILL SAY TO THIS MOUNTAIN,'MOVE FROM HERE TO THERE,' AND IT WILL MOVE; AND NOTHING WILL BE IMPOSSIBLE FOR YOU.(MATTHEW 17:20)

> KEEP THE FAITH...WE WILL DEFEAT THIS GIANT AND GOD WILL UPHOLD US AND KEEP HIS PROMISES.

> REMEMBER......NOTHING IS IMPOSSIBLE WHEN YOU PUT YOUR TRUST IN GOD!

7/17/14 – Constructive Act #119 – Ride The Roller Coaster

Sometimes you just have to get in the seat, hold on tight, and endure the ride. That's what I feel like I have done these past couple of days. They have not been easy for me and I have re-lived a lot of hours, days and feelings that I could have easily walked away from. I felt I was needed; so instead I took the roller coaster ride and tried my best to help those I knew who were hurting and possibly needed my support. That's what it's like living with and loving an addict.

The hardest part of the ride is that it is NOT natural. It is not something that any parent expects to endure during a lifetime. You can't anticipate the highs and lows. The curves that sling you up against the side and the circles you go around in literally make you sick. There is nothing that can prepare you for the moments you will certainly lose your breath and wonder how you will ever breathe again. The climb to the top feels like it takes a million years. You work so hard to get there slowly and surely and then in seconds, the bottom falls out and you reel into the valley with incredible speed. You spiral out of control until you think you can't take it any longer and then the momentum comes to a halt...just to start the process all over again.

Living the life of a drug addict or being the person who loves that addict more than life itself is the most uncertain time in your life. You can't count on anything other than the ride to continue to take you on a continuous obstacle course. You will always be jumping through hoops and there is always a new obstacle around every corner. Buckle in, hold onto the stability bar and hang on for dear life. And just for the record... Dear Life is NOT a guarantee.

Is there HOPE? Yes, of course; there is always HOPE...But HOPE has to come from within the addict. You can help them with their safety belt; you can tell them to hold on to the bar; you can wrap your arms around them and hold them with all your might...but the EFFORT has to come from them.

When THEY are ready to get OFF of the ride, that is when Recovery begins. It is then and ONLY then that you can walk beside them with both feet on the ground. It is then and only then that they can choose the direction they want to pursue. It is then and only then that both of you can reclaim your lives and begin living again. Its time to get OFF of the Roller Coaster and Reclaim your life. WE CAN DO THIS! GOD GRANT US STRENGTH!

7/18/14 – Constructive Act #120 – The Storm Before The Calm

You've all heard about the "calm before the storm"...but how about the "Storm Before the Calm?" I pray daily that that is what we are experiencing. We are in such a community/national storm right now that I think it is fair to say that our nation is up in arms. I see our community coming together like I witnessed the Nation come together after 9-11. People are scared, children are stressed out and searching for peace, and young adults are dying in record numbers. Opiate/Heroin addiction is a "hot topic" right now and people are investing in it. When there is no "Raging Storm" the immediacy and the resources that are available now will move on to another "Raging Storm." Take advantage of the STORM while resources are available and agencies are eager to invest and help. Timing is everything and now is the time to get help with awareness, prevention, rehabilitation, and CHANGE... WE NEED A SOLUTION. There is a movement going on!

Reaching out for help and resources is harder for some people than others...so keep this in mind.

What I have concluded is there is no solution to opiate/heroin addiction that does not include God Almighty! We are weak and He is strong. What I know that I observed with Davis though, is that he had a hard time believing that he was worthy of that Love. He felt in some way that he had failed God.

When people are scared, they get desperate, and it is exhausting. People of all ages need to understand that God knows what you are going through! Remember, He was the one who said…"Ye who have not sinned…cast the first stone." He is a loving God.

King David wrote these words:

O LORD, YOU HAVE SEARCHED ME AND YOU KNOW ME. YOU KNOW WHEN I SIT AND WHEN I RISE; YOU PERCEIVE MY THOUGHTS FROM AFAR. YOU DISCERN MY GOING OUT AND MY LYING DOWN; YOU ARE FAMILIAR WITH ALL MY WAYS. BEFORE A WORD IS ON MY TONGUE YOU KNOW IT COMPLETELY. (PSALM 139:1-3)

You don't need to hide from God. You CAN'T hide from God. He's the only one who knows the truth about what you are going through. When you go to your dealer, He goes with you. When you reel into oblivion, He is there with you. When you try recovery and go through withdrawal, He is there with you holding your hand. ACKNOWLEDGE HIS PRESENCE!

As of lately it seems there are two ways this opiate/heroin addiction comes to an end. God in His infinite wisdom and mighty power…DELIVERS YOU…or HE brings you HOME. GET YOURSELF RIGHT WITH GOD. Either way, You are going to need HIM…

7/19/14 – Constructive Act #121 – Know The Law

I heard a story this week that made me so angry that I just wanted to cry. Everything that happened was so unnecessary and it was completely avoidable IF…everyone involved had just known the law. First and foremost, when you are in the throes of addiction, whether you are an addict or the family member of an addict, you must know your rights and the laws involved that protect you.

There is a medical amnesty law that was passed in Georgia this past April that protects anyone who makes a phone call, or provides assistance in any way regarding a medical emergency involving illegal drugs from prosecution. The law reads as follows: House Bill: 965/AP

SECTION 1-1. 22 This part shall be known and may be cited as the "Georgia 9-1-1 Medical Amnesty Law." (b) Any person who in good faith seeks medical assistance for a person experiencing or believed to be experiencing a drug overdose shall not be arrested, charged, or prosecuted for a drug violation if the evidence for the arrest, charge, or prosecution of such drug violation resulted solely from seeking such medical assistance. Any person who is experiencing a drug overdose and, in good faith, seeks medical assistance for himself or herself or is the subject of such a request shall not be arrested, charged, or prosecuted for a drug violation if the evidence for the arrest, charge, or prosecution of such drug violation resulted solely from seeking such medical assistance. Any such person shall also not be subject to, if related to the seeking of such medical assistance:

(1) 'Drug overdose' means an acute condition, including, but not limited to, extreme physical illness, decreased level of consciousness, respiratory depression, coma, mania, or death, resulting from the consumption or use of a controlled substance or dangerous drug by the distressed individual in violation of this chapter or that a reasonable person would believe to be resulting from the consumption or use of a controlled substance or dangerous drug by the distressed individual.

(2) 'Drug violation' means: (A) A violation of subsection (a) of Code Section 16-13-30 for possession of a controlled substance if the aggregate weight, including any mixture, is less than four grams of a solid substance, less than one milliliter of liquid substance, or if the substance is placed onto a secondary medium with a combined weight of less than four grams; (B) A violation of paragraph (1) of subsection (j) of Code Section 16-13-30 for possession of less than one ounce of marijuana; or (C) A violation of Code Section 16-13-32.2, relating to possession and use of drug related objects.

(3) 'Medical assistance' means aid provided to a person by a health care professional licensed, registered, or certified under the laws of this state who, acting within his or her lawful scope of practice, may provide diagnosis, treatment, or emergency medical services.

'Seeks medical assistance' means accesses or assists in accessing the 9-1-1 system or otherwise contacts or assists in contacting law enforcement or a poison control center and provides care to a person while awaiting the arrival of medical assistance to aid such person.

Now, please understand that this is a relatively new addition to the GA Narcotics Law and unfortunately, as loudly as advocates are proclaiming this law, there are still a number of police officers in certain police departments in our state that are unfamiliar with it. With that being said, I will tell you about a situation that occurred less than 3 weeks ago in a metro Atlanta suburb.

There were several young people who were using illegal drugs in a location where one of the users passed out. Another one of the users called 911 and stayed on the phone with them until emergency services arrived. This person was giving instructions to a 3rd user who was trying to resuscitate the user who had passed out. Unfortunately, the passed out user died at the scene. What happened next was completely in contradiction to the law. The remaining users were handcuffed, taken into custody and locked into jail. Because they were all very good friends, one of the users could not stop crying and was placed on "suicide watch." She was kept in a cell where all meals were shoved under the door, and this person had no contact with counselors, or any other mental health practitioners, or outsiders for that matter for 3 days. She remained an additional 7 days in the jail before she was released. She was charged on 4 counts and left the jail awaiting a court date.

Now in fairness to the police departments, the majority of new bills that are passed go into effect on July 1st. This bill was so important that it went into effect immediately on April 25th, 2014. It takes a while to get the information out to everyone involved, and for the training in the new law to take place. Yes – mistakes were made, but they were made in "good faith." So – what can be done to prevent this? Print out this "Constructive Act." Carry it with you in your wallet or your purse, and if you were to need it, pull it out and respectfully educate the people who have not had the training or are unfamiliar with it.

Most certainly, the charges will be dropped in this particular case, but the harm was done and cannot be reversed. If you are dealing with the DISEASE of drug addiction in your family... PROTECT YOURSELF AND YOUR LOVED ONES...KNOW THE LAW.

For more information on the "Medical Amnesty Law" — not to be confused with the "Good Samaritan Law" – Google it and read the law in its entirety.

7/20/14 – Constructive Act #122 – Share Your Story

I wanted to start off by saying that this page is awesome and I am glad there is someone out there that cares enough to help educate the public on opiate addiction. Awareness and support are two of the most important things that addicts need. With that said I'll start with my story...

My name is Cameron J., I am 25 years old, and I am a recovering opiate addict. My story begins in 2007 when I was only 18 years old. In order for you to better understand my recovery, I will walk you through the way I started and progressed with this addiction.

I was introduced to opiates when I had my wisdom teeth taken out. For those of you who have had this procedure, you would probably agree that it is very painful. So, obviously my doctor prescribed me medicine that would help with the pain. I was instructed to take 1 pill every 6 hours as needed for pain. At first I followed the directions, took the pill when I was supposed to, and that was that. The pain eventually stopped, but I continued to take the leftover pills.

Since I no longer felt pain from the procedure, I noticed the "high" for the first time. Essentially, it changed my life. However, it was only a matter of time before it changed my life for the worst. Once I started taking the pain medicine, I noticed that they made me feel fearless, confident, and euphoric. At the time the only high I knew of was from marijuana. Had I not been given the pain medicine, I never would have tried to find a "better high." After the bottle of pain medicine from my wisdom teeth ran out, I knew then I would want to seek more. So I did, and I used pain pills here and there for about a year.

At the age of 19 I started dating a girl who was older than I was. When I starting dating this girl, she introduced me to harder pain medicine. Before her, I was not using all the time. I only used when, or if I could find pills. I never would have thought to look for or try other hard pain pills, but the fact that I had someone older than me holding my hand through it, I felt like it was okay. As the relationship progressed, so did my addiction. At first she told me that I probably should not take these pills everyday or I would get addicted. I would just brush it off and say, "Nah, that won't happen to me, I have it under control." Boy was I wrong. It seemed like everyone but me saw that I was an addict. After being on opiates from the time I was 19 to the time I was 21, I had tried every opiate under the sun.

Eventually, doing just the pills, or just heroin was not enough so I started going to the methadone clinic. Methadone is made for people to come off of opiates, however, my addiction was so strong that even after getting a methadone treatment I would just come home and continue the process.

It is a common misconception that addicts are bad people. The reputation of an addict is never good. My goal is to change this image by giving others a better picture of why addicts become just that, addicts. We do not simply wake up one morning and decide to become addicted to drugs. Yes, we ultimately make the decision to take the drug, but that usually stems from a certain problem within ourselves. Most addicts are in search of something to numb their pain. We want to find something that can take away a problem we feel we cannot fix on our own.

There are tons of reasons why people use, my personal reason for using was because of my dad. He was sick from the time I was seven, to the time he died when I was 21. It didn't seem fair. When I began the use of opiates, he was only getting worse. I hated that for him, and I hated it for my mom and brother. I specifically hated it for myself, so I selfishly used opiates to numb the pain. When he died I was well into my addiction and it only made it worse.

RECOVERY:

It took a while after my father's death, but I finally had a revelation and decided that I no longer wanted to live the lifestyle of an addict. So, I quickly sought treatment and started my recovery.

I started using Suboxone (buprenorphine and naloxone), which is used to treat opiate addiction, in March of 2011. Since I have been on Suboxone, I have not touched an opiate. I no longer have the desire to use opiates. I do not have cravings, and I live a much happier and healthier lifestyle. Currently, I have tapered down on Suboxone, and will continue to do so until my body no longer needs the help. The process of Suboxone is lengthy, however, it has been well worth it. If there is one thing I could say to addicts today, it is that Suboxone will save your life. It will be the easiest way to recover and get clean from a drug that once ruled your life. The Suboxone doctors are a huge help, and provide guidance that every addict needs. I cannot stress enough how much it can improve your recovery.

In addition to Suboxone, I currently attend Narcotics Anonymous meetings. These have also been a great form of guidance. Just attending a meeting will help you realize the importance of getting and staying sober. The mere fact that you are not alone in this disease is enough motivation to help yourself.

HOPE:

My experience with addiction has opened several doors. The most important thing I realized is that turning to drugs was not worth it. In the days of my opiate addiction I surrounded myself with terrible influences.

I left my true friends behind for this drug. I am here to tell you that no matter how hard life can be, drugs are never the answer. I learned this the hard way. My advice is to deal with what ever you may be suffering with in a manageable, non-addictive way. There are so many great opportunities for self-help out there. We all have troubles underneath the surface, but think to yourself, is throwing your life away to any kind of drug worth it? I am here to tell you from experience that it is not.

If you have suffered, or if you are suffering from addiction, I want you to know that there is hope. There is hope to get clean, and there is hope to stay clean. Opiates are extremely powerful substances. They can take over your life in an instant. You will become someone you never thought you would be, and the life you once knew will no longer exist. The fact that I, and several others have been able to step away from this evil is tremendous. Surround yourself with people who love and care about you. Create a strong support group. The fact that I have found people in my life who have been able to lead me in the right direction has changed my life. It has given me hope for the future, and it has given me strength and determination to stay opiate-free and clean for the rest of my life. I strongly believe that there is hope for anyone suffering from this disease. Help and guidance is your friend, seek it and do not be afraid.

7/21/14 – Constructive Act # 123 – Let Your Light Shine

Tomorrow is another day… and tomorrow just happens to be a Monday. When people decide to make a change, most of the time, Monday morning seems like the best time to start. People need encouragement when they begin something new – whether it be a job, a diet, a new class, or RECOVERY. So, tomorrow, wherever you go and whoever you see…Encourage them with a smile, a kind word, a positive message or an inspirational word.

Have you ever watched one of those cute little youtube videos with the little babies giggling? Do you notice what happens? Nine times out of ten, you begin laughing and giggling along with the video. It's a proven fact that when people have a positive attitude, they are more successful.

Statistics show that one of the hardest things you will ever do…will be to make a lifestyle change. Addiction is a lifestyle that has one of the lowest success rates when the addict tries to make a change. Have you ever wondered why? There are several reasons. They are physical, mental and emotional.

Physically, the addicts body is craving that next fix and in the case of opiates/ heroin addiction — it is the most severe craving that we know of. The addict knows that in a matter of seven-seconds, they can go to a place of perfect peace. They also know that if they don't get that fix, either by choice or not, that their body will be in horrible pain and that that pain will last for days. Mentally, they have their brain telling them that they are experiencing pain that they could take complete control of just by deciding to use again. Emotionally, there was probably something in their past that had a major role in the reason they started using in the first place. Chances are, that reason has not gone away, and the truth is that it may never go away. So the point is, everything in their being supports the decision to use again.

With all of that being said, the odds are against them to begin with. So, our job is to build them up with smiles, encouragement, kindness, confidence, and love. They are probably the most defeated group of people you can find anywhere when they are in active addiction. So, when you consider that one in ten people are addicts of some kind, chances are you will run into an addict tomorrow. You may never know who it was, where it was or when it was. It's kind of like angels. We know they are among us, but we don't know who they are. So, LET YOUR LIGHT SHINE… Make somebody feel your infectious spirit and help them to become successful. Who knows, you may be the person who gives them the strength to move forward, and in doing so, you may just safe their life.

Here's a giggle to start your Monday morning! Conquer the world today! www.youtube.com/watch?v=L49VXZwfup8

7/22/14 – Constructive Act #124 – Act According To Your Circumstances

If you were told by your doctor that your child only had three months to live, how would you readjust your life? I may not be a doctor, and I certainly don't have a medical degree, but I can tell you as the mother of an addict who is no longer alive, I would have done things very differently if someone had said to me…"Your child only has 3 months to live." I can tell you right now as the mother of an opiate/heroin addict, that if your child is involved with these drugs, consider yourself warned. It may be three days, three weeks, three months or three years, but if your child does not find his or her way into RECOVERY, it will not end well.

In talking with a sweet friend the other day who has gone through the same pain that I have endured over the past year, we both agreed, that if we had been given fair warning, we would have done things so differently.

We would have taken the Family Leave Act, which would have given us three months to stay with our children and actively help them work through their addiction and into RECOVERY. We both also agreed that one of the main problems with gaining support from others for this epidemic is that until you are directly affected, you never believe that it could affect your family.

As long as the goals of the families involved are to protect the addict with silence and anonymity, the problem will not see any improvement. I believe with all of my heart that we have to open up about what is going on with our families and loved ones in the throes of addiction. We have to get over the embarrassment and shame involved with this epidemic and understand that it is a DISEASE and until we treat it as such, nothing will ever change.

Many families are given what I would have considered a gift when their children overdose and have a close call with death or jail. My family was never given that opportunity. Although we did have an incident where we found out that Davis was involved with drugs and taking things that did not belong to him, we were never given that "wake up call" with a near death experience. We did go the Rehab route and were mistakenly convinced that he was working his Recovery in a way that would bring him back to us like we had known him before the drugs. We had no idea of the severe form of addiction that opiates/heroin create. The majority of our research has been done since his death. We would give our lives to be able to have a redo for our child, but that is not an option.

I am telling you now – If you know that your child is involved with prescription opiates or heroin, their days are numbered. Take action now just as you would if a doctor diagnosed your child with any other disease and told you they had three months to live. I wish I had been given this advice from anyone! I paid thousands of dollars for Davis to be in Rehab – and I was never told of the dangers of opiates/heroin. My child was treated as an alcoholic or a child with an eating disorder. Heroin is a different addiction…It is the drug of such a severe addiction that some consider it the drug of NO RETURN!

It i my belief that "NOTHING IS IMPOSSIBLE WHEN YOU PUT YOUR TRUST IN GOD." With that being said, I have come to believe that Recovery without God is next to impossible. I base everything I write on the advice of the addicts who actively communicate with me on the DDF on a daily basis. THEY ARE THE EXPERTS.

7/23/14 – Constructive Act #125 – Regroup and Try Something Different

I'm sure you have all probably heard the definition of insanity…"doing something over and over again and expecting a different result." I hear from many, many families on the DDF – some write openly and others write privately. One thing I do notice with many of the families living through addiction is that they continue to go back to the same Rehabs and they continue to try and solve the problem of addiction using the same strategies over and over again. I think we have to become more aggressive and more inventive with opiate/heroin addiction. Do I know what that means? Of course not! I would be a millionaire ten times over if I did. I wish I did and not for the money…but because the pain and destruction that this specific addiction is causing throughout our country is more destructive than battles and wars that have gone before. Every 19 minutes, someone in our country dies of addiction! WOW…There are more deaths resulting from addiction than car accidents now in our country. We have to do something DIFFERENT!

On our website www.davisdirection.com, we have a section called Rehab Reviews. There are several reviews on there…BUT not nearly enough. When we first rolled the website out, we asked our addicted readers to submit a review of any Rehabilitation Facility that they had gone through. We even opened it up to parents of addicts to do the same. We had very little participation. Over the course of the past week, many of you have been writing in the comments sections about different Rehab centers that you really believe in and where they are located. The problem is that you have not stated WHY you believe in them. What are they doing different? I did notice that many of your posts use the words "long term" and yes – I am seeing that the most successful rehabs are those that require a "long term" stay. I will tell you from experience that a 3 – 4 week stay is not enough to touch an opiate/heroin addict. The craving for the drug has not even begun to subside. Another thing that I think that needs to change is the weekends need to be treated like any other day of the week. Heroin does not discriminate against days of the week! Weekends at the Rehab that Davis went through consisted of total downtime! There were no organized activities and no therapy on the weekends. WHY? The cravings didn't go away on the weekends!

Rehab is just one very minute part of Recovery! Some people come clean and never even step foot in one. As a matter of fact the last stat that I saw on Rehab facilities stated that only 1 in 10 addicts go through some formal type of Rehab center.

So – what else is out there? There are many new medications on the market for addiction now and some of them specifically for opiate/heroin addiction – since it is the fastest growing addiction in our country. There is also a heroin vaccine that is being used with humans now. The animal trials on the vaccine were very promising blocking the opiate high from the get-go! In other words, someone who takes the vaccine will never be able to experience a Heroin High! There is a drug called Ibogaine that is not even available in the US – You have to go to Mexico or Canada for this treatment. It sounds very promising.

From the education/prevention part of this problem, we need to begin to teach YOGA and other stress relieving activities in our physical education/Health classes as early as Elementary School. Children living in the home of an addict – Mother, Father, Aunt, Uncle, Grandparent or older sibling – have more stress than you can ever imagine. I know because I lived through it. I watched the stress that my other children endured throughout the addiction. We have to help them cope with their daily stressors before they turn to self-medication too.

Also – TREAT anxiety and depression. Medication is not the only answer for these. Diet, Therapy, exercise and meditation are different strategies for treating anxiety and depression.

And of course there is the SPIRITUAL side of Recovery! For Christian believers, there is NO POWER on earth that equals the healing power of God. Spend time studying the word or join a Bible study. Go to church! PRAY. Spend alone time with God – HE WILL DELIVER YOU!

Be creative with your Recovery! There are no set answers and what works for one person does not work for another. Find your Recovery Plan and you may have to try something different from you first thought. IT'S OKAY – You've only failed when you stop trying.

7/24/14 – Constructive Act #126 – Challenge Your Faith

"Faith" in the dictionary is defined as a belief that is not based in truth. Whether it be a religious belief or a belief that is based purely out of hope for a better future. Faith is what we are holding onto right now in this war on Opiates/Heroin. My faith comes from God and the belief that He is the one who will show us the way to fight this epidemic.

Higher power that is different from mine and that is your choice, and that is okay. Nevertheless, we are on the same page as far as the outcome that we would like to pursue and regardless of our differences in life in general, we can work toward our goal of opiate/heroin awareness and change together.

Once again my wonderful husband sent me a great article and said that he felt it needed to be aligned with a Constructive Act. Being that he is one of the smartest people I know…I took his advice and I completely agree with him. So here goes…

In our ever changing world, people have become all too consumed with being politically correct and holding back on their own values and opinions because of it. During especially difficult times when the path to change seems virtually unknown and uncertain, the challenge before us becomes how to inspire trust, confidence and loyalty in the people that we want to walk beside us as we seek to educate, prevent, create awareness and facilitate change in the growing crisis of opiate/ heroin addiction. Why do we expect you to follow our page, read our posts, invest in our foundation, share your personal stories and rely upon us to do what we do when we have no proof that it will work? Because we have FAITH.

We have decided to turn a personal tragedy into a positive Foundation that will seek out knowledge, theory, science, and above all ANSWERS and SOLUTIONS to combat this deadly disease of opiate/heroin addiction. When we were gifted with the life of our precious son 21 years ago, of course we never dreamed that he would end up the "poster child" for a Billboard, that we would personally like to see all over the United States, making others aware of the dangers of Heroin. Like any other new parent, we rather saw him as President of the United States one day, and our lives were busy with providing him all of the opportunities to make that happen. However, when personal tragedy hit us in the head with a brick, we immediately were taken back to "what mattered" and "who mattered" and we decided to make a difference for those things and those people. We realized that we couldn't make a nationwide epidemic go away by ourselves, so we reached out to others who were suffering the same "injustice" and those who could possibly experience the same fate in the future. At that point, we "ALL" took a leap in FAITH and tried and will continue to try our best to make a difference.

Last week a couple of posts were taken out of context and I was very upset as people "quoted the DDF" and really didn't quote it at all, but rather entirely used their own words and twisted the meaning of what was said. Being the one who writes the CA's everyday, I dwelled on it, as I have a tendency to do, and I failed to see that out of almost 4,000 daily readers, I had 2 who had twisted the context. Now in any other situation, I would have considered those pretty darn good odds, but it bothered me.

Faith is all I have to go on...I write from the heart and I believe that with the growing awareness and knowledge that we are putting out there regarding this epidemic, we are going to make a difference.

I don't have "PROOF" and I know that I am asking you to jump on board a cause where we are asking you to believe, even when the "tangible proof doesn't exist"...and the reason we are fighting in the first place doesn't even make sense to the majority of people. Why would a bright, intelligent, young person full of potential turn to prescription medications or the dangerous drug called HEROIN?

Please challenge your FAITH and help us at the Davis Direction Foundation to turn this rapidly raging epidemic into a movement of awareness and change that exceeds the growth of this drug that is taking the lives of our children, spouses, siblings and loved ones.

Next week I will return to work to complete my journey of 30 years of public school service which will end on November 30th. I will be working double duty until then and I'm sure mistakes will be made and things of lesser importance will be placed on a back burner. Please don't hesitate to "re-email" me or "remind" me of things that you notice might need attention. I could use the help. Have FAITH in our Foundation – because it belongs to everyone of us who believe in the SOLUTION to Opiate/Heroin addiction and abuse. Don't wait to become involved until you are hit in the head with a brick. WE WILL MAKE A DIFFERENCE.

TOMORROW I will be compiling a new list of different Rehabs that people have mentioned lately. Please check back to see which ones have been recommended.

7/25/14 – Constructive Act #127 – Write a Rehab Review

Last week was a terrible week in the fight against opiate/heroin addiction. So much tragedy surrounding the week and filling every person with sadness and gloom. Out of the stories of last week, many out there saw a need to find a good Rehab facility and wrote in offering the names of many. I have compiled the names and have looked for links to websites. I will post them and then I will also post resources that were shared as well. I have not personally researched all of them, but what I did look at seemed worth the time I invested. So, If you were one of the ones who submitted a name or a resource, PLEASE consider writing a "Rehab Review" offering your thoughts and sending them to me at info@davisdirection.com. I will post them on the website at www.davisdirection.com.

We have asked for Reviews before, but people are apprehensive to write them. Please write what you know and you can keep your offerings factual. Write about education, therapy, # of patients accepted, co-ed or not, finances, cleanliness, downtime, success rate, wait time, etc... You can write anonymously or you can include your name — either way is fine. You can go to the website and look for examples if you like. I would really like to try to step-up this part of our website as a service for other families looking for treatment.

If you are reading this post and you have information or experience with any of these Rehabs or Resources, please chime in in the comments section below and let us know what your experience has been. If you have a different Rehab or Resource to share, please feel free to post that as well. It will take all of us working together to find the solutions.

7/26/14 – Constructive Act #128 – Pause to Understand P.A.W.S.

And I'm not talking about the pet organization. I'm talking about POST ACUTE WITHDRAWAL SYNDROME. Most of you have heard me say or have read somewhere that Opiates/Heroin addiction is the most severe form of addiction that we know of. Because you can reach a place of perfect peace in 7 seconds or less and because withdrawal from these drugs is so painful and excruciating, it seems almost impossible to quit. Even when you have entered Recovery and have been there for months, the drug keeps calling your name! The epidemic continues to rage because it is fueled by the fire of withdrawal.

I'M NOT GOING TO REINVENT THE WHEEL ON THIS ONE! I have found the perfect website to explain the syndrome. It includes the explanation of what exactly it is; then it gives you the symptoms as well as strategies to use as well as tools that will equip you with the means to fight back against withdrawal.

I lost my Sweet Davis because he couldn't fight the withdrawal. I was not equipped with the knowledge to help him. There were things I could have helped with such as Nutrition during withdrawal. Educate yourselves – whether you are the addict or the person who supports the addict. KNOWLEDGE IS POWER. Please read this VERY comprehensive website. whatmesober.com/paws/

On this the first day of her third year of Sobriety…Congratulations to Brandy W. This story will surely save lives. UNBELIEVABLE… Thank you Brandy…You may never know the impact of sharing this story.

My sobriety date is July 26, 2012. Before coming into the Extension, I was what one may consider as "doomed". I came from a "split" dysfunctional family. Don't feel, don't talk, be seen not heard… out of sight, out of mind and everything must be perfect to the outside world was deeply ingrained.
My father was an alcoholic and cocaine addict who was extremely abusive in every sense of the word, emotional, physical, sexual, mental and verbal . My mother was a person that the community looked up to. My mom, who became a single mother did the best she could do. However, my dreams were smashed at an early age… and it took quite some time for me to be able to recall anything positive from my childhood. I had a lot of mixed messages and jaded perceptions.

At 9 years old, I started stealing from gas stations. I can now say it was a "payback" thing to get back at my mom. At 13 years old, I started actively using cocaine. At this time I would manipulate my mom into dropping me off at the skating rink ... I've never skated, in fact, I've probably only put on a pair of skates once if that. The only reason I went and wanted to go to the skating rink was to get high in the bathroom. Things escalated quickly and I lost what little of myself I had.

After cocaine I went to meth and anything else I could get my hands on. I was such a lost, confused, and angry little girl. I went through life just trying to cope and blend in. At 16 I had a couple of shots at modeling but those fell apart due to my drug use. Then... I decided I wanted to be a "thug" on the streets. When I hit the streets, I hit them hard. Criminal activity became a way of life and I viewed it as being self-sufficient. I absolutely loved and lusted after the fast paced lifestyle. Another form of addiction, another high. I was certain that I was going to die in the streets. I never thought I would make it out. My motto was "Go big or go home, nothing little... make the time worth it" ... I did a lot of time behind bars, hindsight is 20/20... it wasn't worth it. Every time I went to jail it was like a family reunion... instead of the roaches singing "We are family" the cons shouted it from their bunks. The jailers, the DA, the nurses, and the judges all knew me by first name... no last name needed. Each time I was incarcerated my favorite line was " I'm sorry, I will never do it again"... 3 weeks would be pushing it but you can bet I was right back behind those bars.

The justice system was my way of life since I was about 16... Up until recently, last month to be exact, I've always had 3 probations in different counties running at the same time... now I'm down to 1. THAT IS HUGE! I was the type of addict that would steal from you and then "help" you look for whatever it was... or I would wait until you went out of town or out to dinner even, sell your furniture out of your house like you wouldn't miss it when you returned. Of course my drug use increased and behaviors were off the charts.

At 21, I had my son who is now 7. I have been in and out of his life, no consistency what so ever. My mother and her husband stepped into the parental role when he was about 2 years old. I couldn't stop using, I couldn't give up the lifestyle... I adored the chaos. I was a perfect definition of a chaos junkie... if chaos wasn't present, I could and would create it.

I can recall many nights laying on the floor withdrawing from the opiates praying and screaming to die. Fox hole type prayers were my favorite while laying in the floor thinking I was dying from heroin... "Please God, if there is a God help stop these withdrawals..." "Please God, make it stop I will never use again". At this point death was okay with me, in fact... death was welcomed. "If there's a GOD, TAKE ME, TAKE ME NOW... I can't do this..."

There were times where I had overdosed and the only way I knew was due to the fact my chest had been beaten black and blue by the person that was living with me at the time. I entered The Extension in 2009, ironically exactly 3 years before my sobriety date. I wasn't ready, at all. Self run riot all the way. I finally got discharged for not following the rules. I broke all their standards, guidelines and rules... made my own, and broke those too. So I went out and started digging my bottom deeper and deeper, playing with death. Life was a gamble and life dealt me some messed up cards.

Finally after losing my family, having minimal contact, if any, with my son, countless time behind bars and losing every bit of myself in any shape, form or fashion, the gift of desperation was in full effect. I returned to The Extension, completely and utterly broken.

Courage isn't the absence of fear, I now know what that truly means... that was the most fearful day for me... walking back through those doors was the most courageous thing I've done. My freedom of choice was given back... freedom, something I didn't have the true concept of, was there. While at The Extension I was able to learn what made me tick. The opportunity to look inward and upward instead of outward and downward. Finally enlightened to the fact that I wasn't a bad person, I was a sick person.

Addiction is a disease much like cancer. I gained insight into what boundaries were and how to utilize them. The importance of communication and interaction with others in a healthy manner which is a necessity in everyday life. Most have a jaded perception about relationships and trust... I never knew what genuine, real relationships were about and I was able to experience my first while at The Extension.

I think the most useful group/class for me was Relapse Prevention. I carry that book everywhere! In school I was taught that knowledge is power; well I'm inclined
to believe that is true. Relapse doesn't just happen, many components lead up to the actual relapse. Relapse occurs in the brain before the actual using begins. Awareness about the disease, not just about the actual drug use, is a vital part.

While at The Extension, I actively started working the 12 steps and the principles behind them and began my journey in recovery. When it came to the principles and the steps, like most I know, I made it harder than it had to be. I had to start by making little changes. "If nothing changes, nothings changes"... for myself stopping at the crosswalk and waiting on that little man to come up was huge. Somewhere along the process I became a productive member of society. I was employable even with my lengthy criminal record, which is longer than some side streets. I gained the true meaning of being self sufficient and responsible. I built self esteem, self worth and self respect – qualities and characteristics I never had before. My recovery has opened more doors than my addiction ever slammed shut. Addiction has a domino effect – it impacts every one that is in contact with the addict... I'd like to view my recovery the same way. Liabilities turned into assets. The Extension is my foundation; I visit frequently. Watching things "click" and the life come to a person who was dead when they came into the doors is probably the greatest gift.

I'm currently sponsoring 3 women. I can only hope I help and assist them as much as they help and assist me. My relationship with my family is honest and progressing daily. The slogan "Time takes time" is a perfect fit. I'm a parent now, whereas before I was in and out and never really present. I experience my son's witty and comical responses and watch him grow daily. I'm active in his school and activities...a total baseball mom. Most importantly, I can impact his life in a positive way. I'm a woman — no longer a scared little girl; I have a voice; I am worthy. I strive to give back to my community and to be involved. Currently I participate in a youth outreach program, it's amazing!

My dreams have been awakened. I want to assist other addicts and open the pathway to a life they never knew existed. I was asked some time ago if I considered myself a success. I myself am NOT a success and I refuse to allow my ego to tell my otherwise. I have an addict's mind. What is successful: The Extension, the program and my Higher Power. I am lucky enough to live two lives, grow, evolve, improve, help others and go to sleep with a clear conscience. That is purposeful, that is success. Just because one is breathing doesn't mean they're alive... I am alive... grateful to be alive.
– Brandy W.

7/28/14 – Constructive Act #130 – Never Use Alone

I hate to use a negative word in a Constructive Act – but I couldn't think of a better or more direct way to get this one across. Just like in swimming, there is the"buddy policy" – it is put into practice for a very good reason. It is meant to save lives. I'm certainly not suggesting here that you should use with a buddy, or that you should use at all for that matter. But, what I am saying is that you should never use alone and put yourself in a situation where if you overdosed, no one would be around to find you.

I can't help but think about Davis and the fact that he used alone in his car in a dark parking lot behind a building. Although he was in a very busy strip mall shopping center, he chose to park behind a restaurant close to the dumpsters where others may not choose to park. He was alone and no one knew where he was. He stayed in his car for over 22 hours until he was found.

I know there will always be a lot of "What ifs" but the fact remains, he chose not to put himself in a situation where he would be found if the worse case scenario came to fruition. And, of course it did. Had he come home to use, or if he had been with others, or even if he had gone into the bathroom of the restaurant instead of the parking lot alone in his car, he might have been rescued. He did not intend on dying that night alone in his car. There were too many facts that proved that. He expected to use, come home and go about his life. He was trying to get his life together, but he got caught up in the addiction and made a mistake that cost him his life.

I'm not naive enough to believe that just because someone says to stop using that addicts will stop using. We all know that it does not work that way. So, when you use prescription drugs illegally or you use heroin, if your intention it to live, then it is vitally important that you use in a place that if something goes horribly wrong that you will be found.

Today in the "SHARE YOUR STORY SUNDAY" Brandy said that she was completely broken when she decided to make a change. Someone even commented on the fact that all too often, people die before they are broken enough to choose recovery. In the first Symposium that we had on June 3rd, Dr. Sam Matthews, a DDF Director, made it very clear that the elevator of life goes ALL THE WAY to the BOTTOM...BUT...YOU CAN GET OFF ON EVERY FLOOR. You don't have to wait until you hit rock bottom. Learn from the stories of others like Brandy. Make a conscious choice to get off of the elevator before you get to the bottom. Begin working your way back up to the top, there are plenty of people out there who are just waiting to help you on your journey to RECOVERY! There is HOPE; There is FREEDOM; There is LIFE... Choose to LIVE and help others do the same. GODSPEED on your journey.

7/29/14 – Constructive Act #131 – Make a Phone Call

That's all… just make one phone call. Make it to someone that you have lost touch with and just check in with them. Reconnect and make sure they are doing well. Sometimes when people fall off the social scene, it's because they are working so hard to take care of themselves or someone that they love. Let them hear a live voice on the other end – no texting or emails…talk to them so there will be no miscommunication.

If you cannot get in touch with them using the cell phone, try a house phone or go by the house and just say hello. This new age communication often leaves a lot to be desired and also leaves a lot of things unspoken. One of the first things an addict loses is his or her phone. In most Rehabs, the first things they ask an addict to do is leave their phone behind. They won't even let you bring it into the facility in most cases.
I know that when Davis discreetly entered Rehab, there were many texts and messages that came to his phone and his computer. Several attempts were made by individuals to touch base with him. After they received no response, instead of calling the house phone or dropping by the house, they just stopped communicating altogether. It was kind of like if I can't get a response, I'll just move on to another friend who will reciprocate with the texts or messages.

Sadly, the only people who continued to send messages and texts were those who were trying to push drugs or collect money. The rest of the "friends" just chalked up no response to no response and went on about their lives. How sad! I know that so many people said to me…"If I had only known, I would have reached out to Davis and tried to make a difference."

I'm sure that was true. I guess what I am trying to say is that if you feel something is different and you try numerous times to get a response from someone who has responded to you in the past, but for some strange reason just stops responding… Find out WHY! Friends don't usually just ignore friends without a reason.

Opiate/Heroin addiction is an epidemic in our nation. More people are dying from overdoses from drug addiction than are dying in car wrecks now in our country. Don't assume when your friend stops responding to you for no reason that everything is okay… if they are truly your friend…Check on them and just let them know they are important to you and that you are concerned. The same things goes for the loved ones of the addicts. They spend so much of their time trying to help their child, spouse, brother, sister, parent or whomever, that they lose touch with the outside world. Remember the old song…Reach out and Touch someone you love – That's what an addict needs – A LOVING TOUCH, not a text with no follow-up!

7/30/14 – Constructive Act #132 – Give And Take

It's really a simple concept…sometimes you give and sometimes you take. If you think about it, if no one ever gave, then no one could ever take and vice versa. So – why is it so hard for some people to "TAKE?" I have found throughout my life that it's much harder for good people to "take" that it is for them to "give." Giving never seems to be a problem for most people. Some people will even give when they really don't have enough to share…but they give anyway! Taking is not always so easy – there seems to be a stigma that goes along with "taking."

Many times when people are going through the most trying times in their lives, they don't share their problems with others. When they could really use help in many ways, they never let any one know that they are in need. They don't want to "take" from others to help themselves. A lot of time I know there is pride involved, but pride is usually preceded by shame and embarrassment that a person or family has problems in the first place.

I have been very busy trying to plan this golf tournament and get donations for the Silent Auction. Sometimes it's still very hard to "ASK" for help. Even though I know that my friends and family… and I'm finding out even STRANGERS… are wanting to help and do whatever they can to make this Foundation a SUCCESS. My heart has been touched in SO many ways. I've reconnected with old friends, I've made new friends, and I've of course had my true friends beside me every step of the way.
Some people will not take NO for an answer when they are trying to help make a difference, and you do not know what that means to a person receiving the gifts. It is still VERY humbling to accept the fact that I need help. This job is bigger than me and I am not capable of doing this alone. When I rally help, I am still always afraid of the word "NO" – and it's not because I won't get help from a specific person, but it's the fact that I may have offended someone by asking.

I started thinking about this in relationship to Davis and other young adults – or anyone for that matter – who is using. I remember how extremely hard it was for him to finally break down and ask for help. Even though we were trying our best to help him in the ways that we thought were correct, he was ashamed to accept our help. I have asked myself over and over again why that is and I keep coming up with the same answer over and over again. He did not feel "worthy" of our help or anyone's help. He felt like he was a burden to everyone – even though he knew every one of us in the family would have laid down to die for him. Accepting help is HARD!

Shame is a terrible enemy. It keeps addicts from getting the help and care that they need. They will "take" from you behind your back because they are too embarrassed to ask you for help or tell you they are feeling "less than" and in need, to your face. HELP THEM ANYWAY! Don't take NO for an answer. Drive them to counseling and stay with them, visit Rehabs with them and help them choose one, take them to church with you, read self-help articles aloud to them. If you know they are using, it's not important that you make them admit it or even find their stash. EDUCATE them and GIVE them the best you have. Make them TAKE your help by not allowing them to refuse. Inform them of new options that are in the news every day!

Now I know that I have said on numerous occasions that it is the addict has to make the EFFORT and decide to enter RECOVERY. I'm not contradicting that in what I'm saying. All I am saying is that they NEED someone along the way to walk beside them who WILL NOT TAKE NO for an answer. Help them to overcome their shame and guilt and remind them of their WORTH! That is the biggest struggle! Try your best to MAKE THEM "TAKE!" It will be the hardest thing you ever figure out how to do.

7/31/14 – Constructive Act #133 – Keep a Box of Kudos

Twenty-eight years ago when I was hired in Cobb County as a first grade teacher, my awesome principal told me to keep a box of every nice note that anyone ever wrote to me.

Being young and impressionable, I brought my box to school the very next day. It was a beautiful Jessica McClintock gift box my husband had given to me. I still have that box to this day and for the last 28 years, I have been filling it with notes from parents, students, administrators, colleagues, community leaders and family members. I keep it at school on my shelf and every now and again, I NEED to take it off the shelf and read those kind and meaningful notes that were written from the hearts of people that I cared very much for.

Life is full of ups and downs and every day will not be a day that we will want to write home about. We have to learn the life skill of taking the good along with the not so good and learn to put it into perspective and move onward through life. There will be days when we are down in the dumps for whatever reason and we need to learn how to rise above. That's where our box of "KUDOS" can come in very handy. Take it off the shelf and read as many of them as is necessary to remind you about all of

your special qualities and about all the times that you were there for someone when they needed you to help them. Allow them to return the favor... by re-reading their heartfelt note of a time that you used your gifts and talents to help them rise above.

Re-reading my notes from my "KUDOS" box is what finally convinced me to become a Counselor. I decided that it felt great to genuinely help others and that some people thought that I had a gift for it. So, I went back to school and chased my dream of helping others. My box of notes gave me strength when I needed it and helped me to remember that when I failed or made a mistake that it wasn't the end of the world. They reminded me that on any given day, the tables would turn and I would be the one making someone else feel good about himself or herself.

Your box of KUDOS will do the same for you whenever you need it. So many times when we are in the valleys of life, we forget of all the wonderful things that we have accomplished in our lives. The box of heartfelt notes and sentiments will remind you of exactly what you mean to someone in your past or even in your present. The notes will remind you that you are a worthy human being who has the capacity to change the course of life for another person. It will remind you of a time when you were in your prime and being a productive person making a difference. It will make you feel warm inside and perhaps even bring tears to your eyes as you reminisce over the wonderful joy that you've brought to others throughout your life.

Find a special box TODAY and make it YOUR box of KUDOS. You probably already have a note or two that you kept because it made you feel good. Put them in your box...but make sure to re-read them before you do. YOU ARE WORTHY!

I have posted one of my most cherished notes – one I received from Davis after his week on the oil rigs in the summer of 2012, before his death. His Dad and I had given his room a makeover while he was gone.

8/1/14 – Constructive Act #134 – Wake Up and Smell The Coffee

Well it happened today. My 14 year old was offered prescription medication from another person slightly older than she is. Am I shocked? Not really. Am I mad? I can't decide. Am I going to do something about it? You bet I am!!!

You're probably asking yourself right about now why I can't decide if I am mad? The answer to that is because I"m not sure the other child knew what she was doing. Did she know what she had. Did she know that offering prescription narcotics is a criminal offense? Did she know that what she had in her purse is extremely addictive? Did she know that she needs to stop taking those meds when

106

the pain they were prescribed for becomes manageable? Did she know that she needs to return those extra pills to a dropbox? My gut tells me probably not, but my head says…"ARE YOU KIDDING ME?"

When the statistics are telling us that a person dies every nineteen minutes from a drug overdose and we know that there are more deaths that are related to prescription drug abuse than there are car accident deaths now, it is hard to believe that parents are not policing these drugs with an overpowering sense of authority. I just saw on the news where 3 teenagers are being charged in the heroin death of a beautiful young lady, because they did heroin together and she died of an overdose. They waited 10 hours to make a call to someone that she had died. They are still looking for who supplied the heroin. Now I know these kids and even the suppliers probably did not start with heroin. They probably started with prescription drug meds that weren't theirs. And the dealer probably did not start by dealing heroin either. I would assume he or she started off dealing something much less potent. So – going back to my questions about the one who offered drugs to my child yesterday…Where is she in the process…OR…is she even in the process?Either way, I'm going to help her. I can only hope and pray that she doesn't have a clue and neither do her parents about the implications of what happened yesterday. I can only hope and pray that when she offered those meds to my child that she was thinking that she only genuinely wanted to help her with her minor muscle pain. I can only hope and pray that she will listen with an open heart as will her parents and they will understand the epidemic as we all do if you are one of the regular DDF readers. AWARENESS, EDUCATION, CHANGE, and PREVENTION are our goals. I would be such a hypocrite if I sat back and just SHOOK MY HEAD! GOD GIVE ME STRENGTH!

8/2/14 – Constructive Act #135 – Rescue Your Individuality

I Believe that all too often in life people become what they are expected to become or what they are encouraged to become or even worse…what they think their parents want them to become. In this crazy world in which we live, there is so much pressure surrounding what happens to a child when they are done with college, and their path is not so clear anymore. Now they have choices and they are not being told what the next step is – except to get a job. What a frightening time in the life of a kid who has been told every move to make up to this point.

Even in college, you are told every class to take and what year to take it in. That's great if you know exactly what you want to do when you get out of school, but what about those kids who don't really know. I know I obtained 3 degrees before I really decided what I wanted to do in life. Now, especially in the state of GA, with the HOPE scholarship, you don't waste classes taking them just to see if it is something you like, because that eats up the money in your scholarship. You are only given the exact number of class hours that it takes to get the degree that you have chosen.

Then when you do get out of college and you are entering your first job, many times due to accountability measures put in place, that degree you got and possibly went into serious debt for didn't help you at all because you have to do things the way the company tells you via some kind of computer program or online "fill in the blank" one size fits all, cookie cutter system chosen by someone else because it works for them.

WHEW – what a way to lose your individuality. All this time you went to school and were told to think outside the box, and use your higher order thinking skills, you thought you were preparing yourself for the outside world. Little did you know that you would enter the world of conformity! Conform to this and conform to that and do as I say, not as I do. WHAT A DISAPPOINTMENT. Real life is not really that different from school.

People have lost their individuality because there is no longer time to get to know one another, interact as individuals, learn your common traits and "BECOME SOMEONE."

We are an email, or a username. We are a number or a symbol. We have become anything but human because we are all too busy measuring our accountability. Enough is Enough. When can people just be individuals with personality and get the job done that they were hired to do? IT'S NO WONDER OUR KIDS ARE STRESSED OUT AND HAVE TURNED TO DRUGS!

The Wall Street Journal recently published an article about how truckers can no longer veer from their schedules because they have computerized programs inside their trucks scheduling every stop, bathroom break, gas fill-up, snack and drink stop. No time to be nice to others and have a conversation along the way. They will never meet a new friend or network with others for different opportunities because of the micro-management involved in companies now.

I'm going to get off of my high horse now and stop the rave so that I can go and trade my high efficiency washing machine in for an old fashioned, agitating, fill with water to the top, in order to get the job done REAL MACHINE!!! Food for thought!

8/3/14 – Constructive Act # 136 – Share Your Story

This week, the story of addiction is being shared anonymously because of the children involved. The thing I want everyone to see from this story is that this person began his addiction at the age of 32! We have talked about the age of opiate/heroin addiction being on average the addiction of 18 – 36 year olds. It's not just young kids... it's adults as well under stress and trying to find a way to cope! Thank you for sharing this story with us today.

Hi, I just wanted to share with you that your organization is WONDERFUL! I remember being in high school way back in 1996 and this type of epidemic did not exist. I read your constructive Acts daily...they have helped me a different type of way. I'm a mom to 3 younger children with one on the way...My husband currently lives with his parents due to opiate pain pill addiction (oxies, roxies, you name it). Over the past 3 years I have endured so many of the things you write about!! We tried everything, inpatient, outpatient, the list goes on like you know.
I have not suffered a loss like you, I cannot imagine and admire you for your strength. I do feel like I lost my husband, best friend, the guy that graduated with me back in '96 from Norcross High School...just lost him in a different way(lost him to the disease of addiction that is headed to divorce). I drew the line in the sand...you cannot bring pills into the house with little innocent children. I would wake up to a stranger some days and the kids would be frightened because their strong, loving, kind Daddy was a sick monster in withdrawal on the couch.

Each day I pray, that somehow, someway, before the divorce is final, he finds his way back to us and chooses family over pills.

My job now after 3 years of trying endlessly to help is to take care of myself and the kids...because it affected me so badly there was a point I was so depressed I could hardly get out of bed.

When we married, the pills were not a part of my husbands life yet, they were introduced by an old high school friend and the nightmare began from there...at the age of 32.

I have thought about writing you for sometime, but I didn't have the strength because my situation is different...yet your foundation has been my hope. God Bless you.

8/4/14 – Constructive Act #137 – Take an Interest Inventory

It's an age-old tool that has been around for a long time, but people rarely use them unless they are offered in a therapy session or through a school class. They are available online and you can take them in the comfort of your own home or office. You can get specific job results or you can get generalized categories of what field you might enjoy.

I have included 2 links for inventories that will take about 15 minutes each. See if you are working in the right field or if you are training in the right field. You might be surprised at your results. You might even make some changes based on your results. At the very least, look into your results and see if you can glean anything from them.

A couple of days ago when I posted about "rescuing your individuality," there were some comments that were full of emotion. Rightly so! We have become a world that places way too much emphasis on the wrong things. Who makes the most money? Who has the most material things? Who has the highest job title? Who is blue collar and who is white collar? It seems somewhere along the way we forgot to ask the question...Who is the happiest in their life?

My Daddy always had a saying for when I was growing up and I would be intimidated by someone. He would say..."He puts his pants on one leg at a time!" or "She puts her pants on one leg at a time!" Either way, the lesson was the same. Not one of us is any better than the rest of us. Yes, — there will always be judgmental people out there and I'm sure that most of us will have to admit to being one of them at some point in our life. But, in the end we answer to one God and we answer to Him alone!

Find out what will make you happy and spend the rest of your life doing it. Be productive enough to put a roof over your head and food on the table. The rest is just not that important when it's all said and done. Life is short, but it need not be shorter than it is supposed to be because in your stress and discomfort you turn to addictive substances. If you become that stressed out, take a step back and re-examine your motives and the life you are leading. Figure out how to remove the stress and spend the rest of your life doing what feels RIGHT and GOOD.

checkoutacollege.com/explorecareers/interestsurvey.aspx
www.mynextmove.org/explore/ip

8/5/14 – Constructive Act #138 – It's Okay to Cry

I don't like to cry. I think crying is a sign of weakness and I try hard not to ever cry. It's embarrassing to cry and I would rather be strong and brave. But, the truth of the matter is in the last 5 months I have cried more tears than I have probably cried during all the rest of my life. In fact, I am crying right now as I write this post. The tears just seem to fall from my eyes sometimes and there is no stopping them. Today is an anniversary – It's been 5 months since we lost him and I miss him more and more each passing day.

I just want to sit beside him and be near him. I want to smell his cologne and look at his chewed up fingernails. I want to laugh with him at Uncle Si and stay up late just to talk to him. I want to apologize to him for not understanding while he was alive what he was going through and for not investing the time to help him because I didn't understand what Heroin was and how it affected people. I want to write a post for him that means something and helps him like it helps others who write to me that I help them. I want a do-over that I will never get! So I cry – and it's okay! It feels weak and embarrassing, but it makes me humble and teaches me to turn to God for comfort. I feel better when I finish and then I have the strength to keep on keeping on for the good of others who need help.

I cry when I ride down the street and his billboard comes up unexpectedly and I feel like he is here on earth again. It really kind of takes my breath away. I cry when something happens in our family and our WHOLE family isn't here to celebrate or to grieve together. I cry because there is a void that cannot be filled no matter what I do. I cry on the first day of school because he would have started his senior year of college this fall and instead, he sits on my mantle and he will never graduate from college. I cry because if I can't take his picture for the first day of school, I don't want any pictures and I don't want to see anyone else's either. I cry because I am planning and organizing a huge golf tournament which he would have, and should have been playing in and helping with and he would have, because he was a servant leader!

I cry because I get frustrated with the computer and he is not here to help me. He always made everything right! God knows how I miss my boy and it just never gets any easier. I cry when everyone goes to bed because I don't like for them to see my cry. It makes them sad and then they get upset. I cry because I got the chance to love one of the greatest kids on earth for almost 21 years. I cry because it was better to have loved and lost than to have never loved at all. But, that doesn't mean it doesn't hurt to love and lose. I cry because I can't help it – It just happens and IT'S OKAY TO CRY!

8/6/14 – Constructive Act #139 – Plan an Event

That's right – You can do it. Plan an event in your community to bring AWARENESS to the epidemic of Opiate/Heroin addiction. There is an event that would be awesome to participate in and one that could be easily planned in any community and it's called the "LIGHTS OF HOPE."

On September 1st, from 9:00 – 9:15 – "LIGHTS OF HOPE" is planned to go on across the nation. It's a candle lighting service to light 3 candles. One is for an addict who is using, one is for an addict in Recovery, and the 3rd is for an addict who will forever be remembered and loved.

I am going to plan the service for the Davis Direction Foundation and it will be held locally. The service should take no longer than 15 minutes and it is just a way to pledge support and show the addicts and "Recovery Resources" in attendance that we accept them and understand that they have a disease. You can sing a song, say a prayer, read a poem or just tell about the 3 people that you honor and why you honor them.

This is not a hard event to plan, you just need some candles, some lighters and some love in the service. That's all! So no matter where you are, and no matter how large or small you want your event to be, it's something that can be done wherever you are. You might want to have a simple neighborhood event. You might want to host an event at your church or at your school. You might want to plan your event at a local park or in a town square.

Let's plan these events all over and then post pictures about how we brought AWARENESS to this epidemic and then how we plan to bring about CHANGE. Together we can make it happen! Let's LIGHT up the Nation on the evening of September 1st as we participate in the "LIGHTS OF HOPE" sponsored by "The Addicts MOM." Keep watching the DDF for the announcement of our "Lights of HOPE."

8/7/14 – Constructive Act #140 –Explore a Website

The other day I posted an article from Molly, that told of a story about her cousin, Jeffrey who had struggled with prescription opiate addiction and eventually died from an overdose. The story was posted on Attorney General Sam Olens' website.

The website had many other very good articles, tips, statistics, and solutions for prescription drug abuse. I probably spent over an hour going through the site looking at everything available under the "Prescription Drug" tab. I thought about taking several pieces of it and including them in the "constructive acts" in the coming days. Instead, I decided to just make the "Constructive Act" to explore a website and use this very good site as the example.

My hat is off to Sam Olens – GA Attorney General – for recognizing this epidemic as a "Key Issue" and for putting such a great site together to explain it to his constituents. The only thing that I think should have been added to the site is the fact that when addicts run out of money using Prescription drugs, they often turn to Heroin because of the price and availability.

Many of you know already from reading the DDF, that there was a protective coating put on prescription opiates several years ago in order to address the problem of abuse, however, it drove the price of each pill up making it unaffordable to most prescription drug addicts. Being addicted and out of money for drugs, many of them turned to heroin which was sold on every street corner for $10 or less every day of the week. This is why the Heroin problem spiraled out of control.

Take a look at this very comprehensive website because there is a statistic that suggests that 80% of all heroin users began their drugs abuse with prescription drugs. Every parent in our nation should go to this website and read every word.

KNOWLEDGE IS POWER!
GREAT JOB MR. ATTORNEY GENERAL!

law.ga.gov/prescription-drug-abuse

8/8/14 – Constructive Act #141 – Re-read The Little Engine That Could

And I do hope that it is a RE -READ and not a first time read for all of you. One of the greatest stories ever written. A story of motivation and positive thinking written in the simplest form, yet having the most complex lesson in life......this story is magnificent. I can't imagine living a childhood void of this little book. As a first grade teacher when I began my education career, it was a staple in my classroom.

I feel like I could use a good dose of the book right now in my life. I'm in the twilight of my career as a public school counselor and in the beginning of my life as a co-founder of a Foundation to make others aware of the perils that took my son from me – opiates/heroin. I'm burning the candles at both ends as they say... and I have to keep telling myself...I think I can ...I think I can...I think I can.

Sometimes in life when we get to the most difficult chapters and the darkest valleys, we have to resort back to the lessons we learned early on to get us through, and this little book held one of them for me. For an addict, perhaps it could help you through recovery. It's all about self-talk and positive thinking which is a huge part of recovery. It's about believing in yourself and what you have chosen to do in order to reach your goals. It's about being bigger than the problems you are facing and mustering up all the strength to make it to the top of the hill so that the view on the other side is blissful.

If you don't own a copy of this great little story by Watty Piper, go out today and buy a copy and keep it with you as you work through your recovery. Read it every day. Memorize the important lines and the sayings that you need to repeat to yourself when you are feeling the cravings of the past closing in on you. Imagine yourself as that sweet little engine that would let nothing stand between himself and success.

We're coming up on National Recovery Month in September. Position yourself now to be ready to take that leap of faith on September 1st, 2014.

Step into recovery and into a life that will put the past behind you. Find a support network, a church that embraces its people – all of them – and a friend or two who will be there for you on your journey. Look into all the options – drug therapy, Vivitrol, Rehab, individual therapy, group therapy…Decide now what route you will take and be ready to "THINK YOU CAN."

8/9/14 – Constructive Act #142 – Mark Your Calendar

There are people on the DDF everyday who are asking "How can I help?" "What can I do?" "Is there anything you need?" Well…as a matter of fact…"YES THERE IS!" I need all of you to mark your calendars now to attend two events! I will list them below and tell you how you can help and what you can do! So my friends, it's time to put your "Energy" where your mouth is and take action!

FIRST EVENT: Monday evening September 1st, Kennesaw Mountain High School Front Lawn, 9:00 – 9:15 p.m. We will participate in the "National Lights of Hope" ceremony sponsored by "The Addict's Mom" organization. Here's what you need to do. Bring 4 candles, a lighter and a spirit of HOPE. We will light one candle in support of addicts, one candle in support of a person in Recovery and one candle in memory of someone who lost the battle. We are adding a fourth candle for the families of addicts because they suffer and need support as well.

We will light a candle in MEMORY of Davis Henry Owen, the Namesake of the Davis Direction Foundation. We will light a candle in support of Joshua Pierce Ruzbacki – who is currently in RECOVERY at the Jericho House. We will light a candle in support of opiate/heroin ADDICTS everywhere in hopes that they will soon be in Recovery. Last but not least, we will light a candle in support of all FAMILIES who love and support a family member suffering with addiction.

If you would like the name of your loved one read aloud at our ceremony, please send me their name and we will honor them as well. We will read names for 2 categories only…The Memory candle and the Recovery candle. We will have a moment of silence for all Addicts and all Families.

This event will kick-off National RECOVERY month – which is the month of September.

SECOND EVENT: "The Continuum of Care Symposium" Wednesday Night October 8th, from 7:00 – 9:00 at Marietta High School. You may have joined us at our first Symposium on June 3rd at MHS for "Taking Aim at Addiction" which was our 1st in a series of 4 Symposiums that will take place this year. We had over 400 in attendance and focused on our goals of AWARENESS and CHANGE. At our October Symposium, we will be hosting a REHAB/FOUNDATION fair and we are inviting any rehab facility or active foundation dealing with opiate/heroin addiction in the country to set up a table and share their information with those in attendance. If you know of a Rehab facility or Foundation meeting the needs of our cause that you would like to attend our Symposium, please share our information with them. Our keynote speaker for the "Continuum of Care" will be Ms. Teresa Johnston, Director of the Center for Young Adult Addiction and Recovery at Kennesaw State University. We will also hear from Dr. Harold McLendon, DDF Board member and WellStar Physician, regarding the properties of prescription drugs and Heroin. Tanya Smith will be sharing her personal journey of loving and losing her daughter to addiction. This event will be INFORMATIVE and POWERFUL!

Make plans NOW to attend both events and spread the word. Help the DDF to realize the number 1 goal of AWARENESS... Knowledge is POWER and we need to educate the community and the nation. You man not have an addict in need today, but tomorrow may not be so kind. Don't think this could never happen to you...That's what I thought. PLEASE SHARE THIS POST!

8/10/14 – Constructive Act #143 – Share Your Story

This story needs no explanation...Read carefully this incredible journey of HOPE and RECOVERY! What a Blessing it is to have this amazing Child of God share it with us!

I grew up with two amazing parents & a younger brother. Our home was centered around strong Christian values & principles. We were at church pretty much every time the doors were open. My surroundings were secure, I was loved & I knew it. My faith was tested when I was junior in high school. I received a call that my dad had become ill & was rushed to the hospital. My dad was my everything, he was my hero & the greatest man I ever knew. I prayed desperately for God to heal him & I believed he would. Two hours later, he passed. I can't explain how much I hurt. It rocked my foundation & shattered my world. I became angry with God & felt abandoned.

Life marched on & we moved closer to be with family. A decision I was unhappy about. I married at 20 & had a son a couple of years later. My life felt complete. Several years later we were blessed with a daughter & once again I had a family of four. I was blessed with a wonderful family, great job, home & by the worlds standards I was successful. But, I was still empty. I was & still am a very hard worker. It's that addictive nature I have that I tend to overdo anything I enjoy. Enough of something good just doesn't always exist for me.

I began to have some health issues & sought a Dr. for treatment. He prescribed Vicodin. I'd had pain meds before and always liked the feeling. But, this time it was like finding a new friend, a new friend that could help me deal with life. I didn't just like it, I loved it! I felt liked superwoman, I could conquer my day & have energy to spare. Soon after, I learned ways to get more & more & after a referral I ended up at a pain clinic. Wow! I felt I hit the jackpot. This Dr. also started me on Xanax, another med that became a drug of choice. Within the first month I was abusing my pills. If the bottle said 1 every 6 hours, I took 2 or 3. I have never been a rule follower. More was always better to me. I took drastic measures in chasing these pills. I have lied, cheated, stolen & for years bought pills from a dealer to satisfy my hunger for this high I received from these pills. I did things I never dreamed I would do.

After 5 years of this my family forced me into a detox hospital & I played that game for 3 days. I had a goal when I came out & that was not to change my life & live sober but, to now begin to use my pills correctly. I was going to do it right this time. I convinced my family that was a good idea & I was high within 24 hours of leaving the hospital. I wish I had reached my bottom then because the next 2 years were awful.

My son, 17 years of age began to follow my path through addiction. He was an amazing athlete, smart & well liked. He is & was a great guy. He had to have a surgery & received pain meds for 2 weeks. He knew I had a problem with them & it didn't take him long to realize he liked that feeling of being able to numb everything. He had teenage stresses & pressure & used the meds just as I did, to escape life. At the age of 18, he over dosed on my meds. He was constantly stealing meds from me. I knew he had a problem & I had no idea how to help him nor myself. He survived that night & went to a 7 day detox (the exact one I had been in). He relapsed immediately. How could he not, he had a mom that kept these pills in the home. I told myself it was okay for me to have them because these were my prescriptions with my name on the bottle. Leaving out the fact that I bought pills to continually keep them filled.

The next year was horrible. I had several seizures, lost my business, my marriage was not good, my daughter was living in this mess & my son hated me for allowing this demon into our lives. Our home was chaos to say the least. I knew that I couldn't stop using on my own & honestly didn't know if I wanted to. One Friday night, I had run out of pills & pretty much out of money. I was tired, tired of living & tired of chasing these pills. It wasn't fun anymore I no longer felt the high I once had, It had become purely survival. I was living day by day trying not to detox. I was hopeless, devastated & miserable. I was a prisoner & I didn't see a way I could live without these pills. I prayed to die, I
begged to die. I gathered my family, packed my bags & went back to the detox hospital. I walked in shattered & I spent that night praying & begging

God to save me. I realized I had lived my life being angry & resentful of my dad's death. I asked God for his forgiveness & I surrendered my life to him. All that I was, which seemed like nothing more than flesh & bones. He removed the obsession over pills almost immediately however, the physical pain & emotional pain, I had to walk through. He became my eyes when I couldn't see & my legs when I couldn't walk. He met my needs each day & placed people in my life to help me in my recovery. He taught me how to forgive myself & let the past go. I came out of detox & threw myself into recovery. Celebrate Recovery, AA, & NA. I sometimes went to 3 meetings a day. I use to judge drug addicts and think, "Why can't you just say no"? The very people I judged, help to selflessly save my life. God continually put people in my life that helped pave my road to recovery. Learning to live clean & sober was challenging. It's no joke & the hardest thing I've ever been through. I had to surround myself with people like me that understood what I was going through.

My son was slower paced. He got clean the day after me but, refused to really work a program. He was depressed & hid out in his room. He was lonely & broken. The only thing I knew to do was love him, pray for him, lead by example & never give up on him. I did a lot of things wrong, I begged too much, I yelled too much, I enabled him, I did all I knew & it really didn't make a difference. He got up one Sunday & decided to attend church with us. That morning, God changed his heart. He was saved that day & began a new life. Today he is very involved in celebrating recovery & shares his testimony often to young people. He is now attending seminary & is getting ready to leave on his third mission trip. His life, like mine, is surrounded around recovery. God took what I saw as impossible & made it possible. Matthew 19:26

Even though I have been blessed with nearly 3 years sobriety, life is not always easy. I have had MANY ups & downs. I've learned to live in the moment, doing one day at a time. I know & believe today that I'm not facing this alone. Addiction has humbled me & also given me purpose. Without God, my sponsor, a recovery program, the 12 steps, an awesome therapist, & a family that refused to give up on me, I would not be clean today. I share my story today & I pray it provides hope. My son & I go weekly into the detox center that we were both in & share our story. You see, God took my mess & uses it for good. I'm overwhelmed with that amount of grace & mercy! My chains are gone, I've been set free! I owe Him nothing short off all I am & that would never be enough. I'll spend my days sharing my story until I meet him face to face! – Jeremiah 29:1

8/11/14 – Constructive Act #144 – Never Look Back

So many times in life, we lose our position and our courage by simply looking over our shoulder. Looking back takes our eyes off of the prize and our focus off of the goal. NEVER LOOK BACK. Remember what happened to Lot's wife when she looked back in the Bible? She turned into a pillar of salt. She was gone in the blink of an eye, stricken dead! Keep your eyes on the prize and keep "Moving onward through life...Looking upward to God."

Will we make mistakes? Will we lapse and re-lapse? In most cases...Yes we will, but that does not mean that we have failed. It simply means that we lost our footing and slowed down a little...but don't make it worse by looking back! You have to learn to focus on what really matters and that is RECOVERY.

It is fitting in life that we try to reach "milestones." Have you ever wondered why they call it a milestone? One of the most coveted wins in racing is that of the fastest MILE. What an honor it would be to hold the title of running the fastest mile in history. In 1954, Roger Bannister became the first man in history to run the mile in less than four minutes. Two months later, John Landy broke his record by 1.4 seconds. A month later, the two men met to run the historic race for the title of "the fastest mile."

Moving into the final lap, Landy was in the lead and looking like the final winner... BUT – he took his eyes off of the prize and his focus off of the goal.

He looked back to see where Bannister was! In the blink of an eye, Bannister took the lead and won the race. Landy later told a reporter at the race..."If I hadn't looked back, I would have won!"

STOP LOOKING BACK! Move forward and if you slow down a time or two, get right back in the race and COMPETE! No one ever said Recovery would be easy, instead...it's quite the opposite. Don't allow yourself to become consumed with the minute details of daily life in a way that it takes your focus off of what really matters. Your RECOVERY is what really matters and GOD will walk beside you keeping the distractions at bay.

Don't sweat the small stuff and you WILL find Victory over your addiction as you cross the FINISH LINE!

8/12/14 – Constructive Act #145 – Help Us Make This Go Viral

So proud to bring to you our very first PUBLICATION!

Thank you to Dan Frisbie for giving of his time and talent for this very important cause! PLEASE SHARE!
SearchYouTube for Davis Direction Foundation.

8/13/14 – Constructive Act #146 – Pay Attention

Pay attention – even if you don't have a dog in this fight! I don't really like this saying "dog in this fight"…but I don't really know how else to say it. People who have not been directly affected – "YET" – are not paying attention, and then when it happens to them…IT'S TOO LATE! This is one area that we COULD have control over, and we need to try harder. It's like someone said to me last week…"You can turn your back today, but tomorrow, your child's best friend may be the heroin addict in the classroom, the workplace, the civic club, or even the church." It may not be your child, but it could be your nephew, your cousin, your grandson, your aunt/uncle, or even your spouse.

For me, it was too late when I began to pay attention! My sweet son was already addicted and desperately in the throes of addiction! I didn't know the warning signs, the lies, the deceit, the denial that I would become a part of. I had no idea of the severity of opiate/heroin addiction. I seriously didn't have a clue and I kept thinking it was a phase and we would work through it and come out victorious on the other side. Boy…was I wrong.

I'm so excited to see the churches begin to understand and become involved. I think it is vitally important that the young people who are already addicted understand without reservation that the churches are opening their doors and shedding their judgmental overtones to embrace the people with the disease of addiction. God wants us to come together and rescue these precious people. They cannot do it alone; they need the support of all of us and especially they need the merciful and unchanging love of God! So many times as I read "Share your story Sunday" I hear the unyielding praises to God for helping these kids come out on the other side. I hear over and over again how God has stepped in and literally given these precious addicts control over their addiction.

God promises us in the Bible that He will be with us every step of the way and He will never leave us or forsake us. Now is the time to claim that Promise and lean on Him for His unchanging love and security. These precious children of God need to surround themselves with people who have the love of God in their hearts and learn from them how God can help them in this life and love them forever in the next.

You may not have a reason to read another word on the DDF at this point in your life, but as I have said over and over……"Knowledge is Power" and the more you know the more you have prepared yourself to help your loved one when the time occurs. DON'T WAIT until it's too late to become involved with this epidemic. Just like the flu or ebola recently…No one expects to be the next victim. Prepare yourself and make plans and take precautions. It is better to be prepared and never have an opportunity, than it is to have an opportunity and not be prepared! Don't miss the opportunity to save a life and help an addict – The next addict…MIGHT JUST BE YOURS!

8/14/14 – Constructive Act #147 – Protect Your Goals

We've talked a lot about goals and dreams and how they are involved in Recovery. We set goals and we dream dreams. Our dreams are often realized because we have met our goals and achieved success. Some goals are easier to achieve than others and some are a real stretch as we try over and over again to attain some measure of progress.

If a goal is achieved easily, without much effort…is it really a goal at all? Perhaps it is something that we were comfortable with in the first place but needed to accomplish within a certain time frame. A goal should require effort, time, ingenuity, and thought provoking ideas. It should not be easy…because if it were, it would not be much of a goal at all.

In "The Leader In Me" workbook published by Franklin Covey Education, there is a percentage attached to the likelihood of achieving your goal. In other words, there are things that you can do to "Protect Your Goals" and ensure that they are attained.

• Hear an idea you like. 10%
• Consciously decide to adopt the idea. 25%
• Decide when you will do it. 40%
• Plan when you will do it. 50%
• Commit to someone else that you will do it. 65%
• Make an appt. to report your progress with that person. 95%

It is a proven fact that people who regularly set goals are more successful than people who do not set goals. I also believe that addicts in recovery realize more success if they are actively setting goals to achieve. That goal may be nothing more than living for the moment, or living by the Serenity Prayer. But… to an opiate/heroin addict, those 2 goals require effort, time, ingenuity, and thought provoking ideas to help them make it through each day. If you are an addict entering recovery or an addict in recovery, take a look at the Covey model and try to incorporate it into your goal setting regimen and see if it helps. Find an accountability partner or a sponsor and make a commitment to that person to give 100% effort.

Sometimes the goals we set may be too lofty because we are often harder on ourselves than we are on others. Occasionally, we want things to happen too quickly and we forget that our problems didn't happen overnight and that we won't be able to fix them overnight. Find your happy goal-setting medium and get started with setting reasonable and achievable goals toward your RECOVERY!

8/15/14 – Constructive Act #148 – Start the Dialogue

How do you start a conversation about Heroin? It's not like making small talk or talking about the weather. It's not considered southern hospitality or even being cordial to talk about heroin. It's a hard conversation to begin and it carries lots of embarrassment and shame with it.

Start it anyway! It may save a life. This CA comes from one of my best friends in the world. She is the Laverne to my Shirley! She was with me the last time I saw my sweet Davis alive and she is involved in this cause whole-heartedly! She knows my heart and she is my inspiration. She finds a way to start the conversation because she knows she may be saving a life every time she begins it.

Last week she was sitting with her daughter waiting on her senior portrait session for over an hour. Being the observant person that she is, she noticed that one of the parents was browsing through an old yearbook from Kennesaw Mountain High School and she also noticed that she was on one of the pages that my son was on. She was on the "Hall of Fame" page and Davis was there in all of his splendor. She leans over to the lady and says ..."Oh I know him – that's Davis Owen. He was a great kid." "WAS" being the word to begin the conversation. She began to tell the story and let this mother know how prevalent heroin is in our community and that it is taking the lives of intelligent, outgoing, popular, amazing kids...Davis was one of them.

She's not embarrassed or ashamed to talk about her best friend's child who died of an overdose. She knows that by opening the dialogue of opiate/heroin addiction that she can educate ignorant people who still believe that heroin addicts come out from under the bridges of major interstates. She knows that opiate/heroin addiction knows no boundaries and that it does not discriminate based on race, socio-economic status, gender, or social status. She also knows that the conversation that she initiates today may save the life of an addict tomorrow. She also knows that the dialogue that she begins with her own kids regarding opiate/ heroin addiction will give them the tools that they need to "NEVER ...NOT EVEN ONCE" take an opiate.

She is humble, she is not proud, she is intelligent enough to know that even though she does not have a "dog in this fight" today... that tomorrow is another day and she is doing everything that she can to educate and prepare her own children to deal with this epidemic. She is an amazing friend who has embraced this epidemic with me and works as hard as she can to make a difference for other kids. She is a role model for community service and she is an advocate for kids – even opiate/heroin addicts.

My daughter called me this afternoon with a sad story of suicide and then made a profound statement that she had heard one of her friends state. She said..."Isn't it strange that people are often times NOT willing to die for their own beliefs, BUT, they are willing to make judgmental statements that cause other people to take their own lives because of the stigma that is implied." WOW – FOOD FOR THOUGHT!

Be LOUD and be PROUD and do whatever it takes to create awareness and change regarding opiate/heroin addiction. Be like my great friend who starts the dialogue anyway because she knows that it can't hurt anyone to listen to her conversation, but it may save a life.

8/16/14 – Constructive Act # 149 – "TREAT YOURSELF"

This one is for the families of addicts. We all know how very important it is to take care of yourself especially in times of extreme stress and anxiety. And believe me…When you are living with an active addict…you are living in a constant zone of stress and anxiety. It's like living with anyone else who has a disease where death is imminent if you don't receive the proper care or medication to keep the disease in check.

When the addict is out of your sight and I mean even in the next room, you live in constant fear of what they are doing and who they are communicating with. When they are sleeping, even if it is under your own roof…you constantly wonder if they will be alive when you wake up in the morning. If they are with you, you are analyzing their every move trying to figure out whether or not they are high or if they are in need of a fix, or if they are truly still in recovery. This disease never lets up. Yes – it can go into remission…that's called recovery – but there's always the fear that it will show back up.

When they leave your home, or if they live apart from you, you always get that lump in your throat or that empty feeling in the pit of your stomach when the phone rings or the doorbell rings. If you let your thoughts wander during the day, you can create scenarios in your own mind that would make the scenes in "Final Destination" pale in comparison. There is "no rest for the weary" because – there is "no rest for the wicked."

So – somewhere along the way…you have to make a conscious effort to "treat yourself." You have to put it in God's capable hands for an hour, a day, or even for a week so that you can refresh yourself and renew your spirit. You need alone time with God and with each other. You will find out no matter how hard you try… unless you are handcuffing your addict to the wrought iron stairwell when you leave…(and don't think the idea did not cross my mind)…you have no control over their actions. Don't give up everything else you have going for your family in order to prove me wrong on this one…it won't happen!

Families have been torn apart over how to handle the addict that every member of the family loves unconditionally. Because there is no perfect answer, everyone has to figure it out on their own. Marriages have dissolved, non-addicted children have moved away from home to get away from the stress, parents have turned their backs all in the name of love and recovery. Don't get me wrong turning their backs was probably the hardest thing they have ever done and they did it as the ultimate sacrifice…BUT…nonetheless, they lost contact – sometimes for years or ultimately until they received that last phone call or doorbell ring.

My point is…that as it stands right now, nothing you can do will change the fact that the addict has to make the changes for himself or herself. So – in the meantime, don't let them ruin the good things you have going on in your families and in your lives. TREAT YOURSELF; and in doing so, refresh your mind and body while you renew your spirit, your faith and your trust in God. You will be a better person for it and you might just preserve the rest of your family in doing so.

8/17/14 – Constructive Act #150 – Share Your Story

This is a little different story. A mother write her feelings to her son in a letter of desperation regarding his situation. I know this Mom is sharing the doubts that any one of us mothers of addicts can relate to… Please read her story. For her there was a happy ending, and we rejoice. You never know what one act may be the act that will bring your child back to you…Try everything and stop at nothing…IT IS A DISEASE!

THE LETTER:

I wrote this letter to my son 1 year ago, he was new in recovery and had his first (and last) relapse. He had told me he was considering stopping treatment. His response to this letter was life changing. He called me a few days later and sincerely apologized for backing me into a corner, acknowledging how his behavior left me with no alternatives. I am so proud to say it has been 1 year since he has used. I am passing this on as I know to we'll how helpless a parent feels but I have my son, opiate free today and I know that I was a critical part in that…

I keep telling myself that I have done everything that I can do to help u, to save your life, and I can't help but to think if u overdose and die from this heroin addiction will what I have done for u still seem like "everything". No good mother should have to have this battle. I tell myself that somewhere inside u, u love me, u want me in your life, u want to have a life that is honorable and productive.

I can't change the past, I can't go back and re-do the things I have done, I honestly don't know what I would change anyway. All I can do is move forward, trust my love for u and know that being your mother has been the toughest job I'll ever love.

You have made choices in your life that have led u away from me and the life I had envisioned for u. These r your choices not mine. I have to live with my own guilt and failures.

I have to learn how to survive in this world without being able to breathe. You are and will always be my life, my love, the air in my lungs. I, like you, may not survive this horrible addiction, it breaks my heart to know that the thing I have tried so hard to escape as far back as my memories will allow me to go is the thing that may ultimately be my demise.

I chose you 21 years ago, I gave up my life as I knew it. For the past 21 years I have tried to be the best mom I could be, I tried to set a good example for you, I tried to give you everything I never had growing up. I frequently feel I'm not good enough, that my efforts fall short but yet I persevere knowing that I am enough for my boys. They need me to be the best, they deserve the best, they r worth it.

I can tell you that I am in a place that I have never been, I can't see the light, I am struggling to find the will to go on. We all make hard choices everyday, these choices affect not only ourselves but the ones that love us most. I would rip my beating heart from my chest and happily hand it over to u if that would help you. I realize now that I am powerless over this addiction, more so than maybe even you.

I will as always continue to love u no matter what but please understand that should you choose to live the life of an active addict it will not be in the presence of me. You will force me to stop providing any means of support to you. I will be forced to deal with the fact that any support given to u may kill you. I want more than anything to be part of your life, I will not contribute to your death. I thought it was only fair to share how I feel and how your choices will effect us both. I am at the end of the rope, I'm sorry that I can't hold on anymore Jordan. Know that no mother has ever loved her son as much as I love you, no matter what happens don't forget that.

8/18/14 – Constructive Act #151 – Time To Share

Ever so often, we take time to ask that you share our Facebook page with friends from all over the Nation and the World. Each time that we do this, we get new followers who help us spread awareness about opiate/heroin addiction. It is of vital importance to us that everyone understand our goals and beliefs. It is through awareness and education that we will accomplish change. So, with that being said, here is our mission statement and our beliefs.

Our Mission Statement:

The mission of the Davis Direction Foundation is to serve as a role model in our community in order to become a national resource for Opiate/HEROIN ADDICTION awareness and change. We will strive to remove the outdated stigma of opiate addicts and revamp the rehabilitation process to appropriately address the disease of Opiate/Heroin Addiction as one of the most severe forms of addiction. We will support recovery.

Our Beliefs:

- We believe recovery is real.
- We believe that collectively we can make a difference.
- We believe that the optimal answer to opiate/heroin addiction is prevention.
- We believe that heroin causes one of the most severe forms of addiction.
- We believe that we must make heroin a public conversation in order to make a difference.
- We believe that the stigma of a HEROIN ADDICT and rehabilitation for them is outdated and needs to be changed.
- We believe that legislative changes need to be made in certain areas.
- We believe that addiction of all kinds is a disease.

Our billboard campaign – Thanks to CBS OUTDOORS and FAIRWAY OUTDOORS who just recently joined us in our fight against opiate/heroin, has reached out to families all over Atlanta. Now we are trying to get outside of the Atlanta Area with our Billboards in order to spread our message. The Graphic art has been donated – thanks to Jason Gribble, of Formetco Inc., and is ready for anyone who can find donated space on a digital billboard in our Nation. One phone call is all I had to make and thanks to Doug Penner of CBS OUTDOORS, he had us up and running in a matter of hours. You can do the same. Look in your area for Billboard companies and MAKE IT HAPPEN! Message me or write in the comments below and I will send you the Billboard artwork for any company who is willing to donate space in order to create awareness for this horrific epidemic. Atlanta is saving lives because of the generous donation of Billboard space!!!

8/19/14 – Constructive Act #152 – Reach Out to Rehab and Recovery

On October 8th, 2014, we will deliver our second Symposium – "The Continuum of Care" at Marietta High School from 7:00 – 9:00 pm. This event will be fantastic as we will be hosting a "REHAB AND RECOVERY FAIR. It will be run like a college or job fair with comparative information, literature to hand out, drug kits, test stix and Naloxone prescriptions.

You don't want to miss this event. It will be every bit as awesome as the first one with even more giveaways and powerful testimony. The event is open for all Rehab and Recovery facilities; we are neither discriminating nor endorsing any facilities, just exposing and allowing them marketing privileges.

Help make this event AWESOME by handing out the invitation letter to ANY and ALL Rehab and Recovery facilities. Thanks for your help! Fell free to copy and paste the letter – OR share this post on your own page. Thanks for all that you do…

August 15, 2014
Dear Recovery Vendor:

On October 8th, 2014, the Davis Direction Foundation along with Marietta High School (MHS) in Cobb County GA, will be hosting our second Symposium in a series of four, on the topic of the "Continuum of Care" for opiate/heroin addiction. We are excited to announce that we will also be hosting a Recovery Fair in the lobby of the Marietta Performing Arts Building at MHS. It will be run in the same fashion as a college or job fair. Each vendor will be provided with table space to share their services in the area of opiate/heroin addiction. Please understand that we are specifically dealing with opiate/heroin addiction due to the rising number of deaths and overdoses in our community and the nation. Please do not reserve table space unless you have a service to offer regarding this particular addiction.

You are invited to enter through the lobby doors beginning at 5:00 pm to set up and prepare to talk with our Symposium guests. We would ask that you bring as many hands-on resources as possible to share with parents and family members dealing with addicted loved ones. It is very intimidating to purchase these items in stores without any prior knowledge of which brand or what information you expect to receive from the purchase of the item. We would like for parents to see up to date information, drug tests, stress toys, yoga balls, herbal and all natural products that help an addict in recovery. Anything and everything that you think would educate the loved one of an addict is what we would like to share at our Recovery Fair.

Please come equipped with information about your facility, or practice so that parents and loved ones can leave with a comparison of facilities in order to choose the best resource of Recovery for their addict. Handouts and brochures would be wonderful. We know that all the information will be overwhelming for our guests, so the more information they can leave with, the better.

Please contact the Davis Direction Foundation at: info@davisdirection.com in order to reserve space at our Recovery Fair. We are hoping for an audience of 600

– 700 people. We are welcoming Rehab facilities from all over the nation due to the fact that often times families like to send their addicts far from home in order to get the best possible care in the best possible setting. Sending an addict far from home often reduces the "flight factor" from the facility. We are asking for a donation in keeping with your financial ability as opposed to charging a fee to participate. Please let us know no later than October 1st if you are planning to participate in our October 8th Recovery Fair. We will have your table ready and waiting for you.

8/20/14 – Constructive Act #153 – Allow Life to Happen

I was talking to a friend of mine today who has been my friend for almost 30 years and we have both raised multiple children in the public school system. We came to the conclusion that we put way too much pressure on kids to "Have a Plan." Then, when that plan doesn't work out, the kids often don't know how to handle the aftermath.

In recent years, we have gone so far as to ask our 8th graders to choose a college/career path and choose high school classes accordingly. DID YOU KNOW…"About 80 percent of students in the United States end up changing their major at least once, according to the National Center for Education Statistics. On average, college students change their major at least three times over the course of their college career."

So if the above statement is true…How in the heck do we expect 8th graders to choose a career path? Which leads me to my next point…… Why do the adults in charge of extra curricular activities not like to share their students with other adults and activities? Somewhere along the way, we have lost the art of "developing" children and we have moved toward "owning" them. Nobody wants to share a talented child with another sport, club, performance group, etc… The adults involved all want to "lay claims" to particular children who by all calculations are very talented in specific areas. The question remains…How do we know they are not talented in other areas? And…more importantly, how do THEY know that are not talented in other areas if they are not allowed to try them out? Shouldn't school be a safe place to try out different areas of interest? I personally believe that we are doing children a huge disservice by "making them choose" areas of interest at such a young age.

"Choosing," in and of itself, is stressful and creates a great deal of pressure. Young people are worried about hurting feelings, disappointing adults, going in different directions from their friends, and failure. WOW – that's huge for a young person. As adults, it is our job to create a safe place for our kids to explore different avenues. I don't feel like we are doing so hot in this area.

I have to pay a huge compliment to a dear friend of mine, Mrs. Leigh Colburn, Principal of Marietta High School. She is also a board member on the Davis Direction Foundation, and a huge advocate in the fight against opiate/heroin addiction. Being the principal, she has a responsibility and is in a position to do what she feels is right for kids. So, when she has a student who wants to participate in 2 sports, 2 extra curricular activities, 2 competitive events, she calls the ADULTS together and asks them to work things out in the best interest of the child. She is of the belief that if the child wants to try to participate in ongoing activities that may have scheduling conflicts, it is our job as educators to work it out for the kids. We have to provide that opportunity. WE HAVE TO TEACH THEM TO ALLOW LIFE TO HAPPEN. We have to encourage them to try new things and see how they feel about them. It's the same philosophy as "Green Eggs and Ham" – You never know until you try.

That "PLAN" that we have imposed upon our children and our students is getting in the way of LIFE! We are inviting them to feel failure because the plan might have been flawed from the beginning. Routines are good for kids and general expectations are good as well, but we have to draw the line at creating "PLANS" at such a young age. The best lesson we can teach our kids is to relax and ALLOW LIFE TO HAPPEN. Learn to roll with the punches and bounce back when things don't work out as planned. Sometimes the most beautiful things in life are the things that happen spontaneously…"Learn to allow Life to Happen."

8/21/14- Constructive Act #154 – Write a Thank You Note

It's community service day folks. It's time to say "THANK YOU" to the people who put their lives on the line everyday to make arrests and get the dangerous evil drug – HEROIN – off of the streets and out of our community. We sit back and say that it should happen and that it even needs to happen. Then when it does what do we do? Lots of us say – "well, it's about time!"

Well – I say "It's about time we say "THANK YOU!"

MCS is the unit in Cobb County and Marietta City that joins forces to combat Narcotics. They put themselves out there in ways we as mothers, fathers and siblings would die a thousand deaths if we thought our children were in the same situations. They purposely put themselves in situations to understand the process and find the dealers. They go undercover and work covert operations in order to SAVE OUR CHILDREN! That – at the very least deserves a THANK YOU!

You can send your cards to:
MCS
185 Roswell St.
Marietta, Ga. 30090-9650

Let them know how much you appreciate their efforts on behalf of your families, your addicted children and all the broken hearts of parents who are working so hard to eradicate this DISEASE! Show them your support and let them feel the community support that is behind them everyday.

This unit is the equivalent of the front lines in any war or major battle. The guns involved with drugs are second to none and in many cases more powerful than issued to any soldier. Not only should we ALL write THANK YOU notes to these awesome officers, but we should keep them in our prayers as well.

Working TOGETHER, we will be able to facilitate change and make everyone AWARE of the dangers of everything involved in this war on Prescription opiates/heroin. It takes a village to raise a child…BUT it takes a village WITH an MCS unit to fight a war on drugs!

THANK YOU MCS for putting yourselves on the line EVERYDAY to keep our children and family members SAFE. You are doing a FANTASTIC JOB and YOU ARE MAKING A DIFFERENCE!

8/22/14 – Constructive Act #155 – Keep The Faith (Revisited)

I have to remind myself of this so many times throughout this journey. There are days that I still hope to awaken from this nightmare and say…"WOW – I just had the worst dream." On those days I have to really focus on what is good and happy and right with my family and the world around me. I have to surround myself with lifelong friends and remember the good and put the unthinkable in a dark place in the back of my mind. I have to turn to God and "KEEP THE FAITH."

For those of you who know me well and are friends with me on my personal FB page, I wrote a post last week that said "Going to get my Boy!" I was headed down to Hartsfield -Jackson to get my middle son who was on his way home from India. I was going to ride right down their walk up to the pick up area and collect Connor and bring him home. It was AWESOME! He was home and he was safe and he was mine!

I couldn't help but think that I also wanted to get into my huge SUV and drive straight to the gates of Heaven. I wanted to put my pick-up # on the dash, roll down the passenger's side window and say…"Hello St. Peter, would you please let God know that I am here to pick-up Davis Owen." "It's time for him to come home."

Every time I look at that status on my page, my heart skips a beat and I struggle for that next breath. I WANT TO GO GET MY BOY!

IT'S TIME FOR HIM TO COME HOME! It's those days that I have to rely on my faith to keep me grounded and to dry up those tears in my eyes that make them swell until the world around me is so blurry that I can't even see. I can't even imagine what people do who lose a child and they don't have God to help them re-focus on life without their precious gift.

I focus on the fact that I will see him again one day and I try to rationalize the irrational by thinking that people who defect from their countries to seek freedom often times have to leave their family members behind knowing that they will never see them again in this lifetime. It's on those days that I pretend that he just defected to another country called Heaven. He's still here; He just moved away to Heaven. I will never see him again in my home or be able to go and get him and bring him back...BUT, my faith allows me to know that I WILL see him again one day...I will just have to travel to his home – his glorious, beautiful, and perfect home in that land far away called HEAVEN! I will "KEEP THE FAITH."

8/23/14 – Constructive Act #156 – Flash That Beautiful Smile

It's true that we all love to have a beautiful smile and beautiful teeth. As parents, we often spend a small fortune putting braces on our children in order for them to feel confident when they smile, talk or simply open their mouths. That's why it is a no-brainer when wisdom teeth begin to push their way to the surface, that we call the oral surgeon and schedule that surgery to keep the teeth in perfect order. We don't want those wisdom teeth to crowd that beautifully symmetrical smile that we purchased for upwards of two years.

STOP RIGHT THERE! Let me just tell you that what you may read publicly on the DDF is only a small fraction of what comes in through private messages and emails. I would say beyond a shadow of a doubt… that hands down, more young adults become addicted to pain killers because of wisdom teeth removal than any other single factor according to what I have been told through our foundation. Parents write in on a daily basis with heart-wrenching stories of how their children became addicted to pain killers,......which led to heroin, over and over again. More often than not, the recurring theme that I read about is the fact that wisdom teeth removal was the beginning of addiction for these young adults.

The complaint is, that the oral surgeons allowed their children to leave with a prescription of 30 – 35 hydrocodone pills for what is usually only one, or at most two days, of unbearable pain. The parents state further that their children could have more than likely gotten by on Advil or some other alternative to narcotic drugs.

Here again, we trust the doctors and do not question the fact that they prescribe opiates for pain that could probably be managed without them. There are alternative drugs – that are NOT narcotics – that could just as easily be prescribed without the threat of addiction.

Parents – BE ADVOCATES FOR YOUR CHILDREN – Don't allow any doctors to routinely prescribe narcotics for them. Ask them to start with lesser drugs that will have a pain reducing effect without the risk of addiction. Speak openly with them and if they don't respect your questions or concerns......... shop around for a new doctor. If after trying a non-narcotic drug, your child is still in excruciating pain, ask for only a day or two worth of narcotics. If your prescription is written for more, the pharmacist does not have any control over how he can fill it. He must fill it as written. So make sure before you leave the Dr.'s office that your prescription is for only a couple of days worth of opiates. Not a pill more!

Discuss with your child the dangers of taking narcotic drugs when having their wisdom teeth out. Help them to understand a lifetime of addiction is NEVER worth the lack of short-term pain! Look for natural remedies and alternative pain relievers like ice, heat and pure vanilla. Work with your children to make informed decisions and steer clear from dangerous drugs such as narcotics! WE HAVE GOT TO CHANGE THIS MIND – SET!

8/24/14 – Constructive Act #157 – Share Your Story

I know this is not a story from a DDF reader, but these are real stories from real people who have been heroin users.

I don't know what their status is today, but they give a very real perspective of being a heroin addict. If you are a DDF reader, and you would like to share your story in order to help others, please write to me in a private message and you can be our next Sunday story.

www.drugfreeworld.org/real-life-stories/heroin.html

8/25/14 – Constructive Act # 158 – "ASK THE EXPERTS"

You have heard me say before that is we are ever going to make any progress in stopping this deadly opiate/heroin addiction, we will have to talk with the addicts who are taking the drugs. They are the experts. We have to find out who they are and why they are making the decisions they are making. I have also mentioned that I think a lot of drug use is directly related to stress and expectations that are put upon others. With all of that being said…We need those of you who have been addicted to opiates/heroin to PLEASE TAKE THE SURVEY. If you have someone you know that has been addicted to opiates/heroin, please ask them to go on to the DDF and take the survey. Our goal is to have research to report at the October Symposium.

PLEASE TAKE THE FOLLOWING SURVEY IF YOU HAVE OR ARE CURRENTLY ADDICTED TO OPIATES/HEROIN.

This will be the first official piece of research for the DDF.

docs.google.com/forms/d/1drJFKljwt-
VVZF9A2Ap3qx8Y_DEVBkThTHMhUW9008c/viewform

8/26/14 – Constructive Act #159 – Learn to Trust Again

For the families of an addict and for the addict as well, this is probably one of the hardest concepts to achieve because of the lack of trust you have endured throughout the addiction journey. If you have traveled this journey you will understand this post, and if you have not traveled this journey, you will think you understand, but you don't have a clue! I don't say that to make you feel less than, but the fact of the matter is that you cannot imagine the level of distrust you will experience once you have loved and exhausted every ounce of your soul in a beloved addict.

As I sit here and try to compose this Constructive Act, I am at a loss for words to describe the hurt, the pain and the absolute absence of logic that accompanies life with an addict. To lose the trust you have for your child, your spouse, your lifelong love and the piece of your heart that you hold so dear is beyond understanding. To see a physically functioning human being that is seemingly making choices to destroy his or her life and robbing you blind in the process cannot be explained. You lose faith and at times forget to trust in God.

To trust again in any way, shape, form or fashion becomes next to impossible. You don't trust yourself to begin with. You begin questioning yourself and your sanity first and foremost. You want so badly to believe the one you love, that you question yourself and your organization and memory. For weeks after Davis died, I was still looking for missing jewelry hoping that I had misplaced it or put it in a different spot and forgotten where that spot was. You become suspicious of every motive, every act of kindness and everything that is out of the precise ordinary. You trust no one!

You put up walls and barriers to protect yourself and your feelings. You learn to rely solely on yourself so that "trust" doesn't come up in a relationship or in a friendship. You work twice as hard and sleep half as much because you don't want to stop and think about your life and your situation. You continue to unconditionally love your addict with your entire heart and soul and lose trust that anyone else can do the same. You distrust everyone's motives and sacrifices. You become cold and hard in order to survive. The lack of trust takes away your inner soul.

So how do you learn to trust again? Baby steps...you just put one foot in front of the other. Start by sharing your story and realizing that you are not the only one who has walked a mile in your shoes. Addiction has destroyed many wonderful families because of the fact that finding trust again is so very difficult. Start with your trust in God. God in His infinite wisdom will take care of each and every addict in a way that we may never understand, but He will sustain us. Start with spending time with your immediate family members and learning the new normal that has become your family destiny. Find a way to break down the barriers and tear down the walls in order to learn to trust again. Trust is vital to relationships and relationships are vital to survival. Melt into someone's arms and learn dependence once again. Let someone else take the lead as you re-learn to love and trust. Your soul depends on it.

8/27/14 – Constructive Act #160 – Think Outside of the Box

I remember many times when Michael was coaching baseball hearing him say to his struggling batters... "Why do you keep stepping up to the plate, doing the exact same thing and expect different results?" In other words if you don't make adjustments, there will be no changes. Sometimes the hardest things in the world to do... is try something different. Albert Einstein said..."Insanity is doing the same thing over and over again and expecting different results."

I think there are just absolute habits that we have that we don't even have a clue as to how to change. Even if we wanted to, we don't know how to begin. I think that's where we are with this Opiate/Heroin epidemic. We keep trying to address drugs in the same ways we have for years and it didn't work then and it's not working now. We keep thinking that it can't happen to "us." We keep trying to keep it a secret because it's shameful and embarrassing. We keep telling our kids to stay away from drugs and if they are taking them... to just stop. We keep going to traditional Rehab and we continue to Relapse when we get out.

ARE WE INSANE?

We have got to realize that this is a DISEASE. Why are we not treating it like other diseases? How many addicts have gone to their doctors for their addiction? Why is insurance not covering this disease like it covers other diseases? Did someone fail to count the opiate receptors in our brains and find that there were twice as many as any other receptors? Are we putting people with other diseases in jail in record numbers? And I know what you are saying in the back of your brain...BUT addicts cheat, steal, lie and feed their disease. Well...sugar is the number 1 fuel for cancer, but do we put people with cancer in jail for eating sugar? Do we condemn them for eating sugar? Because in doing so, they are contributing to their disease. It is a conscious choice. They may not steal the sugar or even lie to get it, but nonetheless, eating sugar contributes to the disease.

Some of you probably think I have lost my mind at this point, but I am just thinking outside of the box! I'm stepping outside of my comfort zone and making statements that are controversial. I'm tired of being politically correct and not saying what every person who loves an addict is thinking in their private thoughts. Is it really that different? In some countries, narcotics are over the counter drugs. WHAT? Oh yes they are! Believe it or not, those countries don't have nearly the drug problems that we have. WHY? I don't know, but I think that we should try and find out. We have got to stop pointing fingers and instead opening our minds and hearts to help these "sufferers of addiction!" They would give anything in most cases to reverse the addiction and be free of the demons.

My son didn't want to die! Neither did many of your loved ones. PLEASE start speaking out…because at this point what have we got to lose? I've lost the most important thing in the world to me. There is nothing else that I can lose that will ever hurt me any worse. So – I'm ALL in this fight for freedom of addiction. One of my dear friends on the DDF sent me an article last night from a Judge in Ohio who is definitely stepping outside of the box. He is offering addicts Vivitrol shots in place of jail time. WOW – now there's a fine elected official who is willing to step outside of his comfort zone and step up to the plate with a brand new bat! HOORAY for you Judge Peeler! You just hit a home-run in my park!

www.cleveland.com/nation/index.ssf/2014/06/
heroin_addicts_in_ohio_court_o.html

8/28/14 – Constructive Act #161 – Stand Together

Timing is sometimes the most important aspect of getting anything done. When a topic, an issue or an epidemic is at its height in the public eye, that is the time to try and affect change.

The time has come to make our move with opiate/heroin addiction. It is at an all time epidemic high and we cannot allow it to get further out of hand. Our loved ones are dying, our prisons are full with addicts, and families are losing everything all because of prescription drug abuse that leads to heroin.

A friend sent me an article last night that changes the way that hydrocodone is dispensed. The changes include the fact that a person can ONLY get a 90 day prescription filled. HOLY COW – 90 days? Are you kidding me? That's enough hydrocodone to addict several people at once! The restrictions dictate that a doctor is the only one who can call in a refill and that before he or she does that, they must re-examine the patient. Here is a quote from the article:

"Almost seven million Americans abuse controlled-substance prescription medications, including opioid painkillers, resulting in more deaths from prescription drug overdoses than auto accidents," DEA administrator Michele Leonhart said in a statement. "Today's action recognizes that these products are some of the most addictive and potentially dangerous prescription medications available."

AND…doctors are still allowed to dispense a 90 day prescription. WOW! So – after the patients become addicted, they probably won't be allowed to get more of the drugs, because doctors are NOT crazy! So what do you think the patients will do at this point?

You guessed it…Heroin – Here they come!

My point for this post is that NOW is the time we must all stand together and DEMAND change! Doctors are the gatekeepers of these drugs and without prescriptions, they cannot legally be dispensed. There were safeguards set up to track opiate medications that were being dispensed – who was dispensing them and who was receiving them. The problem was that even though the mandate was made by the Government to track this information, there was no funding provided to ensure that it happened. That's NOT good enough! WE need answers from government officials as to why our system has failed to do this.

WE also need answers at to why there are still "pill mills" operating in our state and adjacent states as well for that matter. WE also need answers at to WHY there cannot be a limited number of pills of opiate medication prescribed for minor (not chronic) pain situations and why patients cannot ask for less of a prescription that is prescribed.

Our 3rd symposium will be dealing with the legalities and the legal barriers standing in the way of change. Begin to think of your questions now and the elected officials that you would like to answer them. This is important and it will take time to pull it together. We are looking to January for the 3rd Symposium and we are getting offers from local churches to host the meetings. I am so proud that the churches are getting involved and reaching out! WE need to embrace this issue and let ALL of God's children know that we are here to help…Just like HE instructs us to in the Good Book! CHANGE is COMING……That is one of the goals of the DDF and WE WILL MAKE A DIFFERENCE! STAND WITH US!

8/29/14 – Constructive Act #162 – Mourn The Dead

Yes – unfortunately we have lost another talented, bright, and wonderful child of God. It has taken me back almost 6 months ago to the doorbell ring at my own home. How does a parent make it through the nightmare of losing a child? How do the siblings of the child continue to exist without their precious brother or sister? How do the friends of the beloved addict find the strength to get out of bed and go to school or work and act as if it is just another day in the life of a friend of an opiate/heroin addict? This morning all of these people mentioned will have to figure these things out. They will have to continue their lives without this precious child of God.

The pain and suffering that ensues from the death of the disease of addiction happens all too often now and many of us never see it coming. It catches us off guard and leaves us so very vulnerable. It opens wounds for those of us who have lost a child, sibling, spouse, or loved one, and it creates a hole in the heart for those of you who have been spared the horror up until this point. When will this nightmare stop? When will we figure out the changes that need to be made in order to reverse the statistics and begin moving in a forward direction? There are many of us who are invested in this cause and we are not unintelligent. Let's put our brains together and figure out the direction that we need to pursue.

Today marks the first anniversary of death of a dear friend who lost her beautiful daughter to this epidemic. She is suffering silently today because her heart is broken and can never be healed. But…tomorrow, she will come back fighting because she is selfless enough to know that we have a problem and she does not want others to endure what she and her family have had to endure. She spends hours, day after day trying to make a difference for the children who have lost their way and need to find the path back to freedom.

She is an advocate for children and anyone else suffering from opiate/heroin addiction. We need others who share her passion and our passion to join with us and make a difference.

This venture is not for the faint of heart and not for those who are only halfway invested. We need your whole heart and soul to fight this cause with us. You may not have been directly affected at this point, but if we don't change the direction of this epidemic, it is only a matter of time before you will have your own story to tell.Invest NOW and don't wait until you are standing before God and your friends sharing your story to help others. Donate your time, your resources, your expertise and your money to help us find the solution to this dreaded disease.

Pray for this precious family that they will find peace in the days to come and that they will know that their precious son was a blessing to the world. He had a disease that we have not been able to cure because we do not understand the origins nor the physiology of the disease. Pray that God, in his infinite wisdom, will show us the path that he wishes for us to forge in this journey. Pray that this family will be able to fill the hole in their hearts with the wonderful memories and beautiful thoughts of their precious son who became a victim to this awful epidemic of opiate/heroin addiction. Pray also that you will never know the pain that this family is dealing with tonight. MOURN THE PASSING OF THIS WONDERFUL CHILD OF GOD AND PRAY FOR THE HEALING OF HIS FAMILY.

8/30/14 – Constructive Act #163 – Review Your Plan

As with anything that you work toward, you have to maintain your status. Addiction is no different. This post is for the addicts and the addict's keepers as well. When was the last time you did a "prescription pill check" when was the last time you had the grandparents do a "prescription pill check?" When was the last time you had a sit down conversation with your addict in recovery? When was the last time you told them how proud you were of their continued commitment to their goals? RECOVERY IS MAINTENANCE……How are you managing your maintenance? Are you able to track your addict when they leave the house? Do you own a locked prescription pill container? Are you carrying a Naloxone kit if you are an addict or the parent of an addict? How are you protecting yourself and maintaining your Recovery?

One suggestion for maintaining Recovery is to go to our website and Review the Constructive Acts. There are #163 of them as of today and each of you can hopefully find something imbedded in at least one of them that will speak to you today.

Our website has been up since Davis' 21st birthday on April 27th 2014. It is one of those things that we want to work on and we will work on as funds become available. BUT – our "Constructive Acts" is one of the areas on the website that we HAVE been able to maintain and keep up to date. Re-read them and see if there is something that you can implement that you have forgotten about or perhaps you were not familiar with the DDF until later. Go back to the beginning and look at the titles of each "CA" and see if there is something that you need to work on.

I know that when we were fully aware of Davis' addiction and we were doing our best to help him maintain his Recovery, when things seemed to be going strong and working well, WE GOT LAZY! We would think we were out of the woods and we would let our guard down. ADDICTION IS NEVER FINISHED!!! IT IS A DISEASE!

If you are a cancer patient and you go into remission, the doctor schedules regular "review" check ups to ensure that you are still in remission. They do blood work, and all kinds of other tests to be preventative and look for signs of the disease creeping back in to your body. We MUST do the same thing for the DISEASE of addiction. Heroin especially does such terrible things to your body that you need to be working with a doctor to make sure you are healthy in all other ways. Are all of your organs working properly? Have you been to your dentist for a cleaning and oral health check up? The dentists are often the first doctors to realize there is a problem with addiction. The teeth are one of the first body parts to go!

Last but CERTAINLY not least, remember to VALIDATE your addict and let them know that you realize that they have a DISEASE and that you are on their side! Help them understand their disease and the need for treatment! Love them unconditionally and DON'T GIVE UP ON THEM! They would gladly cure themselves of this disease if they only knew how! Remember that what works for one individual does not necessarily work for another. Before you judge them, LOOK INTO THE MIRROR! Is there something that you have wanted to change about yourself that you have been unable to change? Perhaps your weight, your habits, your level of patience, whatever it is…remember what the GOOD BOOK says…He that is without sin among you, let him first cast a stone. RE-READ AND REVIEW TODAY! It may save a life tomorrow!

8/31/14 – Constructive Act # 164 – Share Your Story

This week the Mom of a using addict is sharing her story…It is the story from the perspective of the "Addict's Keeper" as I have called the loved ones who care for the addicts. It will break your heart and open your eyes to the life of the ones who love the addicts unconditionally and with their WHOLE HEARTS! Please pray for this family as they continue their journey.

Where to begin? My girls call me Mom. My friends call me Deb. My husband calls me honey and my parents call me daughter. I am all those things and mor…I am a mother of a heroin addict.

We are good people. We have jobs. We have a church. Our parents have been married for 50 years. When our kids were little, we had dinner as a family. We provided for our children. We are not the people this was supposed to happen to. THIS CAN HAPPEN TO ANYONE.

She was and is a good girl. She is outgoing. She makes people laugh. So where did it go wrong? We don't' know all the answers and probably never will.

Here is my journey…not from birth, but from the first phone call from the hospital.
May 7th, 2013-About 6 o'clock we got a phone call from Kennestone that our daughter had overdosed on Heroin. Needless to say we went straight there. She

was full of remorse and promised us she would do anything to make herself better...and we believed her.

May 9th-She started outpatient rehab. She got up each morning and went to Cobb Hospital for intense Outpatient Rehab. On her way home each day she stopped at her dealer's house and got her fix. She did not like living at home. She did not like our rules. This lasted a couple of weeks and she left. She literally walked out the front door and down the road with a garbage bag of clothes.

July 2013-We reconnected. We picked her up from where she was living and took her to church on Sunday. We took her out to lunch and dropped her back off. We started to believe in her again. She seemed to be doing better.

We eventually set down some rules and gave her the car back. She got a job. She gave us her paycheck. We paid her bills. She still wasn't living with us but we thought things were better. She visited and took drug tests. She passed every time. All a lie...she was using the whole time. Cheating, stealing and lying.........I didn't see it...I didn't want to. So many in-between stories, it's hard to remember them all. I just know I cried a lot.

Fast forward...It is now January 10th 2014. She has apparently hit her low. We got a call. She wants to go to Detox. Why? Her dealer got arrested and she knew she wouldn't get her fix.

I took her to the hospital. She entered Detox. It was awful. I watched her go through withdrawal in the ER waiting for them to admit her. Pure Hell. Yes they finally admitted her to the hospital only for her to leave AMA on Sunday. She was not ready to quit. Days go by...we wait.

January 16th-We get the call to come get her. She is ready for rehab. We take her the next day. Six days later she decides she doesn't want to be there. She is an adult. Adults don't have to STAY in rehab. If they want to leave, they can. Friends pick her up and she is gone and using once again.

February 5th-We get the next call. She is ready to go back to rehab. We have done our research and are willing to take her. She lasts until the 13th. We get a call...she is no longer welcome there. She can't follow the rules. We are done! We tell the rehab we are not going to pick her up. They take her to a hotel and give her a room for the night and wish her luck. She calls us desperate. We give her a number to a half-way house 2 hours away and tell her to call. She does and they pick her up on Valentine's Day. Everything is starting to come together. We have hope.

Things are going well...Fast forward to June 9th. We get yet another call. She can't follow the rules. She is no longer welcome at the half-way house. She leaves. We don't know where she is. A few days go by and she contacts us again. She needs help. She used again. She is in an extended stay with people she should NOT be hanging around. My husband drives to get her. My heart hurts, my head hurts, but I know this is not my fault. IT IS A DISEASE!

Next rehab- Hoping this will be the last. Thinking it is a good place. She seems happy. We thought this was the place that would heal her…We visited her every other Sunday. Seven hour round trip. We thought we had our girl back. She was on her way and we were happy. Next chapter…Wednesday August 13th- We get a call from the facility. Our daughter cannot follow the rules. We must come and pick her up. I tell my husband. He drives and gets her and brings her home. We have a plan…She will go to a new half-way house on Monday.

Saturday, August 16th-My daughter and I go to the store (CVS). She says she is getting a call…she walks outside to answer and vanishes. Yes…she is gone. I text her and she tells me it is not my fault. She says she just wants to be with friends. She says she just wants to be normal. Contact ends.

Sunday, August 17th-No word. We go to bed worried. 11:35-Call from Kennestone. She overdosed again. We go to the hospital to see our daughter. She is not well. They put her on a 1013 which means she can't leave even though she is an adult. We spend the next few days with her in the hospital. Saturday August 23rd-She finally gets out of the hospital. We pick her up and take her straight to another Rehab. This is where our chapter ends…for now.

Sometimes I wake up and wish it was all a dream. It isn't. It is a disease. It ruins not only the addict, but their family. I have learned so many things a mother NEVER wants to know about her child. We do our best each day. We go to work and we try to be "normal." It is not normal. It consumes your mind every minute of every day. Reach out to the people and resources you have for help. We can't do this alone. Thank you Missy and God bless the families and the addicts. I hope my next chapter is my last, and I hope it's a happy ending.

9/1/14 – Constructive Act #165 – Step Outside Your Comfort Zone

Today will be a huge step outside of my comfort zone as I read the story of addiction and the journey my family endured. The Marietta Daily Journal will publish a story in today's paper about Davis, his addiction, our journey and our Foundation. It was our turn…it was time to share our story. I know it's not Sunday and I'm not writing the story, but I told the story and I agreed for it to be published. Am I nervous? You bet I am. I'm nervous that things will be confused; I'm nervous that things will have been miscommunicated, and I'm nervous that my family will be judged and have to endure nasty comments that will come out in the comments section regarding the article.

It doesn't matter! The fact is that we did live through this disease, and if our story helps one other person, we have made a difference. I can't keep soliciting stories from other people and not be willing to share our story through the darkest valley imaginable. Awareness is the goal of the Davis Direction Foundation and we would be nothing short of hypocrites if we didn't do what we are asking of others. So, today, I will hold my breath as I read the story of my life, my family's life and the horrific epidemic that infected our precious son and ultimately took his life.

It's very hard to allow someone else to tell your story; it will never be quite like you remember it or quite like you would tell it yourself. So – I am beyond thankful that I will have the chance to publish our own story of addiction in a local magazine in November. It will be healing; it will be painful; it will be one of the hardest things I have ever done; but it will be our story and not someone else's interpretation. There will be no comments for us to have to worry about, and no one to blame for misinterpretation.

I was raised to keep family business private and not to share things that were not positive or would present the family in a bad light. We didn't go around airing our "dirty laundry" as it was referred to.

Unless it was an accomplishment, a compliment or something you would want others to share about you…you kept your mouth shut. Plain and simple…We didn't have problems, or at least that's what we wanted others to believe. So – stepping outside of my comfort zone and telling my story next month, will go against everything I was taught as a child. Now I'm not saying that sharing your troubles is a bad thing; it was just something that people of my generation were taught not to do. Maybe if we had come to realize that every family had issues and crosses to bear, our burdens would have been easier to deal with. Maybe we would have received help before things spiraled out of control. Maybe we would have been shunned by our neighbors and our communities, and even asked to leave our church. Maybe…Maybe…Maybe… Who knows and why do I care?

I care because my family is the most important entity on this earth to me and to think that people are sitting back and judging us is still a hard pill to swallow. (I know…bad analogy) Family is sacred and you learn to protect them at all costs. You stick by them and love them in sickness and in health, for richer or poorer until DEATH DO YOU PART.

A part of me feels like I have betrayed my precious child and I have exposed myself as less than the mother I should have been. He was my child; He was my responsibility. There is NOTHING positive about addiction and there is no pretty picture to paint on the other side…if you come out on the other side. Every family that lives through addiction has walked through HELL. PLEASE embrace those that you know are struggling with addiction as we enter this national month of recovery. Step outside of your comfort zone…attend a ceremony or visit with a friend who is dying inside because he or she has no control to change things for his or her addicted loved one. Judge your ability to open your heart and lead by example rather than judging someone else's shortcomings. Take a step outside of your comfort zone and see if you can become more comfortable seeking first to understand.

9/2/14 – Constructive Act # 166 – Allow Support to Become Survival

Last night as I was surrounded by so many people who have supported me through the last 6 months of my life without my precious son, I realized that you guys have been my survival. As many nice things as you say to me on the DDF, it is you who have been my support system and my survival for this first 6 months.

You have allowed me to share my thoughts, my heart and bare my soul to you no matter what the theme may be. I have cried, vented, preached, wondered, thought out loud and thrown ideas out there to you that have possibly seemed quite crazy and you have endured me every step of they way. THANK YOU MY FRIENDS!

I met so many of you who have gone through the same journey that I have over the years, and you were there to support and encourage those of us who share this common thread. I saw and spoke to those of you who have recently lost your children and knew the pain in your hearts. I also saw those of you that I know and have been in contact with who are living with a struggling addict, and I saw and felt the pain in your eyes. I know how hard it was for you to be there last night to support and encourage others, but you were able to survive because of the support of others who are taking the journey with you. What a TERRIBLE bond to have that brings us all together, but it is a means of survival as we support each other through our pain.

Last night, Davis came to me in a dream and he was happy and he was beautiful and buff. He was tan and he was smiling and giving me one of his huge bear hugs. He smiled and laughed and then followed Michael and me to the piano and ask me to play a song for him. The song was "The Way That HE Loves". I know he was trying to tell me how awesome the Love of God is and how much I will come to know it as I share it with him in eternity one day. I have waited for that dream since the day he died and I finally got it last night.

The way that HE loves is so thrilling because…HIS love reaches even me!!!Thank you all for sharing our evening of HOPE! There is HOPE and WE will find it. I love you all and I'm praying for us daily.

9/3/14 – Constructive Act #167 – Keep On Keeping On

I have to admit – I'm exhausted. This weekend was emotionally, mentally and physically exhausting. I feel like I want to go into hiding and not come out until the Spring. I have tons of things that still need to be done, people to call, items to pick up.

I'm over my head with this golf tournament…I have already started making plans for the Oct. Symposium and am actively working on that, I need to write emails, get pricing, make flyers and I'm falling asleep! BUT – I will continue to work because there is a need in our community that is not getting any better. We have an opiate/heroin epidemic that is killing our kids! We cannot rest until we are making progress.

So – We keep on keeping on! This is similar to the life of the addict. The difference is that when I get tired, I go to sleep and rest. When I get overwhelmed, I ask for help because what I'm doing is not illegal, shameful or embarrassing. When plans fall through, I don't panic, I just get busy seeking other alternatives. My choices are endless and my decisions are my own.

Not so with an addict. When their bodies are tired, their brains don't shut down. When they get overwhelmed they panic because there is no one to ask for help. When plans fall through they get desperate and their decisions are NOT their own. They are completely controlled, and obsessed and they turn to self-medicating. They are owned by the drugs and the dealers. They keep on keeping on because they don't know how to stop. They can't stop. They won't stop because the drug won't let go!

I feel like I have learned about the mind of an addict since Davis' death because I can't stop thinking about him. Everything I do is about him, for him, and because of him. I can't stop my brain from thinking about him…HE IS MY ADDICTION! Every smell, every room in my house, every turn in my school, every flower that he planted, every show that he watched, every food that he ate… My brain does not stop! But I don't hurt physically – a broken heart is an emotional hurt. My body does not crave for anything that would make me lie, steal or cheat. So I keep on keeping on because I still have choices with my addiction. I am at peace because I know where my sweet child is. I can readjust and reevaluate and choose a new path. We MUST teach our addicts how to do the same. We must give them the tools, the emotional support and the mental and physical support to obtain Recovery. WE MUST!

We MUST be role models showing kids how to "Dig Deep" into their souls when they need to Keep on Keeping On. This is something we have not taught this generation. We have taught them the "quick fix" and "immediate gratification." They are not used to earning things with long term determination. Addiction is not a "quick fix" or something that can be cured overnight. Recovery is a lifestyle – one that will take determination, commitment, perseverance and skills learned through counseling and research on their parts. There are drug therapies to help them along the way and that's okay –

All medications are NOT bad! Thank God for insulin…it keeps my husband alive everyday. We need to find the new medications that work to keep the addicts alive and keep the DISEASE in remission. We have work to do……se we WILL "KEEP ON KEEPING ON!"

9/4/14 – Constructive Act #168 – Cherish Every Moment

When you are loving an addict and living with an addict, cherish every moment that you have with them and every moment that you get to spend with them, because you never know which of those moments may be your last. As I sit here tonight writing for tomorrow morning, I can't help but think that exactly 6 months ago tonight, I was waiting for my sweet Davis to come home from the Narcotics Anonymous meeting that I thought he had gone to. I was just watching a little television, sitting in my living room all by myself waiting for Davis so I could go to bed and get up for work the next morning. As time passed, my heart grew a little heavier by the minute. At the stroke of midnight, I had a pretty sick feeling in my stomach.

I remember going up to bed around 1:30 waking my husband up to tell him that Davis wasn't home and that I didn't think he was ever coming home again. I remember laying down listening for the garage door to sound, telling me that he was home and that I could go to sleep. I remember dozing in and out, getting up to look out the window to check for his car. I remember getting up at 5:00 a.m. knowing that I would never see him again. I remember the false hope that everyone tried to give me telling me that he was ashamed and couldn't come home because he was embarrassed, but I knew in my heart what the situation was. I remember calling into work saying that I was sick and wouldn't be coming in for work. I remember feeling how very sick I was and knowing it was the worst sick I had ever felt in my entire life. I remember all these things and relive them more often than you will ever know.

Time with an addict is NEVER guaranteed. I know that you could say that for anyone, but saying it for an addict has a different and more intense meaning. Addicts are ticking time bombs; you never know when they will go off and make a mistake that will end their life and life as you know it! They change the dynamics of your entire family and single handedly turn your gut inside out. They are as remorseful as anyone I have ever known, but turn around and do the same things the next day as if nothing had ever happened. Life with an addict is hard to explain to someone who has never lived it, but the thing about that is that more often than not, people know just exactly what you mean. That's because we are experiencing an epidemic in our community, our state and in our nation.

Monday night we listed the names of the sweet family members that had been lost to the disease in our community at our Lights of Hope ceremony. Name for name, there were almost as many as the kids we listed for Recovery. That's a scary thought when you think about it because the statistic is startling when you read it.

For every prescription drug death, there are 10 treatment admissions for abuse, 32 emergency room visits for misuse and abuse, 130 people who abuse or are dependent, and 825 non-medical users. (CDC)

Do you understand what that means? It means that prescription drug /heroin abuse is still very much HUSH-HUSH! No one is talking about it because they are embarrassed! SPEAK-UP and SPEAK-OUT! This horrific epidemic will never end until it is brought out into the open and dealt with. WE have to help these precious children who are suffering silently because their families are too proud to ask for help. YES – I was one of those and I will live with that the rest of my life. Don't make the same mistakes that I did, I have laid them out in front of you raw and unedited. There is no excuse for you making the same mistakes that I did. Let's talk about it…Let's open the dialogue…Let's swallow our pride…Before one more child FALLS victim to this awful DISEASE!

Please pray for me today as I endure the 6 month anniversary of losing my precious Davis – my heart hurts and my soul is numb.

www.cdc.gov/homeandrecreationalsafety/rxbrief/

9/5/14 – Constructive Act #169 – Stay Connected

Every day I hear of new and good things happening in the fight against prescription drug use and heroin. Lawmakers are meeting, civic organizations are asking speakers to speak with them about the issues, churches are getting involved, newspapers are considering it a "Hot Topic, and people in general are tired of kids overdosing and dying. This is a perfect time to be in the fight against opiate/heroin addiction and abuse. Politicians are listening and hearing what we say.

Stay connected politically right now, with elections just a few weeks away (8) figure out who you want to put in office to help us win this war. It's time to start educating yourselves as to what people running for office stand for. Are they concerned? Are they talking about it? Have they taken a stance or made a statement about the problem? LISTEN to what the candidates are saying!!!

I received a phone call from the Lieutenant Governor's office yesterday and the nicest lady graciously declined our offer for Casey Cagle to come and play golf with us Monday week because he is on the campaign trail! I truly understand that – People get criticized for being on the golf course ALL the time when they are elected to do a job. So good for him – But the lady did tell me that Lt Governor Cagle was very concerned about the prescription drug abuse and it is an issue that he has spoken openly about and is deeply disturbed by it. And rightly so – the Lt Gov has children who are of the average age to begin prescription drug use and he would be foolish not to educate himself as to the dangers.

We are looking into Skyping him into the October 8th Symposium to at the very least make a statement about the problem. January will be our big legislative/political Symposium and we are looking now for politicians who are willing to attend and answer questions regarding the misuse and abuse of opiates/heroin. We will ask them what the changes are that they would like to see happen in the community and how far they are willing to invest to see that it happens.

Now is the time to read every article that you can and know the updates, know the cutting edge therapies and come to the October 8th Symposium to learn about the services provided in our community, state and even in the nation addressing Rehab and Recovery. If you are a Rehab/Recovery provider, make arrangements now to set up a booth and talk to the people who will attend the Symposium and let them know what you bring to the table as far as help in our area.

To reserve a table, email us at info@davisdirection.com. We will reserve your spot and allow you to advertise your services and handout information regarding what you do. I have said it over and over again on this site… KNOWLEDGE IS POWER. It will help you keep your loved one alive as we seek for answers to "cure" this disease.

9/6/14 – Constructive Act #170 – Read The Newspaper

I know this is a dying art in this day and age of computer technology, but it never hurts to get a little newspaper ink on those fingers!!! Today, I awakened to the sound of a text message sent by one of the Board members on the DDF telling me to read the "Around Town" section of the MDJ.

Yes – friends, the Davis Direction Foundation has been mentioned yet again this week regarding the epidemic of opiate/heroin addiction in our community! Thank you Leigh Colburn, DDF Board member for answering the call of the Rotary Club to promote awareness and affect change.

This was an excellent article and extremely accurate. The article speaks about Rick Allen's presentation to the civic club reporting the facts and statistics regarding opiate/heroin use among people in our community. Mr. Allen is the Director for the DEA in Georgia. He was also our keynote speaker at the June Symposium. Once again he accurately and "in real time" depicted the state of our community regarding this epidemic. It's frightening and something needs to be done. He reported that due to recent restrictions placed on prescription drugs, we could quite possibly see a rise in the use of heroin.

Could it be your child? Could it be your child's best friend? Could it be your sister, brother, nephew, or niece? NO ONE IS IMMUNE! Please read the paper and keep up with current events related to this crisis. I know that the Marietta Daily Journal has planned to do upcoming articles that are related because they realize the importance of this issue. The reporters, photographers and editors there all have families of their own! They have realized the dangers and are on board in bringing you – the readers – up to date on every angle of this epidemic.

Last week – I received another text from yet another Board member – Dr. Sam Matthews – who was telling me the Wall Street Journal had published an article on Naloxone, explaining the properties and how it was being used to address this National crisis. Naloxone – also referred to as Naloxone – is the drug that brings an overdosed person out of the overdose and buys them about 45 minutes to an hour to get to the hospital for life-saving medical help. It was another great article in the NEWSPAPER helping people to understand the implications of opiate/heroin addiction. We will have Naloxone available at the October 8th Symposium thanks to the diligent work of the DDF Board Members, one of whom is our Medical Director, Dr. Harold McLendon.

I'm quite sure if you pick up any newspaper for a solid week and read it from cover page to last page, you would find something about opiate/heroin addiction. I know the recent bust with 46 arrests was published in several Atlanta newspapers. Stay up to date and informed. "Knowledge is POWER" as I have stated almost weekly. I think I'll go ahead and make that one an acronym – "KIP"

I'm going to end this "CA" here so that I can run out and pick up my MDJ. I'm going to subscribe either online or for the "driveway" issue. Either way, I'm going to stay informed. "KIP"

9/7/14 – Constructive Act #171 – Share Your Story

This kid is AMAZING – He has recently entered recovery after a very scary experience! I have never seen a recovering addict work it so bravely. He attended the Lights of Hope ceremony and came right up to me and introduced himself. Iknew him from corresponding with him on the DDF messages. He stole my heart! He has embraced the DDF and calls us "His Family." Now – that's what it's all about! Xxooo – Love you Tanner!

My story...

I would like to start off by saying i am honored to share my story with you all. My name is Tanner L. and I am a grateful recovering heroin addict. My story really starts off six years ago when i was only 14 years old. My parents had just split up and i used that as an excuse to "self-medicate" myself with drugs.

It all started with smoking pot and as i grew i became more experimental with pain pills and other forms of pills. Using drugs began to interfere with my school work and really led up to me having zero motivation to succeed. I found myself hanging with the wrong friends, getting into constant trouble with the police, my family, and my school. I never admitted i had an issue. Always thought i could manage my using. My mother tried multiple times to get me into treatment but refused to cooperate with them.

I had a tendency to run away from my problems and not face them like many addicts. As i finished high school i found myself in the mist of the club scene. Using club drugs regularly. I was stealing from my family, lying about where i was, what i was doing. My life became a game of how I'm gonna get my next high. I was seriously in denial about myself and became very selfish. I "had it under control"... not knowing the damage i was doing to myself, my family, and my few real friends i had left. Unfortunately i was kicked out of the house and spent many months homeless living from house to house. A kid brought me in to his home who is a heroin addict and this is when i hit rock bottom.

I tried heroin and my life was revolving around the drug. At the time i was working two jobs to pay my spot in his home and to maintain my addiction. I couldn't wake up not in pain... i couldn't go to work if i didn't have some to get high before i went in so i wouldn't be sick. My life was unmanageable. I "needed" the drug... it was like no other drug i had done. It had complete an utter control over me.

On June 17th 2014, i overdosed in the home of where i had been living. I was unconscious, and Thank my higher power my roommate had passed by the room I was in and immediately dialed 911. I was administered Naloxone by Cherokee County EMS and came right back to life.

Through my experience I had spoken to a higher power that was telling me I will give you one more shot... I was treated for aspiration pneumonia and kept on close watch because of my overdose. I voluntarily went to Highland Rivers rehabilitation where I spent a month and a half in intensive treatment.

Today i am so blessed where I am. And the new life I am living. It's an ongoing struggle to fight, better yet, manage my addiction. I consistently attend Narcotics

Anonymous meetings as well as stay connected to the Davis Direction Foundation. I currently have a fundraiser up and running through my job that is helping raise money to donate to "MY" DDF family. I'm still learning new ways to give back to my community but spreading awareness about heroin/opiate addiction is my number one goal.

I plan to attend college in the Spring and study to become a drug addictions counselor in the future. My destiny is to help fellow addicts and make an impact, even if its one person, a chain reaction makes a difference! Finally i would like to state that if you know an addict in recovery or one actively using. Here it from me, do NOT give up! We are beautiful people under the skin of our addiction. Love them, cherish every moment with them. This is a disease, an epidemic. And I'm blessed to share my story for the rest of my time. I love you all who are a part of my life. And God Bless the families and addicts everywhere. We at DDF are here for you.

9/8/14 – Constructive Act #172 – Question The Security

Tonight we sadly posted on the DDF about an addict we have had in our fold who OD'd WHILE IN A REHAB FACILITY. Yes – you read that right and in all caps because I am screaming!!! What are we dealing with when we are paying thousands of dollars… and the very institutions that we are paying it to are allowing the drugs inside their walls?

I was extremely concerned about this very issue when Davis was in Rehab. Although the paperwork they provide to families when entering the facility sounds good and right, what really happens is extremely different and it's time to start calling these places out.

When we went for Sunday morning visits to attend meetings and worship with others, we were supposed to sign in and be recognized.

NEVER once did we see anyone who was physically manning a sign in sheet or even providing one for that matter. We never signed in except for that first Sunday when I physically sought an employee out and asked where the sign in sheet was and what were we supposed to do as visitors? She simply pointed me to a desk with a clipboard on it and went on about her business.

When we visited on family meeting night during the week, we entered the young adult facility and more often than not, no one was at the front desk and we NEVER signed in. SECURITY WAS TOO RELAXED! We were not ever checked for cell phones, bags, coats, or anything else that would have been an avenue to carry in drugs. Davis was allowed to come to our car and hang out with us unattended. We could walk all over campus with him, and nobody cared or checked us out. How did they know we were not bringing in drugs or other contraband items? After all, we had 4 other teenage kids with us on most visits.

During Sunday morning meetings, we constantly saw kids with their parents cell phones and kids with their own cell phones that parents had brought to them. There was little to zero security at this particular facility. Half the time, the weekend staff member never showed up to walk with these kids and never interacted with them. He was just a glorified babysitter in my opinion. They were supposed to check any bags we brought to Davis and we had to ask them to make sure they would check them. We could have easily brought them straight in and no one would have ever questioned it.

For the record I was paying $3,900.00 per week for this kind of negligence. Don't ask me why I didn't demand better security. I just walked around like a little vulnerable parent at the mercy of all that was happening – Good or Bad! I'm ashamed to admit that now, but it is true. Drugs could have easily been smuggled into this place and no one would have ever known. They didn't drug test nearly enough and I don't know why.

As you can see from tonight's post, SECURITY is of the utmost importance. ASK QUESTIONS! DEMAND ANSWERS! And if you don't get them to your satisfaction, change facilities. If you are invested in helping your addict, make sure they are INVESTED in helping them too! NO SECURITY = DRUGS

9/9/14 – Constructive Act #173 – Practice What You Preach

This is an old saying that most of us have heard for the better part of our lives. This is also an old saying that most of us can be accused of not doing at some point in our lives.

It was probably the reason that the other old saying "Do as I say...Not as I do" was first spoken. These are hard words to live by because most of us have a vision of what we want our lives to be like and the values and morals we want to practice throughout our time here on earth, but it easier said than done.

A common conversation continues to come up as addiction is discussed throughout our community. If you directly ask most people whether or not addiction is a disease, the majority of people will say unequivocally "yes." The reason for this is that most of us have an addict that we know and love in our families and we have witnessed first hand the trials and tribulations of personal struggle within the addict. I know personally that watching my precious Davis struggle with the battle of addiction was one of the most heartbreaking experiences of my life. Knowing the conflict between the brain and the heart and seeing it openly exposed was almost unbearable. I still have very painful scenarios in my memory of this heartbreaking disease and the battles that ensue.

I know that there are plenty of parents out there who are telling their children over and over again about the perils of drugs and other addictions, while at the same time indulging in addictions on a functional level. Are you practicing what you are preaching? You do realize that the only difference between that first drink, or that first opiate prescription is the fact that there are some of us on this earth who are genetically predisposed to addiction and others of us who have been spared. "Therefore by the Grace of God go I."

So – I will ask you – all of you – many of you who have agreed with me through comments and posts on this very page, Are you practicing what you preach? Are your medicine cabinets cleaned out? Are your opiate medications or all of your prescribed medications for that matter locked up and out of reach of the experimental aged children in your home – 12 – 17? Are you drinking and driving in front of your children? Yes – even one drink? Is there anything in your life that you need to reevaluate as you look in the mirror every morning?

I would venture to say that 99.9% of all children love and look up to their parents with unconditional admiration. We are our children's first link to knowing how to handle situations. Our behavior will more than likely at some point become their behavior. Having been a counselor for almost 30 years, I understand repeated cycles of behavior.

Make sure that your behaviors are worth repeating. If addiction runs in your family, and if you look long and hard enough you WILL find it, make sure your kids know that you cannot predict which drink or which pill will be the one that turns the cucumber into a pickle! "Practice what you Preach"...without DISCLAIMERS!!!

9/10/14 – Constructive Act #174 – Contribute When You Can

We are coming up on our very first major fundraiser. This is so important because raising funds is what allows us to concentrate our efforts to help those who need help to endure and find a solution for the epidemic of opiate/heroin addiction. The families of the addicts find themselves just trying to survive the experience while the addicts in most cases actively seek a solution but find that the solutions that others place on the table in fact aren't solutions at all in most cases.

Most of you know that the mission of the Davis Direction Foundation is to promote awareness, affect change, and keep the users alive until we can find appropriate solutions that work. So – with that in mind, I will lay out some of our initiatives that will allow us to stay true to our mission. We are preparing informational packets to hand out to people who come into the hospitals who have overdosed. The packets include information explaining the disease of opiate/heroin addiction and why it is the most severe form of addiction that we know. It also explains heroin and the history and properties of the drug. The packet will include resources that the families, deep in the throes of addiction, can utilize for support and encouragement. It will provide the different ways to access the Davis Direction Foundation so that these families can stay up to date with current information and support opportunities.

We are also going to hand out Naloxone at our upcoming Symposiums. We are very excited to announce that we will have the Naloxone kits available at the October Symposium. We will have trainers available to explain to the families and friends of addicts how to use the kits to bring an addict out of the overdose and save their lives. These kits are very affordable, but a major expense when you realize the epidemic proportions that are needed to hand out. This initiative will be a major expense for us. It will also be one of our most important offerings as a Foundation.

We will continue to create public awareness through the preparation and passing out of literature regarding our Foundation and the epidemic our community is experiencing.

We will actively be in the community at appropriate places to distribute awareness pieces such as our new rubber bracelets and to share our information. We are looking into partnering with local pharmacies to hand out information regarding the specific prescription drugs that can lead to addiction. Many people don't know the names of the drugs that contain hydrocodone, Oxycodone and other ingredients that have addictive properties. They don't know when they walk out of the pharmacy that they are carrying a potentially dangerous drug that is taking the lives of our family members. We will actively educate the community and beyond regarding this issue.

Last but not least, we will continue to have the educational symposiums with speakers and organizations who are in attendance to share their services and knowledge in order to affect change regarding this epidemic. We will be an active legislative force affecting necessary change in order to protect our families and their loved ones. We will continue with our public billboard campaign putting a powerful message out there in hopes of opening the door to public conversation about opiates and heroin.

All of these efforts take money and that is where the money you are so generously donating to our Foundation will be spent. We guard every dollar with our hearts as well as our brains as a Foundation and we spend in line with our mission and goals that we have outlined above. So – please contribute when you can and what you can. No donation is too small and every donation will be used to address the mission and beliefs of the DDF. We are forever grateful for every donation Thank you for your generosity.

9/11/14 – Constructive Act # 175 – Humble Yourself

Sometimes I change tracks in my head just because of something I read that speaks to me. This morning is one of those times. I was all ready to write a different CA and when I read my email I suddenly thought to myself that I needed to write something other than I had planned. I woke up this morning to my daily devotional and for some reason read it first before I started writing. It was all about humbling yourselves and not judging others.

I know that whenever we talk about all the statistics regarding prescription drugs and heroin someone always says…"And those are just the ones we know about who are admitting they use." This means that the numbers are probably way more that we know and the statistics are way higher than what we see in print. What keeps these addicts from admitting their use and reaching out for help? PRIDE!

I've decided that PRIDE works two ways. First and foremost, Davis had gotten himself into something that he had lost all control of. It's hard to lose total control of something when you are an intelligent person. It makes you feel vulnerable and stupid. Secondly, if you are on the outside looking in, many of us become judgmental and create stumbling blocks or obstacles that get in the way of these people who are suffering with addiction. Since the addicts can't get inside anyone's head to know their thoughts, they began to assume that everyone is judging them and they have nowhere to turn for help. Maybe they did reach out to someone who happened to be judgmental and they felt rejected and began to withdraw. For whatever reason, addicts are not usually very forthcoming with their addiction.

This needs to change! The Bible says…

> HUMBLE YOURSELF BEFORE THE LORD AND HE WILL LIFT YOU UP. (JAMES 4:10) FOR THE LORD TAKES DELIGHT IN HIS PEOPLE; HE CROWNS THE HUMBLE WITH SALVATION. GOD OPPOSES THE PROUD BUT GIVES GRACE TO THE HUMBLE. (JAMES 4:6)

If you are an Addict, God is asking you to come to Him for help. He is waiting with open arms to receive you into his fold. If you are a Christian already and have wondered away from God, He is waiting again with open arms for you to come back to Him. He is "OPPOSED" to those who are judgmental and making you feel that you are less than. As a matter of fact, He even says MANY WHO ARE FIRST WILL BE LAST, AND MANY WHO ARE LAST WILL BE FIRST.

(MATTHEW 19:30). God has reserved the right to be the FINAL JUDGE. It is He and He alone who decides what is in your heart. NEVER let anyone else make you feel like you are not worthy of God's love. YOU ARE WORTHY AND GOD LOVES YOU.

The Faith community needs to step up and get involved in this opiate epidemic. We are not doing enough to support God's children who are suffering with the disease of addiction. I believe in my heart that the solution to this epidemic is GOD! We are medically trying to treat the disease and not looking enough at the cause. The way to break the cycle of disease is to eliminate the cause. Why are kids turning to drugs in the first place? Stress and anxiety...Pressures in a world that is harsh...Expectations that are internal and the feelings of not being good enough...So many reasons are out there and we have to encourage those suffering with addiction to humble themselves and turn to God. At the same time, we have to encourage those who don't understand the disease of addiction to humble themselves and stop judging others which creates a vicious cycle of withdrawal and lack of help for those who need it. Everyone...PRACTICE HUMILITY.

PRIDE GOES BEFORE DESTRUCTION, AND A HAUGHTY
SPIRIT BEFORE A FALL. (PROVERBS 16:22 *NIV)

9/12/14 – 9Constructive Act #176 – Pick Your Role

In the world of addiction, EVERYONE has a role. It can be an active role or a passive role, but EVERYONE has a role. You may not realize it yet, but one day you will. Some roles are obvious and others not so much. You may not even realize that you have a role until it is too late.

There are the addicts, there are the families of addicts, there are the Rehabs, the doctors, the law enforcement agencies, the lawmakers, the advocates, the teachers, and the innocent victims. Have you seen your role yet? If not, perhaps one day you will find out that you are the parent of an innocent victim, or worse...the child of an innocent victim. One way or another I can almost guarantee you that before your life is over, you will have been touched in some way by the DISEASE of addiction.

A friend of mine called me this afternoon and said, "I have a Constructive Act for you and you're not going to believe it." "You need to tell people to call 911 without hesitation." She then proceeded to tell me about a story that a teacher told her this week about an incident that happened at a local strip mall of mostly eating establishments. As this teacher was walking by a restaurant, she heard a rapping on the window and saw a lady inside motioning for her to come in. So she went in and the merchant inside told her to watch this young lady in a car in the parking lot. She was swaying back and forth in her car and the merchant told the teacher that she thought something might be wrong with her. Without hesitation, the teacher told her to call 911. The merchant was unsure about doing that. She said "I've never done that before." "Do I have to give them my name?" "Is there a charge to call 911 if they come out to help you?" I don't know for sure, but I didn't get the impression that this merchant was very young. She was just very unsure about making the call to save a life or get this young woman out of her car and out from behind the wheel.

The teacher offered to make the call for the lady, but the lady finally called herself. Long story short, the woman's mother showed up when the emergency vehicles called her to make her aware of the situation, and told them the girl had been struggling with addiction and was high on meth. NOW...If you don't think that this merchant had a role and an obligation to help in this situation...THINK AGAIN! What if she had ignored the situation and allowed the young woman to drive away high on meth? What if, GOD forbid, she lost consciousness behind the wheel and hit your loved one in a head-on collision therefore taking away your ability to "PICK YOUR ROLE" because your role had been chosen for you? EVERYONE HAS A ROLE!

Understand that we are in the midst of an epidemic! Don't hesitate to err on the side of caution by calling 911 or blowing the horn at a car that is parked with someone asleep inside. You don't have to be right...You just have to be involved. Remember, your lack of action could cause a different action and it might be one that ends in the loss of life. When there is an epidemic among us, people take precautions...Look at all the precautions that Emory has been taking when treating the Ebola patients when they come into our community for treatment. They take all the precautions they can to prevent the spread of the deadly Ebola virus. Well, the Disease of Addiction is much more widespread than Ebola, so why would anyone want to leave themselves unprotected? Why would you put your own kids at-risk by not involving yourself in a situation where all you have to do is make a phone call. Leave the rest up to the trained professionals of 911. Invest in our community..."PICK YOUR ROLE" while you still have a choice!

9/13/14 – Constructive Act #177 – Take Care of Your Team

It's College football day and everybody has a team – even if you didn't go to college at your team's institution! EVERYBODY HAS A TEAM and we all invest in our team. We wear their jerseys, we buy their jewelry, we buy season tickets and flags for the cars. We all have a mascot or 2 hanging around the house and we all post our pictures on Facebook when we are with our team! GO –FIGHT–WIN –

Are you investing in your family team? Yes – I have regrets in this area and I'll tell you why! As a counselor and as a MOM – I began to think my job was coming to a close after my children turned 18.

I felt like if they needed me after that point, they would come to me and seek my guidance or that of my husband.

I had done the teaching and the rearing. I had instilled the values and had them in Sunday School every Sunday. I had helped them maintain their grades through high school and helped them complete their college apps. They were where they needed to be and life was good!

Generation "Y" as I have spoken about many times, comes with a whole new level of adulthood. Whereas, in our generation, we were pretty solid when we left for college to go and find our place in the world, it is so different for our kids. First and foremost, we are in a position in our society where jobs are not as easy to come by and lots of our kids have chosen to stay in school and get an advanced degree. That makes it even harder to get a job in some cases because the entry level salary expected is not available in lots of cases. Generation "Y" also expects pats on the back, promotions, and titles that it took years for us to achieve. Because they were given trophies and "titles" at every level of their education and extra curricular involvement , their expectation in the adult world of work is very skewed. What we saw as "Paying our dues" is often times considered "failure" to them.

When we entered college, the fields of study were still very stereotypical for the most part, and our choices were somewhat limited according to the University we chose. And it was "OKAY" to choose not to go to college if that was what we wanted. Now, the fields of study are so wide open – I don't even know what some of them are, and I even know of a friend who got to "make up" his own college degree and they are configuring it as he progresses through it. I will equate this to having too many choices. It's like going into a mall vs. a dress shop. Sometimes there are too many choices and life becomes overwhelming. Davis, I know, felt a great deal of stress in this area because he didn't have a strong calling for a specific career. This was very stressful for him.

With all of this being said, life now poses a whole new era of parenting for our generation. The average age of prescription drug addiction is now 18 – 36 years of age, with experimentation beginning as young as 12. So – I go back to my original statement…How are you investing in your team? Maybe it's time to stay a little more involved for a little bit longer. Instead of baby-proofing our homes…we need to opiate-proof them. Buy a lock box for meds, return our meds to drop-boxes, don't fill prescriptions for opiates that you can get by without. Continue to have those "educational" conversations around the dinner table regarding life situations and how to handle them.

And for that matter…Continue to have those family dinners!!! The "OWEN 7" has made some changes in our home. We've taken a step back and re-visited some practices that were in need of some revision. Continue to include your ENTIRE family in outings and vacations. PROTECT YOUR TEAM! Cheer for your team. Keep a check on their health and sanity. If you are in doubt of a member and their health, have that member take a drug test. If you are in doubt of a member and their sanity, have that member speak with a counselor or psychiatrist. If that member is sick…Get them to a doctor! Invest in your team…GO – FIGHT – WIN!!! In the grand scheme of things, your FAMILY TEAM is the most important TEAM of all!

9/14/14 – Constructive Act #178 – Share Your Story

This precious Mom needs our prayers. She wanted to tell her story so badly, she texted it on a phone because she no longer has a computer due to her son taking all she had. She knows it's a DISEASE and she continues to try to find ways to help him. There is no love like a mother's love… Please read her story.

My son had always been a quiet child… always by my side …he never got into trouble at school always made good grades and in high school made 3rd highest score on his PSAT …my husband and I found his interest …was sports. He got involved in a sport where he could excel and he did. He won many trophies because he was good at his sport. His problems with heroin didn't start until he was 17 …he had stopped racing and had free weekends…he began to make new friends at school and I remember being glad he had come out of his shell …I thought it was a good thing…but what I didn't know was the friends he had made were not who I thought they were…they were older than him …I never thought anything was wrong …but later realized that right under my roof…these kids introduced him to heroin.

A few months later …the day I will never forget…2 detectives knocked on my door and told me that they were arresting my son for stolen property and he had sold it to a recycling business…and wanted to go to his high school to arrest him…I believe that was the day I was so caught off guard …I couldn't understand he was such a good kid he had no problems that I knew of ? That day …they told me something that shattered my world …after they left I was in such shock… I remember sobbing asking God how this could have happened ? Why ? And that was the beginning of my journey through hell with my son and his heroin addiction.

We put him in a rehab for 6 weeks hoping that would cure him when he completed the program I sent him to live with his grandfather to get him away from his old friends. He seemed to be doing great for awhile had a job… until his grandfather found out he had stolen thousands of dollars worth of checks and he had forged them... he was then sent to his father's where he also started to pawn whatever he could for his addiction ...take in mind this was a child that everyone adored. I had no idea what was about to happen... my entire family was about to go through a living nightmare.

We sent him to a doctor to prescribe suboxone... maybe that was the answer ? That would cure him I thought ? But it seemed that was not the answer ...because he continued on this path to destruction with heroin and Oxycodone. He was passed back and forth to his father and I he'd pawn everything he could there ... and so my cousin would always go pay to get everything out of pawn ...My rings My camera anything of value... he would lie to everyone he would take hundreds of dollars he would charge $1000 on my cousins credit cards ...I felt helpless...I promised myself ... I will do everything I can to save my son ... I remember I would see his head bobbing at night and I knew ...it was so serious... so I called his father and told him to come get him. His father would come and get him he would go thru withdrawals and sit for a week at a time .,over and over... always to return to his addiction.

The money didn't mean anything to me I always told him I would sell everything I had to save him... but it seemed that everything I had... would not save him from the addiction . I went to Church prayer meetings to help myself and they did help me they helped me to understand I was co=dependent that I could not change him ...I couldn't fix him... his addiction not only affected me, his addiction affected everyone around him, everyone that loved him all the family members that loved him. He would lie to get money; he would do anything he could to feed that addiction he actually slept in his truck. He lived in this truck for a few weeks because he kept stealing from everyone.

This child was not my child anymore he was not the sweet child that I knew ...and I'd pray to God every night for him. There were nights when I wondered when he left would he make it till tomorrow? I remember one night laying on the floor in my bedroom asking God to take me because if he didn't make it I would never make it... and as I was praying that very night ...my son walked through the front door and I knew that God had given me a sign that he would make it... I had been ready to end it all but I could not leave my baby boy ...he continued to be passed around from family member to family member because he was still stealing...from one or the other ...he would pawn ...

I'm sure over a period of a few years we'd spent over 50,000 including everything from family. We tried everything in our power to help him from his heroin addiction......we all begged him "please go to rehab" I had been begging him; so had my family members but he always assured us "saying I can do this on my own" so we went thru many more times with him going through withdrawals then one time at my house he was going through withdrawals once again ...for a week...and

I told him" son, I said you know what's out there waiting on you"? When you leave here… it's the world… and I hope you're prepared to deal with the world.

There were many times like that …"I'm clean now I'll be ok "well soon … I'd find out he wasn't… he had gone right back to the addiction then one day recently I found out he had charged $3,200. on my cousins credit card and that's when I decided this has got to stop …, I had him put in jail it was the hardest decision I ever made… but no one including his father would do it …it had to be My decision it was on my shoulders …so I had him arrested.

When I went to visit him he said a man came up to him and spoke to him and told him "son your clean cut you're a nice looking kid and your family loves you" what are you doing in here? My son asked him" how many jails had he been in?" and he said "you name it I've been in every jail" sometimes I wonder if he was an angel he told my son that he would never make it in jail which helped because it scared my son so much. Maybe that would change him! I thought, but as soon as he got out a week later he went back to it…it did not stop his addiction.

I found out about a methadone clinic recently and he's been on a methadone program and it seems to be helping him with the craving he is working and he seems to be healthier than he has been in years. I am proud of him and so many ways but I don't like the fact that he still has to be on a methadone program but it is better than him stealing thousands of dollars and whisking jail… it is been a long hard treacherous road.

I'm telling you this addiction knows no bounds. He was, and is a wonderful kid and now I'm actually seeing him come back some ways but is also because of the methadone program that he is in now. I hope and pray that this is the answer but God tells me there are no answers no right answers to this addiction.

I did pray and pray and pray everyday besides my son I guess sometimes it just means but there is a purpose I don't know I don't know why my son has made it I don't know why my son has lived through what he is been through but he has I suppose the methadone program has helped me in a way.

I am NOT saying that is the answer I'm saying there are no answers but I do know that prayer and God working in their lives does work. So many prayers to all that are out there struggling with their children's addictions. All I can tell you is keep fighting keep trying everything in your power. If it be rehab, if it be suboxone, if it be any kind of program that you can get them on… and just keep trying because I don't know the answers. Only God may, but I do know one thing don't ever give up. Sometimes we have to accept the facts but maybe our children don't make it but we also know it's nice to have the Davis Direction Foundation because this will become a forefront in this country and they will all see that drugs harm every class, not just the poor. My son was brought up that when I got home he was given every opportunity and everything that any child could want but that did not stop the addiction in his life. I am happy to say we are blessed that he seems to be doing better but its only been a couple months on the methadone program. The program seems to be helping the cravings. I am only saying don't give up hope. Hope is what keeps us going; hope is all we have, prayers, prayers, prayers!

Thank you for reading I hope this might help someone I don't have all the answers … there is no right answer to this but I know there is a purpose. There's a purpose for everything that happens in our lives like the Davis Direction Foundations and their beautiful child … I'm so happy to be a part of it now because I really believe that getting awareness out to parents... maybe we can help because we have been through it. There should be programs for these kids I don't know of any that have worked for my son except the methadone program but it's only been a short time, a couple of months. I still feel on the edge hoping and praying this might be the answer? I encourage him to stay in the program because he has gotten better but I also wonder because I never know what the future will hold but I always hold on to hope … I cannot say I know the answers because I don't because each child is different. What may help one may not help another …I don't have the answer to cure a child from addiction to heroin or Oxycodone…all I can say to the mother's and families dealing with this demon of an addicted child, Don't give up …do everything …if it's rehab then rehab...if it's doctors…then doctors…if it's anything try it …try it ALL …but most of all…pray, pray, pray, constantly …

9/15/14 – Constructive Act #179 – Roll With The Punches

Sometimes that old devil just tries his best to get in the way! No matter how hard you have tried to put things into motion for a smooth flow, things just don't go according to plan.

It's OKAY! It's times like this when you have just got to put things into perspective and ask yourself…"Am I surrounded by love?" Do I have my family with me?" "Are my friends there for me in my time of need?" If you can answer yes to all of these, then you are one of the lucky ones!

For weeks now, we have been planning "A Day for Davis." We have dotted our i's and crossed our t's and things have fallen into place with such ease that it has been almost easy. This community has been one of the most giving communities in the world. I am proud to live in Cobb County where the people jump in and understand the cause and invest in the future.

Today, when we were running around attending to last minute details and picking up last minute items, something strange started happening at our home. The lights started flickering, and all of the sudden the appliances started popping and the house started smoking and smelling of electrical flavor. Needless to say, the whole panel was blown and it had to do with underground wires and defects going back to the beginning of the home being built. We probably lost the majority of our appliances and we will have a lot of work to do to make things right again. The intercom started coming on and the radio started playing and the house took on a mind of its own. We called some of our friends who called some of their friends and before you could shake a stick, we had a certified electrician – "owner of the company" at our door. He was amazing and very thorough, but he had his limits. In other words, there was nothing he could do to keep us in the house tonight. So – needless to say, we packed up the golf tournament, ourselves, and our deflated egos and moved into a hotel.

Yes, – I was overwhelmed, and the waterworks went into overtime…BUT – I'm surrounded by love, I have my family with me and my friends are here for me! What more could a girl ask for? Tomorrow will come and go and we will have an awesome day, because the people coming to the tournament and silent auction are coming to support the cause of opiate/heroin addiction. They are coming because they loved Davis, they know there is an epidemic in our nation and they realize that addiction knows no boundaries.

Tomorrow, I will be surrounded by the people that I love, the friends that I need, and the spirit of hope! Tomorrow will be an awesome day, an awesome tournament, and an awesome "Day for Davis." And as my Daddy used to say…"the devil can kiss my foot!" See you all tomorrow!

9/16/14 – Constructive Act #180 – Measure Your Success

In this world of accountability, people are always trying to come up with ways to measure success. So, we come to the question of…"How do you measure your success?" We could take a lot of different approaches on this one – but traditionally everyone thinks of a money amount when talking about a fundraising event. So – to begin with, without being down to the penny, it appears that we may have cleared around $15,000.00 yesterday! We consider that a HUGE success for the first year and our first fundraising event. We also consider that a HUGE success since we pulled it off 5 1/2 months after becoming a Foundation.

The money is only one small way to measure success. As a Foundation we try to look at the bigger picture and measure success in other ways. Yesterday, we educated 60 golfers about the perils of opiate/heroin addiction. Every golfer went home with a pamphlet in their golf bag as well as a rubber bracelet with the Davis Direction Logo on it and the words – Narcotics…Never…Not Once!

We provided a place for families who lost children to this horrific disease to come and heal by working or making a purchase at the silent auction or by simply making a donation to the DDF. We had one precious mother show up who had lost her son eleven years ago. She had heard about the golf tournament and the silent auction and wanted to come and be a part of it. Several of us spoke with her and listened to her story. Eleven years later, she still needed to try and fill that hole in her heart, so she chose to come and spend part of her day with us. We had families donate their addicted member's sports items for the auction hoping to keep other children from going down the same path. Families of children going through active addiction came to help in hopes of raising money to address awareness and change. Families of children in Recovery came because they live in fear everyday knowing the statistics of lapse and relapse associated with opiate/ heroin addiction. Parents of children ages 12 – 36 came because they know that their kids are surrounded by other kids who are addicted or will become addicted to prescription drugs and they are trying to educate themselves in order to prevent their kids from becoming a statistic. They know that no one is immune and they work hard everyday for the cause.

Community members graced us with their presence because they realize that the Foundation is working hard to prevent the spread of opiate/heroin addiction in our community. The Cobb Community Foundation was represented as well as prominent members of our Faith Community and our Corporate community. We networked with these individuals and have gained new perspectives and connections to help our Foundation become even better. We got commitments for next year from people who helped this year, as well as ideas about others we could involve and bring on board. Sixty corporations, businesses and/or individuals purchased hole sponsorships or made donations to support the Foundation.

There's an old saying "Make new friends, but keep the old, one is silver and the other gold!" The Foundation was truly surrounded by silver and gold yesterday. Friends of every Board member showed up to help support the cause. We are so blessed with our friends. Even though, they may have no personal connection to the disease, they know how prevalent it is in our community and they are making an investment to help others. Friends of the Foundation helped us to achieve overwhelming success yesterday.

Last but not least, we opened a door for addicts in RECOVERY to "GIVE BACK" through donations or service. They were able to sit on the other side of addiction and help to save lives. They bought hole sponsorships, put stakes in signs, and carried box after box to load cars and trucks to be taken to the event. They literally made themselves available for anything and everything that needed to be done for the cause.

"How do you measure success?" Yesterday, there is no yardstick long enough to measure the success that we were blessed with. Yesterday, thanks to the efforts of so many friends, families, and community members...Our success was immeasurable! "A Day for Davis" was overwhelmingly amazing and I'm sure he was smiling down! Thank you one and all.

9/17/14 – Constructive Act #181 – Get Creative and Save Lives

Georgia Attorney General Sam Olens has partnered with several abuse prevention groups and state agencies to sponsor the "We're Not Gonna Take It" video contest that will run September 15 – October 31, 2014. The contest is designed for Georgia high school students to raise awareness and encourage teenagers to live a healthy lifestyle by rejecting prescription drug abuse.

I have said it before and I'll say it again, the addicts are the experts on the issue of opiate/heroin addiction. So – who better to create a winning video for the Attorney General's video contest about prescription drug abuse.

We all know that we are losing the some of the brightest and best to this deadly disease, and often times they are the most creative as well. They are so creative and gifted that their brains never shut down and often times that's why they turn to the medicine cabinet for help. They are exhausted and they seek a way to self-medicate in order to get much needed rest.

Families of addicts can get involved if you have a high school student by helping to help others realize what the families go through when one of their members is sick. The addict is so sick that they rarely consider what their disease is doing to the rest of the family. They are often in such denial that they won't even admit they have a problem until it is too late – they are already deep in the throes of addiction.

High school health teachers can get involved by requiring your classes to get involved. Have them write scripts including latest statistics and names of pills that are being dangerously abused. Have them do the research on the ages of kids experimenting with prescription opiates and the number of deaths in each age group. Have them present their videos to the rest of the class or find a Middle School and ask if you can educate their students by running the 30 second videos on the morning announcements each morning.

Community members can get involved by offering to show the videos at civic meetings, city council meetings, anywhere there is a meeting with a screen and a projector with the capability for doing this. The DDF will commit right here and now to show the top 3 winning videos at our January symposium during the transition of speakers. We will highlight the kids who wrote and produced the videos as well. We will also post a link to them on our FB page and website! Hopefully by January we will have well over 5000 "Likes," or daily readers as I like to think about them, on our Facebook page.

Polish up the lens on the iPhone or grab a video camera and get started saving lives. The more participation, the more education! this can only be a good thing. Below I have posted a link with past winners from the state of Kentucky. Let's show them that GEORGIA is a contender when it comes to creativity and brilliance.

ag.ky.gov/rxabuse/Pages/rxpsacontest.aspx

9/18/14 – Constructive Act #182 – Breaking Bold

Sometimes I think the world is not ready to hear what I have to say! I want to be very philosophical and then again I want to make analogies that I'm sure would offend others. But, when you have lost a child, you have thoughts that others don't have because there is a part of you that knows you have nothing left to lose. Sometimes my thoughts even shock and perplex me! I think to myself did I really just think that…but I did and I can justify every thought that comes into my head. It might not make sense to you, but I bet every parent that has ever lost a child to opiate/heroin addiction would stand up and applaud!

Obviously what we are doing and what we are teaching our young students coming up through the ranks is not working If it were, we would see a decline in drug abuse and we are not seeing it. So, I begin to think what if we… and what if they… and outrageous thoughts begin to enter my head. What if we didn't patrol drugs at all? After all, God put them on the earth and he must have had some intended use for them. Right? And if you are in pain that requires prescription opiates…then why not go to the hospital and receive them intravenously? That way, nobody gets pills – but how fair is that to people in chronic pain whose quality of life if worse than ever without pain management? How about… what if all drug abusers were court ordered to rehab rather than the prison systems – where I hear drug dealers are still making money in spite of the situation.

It's time for BOLD measures if we are going to make a difference. I'm tired of doing the same old thing and thinking it's going to work. There are some articles out there that have some really "outside the box" ideas and I'm going to start posting them. People have got to start thinking differently about the state of our nation when it comes to opiate/heroin abuse. Every 19 minutes a child dies from this disease and according to the CDC, at last count, there were 669,000 people in the US on heroin alone. And that statistic is almost 2 years old! For the first time in history, prescription drug overdose deaths are outnumbering automobile accident deaths. WAKE UP AMERICA! We are in crisis. It shouldn't take 2 buildings to fall from their foundation for us to realize a national crisis!!!

Make sure you are in attendance at the Oct. 8th Symposium at Marietta High School where our Medical Director, Dr. Harold McLendon, discusses new and "outside the box" drug therapies, one of which is not even legal inside the United States.

As of right now, you have to go to Mexico or Canada to receive this treatment. And WHY in the world is the price of Naloxone so high and the price is going even higher right when laws begin to pass that everyone can have it? Is this Pharmaceutical PRICE GOUGING? Isn't that ILLEGAL? Is Harm Reduction really what it says it is, or is it going to become a money making business? Why is Vivitrol therapy outrageously expensive – over $1,000.00 per month for one injection? Do we really want our nation to get help for this crisis? It doesn't appear so! Why is insurance not behind this disease? I think the answer to that is because we don't treat it like a disease ourselves…Have you gone to the doctor for help? Does your personal physician know that you are an addict? If not, then shame on you! WE have to help ourselves before we will see change. ADVOCATE…Don't take no for an answer! Make people do the right thing! We don't need to be a part of BREAKING BAD…BUT – we do need to be a part of BREAKING BOLD!!! We MUST stand UNITED for our children and their children…WE MUST!

9/19/14 – Constructive Act #183 – Go To The Doctor

This post is a continuation of yesterday's post in a way. If you are an addict, and you have not been to the doctor, then shame on you. This is where we have to make a decision of what we believe about addiction. If you truly believe addiction is a DISEASE – and I do – and research supports this belief – then GO TO THE DOCTOR!

If you found out you had any other disease in the world, what is the first thing you would do? I certainly can't speak for everyone, but I know that when my husband began suffering with symptoms of diabetes, we were headed to the doctor. Several people in my extended family have had the symptoms of high blood pressure and they too, went to the doctor. Friends have had Cancer, Alzheimers, Asthma, Chron's…any other disease you can name and where do they all end up? That's right – at the DOCTOR!

So, the question is…Why do people with the Disease of Addiction NOT go to the doctor. The answer to that is simple – they are embarrassed and ashamed and they are afraid others will find out. Now, I can't promise you that other people won't find out, but if they find out from the doctor's office, then that office is going to be in a lot of trouble and you will likely have all the money you need to consider Rehab!

HIPAA is the federal Health Insurance Portability and Accountability Act of 1996. The primary goal of the law is to make it easier for people to keep health insurance, protect the confidentiality and security of healthcare information, and help the healthcare industry control administrative costs. HIPAA provides for the protection of individually identifiable health information that is transmitted or maintained in any form or medium. The privacy rules affect the day-to-day business operations of all organizations that provide medical care and maintain personal health information.

Confidentiality is one of the core duties of medical practice. It requires health care providers to keep a patient's personal health information private unless consent to release the information is provided by the patient. HIPAA requires the following entities to comply:

Health Care Providers: Any provider of medical or other Health Services that bills or is paid for healthcare in the normal course of business. Health care includes preventive, diagnostic, therapeutic, rehabilitative, maintenance, or palliative care, and counseling, services, assessment, or procedure with respect to the physical or mental condition, or functional status of an individual.

Now that confidentiality is out of the way, you need to realize that opiate medication – ESPECIALLY HEROIN – does a real job on your organs! Chronic users may develop collapsed veins, infection of the heart lining and valves, abscesses, constipation and gastrointestinal cramping, and liver or kidney disease. Pulmonary complications, including various types of pneumonia, may result from the poor health of the user as well as from heroin's effects on breathing. (Partnership for Drug Free Kids) Heroin also takes a toll on teeth and gums directly and indirectly.

Needless to say, there are multiple reasons to go to the doctor if you are abusing or addicted to opiates/heroin. Get the help you need with total confidence that your doctor will not be sharing the details of your care. Treat this DISEASE like any other disease and get the help that might just save your life and get you into Recovery. Many times doctors are able to treat the underlying causes – depression and anxiety – that lead to self medication that eventually lead to heroin use. TRUST YOUR DOCTOR – SEEK MEDICAL HELP!

9/20/14 – Constructive Act #184 – Reflect from Time to Time

Every time I'm at the ocean, it's just seems like the proper time to reflect. I don't know if it's the time I miss Davis the most because I never come without all of my children, or because I look out across the ocean and I begin to understand something about eternity. Listening to the breaking waves, watching schools of manta rays swim across the shoreline and birds landing on the balcony where I'm writing this morning all remind me of God's infinite plan. Looking toward the horizon reminds me of the endless grace and mercy God has for each of us, and knowing that it never ends is comforting.

Today's post is the first day of the second half of the year since Davis was called home. I rounded up to "183" for the first half and now we begin the second half with day "184." I am in the second half of my life being that I am in my fifties, and I have lots of things to reflect upon. I know that many of you have asked that I put all of my "Constructive Acts" into a book and publish it for others to find comfort in. I have decided that "if" I do that...I will do it in two parts. The first book will be titled "The First Half of the First Year Without My First Born Son." Davis and I had a thing about numbers. He had lots of my OCD tendencies and we both counted things. Numbers were important to us and I'm not sure why. Our favorite number was "4". It was a lucky number for us and it always was somehow in numbers that we picked. If we couldn't pick 4, then we picked 16 (4×4) or 24 or 44 or something with 4 in it. I'm not sure why except that it made us feel better. Davis and I were kind of silly like that – even when listening to the tv, the volume was on a "4" number...24, 34, 44 if we wanted it really loud and 64 for sports. It was on 14 if I was trying to be quiet in the morning before everyone else woke up. It's kind of funny what is important to people and the memories you have when they are gone, but every time I see the number "4" I think of my sweet boy and how much I miss him.

I look out to the horizon and I wonder where Heaven is. Where exactly is this beautiful place that my son has gone to? What is it like there? Does he live with my Dad and Granny? Has he made new friends? Does he get to see snow ever again and ride dirt bikes? Does he get to see foreign countries from above and the beautiful and exotic animals that God created? I wonder about so many things, but mostly I wonder about the conversations that he has with God. I wonder how God gets around to seeing everyone and how he spends time with all His children. I think about all the Catholic people who would love to see the Pope and I know some never see him. Then I multiply all the people of all Christian religions who love Jesus and God and are already in eternity and want to spend time with GOD and I wonder how they do it? Then I wonder WHY I wonder all these things? I know I will never have the answers until I am there.

I do have answers to a few things though that I didn't have answers to before this year. I do know that God will love you through the unimaginable and He will give you the strength and purpose to move forward with your life. He will teach you how to move on by spending time with Him and listening and watching for signs along the way. He will send you sweet reminders and new ways to look at old things. He will "grant you the serenity to accept the things you cannot change, the courage to change the things you can, and the wisdom to know the difference. He will allow you to live one day at a time, enjoying one moment at a time, learning to accept hardships as the pathway to peace."

I learned that I am a member of the most awesome family in the world. The Owen "7" continues to function with love and acceptance of one another, allowing each other to work through his or her grief in the way that works individually. We support each other up close and personal or from a distance and we've learned how to know when and what each other needs. We've all managed to continue our journey on this earth with Davis in our hearts and not by our sides. We've all learned that tears are okay and that grief presents itself in different ways at different times. We've all learned that sometimes we need to put less important things aside and gather around one of our members to support his or her journey of grief. We've learned when to be near and when to back off. The most important thing that we have learned however, is that we are still the Owen "7" and that we were and are meant to be together.

As a Counselor, I've learned there is no pattern, rhyme or reason to grief as some might suggest. Grief is a not a process…it is an individual journey. Sometimes it's brought on by a smell, a red bird, a number or a familiar look on an unfamiliar face. It can be funny, it can be frightening, it can make you angry or melancholy. It just is whatever it is and you don't know what it is until it happens. Sometimes it happens at the most inopportune time and that can be unfortunate and all exposing. But you get through the bad spot and move on.

Reflection always seems to be calming for me. It makes me feel closer to God and more appreciative of everything I have and had. I would not take anything for the 20 years I had my precious Davis. I know he is my guardian angel and I know he has had an opportunity to speak with God. He always found a way to do what needed to be done. I know he is asking God to help us fix this terrible epidemic of opiate/heroin addiction. He is my hope, my pride and joy, and my forever firstborn son! I love you Davis Henry Owen…heart and soul!

Xxooo – Mom

9/21/14 – Constructive Act #185 – Share Your Story

This story comes from a young man in our community who has decided to make a difference. He brings HOPE in that he has had years of recovery and is still going strong! Way to go Trey!

I grew up in the suburbs of Atlanta. I am a family man with a wife and 3 great kids. I love sports and I'm from Georgia, I'm a homer so I love the Dawgs, Falcons, and the Braves. Oh and I am a drug addict and an alcoholic. By the Grace of God and by the tools provided to me by 12 step programs, I have been clean and sober since September 26th, 1989. My life turned around way PAST 180 degrees if that is possible!

I started smoking weed and drinking in High School. I ruined many opportunities made possible by my Mom and Dad. They taught me the value of an education and gave me many opportunities after high school to further my education that I squandered. My addictions got a hold of me by the time I finished high school and I was not able to accomplish what I did want in my life until years later when harder drugs brought me to my knees, literally and figuratively. I made a series of poor choices without any real consideration about the decision to drink or drug. Until it was too late for me to choose. That resulting in my becoming an addict and alcoholic. By the Grace of God I escaped a longer life of misery or death. I give all credit to God and 12 step programs. And without "The Program" I doubt I would be alive today. I also credit the 12 steps to leading me to my Relationship with God.

I am one of the lucky ones. In 2000 I lost my friend of almost 30 years to a heroin overdose. He knew the sober life before I did, but the Friday before mothers' day he relapsed after some significant clean time. Sometime that night or the next morning, I lost my oldest friend. He was like my little brother. He is but one of many who I watched either Drugs or Alcohol kill and I still see,know many who are still suffering.

I have been very blessed to work with kids in my passions, tennis and our snow sports programs for many years now and this summer while leading our first Outdoor Adventure Tour program, I spent lots of quality time with a handful of great kids each week. It was an amazing experience. After the tours ended I was left with a thought that I really needed to share my story with kids/teens specifically, about the most important decision they will ever make as a young person growing up. That is when I decided to start a program to reach kids.

PREVENT DEFENSE is an addiction prevention program we are bringing to students in health and/or PE classes in as many schools as possible this year. We are doing so with my personal experience(and eventually others as well) with the consequences of that first wrong decision to try drugs and or consume alcohol while a student. Those students who drink alcohol and/or smoke marijuana have a 650% greater chance of becoming an addict or alcoholics than those who wait until the legal drinking age. Last Friday was our debut at Kell High in Cobb. It was incredibly well received by the students. I received emails from students asking for help as well as wanting TO HELP. Please visit our Facebook Page and "Like" and please remember that there is a real War that we need to fight here on 2 fronts. Treatment for those afflicted with addiction and in prevention. Let love those who need the help and let's reduce the need for treatment by bringing the reality of this disease face to face to our kids!

We are very young program but very committed to the cause and working with as many established Prevention, Awareness and Treatment programs as possible.As a tribute to my friend I state that if Kids Just Have More Insight, Information, Interest, more will make a better decision about drinking or drugging as a teen. (hopefully as an adult also)

My Name is Trey and I am a recovered Addict and Alcoholic

9/22/14 – Constructive Act #186 – Describe Normal

As I was driving back home from the beach this afternoon, I thought to myself, "Wow – it will be nice to get back to NORMAL." Then I thought "NORMAL" will never be the same for me again. NORMAL means having 5 kids to take care of, loving them, taking care of their needs, being there for them, all the things I am supposed to do and…now there are only 4. NORMAL is not NORMAL ever again. So what is NORMAL? Does it change? Is it really even a thing? Does it exist? Not for me anymore. As far as I'm concerned, there is no such thing.

My life is completely abnormal now. It is not what I wanted or expected or ever even dreamed of. I never considered my life could be or would be anything outside of NORMAL. Now, NORMAL is in the past and does not exist. What is your normal? Is it here today… but maybe gone tomorrow? Have you ever even experienced it? Maybe you are one of the ones who never knew NORMAL. Maybe NORMAL for you was so dysfunctional that you thought abnormal was NORMAL to begin with.

The life of an addict or the family of an addict is anything but NORMAL. I went on vacation the last half of this week with just my children because my husband is in the busy season of his work. That in itself was abnormal! We've never left Michael at home before, but this college visit could not wait and we were so close to the beach that it just seemed like the right thing to do. It was much needed and it
was very relaxing. During the week, I was contacted by a couple of families who were going through ABNORMAL things and they reached out to the DDF for help. I'm glad that the DDF has had that impact on families and that we are considered a place to turn. But, the fact remains that these families needed help because they felt what was going on in their lives was not NORMAL.

Who decides NORMAL? Who gets to say what is normal and what is not? Describe NORMAL! Life is always about expectations and the expectations are changing everyday. What we as a generation expect of our kids, may not be in their best interest for this ever changing social media kind of world that we live in. Is college really the NORMAL thing to do, or can life be NORMAL if our kids are allowed to forge their own paths with or without education?

When you honestly look at this epidemic of prescription drug abuse and opiate/ heroin addiction, who are we looking at? The research suggests that we are looking at white middle class suburban families. These are traditionally the families that have expectations that our kids will go to college and graduate with degrees. Is this NORMAL? Are we creating stress that our kids are ill equipped to handle? Do we get to decide what will make them happy and constitute a great life for them? This trip was a little different for us. We talked about college, because that's what my son wants to do, but I also told him that if he didn't want to go that was okay too! I've NEVER said that in my life! I'm not even sure that I believe it! It's certainly not how I was raised, but I was not raised in the same environment that my kids were raised in. Life was so much simpler then! It was NORMAL! There's a new show out that all the kids love and I'm not sure why…It's called "Orange is the New Black"…Is that NORMAL?

9/23/14 – Constructive Act #187 – Help Us Out Here

On October 8th, the DDF will bring another Symposium to the wonderful people of our community. This Symposium will be on the "Continuum of Care" and will once again take place at Marietta High School beginning at 7:00 pm. Dr. Teresa Johnston of Kennesaw State University will be our keynote speaker and our own DDF Medical Director – Dr. Harold McLendon will be speaking on the properties of opiates and the drug therapies available to combat the addiction. We are excited for the knowledge we will be bringing you at this event.

We will also be handing out Naloxone kits to those in need on this night. We have decided to expand our mission to include keeping addicts alive until we can provide a better solution to the horrific addiction and epidemic that we are suffering through. There is not one incredible, sure-fire, absolute solution and we are intelligent enough to realize this. With this being said, we are committed to keeping opiate/heroin addicts alive until we can offer a more comprehensive solution that will allow addicts to enter recovery and stay there.

Here comes the part where we need your help and you can contribute to helping the DDF help others. Reach out to the Rehab and Recovery facilities that you are aware of and invite them to our event. We will be hosting a Rehabilitation and Recovery Vendor Fair for this event and we are in need of vendors who offer services in the area of opiate/heroin addiction. We already have many vendors who are registered to show up and talk to the attendees about what they have to offer. For a donation based on what they are able to contribute, we will set up a table and allow them to market and advertise their services. We have vendors from as far away as Boynton Beach, Florida who have already made their donations and reserved table space. Marietta PD will have a table to show families of addicts the tests that you can purchase to check for opiates in the body. We also will have

Quest Diagnostics to market their new test to Doctors. Their test will allow for prescription drug monitoring. We need Rehab centers, halfway houses, IOP's and any organizations who have something to offer in the way of Recovery. Private practices as well as Counselors, psychiatrists, and therapists are welcomed too.

If you would like to make a donation and reserve table space, please send an email to Davisdirectionfoundation@gmail.com. We would love to have you join us not only for the night , but also for the fight against opiate/heroin addiction. We will send you our vendor letter and the instructions for joining us for the night. WE WILL MAKE A DIFFERENCE!

9/24/14 – Constructive Act #188 – Forge Ahead With Full Speed

I truly feel like the DDF is on a roll! I know last time I felt like that, the Devil took a swat at us and shorted the ground wire in my house the night before the golf tournament. Poltergeists revisited!!! But we survived that situation and now we are moving onward!!! We had several great things happen today. I know that just like all the other things that God has blessed us with, He is truly watching over us now as we plan for the upcoming Symposium. The "Continuum of Care" Symposium and "Rehab/Recovery Fair" will take place on October 8th at Marietta High School beginning at 7:00 pm. Please make plans to join us now for this powerful and informative event.

Today, we received word from the VP of Sales at the company that manufactures Vivitrol, that he will be in attendance for the Symposium and he will set up a table

and be available to help families with the understanding required to have a child on this opiate drug therapy. We also received word from Quest Diagnostics that they will be debuting their new Prescription Drug Monitoring kit at our Symposium for doctors to screen patients for opiate use before prescribing other drugs. These are two hugely significant events that will provide a wealth of knowledge for people in attendance at the Symposium.

We have people from as far away as Massachusetts and Florida who have registered to attend our event and set up a table to advertise and display their services. This is Fantastic. We need to know what people are offering in the way of Rehab and Recovery and be able to distinguish between the services provided. We have Rehab facilities from as far away as Boynton Beach, Florida. Many times families like to take their child to a facility where they know the child is not going to try and run. So, we need to have choices from Rehabs that are not close in proximity to us.

We are still taking reservations from vendors for Rehab facilities and private practice psychologists and psychiatrists. Research shows that individual therapists are the #1 entity in helping addicts reach recovery. Only 10% of people who are deep in the throes of addiction ever reach out to Rehab facilities anyway. So, with that being said, let's see if we can get some private practice Counselors to come and set up a booth.

This Symposium and Rehab/Recovery Fair is going to be amazing. We will have the DDF training and handing out Naloxone kits, the Marietta PD training parents in how to use over the counter drug kits – as well as giving out kits to be used at home, and other vendors handing out their printed materials for you to take home and thoroughly examine before making a rehab choice.

I've said this more than once…"KNOWLEDGE IS POWER"…come to this Symposium to gain your power and see all of the up and coming solutions to deal with opiate/heroin addiction.

9/25/14 – Constructive Act #189 – Realize that People are Just People

Does a "title" really change what you are, or who you are? Does studying a discipline and getting a degree or a title make you somehow superior to others? Does being the "Boss" make you something that others think they are not? What really matters when considering a person's character and deciding how you want to align yourself with that person? Is it something they have achieved or rather what they stand for internally? Is it what's in their heart or what's in their head? I know how I answer that question.

My Daddy always taught me that "People put their pants on one leg at a time." You have probably heard me say this before on the DDF, but I want to really examine it in this CA. What does it mean? Why did he feel that it was so important for me to know that? I understand now that it directly affects how you feel about yourself and what you think you can accomplish. I have learned to question almost everything in my life because I have learned that many people think they are the authority when they have only become a "legend in their own mind." Just because the boss is the boss doesn't mean that he or she is always right or that their way of thinking is the only way of thinking. Yes, you must learn to work with the boss if you value your job, but at what point do you stand up and say… "The way the Boss believes is compromising my character?" At what point do you say… "The Doctor told me to do this, but I don't really believe in that school of thought so I am seeking a second opinion or perhaps even changing doctors."

There is a very widely accepted idea out in the world that says to "follow your gut." Why is it so hard to follow your gut and stand up for what you believe in and stand your ground? The answer to that is very simple…It's a lack of confidence. Some people exude confidence and others cower at the thought of having an opinion. Some people have the overbearing effect that dares others to question their opinions or beliefs. NEVER QUESTION YOURSELF when it comes to your beliefs and values. Choose what you want to believe and then stand up for it. Some of the greatest forward thinkers of the world were thought to be idiots by people who were closed – minded.

I had a colleague of mine come into my office today and say that if she were to tell her Doctor that she was addicted to prescription drugs that her Doctor would probably ask her to leave the practice. Now whether that is true or not, if you have that feeling about your doctor, then you need to find a new doctor. Please understand one thing, when you are paying a doctor to take care of you, YOU ARE THE BOSS! You have hired the doctor to provide a service for you. If you are not receiving the service that you expect, you need to find the right service for you.

Take charge of your life; be your own advocate! Step outside of your comfort zone and take care of your needs. It could save your life. Remember that everyone of us was born NAKED! What happened after that is what shaped us and made us who we are. It's never too late to change. LOVE YOURSELF enough to value your own thoughts and never let others' thoughts dictate how you feel about yourself. You are WORTHY, you are CAPABLE, you are UNIQUE, and you are a child of the KING! ACT LIKE IT!

9/26/14 – Constructive Act #190 – Learn It's Okay to Feel All Feelings

As I took my seat on the only fair ride that I will ride (the bench) last night, I had the front row view of everyone at the fair. As people passed me by, while I sat and waited for the kids to ride ALL the rides they love to ride, I realized I was one of the "scared" ones. There's no way that I will ever get on a ride at the fair because it's engrained in my brain that those rides go up at the creation of human hands in a matter of hours. I'm too afraid that bolts may not have been tightened properly and pieces may have been put in the wrong places, and parts could even be missing! YEP – I'm a SCAREDY CAT!!! My kids continue to try and get me on those rides every time we go, because they don't think I should be scared!

I sat on my bench and I watched the kids ride their rides and I took pictures and I even participated in the Pig Races!!! I raised my hand to claim a PIG to cheer on to victory (That's the part where I embarrassed my kids). Well – The man chose me; My pig won and I got a blue ribbon! And all this time…the only thought that kept running through my head was…"Davis would have loved this." I missed him the whole night long and he should have been there! In my thoughts, I convinced myself that he was watching us from Heaven and laughing at us and sharing in our fun. I don't know if that happens in Heaven or not, but it makes me feel better to think that it does. It gets me back to the "feel good" state of mind.

The point is that all the while that we are on earth – we find ways to SELF-SOOTHE! We even teach our babies to self-soothe from the cradle by letting them cry for a while, going back in and putting a pacifier in their mouths, or teaching them to find their thumbs. We spend our whole lives trying to teach our kids how to "numb" the feelings that they don't want to have or change the feelings that are not positive. How many times have you told your kids to "just ignore things." We engrain the principal of "feeling good" into our kids' brains, and it teaches them that if they are not feeling good and positive, SOMETHING IS WRONG.

So – Why are we so surprised, when they begin to self-medicate? As parents, we need to help our kids learn to deal with ALL of their feelings. We all too often try to "make things better" by getting our kids back to their "feel-good" state of mind. When they are lonely, we go and get a friend for them; When they are sad, we try to take their minds off of their sadness by going out, or buying them gifts or toys to take their minds off of their sadness. How many times as a parent have you just sat and cried, or been gloomy with your children and taught them that it was okay? Life is full of disappointments and we all must learn to deal with them and have "bad days." When they are angry or upset, we send them to their rooms until they can come out and be happy again! I just don't think we are teaching our kids to FEEL ALL FEELINGS. I feel like we are teaching kids they are only OKAY when they are happy. Teach them to journal, or express themselves through art or poetry. Teach them to create something out of supplies from nature. Teach them it's okay to spend time with negative feelings and that some of the most beautiful works of art or literature have come from a painful times in a person's life. Teach them that medication is not for emotions. Now, that's not saying that a child never needs to be treated for depression or anxiety, but it should never be the first line of defense. We need to teach our children how to be unhappy…It's a life-skill and it's OKAY! Yes – I realize the goal is always to get back to the positive feelings in our lives…BUT – there will be valleys and they cannot always be overcome in a short period of time. THAT'S OKAY, and its REAL.

9/27/14 – Constructive Act #191 – Work Together

Michael and I just finished watching the story of Nickola Tesla – whom I doubt many of you are familiar with. He is responsible for the electricity that lights up your homes and businesses. You may have thought Thomas Edison was responsible for that, but once again, the learning that you received from the history books may have been a little off. Edison was responsible for the direct current and Tesla was responsible for the alternate current – AC. Both men were brilliant, but refused to work together. Just think what might have come to fruition if they had put their brilliant brains together!

This "CA" may be a little premature – but here goes anyway. We are currently working with a volunteer from Tennessee to open the first chapter of the "DDF" in the state of Tennessee. The details have not been finalized, but we are excited beyond belief that there is interest and desire to "WORK TOGETHER" to help fight this epidemic occurring throughout the nation. Yes – one of our mission statement goals is to become a "National Resource and Role Model" for other communities to emulate. We are so honored that Tennessee has reached out to us to begin this process.

We are as transparent as a Foundation that you will ever know and our only goal is too eradicate the disease of opiate/heroin addiction from the face of the earth. It is robbing us of our children, our grandchildren, our siblings and ultimately our future. We must "WORK TOGETHER" to find a way to stop it. I have said it before and I will say it again…"If we can put a man on the moon, certainly we can find a way to fight opiate/heroin addiction." The fact that this epidemic is claiming the lives of more individuals than car accidents now is incomprehensible to me. How can this be?

With the recent funds that we gained from the first golf tournament, we will be looking for an individual to bring our website up to speed, getting our informational resource packets out to hospitals and rehab facilities, and continuing our billboard campaign that has been run completely from the donations of CBS OUTDOORS and Jason Gribble – the graphic artist behind the design. Both of these men will be honored at the upcoming Symposium for their contributions to the cause. We are so very fortunate that the accomplishments we have made to date are almost entirely the gifts of community members and in-kind donations. We would be nothing without the ability to work with others in our community to promote awareness and affect change.

There are 2 things we need your help with and anyone can help. We need you to reach out to Rehab and Recovery Facilities to join us on October 8th at Marietta High School for our "Continuum of Care" Symposium beginning at 7:00 pm, and we need you to begin considering if you could be the volunteer who would head up a "DDF" chapter in your state. We, as a foundation, need to move because the time is right. There are some decisions being made that I believe are going to make heroin even more desirable in the future – such as the recent restrictions being put on Hydrocodone. Sometimes, I think we fail to look at the long-term implications and go for the quick fix.

I have included our Mission Statement so that all of you reading this "CA" will know exactly what we are hoping to accomplish. I will share it in a separate post today and ask that you share it all over the Nation. It's time to move and move NOW – One more life lost to this horrific disease is ONE LIFE TOO MANY! JOIN US NOW!

DDF Mission Statement:

The mission of the Davis Direction Foundation is to serve as a role model in our community in order to become a national resource for Opiate/Heroin Addiction awareness and change. We will strive to remove the outdated stigma of opiate addicts and revamp the rehabilitation process to appropriately address the disease of Opiate/Heroin Addiction as one of the most severe forms of addiction. We will provide direct assistance and services to individuals, family members, or others at risk of experiencing an opioid related overdose including but not limited to providing opioid antagonists. We will support recovery.

Pray with us and for us as we strive to "WORK TOGETHER" as a nation to combat this disease that is robbing us of so many of the brightest and best of God's precious children.

> AGAIN I SAY UNTO YOU, THAT IF TWO OF YOU SHALL AGREE ON EARTH AS TOUCHING ANY THING THAT THEY SHALL ASK, IT SHALL BE DONE FOR THEM OF MY FATHER WHICH IS IN HEAVEN. FOR WHERE TWO OR THREE ARE GATHERED IN MY NAME, THEIR AM I IN THE MIDST OF THEM. (MATTHEW 18:19-20)

9/28/14 – Constructive Act #192 – Share Your Story

Here is a story from a 23 year Veteran. There is HOPE in RECOVERY. 23 years CLEAN and SOBER! Congratulations to Lisa. Here is her story:

Hi. My name is Lisa I live in Acworth and moved here from Connecticut. I was born and raised in Bronx, N.Y. and have been sober for 23 years. I am only 45 years old and married a Godly man and have two beautiful daughters. I met my husband in AA. Let me start by telling you who I am, where I have been and how I arrived where I am today.

I started using drugs and drinking alcohol at the age of 16.I used and abused various types of drugs such as: acid, cocaine, alcohol, etc. Just to name a few. I found myself in extremely volatile and dangerous situations, simply in order to attain more drugs. All while hiding this from my parents and family. I would lie, steal cheat and expose myself more than I thought I ever would in my life. By the time I was 22 yrs old I lost several jobs, had sex, had an abortion all because I wanted to do more drugs. However God had a bigger better plan for me as he began to save my life. I found myself in rehab for 30 days, I learned in fact that I had a disease. I began to realize I wasn't a bad person trying to get good, I was a sick person trying to get well.

God gave me a new life today. I am 23 years sober by the Grace of God. I have a husband who loves me. God also blessed me with two beautiful daughters. I also share my story to many people that one day it will help someone who is struggling. I saw many of my friends lose their lives to drugs and alcohol and why God saved me I don't question, but try to be grateful everyday for my life and hopefully save a life today.

I want to show my daughters they can live a life without drugs and alcohol, and I continue to go to God for help first and he will continue to bless me and my family.

I feel truly blessed to be working part time, while I continue to maintain my sobriety be with my family and have a loving relationship with my husband.

9/29/14 – Constructive Act #193 – Invite A Friend To The Symposium

On October 8th beginning at 7:00 pm at Marietta High School, The Davis Direction Foundation will host the 2nd, in a series of 4, opiate/heroin Symposium. Did you know that everyday 2,000 teens abuse a prescription drug for the first time? That right there is enough of a reason that you should be at the Symposium to educate yourself and protect your children. Every 19 minutes someone in our country dies of a drug overdose. More people now die each year from accidental drug overdose than in auto accidents. I could go on and on, but do you really still need to be convinced?

I lost a son because I was so uneducated in the area of prescription drug abuse. If I had known the dangers, I would have had my medicine cabinet cleaned out and I would have warned my kids about "friends" who want to share prescribed drugs. Yes – kids think if it is prescribed by a doctor, it must be okay to take. My kids knew full well the dangers of illegal drugs, but what they didn't know was that you could become completely addicted to Prescribed drugs that would lead to illegal drugs once you were addicted.

At the Symposium, we will have awesome speakers, drug reps from companies sharing their knowledge about drug therapies and drug antagonists. We will have Marietta PD explaining how to choose and give a drug test to your child. We will have Quest Diagnostics, marketing a test for Dr.'s to administer in their offices to see exactly what patients are already on when they come into the office. We will have Rehabs, and Realtors who sponsor kids in Rehabs. We will have private practice counselors and therapists as well as all natural remedies to help a child through the withdrawal of opiates as they enter recovery.

It is not too late to get on board as a vendor and it is certainly not too late to put the date on your calendar and bring a friend. Don't wait until you are dealing with addiction in your own family to start attending these symposiums. Forewarned is Forearmed! Knowledge is POWER! Contact us at   info@davisdirection.com to participate.

The Davis Direction Foundation will be handing out information about our Foundation as well as handing out Naloxone nasal kits for the families who need them. We will have on site training by our Board of Directors. This is a meeting you cannot afford to miss. Prioritize your family and your friends by being present with a friend or neighbor by your side. You will be shocked at the information you will hear and you will be forever indebted for the knowledge you will gain. The life you may learn to save could be your own child or family member. Experimentation begins as early as 12 years old and the age group most likely to die from a prescription drug overdose is 45 to 54 years old. Georgia has the 36th Highest Drug Overdose Mortality Rate in the United States. Come to our Symposium to find out how we can work together to change these statistics.

9/30/14 – Constructive Act #194 – Share Information

Yesterday was a day of incredible pain for a couple of us in the DDF leadership. The Moms of several addicts called us asking for help and prayers because they felt they had turned down a Dead End Street. Their children had relapsed and there seems to be nowhere to turn. Rehabs have been exhausted, parents have been told at every level to turn their children away if they come home and the question then becomes "Home or Homeless?"

Rehabs have become so expensive that the price alone makes them very exclusionary. Nothing else takes place "daily" that the addicts can participate in so that they are protected from themselves and others who might be using that lasts longer than an hour and can be individually attentive. Lots of times opiate/heroin addicts end up in AA meetings that basically are not meeting their needs. So where do they go for services? There is no such thing as "Public" Rehab. If you need healthcare at a public hospital, you cannot be turned away on the basis to pay. Rehab needs to be more affordable for people who need the services. Anne Fletcher suggests in her book "Inside Rehab" that only 10% of addicts ever step foot inside of Rehab. That's because they are the ones who can afford it. I truly believe that ALL addicts eventually want help. Addiction is a DISEASE that is put on a different scale than all other diseases and getting help when you are an addict is as messed up as addiction itself.

Can you name another disease where insurance, after an average of 21 – 28, days denies the patient? Can you imagine the outrage if a diabetic was turned down by insurance after 21 days of the disease and told to come back the next year and get

21 more days of treatment? How about a cancer patient or a patient with high blood pressure? In Pennsylvania, a law was passed so that Doctors could have the say regarding insurance and when treatment services would stop. Aren't Doctors the ones who have had the training and the education to evaluate the disease in the first place? What training do insurance agencies or agents have that allows them to decide when a disease is not worthy of further treatment?

Why has Naloxone – the opiate/heroin antagonist – been around for years and we are having to fight like dogs to get it into the hands of addicts and their families? There are so many questions that surround the whole arena of addiction that I feel like this post is just one big question rather than any answers or suggestions. Different states around the nation have put legislation into place and have passed laws that affect drug trafficking. Why on earth are there still states out there that do not have "The Good Samaritan Law" in place? We have to become UNITED in this cause and every Foundation working toward opiate/heroin addiction and treatment needs to be transparent! If the DDF has put something into place that you want to know about…Pick up the phone and ask…678-725-1298…shoot us an email and we will answer…come to the Oct. 8th Symposium and glean information from the BEST around with our speakers and representatives. WE WANT TO SHARE!

If you are working toward this cause and you have something in place that works…You need to be shouting from the Mountain Tops!!! That is the only way that we will be able to address the epidemic and eradicate it! If you are a Foundation and you see something that works going on in another Foundation then you need to feel comfortable enough to ask about it. Information regarding this epidemic CANNOT BE EXCLUSIONARY. If your organization is keeping deals and or information secretive, then you should re-evaluate your motives and decide if you are truly in it to save lives, promote awareness and affect change!

The Goal of the DDF is to become a National Resource based on what we are doing in our own community to promote awareness and affect change. We want people all over the Nation reading our daily posts and visiting our website and Facebook page. We want you to notice that on the website we have a place where we list other Foundations so that you can have access and be aware of them as well. We post articles from others and we participate in ceremonies that are promoted by other Foundations. When we see something that we feel is a good idea or is working to help families in the throes of addiction, we go with it – We're NOT trying to re-invent the wheel here – WE ARE TRYING TO SAVE LIVES!

10/1/14 – Constructive Act #195 – Consider The Addict

They are the Chosen Children. They are the ones with the Addiction Gene. Did you ever wonder why them and not you? I know I have. I'm quite sure that these chosen children didn't say…"God – I volunteer to have the addiction gene – I know someone has to have it apparently, and I will be the one!" No – that is a disease, as is any disease, that no one wants to be plagued with. With other diseases – even birth defects – others look on and say…"Poor thing, Why did this have to happen to them?" Or better yet…"Why did this have to happen to anyone?"

With addiction comes blame and persecution. It's like somehow others believe that these addicts chose their DISEASE. Any study of Neuroscience suggests that Addiction is a disease that 50% (the only number I have seen) is believed to be genetic. So then the question becomes "Why them and not me?"

Raise your hand if you have ever had a drink? Raise your hand if you have ever been given a prescription of pain pills? Did you really stop to do the math in your head that you were playing Russian Roulette and that 1 out of 10 people in this nation are addicts? Or, like most people, did you just think, the good Doctor gave me this prescription in good faith and it must be fine. There are so many times in my own life that I have done both and by the grace of God, I was spared the genetic make-up to be an addict. 8 major operations in my life – 5 of which were c-sections and each time, I went home with a prescription of pain medication which I needed to help me get through the healing process. Now I stop and ask myself often……"What if I had been an addict?"

Are these chosen children mean? Are they stupid? Are they uncaring and unloving? Are they outcasts and pariah? NO – for the most part, they are some of the brightest, funniest, loving and caring children on the planet. They are the ones who will give you the shirt off of their back and go out of their way to help and care for those in need. They are the ones who will give the homeless people holding the signs a dollar out of their pocket – even if it is their last. They are the ones who will stop and share their water with a stray dog. They are the ones who will half their candy bars, cookies or sodas with you. They are the ones who can sense when something is wrong and when someone needs a friend. They don't stop there, they act on their senses and do something to help that friend – or stranger.

When Davis died, stories from his friends flooded my Facebook and mailbox. His friends came to me and told me things in person that made my heart swell with pride knowing the person that he was. He was the one who never made fun of others…He helped them overcome their shortcomings whether it was being shy, being a poor reader, needing help in math, Davis was often the child in the classroom who was helping others at the request of the teacher because he would finish first and it was usually correct. I can name many friends that he helped along the way. Many of them have written to me and reminded me of the ways he helped them. He never judged them or talked about them, he just helped them and then went on about his way.

He was the "animal rescuer" of the family. He would often come home with a stray kitten or puppy and he wouldn't stop until he had found them a home or convinced his Dad and I that we had to keep them. To this very day – we have a cat named "Boo" that showed up close to Halloween and Davis secretly took him inside and bonded with him because at the time, he was so conflicted that he needed a friend. He wrote about his cat on his Facebook and this is what he said:

"During one of the most challenging chapters in my life…This stray cat shows up at my door, freezing cold, malnourished, and clearly hurt. After giving him food and water, a name, and a nice heat blanket to sleep on for the past few days, he has become my new best friend, and has shown me the meaning of love in its most pure and simple form. Thank you Boo, for your coincidental and influential presence in my life. Who else could possibly lay here as I simultaneously watch Reno 911 and play Pokemon, and not make one single judgmental comment?"

Needless to say, "Boo" is still a resident of our home and comes and goes freely, sleeping in a bed with whomever is the lucky one for the night. She gives us comfort and a purpose to carry on, reminding us daily of the huge heart Davis had for those less fortunate than he. She reminds us that Davis rescued others whenever he could – including animals – and that now it is the mission of the Davis Direction Foundation to "rescue" the chosen children from addiction. We must find a way, a solution, and a new path for those struggling daily. THEREFORE BY THE GRACE OF GOD GO I.

10/2/14 – Constructive Act #196 – Save The Date

I am proud beyond words that my home church, Marietta First United Methodist Church, is leading the way as a role model in our community to address addiction as we search for answers and solutions to address the opiate/heroin addiction epidemic. Mark your calendars now for SUNDAY, OCTOBER 26TH – BOTH SERVICES 9:00 AND 11:15 for the "HOPE AND HEALING" service open to all families affected by addiction. We will offer special prayers for individuals and families who have been touched by addiction of any kind. Following our 11:15 worship service, we will have an open luncheon for anyone who has been impacted by this issue. There will also be a drug take-back box on campus all morning as an opportunity to safely dispose of unused prescription drugs. WOW – I know Jesus is proud that we are openly extending our arms and opening our doors in an effort to embrace God's children who are struggling with the disease of addiction.

I think it is very apropos that we are offering this service at the beginning of RED RIBBON WEEK. Red Ribbon Week began in 1985 and is sponsored by the National Family Partnership. It is an effort to address the death and destruction caused by drugs in our country. What better time to make a statement in the community regarding awareness and change? The Bible teaches us " You are a lamp unto my feet and a light unto my path." God has laid out a path for us and we need to pray for guidance along the way. The Church offers a community of Faith to help us find that path. The Church is here to support us, whatever our needs might be. They are our prayer partners, our supporters, our encouragers, and our light in the midst of darkness. Open your hearts and allow the church to be there for you if you are struggling with addiction. We will accompany you and your loved ones without shame as we continue this journey together and help you find your way into recovery.

The 2014 Red Ribbon Campaign theme is "LOVE YOURSELF." Marietta First United Methodist Church is a church full of Love and Hope and I know that we are ready and waiting to embrace anyone with any need in our community. After the 11:15 worship service on the Day of "Hope and Healing," please plan to join us downstairs in the fellowship dining room for lunch and fellowship. We want to get to know you better and we will be asking you to help us determine the needs related to addiction that we can address. We will ask families that have been affected by addiction to complete an informal Needs Assessment that we will use to put other things in place for you through the year and possibly even on a weekly basis. We are here to serve you, and your family knows more about what you need than anyone else. I know that there were things that my family felt like we needed when we were living in the throes of addiction and they were not available.

For our family, we had a need to be together as a family for worship. We could only do that through a formal worship service and that was great, but we would have liked a smaller group setting with other families going through what we were going through to help us and inspire us and allow us to smile and enjoy the company of others without worrying about what we were trying to hide for fear of judgement. We would have liked a place to go that could have helped to educate us about offerings in the community related to the disease of addiction. There were so many things that we didn't know that we didn't know. If we could have been in a networking group, we may have learned things that we didn't to know to ask about.We would have enjoyed a class to remind us of the miracles God performed in the Bible and the leaders in the Bible that made bad choices, but God forgave them and blessed them when they returned to Him. There were times when we needed someone to say to us, "We've been down the path you are traveling and there is HOPE and HEALING on the other side."

We are doing our best to address a nationwide need that affects 1 of every 10 people alive. Please don't feel alone in this epidemic. In the research that I have done since the death of my sweet Davis, I have not found one family that has NOT been affected by addiction when they look into their extended families.

Please save the date and plan to spend it with the entire congregation of MFUMC, as we dedicate a day for HOPE and HEALING. Be thinking about the needs of your family and how we can address those needs and accompany you along your journey.

You will be our HONORED GUESTS and we will serve you and your families not only because WE want to, but because GOD wants us to. We are looking forward to a wonderful day of worship with you. I know my family still has some healing to do and I am personally looking forward to this day.

10/3/14 – Constructive Act #197 – Take a Look at What Works and What Doesn't

For years, our Nation has come up with campaign after campaign for Drug Abuse and Prevention. Programs such as Drug Abuse Resistance Education – "DARE" and "Just Say No" did not produce positive results. In the famous words of Dr.

Phil – "How's that working for you?" The answer to that question has to be – Not so well! So – we have to take a serious look at what's working and what's not working and why? The current school of thought is that the best prevention factors include community, religion, athletic involvement, parental involvement in schools or other social arenas with children, and healthy and stimulating alternative activities. So – in other words, get active with your kids and take them to church.

For years, research has suggested that children whose parents are involved in the school system do better in school. As a school counselor for 26 years and an educator for 8 years prior to that, I have found the above statement to be true. The children who have active parents in the schools are the students who perform better than those whose parents never show up. So I think it only makes sense that children whose parents are involved in the community, church, athletics, extra curricular activities and school are more likely to succeed socially and emotionally. Now of course there will always be the exceptions, just as I consider Davis to be the exception – because I know that our family has always been involved in all of the above mentioned activities. So what happened in his case? Who knows? We may never have all the answers, but I think involvement in your child's life in any and every aspect of their activities is only a good thing.

So, look at your own situation. What are you doing with your child? If you consider that drug experimentation begins as young as 12 years old and continues through age 17, and if you consider that every day, 2000 teens abuse a prescription drug for the first time, it would seem to me, that instead of backing off when your child goes to middle school, you should jump in head first and be at every event you are invited to. I remember the first year my daughter went to middle school. She came home one day and told me that there was a drug dog there and that the police had gone into the bathroom and pulled the ceiling tiles back and taken drugs out of the ceiling of the school. I couldn't believe what I was hearing. Then when that same daughter went to High School over 10 years ago, it wasn't uncommon for her to come home and tell me about kids who had been suspended for being caught with pot or other illegal substances at school. This is not something new that has just started happening. I can even remember when I was in High School that kids would come into the classrooms stoned.

Community, religion, athletics, school and other social arenas include a lot of activities and a lot of events. Do you try to participate in all of these things? Do your kids participate with you in these events? If we are truly talking about prevention, ask yourself – "When was the last time we did anything as a family?" I know one of the things that seldom happens anywhere anymore because of after school schedules and work related obligations is the "family dinner." Everyone is going in a different direction on a different time schedule. We do go to church as a family and we do community service once a month as a family. My husband and I try our best to attend school meetings like open house and of course we are there when our children perform. But I will tell you that we don't always attend meetings for our younger children that we have attended already for our older children.

In all fairness to families and parents of school aged children, I do feel like meetings are overdone. If you need to get the word out about anything… somebody calls a meeting. I feel like meetings should be reserved for very important issues and that if you have a meeting and people leave feeling like the meeting was a waste of time, then the chances that they will come to a future meeting are very slim. This is the age of technological information…use it when you can. Reserve meetings for face to face importance and make them worthwhile.

The point is – you need to Get Involved if you are not involved and you need to Stay Involved if you are already involved. Just because your children are growing up and are verbal enough to tell you what happens and what you need to know doesn't mean you should parent from a distance. Be there for your kids — until they are grown and out the door!

10/4/14 – Constructive Act #198 – Prepare Yourself For Action

This past week I mentioned earlier that there were several families that I know of who were dealing with relapse with their loved ones who are addicts. One of them approached me about getting a Naloxone kit. I did have one "syringe" kit left and I told her she was welcome to come and get it. "Syringe" kits come with a whole new set of criteria and worries. So, I would suggest that if you have a kit of any kind that you prepare yourself not only physically to move into action, but you MUST prepare yourself mentally an psychologically as well. The Counselor in me thinks immediately of visualization techniques for this preparation. You must go over in your mind what you will do from beginning to end and you must see it —

yes the worst case scenario – you have to see it in your mind if you are truly going to prepare yourself to successfully use a Naloxone kit.

First and foremost, you must get the training you need from someone who knows and has been trained to train others. Our own DDF Director, Tanya Smith, will be providing this training – first to all of the DDF Board Members, and then to the families who receive kits on Wednesday night at the Symposium. She is certainly an expert in this area and if you are present Wednesday night to receive a kit, you will certainly learn from the best. This will be the physical training and preparation. That is not something that you can do alone – You must have someone else teach you how to administer the Drug.

Secondly, you must prepare yourself mentally and psychologically. Consider this scenario with a syringe kit: A panic-stricken mother finds her child unconscious, barely breathing and non-responsive. She is expected to a.) call 911; b.) maintain the presence of mind to locate the recovery kit, open it and follow directions c.) Remove one vial, flip off the top, remove the cover from the needle, draw back the needle about 1/3 way, inject the needle into the vial, insert the air into the vial, draw the plunger back to fill the syringe to the 1.0 ml mark, (ideally expelling any excess air without expelling the drug) and inject d.) place the cover of the needle back on the needle and, VERY IMPORTANT, d.) do so without sticking herself with the needle e.) patiently wait two minutes and calmly repeat, i.e. the "patient" has not responded and therefore the mother assumes death is imminent...as it may well be.

Now if you think this scenario can be accomplished without mental and psychological preparation – THINK AGAIN!!! You should go over and over this specific scenario in your mind all the while visualizing YOUR CHILD as the victim! YES – Put a face on the victim and YES – consider the fact that you may be too late after the first injection – and YES – consider the fact that you may not be successful at all. This is the only way you will survive this scenario. The Nasal kits are much more "user friendly" but there is still Mental and Psychological preparation to be done.

Hopefully you will never have to experience the above scene, and if you do, hopefully you will be successful and your child will survive the Overdose and get to the hospital in time to live. Hopefully your child is not a "closet user" like mine was and go off to a secluded location or wait until everyone is asleep at night to use and no one will ever be there for them in time to save them. But you need to process every possible scenario if you are in possession of a Naloxone kit. You must be prepared at the drop of a "body" to Move into ACTION and you must know the steps to take, like the back of your hand, if you are expecting to experience a successful "Bring-back."

More and more families are getting these kits and more and more doctors are beginning to write prescriptions for them. As a result, the price is sky-rocketing. It has literally doubled in the past month. There is a "supply and demand" shortage that is causing a bit of a panic with families trying to get their hands on a kit. Plan now to get your kit if you are living with an addict. With the correct Physical, Mental and Psychological preparation, your addict's chances of survival will be much greater.

10/5/14 – Constructive Act #199 – Share Your Story

Today a young lady that I admire so much has decided to share her story. She had chosen to share anonymously for several reasons. I'm proud of the woman she has become and proud to know her for the past several years. Thank you for opening your heart and sharing your story…Here is her story:

I look back over the eight years I've been sober and it's still hard for me to believe. I'm not supposed to be sober. I'm not supposed to be happy, joyous and free. I'm supposed to be the drunk, wasted loser I had been for so many years.

Maybe it would be easier for me to say I was abused, traumatized, or mistreated in some way as a child, but I cannot. I had a lovely childhood. I was involved in sports, music, my community. I had friends, a family who loved me and I got good grades.

This may sound strange to a person who isn't an addict, but I knew I wanted to get drunk long before my first sip of alcohol.
I began drinking at age thirteen, and I never wanted to stop. Heavy drinking was commonplace amongst my peers, and although drinking and drug use was the norm, most kids in my hometown managed to be successful.

Heavy drinking was no longer enough for me, so I began smoking marijuana regularly and also began using cocaine. After graduating high school, I went off to college and continued my hard-partying ways.

Somehow I managed to graduate from college, but my partying lifestyle didn't subside; in fact, it only became worse. I got my first DUI when I was in my early twenties. For most, this would've been the wake-up call needed to stop a person from making an even bigger mess of her life, but not an addict. My first DUI didn't curb my drinking at all.

It was during the years between my first and second DUIs that my cocaine use became out of control. It was during these years, that my life had become truly unmanageable. I ended up in places and drank and used with people I never would've imagined. My life had completely spiraled out of control.

I was arrested for my second DUI. This arrest was the turning point in my life. This DUI is what led me to AA. It was within the walls of Alcoholics Anonymous and through the people there, that I was able to turn my life over to God.

Today I look around at this second chance at life and I have to remember that it's the first drink that gets me drunk; not the fifth, not the seventh, not the tenth. The first. If I don't pick up that first drink, it is impossible for me to get drunk.As long as I remember I am an alcoholic, to keep maintain a healthy fear of ever picking up a drink again, then, only by the grace of God, may I live to see another day sober.

10/6/14 – Constructive Act #200 – Choose Your Direction

As we reach another "Hundred" milestone on the DDF Facebook page and complete "200 Constructive Acts," everyday is still a choice as to what direction each of us will take. Saturday marked the 7th month of being without our precious son and brother, Davis. I think back over all of the decisions and choices I have had to make since his death and I know that with every decision, I choose the direction I will take as I move onward through life. The entire Owen family has made the decision to move forward with our decisions. We have decided to help promote awareness and affect change in the hopes that no other family will ever have to endure the pain that we have endured over the past seven months.

Months ago we could have decided to go back to the life we had before Davis left us, but we knew that would be impossible. When you have a close-knit family like ours, losing a member is like losing a limb. You have to learn new coping skills and accommodations to continue to move forward. There is still a very prominent void in our lives and there always will be – much like a limp when you have lost the function of your leg. It never goes away, but you learn to move forward and keep going, by making adaptations to your lifestyle.

Our life without Davis is different to say the least. We took a family photo last week for an upcoming event, and there was no one there to make us laugh and smile for the picture. Where was the missing jokester who would have inevitably pinched someone on the bottom or said something just a bit risqué to ensure that everyone would have had a natural and sincere smile on their faces? The tutor with the most patience is gone and frustrations run high when we need him for teaching us what came so easily to him. There is an eerie silence where the sing-a-long kid would have been singing on a trip home from a sibling pick-up, or food left on a plate where he would have finished the unfinished meals of all of us. There is a lack of common sense and no longer a "jack of all trades" present when things go awry in the house or the cars. There is no longer the smell of "Polo

Blue" when a handsome fellow shows up ready to leave with the family or the all too familiar bear hug when he hadn't seen you all day. God knows how much we miss him daily and it is a struggle to write about or think about him in this way. He has become our addiction in the fact that we cannot stop the craving to have him back.

In spite of our sorrow and longing for our sweet Davis, we choose each day which direction we will take. Will we continue to move in the direction that helps others and teaches them to do what Davis couldn't, or will we let others figure that out for themselves and make the same mistakes that we made as a family? Will we let others wait too long to learn about addiction, or will we try to teach them now so that they can be proactive and possibly prevent a tragedy? The "Owen 7" would never consider turning our backs when there was even a slight possibility that we could help someone. We will continue "Moving Onward Through Life… Looking Upward to God" just like our motto says. We pray without ceasing and then listen to God for answers.

This epidemic will not cure itself with time; we have to actively come together as a community and each of us has to share our time and talent to help make a difference. When Davis was in rehab, I attended a parent meeting where the question was asked, "What is the latest research on the addiction gene?" The answer offered was that research is ongoing, and the solution is on the edge of completion. Foundations like the DDF are trying relentlessly to keep opiate/heroin addicts alive in order to be around for the ground-breaking research that will bring people to their knees. In the meantime, each of us has to CHOOSE OUR DIRECTION on a daily basis. PLEASE choose to join with us in whatever capacity you are comfortable with, and share your time and your talents, your money and your resources to change the course of opiate/heroin addiction.

If you wait until you are directly affected by this dreaded disease, you will have waited too late. Choose now to take the direction of being prepared and educated so that if and when you are faced with this plague, you will be forewarned and forearmed to deal with it. Knowledge is POWER and POWER will PREVAIL in this fight.

10/7/14 – Constructive Act #201 – Realize You Can't Have It Both Ways

This weekend on Facebook, I saw a story about a very pregnant lady that went into a coffee house and asked to go to the restroom. The young person at the counter denied her entry into the restroom even after the pregnant woman's husband came in and offered to pay for anything on the menu. Apparently the customer behind her in line even told the clerk to give her the code with her purchase and she would give it to the lady. Long story short, the clerk did NOT give the lady a code and she went down the street to another establishment and used the restroom. The manager of the store was later contacted and told the reporter that she was shocked by her employer's behavior which was unacceptable.

Now, at first reading, this story seemed outrageous! In fact, being that pregnant woman 5 times over, I completely agree with the pregnant lady's statement that when the urge hits you, you have to go! Then I began thinking back to my college days and the days that I worked in the local drugstore. As young kids new to the world of work, we did exactly what our bosses told us to do no matter how much it went against our grain and common sense. Our big "catch 22" was cashing checks. Over time, the drugstore I worked in became known as first national bank because all of the college kids came to the drugstore to cash their checks. Now, we had been told as employees that we were not to cash checks and to let the customers know that we could not and would not cash checks. Well, inevitably the person wanting to cash the check would challenge us and go over our heads and ask to speak to the person in charge. There were 4 pharmacists who worked at the drugstore and 3 of them would do exactly what they had told us not to do – they would cash the checks anyway. The fourth one, would back up what they had told us to do and refuse to cash checks. Now I ask you, who do you think I had more respect for? That's right – the pharmacists who realized that he would stick to the policies that he was asking us to run the front lines on! To this day – I still remember "Howard" and I respect him for the position he took to reinforce what he was asking us to do.

It was stressful and degrading to try and present a policy and take abuse from the customers for it, just to have the boss come out from behind the counter and be the hero!

Then I started thinking about the coffee shop situation and I got really angry. I can guarantee you that the young coffee shop employee did not just make up a bathroom policy when he saw a pregnant lady walk through the door. I feel very confident in believing that he was only doing what his employer had asked him to do. I did notice that the employee was not interviewed nor did anyone address his feelings nor quote him regarding the situation. I would also bet that he has taken a great deal of flack over this situation in his own community and that he feels stabbed in the back. The media may not have named him, but I'm sure everyone in the community where he lives knows exactly who he is and what he did. We teach kids in schools that they are to do as they are told. We don't teach common sense and we put consequences in place for those people who cannot follow the rules as they are written. We are creating a group of kids who do what they are told without question and they stick to their guns because they don't want to be fired for not doing what the boss has asked them to do. Then when the rules in place create a problem, the kids are the first ones to be thrown under the bus!

How stressful that we are putting kids in this position. Shame on us as adults.

Now I can't tell you for sure that this is what happened, but it would not surprise me if it were not too far from the truth. It's no wonder that kids are looking to self-medicate in this day and time. Everyone wants to protect himself or herself, just as this manager covered herself with the media. What ever happened to backing up your employees?

As adults, we need to consider very carefully what we are asking our young employers to do. If we are not going to stand behind them and back them up when they are doing as we asked them to do, then don't ask them in the first place. The average age of a heroin addict is 18 – 36—the age of kids as they begin working. We need to mentor kids and support them into the world of work. I often feel like we just treat them like they have all the answers when they begin a job. They are still young; they are still naïve; we have not taught them to think strategically and make decisions on their own. We are the captains of the ships, and don't forget—a good captain always goes down with the ship! Don't create more stress for a kid. They have enough of it as it is. We have lost the art of letting a kid be a kid in our society. We need to figure out how to get it back!

10/8/14 – Constructive Act #202 – Grab a Friend and Join Us

The Continuum of Care is perhaps the most important part of Recovery. It is in fact how to stay in recovery. We have some great speakers, some powerful new information and 22 vendors committed to sharing the evening with us to answer your questions and share their services. You don't want to miss this event. Marietta High School at 7:00 pm until we are done! Our vendors include:

INTOACTION TREATMENT
VIVITROL
SOOTHEDRAWAL
EVERGREEN COUNSELING LLC
MARIETTA POLICE DEPT./MCS
Naloxone TRAINING AND GIVE OUT – DDF
REALTORS 4 REHAB
TALBOTT RECOVERY
FOUNDATIONS
CELEBRATE RECOVERY
QUEST DIAGNOSTICS
INSIGHT PROGRAM
JERICHO HOUSE
NORTHWEST GA BEHAVIORAL HEALTH
DAVIS DIRECTION FOUNDATION
KIM KIRIUP – THE MILTON THERAPIST
BRIDGES OF HOPE

PREVENT DEFENSE
THE ADDICT'S MOM – GA CHAPTER
METRO ATLANTA RECOVERY RESIDENCES
HEALTHQWEST
GRACE GIRL BEADS will have jewelry available for purchase and you can purchase the DDF rubber bracelets 4/$1.00. The Naloxone will be available at no cost, but we will be accepting donations. Please consider a donation to the Davis Direction Foundation to help promote awareness and affect change in the midst of this horrible epidemic that we are experiencing nationwide. The CDC came out with new statistics this week that said in 28 states the overdose death rate for opiate/heroin addiction had doubled since 2012. We must work together and we must get started now. Thank you for your constant encouragement as we move forward through this crisis. The DDF is looking forward to a HUGE night tonight. Don't miss out on all of the knowledge tonight. Knowledge is POWER! Please share this post one more time! Let's fill the Marietta Performing Arts Center to capacity.

10/9/14 – Constructive Act #203 – Take Time To Evaluate

As an educator and counselor for the last 33 years, I have learned the importance of evaluating performance and learning to let data drive the mission. With that being said, I want to do a public "self-evaluation" of sorts of last night's Symposium. First and foremost, I will tell you up front that without a doubt, everyone involved gets an A+ for the night. Our speakers were amazing, our vendors were informative and passionate, our Organization and Fundraising Committee was awesome; the Facility was Beautiful and the Board could not have been more involved! So, let's break that down and really evaluate what that means.

We'll start with the facility. Thank you to Leigh Colburn, DDF Board of Directors, for hosting us at the Marietta Performing Arts Center at Marietta High School. The facility was well prepared for us and beautifully put together. There was absolutely no issue with us asking for 4 more tables to be set up due to the 4 new vendors that we acquired during the day on Wednesday. The custodial staff was friendly and courteous to all of our vendors and accommodated each request with a wonderful attitude. The facility was clean and each vendor table was beautifully skirted in the Blue Devil color of Marietta. The lighting and sound was readjusted for each speaker and there were absolutely zero glitches! Thank you to the facility staff – job well done!

Next, my hat is off to the AWESOME Organization and Fundraising Committee. Deb Ross, Bev Pleinis, Patti Zaino and Andrea Atkinson are amazing FRIENDS and hard workers. When they saw me pull up in the "Big Car" out the door they came and began the daunting task of unloading my madness to which there was no method.

They had signs on vendor tables, pumpkins filled with candy, jewelry table set up, iPad ready to accept sales and donations, all the while welcoming each guest who came through the door and answering their questions and fielding their concerns. While I was speaking with vendors, parents, addicts and community activists, they were cleaning up after the Symposium and vendor fair. They had me loaded up and ready to pull out of the parking lot 30 minutes before I finished my last conversation. "Mind Readers" could not have done a better and more thorough job. I would be completely lost without these ladies – they are truly the "Wind Beneath my Wings." I love you all and you are INCREDIBLE.

The 25 vendors who were in attendance last night could not have represented themselves in a more professional manner. Not one of them had a single complaint, and they all had something unique and worthwhile to offer to the crowd. There were beautiful displays with brochures of powerful and specific information. They greeted guests with compassionate hearts of service. Each vendor stayed until the last guest had left and they all cleaned up after themselves and left their vendor space as they found it. They were most appreciative of the opportunity to share and market their services to the crowd. Thank you to each and every vendor for caring enough to show up! What you did beyond that was truly above and beyond the call of community service. You get the highest marks for your preparation and presentation.

Last but certainly not least, our speakers outdid themselves. Tanya Smith told a heart-wrenching story of her daughter's journey through opiates that ended tragically. She shared the best and the worst of the story. She laid it out there for everyone to see in order to understand the disease of addiction. Dr. Harold McLendon was magnificent in his delivery of the perils of opiates and the choices of drug therapies. Everyone in the audience understood in layman's terms what he was saying and exactly what he meant. He left no stone unturned as to the exact details of how opiates act and react in the body and brain.

He eloquently described the differences in the different drug therapies available and even talked about one therapy not available in the US but gaining momentum in Mexico and Canada. Dr. Jeff Stoddard joined us from MA where he serves ad VP of Alkermes Inc, and went into depth about Vivitrol and why such a drug therapy could be instrumental in recovery. He told how it worked and why it worked. He actually served in a dual-role last night as a speaker and a vendor.

Speaking through song last night, Shelbea Owen and Zachary Seabaugh brought many to tears last night as they sang "Blessings." I don't know of a song that could be more aligned with the disease of addiction than this one.

"And what if trials of this life the rain, the storms, the hardest nights are your mercies in disguise?"

I cannot think of a song that better describes the feelings and questions of an addict or an addict's family and loved ones. Shelbea and Zach did a beautiful job delivering a powerful message. Their hearts were pure and their intentions were purposeful.

Our Speakers were truly second to none last night. Thank you one and all! So with the "self-evaluation" completed with flying colors, how does the data drive the mission? Continued awareness, continued change and continued life-saving measures as funds allow. We are on the right track and we need more of the same —MUCH MORE! Please continue to stand with us and fight with us and continue to give when and where you can. Our mission is clear and our work is cut out for us. Thank you for being there for us.

10/10/14 – Constructive Act # 204 – Don't Hide Behind Addiction

This is one of the many things that struck a chord with me on Wednesday night when our DDF Medical Director, Dr. Harold McLendon, was speaking at the Symposium about the properties of opiates and the drug therapies involved. He said to "stop hiding behind addiction and get help." I know I have said before if you are an addict, you need to go to the doctor and receive treatment. This is so important. Please forget about the way that anyone else may think or talk about addiction; it is only their ignorance that makes them say things. People don't know what they don't know. If you are an addict, you are in good company among plenty of other good people who are going through the same things as you are. 1 in every 10 people is right there with you. It's people of all ages, and all socioeconomic backgrounds who share this disease and who need help from the medical community.

I wish every doctor in our nation could have heard Dr. McLendon's presentation, and I wish every doctor in our nation would invest half as much time and energy as Dr. McLendon has in trying to help the addicts in our community. And I will put it our there for every doctor who reads this post—one thing that Dr. McLendon wanted everyone to know is that "Addiction has NOTHING to do with will power." You cannot will yourself out of addiction! Just as any person with diabetes or cancer cannot will themselves well, Addiction is a DISEASE. So – go to the doctor. Stop hiding because you received a gene at birth that went into override when you took a prescription medication that may or may not have been prescribed to you. Many people are victims of prescription drug addiction because perhaps they needed pain relief at some point and were actually given a prescription that they became addicted to. Others took a prescription because they found it in the medicine cabinet and they were self-medicating for a pain need or needed to sleep. We have become a pill-popping society because we have been taught to look for a quick fix. Whatever happened to the old saying, "no pain – no gain?" We're often too quick to try and fix something instead of trying to work through it. As a result, we are now in a crisis in our country because we are experiencing an epidemic of opiate/heroin addiction.

I wish I had the answer of how to make this epidemic publicly acceptable to talk about and publicly acceptable to get treatment for. I wish I knew how to take away the "Judgmental Gene" from everyone who may have formed judgments about prescription opiates/heroin and the people who are addicted to them. I wish everyone would live by the verse in the Bible found in Matthew 7:5 – "You hypocrite, first take the plank out of your own eye, and then you will see clearly to remove the speck from your brother's eye." Possibly the only thing socially worse than the "Addiction Gene" is the "Judgmental Gene!" The people with the "Judgmental Gene" are keeping the addicts and their families from seeking the help they need to enter Recovery.

Every doctor with a prescription pad has the capacity and legal right to write a prescription for Naloxone – the opiate antagonist that is saving lives and giving addicts a second chance. If you are a doctor and you are reading this, please know that one in every 10 of your patients is an addict of some kind. Many of them between the ages of 18 and 36 are opiate/heroin addicts. PLEASE HELP THEM! Help them compassionately and without judgmental undertones just as you would help them with any other disease. If you are unaware of Naloxone and that you can now write a prescription for it, do your research and understand the epidemic that is now claiming more lives than car accidents in our country. DO YOUR JOB! HELP SAVE LIVES! If you are an addict and you don't have a doctor willing to invest compassionately who understands what it means to be addicted to opiates/ heroin, then find a new doctor.

STOP HIDING BEHIND ADDICTION! There is no shame in asking for help! People hide because they are ashamed and embarrassed about issues and things beyond their control. If you know an addict suffering with addiction that is not asking for help, reach out to that person and encourage them to get the help they need and deserve. Let them know that they have nothing to be ashamed of or embarrassed about and that they are WORTHY of HELP and LOVE.

10/11/14 – Constructive Act #205 – Connect

Wherever I go these days, if I stay for long enough, or if people in the community know my story and what happened to our family, they instantly tell me of their connection to us and we feel a special bond because of it. I will tell you that I had no idea how vast opiate/heroin addiction was before I became involuntarily involved in it. I had no idea how many wonderful people were addicted or how many wonderful families were dealing with the same thing I was dealing with. I have met "Salt of the Earth" families through this disease and I have connected to each and every one of them. I wish that Davis could have had the opportunity to meet and connect with all of the beautiful and wonderful families that I have met over the last 7 months because if he had, I know he would still be here.

Yesterday, one of my beautiful and wonderful new friends asked for prayers on his Facebook for his Grandmother who is in failing health and I told him I would pray for her and him as well. He wrote me back and told me "I love you." My heart melted because that's the way Davis was. My family is a family that ends every goodbye, every night and every time we separate from one another with – "I love you." Those were the last words that Davis and I shared with each other. I met this young man – who is absolutely adorable by the way – only once at the "Lights of Hope" ceremony and he gave me a great big BEAR HUG and a beautiful and huge smile. It was quite obvious that he was proud of himself and his accomplishments. I'm proud of him too. We are CONNECTED! I am there for him and I know he knows it!

There is a beautiful and wonderful mother that I met for the first time at Wednesday night's Symposium that I feel like I have known for years. We have exchanged emails, text messages and prayers for her sweet daughter who is in Recovery and is doing well. We met through heroin. We have spoken early in the morning, (I'm talking before the roosters) and we have spoken late into the night on occasions when each of us needed someone to be there for the other. We are connected.

There is a board member that I share a common bond with. We have both lost our children to heroin and we know the hole in each other's hearts. We often even have the same thoughts at the same times and we laugh at and with each other. In a matter of days, we knew that we had a bond that we shared and that we needed each other. Both of us are strong women, who know the weakness of the other because of the experience we have been through with our precious children. We are CONNECTED.

After Davis left rehab, they told him since he was not going through their particular "halfway house" that he could no longer be connected to them or anyone who came to their program on their campus. They in essence took all of his connections away, even though he was attending an out-patient rehab that they had recommended and facilitated him getting admitted to. They had zero security measures in place to check anyone who came through the doors for any of their meetings, but they purposely removed all of my child's connections that he had made and bonded with over the last 3 weeks that he had been in rehab. They also recommended that we not give him his phone back for a while due to the "several" connections that may not be good ones. Well okay – I understand that, but what about the many, many good and necessary connections? Why would you do that to someone? It was like they sabotaged him from the beginning.

CONNECTIONS are what keep you going and get you through the hard times. When I went through Davis's things after his death, I found the names and numbers of all his friends in rehab. They were on torn piece of paper because he did not have his phone to put them into. He kept each and every one! I wish so badly I had never taken his phone away. They all came to his memorial service because they felt connected to him even in death. I wish I had known that I "didn't know what I didn't know!"

It was such a beautiful thing watching people become connected at the Symposium on Wednesday evening. Unfortunately and fortunately too, we are an ever growing community of connections. Let's be there for each other, and each other's addicts as well as the entire community. Let's stand and fight, educate, network, encourage and love each other through the nightmare of this disease. We are the ones who will pave the way and change the course of opiate/heroin addiction. I am by no means saying that we are exclusive because we have the opiate/heroin connection. We are exclusive because we are fighting to rid this nation of it. So, please, whether or not you are actively fighting for a loved one now, learn everything you can so that you, unlike me, will never have to say "I wish I had known that 'I didn't know what I didn't know.'" I love you all!

10/12/14 – Constructive Act #206 – Share Your Story

Today's story comes from one of the vendors at the Symposium last Wednesday. Andrey Rossin – from INTOACTION in Boynton Beach, FL met a group of graduates from our community for the Symposium. He also brought an entire tri-fold of stories from addicts still in Recovery at his facility. Each one of them is compelling and heart wrenching. Today we will hear the story of a young woman who is doing well and enjoying her new-found freedom from addiction. Here is her story:

I was born and raised in Kennesaw, Georgia. My parents were and still are very loving and caring towards my brothers and me. They provided anything I could've ever asked for and more. I started cheerleading at a young age, and continued on to do competition cheerleading for the Stingray All Stars throughout my middle school years. Schoolwork, making straight A's and determination to do well in every aspect of my life was always my top priority. I had a good group of girl friends until I decided to hang out with the older crowd because I thought it was the "cool" thing to do. By my 8th grade year, my older brother began selling oxycontin. My best friend was into drinking alcohol and smoking marijuana and that's when my life started to change.

I was constantly getting suspended from school, sneaking out of my house, and hanging out with guys that were way too old for me. I stopped listening to my parents continue to teach me right from wrong and decided I knew how to live my life at age 14. When I was 15 years old, I tried oxycontin for the first time due to peer pressure from a loved one, and that started a horrible downhill spiral. OPIATES TOOK A GRIP ON MY LIFE THAT NO OTHER DRUG OR ALCOHOL HAD DONE BEFORE. I fell in love. I went to 3 different high schools, didn't walk with my graduating class, and barely passed due to my using. I stopped working at a normal job and became a dancer at a nightclub. All my morals, values and self-respect were thrown out the window. I didn't care about anything before or after my next fix. By the time I was 19, I was shooting up heroin and doing any other drug I could get my hands on via IV usage. I was absolutely miserable. I was a walking zombie. There was no life in me at all.

I couldn't decide if taking my own life would be better than living the one I was choosing to live or not. I was a slave to heroin when I turned 21. I went to treatment for the first time. I wasn't ready to give up using heroin and change my life, so I thought of every excuse to leave and relapse. A few months after rehab, I went to jail for a probation violation. I decided I couldn't keep slowly letting heroin kill me and destroy everything in my path, so I called a friend for help. I made the decision to come to INTOACTION at the end of April 2014. When I got to INTOACTION, I was hopeless. I didn't think I was ever going to be able to live a normal positive fulfilling life. As time went on, that changed.

Today I am full of happiness and smiles. I have rebuilt great relationships with people I stole from, lied to or cheated. My parents and brothers are supportive in every way possible regarding my recovery. I rely on God to help me through every single day, clean and sober. I'm able to help other people today and have gratitude towards even the little things in life that went so unnoticed when I was using.

I owe my life to INTOACTION. I have future plans to open my own ministry and share my story in hopes to bring other addicts and people who have struggled, toward my amazing loving God and to the recovery process. I wouldn't trade my worst day sober for my best day high. I'm the girl I was 10 years ago, motivated, dedicated and hardworking. But now I grow more and more selfless and humble every single day. Thank you INTOACTION. I love you guys!

Emily P. – Sobriety date May 3rd, 2014.

10/13/14 – Constructive Act #207 – Be a Part of The Solution

When there is a crisis taking place, people often become scared or even a little panicked. Those people who think they are safe often times have a false sense of security because of their ignorance. Now, please understand "Ignorance" is not a mean or derogatory term, it simply means that you don't know what you don't know. If you are not part of the solution, then maybe you're not part of the problem, but perhaps you are standing in the way of others who are actively seeking a solution.

At the Tech game on Saturday, for the first time that anyone I spoke with could remember, the stadium had to be evacuated due to an impending storm that contained heavy lightning. The announcer asked people to begin moving into the underside of the stadium out of the elements and to do so in an orderly fashion. People began moving into the hallways of the stadium, but as people were entering the underside through the section awnings, others had stopped and started standing alongside the walls of the awnings just outside of harms way. These people were stopping others from getting to safety because now they were blocking the exits. People began to shout at them that they needed to continue to move into the underside of the stadium, but they just stood silently and didn't budge. Now these were not young kids who didn't know any better, they were people that looked to be in their sixties and seventies. These were people who most likely had children and grandchildren. They were certainly not being part of the solution, but the problem was they were standing in the way of others who were looking for a solution. They were preventing people from getting out of harm's way because they were being selfish and outright rude. In other words, in this case, they didn't care if others were struck by lightning, because it didn't affect them. Let me assure you that if a pop of lightning had come even a little close to the stadium, those people would have been the first people who were trampled due to their decisions about how they chose to deal with the situation.

This is kind of like the opiate/heroin epidemic in that people have a false sense of security because they are not directly affected by the epidemic as of right now. They are immediately out of harm's way, at least for the time being. Maybe they are not living with an addict or they themselves are not an addict, but that does not mean they are completely safe or out of harm's way. Addicts are on the roads driving under the influence of opiates and heroin. Addicts are robbing people of valuables and taking medications that may be necessary for people with chronic conditions. It's all part of the disease – they will do whatever it takes to get what they need. They are not typically violent people, but they can certainly create the scenario for death and destruction with the reactions caused by their actions. We have a problem and everyone is potentially at risk. Wherever you are, if you are in a crowd of people, consider the fact that one in every 10 people is an addict. How can you think that you would not possibly be affected by this epidemic?

Be a part of the solution. If you have to take opiate medication, keep it under lock and key. Dispose of it when you are done with it. Take it to a drug drop box and get it out of your homes and vehicles. If you are living with an addict, help them seek out long term care for their addiction so they can overcome the disease and put it in remission. If your young child or teenager is given an opiate prescription, monitor the dosage closely and when they no longer need it because the pain can be relieved with a lesser medication, get rid of it. Know the names of all opiate medications and ask the doctors for an alternative if you can get by without the opiate. Don't be ashamed and embarrassed by this disease; seek information openly and honestly. Talk with your doctors and educate family members – including elementary age children. What you teach them now could influence their behaviors in the future.

Opiate and heroin addiction is a problem that potentially affects everyone. Directly or indirectly, you may have already been affected and not know it. Protect yourselves and your families through awareness and knowledge. Know the dangers and be aware of the potential situations that could cause a problem. Be a part of the solution and whatever you do, don't stand in the way of others who are actively seeking a solution.

10/14/14 – Constructive Act #208 – Check Their Pupils

Last week at the Symposium, I learned something that I had never heard before. It was something so basic that I wish I had known living with an opiate addict.

During Dr. McLendon's presentation, he taught us that if you are using opiates that your body will become tolerant over time to the medication. You will need more and more to get the same effect that you received when you first started using. One pill may turn into four and so on. The effects of the drug will lessen over time and the addict will take more and more to achieve the high. This is one reason that people overdose. Also, when you stop the medication for any period of time, you will need less to get the high when you start taking again. This is one of the reasons people overdose on heroin. They think they can take the amount they used to take after they have stopped for a while, and it is too much. An overdose will occur because your body cannot tolerate such a large amount after you have been clean for any period of time.

The part that I did not know, is that no matter how long and how tolerant you have become, one thing never changes. When you are actively high on opiates, your pupils will constrict. They will be tiny pinpoints and they will not react to light and dark. This is one of the reasons an addict will not look you in the eye. The eyes are a dead giveaway for an opiate addict. All those days, that I suspected that Davis might have been high, all I would have needed to do would have been to check his pupils. I'm sure I thought his eyes looked different, but I could not figure out what is was. I do remember going to rehab and looking at him after he had been there for his first week and thinking how beautiful his eyes were. They were bright and beautiful and the green color was so vivid and pure. I had not seen them like that in a while, but I did not realize it until I saw him that day.

I found the following information on "Erowid", a website that many addicts use for drug information and information regarding experiences from drug use. It is in direct agreement with what Dr. McLendon was teaching last week at the Symposium.

"Heroin, like other opioids and opiates, actually causes pupils to constrict (get smaller), not dilate (get bigger), after use. This constriction, called miosis, is a sign of opiate inebriation that law enforcement looks for in areas with high heroin and other opioid/opiate abuse.

Many other drugs–like stimulants and classic psychedelics–produce extreme pupillary dilation, causing the pupils to get larger. This effect is called mydriasis. However, drugs that bind to opioid receptors (as agonists, like heroin) have the opposite effect and produce miosis.

The duration that pupils are constricted is directly affected by the half-life of the drug and its metabolites. Heroin and its metabolites (including morphine, 6-monoacetylmorphine, and the gluconurides) have relatively short durations, resulting in pupil constriction for roughly four to five hours after use."

References #1. Goldberger BA, Cone EJ, Grant TM, et al. "Disposition of Heroin and Its Metabolites in Heroin-Related Deaths". J Anal Toxicol. 1994;18(1):22-8.

If you are concerned about your addict using opiates, check their eyes. This symptom of addiction is never changing. It is a dead giveaway and something I had never known and never been told until last week. I wish I had known. Drug kits are expensive and not always on hand. They can also be manipulated and cheated on – especially if not taken in the presence of another person, which becomes a huge privacy issue. The "eye-check" is free and cannot be manipulated or tampered with.

We all long to know if our addicts are still using or not and unfortunately they are not always forthcoming about their continued use. We want to know because we care and we know they are in danger if they are high. We love them unconditionally and all we want is to have them back in our lives DRUG – FREE.

10/15/14 – Constructive Act #209 – Make A Plan Today

I know I have said this before, but I don't think people understand how vital it is to that moment in time when decisions have to be made and the life of a child, sibling, parent, friend or spouse hangs in the balance. Last night I had a panicked message to call a sweet grandmother who had been dealing with her precious grandson for months related to heroin addiction. Her grandson had been doing better than in the past, but he was still an addict. This morning I awakened to a text message from the sweet relative of an addict whose cousin had just given birth to a precious baby and the daddy was apparently shooting heroin. These people now need answers and they need them now. Just as a cancer patient who comes out of remission goes immediately back to the doctor for treatment, and addict has to have the same kind of plan. There's no time to start the research now – Now is the time for action.

I certainly don't have the answers for these people, but I can give them options, which is what I did. The options that are right for some people are not necessarily right for others, but you need to know what your choices are and then put them in some kind of order to be able to use them. I would suggest keeping a notebook of options and add to them as you see something added to the DDF or any other sites that you keep up with. First and foremost as I have always said… Get a Doctor! Ask your doctor if your addict gets to a point where they need medical care. Will they be able to treat them and could they allow them to detox in a hospital? When your addict is at the end of the line and out of control, where will you take them? You have to know the answer to this question. You have to know what the rules and laws are regarding these places as well. For the most part, an addict over the age of 18 has the right to check in and out of places at will. You will have no control over this and you need to know this now. You won't even be able to get any information unless your addict will sign a release for the doctor or facility allowing them to speak with you.

Have a plan for the following questions:

If you find your loved one has overdosed, who is your first phone call to? Of course the answer to this one is 911. Hopefully, you have a Naloxone kit in your possession that you know how to use. Still call 911 first, have them in route and then use the kit.

Which hospital do you want your loved one transported to? This is your choice and you only have 30 – 90 minutes to work with here. Know where you are going.

Where do you want your loved one to detox? This is the period of withdrawal that each addict must go through before they can enter rehabilitation facilities. Some rehabs offer this process on site, other do not.

What rehab will you use – or will you even use a rehab facility? Some have specific opiate/heroin protocols that are in place and others do not. Know how the facility you are using treats opiate addiction. It must be treated differently than other addictions and it must be treated long-term. If I had decisions to make over again, I would look for a facility with a minimum stay of 6 months to a year. This is active treatment – NOT a halfway house. Understand why opiate/heroin addiction is a more severe form of addiction and why it needs to be treated differently.

Do you have the name of an individual counselor? Know the credentials of your counselor. People who have 6 weeks of training can get an addiction counseling certificate and frame it just like an addiction counselor with a Master's degree from a respected college or university. Beware of Addiction Counselors – do your homework in this area.

What will your insurance cover? If you don't have insurance, know where you can take your loved one that will take them anyway. These places are out there – I posted one yesterday on the DDF.

Lastly, and certainly most painful, pick a funeral home or crematory. Sometimes, unfortunately, you have to bypass all of the above questions and this is the only one you get to answer – as in my case.

Loved ones are dying in record numbers due to opiate/heroin addiction. This is a fact! More people are dying of addiction now than are dying in car accidents in our country. Every 19 minutes an addict dies. These are the FACTS! You must have a PLAN.

If you are not dealing with an active addict, start now to understand the disease of opiate/heroin addiction. It is the fastest growing epidemic in our country today. Quit worrying about EBOLA and the scare it has created and begin worrying about something that is much more likely to affect your family in some way. Prevention is the greatest cure – do your teaching and preparation now to protect your loved ones and your friends. INVEST IN A PLAN FOR PREVENTION AND A PLAN OF ACTION! YOUR LOVED ONE'S LIFE MAY DEPEND ON IT.

10/16/14 – Constructive Act #210 – Tell Your Story

Every Sunday, the DDF posts a story from someone who has had some experience with opiate/heroin. It was designed to show others that hope and recovery is attainable and that there are pathways to follow that can help. In my opinion, it has been a huge success and it has done more to help others than first imagined. People have poured out their hearts and let others know how desperate they were and how awful their situations were before they turned them around. I have read some stories that have just absolutely blown my mind and I can't imagine the fortitude that these addicts must come up with in order to survive. But – it happens, they do it, and they live to TELL THEIR STORIES!

It's amazing and inspiring to hear a story from someone who has been there done that. It is valid; it is reassuring; it is important to other addicts; it is respected by others; it lends hope and a future for other addicts and families. It is necessary! If you are an addict and you have not told your story, it's time to begin helping others. If you have lost a child or loved one to this awful epidemic, it's time to tell your story and help others. If you are suffering through a painful journey with an addict and you are sad and forlorn, it's time to tell your story and help others realize they are not alone. Too many people are suffering silently because they think they are all alone and they have no one who would understand. That is so far from the truth and we all know it, but I have found in talking with the addicts that they feel all alone when they are going through this – especially when they relapse.

By telling your story, you will help others realize that a lapse or a relapse is just a "bump in the road" if you can find your way back to recovery quickly. Everyone makes mistakes and with this particular addiction, the average addicts relapses 6-7 times before they can enter recovery more successfully. YOU ARE NOT ALONE!

I think sometimes when people leave a certain lifestyle behind and they turn the corner to success in life, in family and in general, they want to leave the other life behind in so many ways. It's kind of like, if they don't talk about it, then it never happened. BUT – it did happen and you now have a gift that can be used to help others. It is with all of the addicts who have entered successful recovery that we will find the answers to help others and that is why it is so important to TELL YOUR STORY! Your key unlocks the future to a new life for others!

We will continue to post "Share Your Story Sunday" because it is the only day of the week when addicts or "The keeper of the addicts" gets to tell his/her story. It is important; it brings comments from others that validate the process and the addict, and it offers hope and a new life for active addicts. If you are willing to share your story with others in an effort to help them, please send me your story to info@davisdirection.com. You can tell me if you would like it to be anonymous or if you are ready to put your name on it and own it. There is no shame in recovery, but I do understand when people with small children are not ready to expose a past lifestyle, or when people have other reasons for protecting their identity for the time being. Sometimes the time is just not right to add your name and I get that! We will post your story anonymously – just make sure I know how you would like for me to post it.

This week I will be sharing the story of Andrey Rossin – the owner of Into Action – a Rehab facility in Boynton Beach, Florida that has helped many of our local young adults find their way into recovery. They had a huge show of support for their facility and for Andrey as well at the Symposium on October 8th. Several of them have already sent me their stories and I am waiting for others to follow.

I have always said that the addicts are the experts in this area, and they are the ones who will help us find our way out of this epidemic. The experts are growing in number in more ways than one. Yes – the epidemic rages on and people continue to die—but in our community, the experts are growing in number in a different way. They are helping others find their way into recovery and they are speaking out and sharing their stories. They are putting beautiful faces and names on their disease and it is offering hope for others. Keep up the good work! You are making a difference. TELL YOUR STORY… it may just save a life.

10/17/14 – Constructive Act #211 – Make a Wish

I saw the # 11 on this CA and I immediately thought of 11:11 and how people always make wishes at that time and so I went with it. Here's my wish – "I wish that people would become as preventative and concerned about the prescription drug abuse and opiate/heroin abuse in our country as they are concerned about Ebola!" I know you are not supposed to tell your wishes – but I've told everything else on the DDF – so it just seemed like the right thing to do. I saw yesterday where Dekalb County School System had even made new rules about admission into their schools for people who were coming from the African regions.

All the news stations are starting with the Ebola virus and the ONE or TWO people who have been affected by it. They are giving advice about how to protect yourselves and the precautions to take if you don't want to get the virus. DON'T THEY KNOW THAT A PERSON IN OUR COUNTRY DIES EVERY 19 MINUTES FROM PRESCRIPTION DRUG, OPIATE AND HEROIN ADDICTION? YES I AM SCREAMING!

As a matter of fact, one of the DDF board members sent this statistic to me yesterday. The CDC is reporting there have been 4,500 Ebola deaths WORLDWIDE. The same news media and CDC have estimated that opiate/heroin related deaths in America could possibly hit 35,000 in the 28 reporting states and 50,000 NATIONWIDE. According to this statistic, you should be shaking in your boots about prevention for opiate/heroin related deaths and put Ebola on the back burner for now! I'm quite sure that Africa's top story on their news channels is NOT opiate/heroin addiction.

In order to be preventative for the opiate/heroin addiction, CLEAN OUT YOUR MEDICINE CABINETS! Take old and unused prescriptions to a drug dropbox. Marietta Police Department has a dropbox available 24/7 and Marietta First United Methodist Church will have one available for Sunday Services on October 26th, at 9:00 and 11:15. Don't allow your teenage children to carry their pain killer prescriptions around in their pocketbooks or bookbags. I told this story earlier this summer, but I'll tell it again. This summer while working on a show, my 14 year old daughter was offered prescription pain pills from another teenager who had been prescribed an opiate for an injury. She was asking for Advil for a headache and quite innocently was offered these instead. The other child was just trying to help her and since she didn't have Advil – she offered her something even better. I'm quite sure it was innocent and the other child was just as ignorant about prescription pain pills as most of them are. But, as a parent, why in the world would you allow your child to carry these around in your purse? If you are in this much pain, you need to be at home in bed. If you are out actively participating in activities, you OBVIOUSLY don't need prescription opiates to get by!

Ask your doctor about ALL of your prescriptions. Know what you are going to get at the pharmacy before you leave your doctor's office. Ask – "Is this an opiate prescription?" If it is, ask about alternatives. Decide about the level of pain you are willing to endure. Can you stand a little pain? Will Advil or Tylenol be enough to manage your pain? If so, opt out of the prescription med and go with the safe alternative. GET CONCERNED! Opiate/Heroin addiction is a much worse epidemic in our country than Ebola! Let's start acting like it. Red Ribbon Week is coming up in the public school systems all over the nation! Call and ask your child's school what they are doing to address Prescription Drug Abuse during this week, Oct. 26th – Nov. 2nd. Be proactive! Tell your child's school that everyday in our country 2000 teenagers try prescription drugs illegally for the first time! Every 19 minutes a person dies from opiate/heroin addiction in our country. Addiction now claims more lives in our country than car accidents! Let's put our epidemics into perspective here. The crisis in our country is opiate/heroin addiction – NOT EBOLA!

10/18/14 – Constructive Act #212 – Cherish Every Moment (Revisited)

When you are living with an active addict, and according to statistics 1 out of every 10 of us are, understand that there will be good times and bad times. Not every moment is terrible and tragic. Over the past year and a half that we knew Davis was using before he died, there were many moments that we felt sure he had recovered and that he was coming back to us and that life would return to normal. I wish I had taken more pictures, grabbed more hugs, had more conversations, and just spent more time hanging out with him. Those are the times that are so confusing to people. The addict just seems absolutely alright. Opiate/heroin addicts are highly functional especially if they are using at night and are functioning during the day at a job or going to school. The whole community was in shock when they found out that Davis had died of a drug overdose. There have been reports of doctors, nurses, teachers and other professional people in every field using and functioning all over our nation. Granted, they can't keep it up forever, and it will catch up with them, but the point is that there are moments to be cherished when you live with an addict.

I cherish each hug, especially the last one I ever got, each conversation, each shopping trip, each errand he ran with me, each meal he ate and thanked us for, each time we went to church and to the nursing home, each time we shared a holiday, each time I got to wake him up and tell him "Good Morning," each time I had the opportunity to pray with him or have a deep religious conversation, each time we attended a function for another family member, each birthday we celebrated, each time we went out for dinner, each time we watched Duck Dynasty, each time he showed me new pictures of sweet Emma, each time we delivered Thanksgiving meals, each time we worked in the yard, each time we folded laundry together, each time he sat with me in my office because he had a few minutes to spare before he began work, and especially each time he walked through that back door whistling and swinging his keys.

I try so hard to forget the hard times because I know that he was not himself and that the disease had taken a part of him away from us. We posted a sign we found in a magazine on his bedroom door when he left for rehab that still hangs on his door that says "We Want You Back." It's still there although now it takes on a whole new meaning. I wonder sometimes how different it is that I go through everyday functioning like the person that I was before I lost him, getting up in the morning, going to work, coming home and doing the things a mom does, picking up kids who can't drive and attending functions in the evenings. But, almost every night, when my head hits that pillow, I become that helpless person that can't fight any longer and the tears begin to swell and the breathing becomes so labored, the body begins to shake and I begin to pray. I thank God for holding my baby and taking him out of his bondage. I have to remember that he is at peace in the arms of God, spending time with my Daddy and my Granny. This part never gets any easier. Sometimes, you just have to shut down and take a couple of days for yourself and be alone because you can't continue to function like nothing ever happened. Yes, life goes on and certain days are harder than others. I can assure you though, that all of the "firsts" consist of 365 days – not just Holidays! Every day of the year that I am without him is a "First." Today is the "FIRST" October 18th that I have been without him, and it's no easier or harder than any other day of the year. It just has a different significance. The changing seasons bring on difficult times because with each season, new memories are realized. Moving into fall brings on a whole new set of visuals – clothes, pumpkin patches, raking leaves, pumpkin pie, "Kilt Squad," and the list goes on and on.

CHERISH EVERY MOMENT—it could be the last moment. Take pictures; take time; savor each experience, and keep a journal. As soon as Davis died, I wrote pages and pages of what our last days together were like. I read it often because I never want to forget. Moving into the Holiday season won't be easy, because traditionally we take more pictures and have more traditions, but realistically, each individual holiday will be no different than today – Saturday October 18th – I miss you sweet angel... every minute of every day. Xxooo

10/19/14 – Constructive Act #213 – Share Your Story

Today, Andrey Rosin – Owner of "IntoAction" Treatment Center in Boynton Beach FL, shares his story. He came and set up a booth in our vendor fair at the October Symposium and couldn't wait to share his program with everyone there. He has helped many young people in our community and they say, "He saved their lives!" Thank you for sharing, Andrey!

My story.

I am a hopeless variety alcoholic and addict. In my family everybody drinks, but only I have a problem or at least all the focus is on me… but really I did not have any problems; it was all you! People were telling me I got problems that I did not seem to have. Crazy you say, not really that was my life-always depressed and suicidal from the age of 13. I am the poster for the bipolar disorder, and the one with constant burning desire—whenever I wanted my fix, there was no stopping ,no looking back, always agitated and hyper.

First alcohol black-out at the age of 13, by the age of 19 I was a full blown alcoholic and was using anything I could put my hands on. By the age of 22-23, I turned IV user and by the age of 29 had numerous overdoses and was using crack and heroin on a constant basis. October 2006 at the age of 29, I slid into coma. I was delivered from my dopeman room straight into Miami Cedars Hospital. The fight for my life just began—it lasted three days during which my then girlfriend and parents were told to say farewell since organs will start slow shut off process. Then I had started coming back to life. "Wow", you would say, did I jump up and asked for help, no and no for what? I knew what I needed… just a detox would help.

And that's where spiritual experiences started occurring; someone that I knew from a long time ago in Boston came into my life and told me he would take me into 90 day program in Delray. Go or not go was really not a question I wanted to please my relatives, to pacify them and in the end I was really badly mangled. Half of my body barely functioned and was numb for a while, so I went. Within the first couple weeks I was brought into a meeting that turned my world around.

First time I saw people that had recovered or at least that's what they said. They had something I wanted. There was content and happiness that radiated from them that was very different. I had been so used to people whining, crying, bitching and complaining in the AA/NA meetings that was an experience in itself. I was not allowed to share (haha) like I really wanted to. There was nothing I could say anyway. But I was told that if I don't know the solution all I would be doing was mumbling about the problem and no one needs to hear that. There, the approach was so fresh and new that something like a little hope started inside of me. I had asked my friend at my second meeting, "What am I to do," and he simply put it, "You must ask one to become my sponsor-a guide in recovery." Huh, who and how the heck would I know? He ended up pushing me toward someone leaving the group and telling me to take action. I ran and asked the guy. The young guy turned around and told me it would be an honor and a privilege to bring me through the process. I was aghast. Then he gave me a set of instructions and I went on to work. Yes to work—really to work and I wrote 5-6 hours daily while being at that center cause I knew the moment I would leave, all the work will be out the window.

I can go on and on about this process The result is visible—the obsession and desire to drink and use left me before the end of the treatment and that is a miracle, absolute miracle! It never came back!

Even more since then I have started sponsoring guys one by one and bringing them through the process and have seen a few change and recover since! 2011 is the year I went into a new journey and started planning "IntoAction Treatment." 2012, February 6th our first client flew in from Atlanta (now you know why I am so attached to Georgia). Since then we have had 68 planted trees—yes we plant a tree once you complete the program and all of our guys work closely with sponsors and go through the process in order to get better as well as have attentive therapists that address all the underlying issues.

It really has been a blessing to be a part of this journey and see others change. Thank you for allowing me to share my story here. Today I know just like I know my name is Andrey… I can be free and happy without the fix – because I am!

10/20/14 – Constructive Act #214 – Attend an Event

Every time I read a "Share Your Story Sunday," there seems to be an event or a single experience that becomes the "Aha" moment for the addict. More times than not, it seems to be a spiritual meeting or experience where God speaks to an addict and lets them know that He is always there for them waiting for them to accept His help and forgiveness. I am so personally proud that my home church – Marietta First United Methodist Church – is taking a stand in the community to love and accept the disease of addiction and all of those families who have been affected by it, by embracing them in a Service of Hope and Healing this Sunday, October 26th, 2014.

Nest Sunday at both services – 9:00 and 11:15 – Dr. Sam Matthews – Senior Pastor at our church will be preaching a sermon that addresses the disease of addiction. Dr. Sam and his family have been personally affected by the disease of addiction, and they share a passion and an understanding of the disease and how it affects addicts and families of addicts. He is a humble servant of God and a Director on the Davis Direction Foundation. He is teaching his congregation to follow the word of God and to open their hearts and their fellowship to support and embrace these families affected by this disease. Following the 11:15 worship service, all individuals and families who need support working through these issues are invited to join us for lunch in the fellowship hall for an additional means of support.

We will be asking you to complete a needs assessment to help us decide as a congregation how we can best support you and show you the love of Jesus. We want to provide you with the meetings and activities that you feel will help you as you enter or follow your journey into recovery. Many of you have already sent emails or Facebook messages asking us to meet you or sit with you on this Sunday. The Owen family and the Davis Direction Foundation Board would consider it an honor to host you as our guest and sit with you and beside you during this service. We will meet you out in the front of the church and personally walk you in and sit with you for this service of Hope and Healing. The DDF Board is hoping that you will take advantage of this opportunity and reach out to us and tell us what your needs are. We are open to hear what you are saying and open to serve in the areas that you establish need.

Please come and worship with us as we celebrate the love of Jesus and the rejoicing we feel when one sinner repents. There is not one of us in the church who does not need forgiveness and not one of us who realizes that there is not any degree of sin in God's eyes. Hebrews 8:12 tells us that "God will be merciful toward their iniquities, and will remember their sins no more." God is so merciful and is waiting to help us and heal us. We are listening to God and wanting to serve in a way that pleases Him as we help His children work through the disease of addiction.

As we enter Red Ribbon Week, Nationally – October 26th – Nov. 2nd, join with us as we try to make a difference in our community. Marietta First United Methodist Church will have a Drug Dropbox in place this Sunday in an effort to be preventative for families throughout our community. Our Hope and Healing Service and our Lunch after the service is especially for YOU! We love you and we embrace you and we want to make a difference in your life. Please allow us this opportunity as we reach out and do the things that we hear God calling us to do.

10/21/14 – Constructive Act #215 – Offer Hospitality

Red Ribbon Week will officially start on the 23rd of October and run through Halloween night. The Red Ribbon Campaign was begun almost 30 years ago to address the killing and destruction caused by drugs in America. If it had begun this year in America – I think the wording would be a little different. I think it would say – the "Death and "Destruction" caused by drugs in America. Schools and businesses all over our nation are doing something to promote drug awareness and hopefully prevent people of all ages from ever touching illegal drugs. But, what about the people who are already deep in the throes of addiction and are desperately searching for answers and solutions? As much as I agree that prevention is the best solution, I'm not naïve enough to believe that our work to help those already suffering from the disease of addiction will not last for generations to come. For those people, offering hospitality may be one of the kindest acts you can do for them. Showing them respect and love may do more to change their life than any one single factor that you can control.

This is one disease that the person who has it, has to do the majority of the work. It's not like a disease that you can go to the doctor for and get the medications that make your body function as it did prior to the disease. There are no medications that take you "back to normal" or equalize the chemistry of your body so that it functions normally until you take another dose, like in diabetes. The addict has to fight the struggle going on mentally inside of the brain as well as the physical symptoms. Davis talked regularly about those people in his life who were "nice" to him. It was as if he felt like he didn't deserve to be treated nicely and when someone was nice to him in any way, it touched him deeply. It did not go unnoticed. Throughout his life as an addict, he always had time to help someone, or lend a helping hand in any situation. He was never judgmental and he would give you the time of day as if it were his only job on earth. He was just NICE to people. I think sometimes he was that way because it meant so much to him when others treated him with respect and showed him kindness.

I often have mixed emotions about campaigns that last for a week throughout the year because people participate during that week and think they are good to go until that particular week rolls around the next year. Every week should be Red Ribbon Week in our nation. Have you heard the statistic that the DEA director stated at our first Symposium? He said that less than 5% of people in the world live in America, but, those 5% consume over 95% of all opiate prescriptions in the world! That is STAGGERING! We should be promoting awareness 365 days a year with statistics like that.

So what can you do to make every day a Red Ribbon Day in America? I truly believe that people are inherently good and that until things go so terribly wrong for them, and the stress of life consumes their thoughts and actions, that most people are happy and drug free. Then, sometimes, through no fault of their own, something happens and causes physical or mental and emotional pain that is addressed through medication and thus a life of addiction unfolds.

On a daily basis, show hospitality! Be nice to others—you never know the crosses they bear and the things they have been through or are going through. Speak to

211

everyone and offer a smile. Take the high road and be the bigger person! Truly be a SERVANT of God. If you are in a leadership role, be a servant leader. Do nice things for others and role model the way you would like to be treated – ALWAYS! Your act of kindness may be the last act someone who is an addict experiences on this earth. I often wonder, who was nice to Davis on the night that he died? I hope someone was!

10/22/14 – Constructive Act #216 – Know the First Offender Act

For the most part, if a person does opiates/heroin for any length of time, they will end up in jail. Many people who write to me on the DDF have either been in jail, or have a loved one in jail. However, research is telling us that jail is not the best like anyone else who breaks the law for now. When they finally serve their time and get out of jail, trying to find a job brings on new challenges. With a background check being done for most companies these days, problems arise when the background check comes in and shows that the person is a felon. Who wants to hire a felon?

Do you know what the First Offender Act says? Here is the legal definition of the law: Georgia First Offender Act The First Offender Act is an alternative sentencing mechanism that allows someone to accept responsibility for a mistake, pay his or debt to society, and avoid the label "Convicted Felon".

Now, there are certain violations of the law that are not covered under the First Offenders Act:

What Crimes are not available for First Offender Treatment? First Offender Sentencing is not available to defendants in the following classes of cases:
(1) A serious violent felony as defined in Code Section 17-10- 6.1;
(2) A sexual offense as defined in Code Section 17-10-6.2;
(3) Sexual exploitation of a minor as defined in Code Section 16-12-100;
(4) Electronically furnishing obscene material to a minor as defined in Code Section 16-12-100.1; or
(5) Computer pornography and child exploitation, as defined in Code Section 16-12-100.2.
There are also certain consequences that are stipulated if the person breaks the law again during the time they are serving under the First Offender Act.

The First Offender Act is a "double-edged" sword. Under O.C.G.A. § 42-8-60, "upon violation by the defendant of the terms of probation, upon a conviction for another crime during the period of probation, or upon the court determining that the defendant is or was not eligible for sentencing under this article, the court may enter an adjudication of guilt and proceed as otherwise provided by law."

What happens if I violate the terms of probation?

Upon a revocation of a defendant previously sentenced under the First Offender Act, the Court that sentenced the defendant may re-sentence him/her to the maximum sentence penalty allowable under the law.

This is another one of those situations that you need to familiarize yourself with if you are an addict or "an addict's keeper." I personally know people who have used the law to change their lives for the better and get awesome jobs and provide for families. It is designed to help people and when used correctly and in recovery, I think it is a very good opportunity to change your circumstances.

This post was written because of a private message that I received this week from an "addict's keeper" who was trying to help a loved one. It is good information – that I mostly "copied and pasted" because the information is extremely technical and I didn't want to get it wrong.

On the flip side of all of this, sometimes jail saves an addict's life! I have heard on more than one occasion that having a child in jail was a blessing because it allowed them to get their life back together and forced them to stop using. And on the flip side of that, I have also heard that the jails are full of drugs. I have no experience with "jail" to know what really happens behind bars as I know some of you do, but I do know that it is a system that needs to be looked at further where drugs are concerned.

10/23/14 – Constructive Act #217 – Be A Mentor

For those of us in our middle aged time of life, I think we are the generation that gets to look back and see such extreme differences in our childhoods as compared to the childhoods that our children are living. One of the biggest differences that I see is the fact that children don't really have relationships with other adults like we did when we were growing up. I can think of several families either in my neighborhood or in my church that the parents were like a second set of parents to me. I could have gone to those people in a time of need or stress in my life, and they would have helped me with whatever I needed. Social media has taken over our children and whereas we would have begun being included in more adult conversations as we entered high school, kids now are happy to stay in the car, or sit in a secluded spot and "visit" on their cell phones, while the adults visit with each other.

If you think about jobs that we have now, people come and go in companies so quickly that young people don't really have mentors like we did when we began our jobs. I know my first principal in Cobb County took me under her wing as a young teacher and was there for me in life 24/7 – 365. She didn't stop caring when the bell rang, she was there for me as a life coach, mentor and a friend. When Davis died, she was one of the first people to show up at my house and she left me a note on the family white board that is still there. I haven't been able to erase it, because she means so much to me. She came back a couple of weeks later to check on me and sat with me for a couple of hours imparting her wisdom and sharing her love. She was my mentor. I stayed with her for 6 years as a teacher, until she left to take a year off with her second child when she was born. In my eyes, she was never replaced professionally nor personally.

Young people today need older people in their lives! They need people aside from their parents who care and are there for them around the clock. This is such a fast paced world in which we live, that people are sometimes so consumed in their own lives, that they don't make the time to form relationships with the "new" people. People don't have others over to dinner like when we were growing up. They just meet at restaurants now. They don't have families over to share their homes and their important treasures/history inside their homes. My children have their friends over and they go to their friends' homes, but as families, we don't visit each other like my family did when I was growing up. Out of the 5 children that I have, we have a "family" relationship with 1 family that I met through my children where we actually visit in each other's homes. This is one thing we need to bring back in our society.

Families need families! When we were growing up, families seemed to live closer together. I know we ate lunch with my Granny every Sunday after church and my cousins came over as well. Now, families move away from each other and cousins grow up states away from each other. My own kids only see their cousins on Thanksgiving and Christmas. We have never replaced those connections in our society. It has changed who we are.

Reach out to people in your paths. If you are with someone every day and you are not available to them in ways that differ from the job, get to know them. See if you can reach out to them emotionally and personally. Be a friend. Be a mentor. Make a difference and be someone who can help someone in need. I'm not talking about money or material things, I'm talking about an emotional connection—or a source of advice. Wisdom comes with experience and cannot be replaced by anything else. Share your wisdom with someone today; let them know you care enough to be there for them 24/7 – 365. It could make a difference in someone's life.

10/24/14 – Constructive Act #218 – Prepare Yourself Mentally

Living with a loved one affected by addiction is not an easy life and it requires lots of mental preparation on your part. If you happen to be the "addict's keeper," then you are never quite sure what you will come home to or what you will be called away from. The night that our nightmare came to a physical end, we only had one child at home. We had to figure out how to find and inform 3 other children – 2 of whom were away at school and the other was at a rehearsal for an upcoming show. We had no plan, and quite frankly we had not talked about the real possibility that Davis might die and how we would handle that. It was just one of those things that kept trying to creep up in your brain, and you just kept pushing it to the back every time. I thought we would be able to protect our other children from the addiction by keeping them as far away from it as possible. We tried so hard to keep their lives normal while we tried to handle the disease of addiction. Just as in other diseases, often times the healthy children are left out of things because you are either trying to protect them or there is just simply not "enough of you" to go around.

Looking back, we should have sat the other children down and explained to them out loud what could possibly happen and how they would have wanted us to handle that situation if it did happen. It's one thing to know it in your head and your heart, but quite another to hear it out loud being confirmed by a person who truly believes what they are saying. My oldest child got a phone call that night, because we could not find anyone to go and knock on her door and bring her home to us. She grew up that night in so many ways. She had to pick up the other 2 children and bring them home so that we would all be together as a family. Her heart was breaking from losing her best friend and yet she had to jump into action and truly play an adult part in the scene unfolding. She handled it like a champ, but I know it is a night she will never forget and I wish so many times that we had had a plan to follow so that it could have been different.

On the other hand, I thank God everyday that none of my children nor Michael and I had to find Davis dead. I don't truly think there is a way to prepare yourself for that. Knowing that it could happen and then it actually happening are two totally different things, but God was merciful to us in that way. If I had to tell you one thing to prepare yourself and your other children for though, it would be that exact event. It happens so often and I have not heard of any family or friend yet who actually had prepared for it to happen to them and actually had a plan for how to handle it.

Mental preparation is a blessing in so many ways. Although God built in a system called "shock" to help us through those kinds of events, having a plan and being mentally prepared are still such solid abilities to fall back on. As a Counselor and a mother, I cringe at the thought of my 14-year-old daughter having found her brother and trying to figure out what to do and how to handle the situation. What if she had been alone and had to go through that all by herself? It could have easily happened and I'm ashamed that I did not prepare her or any others for the situation. So many times all of the focus is on the addicted loved one and not on the others who are living through the nightmare.

Do yourself and the rest of your family a favor and prepare them for the realities of living with an addicted member. It could happen and it does happen—every 19 minutes in our country. Don't be caught having to make decisions and possibly allowing one of your other children to have emotional issues for the rest of his or her life because you did not prepare them mentally and help them with a plan of action. Every person in the throes of opiate/heroin addiction is living through their own hospice—every minute of every day. Maybe that is an idea for helping others, and may or may not happen. A plan could be developed and the family could be taken through a visual journey to prepare themselves mentally for the worst case scenario. I hope that none of you will ever have to experience the end of the physical journey, but someone does... every 19 minutes.

10/25/14 – Constructive Act #219 – Phone a Friend

Phone a friend and invite them to church This is a great thing to do wherever you are in our nation – BUT especially tomorrow in Cobb County at Marietta First United Methodist Church at 56 Whitlock Ave. in Marietta, GA. Tomorrow is the service of Hope and Healing and will speak to the families and the individuals who have been affected by addiction. There will be 2 services, one at 9:00 and the other at 11:15. Afterward, there will be a luncheon served, where you will hear more about what is available through our church and in our community to support you along your journey. You will hear stories about the journeys of others and there will be a time for you to ask questions and also hear about what is presently in place at Marietta First United Methodist. You will also be invited to complete a Needs Assessment asking about your specific needs in order that we can address the needs that are not currently being addressed, or help you find a place that will help.

It will be a great day with beautiful songs, meaningful scripture, and a message that will speak to your heart and give you strength to move onward, looking upward to God. Please join us. If you need transportation, send a private message and we will do our best to arrange transportation for you. There are so many people willing to become involved and already involved who are reaching out to help with this epidemic and make a difference.

Everyone in our nation is involved whether you realize it or not. When one in every ten people is affected by the disease of addiction, everyone else is at risk. Whether it be directly or indirectly, there is no immunity from this epidemic as we know it today. Working together we CAN make a difference and we WILL make a difference. Please join us as Marietta First United Methodist Church leads the way in our community to address this disease by reaching out in love and mercy for the recovery of our loved ones and our nation.

My family and others from the DDF will be outside in front of the church before each service waiting for you to help you find a seat or to sit with you. We are looking forward to this day and we are forever grateful for the understanding and love of MFUMC. Hope to see you tomorrow!

10/26/14 – Constructive Act #220 – Share Your Story

Here is another story from "Into Action" in Boynton Beach, Florida. These kids are going through an amazing rehabilitation facility and they are sharing success. This story is from an individual who graduated rehab, and is experiencing recovery. Here is the story:

I was born and raised in Kennesaw, Ga. I grew up in a somewhat ordinary household, and my younger brother and I were always provided for by my 2 loving parents. I played sports throughout middle school and high school (Harrison High) and was quite involved with a few clubs as well. I had everything I could ask for in my childhood and more. Neither of my parents were alcoholics or addicts, and they worked very hard for all of us. I had my first sip of alcohol when I was 11 years old from stealing from my parent's liquor cabinet. That slowly progressed to weekend drinking in middle school, which then led to marijuana and more alcohol in high school. Later in high school, I was introduced to prescription drugs, one of those being OxyContin.

I started adding friends and losing old ones; my priorities changed and I was no longer involved with clubs or any sports. I was no longer a role model for my little brother and I was no longer a loving caring son to my folks. To say the least, I fell in love with OxyContin and other opiates. I began to do things I swore I would never attempt and became lonelier and lonelier. I managed to get accepted to the University of Mississippi; however, my drug use surely took that opportunity away within a year of attending. I came to a point where I no longer wanted to use but I did not want to stop; I was at a jumping off point in my life. I felt I no longer had a soul, a desire to live, or motivation to do anything without a small blue pill.

I was given the opportunity to go to "Into Action" on a scholarship. I came in there a hopeless scared boy but walked out of their facility a happy young man without a desire or obsession to use opiates or other mind-altering substances. "Into Action" gave me a plan for a way out of addiction, simple instructions, and a blind faith to do so. The staff was so caring and taught me with patience about my malady. I would never recommend anyone I know struggling anywhere else; their primary mission is to see/assist addicts of the hopeless variety get better. Andrey is an angel and has a huge heart and will always give 110% to help the next person.

I owe my life to this place and their grace. Today I have a life I never would have thought after being in the trenches of addiction; I have a career in veterinary medicine and just re-enrolled in school. "Into Action" gave me another chance to grow up and pursue my dreams and ambition. My relationship with my parents is the best it's been in years; I'm closer with my brother than I ever have been. I am truly happy today and know how to handle my problems that appear in life without using or even having the desire to use, which in itself is a miracle. "Into Action" was the final destination for me and truly saved my life.

–Thomas T. 22 years
Sober since March 2013

10/27/14 – Constructive Act #221 – Participate in the Dialogue

After the service of Hope and Healing today, one of the beautiful people who attended said to me, "I just lost it today during the service because you guys were openly talking about, and embracing the conversation of addiction whereas for the last five years I suffered silently, having no one to talk with." We are making progress with this disease and people are beginning to understand the disease of addiction. This young lady was so genuinely happy to hear our congregation participating in a conversation of Hope and Healing that it literally brought her to tears. So many times I still talk with people who want to whisper and talk under their breath because it still feels so wrong to openly discuss the disease of addiction.

ADDICTION IS REAL and it affects 1 out of 10 of us. Not one of us raised our hand at birth and volunteered to host the gene of addiction. It just happens, and then for different reasons and under different circumstances, some of us become addicted while others of us remain unaffected. Just as we talk about diabetes and cancer, we need to begin talking about addiction. We need to have a national fundraiser like the 3-day walk for Breast cancer or the national motorcycle ride for diabetes. We need to have addiction recognized as a disease and we need to raise money for research, awareness and change. We have to TALK about our loved ones, talk about ourselves, and talk about our disease. We have to promote awareness and affect change. WE can no longer sit in silence and expect things to be different. Our time has come and we must act!

Begin asking questions and making comments when the subject comes up and ask your schools what they are doing to combat the epidemic. Ask what programs are available through your church and civic organizations to address the disease of addiction and if none are in place, ask to start one. Ask your drugstore or pharmacists what they are doing to promote opiate addiction awareness and if they are actively counseling patients who have been prescribed opiates. Ask your child's schools if you can put up posters or give out bracelets that promote awareness. Ask your parents' nursing homes if you can put up posters or give out bracelets. There is no age discrimination just as there is no other discrimination. Be proactive in the disease of addiction.

On Tuesday night I will be speaking at one of the Cobb High Schools and they have invited 6 other schools to take part in their evening. Parents are scared and they are beginning to understand that although they are not affected directly at this point, they are indirectly affected and they need to get involved to change the situation. You may not have to get involved for your children, but what about your grandchildren and your other family members? NO ONE IS IMMUNE!

Participate in the dialogue. Start the dialogue and educate yourself to be able to participate in the dialogue intellectually. If you are not at a point where you can participate with wisdom in the dialogue, then it is your responsibility and your job to ask the questions that will bring you up to speed. Don't let ignorance keep you from participating in the conversation. Do it for your children, do it for your parents, do it for your spouse, and do it for yourself.

10/28/14 – Constructive Act #222 – Interpret Things In Your Favor

So much in this life is left up to interpretation and each of us has to draw our own conclusions and decide how we want to interpret the actions of others or the experiences we have. Who's to say whether what we think is right or wrong, it all depends upon how we interpret it—so—I say interpret things in your favor! Whatever it makes you feel—comfort or relief, love or justice, reassurance or a sense of security, interpret things in your favor! You are the one who has to live with your decisions and your thoughts and beliefs. There are so many times that I have to interpret words of others, the events of the past year, dreams, visions, sermons and even thoughts inside of my own head, and I have decided that if I interpret them in my own favor, that it gives me a sense of happiness and it doesn't hurt anyone else. It allows me to continue my journey moving onward, looking upward to God.

Being the analytical person that I am, I spend way too much time trying to create a purpose for everything that happens and looking at all angles of the situation. Sometimes it drive me crazy and I way "over think" the situation to try to give it some meaning. Sometimes it just is what it is! I have had a couple of dreams since Davis died and I know that he needed for me to know something. The first one was a dream where he came to me and told me that I needed to stop looking for a bracelet that I had been looking for. He told me that he had taken it and used it for drug money and that I needed to stop looking for it because it was gone. He told me that he was sorry and that he wanted me to know that. He was very remorseful and he needed me to realize the extent of the disease so that I could help others. That is my interpretation of the dream and it was pretty easy and purposeful.

The second dream was a bit more confusing! Davis had come home, but we all knew he was visiting from Heaven and he asked me to play him a song on the piano. The song was "The Way That He Loves." I didn't really understand why he wanted to hear that song, but I sat down at the piano and I played it for him anyway. I started looking at the song and reading the words and the more I read, the more I knew that he was telling me all about the love of Jesus and how beautiful and thrilling it was. He needed for me to realize that the love of Jesus was so much more than we could ever realize on earth, but that when you get to Heaven, you see it and feel it and experience it and it is EVERYTHING! We had been planning the service of Hope and Healing at the time, and I believe it was Davis' contribution to the service. He wanted everyone there to know the love of Jesus and the way that He loves. I asked Bryan Black – the Minister of Music at MFUMC to please let Shelbea sing the song for the service and of course he agreed. She sang the song and after she was done at the 11:15 service, I heard someone from the back of the congregation say "WOW" – and I knew that it was about the message of the song. It touched someone and they realized that God's love is so amazing!

I see cardinals at my bird feeders and I think that sometimes they are Davis coming to check on things. One day I read on a friends FB page that cardinals are God's messengers coming back to check on their loved ones. I choose to believe this and interpret it in my favor, because it makes me happy. It makes me smile and it allows me to go on and live my life in a way that supports my family and allows me to understand that God's blessings don't always come in packages with bows and ribbon. Sometimes God's blessings are "hard-to-learn lessons" that makes us dig deep into our faith to understand. I have to trust that God is in control and that His decisions are supreme. I also feel the presence of Davis in the most intricate situations and I find myself asking myself what really matters and why I will choose the decision that I will choose to solve a problem or support a solution. I have said on many occasions that after I lost a child, nothing seemed to matter in the way that it might have before the loss. It helps to put things into perspective and allows me to concentrate on what REALLY matters in life. Sometimes things that I might have fought for before the loss are completely insignificant to me now.

Losing a child, tragically or not, makes you a different person. It's up to you how that different person will present the new image and it's up to you how you will move forward. But I do know one thing for sure, if you allow yourself to INTERPRET THINGS IN YOUR FAVOR, you can move forward with a healthy and healing attitude and possibly make a difference for others. That's what I have chosen to do and I'm glad that God has granted me that opportunity.

10/29/14 – Constructive Act #223 – Listen With Your Whole Heart

Last night I had the distinct privilege of hearing one of my favorite "Recovery Resources" tell her story for the very first time and it was a true blessing in my life. Listening with my whole heart allowed me to hear things I may not have heard otherwise. She stood proudly and bared her soul in front of friends, strangers and God. She was MAGNIFICENT and she made a lasting impression on everyone who showed up to hear her story. She started from the very beginning and took the listeners through every decision and bad choice she ever made and told them why she made it. As I sat and listened, I thought to myself "How in the world does common sense compete with a drug that seemingly has super powers?"

As I continued to listen with my whole heart, I heard the story go from a wonderful beginning to a morbid ending, though death was escaped. I heard her describe how the drugs take on a personality of their own and compete for your very soul. When a young person is trying so very hard to be invincible and begin a career with a future, how does a sober member of society combat the enemy? Hearing how the drug gives confidence, makes your body image all better, and triples your energy almost convinces you that you should try it yourself. This is the BEAST that we are dealing with.

How do you lead a person considering drugs further down the journey into the dark zone and show them that it never ends well? There will always be those people early enough in their journey that will describe the super powers of drugs and the undeniable positive change they will have on your life. Whether they will give you super energy and allow you to do the job of three people in half the time or allow you to escape the stressors of daily life and slip into utopia, there will always be the people out there who will lead you down the road of destruction because they have not yet rounded the curve. How do you teach a potential drug user to look far enough into the future to see how the story ends? This is the million dollar question.

I listened with my whole heart and heard how she was enticed to take drugs in order to focus long enough and hard enough to stay up all night and cram for a test and still have enough energy to laugh, have fun and skip a night of sleep. It not only got her the grade she wanted but it also allowed her to triple her productivity and become the Goddess of Production! The more she produced, the more pills she had to take and the more pills she took, the more abuse her body endured. Finally she was working as hard if not harder to allow her body to rest as she was to force her body to produce. It became a vicious cycle and consumed her life and her soul. She ended up spinning out on a rainy night on a slick highway nearly killing herself and others before she was able to see the destructive road down which she was traveling.

You are probably asking yourself about now just how long this process might have taken... how about 6 years? Yep—that's how long the process took and how long the addiction lured her soul before she had a wake-up call. What if she had not spun out on that rainy road on that dark night? Would she still have been able to disguise her addiction for a super power of Productivity?

How can we help kids paint this picture in the reverse order? That's what we have to figure out. It won't be easy, and it won't happen overnight! BUT, IT HAS TO HAPPEN! When we as sober adults begin to listen with out whole hearts, we will hear the cry of the children for help. We will hear and we must heed the cry and all get on board to protect the innocence and invincible attitudes of our youth. We have to help them channel their energy back into logical expectations and to re-route society into logical demands. Everything cannot and should not be a competition. We have to teach the children to decide what they want to invest in and how much they are willing to invest. We need to teach them to draw lines and NOT step over them. Stepping over is what is costing lives! It's okay to be average, it's okay to have an average income, and it's okay to have just enough to be happy! Life is too short for anything else. LISTEN WITH YOUR WHOLE HEART, and you will hear exactly what you need to know about each individual child and what he or she is willing to sacrifice. What a beautiful evening, listening to a lost and confused soul find her way into recovery. 10 months in and going STRONG… now that's an Energizer Bunny!

10/30/14 – Constructive Act #224 – Endure The Lemons

Sometimes it's just not possible to take lemons and make lemonade. You have to endure the lemons for a period of time and work through situations that have been put before you. Maybe you need to go through Detox, or maybe you are mourning the life of someone that you loved so dearly that lemonade is just not a possibility at this moment. That's okay – Sometimes you just have to endure the lemons. Things will be sour for a while before you can make them sweet again. I remember as a young couple taking all of the kids on vacation. They played this game in the car called "sweet or sour" and they tried to get passengers in passing cars to smile and wave at them. If they smiled and waved, they were sweet, but if they did not, they were sour. It always surprised me how many people did not actually smile and wave at my adoring kids! Haha—but I know that sometimes people are in a place where they are just having to endure the lemons until they can find the ingredients of life to change the recipe.

Opiate and Heroin addiction, or addiction in general, can do that to people. It puts them and often times their families in a "sour" place in life and they have to endure the journey there until they can come to terms with it or find a way to change it. It is one of the most sour places of life in my opinion. It sticks with you until you think you absolutely cannot breathe one more breath. The good thing about the low places in life though is that NOTHING can separate us from the love of God—no matter how sour it gets. I know when Davis died, life was so sour that I didn't even know if I could continue to breathe. There was a place in the Bible that I would go to read and it gave me great strength through the darkest days of my life. Romans 8: 38-39 gave me more comfort than anything else I could grasp.

"38 For I am persuaded, that neither death, nor life, nor angels, nor principalities, nor powers, nor things present, nor things to come, 39 Nor height, nor depth, nor any other creature, shall be able to separate us from the love of God, which is in Christ Jesus our Lord."

Not only did it give me strength, but it gave me great comfort to know that NOTHING was able to separate Davis from the love of God either.

Turning to the Bible in times of heartache has been such a source of strength for me, and more so than anything else in my life, the Bible has helped me to endure the lemons of life. There are so many promises that I hold onto and so many words from Jesus that I take with me everyday of my life that get me through. Next week will be 8 months that we have been without Davis and sometimes I think each day gets harder and harder as it becomes more real and more forever!

Red Ribbon Week has probably been one of the most emotional weeks of my life since his passing. Although I know it is a great opportunity to help others and to get the word out there about drugs and the dangers they entail, it has also been a constant reminder to me that people die from drugs. My son died from drugs and that will never change. There's no way to say it and make it sound good or honorable. He died from drugs and it was a tragedy.

The past 8 months has been a sour time for my family, but we have endured it and we will continue to endure the loss forever. There have been "sweet" moments and even "sweet" days, but God gets us through the "sour," because NOTHING can separate us from His love—even on the "sourest" of days. Thank you God for your enduring love that makes our lives a little sweeter everyday.

10/31/14 – Constructive Act # 225 – Plan Now For The Holidays

Traditionally Halloween marks the date when we begin to make Holiday decisions regarding Thanksgiving and Christmas. We begin to decide whose house we will go to for Thanksgiving and where we will spend our Christmas holidays. A recovering addict needs to be included in these decisions. They need to prepare themselves for possible "triggers" they will encounter throughout the season especially if it includes a trip back to a place where they were actively using. Also, if you are visiting in Grandparents' homes, or anywhere other then your own home, make sure all medications are locked up and out of sight. Don't leave things to chance.

Take precautions, safety proof for addiction, and respect the recovering addicts' decisions; they have learned to guard themselves and protect against their triggers.

If you are spending any time with a recovering addict—especially one who is early into recovery, you need to understand drug triggers. According to The Palm Beach Institute, "Drug triggers can be categorized into three main categories: environmental triggers, re-exposure triggers and stress triggers. Environmental triggers can include those places and events that can induce thoughts and cravings. Those physical places can include bars, parks, street corners, houses or other places in which a recovering addict's drug and alcohol use took place. Re-exposure triggers refer to specific events or circumstances that bring the recovering person into proximity to drug and alcohol use. Stress triggers are those triggers that are closely tied to a recovering addict's re-entry into the regular world after treatment. A recovering person may have insufficient skills for handling the social and peer pressures regarding use and may also have insufficient skills in regard to handling both negative emotions and interpersonal conflict. Those stresses may lead an individual back to drug use since the use of drugs was seen as a coping and calming mechanism."

The holidays can certainly bring on a great deal of stress for any of us, but especially for someone who may be working hard to maintain his or her sobriety. If you are a recovering addict, be proactive and start now to develop a plan for dealing with the triggers. Make sure that you are adopting a healthier diet and lifestyle in recovery. Putting the right nutrients in your body not only takes care of the physical side of things but feeling good also provides mental stability as well. Take up a hobby or carry a good book with you wherever you go. It will keep your mind off of things from the past and allow you to concentrate on healthier more productive things.

Here is a good strategy for getting past a trigger from The Palm Beach Institute: "A technique that is often employed is what is called 'urge surfing.' With this technique the recovering addict can visualize the craving as a wave that has to be ridden from the top of it until it crests."

Most importantly in getting through the holidays, if you are in recovery or spending time with a recovering addict, make sure the avenue for communication is wide open. "Being able to talk to family, friends and those in recovery about cravings and drug triggers is essential. Being able to be open about those feelings of using can provide catharsis and release and help to restore honesty."

The holidays are a time for family, friends and fun. If you are a recovering addict's family member or parent, help them prepare for the holidays by laying the foundation for open communication and by utilizing proactive planning. This will reduce the stress for both of you and your recovering addict will feel the love and support that you are offering by helping them to protect themselves.

11/1/14 – Constructive Act #226 – Find Out What You Don't Know

I just spent the last 30 minutes on a phone call with a friend from my past helping her come to terms with her life situation: living with a 26-year-old opiate/heroin addict. I spoke from my heart and she spoke from her heart, and we both knew that no matter how much we knew and shared with each other, no one has the answers for heroin addicts. How do you turn your back on you own child—no matter the age—and tell them you understand they have a disease, but you cannot help them with it, and "Good luck"? As a mother, I know no one is ready and willing to hear this! I know for a fact, if I had thrown my child out of the house and into the streets, he would have ended up with his dealer. He would have ended up with his dealer, robbing and stealing to get what he needed. That's how strong the addiction and the obsession is. It's not a choice and will power is not an option. If I had a "do-over" I would look to medical solutions such as Suboxone, Vivitrol, or Naltrexone implants. I would have walked out of Rehab with him and gone straight to the Doctor's office for a Vivitrol shot. I would not have even considered asking my sweet child to go cold-turkey and suck it up! That's asking the impossible from what I have learned. Asking an IV heroin addict to stop in any way, shape, form or fashion, is just RIDICULOUS!

I also learned from talking with my sweet friend from the past that the biggest problem out there is that people still don't know what they don't know. I'm telling her about Vivitrol and Naloxone kits, and she is listening to me and saying that she had no idea that these options were even available and she needs to know more about what I know. How is it possible that people still don't know about Naloxone kits and the Vivitrol shot? That blows my mind! The two most important advances in opiate/heroin addiction and people deep in the throes of the addiction don't know of either option. How can this be? I'm blown away by the lack of awareness in the midst of an epidemic. I am blown away, but by the same token, I was one of the ones who knew nothing and my own son was an opiate/heroin addict. I knew nothing until it was too late for me. He was dead and he was gone forever. There are no "do-overs" with heroin.

When I say to educate yourselves and plan now for how you will handle this situation, I cannot stress this enough. Just as people planned for polio back in the day, people need to plan to prevent opiate/heroin addiction now. It is real; it is available; it is an epidemic... What are you waiting for? Start with your young children. Don't wait for the school system to educate them about this problem. Don't wait for society to kick in and try through media campaigns to fix this for us. Sit down with your own kids and actively discuss this opiate/heroin epidemic and show them the "bliss to death" scenario they will be choosing to deal with. Make it real and make it authentic for them.

I guess I'm starting to panic a bit as I get phone calls and emails regarding the precious children of our community. Parents and the "Addicts' Keepers" are reaching out to the DDF wanting to know how to "fix" this epidemic and all I can say is that there are no known "absolute" solutions now, but we are actively working on them. It just seems like such a lame answer and such a cop-out for genuine people who are searching for valid solutions. The answers as we know them now are just not sufficient for the epidemic that we are experiencing. If you live in this area, in a very few short days, a magazine will be delivered to your door with the picture of my family—"The Owen 7"—on the front cover, and my story, completely written by me, will be inside the issue. Please read it, read it to your children and have a discussion about it. Put a name and a face and a community on the destruction of this epidemic. Prevention will ALWAYS be the best cure, but for some it is too late for prevention and for those we are actively searching for a solution. There is no cure; it is a disease and once you become a pickle, you can never be a cucumber again. But given the right care, you can be the best and healthiest pickle in the jar, and you can last for a very long time! Hopefully one day, there will be a "cure" for this disease. From what I know, we are very close to identifying the addiction gene, and maybe just maybe, one day there will be a "magical restoration solution" that can take the pickle back to a cucumber again and that is what I continue to pray for everyday!

11/2/14 – Constructive Act #227 – Share Your Story

Here is another story from a young man who attended Into Action Treatment Center in Boynton Beach Florida. He was from Acworth, Ga when he left to be at Boynton Beach. Andrey, the Director of Into Action has made it a point to get the guys and gals from his treatment center to share their stories with us and for this we thank him.

Here is Ryne's story:

First of all I was raised in what I would consider your perfect American Family. I'm the oldest of 3, with a mother and father that loved us unconditionally and gave us everything we ever needed. I moved to Acworth right before my 8th grade school year because of my dad's job.

Immediately I got mixed in with the wrong crowd. I would consider myself the class clown (people-pleaser). I stayed in trouble throughout my school career. I took my first sip of alcohol when I was 7 years old. My dad had let me taste his beer. I remember it to this day. It was a Coors light, and I didn't hate it or love it, I just thought it was cool. I mean, he was my dad and I looked up to him.

Later on it turned into stealing liquor from my parent's cabinet and replacing it with water. Soon came the marijuana and oxycontin. At first it was an occasional thing but I absolutely loved the way it made me feel. Eventually, after the crackdown on pain medication, I was quickly introduced to IV heroin. It was more effective and cheaper. I'm sure you are thinking that's when things went down hill really quickly and let me tell you... YES THEY DID!

I had begun a downward spiral landing myself in jail numerous times, treatment twice and countless IOPs (intensive outpatient facilities) and therapists. I wanted to die, but was too much of a coward so I continued doing the only think I knew disappointing loved ones and shooting dope.

Then by the grace of what I know and consider GOD, I found Andrey and Into Action. With a cut out, clear process, Into Action pushed me to get a sponsor and work the steps how they are laid out in the Big Book of AA. Into Action guided me to learn to finally move on from any past and finally love myself. I had become the man I couldn't have dreamt of being. The staff at Into Action and Andrey really do care and will love you until you learn to love yourself. I am forever grateful to them and would recommend the facility to anybody struggling and looking for a way out.

My name is Ryne S. and I'm 25 years old and 15 months clean and sober.

11/3/14 – Constructive Act #228 – Honor Your Addict

Yesterday in my church was "All Saints Sunday." It was the Sunday in church that the 'Honored Dead" were named and a bell was rung for them. My family stood in honor of Davis and a bell was rung on his behalf. The ceremony was called the "Naming of the Honored Dead." We stood proudly as we remembered our precious son and brother as he was honored with the ringing of the bell. The preacher talked about how people have come before us and people will continue to come after us, but the church will remain steadfast in the midst of change. We were asked to remember those loved ones who have died in the past year and how they had touched our lives and made us better people for having known them.

The choir sang an anthem with a beautiful message:

"Good shepherd of my soul, come dwell within me; take all I am and mold your likeness in me. Before the cross of Christ, this is my sacrifice: a life laid down and ready to follow. The troubled find their peace in true surrender; the prisoners their release from chains of anger. In springs of living grace, I find a resting place to rise refreshed, determined to follow. I'll walk this narrow road with Christ before me, where thorns and thistles grow and cords ensnare me. Though doubted and denied, He never leaves my side, but lifts my head and calls me to follow. And when my days are gone, my strength is failing, He'll carry me along through death's unveiling. Earth's struggles overcome, heaven's journey just begun, to search Christ's depths and ever to follow."

It was such a beautiful service, but right in the middle of the service, a fire alarm went off and the entire congregation had to evacuate. In the midst of such a beautiful service it reminded me of the beautiful life that I spent with my sweet child for the first 18 years of his life. It was a fairy tale beginning and he was everything that any parent could have ever hoped for. He was the perfect big brother and role model for his younger siblings and the perfect best friend for his big sister. Then in the midst of his fairy tale life, the alarm went off and all of the sudden he was an opiate/heroin addict and the fairy tale life that we knew and loved had come to an end. We evacuated life as we knew it and our fairy tale existence was forever lost.

There were no real warning signs for us and it happened all of a sudden. We were caught unaware and left out in the cold. Just like the fire alarm at the church this morning, we were left standing out in the cold wondering where the tragedy had begun and what could be done about it. We all looked around aimlessly waiting for answers from others and waiting for the all clear sign to be heard so that we would know the crisis was over and it was safe to resume life as we knew it. Unfortunately, for our family, our "all- clear" sign never came and instead we had to cremate one of our members.

We miss him everyday and we know and love him for the ways he made us better. So we honored him yesterday with our presence and our "standing in recognition" when his name was called and his bell was rung. It felt wonderful because he was remembered but devastating because he was gone as we stood proudly in honor of our beloved son and brother. We honored him in our hearts and in our memories yesterday at church and it was an honor and a privilege to recognize him and the impact he had on each of our lives. He touched each of us and made us better individuals for having known and loved him. We are who we are because he was in our lives and he added meaning and purpose to each of us. He taught us things in life and he taught us things in death. He made us who we are and we will forever hold him in our hearts until we meet again.

Hopefully you have not lost a loved one to addiction, but if you have a loved one who is suffering from addiction, take the opportunity to let them know the impact they have had on your life and how you are a better person for having known them. Encourage them by reminding them of their strengths, and support them by realizing and accepting their shortcomings as an addict and reminding them that it is a disease and you are there for them on their journey. I only wish my journey with my beloved son had been a little longer and had concluded with a happier ending.

11/4/14 – Constructive Act #229 – Exercise Your Right To Vote

Today in Cobb County—and other communities across the nation—it is election day. Men and women throughout the ages fought and died for you to have this privilege. If you are of age and not registered to vote, shame on you! But if you are registered and choose not to vote, that's even worse. Polls open at 7:00 am and close at 7:00 pm and you need to be there to cast your vote and have a say in your community and your state.

The DDF cannot and will not endorse any candidate, but I can tell you a few facts about some of the things going on in our community involving the prescription drug epidemic. Beginning with Governor Deal, on April 24, 2014—Governor Nathan Deal Signed the 911 Medical Amnesty/Naloxone Law. This law, better known as the Good Samaritan Law, provides amnesty for those people who call for help or seek help for someone who is in physical duress due to a drug overdose. It further allows Naloxone to be prescribed and given out to people who may be in need of having one. This law is the reason that we were able to hand out the Naloxone kits at the October Symposium and it is the reason that we will be able to hand them out again at the January Symposium.

Attorney General, Sam Olens, will be our January 15, Symposium speaker; the title of the Symposium will be "Laws, Limits and Loopholes." Sam is a daily reader of the DDF and has "liked" our Facebook page. His office just finished a competition for the youth of our community in which they were encouraged to create and submit 30 second videos warning of the perils of prescription drugs taken illegally. He was also quoted in the Marietta Daily Journal on several occasions lately voicing his concerns over this crisis. He is invested in helping us find a solution and making some changes that will save lives that are being lost because of opiates/heroin.

State Representative, Sam Teasley, also attended our October Symposium. He serves House District 37 which includes a large portion of Marietta City limits with some unincorporated Cobb County to both the west and northeast of the city limits. There are many great candidates on the ballot today and I'm sure some of the others are concerned and invested in the epidemic of prescription drugs that lead to heroin use and how they are affecting our community. Get out and vote and then not only do you have you have the right, but you also have the responsibility to hold your elected official's feet to the fire to work hard and make a difference in our community. We need our voices to be heard in the coming weeks, months, and years and we have to earn the right to be heard by exercising our right to VOTE! See you at the polls!

11/5/14 – Constructive Act #230 – Enjoy The Dividends

Every day as I get home from work and sit down to begin work on the DDF, I get messages that concern me, messages that are filled with desperation, messages searching for information, but my favorite messages are those that are from the people who are in recovery and celebrating milestones. I hear things lik, "I have 90 days of sobriety" or "I have 6 months clean" or "today marks my first year in recovery." These messages bring joy to my heart and my heart swells with pride for these people who are working so hard and are able to enjoy the dividends.

Yesterday was one of those days for the DDF. Yesterday marked 8 months that we have been on this earth without Davis. Every time the 4th of the month rolls around, we add another month to our journey of grief. But, our family has survived and we have been able to focus on doing what we feel God has called us to do through the Davis Direction Foundation. Yesterday was also a day that we got to enjoy some of the dividends of our hard work. The DDF got word of our first Naloxone kit save. One of our kits that was handed out at the October Symposium was used to save a life and for that we are celebrating. Yesterday, our Charles Schwab account was opened and we received our very first shares of stock as a donation. Watch the FB page and the website for how all of that will work. Yesterday, several of the candidates who have been strong supporters of the DDF were elected to a second term and that was a celebration for us as well. Yesterday we delivered the last of the DDF rubber bracelets that were ordered and we placed over 10,000 bracelets on the arms of people in our community to promote awareness. Yesterday, "Our Town" magazine was delivered to a majority of the 50,000 homes in our community that are on the mailing list to receive it. One entire page in the magazine is devoted to the DDF and the work that is being done in our community to promote awareness, affect change and save lives. Today we are enjoying the dividends of our hard work and celebrating our accomplishments.

Some days I feel completely overwhelmed in a good way because I feel like the DDF was one of those internet entities that was rolled out there and we were completely unprepared for what would happen next. It took off with such steam and force, that we are behind the 8 ball and always working hard to catch up. This week alone, we have hired a website consultant and are in meetings to make our website worthy of the people who need to use it for information and insight. We have opened our 3rd account to be able to accept donations and make investments in order to do what we need to do to adhere to our mission statement. We have placed a second order for Naloxone kits in order to provide them at the January Symposium. We are actively working on a contract for state chapters of the DDF to open across the nation. We will receive our first annual dated Christmas Ornament in order to raise money and we will begin shipping those out. We will continue to actively add names and addresses to our mailing list. Next week, we will send 2 of our Board members to an investment seminar to make sure we are making the most of our contributions so that we can make the most difference according to our Foundation. We are currently working on a 2015 Budget including short term, mid-term and long term goals that we will work toward, all in alignment with our mission statement. We are filing for our own 501(c)(3) next week so that we can do things in addition to the things that are allowed by the Cobb Community Foundation that we will continue to be a part of. We will have our 5th DDF Board meeting over a period of 7 months making plans for becoming a better Foundation. We are "moving and shaking" and we are enjoying the dividends of our hard work.

If you are an addict in recovery, you need to sit down with a pencil and paper and do what I just did above. List the things you have been able to accomplish since you have put your mind and heart into your recovery. Sure, you may have had some setbacks and disappointments, but they do not define you! Keep "moving and shaking" in your recovery and don't forget to enjoy the dividends, and celebrate the accomplishments. If you have even one day in recovery, list the good things that happened in that one day! It's a beginning and it will only lead to greater things. The DDF is here for you along your journey. Let us know what you need and we will do what we can to make it happen!

11/6/14 – Constructive Act #231 – Realize Dr. Phil is Not The Heroin Hero

Last night as Michael settled down to do his research as he does every night for the DDF, Dr. Phil's show regarding heroin addiction popped up as one of the first links. He began watching this show and then sent it to me to watch. This morning, we were both still as angry as we could be that he would stoop to "ratings" to dramatize and sensationalize this DISEASE and set back the efforts of every organization in existence to try and find a solution for the addicts and their families who are deep in the throes of opiate/heroin addiction. First of all let me say that the words "God" and "Disease" were not mentioned even once throughout the entire show. Secondly, even though he did say that no one was immune, he chose a family with not one, but three heroin addicts and a mother who openly snorted cocaine and was daily handing her three daughters money for their addiction to get them to "leave her alone." And finally, in my training as a Counselor, the word Counselor has always been synonymous with the word Helper. Yesterday's show did very little, if anything, to help the addict or the families of addicts who are trying their best to do their best with the available and affordable resources that they can find.

To talk about opiate/heroin addiction in a conversation void of the word "disease" is just absolutely wrong. Enough research and documentation has been done that proves that an addiction gene is involved as well as other biological, environmental and developmental factors. Addiction is a brain disease and it should be treated as such. To go into all the research involved in this disease would be impossible in just one "CA" post, but rest assured it is a disease, and to address the problem without noting this is just ludicrous. To leave God out of the conversation is also very disturbing to me. Even when Dr. Phil turned to one of his chosen Rehab Directors at the end of the show, the guy responded that he was hoping for a "Miraculous Recovery." The word "miraculous" to me indicates that God will be present in this recovery and that without Him, there will be no "Miraculous" recovery. If you read the posts every Sunday, God is such a huge part of opiate/heroin recovery, and to leave Him out of the equation is beyond belief to me.

Dr. Phil did have it right when he stated that no one was immune to this happening in his or her family. With that being said, why in the world did he choose a family with three heroin addicts and a mother who was admittedly a drug addict and openly snorted and could be bribed with cocaine? This is not the "average" family dealing with the epidemic of opiate/heroin addiction. There are those of us that did all, or most of the things we were taught to do by the rehabs available to us. Those rehab facilities were "self-described" to be the "Best in the Southeast," or the "#1 in Recovery Rate." The sad reality is that no-one in this nation has the absolute answers to opiate/heroin addiction. If they did, it would not be the fastest growing epidemic in our nation and addicts would not be dying every 19 minutes and surpassing the death rate of automobile accidents.

Why was so much blame placed in this show? He very definitely placed blame on the parents for enabling these kids and then turned and placed blame on the oldest daughter for funding the habits of her other sisters. He did more to demoralize this family and shame and embarrass them than he did to help them. Heroin addiction cannot be a "blame game." In this show I kept hearing words like "hate," "disgust," "crime," "whore," "junkie," and then the phrase "grow a pair" was used during every commercial break to keep the audience tuned in to the drama. How very sad! Do you really believe that any good and moral man in his right mind would go in search of help, publicly admitting that his child is a heroin addict after watching this show?

Where was the help in this show? Did anyone hear about Vivitrol, or the Naltrexone implant? Did anyone hear of changes in insurance legislation so that those of us who don't have Dr. Phil's money might be able to help our loved ones? Did anyone hear any talk of any resources out there where you can go to find help or any "Living With a Heroin Addict 101" book suggestions? Did anyone notice that Dr. Phil's top three solutions were 1) Rehab 2) Jail and 3) streets? Does Dr. Phil know of the problems that rehabs have with death rates because addicts are continuing to get their "fixes" inside the walls of the rehab facilities? Can Dr. Phil supply us with the government-regulated breakdown of facility evaluations so that we can pick and choose the best ones? No—because it is publicly and virtually non-existent! Does Dr. Phil know that the jails are full of drugs mostly because that's where all of the addicts are now? Ask any addict who has been in prison how easy it was for them to get their fix. Prisoners have a whole "green stamp" system for getting and using drugs behind bars. It's a business within a business of sorts! And then of course we all know what happens on the streets—Addicts die or get additional diseases from living conditions or dirty needles! Did Dr. Phil even mention the life-saving antidote Naloxone that can give a dying addict a second chance?

If Dr. Phil wants to do something to help the ever-growing epidemic of opiate/ heroin addiction in our nation then he needs to provide funding for getting the "Medical Amnesty Law" passed and increased access to Naloxone in all 50 states. He needs to provide funding for drug dogs and training for better security measures in prisons and rehabs that will keep the drugs out. He needs to provide funding for legislation that will recognize Addiction as a disease and require insurance companies to pay for the treatment of addicts, so that they can all have a "fighting chance" as another one of his rehab experts said yesterday. These are just a few suggestions for starters. I could write a book on this!

As for the three sisters and their parents, I would encourage and request that all of the DDF prayers warriors put them at the top of your prayer list. I cannot imagine the humiliation that they suffered at the "voice" of Dr. Phil yesterday. They need our prayers for Hope and Healing and most of all Recovery. Please help us undo the damage by sharing this on your page and restoring Hope and Healing to the families who are searching for answers.

11/7/14 – Constructive Act #232 – Understand That Love Is Not Enough

Everyone wants to believe love is always going to be enough to get you through anything. All of our lives we grew up watching good conquer evil because love won out. We watched stories with happy endings, fairy tales, cartoons, and especially the Disney movies where love always conquers everything. Opiate/ heroin addiction is different. Love is not enough because there is a brain change going on and the person that you have loved and longed for throughout the addiction is not really the person that you are dealing with anymore.

Anyone who knew Davis knew that he loved life, his family, and his friends with his whole heart. Before the drugs, Davis' love was focused on all of the right things. He loved God, his family, his friends and life in general. He genuinely loved others and would do anything to help someone in need. He was the one when we saw a homeless person on the side of the road holding up a sign that would begin to ask what we had in the car that we could give to them. Whether it was a bottle of water, a pack of crackers or a piece of fruit, he usually came up with some sort of offering.

Once the drugs took over, he loved the drugs more than anything else. He wanted to be able to give them up. He told us on more than one occasion that he wished he had never ever taken anything. He told us that we would never understand what it felt like to be so conflicted on the inside knowing what he really wanted to do but not being able to do it. He told his brothers and his sisters that they had the same propensity as he did to become an addict and that he never wanted them to ever take anything. In fact, that was the last conversation that he ever had with his older sister Chelsea. As a family we found out that he was right, we never knew how conflicted that he was on the inside and what control the drugs had over every ounce of his being. If love had been enough, he would have been able to come back to us and to his precious daughter that he loved more than life itself. But love is not enough when a person becomes an opiate/heroin addict. Deep in the throes of addiction, the person that you have always known and loved is not the person that you are dealing with anymore. The brain changes that have taken place due to the drugs have turned them into someone else.

Detox, intensive therapy and the love of God is what can bring them back, but it has to be a combination of many things and sometimes they may not get the combination right at first. Many of these addicts even need drug therapy to help them with their journey of recovery. Drugs like Vivitrol and Naltrexone implants may be necessary to block the opiate high and provide a psychological advantage that allows the addict to understand that no matter what they take, it will be a waste of money and time because the opiate receptors will be blocked by the drug therapy. The intensive therapy may come in the form of individual therapy, group therapy or even a residential treatment center followed by a halfway house. Sometimes it takes years and actually addiction is something that an addict will battle for the rest of his or her life.

There is a pill that we are praying for that is in the research stages that will hopefully re-set the opiate receptors and put them back to their pre-drug condition. This pill would revolutionize drug addiction as we know it. It would work similar to the Ibogaine therapy that is now available in Mexico and Canada that has hallucinogenic properties that keep it from being legal in the United States. It would in fact take the pickle back to the cucumber! Please begin to pray with us that this research will move quickly and successfully and that very soon we will have an "absolute" answer for those people who have been afflicted by the disease of opiate/heroin addiction.

11/8/14 – Constructive Act #233 – Never Lose Hope

One thing that an addict and an "addict's keeper" and the family members and loved ones of addicts must never lose is HOPE! When you lose hope you lose everything. I just feel like so much good is happening for those deep in the throes of opiate/heroin addiction right now that everyone needs to focus on the future and hang on with everything you can muster. When you have top billing in the area of "cause of deaths" in the United States, you have to realize that people are beginning to pay attention. Addiction now out numbers automobile accidents as the #1 cause of death in the United States. These are the kind of statistics and charts that wake people up and open their eyes to things they may not have realized or even accepted as of yet. This is the kind of information that offers HOPE to the people who are suffering from the leading cause of death in the United States, because people always try to tackle the biggest problems with the most energy. You have to know that there is HOPE and you have to know that we are trying our best to help find that HOPE for families across our nation.

If you are suffering from opiate/heroin addiction, PLEASE seek help that will allow you to hang on until we figure out some things. There are many drug therapies in place and several opiate blockers as well as rehab clinics and group therapies that will give you strength and help you stay the course until we find some solid answers. There are churches out there that are opening their doors and their hearts to help individuals as well as families who need support during the time of crisis as it relates to addiction. There are books and articles and even YouTube videos that provide information and inspiration that will give you HOPE and allow healing to take place and hopefully lead you into recovery. There are designated websites and Facebook pages just like the Davis Direction Foundation that are designed to reach out to addicts and their families to help you and others understand the severity and complications associated with the disease of opiate/heroin addiction. There is HOPE, but you have to be willing to search for it and then apply it to your life.

Personally, I believe in fate; I believe in karma; I believe that things happen for a reason and I believe that God sends messages to us in the strangest ways sometimes. Today I unwrapped a Chinese Fortune cookie and my fortune read, "Your present plans are going to succeed." Well remember last week when I wrote to "INTERPRET THINGS IN YOUR FAVOR?" well today I decided to interpret my fortune in my favor. I know that my fortune was related to the DDF; I know this because I believe in HOPE. Hope is what keeps us "Moving onward through life... Looking upward to God."

In the 13th chapter of 1st Corinthians, Paul says, "12 For now we see through a glass, darkly; but then face to face: now I know in part; but then shall I know even as also I am known. 13 And now abideth faith, hope, charity, these three; but the greatest of these is charity.

People have been holding onto HOPE for as long as anyone can remember, and Paul categorized it as one of the three remaining things. Surely there is a reason for this. Hold on to your hope, and pray that there is an answer for this epidemic that is closer than we know. Never lose hope.

11/9/14 – Constructive Act #234 – Share Your Story

This week's story comes from a husband and a father who truly was a desperate man. Hearing this story not only rips your heart out, but it also gives you so much HOPE if you are still deep in the throes of opiate/heroin addiction.

Here is his story:

My journey through God's eyes: It was not too long ago I had already planned my death. I had moved out of the house because my wife did not trust me anymore. I had lost my job and most of my friends. Eventually things got so bad, my wife let me move back in the house but not in our room. I was in the guest room and that did not make me happy because I knew she did not want me there and I knew it was only a matter of time before she was going to make me move out of the house. She knew and I knew that I was still doing drugs. So, I had made up my mind when that happened, I was going over to the old man's house where I was living the first time my wife threw me out, get his gun out of his room and blow my brains out. That's how far I had let drugs take over my mind. They made me feel like I had nothing to live for but God knew I had everything to live for......my wife, my life, my children and most of all for Jesus Christ.

Just when I thought it was all over, God spoke to me and told me... "do not speak of killing yourself again, because I have a better plan for you." My mind was saying , "Thank you God," but my body was saying, "You can't do this; you know you need drugs to survive." I didn't know it but at that moment God had already taken over my life. He was leading the way for me, so I picked up the phone and I called the Into Action treatment center and the next day I was on my way. I had nothing to lose... so why not?

Before that day I had never been on an airplane before and I always said I would never get on an airplane, but for some reason I had no fear of getting on that airplane. I do know now it was God helping me along the way. So when I got to the Into Action, I said, "Well, here I am again" because I had already been to the The Recovery Place in 2010 and I thought it was going to be the same old thing. Little did I know that God had a bigger plan for me.

When I first got there and went into that room, I felt the presence of God and it made me feel so good and relaxed that I could forget about everything around me. Then about 10 days after I got there a man named Bobby came for treatment. He and I hit it off very well. That was the first time I realized that if you give God time, He will deliver. So every morning I would get up and go to my classes and everyday I started to notice that I wanted to go to class more and more not knowing that God was leading me in the right direction the whole time. One night we watched a movie called Passion of the Christ. When I saw what Jesus did for me, it made me very ashamed that I had not done more for my God and Jesus.

So, when I got back to my room, I got on my knees and said "God, please forgive me for not serving you the way I should," and at that moment I felt God come down in me. I thought I was going to bust open inside. I felt all my troubles leave me and at once it was like He said, "Give it all to Me my son, and you will not have to worry about it again." My life changed right then. See when I was doing drugs, I had lost contact with God. All the people I thought were against me were leading me on the right path. I would lie to my wife knowing the whole time she knew what was going on because she asked God to show her when I was doing drugs and He did. Even though she knew, I would still do drugs, not because I wanted to, but my body would tell my mind that I needed drugs.

See, that is what happens when you take God out of your life. You lose all control, but by me giving my will back to God and getting on my knees every night, I now have control through God's eyes and now I can live in peace for the rest of my life. Thank you, God and Into Action Treatment Center for being there for me.

David Thaxton

11/10/14 – Constructive Act #235 – Remain Calm and Proceed With Caution

Well the time has come that I have dreaded for many months now and decisions have to be made. The Holidays are upon us and we are faced with the decision of breaking with tradition or continuing to do what we have always done, knowing every step of the way that my thoughts will be spinning with the absence of my precious Davis. It's not just my decision, it's a family decision and the 6 of us have to come to consensus on how we want to handle this holiday season. Some decisions are easier than others—like the things we will do in his memory. But those things are new and in addition to the other things. Those things will be healing and will be active additions to a response for filling a void that we all will have. It's the things that we have done for the past 20 years where we will miss his presence and have to decide whether or not we will forego the tradition or replace his part. It's heartbreaking and hard to approach without falling apart, but we all know one thing for sure. In just 17 short days, Thanksgiving will be here and we will thank God for allowing us 20 years with one of the most lovable, and unforgettable treasures of His kingdom, and we will beg Him for the strength to help us through the day.

In some ways, I want to sleep through the day and never get out of bed. I want the day to come and go and the day after to be here and I go on with my life as if the holiday never happened. I want to ignore Thanksgiving!

But, I know that the Bible says to Praise God in all things and I want to obey the word. How do I say "Thank you, God, for choosing my child?" How do I praise His name over the circumstances of the past year? That's a hard one for me and for the rest of my family as well. How do any of us praise God for the addiction gene and the misery it has caused throughout centuries of time? How do we continue to praise God for the destruction that it continues to cause for families all over our nation? How do we say "Thank you, God" on Thanksgiving day?

Well, I don't know where or when or even who we will be amongst on November 27th 2014, but I do know one thing for sure. I will say "Thank you God for allowing me to be the mother of one of the most beautiful souls that ever walked the face of the earth. Thank you for the beautiful memories and for the lessons I learned from this wonderful young man. Thank you for the 20 Thanksgivings before that we shared our traditions and thanked you together. Thank you for the lives that he touched and the friends he made. Thank you that he made a difference on this earth and that he continues to make a difference even in death. Thank you for your plan of salvation that allowed you to take him home and that allows me and mine to meet him on the other side one day. Thank you that his body is whole again and that he is no longer suffering from the disease of addiction. Thank you, God that I can now realize that it is better to have loved and lost than to have never loved at all. Thank you, God that you gave me 5 other beautiful people to walk this journey with that loved him and miss him every ounce as much as I do. Thank you, God, for Davis Henry Owen. The world was a better place because he was in it."

I'm not alone in this predicament, other families stand with mine this holiday season missing a loved one or dealing with the disease of addiction as they sit down at the Thanksgiving table to thank God for ALL things. We don't have all the answers and none of us for certain understand God's plan as it unfolds before our very eyes and hearts. But, we must have faith in the plan and in the word. We must remain calm and proceed with caution, listening every step of the way to God's voice so that when He speaks we will hear. We will hear how He wants us to make a difference moving forward helping others with this disease. We are all here for a purpose and I'm sure I have found my purpose in life. I am listening and trying with every ounce of my being to heed God's word and help others who are going down a path that my family has gone down before. We obviously made mistakes, but we are laying it all out so that hopefully others can learn from our mistakes and have a different outcome.

Reach out to others this holiday season and let them know that you are here for them and that you don't judge them, but rather you thank God that he spared you and your family from the horrors of addiction. No one is immune and just because you are free from the disease of addiction this holiday season, doesn't mean that you will remain free from addiction in your family. Take time to learn what you don't know moving forward so that you can hopefully prevent what happened in my family from happening in yours.

We will thank God for each other this Thanksgiving and no matter where we are or who we are with, we will hold each other tightly and remember the one we can't hold physically, but we can hold forever in our hearts. We will thank God for you Davis, and we will forever be grateful that for 20 beautiful and very short years you were in our physical fold and we will forever more long for that touch. Remain calm and proceed with caution as you thank God for all of your many blessings; that's what the "Owen 7" will be doing for Thanksgiving

11/11/14 – Constructive Act #236 – Dream Big and Make It Happen

This past week, the DDF Board of Directors met and we talked about a business plan and our short term, mid term and long term goals. What do we see in our future and how do we see our Foundation making a difference in 2 years, 5 years and in 10 years? WOW—a lot can happen in that amount of time. In fact, 10 years would have been half a lifetime for Davis. No person has the true capacity to see down the road to 10 years time, but people have been known and revered for their ability to use their forward thinking skills to orchestrate the future and how people can make a difference. The DDF Board talked about some great ideas and some projects that we hope will one day come to fruition. We are developing a business plan, and then marketing strategies to make sure that we can produce and finance a plan that will allow us to reach our mission of promoting awareness, affecting change and saving lives until we can reach a solid solution to address this epidemic.

As a Counselor and teaching kids to "brainstorm," we always say, "the sky's the limit." In other words, there are no bad answers or no limits in the brainstorming process. Anything goes and that is often the way that you get "out-of-the-box" thinking and answers. Someone's funniest or most outrageous answers spark an idea in someone else's train of thought and then all of a sudden, someone has a great idea to address a problem. It's a process that is designed to help a group of people come up with a solution that couldn't have been thought of without a group effort. It's building upon the thought processes of others, and it works!

Some of our ideas included a Christmas Eve "Lighting of the Way" ceremony, a National Conference in the next year or so and even a Rehab Center or a halfway house. These are just some of our "Pie in the Sky" ideas and efforts that we think would have a huge impact on the future of opiate/heroin addiction. Will they all happen? We don't know, but they have been thrown out there because one or more of us thought it could and possibly should happen.

Dream BIG—and if you are an addict, then this includes you! What have you always wanted to become? Do you have a vision and a place you go inside your head that makes you successful or makes you at peace? If the answer is "yes", then let's figure out together how to make it happen. If the answer is "no", then let's figure out how to make the answer "yes" and get you moving in the right direction. I've been told all throughout my life, and I could probably go to "Google" right now and find any number of studies to support the fact that people who "dream big" and "set goals" are the people who succeed in life. I do know more than a few people through the DDF who have "come back" from a drug filled life to become successful and make a great living while raising a family and sharing a beautiful marriage. I also know of others, in the late 50's and 60's who are still living in the parents' basements, still on drugs being supported by society in some way and wondering when they will—or even wishing to die.

We all have choices in life, and choosing to be "drug-free" is just the beginning. There are organizations and establishments out there who are committed to helping addicts and their families. There are therapies out there that are new and cutting edge that you can put in place to try and enter into recovery. Different things work for different people, but if you are not actively trying...... nothing will work. Reach out to the DDF if you are in need of help and let us offer resources and information that could possibly help you find your way back. We have made it a calling and a mission to help those who are affected by opiate/heroin addiction. Let us do what we have chosen to do by helping you to "dream big" and then helping you make those dreams come true.

11/12/14 – Constructive Act #237 – Allow Answers

Questions and answers are the source of how data is gathered in the opiate/heroin epidemic. Statistics already tell us that 12-17 year olds are the youngest group to experiment with these drugs. We know this because children are self-reporting as well as being hospitalized for overdose. If we already know this information, then shouldn't the education and the prevention programs be aimed at this age group? We have to find out what they know in order to combat the epidemic that we are experiencing today. Yesterday on the news program I was watching, I saw a mother who was upset that her child had an opportunity to participate in a questionnaire. The questionnaire had questions about illegal drugs and even specifically mentioned meth and cocaine. The Mom thought that her child didn't even know what meth was and that the questions were "unacceptable by any means." She further thought that the survey could peek his interest in drugs and he might fall prey to peer pressure to participate. So, long story short, she "opted out" for her son and he did not participate.

Now for all of my local readers, this happened in Cherokee County—where they had several overdose deaths last week due to opiate/heroin abuse. No—they were not 12 year olds that died, but 12 year old have died in our nation from opiate/ heroin use. In addition, the DDF is a strong believer in the fact that prevention will always be the best solution. The mother was concerned that her child did not know about specific drugs. To me, if you have a 12 year old who does not know about meth and opiates, then your child is in more danger that the kids who do know about these drugs and know what to look for and what to avoid. The kids who have had these hard conversations with their parents are way ahead of the curve than the kids who are not. I'll never forget the first time my daughter came home in 6th grade and told me of the officers and the drug dogs who came to her Cobb County Middle School and found pot stashed in the bathroom above the ceiling tiles. I was mortified! But, my daughter knew what pot or marijuana was and that it was smoked or baked in brownies and that she needed to be aware of the fact that it did exist.

I've said this on more than one occasion, but my 14 year old daughter was offered prescription medication this past summer as a gesture of compassion because she was asking for Advil. The girl who offered it to her was completely unaware that her orthopedic pain prescription was not a medicine that could be "legally" shared due to the dangers of addiction and overdose. Thank God my daughter knew better than to accept any prescription drugs from anyone other than a doctor for her own treatment.

I will tell you as a counselor what I tell other parents about opting out of any program offered through the school system. First and foremost, the school system has chosen the specific age group because of a need that has been determined through research. Secondly and perhaps more importantly, if your child is not allowed to participate in a program that is offered to his or her classmates school-wide, you can rest assured that as soon as there is any free time such as recess or lunch, they will be inquiring about what they missed. As a result, your child will get the watered down and possibly incorrect version of the content of the program because they will be getting it second-hand from another classmate! So your real choice is not do you want your child to participate, but rather, who do you want your child to hear the message from—a trained and approved teacher/speaker, or another child in his or her grade? I know what I would choose.

Now I will tell you this. When programs are offered to your child and there is an opt-out opportunity, parents are, more often than not, invited to preview the program or preview the survey. The percentage of parents who actually take advantage of this preview opportunity is usually less than 1% at my school. So I'm advocating, that parents need to be more involved and more purposeful in having the hard conversations that should take place at home regarding the content of the lesson or survey that will be administered at the school.

Ideally, the school is only reinforcing what the parents have previously taught at home. Unfortunately, in many cases, this is not the way it occurs. Parents, please understand, if the school system is using precious instructional time to have the kids participate in a survey or attend a lesson of importance, then there is a reason a good reason. So please allow your kids to ANSWER the questions and participate in the lessons. They will be supervised during the process and provided opportunities to ask questions or express concerns to the person in charge of the process. If that person deems it necessary for the child to have further discussion regarding the issue, they will direct them to the correct person and in most cases, give the parents a call.

11/13/14 – Constructive Act #238 – Remember The Seasons Change

Remember The Seasons Change and Life Goes On.

I was awakened early this morning around 3:37 am by the sound of my weather alert, notifying me that Kennesaw, GA was included in a freeze warning. Any other year, my first thought would have been of my beautiful ferns still out on my front porch or the orchids on the back deck, but not this year. This year, my first thought was about the addicts out there who came from beautiful and loving homes, whose loved ones have decided to use tough love and told them to leave. I, along with plenty others at 3:37 a.m. when the alarm went off, or perhaps those up north who are feeling the Polar Blast this week, or those who are maybe shoveling out from underneath a foot of snow, am wondering, where are the children? I paused to say a prayer for them and asked God to keep them warm and safe and hopefully lead them to seek shelter in the form of a rehab center or a church shelter.I worried about the children who have been sleeping out under the stars in the warmer weather, I wondered if they had blankets or hats and gloves. I worried that they may be freezing, maybe literally to death. Living with an addict will change your life forever.

The changing seasons are the worst for me. I have to deal with new memories and replace the things that my sweet Davis used to take care of for me. He would always bring the firewood to the deck and he loved a fire going in the fireplace, so he was the one who would start the fires and have them warm and cozy when I would get home. He was the one who would bundle up and make us laugh with his funny "mad bomber hats" or his "pigtail" hats as I called them. He loved his hats and he loved his "heat" blankets as he called them. About this time every year, we would go in search of a new "heat blanket" because he loved being warm and cozy better than anyone in the family. He would wear fuzzy socks and even fuzzy, furry, funny slippers. He did not like to be cold ever!

His friends in rehab knew this about him. They still talk about the times that he would walk through the halls with a cup of coffee in each hand—not sure if he needed that much coffee or if he was just trying to keep both hands warm. His roommate was so happy that Davis was in the room with him, because they were like two old men keeping the room so warm that others couldn't even stay in there with them. But they liked it warm and cozy, and they liked that they had that in common. The friends at Rehab loved Davis' hats. Anyone who ever knew Davis knew that he liked to be warm! He didn't care how hot it got in the summertime, but in the winter, he hated to be cold! He asked me to bring him extra warm clothing—hats, gloves, jackets, so that he was sure that everyone would have something to stay warm. He loved to share.

I think this is a good time of year to try and convince your loved ones in addiction to enter a recovery center or to get a counselor and begin intense therapy. It's a time of year when the elements of the world are unkind to the homeless and people die when they have no protection. It's a brutal time for those who have nowhere to turn. It's times like these when I wish the DDF were way further down the road in our long-term journey so that we had a place to offer these children to turn. I worry about them and I can't help it. God has laid this on my heart and it is my focus now. I watched Davis take care of "Boo the Cat" when the elements turned harsh outside and he knew he wouldn't survive the winter without shelter from the storms. Davis taught me a lot of things—things that sometimes I didn't even know he was teaching me until I take a look back and see how he modeled things that I can put into place in the future.

Please, if you are reading this post and you are still looking to make donations before the end of the year, consider donating to the DDF so that our long-term journey can come to fruition sooner than later. You can go to our website and donate through the online donations that are set up for credit cards or Paypal, or you can send a check to Cobb Community Foundation at P.O. Box 671868 Marietta, GA 30006-0032 made out to the Davis Direction Foundation. This money will allow us to promote awareness, affect change and save lives through life-saving medical kits that we hand out. It will also allow us to invest in our mid term and long term goals that we are actively planning to pursue. Help us to put an end to the heartache and begin the healing process—Help us to provide hope. No donation is too small. Every penny when added to another penny becomes a work in progress; that's what the DDF is—a work in progress. Please consider helping us progress along our journey.

Our website is www.davisdirection.com. We are currently undergoing an intensive website upgrade. Very soon you will be able to see the difference and the changes made by "524 Creative" our new web developer. We will have a beautiful, informative and powerful website that will be in place by the first of the year and we are excited to be able to offer this to people who need us and count on us. Godspeed.

11/14/14 – Constructive Act #239 – Read and Reread

Read and Reread Until You Understand.

The world of opiate/heroin addiction is a complicated one! When trying to understand the addiction as a disease, sometimes the words and terminology used are not always in layman's terms. Sometimes you need to get the dictionary and the computer out and have them at your fingertips in order to breakdown articles for thorough understanding. I don't always have the patience to do that, but there are quite a few members of the DDF that do have this skill and my husband is one of them. He does most of the research for the DDF and this week he ran across an article that was very informative and powerful. He sent it to the rest of the Board members and even made a phone call to our Medical Director to try and understand just exactly what the article was saying. He has an uncanny ability of reading and rereading things until he can completely grasp the true meaning of the article and then he can in turn break it down for people like me who need the layman version. I have asked him to summarize this article for the DDF Facebook page in order that people can read and understand the progress that we are making toward understanding what addicts are going through and how the medical community is responding. I'm not trying in anyway to insult anyone's intelligence, but sometimes, people just don't have the time to look up everything they need to find in order to understand what someone is trying to say.

There have been some real breakthroughs just this week with the fact that people are actually beginning to talk about the fact that people with mental illness— anxiety, depression, bi-polar, ADHD, OCD—and other mental illnesses as well are actually ending up in jail twice as much as people who are not suffering with these issues. Many times it is due to the fact that they are self-medicating, often with opiates. WSB-TV actually did a segment on this yesterday calling the jails the new asylum rather than a place of incarceration. As a society this seriously needs to be addressed and articles like the one that will follow are the kinds of articles where the research will be found to support this.

I will tell you up front that this is a very long but necessary post that people need to understand. Maybe you want to save it until tomorrow when you have more time over the weekend to try and comprehend what the article is saying. Please READ and REREAD so that you can be an advocate for the addicts who are suffering from opiate/heroin addiction. I will provide the link for the entire article at the end of this post, but first, some of the highlights with Michael's translation that he wrote at my request so that I could better understand. This is one of those articles that you need to pass along to the Dr's in your life so that they can be in on the conversation.

Michael, my husband says, "I am not translating the whole thing and I do not pretend to be a doctor or expert on any of this. I am simply trying to point out what I think to be some of the obvious:"

(THE ORIGINAL ARTICLE)

A significant minority of the population only feel truly well on opioids. In effect, they self-medicate, taking responsibility for their own mental health in defiance of medical orthodoxy.

It would indeed be extraordinary if – alone among the neurotransmitter systems of the brain – the endogenous opioid families were immune from dysfunction. Enkephalins are critical to "basal hedonic tone" i.e. whether we naturally feel happy or sad. Yet the therapeutic implications of a recognition that dysfunctional endogenous opioid systems underlie a spectrum of anxiety disorders and depression are too radical – at present – for the medical establishment to contemplate. In consequence, the use ofopioid based pharmacotherapies for "psychological" pain is officially taboo. The unique efficacy of opioids in banishing mental distress is neglected. Their unrivaled efficacy in treating "physical" nociceptive pain is grudgingly accepted.Later this century and beyond, however, the development of highly selective, site-specific designer drugs and innovative gene-therapies may enhance our native opioid function and revolutionize mental health. Therapeutic intervention targeted on the opioid pathways will potentially enrich the quality of life of even the nominally "well", not least because – by the more enlightened health standards of posterity – we may all be reckoned mentally ill.

Today, by contrast, immense energy is devoted by the authorities into persecuting "illicit" narcotic users. Many drug-"abusers" feel well thanks only to the "non-therapeutic" use of opioids. They are stigmatized, pilloried and criminalized in a futileWar Against Drugs. In the "Inquisition against pleasure", victims of medically sanctioned human-rights abuses – e.g., the hundreds of thousands of drug "offenders" incarcerated in the American gulag – are officially supposed to believe their malaise-ridden drug-naïve states were "normal", "natural" and mentally healthy. In the course of our ill-conceived Drug War, vast resources are dissipated by the state-apparatus in an effort to choke off narcotic production and supply. When these efforts are temporarily successful, drug-deprivation makes the habitual opioid user feel ill; [s]he "cold-turkeys" with characteristic irritability, anhedonia, depression, sickness behavior and sometimes raw physical pain. The ill-effects felt from involuntary deprivation of opioids are taken to demonstrate the likely ill-effects of legalized access, a paradox that might be thought labored were its human costs not so tragic.

When caught up in the criminal justice system, users may be pressured into taking opioid antagonists like naltrexone (Trexan). Such drugs can induce dysphoria and suicidal despair. At best, their use subtly diminishes the victim's capacity ever to feel well. Meanwhile Chinese military surgeons have developed (2003) a new treatment weapon against narcotic users: surgical destruction of the pleasure centers. Western doctors are said to be following these procedures with interest, but are more likely to achieve their functional equivalent by non-surgical means.Even where it is acknowledged that many opioid users have a pre-existing anxiety or depressive disorder in urgent need of relief, those so afflicted are fobbed off with often third-rate psychotropics instead. For a start, the monoamine hypothesis of depression – and the new classes of drug it has spawned (SSRIs, NARIs, SNRIs, NaSSAs, RIMAs etc to complement the dirty old tricyclics and irreversible unselective MAOIs) – is radically incomplete. A minority of people, admittedly, find such drugs effective.

Often taking a licensed antidepressant is better than nothing at all – perhaps in part because of their positive effects on endogenous opioid peptide release. Yet even in the context of controlled clinical trials with relatively high dosage-regimens and artificially good rates of patient-compliance, it's rare for response-rates to reach more than 70%. Rates of full remission of depressive symptoms are far lower, perhaps 25-30%. Out "in the field", the picture is worse still. Adverse side-effects are common. Response may take weeks. Withdrawal reactions can be unpleasant.

A recognition of the crucial role of dopamine, and selective dopamine reuptake blockers, in sub-types of depressive mood-disorders might push response and remission rates higher. The mesolimbic dopamine system is critical to vitality, motivation,libido and a capacity to anticipate reward. Dopaminergics can also act as analgesics. They can also reverse the apathetic sedation induced by some antidepressants and opioid agonists. Yet the FDA stymies the licensing of effective dopamine reuptake-blocking mood-brighteners at home; and applies pressure to deny access to them abroad. This is because of worries about their (sometimes) faster efficacy – and mild psycho-stimulant effect – raise the specter of "abuse-potential"; and proscription, persecution and indiction are favored over consumer education. For Big Brother knows best.

More controversially, adding customized opioids, enkephalinase-inhibitors and kappa-antagonists to our therapeutic armamentarium may prove critical to boosting response- and remission-rates towards 100% in the decades ahead. Crudely, whereas dopamine mediates "wanting", mu opioid agonists mediate "liking". Both systems can be fruitfully enhanced. Depressive and dysthymic people often suffer from a dysfunctional opioid system and anhedonia – an incapacity to experience pleasure. Sometimes orthodox "antidepressants" may even make them feel worse. Yet controlled clinical trials of designer narcotics for refractory and/or melancholic depression, let alone their use by "normal" people with "ordinary" mood-disorders, are not imminent.

In the short-to-medium term, then, we need better-targeted opioids, safer and more site-specific than the present crop. Smarter opioids can potentially be combined with cholecystokinin antagonists (e.g. proglumide); nitric oxide (NO) synthase inhibitors;peroxynitrite-blockers; and also, perhaps, better-designed NMDA receptor antagonists – co-analgesics with potentialantidepressant efficacy that inhibit the onset of tolerance. Although mu receptor agonists are the best analgesics and euphoriants, selective delta receptor agonists and enkephalinase inhibitors may prove clinically valuable antidepressants. The development of centrally active and more selective kappa antagonists – which block the endogenous excess production and reuptake of dynorphin underlying many depressive and anxiety disorders – is also a priority. Orally active JDTic, a potent, exceedingly long-acting selective kappa antagonist, is currently undergoing preclinical testing. Kappa Therapeutics, the world's first conference dedicated to the kappa opioid receptor, was held in Seattle July 2011. In the meantime, Buprenorphine (Buprenex, Temgesic, Subutex), for instance, is certainly no panacea; but it would probably benefit a far wider section of the population than its current restriction to use in "detoxifying" heroin-addicts. Its role as a mixed mu agonist reduces buprenorphine's addictive potential as a euphoriant while increasing its safety in overdose. Buprenorphine's kappa receptor antagonism may contribute to its superior efficacy as an antidepressant. Even the humble codeine analogue tramadol (Ultram), a selective partial mu agonist analgesic with noradrenaline and serotonin reuptake inhibiting properties, can serve as a usefulmood-brightening stopgap. Weak but non-negligible kappa agonism limits its therapeutic benefit. But contemporary medico-legalopiophobia ensures such usage remains strictly off-label.

(TRANSLATED for easier understanding BY MICHAEL OWEN)

A significant minority of the population only feel truly well on opioids; therefore, they self-medicate, taking responsibility for their own mental health against the advice, beliefs, dogma and convictions of the medical community at large.

Wouldn't it be great if the human system that is responsible for pain management, anxiety, depression and what we consider to be normal emotional health, was free of defects and malfunctions. Enkephalins are responsible for encoding and processing of harmful stimuli in the nervous system and, therefore, the ability of a body to sense potential harm. Skin, joints, and body organs are all receptors in this process. The understanding that a dysfunctional pain management system in the our body may be responsible for many disorders and yet deserving of therapeutic recognition/remedies is a little extreme for the medical community to accept; it is taboo to use drugs to remedy these dysfunctions like we use Ritalin to treat ADD.

The use of opioids to produce a desired effect or outcome in treating dysfunctions, distress, and mental pain is neglected. They are grudgingly accepted in treating "physical" ailments and pain, but not necessarily the aforementioned dysfunctions.

Instead, we spend our time, energy and resources devoted to persecuting narcotic users; simply put, many users (many labeled drug abusers) are taking matters into their own hands to treat their ailments. They are then stigmatized, pilloried and criminalized in an on-going never ending futile

War Against Drugs. In the course society's Drug War, vast resources are exhausted by the state-apparatus in an effort to choke off narcotic production and supply. When these efforts produced temporary results, the ill-effects felt from involuntary deprivation of opioids are taken to demonstrate the likely ill-effects of legalized access; a contradictory way of bringing forth facts to support the continued suppression and denial of pharmacotherapies for "psychological" pain.

Of course there are many opioid users that have been acknowledged by the medical community to have dysfunctions which may need some type of attention or treatment. However, in many of these cases, the person is relegated to socially inferior levels of treatment compared to the ailment. For instance, the hypothesis of chemical imbalances causing depression have led to a new class of drugs. Admittedly, taking such chemical altering drugs is better than nothing at all. Often taking a licensed antidepressant is better than nothing at all—perhaps in part because of their positive effects on endogenous opioid peptide release. Yet even in the context of controlled clinical trials with relatively high dosage-regimens and artificially good rates of patient-compliance, it's rare for response-rates to reach more than 70%. Rates of full remission of depressive symptoms are far lower, perhaps 25-30%. Out "in the field", the picture is worse still. Adverse side-effects are common. Response may take weeks. Withdrawal reactions can be unpleasant.In the end, we need better targeted opioids that are safer and more specific to the dysfunction that many users seek to treat/self-medicate. Contemporary attitudes toward pain and the use of opioid analgesics remain barriers to progress in helping opioid users.

11/15/14 – Constructive Act #240 – Spread the Word

If you read the mission statement of the Davis Direction Foundation you will see that first and foremost we are about "promoting awareness" regarding the opiate/heroin epidemic that we are experiencing in our country. It amazes me that people deep in the throes of addiction still do not know the things available to them to help the addicts who are suffering from this disease. It also amazes me at the comments that people continue to write in response to some of the news stories that are posted on the news websites. The DDF has just hired a web developer that is doing the best job possible to make sure that we come up in web searches where people are searching for information on opiate/heroin/prescription drug addiction. It takes time, but we are doing all the right things to make sure that it happens. I have said on many occasions that if you wait until you find out that your loved one is an addict, you will be behind the 8 ball in trying to help them into recovery. I have also said on numerous occasions that KNOWLEDGE IS POWER and the more you know, the more proactive you can be in helping your loved one.

Yesterday I had a phone call from a mom who was desperately searching for ways to help her child. She had no idea that there was a drug out there that would block the "opiate high." There is new and powerful information coming out every day to combat this epidemic and unless you are tied into a website like ours, or you are actively doing your own research, you will miss things. There is a drug called naltrexone that will block the opiate high and it comes in the form of a shot called Vivitrol and an implant that you can find out about at "Start Fresh Recovery." Here is an excerpt from their website: "Addiction is a complex brain disease that requires a medically based, comprehensive approach to treat the physical cravings as well as the psychological, emotional, behavioral, and nutritional aspect of the disease. For most patients, we use a subcutaneously placed, time-released implant of the FDA-approved medication, Naltrexone. With cravings out of the way (for 6-12 months in most cases,) our patients are finally able to be productively receptive to the psychological and behavioral aspect of their recovery. Untethered from the intrusive and compulsive urges to drink or use, our patients participate in an intensive and personalized, outpatient, one-on-one counseling/life coaching program in a private environment."

If we had known what we now know, when we left the rehabilitation facility with Davis as he was discharged, we would have had an appointment to either get an implant or a Vivitrol injection before we ever came home. It just gives the addict a fighting chance. I know that these options are expensive and that every addict or family may not be able to afford them. Insurance is beginning to come around and include these medications and if yours does not, then you need to fight for it. Make phone calls to vendors and legislators! Don't stop fighting. This disease is real and we need to see changes. Change WILL happen—I just hope that it happens quickly enough to help your loved one. The only way that will happen is if we all stand together and demand change. I for one am tired of hearing stories about addicts who are desperately trying to get help and they are being turned away at every facility because they either don't have insurance or they won't treat them because addiction is not considered a "life-threatening" situation. Well I can tell you without hesitation that it was a "life-threatening" situation for my child and it didn't end well.

Please INVITE your friends and family members to "LIKE" the Davis Direction Foundation on Facebook and go to our website often to help us gain the frequency that we need to become a "first page" Google search. I would personally like to see the Facebook page reach 5,000 likes by the end of the year. The more people that we have involved in our cause, the more noise that we can make in our own community as well as the rest of the nation. The more noise we make, the more recognition we will get for the epidemic that is claiming the lives of our children at the rate of 1 every 19 minutes. Addiction is now claiming more lives than car accidents in the United States. If every member of our Facebook page would just invite one person, we would be at almost 9,000 people who knew about our page.

I am often asked, "What can I do to help?"—well here is the answer, and it doesn't cost a dime. Invite others to like our page and visit our website! It WILL make a difference, and if just a handful of those people make a donation to the DDF, then it is money that we didn't have to begin with and it will be money that we can spend to "promote awareness, affect change and save lives." It is time to MOVE and it is time to SPREAD THE WORD. Help us MAKE A DIFFERENCE. It could be your friend, your family member, your sibling, your spouse, your unborn grandchild, or even the one that is destined to cure cancer that you save! SPREAD THE WORD!

11/16/14 – Constructive Act #241 – Share Your Story

This is one powerful story! If you don't think there is hope, read this one. This is one determined person now sharing his life with one lucky woman! I'm sure their 3 kids are happy and healthy and full of love as well. IT CAN BE DONE!

Here is his story:

All I can remember is the catheter being removed, feeling an IV in my arm, and being handcuffed to the bed in the hospital room. I was told I had died and had been brought back. All the while, a police officer continued asking, "Where'd you get it?" For most people, this would've been rock bottom, but not me. My drug use continued for another two years.

I was 21 years of age, I was arrested and charged with felony possession and distribution of marijuana. In my case, marijuana was only the tip of the iceberg. I was using any drug I could get my hands on. I lived a party lifestyle, going to clubs and doing recreational drugs. I had been living this way for so long, I knew no other way. I woke up every morning thinking about how I could get my next fix. My friends during this time were enablers. None of us had what would be considered real jobs; we had no ambitions and only enjoyed partying. I, in NO way, blame my friends for my actions, but I mention these "friends" because I chose to surround myself with people who were equally embedded in the same drug-filled life as I was living.

After my arrest I lost everything. I had no money, no job and my car repossessed. I was lucky to get a job doing construction work. I had distanced myself from my parents and family, and hadn't had contact with them for two or so years.

I found a job after my arrest, for a family owned flooring business installing hardwood floors. My boss lived close enough to me that she was able to pick me up and drop me off at my house, or wherever I happened to be staying that night.

I was able to turn my flooring job into an apprenticeship. I travelled the southeast working on large commercial jobs: hotels, restaurants, and condos. I was finally able to lead a somewhat productive lifestyle at this time because I was forced into sobriety by the law.I was found guilty and convicted in the fall of 2000. My punishment was three years of probation, fines, and 20 voluntary confinement weekends in jail. I was able to keep my job traveling while fulfilling my probation requirements. In my case, I didn't go to rehab, but I began to surround myself with "winners" and I began to allow God to creep back into my life.

During this time I lost all contact with old friends and I lived a healthy, drug-free lifestyle. I finally felt as though I was doing something good.

Upon completion of my probation, I stopped traveling and started my own business. I also continued to invite God into my life more and more each day.

I knew I had wasted many years living for drugs, but I needed to continue to move forward. I decided that I needed to go to school to get a better job. I went to Chattahoochee Technical College and graduated in nine quarters with an associates degree. I then transferred to Kennesaw State University and graduated with a B.B.A.

While attending KSU, I worked a few internships and became a member of several prestigious collegiate organizations. I also made presidents' and deans' list, all while working full-time.

I met my wife a few months before I started my college journey, the newest chapter of my drug-free lifestyle. My wife and I have been married for five years, have a beautiful family, and live a clean, happy and healthy lifestyle.

When I was arrested, I was mad at the police and the judge for my sentence. As time has gone by, I have realized that it was probably one of the best things that has ever happened to me. I was able to change my life, learn a skill set, earn two degrees, find the woman I love, and have three children with her. Of course, I may have been able to do all this without having been arrested but sometimes people must learn the hard way—and learn I did! Today I have a good, stable, and satisfying life for which I am eternally grateful.

11/17/14 – Constructive Act #242 – Expect the Empties

The "empties" are the things that are giving me the hardest time right now. I have decisions to make regarding the holidays—Thanksgiving and Christmas—and Thank God, my friends and family are offering me a way out. I know that if I were to go to Thanksgiving the way I have gone to Thanksgiving for the past 20 years, all I would see were the "empties." The "empty seat" in the car on the way down, the "empty seat" at the table, the "empty hand" offering Sonny Boy, the horse, apples for dinner, the "empty space" on the couch after dinner when everyone sleeps, and the "empty space" in my heart when I sit with my family at the Thanksgiving celebration. I can't do that! It's plain and simple and really quite obvious! MY SON IS GONE! I can't pretend that I can sit and do things the way I have done them for the past 20 years. Why would anyone think that I could. Thank God that I have family members and friends that have offered me a way out.

Already I am feeling the holiday depression. I start to think about what is to come and I experience shortness of breath, I feel nauseous, and I have a hard time drawing my next breath. The tears start to fall and I have NO control over my own emotions. My eyes burn, my throat constricts, and my heart breaks. I realize that a broken heart doesn't always kill you!

So—what do we do? We do something that is completely out of the norm and something that will keep us completely busy for the duration of the holidays. We go on vacation! We have decided as a family, to go away and be alone in a different setting, a different state and a different tradition. Maybe we will eat fast food, or maybe we will have a sandwich or even a can of soup—but we will not see an "empty" everything because we know where and when Davis would be missing. Maybe next year we will be able to return to the everything, and as long as we have our immediate family with us, we will survive. We will spend time with God, instead of extended family and we will connect with our feelings and reach deep into our souls and search for the strength to move forward.

For the past 8 months, there have been one set of footprints in the sand, and we expect that to be the norm for some time. God has carried us for the past 8 months and He has given us the strength to do what we needed to do to survive and help others. We have been able to experience healing through helping others and it has felt good. We feel a connection with Davis in doing for others what we couldn't do for him.

My "little buddy" will be with me forever in my heart, but to be around the "empties" this year is just not something that I can bear. My heart is broken, my soul is empty and my spirit if fragile. I need to be renewed. I will go to the ocean and speak to God! I know He is there—I feel closer to Him there, than anywhere else on earth.He will hear me, and He will fill my soul and I will be renewed. I will be able to carry on and take care of others and give them the best of me.

I know there are others, plenty of them, in the same situation as I am in and I know they are searching for answers to help them through this time as well. Do your best to make your situation work for you and know full well that you will face the "empties." It will be hard; in fact, it will be brutal and I truly don't know if it will ever be any easier. The only thing that I can hope for is that through helping others, we will find peace and the "empties" will be filled with HOPE for others as we do everything we can do to make sure that others don't have to endure the pain that we will forever deal with. Serving God is a way to mend our hearts, and mended hearts will allow us to continue "moving onward through life… looking upward to God."

11/18/14 – Constructive Act #243 – Start Collecting Now

The holidays bring about different circumstances for different people. Just as I have written about the grieving families over the past couple of weeks, there will also be families who are deep in the throes of addiction and the addicts themselves who will be forced to endure another holiday season and navigate through the best way they can. These families will be on pins and needles because planning sometimes becomes a tireless effort, and the addicts often times find themselves with nowhere to go because they have exhausted all of their choices and many times the families have chosen the route of "tough love." Many addicts will be on the streets and in the shelters this holiday season cold and all alone. For some of them, maybe just maybe, it will be their "turning point" or their "rock bottom," and they will decide to enter recovery. For others, it will just be another day of finding their next high, all the while searching for the HOPE they need to turn their lives around.

Last Christmas, as we joined our extended family for Christmas Dinner and a day of celebration, I looked around and noticed that Davis was not with us. I naturally got up and began looking for him and I found him out on the front porch rocking in a rocking chair… cold and alone. I asked him why he was not inside with the rest of the family and I will never forget the words he said to me. He said, "Everybody in there knows what I am." At that point in time, I assured him that no one knew that he was actively addicted to opiates and that they loved him and cared for him. I further reassured him that even if they had known, it would not have changed their love for him. The point that I am making is that our loved ones in active addiction have a very low self-esteem and an even greater sense of insecurity. The deeper into addiction they go, the worse these feelings become and the only way they ever feel "worth" at all is by getting high and eluding reality. Our job is to bring them back into the fold and let them know we love them unconditionally, but we want them to get well. Put your arms around your loved ones in active addiction and hold them tight and make sure that they hear the words that you love them… it makes a difference.

The Davis Direction Foundation has decided to host an event this Holiday season that will offer hope, healing, warmth and love. We will be rolling this event out on the DDF within the next week when all of the details have been ironed out. But for now, we need your help in collecting a few of the items that we would like to be able to hand out at the event. We need blankets, scarves, gloves, apple cider and styrofoam cups. So, during your Thanksgiving trips to the grocery store, watch for apple cider to be on sale and pick up a couple of gallons for us along with a pack of cups. Also, I have already seen several "fleece blanket" specials in the sale flyers, as well as warm wrap around scarves and gloves. We will also accept gently used, freshly laundered, items in great condition.

We will be partnering with several organizations to make this event a community offering of HOPE. The DDF will announce drop-off locations, partnering organizations, and all the who, what, when, where and why details by the end of next week. We are also working through active meeting sites, and social media pages to advertise our efforts.

Christmas is traditionally the season of giving and this will address a huge community need and provide an opportunity to do just that. Please begin to pray about our event and to ask God to bless our plans and to bring the right people to us. Those who need to know about all the things we have to offer are the ones we are praying will join us.

To all of the DDF active supporters, and there are many of you, please begin to "rally the troops" and start collecting the items that we are asking for. We will be in need of loving, caring and compassionate volunteers to help us bring this event to life.

Stay in touch with the DDF for the details, but for now, START COLLECTING the love offerings we are preparing to share! We need community support

11/19/14 – Constructive Act #244 – Consider The Elements

My house is freezing; it is literally in the 50's! I can only imagine what it must feel like outside all night long when my iPhone says that Kennesaw, GA is 19 degrees with a wind chill of 13 degrees. You may remember a post back in September— the day of the Golf Tournament—when my house exploded! Well, at least all the appliances and electrical things started buzzing, smoking and burning! Well, apparently the heater got zapped just enough to last for a little while longer and then Monday night it absolutely DIED! We called the Home Warranty company and they can't get out here until Thursday! So—in the meantime, we are bundled up in the house with the fireplace going and the space heaters on. We don't leave them running all night because it's just dangerous, and when we wake up in the morning… It's Freezing!

My mind immediately goes to the homeless people this time of year and how they survive. Now, the DDF has gone to great lengths to try and change the stigma of a opiate/heroin addict, and the kind of homes and families they come from. BUT, when the families have exhausted all of their resources and the loved one is still addicted and recovery is not in sight, many of them are told to leave their homes and they do indeed become homeless. Many times we are talking about kids who have lived in the suburbs of Atlanta in upscale subdivisions and suddenly they find themselves on the streets. It's freezing, raining, and they are facing the elements with the clothes that they had on their backs when they left. In many cases, their cell phones have been taken away, or the bills have not been paid, and their cars have run out of gas. With no job and no money and no HOPE…Where do they go and to whom do they turn for help?

I will be completely honest and tell you that I don't have the answers. I do know of addicts and if they drug test the people who come seeking shelter. I will make it my responsibility to find out this week and publish a list of places that they can go or they can be dropped off if that is the route that your family chooses.

Not too long ago, I was walking down Peachtree Street in Atlanta and it was around 9:00 pm. It was windy, chilly and there was a light mist coming from the sky. I noticed that the churches were full of people with blankets and pieces of plastic huddled up in the corners of the front of the buildings where the awning offered some protection from the elements. I passed others wandering aimlessly, possibly looking for an empty corner or unclaimed "awning spot." My heart was breaking as I was walking down the street thinking, "how did it come to this?"

I'm going to go out on a limb and say something that people may not agree with, but I have drawn this conclusion after much thought and research. I do believe that when people have invested their time and energy for many months and even years in trying to change behaviors and "cure" a disease with not a great deal of success, they give up. When they give up, they advise others to give up as well because they don't think anyone can do what they couldn't do. When I sat in the rehab center and I listened to the people in charge tell the loved ones or the "addict's keepers" to turn them away if they left the rehab center and called to be picked up, I knew right there in my heart, I couldn't do that. I believe that the only reason they say that is because they don't have the "real" answer. When you are being paid thousands of dollars to have the answers, you have to come up with something. I would love to see an actual study about the kids who have been "kicked to the curb." Thankfully, Davis did not leave rehab until he was discharged, but I can tell you without hesitation, I would not have left him on the streets in the middle of the winter. I have spoken with many former addicts through email, private messages, phone calls and in person. One question I always ask those in recovery is, "How did you do it?" Very few of them tell me that it was because they were left on the streets and out in the elements. Most of the time it was because they became "sick and tired of being sick and tired." I sat with a recovering addict this week that I have known and loved for years and he told me that his parents never kicked him to the curb. He told me that it was because he knew he was loved that he knew he had something to live for. He is doing fantastic: 3+ years clean, running his own business and helping others on a daily basis.

I won't sit here and tell you that I have the answers, I don't, but I will tell you that the DDF is actively working to find them. We are asking the experts—those in the throes of opiate/heroin addiction to help us help them. They are the ones with the answers. I just pray that we can keep them alive long enough to get the answers from them.

There will be a special on Channel 2 this afternoon at 5:00 pm with Mark Winnie regarding heroin use in Atlanta. Tune in and let's see what they have to say. I also just saw an interview with a representative from Must Ministries that said the Shelter is open from 6 am to 2 pm serving hot coffee and continental breakfast items. You may want to consider dropping off pastries, doughnuts or other breakfast items if you are looking to donate to a shelter.

11/20/14 – Constructive Act #245 – Sacrifice

A sacrifice is defined as a loss or something you give up, usually for the sake of a better cause. It's time to consider what you can give up for the sake of helping to rid our country of this horrific epidemic that we are up to our necks in! If you watched the special yesterday on WSB TV, which for those of you who are not local, is one of the major Atlanta TV stations, then you know that the Fulton County Jail is booking 2-3 heroin addicts a day. That's anywhere from 60-90 heroin addicts a month. Now consider that Fulton is just one of the larger metro Atlanta county jails, but that's a lot of heroin addicts. Consider as well that there are also probably more addicts that are not caught that are still out there driving on our roads and putting others in danger. Did you see the Mom, 26 years old, who was driving on a major Atlanta highway, and crossed all lanes of traffic with her two young children in the back seat, because she was high on heroin? Do you feel safe? These opiate/heroin addicts are not typically violent addicts, they are just addicts who are obsessed with getting their next fix. Yes they are robbers, but they are usually robbing their family and friends, not breaking into random homes with weapons. My point is that we are all at risk because of the danger, and we need to come together as a community to support a solution.

Many times, those affected by addiction received their first opiate prescription from a practicing doctor or dentist for a legitimate injury or surgery. How were they supposed to know that they were carrying the addiction gene and that they would become addicts? Sometimes through no fault of their own, other than trusting a very reputable doctor, these children who had their wisdom teeth out or suffered a sports injury and had to have surgery, became heroin addicts. Now, remember that the pharmaceutical companies claimed that Hydrocodone, Oxycodone, Morphine, and any of the opiate drugs were NON-ADDICTIVE when they were marketing them in the very beginning. You can find article after article regarding this. When people with chronic pain needs received these medications and experienced pain free lives for the first time in years, there was no way to take them back. And that would not have been in their best interest anyway. However, long story short, it brought us to our current state of crisis!

The DDF needs your help in the way of monetary support. We have sponsored 2 Symposiums, and are currently planning for a 3rd on January 15th. We have sponsored one ceremony to kick-off Recovery Month and we have another upcoming event that we are about to announce. We have furnished and continue to furnish addicts and their families with Naloxone kits to reverse the opiate overdose. We have printed materials for distribution, created DDF videos, handed out numerous rubber bracelets, t-shirts, jewelry, and Christmas Ornaments, sponsored a Golf Tournament, created a website which is receiving a major facelift, registered as an Incorporation and filed to become our own 501(c)(3) in addition to remaining a 501(c)(3) fund of the Cobb Community Foundation. All of these things, not to mention the plans that we have for the future, cost money.

Michael and I have decided that during this Christmas season, whatever amount we would have budgeted to spend on Davis this Christmas, we will donate to the DDF. Just as every other board member who is serving on the Davis Direction Foundation, we have already made significant donations to help the cause and we will continue to do so. We are asking you to join us in this endeavor. You can "gift" someone in recovery with a donation made in his or her name to the DDF as well. What a meaningful and lasting gift that would be. We still have our DDF 2014 Christmas Ornament for sale ($12.00) and it would also make a great gift this Christmas.

We have written and will continue to write Grants that will fund some of our efforts, but the majority of the funds as of now have come from the community members who are investing in our cause. For those of you who have contributed, we extend our heart-felt thanks, and for those of you who consider sacrificing to support us, we thank you in advance.

You can go to our website www.davisdirection.com and make a donation with a credit card or Paypal account, We will be set-up with recurring payments when we have our website upgrade completed.

You can personally bring a donation to any of our events. We will always have a DDF fundraising committee member on site to take your donation. We are also set up now with a Charles Schwab account so that we can receive transferred stock, mutual funds, or exchange traded funds. For information regarding this type of donation, please contact Sam Paglioni, Partner, Integer Wealth Advisors Group, LLC, at (770) 974-2787 or by emailing Sam at spaglioni@iwagroup.net.

All donations are tax deductible and you will receive a letter to that effect. Please consider sharing this post on your personal website so that we can get it out there to as many people as possible in order to make a difference in our community and around the Nation. SACRIFICE for the sake of a better cause.

11/21/14 – Constructive Act #246 – Tag 'em and Bag 'em

As awful as this title sounds, I can assure you there is so much truth in it. I'm so tired of hearing that people don't care and the pains of addiction are never real until it happens to you. Unfortunately there is a lot of truth in that thought as well, but I am going to try and bring some reality to the rest of you so that you don't end up like I did, doing my research after the fact, hoping to protect the rest of society from the fate my family has suffered. Whenever there is a suspected drug overdose, you lose your right to take your child and bury them as you wish. They have to be cut open in the back of their heads to check their brains and a V is made in their chest to peel back their skin and check their heart and their internal organs. When you go to pay your last respects in the funeral home, there is blood still in the hair and on the body, because it continues to bleed. There is a crime file put together with pictures taken of the crime scene—hundreds of them. They begin with the crime scene from a distance and then they progress to close ups of the victim—your child—until you see every aspect of their body and their death. Your precious, wonderful, smart, loving and gorgeous child goes from being a living, breathing, human being to being a number that is bagged and tagged with an identification ticket tied around their toe.

How do I know this you ask? Because I forced myself to look at each and every picture of my precious Davis so that I could feel his pain and know that this never needed to happen again to any living soul. I saw him sitting dead in his car from every angle with his drug paraphernalia lying beside him. I saw the contents of his wallet lain out to be accounted for. I saw his precious tear-stained face and followed the trail of the tears that had fallen from his eyes before he died. I saw his mouth opened and the blood that lined his lips. I saw the position of his clinched hands as he must have died and the needle lying in his car beside where he died. I continued to look as they removed him from the car and stretched his dead body out on the cold, hard pavement. I saw where they opened his shirt and showed where the blood had pooled as it does in death. I saw the bag they placed him in and the zipper they would use to close up his dead body for transportation to the morgue. I saw it all and I soaked in every detail because he was my son and I owed it to him. It was the least I could do since I couldn't understand and feel his pain when he tried so hard to help me understand what he was going through. God, this is so hard to write!

I always thought that the worst thing that could happen to a person would be to die alone. No one there to hold your hand as you crossed over to eternity, and yet it happened to my own child. Not too long ago, I saw on Facebook where a father posted his dead child laying on a gurney—dead from an overdose. He wanted to bring reality to others so that it would become a lesson for others to understand. I could not do that and I would not do that, but I sure do understand why he did. He did it so that others would not wait until they had to deal personally with drug addiction, but so that others would understand the need for prevention and drug education. He did it to make a lasting impression on those who thought and still think it could never happen to them. He did it to save lives and protect children. He did it for all the right reasons. What a strong and brave man trying to help others.

It's too late for my child, but it's not too late to make a difference for others. If you wonder why we are working so hard to get our numbers up on the DDF, it's because KNOWLEDGE IS POWER and because YOU DON'T KNOW WHAT YOU DON'T KNOW!

If I had followed a blog because someone had invited me to follow it in the best interest of my family, I may have known some of the things I didn't know and it could have possibly saved the life of my sweet Davis. As long as I have life and breath, I will continue to bring awareness to others of the horrific opiate/heroin crisis that our nation is experiencing, and I will share every awful detail and offer every valuable resource that I know of. We have to find a way to make people care before it happens to them. Literally, it can take less than a day to become addicted to heroin. Tomorrow you could wake up and your life could be changed forever. Knowledge is a gift that I can offer each and every one of you for this holiday season. Please accept my gift and educate yourself so that you can live a long and productive life with all of your children and other loved ones by your side.

11/22/14 – Constructive Act #247 – Embrace People In Your Path

Today has been a crazy busy day, but not without incident and purpose earlier this morning. For those of you who are regular readers, you know that I usually post a little later on Saturday mornings, but not this late. It started this morning with running errands early and getting children where they were supposed to be. After running down to Atlanta twice, we were back in Marietta and pulling into the QT to fill up. As we drove down the street toward the Civic Center, I noticed homeless people all along the street huddled up together and just seemingly hanging out until they could return to a shelter this evening. Turning into the QT, I noticed an elderly person sitting in a walker, hunched over and very still. Michael pulled up to the gas pump and I told him I was going out to check on this person.

I didn't even hesitate, which is unusual for me, because believe it or not, I have always been a little scared of situations like this one. Not this time, I went straight up to this person who turned out to be an elderly lady and began calling to her, asking her if she needed help. She was completely laying in her own lap with a cigarette still in her fingers that had gone out, but not before it burned a hole in her sweat pants. I got no response and I became a little anxious. I had put my Naloxone kit in my pocket just in case I needed it right before I got out of the car. Almost immediately as I started trying to help her, others became aware and started our way. I shook her on the shoulder and then again on the leg all the time asking her if she was all right. Still no response. At this time, I called for Michael to call 911 and he started running toward us with 911 on the phone. As I'm still trying to 'rouse this lady, a young man comes up and absolutely takes charge.

He pulls her back from the shoulders and immediately puts his 2 fingers underneath her neck to check for a pulse and begins calling her by name. "Leddie… Leddie" he calls to her and she begins to raise her head telling us to leave her alone. He begins to tell me that he is an EMT with Grady and that this woman is a "frequent flyer" down at Grady. He also tells me that he usually picks her up in downtown Atlanta and he begins to ask her how she got to Marietta. Of course she has no idea. She is as confused as I am now about what is going on, but I'm extremely grateful that this young man walked up when he did.

Now in the grand scheme of things, I have never used a Naloxone kit, and I knew for sure she didn't fit the profile of an active opiate/heroin addict. But, I also knew I had nothing to lose if I tried to bring her back with the kit, because it cannot hurt you if you are not overdosed. Still, having to make that decision would have caused me great anxiety. So, God sent an angel! He was there to show me how a pro handles a situation like this. Michael and I began to tell him about the Davis Direction Foundation, and what we are actively doing in the area to address opiate/heroin addiction. I asked him for a card and he did not have one—first of all he was NOT on duty and was just being a concerned citizen doing the right thing. He in turn asked me for my card and I went back to the car to get him a card. Of course I was out, I usually have 10 with me, but I have been giving them out at every opportunity. So, instead I gave him a Naloxone kit with all of information on the bag they are packed in. It felt great to put a Naloxone kit in the hands of a professional, especially after the way I witnessed him taking charge of the situation with this mentally ill woman.

That was no accident and no coincidence! God put this young man in our path this morning to show us just what we didn't know. The man was a beautiful role-model and a seasoned veteran in the first responder field. I have no doubt that God knew this man needed a kit for some reason and now he has it. He told me that he would be sending me an email to the DDF and I know he will. He has opened my eyes to the need for a simulated drill at the next Symposium! (Jan 15th 7:00 pm Marietta First United Methodist Church). I also know that the fact that this man was from Grady was no coincidence either. He works down by the bluffs and is certainly down there every time he goes to work. Now, because of our meeting this morning, he will have a kit with him on and off duty and I know that is a part of God's plan.

I know this young man will certainly reach out to us as he was so interested in our organization and how he could help. When he does, I will be asking him to come to the Jan. Symposium to direct our drill! There's nothing like a practice run with an angel!

Whoever you are—and he did tell me his name, but it was not the most important thing at the time, I know we will meet again because he is supposed to be one of the players in the great scheme of things. He wanted to get information regarding our organization so that he could be an advocate for us and continue to help us save lives! Thank you God for yet another blessing for the DDF.

11/23/14 – Constructive Act #248 – Share Your Story

This sweet lady has shared her story from the "sober" point of view. She grew up in a family surrounded by drug addiction and disease. Listen and understand what the sober child goes through growing up... It's heart breaking, but all too often the lifestyle for many.

Here is her story:

My story is a little different from what we normally read on "Share your story Sunday." I'm 51 years old and all varieties of drugs have been (and continue to be) a big part of my life since I was 11. Drugs sucked the life out of my family when I was a child and have caused me to spend many sleepless nights as an adult. I have never even tried marijuana yet I have fought addiction my whole life—just not my own.

I was born in and have lived my entire life in Marietta. When I was 11 I saw my 14 year old brother smoke pot for the first time in our basement and it was on. He had a group of friends in the neighborhood that all seemed to be focused on the same thing, getting high. I don't know what the exact progression of drug use was but I do remember him with handfuls of pills when I was still very young. My parents had no idea what to do. At first they pretended it wasn't happening. Now that I have kids I actually understand how that happens. It's hard to not still see your child as that precious little boy or girl that is wide eyed and innocent. Obviously in the 1970s the resources available for drug addicts were nowhere near what they are now so my parents fought, blamed each other, lectured and begged my brother, paced the floor, separated, got back together all the while assuming that I was fine. After all, the squeaky wheel gets the grease and there really is only so much grease two parents have to give.

As the "good one" I determined that I should be very careful not to cause my parents any more stress than they already had. I tried to take care of everyone and attempted to make everyone get along and like everyone else, didn't have any idea what all of this was doing to me until I was an adult.Just to touch on the highlights of the last 35 years—my parents together, my brother got married, had a baby, lost custody to the baby's aunt, got divorced, got married again, went to prison and then decided to get clean. While this is a blessing and we are all very thankful, he is far from "normal". He lives in a camper and has a small construction business doing minor renovations. He and his girlfriend rescue cats and recently they had 74 cats seized by animal control. I guess his addiction has shifted slightly.

My mother and my ex-husband have both struggled with prescription meds. I know that my son has and probably still smokes pot and I'm not sure what else. He's in college and all I can do is pray and try to gauge what's happening with him based on his grades, our conversations and his willingness to interact with me. I've asked myself regularly over the last 3 or 4 years "how do you know when it's bad enough to take action?" I guess nobody knows the answer to that question until they know it.

I wonder all the time what things would've been like if drugs hadn't been a part of my family's life. I spent a lot of my adult life being angry and resentful for what was taken away. I realize now there's nobody to be angry with. Yes, my brother made the choice to start using drugs but I know now that soon after it was no longer a choice. I know that he would not choose the life he has now and would give anything to have a do-over. I know that my parents didn't know what to do. I know that they were hurting, scared and had no idea where to turn for help. Nobody did anything "to" me for me to be angry about. No matter how much it all hurt me it wasn't aimed at me. I can't take all the credit for all of this awareness; I've had lots of counseling and lots of conversations with God… it's a good thing

He doesn't get tired of listening. We all know you can't love addiction away but I'm convinced that it's necessary if there's any chance for recovery. My parents never gave up on my brother, he always knew he was loved and this is probably why he's still alive. I haven't thought about this but I think I need to tell him that I'm glad he is.

11/24/14 – Constructive Act #249 – Offer Emotional Support

You all probably know by now that I am full of stress as I anticipate the first round of Holidays without my precious son Davis. I know we will make it through because we are strong family with a strong faith. Nonetheless, I'm full of anxiety; but if you ask me how I'm doing, I'm going to tell you that I'm doing fine. Most people do this because that's what we've been conditioned to do and I don't think I would want it any other way quite honestly. If we believe we are fine and can say we are fine—that's half the battle. Please understand I'm speaking about the "Addict's Keepers" or those who have lost their loved ones due to the disease of addiction. We need to be strong and we need to keep moving forward, looking to God for our strength. This is not to say that you don't need to seek help when you are not doing fine and you will know if and when you are in that place. I did wake up this morning with all my fingernails gone on my left hand. That is a sign of anxiety and stress. I know that I sat and bit them off last night while I was watching TV with my daughter. I knew I was doing it when I was doing it, but I could not seem to stop. When I would tell myself to stop, there was always one more little rough spot, or jagged edge that I needed to take care of. So, I woke up to an ugly hand with bitten fingernails this morning. The funny thing is, I'm not a fingernail biter! Funny huh? Not really—just a sign of stress.

Anyway, it started me thinking. How do people who have serious anxiety and depression make it through the holidays? I have always heard that suicide is more frequent during the Holidays and I felt the need to address this on the DDF. So, I got on the internet and started looking for some statistics for this post and lo and behold, I couldn't have been more wrong! December is the least likely month for someone to commit suicide due to anxiety and depression. Below is a quote from the NYU Langone website that was also confirmed on the CDC website.

"Contrary to popular belief, depression and suicide rates do not rise around holidays. The media often inaccurately reports such a link, and also tends to blame suicides during the holiday season on depression or anxiety directly related to the holidays. However, studies have shown that people tend to be less likely to commit suicide during the holiday season, perhaps because of an increase in available emotional support."

I thought about this quote long and hard and then it hit me that what we have been advocating for all along seems to be confirmed here. "Emotional support" is a key component of helping and keeping an addict in recovery. We all know that entering and staying in recovery is ultimately up to the addict, but it doesn't mean that we can't offer and shouldn't offer emotional support along the way. Recently I had a dear friend ask me how to act around her addicted nephew that she would be seeing for an upcoming family event. She didn't know whether to bring it up, act like she didn't know, ignore the fact, or offer support. So, we talked about it for a few minutes and decided, that since most of the family knew the situation, that it was important that she let him know that she had been keeping him in her prayers and that she loved him and was so glad to see him and that she was there for him if he ever needed her. That's offering emotional support. It allows the addict to know that you know they are affected with the disease of addiction, but it doesn't change your love for them. It offers emotional support and HOPE.

Now, I'm certainly not naïve enough, or so much of a "Pollyanna," that I believe we can make everything right for an opiate/heroin addict with a hug and a kiss, kind words and a cherry on top. That's ludicrous! But, lots of family support and encouragement might offer just enough of the courage that they need to enter or remain in Recovery on any given day. If it provides them the courage to get one step closer to the help they need, then the emotional support that we offer is valuable and necessary. Most addicts are at such a low point in their lives that they will tell you they just want to die! Although, the CDC and others proclaim that suicides are not as frequent during the holidays, that doesn't mean that it doesn't happen. So, as I was researching the articles for this post, I also noticed on the CDC website that there are 2 forms of "connectedness" that seem to help with suicide prevention. The first was connectedness with individuals, meaning family and friends. Being able to be around others to keep from being lonely and to have someone to talk to if necessary. The second form of "connectedness" was to that of a community organization, meaning schools and churches. The relationship that develops with these organizations increases an individual's sense of belonging, fosters a sense of personal worth, and provides access to a larger source of support.

The point of this entire post it to encourage people to offer emotional support to families and friends who have dealt with or are currently dealing with addicts during this time of year, as well as the addicts themselves. Just acknowledging that you are thinking about them through a phone call, a text, or a friendly hug if you run into them is a gesture that will long be remembered. You don't even have to bring it up if that makes you uncomfortable; there will be a "silent code of understanding" that will be realized. Don't miss out an opportunity to make a difference. Offer emotional support!

11/25/14 – Constructive Act #250 – Just Live

"THROW CAUTION TO THE WIND... AND JUST LIVE"

Lately, I find myself thinking more and more about the "what ifs." When getting ready to take a trip or doing something out of the ordinary, I think to myself... "What if" it doesn't end well? Not too long ago in the news I saw the story of a very large family on the way to Disney World for the first time. As the 16 year-old son was driving, he apparently fell asleep and had an accident. Five family members were killed—two of which were the Mom and Dad. I suppose that when death has become reality for some of us, we become a little obsessed with it. At least I have. Every time my children go out the door, my mind subconsciously wonders... "What if they never come back?" Every time I plan a trip now, I wonder... "what happens if I never get back home." I guess to an extent, everybody thinks those thoughts, but when you have suffered the loss of a loved one, those thoughts just won't go away.

When I find my thoughts wandering like this, I have to become very philosophical and think in terms of the whole earth and the people who have come before me and the people who will come after me. I have to think that in reality, the day we are born, we begin to die. Some of us procrastinate the process and stick around for a very long time, but others of us barely make it out of the starting gate. That's life and that's the way it has been since the beginning of time. So, I'm no different from anyone else and don't deserve special treatment. The fact that I have already "loved and lost" doesn't really make a difference in the grand scheme of things. God has a plan and His plan trumps mine. You can't run from it and you can't hide from God – so why bother? Those kinds of thoughts make me strong enough to go forward with my plans and submerge the other thoughts deep into the recesses of my mind! Those thoughts and lots of praying!

I know that as my Daddy used to say, "When your number comes up, there's nothing you can do about it." The truth is that our days are numbered from the moment we take our first breath, so we might as well live in the "in between" time. I posted very early in the "CA's" about making a "Bucket List." At the time, I thought it would give an addict a reason to live, I've learned a great deal about addiction since then. I guess the "Bucket List" is more of a reason for the loved ones of those in addiction to have something to look forward to. Living your life as the "Addict's Keeper" is a full-time job filled with worry, heart-ache, tears, and fears. Sometimes you just have to throw caution to the wind and LIVE a little. Life is short even if you are one of those who lives to be a very old person. Sometimes you have to escape and do something for yourself, even if it causes you anxiety in leaving. Find the time to renew your spirit and get in touch with God in a different environment or setting. Leave behind all the chores and expectations of daily living and spend some time with yourself.

There's NOTHING you can do to change addiction. It is a disease and we have not found a cure as of yet. Being in recovery is the same as being in remission, and I know the "Addict's Keeper" always lives in fear of a reoccurrence or relapse. But if we always live in fear, we rob ourselves, our other children and loved ones, as well as our addicts of time that we can make memories and find joy in the present. LIFE IS IN GOD'S CAPABLE HANDS. Enjoy it as much as you can, and find time to "Throw Caution to the Wind... and JUST LIVE!" I'm off to the BEACH!

11/26/14 – Constructive Act # 251 – FIND YOUR PLACE (Revisited)

I guess this could mean a lot of things, at least for me, I know it does. I am at MY PLACE in a lot of ways. The ocean holds for me a special place not only physically but philosophically and emotionally as well as spiritually, and especially the Gulf. Many years ago Davis went on a vacation trip with his best friend Bobby, and ended up on 30A in Florida. We had never really heard of 30A before then, but had seen all of the bumper stickers and wondered what they meant. When he got home, he insisted that we go back and told us it would be the best vacation ever. Chelsea had also been on Spring Break down 30A and agreed that we needed to find a vacation rental at Seacrest Beach on 30A. We rented The Comeback Inn and had the best vacation ever. It was relaxing, beautiful, serene and tranquil. No hustle and bustle, or stress just a little piece of Heaven. So we continue to come back year after year. It has become OUR PLACE.

The ocean is my spiritual and philosophical place; when I look out over the ocean, it seems to be the only length of space that physically separates me from God. I have a feeling that God is just on the other side of the ocean and if I could get in a boat and get to the other end of the horizon, there I would find God. The sand reminds me that I am only a grain in the grand scheme of things and that for the most part I am so very insignificant that the stress and turmoil, pain and heartache that I feel, although very real to me, are totally unimportant to the big picture. The ocean is so Grand, that it reminds me that our nation is only a small part of the universe and it gives me HOPE that since it is such a small piece, that WE CAN MAKE A DIFFERENCE in our own community. It gives me HOPE that since we are dealing with 4.5% of the entire population of the world, that WE CAN MAKE A DIFFERENCE to those people suffering with addiction since they are only 1/10 of the 4.5%. The ocean gives me hope. It is my place!

Then I have to identify My Place in the epidemic of opiate/heroin addiction and figure out My Place and how I can make a difference. I feel like I have been called to invest my time and energy and my heart in helping others come to terms with addiction whether they are the addict or the people who love the addict, or if their lives have been tragically affected by the addict's behavior. I'm not quite sure that anyone is ever educated or trained to lead a cause, rather they are just passionate about what they are trying to do. I remember shortly after Davis died and we had begun the foundation, I made the remark to Chelsea that I wasn't sure if I was qualified to be the leader of the DDF. She told me very quickly that God didn't always call the Qualified but that He always qualifies the Called! So, knowing that, we have sought out and depended on God to show us the way for the Foundation and He has BLESSED us and BLESSED us INDEED!

Now it's time for you to "FIND YOUR PLACE" in the Foundation. Can you be one of the Prayer Warriors? They have been called on multiple times this week and they have shown support, encouragement and compassion at every opportunity. Are you a Daily Reader? Are you trying to educate yourself and others around you in order to promote awareness and affect change? Are you one of the ones who is helping us to reach our 5,000 reader goal by the end of the year? If you are, then you are helping us to carry out our Mission Statement and supporting us in a very important aspect of the organization. Are you supporting us financially? If you are, then you have helped us put many plans in place and spread awareness through printed material and Symposiums. You are allowing us to get Naloxone kits in the hands of those that need them, plus so many other things that have been mentioned lately in other posts. Are you a volunteer? Are you helping us to set up, hand out, and host events? We couldn't do it without you. Are you a Board Member, helping to drive the Mission into Reality? There IS a Place for you in the DDF. Please reach out and FIND YOUR PLACE so that we can continue to promote awareness, affect change and SAVE LIVES! WE NEED EVERY ONE OF YOU!

11/27/14 – Constructive Act #252 – Find a Reason to be Thankful

I remember last Thanksgiving Day—It's a day I will never forget. As we were getting ready to go to the traditional Thanksgiving Dinner, we discovered that Davis had pawned my Daddy's shotguns that the grandsons had inherited to get drug money. That was the day that we truly knew that Davis had a problem. He told us he wanted help and we got him lined up with a Counselor and he told us he was done with drugs. We had no idea and still don't know if he had done heroin at that time or if he was just addicted to what he told us, which was Roxis. I didn't feel like I had a whole lot to be thankful for that day. I felt like God had taken His eye off of my child and let him go astray. I've been praying for my children since the day they were born. I had them all dedicated to the church as babies, and they were all baptized before the age of 10. They were members of their Sunday School classes all of their lives and had some of the most amazing teachers through the years that a person could have ever asked for. Why did God take His eye off of Davis?

I struggled with why God didn't reach down and rescue my sweet son, Davis, for weeks and months, and even after his death I can tell you that sometimes I still don't understand and I may never understand. I never blamed God—I just felt like

I couldn't be mad with God because he had rescued him in a way, just not the way I wanted him rescued. In other words, once again, my plan and God's plan were different. I sit here, yet another Thanksgiving Day, and even though I traveled 300 miles away to remove myself from the "empties," they followed me! My son is still gone and there will indeed be an empty chair at the table. There's an empty bed, an empty voice in the conversation, an empty seat in the car and an empty shopping bag that should have held his treasures. I didn't escape anything, but I did come to a glorious place where I feel so close to God. I feel like here at the ocean I'm as close to God and Davis as I can get until the day I go to my eternal home and see them both. So, am I thankful?

Yes, over the 8 months and 3 weeks that Davis has been gone, I have learned to be thankful for everything in my life. I've learned never to take anything for granted because tomorrow it may not be there anymore. It could be gone from this earth forever. I'm thankful for my family, my friends, for things past and things yet to come. I'm thankful for the lessons that I've learned that have made me who I am. I'm thankful for every experience I've ever had even though one of them broke my heart in two. I'm thankful that Davis is whole again and in the arms of God. I'm thankful that he is not suffering anymore from a disease that we cannot cure as of this moment. I'm thankful that there are people out there who are intelligent enough to understand neuroscience who are actively researching how addiction works and how to cure it.

Most of all, I'm thankful for my God and for the peace that He gives me so that I can continue to function for the rest of this life. I'm thankful for the promises that He makes that let me know that I will be with Him and Davis again. I'm thankful that He put Michael Owen in my life and allowed us to create the "Owen 7." I'm thankful that He has a plan that we don't have to understand, but that we have to realize as it unfolds. I'm thankful that I have 4 children left on this earth who also understand that God's plan is the ultimate plan and that each of them have a personal relationship with Jesus Christ. I'm thankful that He has given every member of my family the strength to move onward in life as they look upward to Him for guidance and peace. I'm thankful that God chose a family for me to be born into that I would never know a day on this earth that I didn't know HIM! I'm thankful that I know now that God NEVER took his eyes off of Davis. I'm thankful for the gift of prayer so that I can talk with God everyday and depend on Him to take care of me, my family and everyone else in need of God's grace. Yes, on this Thanksgiving, I'm thankful, very thankful, and I think that if I can find all of those things to be thankful for considering what my family has been through over the past year… You can find something too.

> 1 Thessalonians 5:18 – "Give thanks in all circumstances; for this is God's will for you in Christ Jesus."

11/28/14 – Constructive Act #253 – Keep It Simple

Davis was the inspiration for this Act. He was never one to "want" for a lot of materialistic things. He just kind of kept it simple and never made it a big deal to have something. Now that's not to say that he didn't have things; his Daddy always made sure that he had the most up to date and best rated sports equipment when he played baseball. I kept him pretty well dressed through the years always making sure that he had clothes to wear if he needed to look impressive, and of course he always had the latest video games! But, for the most part, Davis never asked for "things." He was satisfied with what he had and was always pretty content with simple living. One of the last things that he asked for was a Galaxy 4 phone and that was because he wanted a bigger screen because he used to read a lot of articles on his phone and he liked the bigger screen for reading. For the most part, Davis liked to read short pieces, he didn't really read "books" per se, even though he did like to read a lot.

Even though he didn't read a lot of books, he did choose to read 2 books shortly before he died. The two last books that he chose to read were very philosophical books. He was trying so hard to get well. One of them he was given by one of his dear friends in Rehab. The book was "Si-cology." The book was written by Uncle Si from Duck Dynasty. Davis thought Uncle Si was one of the funniest men he had ever known. We watched a lot of Duck Dynasty before he died and Uncle Si was always his favorite. Si was and still is a simple man. He likes to make people laugh on the show, but in real life, the book he wrote was written to make people think in my opinion. It was also written to inspire. Uncle Si did not lead a privileged life, he had many struggles and he worked hard to overcome and make his way through life doing what was right for his family. I think God is rewarding Si now for all the blood, sweat and tears he had to go through to get where he is today. Davis liked Si because he didn't pretend to be anyone else. He was just a simple man and that was enough for him.

The other book Davis read before his death was "Wild At Heart: Discovering the Secret of a Man's Soul" by John Eldredge. I know he had lots of questions and like I said, he was trying so hard to find the spiritual answers of "how to get well." He knew the road he was going down was a dangerous one and he was looking for the detour back to the main road. What he didn't understand was that there was no quick fix. You have to go back down the road you have traveled and it will take the same amount of time if not longer to get back to the point of origin. It won't be easy because doors that you opened along the way have been closed and locked due to the loss of trust along the way. Bridges have been burned and paths have become tangled and more complex. It CAN be done, but you MUST KEEP IT SIMPLE. There are NO tricks, NO quick fixes, NO underlying meanings, NO short cuts, NO cheats, and NO easy ways. It's pure and SIMPLE: hard work and stay the course.

Maybe the reason so many of the brightest and best are falling to this drug is that these kids are not used to having to work hard for much in their lives because things come so easy to them. They are always beating the system, because for the most part the system if flawed and they have learned the short cuts and quick fixes that we as a society have just continued to keep status quo. They can use technology to change so many things and make them easier and more efficient and often times, they are smarter than the people who are in charge. They think it will be the same way when they try to enter rehab and begin to turn their lives around. Then they come face to face with the demons of opiates and heroin and they are no match for these evil drugs. They have no idea how to handle the situation they are now faced with and they succumb to the overwhelming power of the drugs.

I am in NO way trying to undermine what an addict will go through in order to become clean again. I saw the torment and pain in Davis' eyes. It was indescribable. Some things in life are SIMPLE, and that does not mean EASY. It only means that the answer is not hard to understand. "Drugs" is one of those things. It will be the hardest thing you may ever have to do in your life, but the answer is SIMPLE: You have to STOP using them and use the coping skills you have learned along with your relationship with God to NEVER pick them up again. Yes, there are drugs that can block the high and drugs that can help manage the depression and anxiety and these things are available and can possibly help, but the answer remains simple... STOP, COPE and PRAY! It will be the most COMPLEX, SIMPLE, thing you will ever do. But, IT CAN BE DONE!

11/29/14 – Constructive Act #254 – Mark Your Calendar Again

The DDF will be "Lighting the Way" for Jesus to come into your hearts and into your homes on December 24th, Christmas Eve, from 8:30 p.m.-10:00 p.m. in the Park on Polk St. right behind the Marietta First United Methodist Church on Whitlock Avenue in Marietta, GA. We will be handing out blankets, scarves, hats, gloves and snack bags with a gift from Chick-Fil-A Corporate. We will be serving hot cider and muffins and there will be caroling, scripture reading and beautiful scenery all along the "Way." When you come to the end of the path, you can look back up the hill and see the word HOPE all lit up to inspire those in need of HOPE this Christmas season. We will be spreading the word in various locations to hopefully get the event out there for those who may be out of the house with nowhere to go this Christmas. We know that many addicts end up on the streets and sleeping in cars due to their circumstances and we want to reach out to them and let them know that Jesus is there for them and so is the DDF. For those of you who are the "Addict's Keeper" please plan to come join us, and if your addict is in recovery, this is a great opportunity for them to reach out to others and serve in a way that will make a difference.

For those of you who read the DDF daily and are always looking for opportunities to help, here is your golden opportunity. We are asking for your help in collecting new or gently used blankets, hats, scarves, and gloves as well as apple cider, Styrofoam cups, and mini-muffins. There are several drop-off locations for everything except the muffins, which we will ask for on the day of the event. In Kennesaw, drop off locations are Big Shanty Barber Shop and Eaton Chiropractic, both in downtown Kennesaw on Main Street. Also Keller Williams West (ask for Melissa Krudwig) and they are located at 2651 Dallas Hwy. Marietta, GA 30064. We will announce new locations as they become available.

Parents with children of impressionable age—here is your opportunity to take advantage of the "teachable moment" and explain to your children why this event is necessary. Explain to them that people who take drugs often end up with nothing and nowhere to go. Explain to them that we are handing blankets, hats, gloves and scarves out because many of those addicted to opiates and heroin often end up on the streets, out in the cold because they have spent all of their money on drugs and have sold or pawned everything of value in order to support their habits. Explain to them that many addicts have lied and stolen from their families and their families can no longer let them live in their homes because they continue to take their belongings and sell them. Teach them about the "Point of no Return" with drugs and that the only way many of the addicts even come through Recovery is simply by the Grace of God. Teach them that every 19 seconds, someone dies from a drug overdose and that more people die from prescription drug abuse than car accidents now. Teach them that this is a DISEASE and as of right now there is no cure, but that abstinence from drugs is the only way to make sure you NEVER get the disease.

For those of you, like our family, who have "loved and lost," come out and find comfort in serving and helping others to find their way back. Come out and walk through the candlelit pathway and talk to God asking Him to offer you His perfect peace this holiday season and to spare you the heartbreaking pain that consumes you. Get in touch with your inner soul and experience the beauty of music and scripture in a holy place where you will feel God's presence.

If you cannot make the event, please begin to pray now that we will be able to offer what each person needs that will come to the event. Pray that those who need warmth and sustenance on Christmas Eve will find us. Pray that those who need hearts to be healed from the suffering of loss will find God's healing hand upon them. Pray that those who are suffering from anxiety and depression will find God and the scripture as a means off-dealing with their emotions rather than turning to drugs. Pray that those in Recovery will receive a blessing from the act of service. Pray that all involved are involved because they are passionate about helping those in the throes of opiate/heroin addiction and preventing others from joining them. Pray that God will show mercy toward this epidemic and help the

DDF move in the right DIRECTION – "Moving Onward through Life… Looking Upward to GOD!"

11/30/14 – Constructive Act #255 – Share Your Story

Today I am reposting a post that did not show up on the main feed but was a sideline post. It got lots of response, but I think that it is important that everyone sees what this young man took the initiative to do. I know if it is not posted on the main feed, then the phones don't pick it up and some people don't scroll down the sides.

Underneath that, I will post a cry for help, that I received yesterday afternoon that was responded to in so many ways that the person asking for the help actually identified himself and thanked everyone for help and then drove himself to the hospital to be admitted for detox. People want help and they are looking in the right place when they turn to the DDF. The DDF has a caring, compassionate and highly responsive group of members who are trying to make a difference and it is making a difference! These two have both identified themselves openly and asked openly for help!

First Post:

Adam M
November 18 at 11:27am

I just wanted to share this. I have almost 6 months sober after trying to get sober for the past 3 years now. I haven't been happier ever in my life! It makes me so sad to see people die to this disease. If I can bring any awareness then I'm doing something. I have been through hell and back fighting heroin addiction. I have lied, robbed, and cheated from family and friends. I saw my morals slipping away and tears in loved ones eyes and not even have a care in the world. Heroin sucks and drains the life out of you and makes you become someone that you thought you'd never be. Now sober I look back on all the destruction I've caused and cringe. But at the same time I can start to repair all that destruction. Im so grateful for another chance at a healthy life! Any advice I have is to surround yourself with healthy sober people. Get into a program that can help you meet these kind of people and teach you how to live again. I could go on and on about my story, but my main goal is just to let people know that being sober is amazing and it IS possible. We have all lived the same kind of lives. But I'm here to tell you that you can beat this and recover. Just find something greater than you and put your all into it. Just get outside of yourself and help others and let go of your selfish ways and I promise you will see a difference!

Second Post:

Adam E
Nov 29th, 1:02pm

Hi, my name is Adam E. I'm a heroin addict. I have been battling this disease for several years... I've overdosed multiple times and I am getting worse and worse. I hate what my life has become and I want to stop using. I don't have any financial support from my family and I'm pretty sure my health insurance has run out. I don't know what to do... I need to go to detox and I want to go to treatment. Can you help me? Please, I don't want to die. I feel so alone. My family won't speak to me. Addiction has taken everything from me. I don't want to live like this anymore. If there is anything you can do, please let me know. I need help. I want help. Please...

I will say, that in both cases, the DDF members responded in ways that offered help and acceptance for a Disease that people have succumbed to not realizing how powerful and destructive it could be. Sometimes through no fault of their own but by perhaps taking a prescription that was prescribed for them. Other times maybe they were trying to self-medicate and keep their problems from others. Then there are those who chose to use recreationally. Nonetheless, we help them without judgement and I for one am proud of everyone who helps to get these precious children of God back on their feet... "Moving onward through life...Looking upward to God." Thanks you for your unyielding compassion! DDF members are the BEST!

12/1/14 – Constructive Act #256 – Prepare For The Worst. Hope For The Best

Michael asked me yesterday afternoon if I had ever told Davis that he was going to die, and I said "NO"—but I had told him that "I was prepared for the worst but hoping for the best." There's no way that I could have thought that he would really die. A mother always thinks that her love is enough to conquer everything. I asked Michael if he had ever told Davis that he would die and he said that he told him he would either die or end up in prison. I think that men have a monopoly on reality where death is concerned. I'm not trying to be stereotypical, but I do believe that men are better equipped to deal with the road to destruction. I'm not sure why I really believe this other than the fact that I have seen it happen on numerous occasions. I believe that women are much more positive thinkers than men, and that they think that they can change things in their own minds and make for a better outcome. I know for sure that I think this way. Even though I was scared to death after I found out that Davis had shot up with heroin, I never wanted to allow myself to believe for even a minute that he would die because of it. On the night that he never came home, I knew what had happened, there was no doubt in my mind.

If you believe that your child, or if you believe that you are above the destruction of heroin, think again. Heroin is an entity unto itself and those who are not ready to rid themselves from the destruction of heroin, please consider these things: You or your child will more than likely end up in prison or dead if you are not in rehab or actively working your recovery to get well. I fought that philosophy for a long time, but ultimately found it to be true.

When Michael told Davis that he would either end up in prison or dead, Davis answered with 2 words: "I know." There is a very sad thing about heroin, it takes away the invincibility of most people, but only after it is too late to do anything about it. Most people in their early twenties usually consider themselves to be somewhat invincible. I would suspect most heroin addicts believed in the beginning that they could manage control of themselves if they tried heroin or even took it on occasion. I would even go so far as to say that for a very short time on heroin, most of them thought that they were still in control. But the reality is that they found out very quickly that heroin was in control and that they had lost all control and would have to actively work their recovery every day for the rest of their lives to remain in control of their drug-free lifestyle.

Heroin DOES NOT PLAY! I wish there was a magic way to instill this into the minds of all young people before they ever even considered doing heroin. I know of at least 20 deaths in our area, in the last month, that are a direct result of this deadly drug. I wish there was a "scary component" like a snake strike – something that makes people STOP and back up! People stay away from poisonous snakes and poison in general for that matter! HEROIN IS POISON! IT KILLS! Why are people NOT afraid of heroin? I can only imagine that it is because their minds are so warped from the opiates that are usually taking before someone does heroin that they are not thinking normally.

How do we get the young people to realize that heroin is not a drug you ever try? Everyday, 2000 teenagers try drugs for the first time. Many of these "first tries" lead to heavy drug use and eventually heroin. Many years ago, we made a bold move in the school systems and handed out condoms to the students. Well I can tell you now that if they get to heroin first, there will be no need for the condoms. THINK. THINK outside the box. There must be something that we can do to help young people understand that heorin is different. We need another bold movement that will make a difference. We cannot stop trying to make a difference. We must promote the awareness of opiate/heroin destruction. Prevention is ALWAYS the best answer to any problem. We must work hard now to prevent Heroin use moving forward. It has to stop!

12/2/14 – Constructive Act #257 – Do a Little Research

In January 2015, we will host our 3rd Symposium and the title will be "Laws, Limits and Loopholes." Attorney General, Sam Olens, will be our keynote speaker and we feel very fortunate to have him. As you probably know, Attorney General Olens has been an advocate who is not afraid to speak out about Prescription Drug Abuse. With all of this being said, it is now time to do a little research on your own and come up with questions and concerns that you have come face to face with and would like to see addressed at our next Symposium. There are no limitations to what you can research and ask about, but you will need to make your requests knows before next week when the DDF will meet with Mr. Olens and share with him some of our greatest concerns and issues. We are hoping to address insurance issues, price gouging of life saving medicines, incarceration versus rehabilitation, "addiction counselor" credentials, and governing agencies performing evaluations for rehabs and recovery residences to name a few.

Mr. Olens has been in the forefront of prevention initiatives dealing with prescription drug abuse. He most recently sponsored a video contest for a 30 second commercial speaking out against prescription medications being taken illegally. He asked for High School students to compete for prizes and notoriety.He is deeply concerned about the large numbers of young people turning to self medicating or recreational drug use. He is definitely on board with searching for solutions and now is the time to do your homework and ask your questions. It is not enough to sit back and wait for others to ask the questions for you. All of you on the DDF who have asked questions in your comments and been unhappy with the way things are being handled in the courts and Rehabilitation facilities, it is now the time to ask for your answers. Maybe there are logical explanations that none of us are aware of—we all know that we don't know what we don't know! Then maybe again, there are no specific reasons for the way things are being done and those are the things that we can challenge to become better and more efficient.

We can ask for explanations about laws that we don't understand and we can ask for ways around certain laws that are hindering our progress in the war against drugs. How many of you know about Casey's Law? Well, I'm not going to tell you about it—do a little research and figure it our for yourself! Ask why and when it can be used and why it is not used more often? There must be a reason! Find out what the latest and most effective drugs are and whether or not they are being covered by insurance. If they are not, then why not and what can be done to change this? Have you ever wondered why it is so hard to find a Detox facility for addicts? We have addicts out there begging for help, but unless they have money to pay for their health costs, they must continue to suffer in silence putting the rest of us at risk. Why? Why, why why? Now is the time to get answers! We have an expert at our fingertips who is on our side! Attorney General Olens wants answers too and he is ready, willing and able to help us search for solutions!

Put January 15th at 7:00 pm on your calendar now. Our Symposium will take place at Marietta First United Methodist Church in Marietta. We will meet in the Family Life Hall and we will once again be handing out Naloxone kits to those in need. You don't want to miss this very important Symposium discussing the progress and possibilities for legislation regarding the opiate/heroin epidemic. "Laws, Limits and Loopholes" Don't miss it!

12/3/14 – Constructive Act #258 – Allow Research to Drive Recovery

In the world of education, there is a saying, "The data drives the Instruction." Although it is not always strictly adhered to, whenever it is, there is always a better outcome. When you look at what the research is telling you, everything becomes quite clear. You know what the existing problems are and if you don't adjust your program to address those problems, then you are basically wasting your time. In the world of opiate/heroin addiction, the research is coming in fast and furiously. We need to look at the data and adjust our rehabilitation centers, our recovery residences, our detox facilities and our thinking in general to make our efforts at helping those in the throes of addiction to be the best and most effective efforts.

If you talk with any first time rehab addict, chances are that they worked through a program for a short amount of time—perhaps even less than 30 days. Now a lot of this is due to insurance issues and the fact that even good insurance offers maybe 30 days a calendar year of paid help. I know that insurance wanted to stop paying for Davis after 21 days. At the time, his rehab center suggested that they had done everything they could do for him and they discharged him. I can't say for sure, but looking back, I think it's quite clear, that fighting for insurance to continue to pay takes up a great deal of time and paperwork has to be done, and there are others waiting in the wings to take the vacant spot, so why bother? So many times, as a society we take the easy way out and in the case of opiate/heroin addiction, it is not saving lives!!!

Last night as Michael was doing his regular research, he came across an article in the Huffington Post entitled, "The Condition Many Recovering Addicts and Alcoholics Don't Know About." It was written by Jeanene Swanson and it was published back in Feb 2014. The article goes into great detail about "PAWS," or Post-Acute Withdrawal Syndrome. The research is suggesting that the brain has a tremendous capacity to heal, but that it doesn't heal quickly. The recovery process is different due to the different drugs that were used, but the general rule of thumb is that PAWS symptoms usually peak around four to eight weeks after quitting. That means that the worst cravings and withdrawal symptoms (aside from the immediate physical symptoms: cramping, vomiting, shaking, chills) don't actually appear sometimes for up to 2 months after the addict has been clean. "In essence, withdrawal from drugs of abuse results in a full range of emotional, behavioral and cognitive impairments. Damages to pathways involved in reward, pain relief, stress maintenance, sleep and arousal, learning and memory can have effects that last beyond quitting." And, where are these addicts when all this is taking place? Back out in society with little to no support! RECOVERY FROM OPIATE/HEROIN ADDICTION CANNOT BE ACCOMPLISHED IN 30 DAYS!

The article goes on to talk about drug therapy, methadone, suboxone, naltrexone, and suggests even further that doctors need to get on board with helping their patients through the recovery process. The article says that it is inadvisable to tough out recovery on your own—to begin the process by seeing a medical professional. They can help you through the anxiety and depression that almost always comes with PAWS.

Everyone needs to read this article in its entirety. It is well worth the 10 minutes it will take you to read it and understand what the research is showing. Let the RESEARCH DRIVE THE RECOVERY. You don't have to reinvent the wheel here; just understand the process.

12/4/14 – Constructive ACT #259 – Healing Comes Quicker Through Helping

As I begin this day, the first thought that enters my mind is the thought that today marks 9 months since Davis' death. My family has survived ¾ of a year without our precious Davis. In so many ways the time has flown by and in other ways, it has been the longest 9 months of our lives. We miss him everyday like it was the first day he was gone and we are still dealing with the "firsts" of course. Although, as of now, I can't imagine the "seconds" are any easier, the "firsts" have been and continue to be brutal. Someone once told me that the anticipation of "the day" was worse than the actual day; I have not found that to be true. The days are the worst for me. They are longer and emptier than anything I could have ever imagined.

Helping others through the Foundation has been a saving grace for me. I know that Davis is smiling down on our efforts and so full of pride that we are helping others with the disease he could not seem to escape. I've said it before, but Davis was the kind of person who would have given you the shirt off of his back and his heart was bigger than anyone else's I have ever known. When he saw someone in pain, he hurt with them and he never judged a single soul—unless of course they were being mean to others. He did not like people who were mean to others! He had an especially soft spot for the "Underdog." One of the Special Education teachers at school once told me that Davis could love the children that no one else could seem to love. That was one of the highest compliments that anyone could have ever paid him. All children deserve to be loved and Davis certainly led by example when it came to loving the "hard to love" kids. It made me so happy to watch the kids surround him and vie for his attention when he was working in the After School Program at school. It made me even happier to watch him love them unconditionally!

Davis was a role model when it came to helping others. One of these days, I'm going to compile all the stories of how he helped people that his friends and classmates have shared with me since his death. Even as a young child in elementary school, young adults have written me to tell me how he would help them with their reading, or homework, or how he was nice to them when no one else seemed to care. Stories that I had never heard before seemed to flood my emails and FB messages after his death, telling me of good deeds and acts of kindness that he had performed. People who knew Davis knew that he didn't care about the perception of others when it came to doing the right thing. He would help anyone in need regardless of that person's circumstances or social standing. There was not a pretentious bone in his body. He did not discriminate when it came to the hearts and feelings of others.

If Davis left me with one lesson, it was the lesson of helping others unconditionally and without judgment. He has helped me to heal by helping others come to terms with their disease. Everyday now on the DDF, whether through private messages or comments, or even emails and phone calls, multiple people are reaching out to us for help and answers. We are doing everything in our power to help when and where we are able to help. We make phone calls, plan events, gather supplies that will offer warmth inwardly and outwardly, and we offer a listening ear! We validate the sick and lonely and we tell them we are here for them and God loves them unconditionally! Sometimes when I don't have the strength to move forward, a young man or young woman calls in need of help and that is God's way of helping me put one foot in front of the other. It takes my mind off of my own personal pain and allows me to focus on what is truly important. There are several people in situations as we speak that I am trying to support into recovery and offer information and knowledge about available resources that will help them through their present circumstances. Nothing makes me feel better than to search for answers and offer an ear and an avenue of support. It keeps me moving forward and allows me to breathe when I am searching for my next breath.

There are others who have gone down the dark valley of losing a loved one to an overdose before me that help me on a daily basis and others who have gone behind me. We help each other and realize that our hearts will never be truly whole again in this lifetime. Helping others feels good and it will get you through the tough days like nothing else. It's better than any medication, any "stay busy" task that you can involve yourself in, and any book you can read…yes including the Bible – because helping others is "Living" the Bible! When you are on your last breath, your last tear, your last hope, HELP SOMEONE ELSE. It will renew your strength and allow you to "Move Onward through Life… Looking Upward to

God!" Sometimes you might even look toward the sky and see a star twinkle and know that it was meant for you Xxooo

12/5/14 – Constructive Act #260 – Share Your Successes

Many of you have followed a story that began quite unexpectedly last Saturday with a private message into my inbox. It was a message from a young man named Adam. For those of you who do not know the beginning of the story, I am going to repost the "cry for help" that I received from him.

Hi, my name is Adam E. I'm a heroin addict. I have been battling this disease for several years... I've overdosed multiple times and I am getting worse and worse. I hate what my life has become and I want to stop using. I don't have any financial support from my family and I'm pretty sure my health insurance has run out. I don't know what to do... I need to go to detox and I want to go to treatment. Can you help me? Please, I don't want to die. I feel so alone. My family won't speak to me. Addiction has taken everything from me. I don't want to live like this anymore. If there is anything you can do, please let me know. I need help. I want help. Please...

Any parent who gets a message like this one knows that it pulls the very essence of your soul out of the depths of normalcy. It throws you into high gear and doesn't let you get an ounce of rest until you have resolution. We worked overnight with the help of the awesome DDF readers and into the early morning hours of Sunday even texting during church—Sorry Dr. Sam! By Sunday afternoon, he had been accepted into a local facility to Detox and had begun his journey of recovery. Detox is a relatively short process and for the most part, it is always too short and the addicts are never left in detox long enough to become truly clean. With that being said, it is of vital importance to have a rehab center or a recovery residence lined up to ensure the process of recovery continues without a break in service. So for Adam, the clock was ticking and we were actively helping him to get through to the next step of his recovery.

We spoke with facility after facility, filtering through website after website to try and help Adam find a place to get well. He lined up an interview with a place he had previously received help from and we felt really good about the situation, until the bottom dropped out from under him and he was refused help at this particular facility. Apparently, and in his own words, he had burned a bridge there during a previous stay. We were all devastated and worse than that, we were back to square one! UGH! In the meantime, Adam had reached out to family and friends with no luck of help, which is understandable in so many cases where the addicts have lied, stolen and cheated their way through the family circle. He sat alone and desperate on the front porch of a Marietta Rehab calling out for help and receiving NO answers.

Phone call after phone call was answered by an automated system where we were asked to leave messages. Not a single phone call was returned. We added his name to several waiting lists and filled out several applications. We were very limited in our quest as Adam was dead broke with no insurance. Adam finally found a friend through a 12 step program he had attended who offered him a place to stay while he continued his quest for help. Through an act of fate, one of Adams' friends saw the DDF post and reached out to none other than Andrey Rossin from "Into Action" Treatment Center in Boynton Beach, Florida and told him about Adam. Adam called Andrey and thank God, Adam will be on a bus to Florida tomorrow afternoon and will be picked up by "Into Action" where he has received a scholarship into the program to receive the help he is so desperately searching for.

Andrey represented "Into Action" at the October Symposium and Vendor Fair and has a solid program for opiate/heroin addiction. Many of you had the awesome opportunity to speak personally with Andrey and hear firsthand about his program.

He also brought several of his "success stories" with him and allowed them to speak directly with those who had questions about his program. He is a faithful supporter of the DDF and plans to attend the January Symposium and set up a vendor table once again at the April Symposium and Vendor Fair. Andrey has offered Adam the chance of a lifetime and Adam realizes how lucky he is to have this opportunity offered to him.

Please keep Adam in your prayers and ask God to lay his hands upon Adam's broken spirit and heal him from the addiction he has suffered with for so long. Ask God to heal the broken family and restore peace to them as only He can do. Pray that Adam will realize the path that God has laid before him and walk the straight and narrow that leads to full recovery and a new lease on life.

Adam, the DDF is so proud of you and the steps you are taking to get where you need to be. Your persistence and humble attempts asking for help have paid off. The Davis Direction Foundation supports you to the moon and back! Godspeed on your journey and please keep us informed of the progress you are making. Xxooo Missy, The DDF Board, and the rest of the "almost" 5,000 members strong DDF community!

12/6/14 – Constructive Act #261 – Assigning Blame Accomplishes Nothing

Obviously when a person writes from the heart for any length of time and shares their innermost feelings, it is inevitable that things along the way will be misconstrued or interpreted differently than they were intended to be. On top of misinterpretations, when a person is writing about an issue that has no steadfast answer or solution and continues to throw things out there to offer HOPE, suggestions will have different meaning for different folks and may even frustrate the readers. Then, there is always the possibility that I will be "dead flat wrong" in my writing because I have not "been there – done that" on this journey of opiate/heroin addiction. I realize all of these things, but I continue to write and put personal thoughts out there from my own experience in the hope that something I may say will give another person strength or may even spark a debate that creates more awareness because we all know people love DRAMA! That is the sole reason that I continue to do news interviews and media stories publicly even though it incites public comments from people who have absolutely NO point of reference from which to comment! That is absolutely maddening to me, but the ignorance of others creates great fury from people who do have personal experience who would not otherwise get involved! That creates AWARENESS, which is the main goal of the Davis Direction Foundation.

With that being said, I want to address one issue that I speak about frequently and am very outspoken about in direct contrast (to some places) to others out there who have the platform of a Treatment Center to speak from. We were told point blank and in no uncertain terms that if Davis had a "lapse" after his first Rehabilitation experience, to completely "throw him out." We were not to accept calls, not answer calls, not send money, not continue to pay his bills, (phone, car, food, shelter, etc.) and to leave him "in the streets" to find his way. As parents, we completely disagreed with this philosophy and we did not do this. We were not done trying to help our child and we were not at a point where we had exhausted all avenues of help and rehabilitation. Davis had only been to rehab one time and had only had a couple of individual counselors, and had not been doing drugs for years and years. He was a relatively young drug addict and had NEVER lived away from home. Of course he had stolen, lied and pawned things that we had to buy back, that is a definite part of the disease, but he had not put us into financial ruin and had not financially altered our family lifestyle. Had we put him in the streets as we were "told" to do, I'm certain we would have cremated him much earlier than we did. He would not have survived on the streets under the circumstances at that time.

There is an old saying—some say it is in the Bible00but I don't think so… "that God does not give His children more than they can handle." I think about this old saying often, and I truly believe that God knew that Davis could not have handled 10+ years of living the way he was living and I know for sure that as a family, we would not have survived year after year of living through addiction. There is nothing that prepares you for this life and there are NO WORDS to describe it to someone who doesn't have firsthand experience with opiate/heroin addiction. When I talk about the decisions that our family made, I do not by any stretch of the imagination believe that our decisions should be any other families' decisions. The families of addicts and the "Addicts' Keepers" have to make individual decisions based on their circumstances and personal beliefs. I don't believe there is a family, mother, father, sister, or brother out there who does anything with the intent to harm or hurt their addict. It's like walking to the end of a cliff: you either freeze and just stay frozen for a while or you step back and let someone else take the reins and put it completely in God's capable hands. At that point, God decides! As Christians, we accept that decision or we turn from God and lose our way. That is our decision. Michael and I never felt that we had come to the end of our cliff. We were still approaching the abysmal bottom when Davis left this earth. We have accepted that this was God's decision for our family, and we pray daily that we find the strength and courage to move forward with our lives with His help. We continue to live in honor of Davis, and do what we can to help others. That's what Davis would have wanted.

There are families out there who are standing at the edge of their cliff and their decisions are different. I have NO point of reference from this perspective and I can't even imagine what they go through having done everything they could possibly do and more to help their child, spouse, brother or sister. They are exhausted from the fight and they are numb. I've been told that at this point, you pray for others to do the work that you are no longer physically capable of doing. The money runs out, there is nothing left to take or steal, there are no lies that you haven't heard and the Freudian sense of "trust" that you learned as a child has completely abandoned your brain! I CANNOT IMAGINE! These people have NOT given up on their addicts, there is simply nothing left! An "addict's keeper" finally realizes that short of a miracle from God... there is a point of no return from the human perspective! That's when you have no choice but to "Let GO and Let GOD."

I pray for these families daily and I cannot imagine their pain. There are some things that I truly believe to be worse than death and I believe this to be one of them. During this season of "Christmas Cheer" my heart breaks for families who will spend their first Christmas without their addict, such as mine, but my heart bleeds uncontrollably for those who are exhausted from the fight knowing that it will end one of 2 ways... Recovery or Death! During this time of year and every other time of year, please pray without ceasing and invest in our efforts to find a cure or instill abstinence into those who have never taken opiates. We MUST find solutions and WE WILL. There is HOPE!

12/7/14 – Constructive Act #262 – Share Your Story

Today's story is a little different. Okay... It's a lot different. It's a STORYBOOK of sorts explaining addiction. I am completely out of stories for Sunday's posts – So if you would like to send me one for posting, PLEASE DO! But for today, try to understand this storybook interpretation of just how quickly and horribly it can consume someone.

www.youtube.com/watch?v=HUngLgGRJpo

12/8/14 – Constructive Act # 263 – Remember the Reason for the Season

Anyone who knows me at all, knows that I think Christmas is the most wonderful time of the year! Or, at least I used to think that. I will tell you that this past week has been the hardest week for me since Davis died. In the past, we always had a Christmas tradition that everything was completely decorated before Thanksgiving, but we never turned the lights on until Thanksgiving night. We would turn the TV on the Channel 2 "Lighting of the Macy's Tree" and when the lady hit the high note on "O Holy Night", everyone would man his post and "PLUG IN." Chevy Chase didn't have "nothing" on the "Owen 7." We would light up the house and the neighborhood all in one "high note" second! It was a great tradition and the kids loved it. They loved to bring their friends over and show them our beautifully decorated house and they loved to just be home during Christmas because it was so beautiful. All year long I would look for things to add to the Christmas tradition and would save it for the big light up night. Last night I finally had the biggest "melt down" of all—It was truly like Sally Fields in "Steel Magnolias" except that my moment would have been rated R due to language!

If you remember, I went away the week of Thanksgiving because I knew I could not deal with the traditions of the past. So, I obviously did not get my house ready for Christmas and I was not ready to get my house ready for Christmas. I did not even care about Christmas if you want to know the truth. So, Friday afternoon, when I got home, I began feeling guilty about not decorating for Christmas. I knew in my heart that Davis would have been sad if he had known that he took the joy of Christmas away from us and I knew it wasn't fair to the younger kids that I had done nothing to get ready for the holiday. I began by decorating my mantle. I "hung the stockings by the chimney with care" but it only made the mantle look"bare." Then the discussion turned to "Do we hang his stocking or not?" I chose not to so that I wouldn't have to look at an empty stocking the whole season and be reminded every day and with every look that he was gone. Then the kids wanted it up there. Comments were made like, "Wow—that's sad." And "If you don't hang his stocking, then don't hang mine." "Just take them all down." Everybody all the sudden had an opinion and they were all different.

Then came the tree, one tree, instead of the 5 I usually put up in strategic places. I knew in my heart that there was no way I would be able to decorate the "usual" tree with all the kids handmade ornaments and the symbolic ornaments that marked a period in one of their lives. So instead, I went out yesterday morning and purchased a whole new theme for a Christmas tree that would just be red and gold. None of the ornaments would really mean anything, other than the red birds that remind me of Davis now. I bought plenty of new and beautiful, sparkly, glittery, shiny things to adorn the new themed tree. I even went for white lights this year instead of the multicolored "fun" lights of every past year. I thought the white lights would remind me of a thousand candles lit for my sweet son. It would be a candle light vigil all season. Davis wasn't around to help me with the tree like he always did, so instead I was having to do it all by myself. That did not go well and finally after putting the layers of the tree together out of order and then pulling it completely over to get it apart to reassemble and then putting the base up wrong upon reassembly, when I added the fourth layer the tree collapsed – mind you this is a 9 1/2 foot tree—and I collapsed with it! That's when all "Hell" broke loose! The words began to fly—along with the tree across the living room floor! I was screaming, crying, throwing the pieces of the tree, cursing, and completely melting down because I HATED CHRISTMAS! I WANTED TO DIE! It finally hit me square between the eyes that Davis was never coming home... NEVER!

I went upstairs to my room, slammed the door, and cried for hours! Then I came back downstairs and told Michael I didn't even want a tree! Then a couple minutes later I told him I wanted to blow up the house and the mess I had made trying to put the tree up in the first place, and believe me it was massive! I had pulled over 1200 pre-lit lights off of the tree because I wanted "white lights." Then, Michael calmly got up, put the tree together, cleaned up the entire mess, vacuumed the living room, went upstairs to bed, and texted me the sweetest message of my entire life. He told me that he loved me with all his heart and that he needed me so that he could hold it together and continue to make it through the rest of the season. He couldn't do it without me! I guess men tend to suffer silently whereas women hold it in so long that when they finally let it go, there's no holding back!

The point is that Michael brought it back around to LOVE—and that is what Christmas is all about. The ultimate "LOVE" that was born on Christmas morning, who was born to die so that all of us could have eternal life! Jesus is the Reason for the Season and when we lose sight of that, we lose everything. Because of the birth of Jesus I will see Davis again. Davis is not broken anymore, he is at peace and whole again with our Lord and Savior. Yes, — the one tree will go up with the new theme, the white lights, and I did buy angels, hearts, stars and red birds. Maybe one day, I will have the strength to go back to the "child-made ornament" tree, but for this year, we need a change. The "Owen 7" tree will have celestial bodies and heavenly reminders, which will speak of love and the life everlasting. Merry Christmas everyone! God Bless.

12/9/14 – Constructive Act #264 – Slow Down and Breathe

It doesn't matter where or how you fit into to this puzzle of opiate/heroin addiction, if you are involved even as a prayer warrior, it can become overwhelming and exhausting. There comes a point where you just need to "SLOW DOWN AND BREATHE." As you all have probably guessed from yesterday's post, I am there! So, I have taken the next 3 days off of work, and I let the 9 and ½ foot tree sit idle yesterday except for the first 400 white lights that only covered the first 2 rows of limbs at the very bottom. It's okay! I needed to breathe! As I sit here this morning writing the "CA" for today. I have my first 400 lights glowing around the bottom of the otherwise "bare" tree and that's just fine with me. It's the first 400 candles lit for Davis. I'm taking baby steps and it feels better! I've always been one of those people who jumps into any project with both feet and wild abandon—that philosophy doesn't work with this. I'm learning to slow down and let time do it's thing.

As many of you know, I will be retiring from my Counseling job in an elementary school on Friday the 19th of December. I have been working 2 full-time jobs with the Foundation quickly expanding to much more than a full-time job. So, after 33 years of education and working with children, God is now calling me to a different place in life and I am ready to heed the call and invest much of my time and energy into the Foundation. I will be able to focus on more of what truly needs to be done and to get out there and really begin networking with individuals who can help the cause and save lives. I already have several meetings set up, and the Christmas Eve "Lighting of the Way" as well as the upcoming Symposium in January will allow me to hit the ground running. The Foundation will begin to keep true office hours with a designated phone line that will be answered by a real live person! – ME!

We will see where this all leads and the plan is as it has always been to let God lead in the Direction that He wants us to pursue. Although we are in the process of completing a business plan as all good and successful incorporations do, we will always depend on God to pave the way. I will be meeting with the new Webmasters this week to hopefully get one step closer to rolling out the new website that will be much more user friendly and more up to date with happenings rather than just Constructive Acts and factual information. We are hoping to have a scrolling bulletin board letting you know what we have in the works as well as upcoming events. We are truly about to get down to the business that we are designed to accomplish and we want you on board with us! To make a difference, it will take every one of us at different times and for different events. You do have a place in the Foundation, so take your "breather" now, we are truly about to get cranked up!

Michael and the kids and I are trying our best to figure out our journey this first Christmas without Davis. We are not even so concerned about "new traditions" as we are about just surviving this first year. That will take all of our energy! We are here for each other, and when one of us falls, the others are there to help us up and point us back in the right direction as we continue the journey. Thank God they were there for me yesterday! Now I am gaining strength again and I will be able to be there for them if and when they need me. It's a give and take process that comes from loving and caring for each other, and if you know anything about the "Owen 7" you definitely know that we are all about each other We are about as tight knit as a family can become and we kind of like it that way. When one of struggles for the next breath, another one of us is there to breathe for whomever it is. When we all struggle, it is then that we see one set of "FOOTPRINTS IN THE SAND." We are learning as a family to continue our journey and sometimes it just requires taking time to "SLOW DOWN AND BREATHE." Please continue to remember everyone in this fight in your prayers as I truly believe the recovery that each individual needs whether it be from opiate/heroin addiction or the recovery from the loss of a loved one or even the loss of a "living one" cannot be accomplished without the help of God! He will lead the way in this Foundation and he will lead the way in Recovery. Slow down and sense HIS presence this Holiday season and continue to draw one breath at a time...

12/10/14 – Constructive Act #265 – Find Your Outlet

Some days as I sit here and write my post every morning, I feel just a bit guilty and selfish because, writing makes everything better for me. I have never been one to sit and openly share my feelings through discussion or face to face, but I will admit, it feels good to write them down and get them off my heart. Even as a teenager growing up, I wrote letters, emails, poems, and stories because they have always been my outlet. Writing, planting flowers and plants, and playing the piano make my heart ease up—no matter what the problem is. It can be just a little tug at my heartstrings or it can be a massive epidemic, or it can even be a permanent hole in my heart, but writing, planting or playing the piano, at least temporarily help to ease the pain. All three are things that allow me to think about my feelings. Writing allows me to express my feelings on paper and say things that you may or may not ever see or hear, but I get it off of my chest! Playing the piano when I need an outlet usually means that I will be playing hymns. Hymns really speak to me. You can find one for every emotion, every problem, and every inspirational need. Hymns are great! If you can't play them on the piano, just sit down and read the words sometimes. They will speak to you! Planting plants just lets me get my hands dirty and allows me to begin something that will show results – at least most of the time, but when they don't flourish, it just reminds me that things don't always turn out the way that we might like for them to turn out. It reminds me that I am not in control when it comes to living and growing things and I continue to take the chance anyway. Plants are awesome!

It doesn't matter if you are the addict, the "addict's keeper," the friend of an addict or the loved one of an addict, everyone involved with addiction needs an outlet. One day, when the DDF has it's own recovery residence—and that is a long term goal, we will provide "outlets." I think this is a major downfall of most recovery residences and rehabilitation facilities. They work with the addicts all day long in group settings with very little individual time proportionately, and then when they are done working with them, they have FREE time! I know Davis would either sleep, or read whatever limited materials were available when he was at Rehab. He finally called me and asked me to bring his video gaming system up to the facility for weekend use because there was NOTHING there to do. I did bring it up to the guys and they enjoyed it, but that's one of those mindless, outlets — kind of like watching sit-coms on television. It has its place, but it's not really a productive "outlet."

Michael and I will sit and dream about our "DDF Recovery Residence" and one of the greatest gifts he will be able to offer is to teach young men how to work on cars. That is Michael's "outlet" and I can assure you since Davis' death, he has worked on cars every single weekend and even on the weeknights after he has put in a full day of financial work! It is his "outlet" and when he needs it, it is there for him. From washing them to changing oil, to replacing brakes or entire heating systems, he can fix anything on a car! He saves TONS of money and it gives him something productive to do while he mourns the loss of our precious son. When he gets done with a major repair, he always feels accomplished and he usually makes the statement that Davis would have liked helping him on that repair because working on cars was an outlet for Davis as well. One day while Davis was in rehab, Michael took a big, huge turbo hose in that he had ordered for them to repair Davis' car. Davis lit up like a light bulb and begged Michael not to put it on without him. That was their "outlet" that they shared and I know that Michael feels close to Davis still whenever he works on cars.

Having an "outlet" allows you to get in touch with yourself and your inner feelings. EVERYONE NEEDS AN OUTLET. Whether it is cooking, cleaning, art, sewing, cars, music, electronics, social media, performing …this list could go on and on, everyone needs to have an "outlet." I'm quite sure anyone who has an "outlet" is more mentally and emotionally healthy than someone who does not have an "outlet." If you are not sure what kind of an "outlet" you would like, I will tell you how to get started. Go to a huge bookstore and go to the magazine section. Magazines promote "outlets." You can find a magazine for just about every "outlet" on earth. Find something that sparks your interest and if you don't have the money to buy the magazine, then just sit down on the floor in the aisle and read it! If you decide you don't like it, get up off of the floor and choose another one! Do this until you find something that you really like and then you will know how to get started. The internet is also a great source to help you with your "outlet;" there are you tube videos that allow you to learn just about anything about anything for FREE! I have often said on the DDF and I even wrote an entire post about it: "idle time is the Devil's workshop." An "outlet" prevents that idle time! "FIND YOUR OUTLET."

12/11/14 – Constructive Act #266 – Guard Your Conversations

I have written before on the DDF that my last 3 words to Davis were "I love you." I cannot tell you how lucky I am that those were the last 3 words that I ever spoke to my son. Although, if they had not been, it wouldn't have meant that I loved him any less, it would just have been something else that I would have had to deal with emotionally. It would have been forever and unchangeable. This week alone, I have had several conversations with people who have had conversations that didn't go so well with their addicts, and they are upset about it. I have had conversations with people who have had those hard and ugly conversations (including myself) at some point, but then had the opportunity to have another conversation that ended better and perhaps even ended well. When you love an opiate/heroin addict, you never know when your last conversation will be, and you need to treat every conversation as if it will be your last, remembering all the while, that addiction is a disease.

The ones who love the addicts the most, are the most likely to confront them about their behavior and have those hard and ugly conversations. It's not that we mean to be ugly and harsh, it's just that we know the person that we are dealing with is not the child or loved one that we knew "BD"—before drugs! It's so hard to understand where that person is, and why they can't come back to us. Last night I had a conversation with a couple of friends and we talked about the fact that when you are dealing with opiate/heroin addiction, you are mourning the living. With this disease you begin the mourning process while the addicts are still alive. I know there were many nights that I went to sleep crying when Davis was still alive because I knew that he wasn't my "REAL" Davis. The drugs had altered him and I wanted him back. In fact there is still a sign on his door that I cut out of a magazine that reads, "We Want You Back." I would have given life and limb to have him "whole" again and when you love someone that much, you become passionate and emotional in your dealings with them. You know that what they are telling you is not the truth and all you want to do is get to the bottom of things so that you can begin to help them, but they won't let you. It is the most frustrating feeling in the world and it often leads to anger and raw emotion that leads to nowhere.

Coupled with the above feelings and then the stress of the holidays, things can get out of hand quickly if you lose sight of the fact that "Addiction IS a Disease!" There are so many conflicted feelings for families struggling with addiction during the holidays. The traditional season of "giving" becomes a real issue for families because for the most part, they are out of money due to the fact that addiction is EXPENSIVE. Sometimes you feel like you have spent more that the "fair share" on the addict in the first place and your heart wants to "give" to them, but the money is just not there. You begin to feel guilty because of societal pressures to feel Merry and Jolly and it's just not working for you! You become resentful because, seemingly the addict has robbed the family of the Joy of Christmas. It's just not the same because addiction has taken over your life and your livelihood.

You just want to return to simpler times when the stars aligned and the moon shone brightly.

Rest assured, that if your addict could be granted one wish, or be gifted with one gift that had no stipulations or boundaries, he or she would undoubtedly wish to go back to that first encounter with drugs and decide all over again which way to go. Hindsight is so cruel for opiate/heroin addiction. There is a beautiful song that comes around this time of year entitled "Grown up Christmas List." It's so beautiful and I would think that it is the inner desire of every addict who is struggling with the disease of addiction. (Lyrics by Linda Thompson-Jenner)

"Grown-Up Christmas List"

Do you remember me
I sat upon your knee
I wrote to you with childhood fantasies

Well I'm all grown-up now
And still need help somehow
I'm not a child
But my heart still can dream

So here's my lifelong wish
My grown-up Christmas list
Not for myself
But for a world in need

No more lives torn apart
That wars would never start
And time would heal all hearts
Everyone would have a friend
And right would always win
And love would never end
This is my grown-up Christmas list

As children we believed
The grandest sight to see
Was something lovely
Wrapped beneath our tree

Well heaven surely knows
That packages and bows
Can never heal a hurting human soul

What is this illusion called
The innocence of youth
Maybe only in our blind belief
Can we ever find the truth
No more lives torn apart
That wars would never start
And time would heal all hearts
Everyone would have a friend
And right would always win
And love would never end
This is my grown-up Christmas list

As you spend time with family members and loved ones this Christmas season, remember that addiction is a disease. Remember that every conversation you have with your precious child, your precious spouse, your loving sister or brother, your parent, your best-friend or anyone that you love with your heart and soul could potentially be your last conversation if that person is an opiate/heroin addict. Also, remember that if they could give us the gift of making the holiday season different and "normal" for us, they would. They try everyday to get better; I believe that no one mourns for the lives of the living more than the addicts themselves—they want their lives back. Guard your conversations, speak of love, encouragement and HOPE. As long as they are alive, There is HOPE.

12/12/14 – Constructive Act #267 – Make New Meanings Work For You

For those of you who know me well, you would agree that I am one of the most

analytical people you have ever known. Everything in life needs to have meaning for me and if it doesn't, I usually assign it some kind of meaning so that I can move on with my life. Simple things all the way through to the most complex things must have some type of meaning. In years past, the Christmas tree has had meaning. The multicolor lights were all about fun, and the ornaments represented the history of the "Owen7." We even put a hook on the cork that came out of the Dom Perignon bottle of champagne from our engagement. It was significant in the fact that it was the beginning of our lives together and so in the past, it has hung on the family tree. We purchased the Hallmark ornaments for every significant moment in our lives…first house, first child, new house, anniversary, you name it and it's on our family tree. The tree has traditionally been full of homemade ornaments as well that have signified different times and events in the lives of the kids. It doesn't matter what color, how old, or how deteriorated it is, if it can still hang, in the past it has hung! Then there is my "angel tree," which only had picture frame ornaments with the kids pictures down through the years hanging on it, the "White House" tree — a white tree with the collectible "White House" ornaments, and last but certainly not least, and the most powerful tree – My SNOW tree…thus the reason for the snowy winters of the past! It has only snowflakes and snowmen on white with white lights! If you don't know me, then I think you are beginning to get the picture. Life needs meaning for me!

Now, if you are a regular reader, you will better understand why I had such a fit last week over the Christmas tree—I could not deal with the memories of the trees I had put together in the past and I still had no meaning for a new tree. I was a lost soul with no meaning and I had to go in search of new meaning. It really wasn't about the tree, it was about meaning. Last night, the kids helped me decorate the most beautiful tree ever and when Michael walked in, he smiled and said… It's beautiful!

The meaning of the tree, is all over the place, but it has meaning on multiple levels that will help our family remember and celebrate the important things that we have come face to face with over the past months. The tree colors are red and gold. Red of course symbolizes the blood that was shed on Calvary so all of us could be forgiven for our sins and have eternal life if we believe in Jesus. Gold reminds me of the "Golden Slippers used to walk the Golden Streets" — a song my Daddy always sang when we were growing up. It also reminds me of the "King of Kings" who called my precious Davis home and is now with him. The red and gold ribbon encircling the tree reminds me that God's love flows freely and He wraps His loving arms around his children and holds them close. The circle wreaths on the tree represent the symbol of eternity, no beginning and no end. There are exactly 2000 lights on the tree symbolizing the 2000 teenagers that will try drugs for the first time on a daily basis. 200 of those 2000 – 10% – are red lights symbolizing the 200 of the 2000 who will succumb to addiction. The other 1800 symbolize lighted candles – for those who have passed on or those still struggling. The gold stars remind me of this quote: "Perhaps they are not stars, but rather openings in heaven where the love of our lost ones pour through and shine down on us to let us know they are happy." It wouldn't be my tree if it didn't have golden snowflakes on it. The snowflake is one of God's most fragile creations, but look at what they can do when they stick together. This of course reminds me of the power in numbers and the difference that we are making collectively in the DDF. There is a single drum on the tree, that stands for all of the children out there who beat to the tune of a different drummer—Jesus loves them all unconditionally—there is no room for judgmental feelings. The Red Birds could have a post of their own because of all that they stand for. I see them daily in my backyard and they make me happy. Yes, – I do believe they are visitors and it helps me make it through the bad days. I even talk to them and from time to time I do believe one of them is Davis. It works for me! When you see a red bird in winter, you will prosper in spring. When you hear a Cardinal sing, your sadness will soon be lifted.

When a red bird shows up, help is on the way. I heard a bird sing in the dark of December, A magical thing and sweet to remember. The bows on the branches remind me of the gifts we can offer each other. Any act of kindness, words of encouragement, or prayers offered on someones' behalf are all gifts that we can give daily. It doesn't cost us a penny and it might make a difference to the person on the receiving end. The bells and angels remind me that when acts of kindness are shared and support is offered.

For each and every bell that rings. Another angel gets his wings. It's a Wonderful Life.

There are 4 individually meaningful displays for my family that make our tree extra special. The first display is that of 2 rugged stars made of twisted wire, with a pine cone, natural twine and red bells – They remind me of Davis and Bobby – "Jingle and Jangle" it reminds me of a time when they were inseparable and the best of friends. It makes me smile that my son had a friend who stuck by him even unto death. The second is the display of Elsa and Olaf. This display reminds me how much Davis loved his precious daughter and how goofy he would be with her and how she adored him. The third is the 2014 Davis Direction Foundation ornament that reminds me of the work there is to be done to rid the community and the nation of this horrible epidemic, but it mostly reminds me of HOPE for the future. And last but certainly not least, The "OWEN7" ornament reminds me that we are and will always be a family – even though we reside in different places now… we are FAMILY!

12/13/14 – Constructive Act #268 – Manage With Medication

I'm going to get on a soapbox today and I don't really like to do that, but I'm extremely disappointed over a situation that happened this week. I'm not angry with the addict, I do understand the disease, but when it comes to opiates and heroin, there is a lot of disappointment and despair along the way. It just absolutely comes with the territory. I get that! Here's what I don't get: Vivitrol is

292

available and accessible to anybody who wants it. The website for Vivitrol is vivitrol.com and on the website, you put your zip code in and a list of doctors comes up that are actively stocking the medication and are actively giving the shots. Vivitrol is a proper name for the drug Naltrexone.

"Naltrexone hydrochloride is a pure opioid antagonist. It markedly attenuates or completely blocks, reversibly, the subjective effects of intravenously administered opioids.

When co-administered with morphine, on a chronic basis, Naltrexone hydrochloride blocks the physical dependence to morphine, heroin and other opioids."

The Vivitrol shot lasts for 30 days, but the addict has to be completely detoxed before he or she can get the shot. If they are not completely clean, they will become violently ill. Now, lots of addicts don't have insurance because they are not longer covered under their parents' policies or because they are older than 26, or because they did not register through the government. Whatever the case may be, the shots, in my humble opinion, are medically necessary to treat the disease of opiate/heroin addiction. As a matter of fact, I think that Vivitrol is a saving grace for heroin addicts in the fact that it only works on opiate drugs! It does not work on amphetamines or benzodiazepines. So there is a temporary cure for heroin abuse if you take the medication on a monthly basis. I've said this so many times and it's so true, if I had known about Vivitrol when Davis was struggling with his addiction, that would have been our first priority after detox. So, back to insurance, with or without insurance you need to find a way to come up with the money to get the shot.

You may be sitting here saying, "that's easy for you to say," So let me ask you this, "Do you know how much it costs to bury a child?" Because, I do!

It's way more expensive than a Vivitrol shot, as a matter of fact, you could buy a year's worth of Vivitrol shots for less than you could bury your child. You could buy 3 or 4 Vivitrol shots for the treatment fees you would pay a reputable treatment center over the period of one month. You could sleep at night knowing that your addict is not even capable of getting high and you could even wear your fine jewelry without worrying that it would be stolen as soon as you took it off. Some insurance policies cover the shots at next to nothing and the Vivitrol site has coupon codes and payment plans to help with the cost of the drug. Find a way to get the shots and keep them going for as long as they are necessary. And how long they are necessary is anyone's guess. For now, it is the only "cure" that we know of. Yes, it's temporary, but if repeated every 30 days, it works!

When you think about diseases as a whole, name one that does not have some sort of medicinal support? Diabetics take their insulin, Cancer patients take their chemo and radiation, asthmatics keep their inhalers with them wherever they go. The list goes on and on. So why in the world do we just say to addicts, "Okay here's your diagnosis – you're an addict... So just stop!" That doesn't even make sense! Once again as a society we are talking out of both sides of our mouths. GET OFF THE FENCE. If you believe that it is a disease, then TREAT IT LIKE ONE!

For now, I think this is a GREAT, LIFE-SAVING OPTION! If only I had known. Find the doctor, Find the money, Find the way to help your addict until something better comes along! As long as they stay alive... There is HOPE! www.vivitrol.com

12/14/14 – Constructive Act #269 – Share Your Story

Here is another story from Boynton Beach Florida. Thank you Andrey Rossin for the good job that you are doing down there at Into Action. Thank you as well for helping me out with the Sunday Stories! Thank you Garson for sharing your story this week.

Here is his story:

This time a year ago, it was easy to imagine myself dead. It wasn't a matter of if, but when. I had basically pushed everyone close to me as far away from me as possible. And really, that's how I liked it. If I wasn't close to you I couldn't pull you down with me. Whether or not I actually believed that was the case or not is irrelevant, it affected everyone that loved me. In the year prior to my decision to go to treatment for a severe drug addiction I lost my fiancé and was about to completely be shut off from my family.

And that, was all I had left.

I've heard you have to be in a place of complete and total desperation to want to get clean. I've heard you have to hit your bottom to want to get clean. I've also heard that you have to lose everything to want to get clean. I think these things are all very true, but to me it all comes down to one very simple thing. You have to want it more than you want the drugs. YOU have to want to be clean. And most importantly, NO ONE ELSE can do it for you. They can't make you or convince you otherwise. It's all up to YOU.

I loved getting high more than anything else in the world. More than my music. More than my family. And certainly more than any relationship I ever had. Drugs, more specifically Heroin, were my significant other. But of course, I did them all. I always had a theory that I'd try anything at least once and I succeeded pretty well at that. For over twenty years I mastered the art of being a drug addict or as I liked to call it, "being normal." Drugs helped me escape a reality which I didn't want to have any part of. I was so delusional in fact that I thought no one even noticed when I was high.

Fast forward to a week ago, November 25th. This was my one year anniversary of being clean, the day before my 37th birthday. And what a tremendous birthday it was! I got to spend it with my parents enjoying a day we both thought might never come. I can honestly say that a big part of my success came from the things I learned in my time in treatment at Into Action. Andrey Rossin actually answered my phone call when I finally got up the courage to call someone about my problem. Within a week I was on a plane to South Florida on my way to Detox. After two weeks cleaning out my system of the 160 milligrams of Methadone I was on daily, I finally got to meet Andrey and the Into Action team. I was scared, so scared. Could I do this? Is it really what I wanted? Wouldn't it be easier to just continue to use? These are all valid and terrifying realities when getting clean. Into Action helped me realize there was more to my life than what it had become.

Treatment is not easy for anyone. But it's not supposed to be. Think of the small sacrifice you are making for a chance at actually LIVING the rest of your life! It's worth the risk! Hearing Andrey's story and so many others like his was truly inspiring. Preparing myself for the big jump back into everyday life was a challenge, but Into Action certainly made that transition easier for me. And they made me aware of the dangers to look out for and what to expect. It's not easy like I said, but it's possible. Look at me. Garson C

12/15/14 – Constructive Act #270 – Pass The Butter, Please

I love when I learn lessons from my kids, but I really love when those lessons are things that I have tried to teach them all of my life and then they turn around and remind me of them. Today, we were out shopping and my oldest daughter had chosen a couple of gifts off of an angel tree at work and we were looking around for the things she needed. Being the "Mother" and trying to make sure that "newly employed" Chelsea manages her money responsibly, I suggested that she choose a lesser item in cost for an mp3 player. I told her to get an iPod shuffle which was around $50.00, and after considering it for just a couple of minutes, she decided to go with a full iPod nano, which runs about $100.00 more in price. She still planned to get a couple of additional items that were lesser in value, but she chose to splurge on the mp3 player. Her rationale was that if she were 15 years old and she was hoping for an mp3 player under the Christmas tree, she would be fine with a shuffle, but a nano would make her ecstatic! So, she chose to give the item that would make a difference! She added the butter and that made me proud!

She then told me a story of a Sunday school teacher who taught a lesson in "Giving." She told me that Mr. Beau Wilson taught her that it was more blessed to give than to receive, but he took it a step further and qualified the gift. She said that Beau taught them that as Christians we often give the bread, but just as often, we forget the butter. We don't make it a sacrifice; in other words, we do what we can, so that we don't really feel the impact of what we give instead of going without so that others can experience the gift of love that we need to share. I don't think that any of my friends or family would ever sit idly by and watch someone go without when they were truly in need, but do we put the cherry on top to minister in the way that God calls us to serve?

Now, I will be the first to tell you that there is a huge difference between "needy" and "greedy," but the child that Chelsea chose to get involved with lives in a home and is an orphan. He has no family and will spend Christmas in the home with the other boys. Some of the other boys had such things as "Body wash for men" and "Pro-activ" acne solution on their lists. My personal favorite and the "heart breaker request" was simply for History books. Can you imagine a teenage boy who asks for History books for Christmas? It's hard for me to even think about a 15 year old who does not have a cell phone to listen to his music, but the boy that Chelsea chose obviously did not, so he humbly asked for an mp3 player.

Please locate the event flyer on the DDF and share it on your personal Facebook pages. We need to get the word out that we will be "Lighting the Way" for Jesus to come into the hearts and homes of those struggling with addiction and we will be handing these gift bags out on Christmas Eve for those in need. If your family is supporting a loved one through this unbearable journey, please come and take a walk for HOPE and feel the presence of God along the way. There is so much to be gained from a beautiful and meaningful encounter with God out under the stars, with the moon shining down filling each heart with LOVE and HOPE. Please come and experience the "Lighting of the Way" this Christmas Eve with friends of the Davis Direction Foundation.

12/16/14 – Constructive Act #271 – Just Put One Foot In Front of The Other

I'm working with a precious child right now who thinks he is a failure because he has relapsed. This is such a part of the disease. I have mentioned before on the DDF that statistics say that a heroin addict will go through an average of 6-9 treatment phases before they will have success in recovery—It's part of the disease. So, with that being said, you have only completely failed when you give up on yourself and stop trying. So the question becomes, how do you get started in recovery? You "Just put one foot in front of the other." I have seen a quote lately "The journey of a thousand mile begins with a single step." This is so true. Everybody begins somewhere, but they all begin with a single step. This is why the motto of the Davis Direction Foundation is "Moving onward through life... Looking upward to God." You can only maintain that "onward" direction by putting one foot in front of the other. So, take that step—the DDF is here to support you in your journey.

The Title of this CA comes from one of my all-time favorite Christmas Shows – "Santa Claus is Coming to Town." Kris Kringle is telling the Winter Warlock that he needs to change his ways. One verse of the song goes like this:

> "If you want to change your direction,
> if your time of life is at hand,
> Well, don't be the rule, be the exception...
> A good way to start is to stand!"

> "Put one foot in front of the other
> And soon you'll be walking 'cross the floor.
> You put one foot in front of the other
> And soon you'll be walking out the door."

I'm not trying to trivialize opiate/heroin addiction, but the process is the same and your time of life is truly at hand. If you don't start moving in an onward direction, then you may not be around to move at all. Parents and loved ones can help by gathering information and having it ready and at hand when the addict truly makes the decision to try and get help. It is true that you can't help someone who is not ready for help, but you can help by having the answers to information when the addict becomes ready to take the first step of the journey. There is so much information to sift through and so many questions to find answers to that may become quite overwhelming for addicts who are working with a brain that has been altered because of the drugs. The DDF is currently working on an information sheet to help families and addicts with the information in our community. It is quite a process as we are finding out ourselves as we begin compiling the information.

Many families may be spending time with loved ones during the holidays, and there may be an addict in the family this year that needs encouragement and support – NOT conviction! Please deal with them supportively and with compassion. Help them to understand that recovery is a process that begins with a single step. Help them realize that failure is part of the process and especially part of the disease. Help them to further realize that true failure is only realized when people give up on themselves and stop trying. As long as an addict can stand and put one foot in front of the other, they can work their way into recovery and be successful. It is a PROCESS! Godspeed...

12/17/14 – Constructive Act #272 – Know Your Limits

I'm NOT God and neither is any other parent or loved one who has supported and encouraged an opiate/heroin addict! So many times, I think we try to reach that status or even expect it of ourselves, only to fall short and be disappointed once again. We think that our love can make anything better and can conquer all evils — but Heroin is no match for the human person or the amount of love that we can muster. Opiate/Heroin addiction is not something that can be conquered without divine intervention in my opinion. There are 3 components that must be present when actively seeking recovery—the physical domain, the mental domain and the spiritual domain. One domain cannot achieve recovery without the other two! It is a journey that one must resign oneself to embark upon and although others can be there to support and encourage the addict along the way, we are not a part of any one of the domains.

Over and over again I was so disappointed and hurt that I could not persuade or help Davis to remain in recovery. I was NOT enough! I could not step back enough to realize that it was not about me and that I could not be a part of the recovery equation. Addiction is a solitary disease in that the addict has to choose to enter and remain in recovery. Only the addict can make a choice to leave recovery and re-enter active addiction. Think about it. How many people are actively by your side 24/7 that could challenge your every move and decision. For most of us, the answer in no-one! When you are dealing with an addict, you have to realize your limits! You are only as supportive as the addict will allow you to be!

On the other hand, the addict has to realize his or her limits as well. Heroin is a very powerful entity that knows your name and continues to call upon you to revisit and indulge. Will power is not enough to sustain your convictions against heroin. There must be a spiritual component and in my opinion, it must be God. I get so discouraged when I hear the words "Higher Power" described as anything you need or choose for it to be. Then I get really upset when I hear that some inanimate object is the higher power for someone. Every time I challenge the "Higher Power" words, the person who is in active recovery admits that it is God, but that they refer to it as a Higher Power because that's what they were taught to call God in recovery! Let's call things like they really are—God is God—the creator of the universe and the Father, the Son, Jesus Christ, and the Holy Spirit. He knows NO LIMITS! All things can be accomplished through HIM!

Humans on the other hand have limits! The addicts have their limits; the addict's keepers have their limits and the therapists and rehab centers have their limits! We can only do what we have been trained and taught to do.

WE are NOT GOD! We must learn to yield to God and let Him guide our decisions and our recovery. Only then will we complete the domain cycle and have a plan for recovery with all domains in place realizing their limits. God's love and mercy is Limitless… Call upon Him and His infinite wisdom to show you the way to Recovery.

I had a conversation last night with someone struggling with his addiction. I told him the same thing that I told Davis when he told me he was ashamed and embarrassed to ask God for forgiveness. God sent Jesus to this earth to die on a cross so that we could be forgiven for all of our sins. If you don't ask God's forgiveness, then what Jesus suffered and endured on the cross will go in vain because you don't accept the gift that he sacrificed to save your soul. What Jesus did, He did for YOU! Know your own limits and accept the limitless forgiveness that God is offering and turn your life around. I can do all things through Christ who strengthens me. Philippians 4:13. KNOW YOUR LIMITS!

12/18/14 – Constructive Act #273 – Invest in Your Addict's Recovery

I know that I said yesterday that you can only help your addict if they will allow you to help them, and I do believe that's true. But I do believe that there are ways you can prepare yourself for the chance that they will allow you to help them. An opiate/heroin addict's choice to enter and stay in recovery is theirs and theirs alone, and it will be an active process that, as it stands right now, will last for a lifetime. It won't be easy, but it has been done. Hopefully, down the road, there will be a cure that will re-set the opiate receptors in the brain not allowing you to remember that you have ever been high and not allowing your body to crave what you once knew. We can only hope and pray that that day comes soon!

Several days ago, our DDF Medical Director, Dr. Harold McLendon, Jr. sent me an article to explain the medicinal treatment for opioid detox and recovery. (You can read the article in its entirety on the FB Blog on a Dec. 15th post) At the end of the article, the Dr. who wrote it, also prepared a list of ways to help your addict as they decide to enter recovery. This list is a fantastic list and it is very comprehensive. I think that it is important enough to reproduce in a Constructive Act for those of you who don't pay much attention to the articles or those of you who never made it to the end of the article. Please pay close attention to the second bulleted point—it is the MOST MISUNDERSTOOD part of opiate/heroin addiction. At the end of the list, I included the short bio of the Dr. giving him credit for his work.

"What Is Recovery, and How Can Family and Loved Ones Help?"

Put simply, recovery is restoring the life that was lost during active opioid addiction. As a complement to medication-assisted treatment, there are many ways that family and loved ones can help the person suffering from addiction. Family and significant other involvement is an important part of a recovery program. The following is a list of 10 ways you can help:

• Learning about the disease—the biology, psychology, and sociology of addiction.
• Understanding that addiction is not a problem of poor willpower or poor self-control.
• Understanding that this is a hereditary disease that results in long-term changes in the structure and function of the brain that lead to behaviors that are potentially fatal.
• Learning about the behaviors that occur during addiction, why they occur, and how they can be changed.
• Learning how living and social environments play a key role in triggers, cravings and relapse.
• Learning how easily family members can get drawn unwittingly into supporting their loved one's addiction (co-dependency).
• Encouraging and motivating your loved one to attend and complete treatment even when they don't feel like it.
• Understanding that you cannot make the addict get better, but you are not helpless. You can make changes that promote recovery for your loved one, and for you.
• Participating in support groups that help the family of the addict recover (such as Al-Anon or Nar-Anon).
• Attending the family education sessions with your loved one.

As an American Board of Emergency Medicine (ABEM) certified physician, Dr. Jeffrey Stuckert, M.D. has practiced clinical emergency medicine in Ohio for 29 years. He currently serves as the CEO and Medical Director of Northland, an outpatient drug and alcohol treatment center and The Ridge, an inpatient treatment center near Cincinnati, and has personally attended to more than 70,000 emergency-room patients. Dr. Stuckert has served as Chairman and Medical Director of Emergency Medicine Departments of both the Christ Hospital and Deaconess Hospital for 22 of his 29 years, supervising all clinical personnel and administrative operations of those divisions.

I think it would be a good idea to sit down as a family, if there is an addict in the family, and go over the list together and let your addict know that you are going to do your part to educate yourself about the disease of addiction. Let your addict know that you are going to invest your time and brain power into understanding the how's and why's of opiate/heroin addiction. This would be one of the best gifts that you could give your addict this holiday season. Ask them to help you understand their personal triggers, and explain to them your fears into getting "drawn in" to unknowingly supporting their process.

Lay it out on the table, and don't be afraid of or resistant to open conversation that will allow each family member to better understand the disease of addiction and the role that they play in the process. Understand and discuss the brain changes of the addict and the frustration that comes along with not really knowing who you are dealing with anymore because of the altered personality of the addict. If there are younger children in the home, make sure to include them in the conversation, because they are living through it just like you are and the younger they are when they understand the "life of a drug addict" the more that they will choose sobriety and the philosophy of total abstinence.

I have stated all along that opiate/heroin addiction MUST be a total open and PUBLIC conversation if we are going to make others aware of the disease and if we are going to be able to make a difference. The more awareness we are able to create, the more help we will have in saving a generation of wonderful, bright and beautiful children. Too many children continue to embark on the journey of opiates and too many children continue to die from it. We MUST make everyone aware of the epidemic that we are experiencing in this country and we must work fast. According to Georgia Overdose Prevention, "overdose is the leading cause of preventable injury death in the United States, claiming an average 110 American lives every single day." Time is not in our favor!

12/19/14 – Constructive Act #274 – Experience God's Presence

Somehow at Christmas it just seems like God is ever near and if you stop long enough and wait patiently, you will experience His presence. Maybe all alone as you sit beside the Christmas tree and watch the lights twinkle and shine, or perhaps out under the stars at night, but God is everywhere and He is watching you. You are forever underneath His protective wing, especially if you are an opiate/heroin addict and you are able to read this! Get in touch with God—thank Him for His love and care and ask Him to stay ever near to you this holiday season and always.

Spirituality is so very personal, whatever you and God experience together is forever between the two of you unless you choose to share it. He is the one entity on this earth that you never have to worry about sharing your secrets with and He even knows them before you tell them to Him. You cannot hide from God, so why not experience His presence and bask in the glory of spending a little time with Him this Christmas.

God has brought my family through almost a year without Davis and we have had to stop and feel His presence all along the way. He wraps His loving arms around us and we feel the warmth of his spirit. The other morning as I sat and watched the meteor shower at 5:30 in the morning in the freezing cold chair on my back deck, I felt warm and cozy all wrapped up in my blanket out beneath the stars asking God to take special care of Davis through this first Christmas without us. I know he is at peace and whole again and I know he is waiting patiently for us to meet him on the other side, but I just wanted God to let him know that his stocking is still hung by the chimney with care—yes—I decided to put it back up! I wanted God to let him know that the Davis Direction Ornament is hanging on the Christmas tree front and center and that he is still very much a part of our lives and still very much in all of our hearts even though we can't see or touch him now. I just needed to ask God to give my baby boy a special message that he is still with us in so very many ways. I know God heard my plea and let him know. He sent me a shooting star to tell me so!

On Christmas, we are setting the scene for God's presence to fill a need in your life as you walk through the park behind the First United Methodist Church in Marietta. We will have 1,000 candles burning in luminary bags to "Light the Way" for HOPE this Christmas. When you finish the lighted path, you can turn and look up the hill and see the word HOPE spelled out with luminary bags to remind you that there is HOPE because of God. We will serve hot apple cider so that you can stay warm and there will be me music, scripture and lots of love to share as you experience God's presence. The path will open on Christmas Eve night at 8:30 and will remain open until 10:00 p.m. We will have blankets, hats, scarves and gloves, along with a bag of things to offer HOPE for those in need.

Please come and join us in a beautiful evening beneath God's heavenly sky just to walk and pray, or walk and feel the warmth of God on a cold night, or to hear beautiful voices in the brisk air singing of the love of God and the power He has to offer you to help you make changes in your life. Everyone is welcome, even if you want to walk the beautiful path to offer prayers for others this Christmas. This community needs your prayers, your HOPE and your help if we are ever able to make a difference with this horrible epidemic of opiates/heroin that has invaded our lives and the lives of our loved ones.

Please join with us as we offer our hearts and our help to God in order to make a difference in the lives of those struggling with addiction this year. We need everyone on board and we need everyone to pray.

12/20/14 – Constructive Act # 275 – Do The Math

For those of you who know me well, this is a really scary post coming from me, but the point is that it doesn't take a rocket scientist to see that we have a problem not only in Georgia but throughout the country. As I was watching the news very early this morning I heard a statement that fit right in with this post when the news anchors on Fox News said that "it takes time for laws to catch up with society." Everyone knows that to change laws or to wake people up to what is going on in society, you have to back up your claims with hard data. The DDF has been trying to get hard data from the powers that be for months now and it's not as easy as you might think. So, with that being said, I have come up with some data from comments, private messages and individual posts that have come through the DDF in the past 9 months.

Before I begin, let me put this in perspective for you. The best number that I can find from the CDC is that basically 6,763 people die in the United States each day ––now keep in mind this is a 2010 statistic––but it is the most recent number that I can locate. This past week, Georgia Overdose Prevention.org came out with this statement. "Overdose is the leading cause of preventable injury death in the United States, claiming an average 110 American lives every single day."

So, if you do the math, you will see that basically 1.6% of people who die in the United States on a daily basis are dying from an overdose. Now, coupled with the fact that this statistic comes from an effort to get Senate colleagues to sign onto a strategy to address opiate/heroin death through the use of Naloxone in Georgia, I am assuming that the 110 deaths are opiate/heroin overdose deaths. So, if this is in fact the case, then 1.6% of all deaths in the United States are a direct result of opiate/heroin overdose.

This is outrageous! So, here's another statistic for you. I have done the math on the DDF Facebook page and I can tell you that I come home to an average of 6 private messages per day asking for help for addicts who are suffering from this disease. This is an average, so consider some days there are more messages and some days there are less. But the point is this, our FB page has less members (although we are very proud of our 5,035 "likes" as of today) than the number of people who die in the United States on a daily basis. These are just the desperate people who are reaching out to us to ask for help. For the most part they are the local people because they are requesting the resources in the Metro Atlanta area.

Here is a breakdown of statistics from a gentleman who wrote one day last month from a very small town right outside of Atlanta. "My name is Allen Gardner, III and my son Jason Gardner passed away from a Heroin overdose on 9-20-14, there have been 3 additional deaths since Jason passed just here in Dallas, GA. I was just made aware of this sight and the loss of your son to this dreadful drug. I have been made aware of 7 more deaths from the same way here in the Dallas-Hiram area. This is becoming too much!Again, these are the ones I have been informed about here in Paulding, I hate to say it, but there are probably some I have not heard about. This is 7 in 15 months (1 every 2.14 months), 5 in 118 days (1 every 23 days), 4 in 79 days (1 every19 days)! Totally unacceptable to me. There is NO WAY my family and I can ever begin to heal hearing about another of our community children passing every 19 DAYs to this crap! These kids are not dying in the streets this day and time, they are dying behind the closed doors of their bedrooms in their parents homes. Something more has to be done and fast! A hurting Father Allen Gardner." Dallas, GA had a population in 2013 of 12,415 according to the Census Bureau.

A friend of mine was staying with her mother last month in a Metro Atlanta hospital and during the period of one week, 3 heroin OD's came through resulting in one known death. I could go on and on with these statistics and they are real and current! National and State stats are much harder to come by, but we don't need them to understand that there is a problem that is resulting in epidemic numbers in our community, our state, and our nation.

Our upcoming Symposium in January is going to be dealing with the "Laws, Limits and Loopholes." Attorney General, Sam Olens and Frank Berry, Commissioner from the Ga Dept. of Behavioral Health and Developmental Disabilities, will be tag teaming our keynote address for this event. We will be sending personal invitations to any and all political persons in our state to attend. The Attorney General as well as the Commissioner are definitely on board with the need to address this epidemic in our state and are willing to do whatever it takes to turn things around legally in order to save lives. As I've stated many times, it will take our community collectively to make a difference in this fight! So, plan now to join us for this event and to find out your active part in helping to address the epidemic of opiate/heroin addiction in our community, state and nation! Do the MATH – We are running out of time!

12/21/14 – Constructive Act #276 – Share Your Story

Today we have another story from IntoAction Treatment Facility down in Boynton Beach, Florida. Thank you for sharing your story Nicholas!

Hello All,

My name is Nicholas Labar. Sober since December 30th 2013. I have to express an extreme amount of gratitude towards Into Action Treatment. Not only was I a client there, but I am family as well. Through my journey of numerous treatment centers and countless times trying to get sober Into Action Treatment center showed me I was more than just a number, but a human being. Andrey has a huge heart, one of the biggest I have ever seen in my 22 years of living. Not only is he a great mentor but he showed me that anything was possible. He taught me himself to never give up believing in myself.

Through the strength and courage I found in myself while going through treatment I have accomplished many thing in my short year being sober. Those principles that were planted in my head while being in treatment I still apply to my life today. Needless to say when I walked through those doors I was a broken kid, and today I am a man. A man that has various amounts of goals and aspirations. He believed in me when I couldn't believe in myself. That says a lot about the into action. Because not only is Andrey the owner, He played a key role in my sobriety and never gave up on me. For that I am forever grateful. Today I am successful 22 year old who has a life worth living. A life I wouldn't trade for the world

I give credit to Andrey and the team at into action for me being where I'm at today. Without their faith in me God only knows where I'd be today. They reach out to me on a daily basis and invite me back all of the time. I really am family there. If you want a true testimony of what treatment does, talk to me in person, I'll tell you what is was like before, what happened and what it's like now. Cause if it worked for me, It most certainly can work for you.

Yours truly,
Nicholas L

12/22/14 – Constructive Act #277 – Understand There Will Be Conflict

Life after losing a child just seems to be like a constant state of conflict. Ups and downs, ins and outs, and sometimes inside outs! Yesterday was one of those days for me. Some days everything just becomes personal. Even though I know my faith is solid, I won't lie and tell you that I don't have questions… Lots of them! It all started pretty much as soon as the worship service started yesterday. Don't misunderstand this post; I love my Church! It has been a true Godsend for my family this past year as they have wrapped us in the fold of fellowship and surrounded us with love. But, yesterday was a struggle for me!

Music has always been my therapy; my first degree was in music and I began my career as a music educator. Music speaks to my soul, and yesterday when the menagerie of musical goodness began, my heart immediately became vulnerable. The beautiful handbells, the majestic orchestra, the amazing pipe organ and the ever faithful piano began in unison and I knew I was in trouble. The soloist began singing about angels and the Mother Mary and the Baby Jesus. The memories flooded my mind and took me back to the day that I found out I was having my firstborn son, Davis Henry Owen. No, he was not the divine Son of God, but he was a precious child of God and he was going to be mine. No, he was not placed in a manger at birth; he was placed in my arms and I fell in love. Everything became personal and it was about my little boy, NOT Mary's little baby Jesus. The tears began to roll as I tried to focus on the words of Luke, but the memories outweighed the lesson. I couldn't help it, and I certainly couldn't stop it. I felt guilty and ashamed for letting the burden of my heart take precedence over the Christmas story. Who did I think I was placing the mental pictures of me and my baby above that of the Divine Christ child?

I couldn't sing the hymns, I couldn't speak the words of the congregation and I wanted to walk out! Then, of all days, we had what is usually one of my favorite things happen in the service. We had a baby baptism—of course it was a little boy and he was absolutely gorgeous. Once again, my mind took a turn for the past and I was holding my precious baby boy standing beside my wonderful husband promising God to care for my sweet angel and raise him in the protective fold of the church. It was all about me and my baby boy!

I was still sniffling and tears continued to roll as the preacher kept repeating the most important 5 words of the sermon: "The Lord is with us." The more I heard those 5 words, the more bitter and resentful I became! Where was the Lord on the night Davis died? Had he stepped away from his child? Had he turned his back? Where were His angels that He sends to protect us? I know Davis asked God for help... I heard him as we prayed together.

I just plainly didn't want to keep hearing those words, because I was quite sure the Lord wasn't with Davis when he needed him most on that night when he was all alone. Anger filled my heart on the day that I should have been filled with more love than any other day...the day Love was born. I became so conflicted in my brain that I felt like it was going to explode! My eyes were burning and I couldn't fight back the tears any longer. I just dropped my head and cried! I didn't want to hear anymore!

The service was coming to an end and I was glad! I just wanted to get out of there and go home. I had one more prayer and one more song to get through. I prayed for forgiveness as the preacher prayed for the congregation and I was down to the last song. Once again the soloist began, "He's Got the Whole World in His Hands." Are you kidding me? Was God trying to torture me? Did Davis slip through his fingers? When God made that wonderful "world-wide scoop" of people, was there not enough room for my child to enter his hands? WHAT WENT WRONG? WHERE WAS GOD? WHY MY CHILD?

Don't sing that song to me, it's not true! God doesn't have the whole world in His hands, because my child was left out! STOP SINGING!

I was almost too ashamed to write this post and these words because they sound so awful. I sound so selfish and so resentful. But, I'm human—I have raw emotion that I can't control and thoughts that enter my head that I would just as soon not be there, but they come and I have no control. I couldn't breathe! My family drove away in silence on what should have been one of the most special days of the year —the Sunday before Christmas! What went wrong? Christmas was supposed to be happy and joyful. Christmas was supposed to be fun.

Sometimes it seems so cruel to me that God has all the answers and we have to stay down here on earth and second-guess every decision we make. There are days that I truly need answers and meaning and I can't for the life of me get any. I pray for peace and some days I think God hears my prayers and some days I think He is on vacation! When I sit in the still of the night and I calm down and I gather my thoughts and I put my life on earth into perspective regarding eternity, this journey is so brief. I know that earth is just a minuscule part of God's vast universe and I know that when God made his "world-wide scoop" that Davis WAS in His hands, he was just taken to a different place for now – a place where he has found peace and meaning. Sometimes it's just so hard to trust God's plan as it unfolds. I know in my heart that "the Lord is with us." Some days are just harder than others.

I know at the end of the day that God understands my heart and he hears my pleas for peace and he hears my prayers of forgiveness. I know that He forgives me and I know His heart bears my pain. I also know that he has His loving arms wrapped around Davis, but some days I wish He would just squeeze me a little tighter and take all my pain away. I know grief is a process and I know that my heart and my brain will have seriously conflicting moments, like yesterday. Some days, I just need to understand the plan! God forgive me!

12/23/14 – Constructive Act #278 – Release and Resume

Yesterday I got quite a bit of "stuff" off of my chest and I will admit it felt good. As a Counselor for 25 years, I know one of the most important skills to have is that of validation. People have feelings, just like I did, and they can't help the way they feel – all they are looking for is a little validation. Validation is just acknowledgment... Okay—I hear you! You guys heard me loud and clear yesterday and although it was not pretty, you allowed me my feelings and you embraced me as a human being. Thank you! I'm in a much better place today because I had the opportunity to RELEASE my feelings and my emotions. Now its time to RESUME my life. Today, I guess I'm writing for myself as much as anyone else out there.

Life is full of ups and downs regardless of your circumstances. The ability to move on is a gift of sorts. Some people don't have that ability and things that happen can put them into a deep dark depression and leave them there for unknown lengths of time. I thank God everyday that I am not one of those people, that to me would be a death sentence on earth. I know there are people out there who suffer from depression and many of them are ones who search for some substance to bring them back to a happier place. I know if I were depressed, I would be searching for something to help me — no doubt! If you are one of those people, don't be ashamed to reach out to the medical community and discuss ways to keep yourself in a better place. I know the place I was on Sunday was not somewhere I would have wanted to remain for any length of time.

I struggled with sleep on Sunday night just because of all the negativity in my day on Sunday, then on Monday, I just kind of went through the motions of the day. Today, I am energetic and looking forward to Christmas Eve night when we "Light the Way for HOPE." Doing things to help and validate others makes me come alive! God calls us to serve and by doing so, I can connect with Him and hopefully strengthen others in the process. It's a win-win situation! I'm also in a creative mood today and I love to do crafty things; it's one of the outlets that I have spoken about in the past. Sometimes, getting yourself back on track takes a little effort on your part. We have to be responsible and accountable for our own sanity and attitudes.

This becomes extremely important and pertinent when you are an "addict's keeper." You cannot let them dictate your personality. You have to remember that they are suffering with a disease and it's NOT personal. Especially at Christmastime, when you want to celebrate, allow yourselves to be happy and try to experience the joy of the season. If you do have one of "those" days, do everything in your power to get yourself back on track as soon as possible. Doing something for others is one of the quickest and most powerful ways to get back on track!

Speaking of doing something for others, PLEASE Plan to come out and join the Davis Direction Foundation as we "Light the Way for HOPE" this Christmas Eve at the Park on Polk Street right behind the Marietta First United Methodist Church. We will have a pathway lit around the entire park with 1,000 luminary lights, carolers along the way, scripture readers, a beautifully simple Nativity scene and the word HOPE illuminated from the hill. The rain is GOING to be GONE by Christmas Eve night when we light up—8:30 pm and we will still be illuminated until 10:00 p.m. There will be guitar playing, carols on the piano and hot apple cider served with mini muffins. For those in need, we will be handing out blankets, hats, scarves, gloves and a bag full of survival items. PLEASE share this event on your page and let others know of the event. I will post a flyer again with the details a little later in the day that you can share on your personal FB pages.

It is designed to be a spiritual experience where you can come to feel God's presence. I envision the sky opening up right at 8:30 so that the stars can shine upon our event—because after all "Perhaps they are not stars, but rather openings in heaven where the love of our lost ones pour through and shine down on us to let us know they are happy." Feel free to bring a picture of your lost ones to place on the tables at the beginning of the path and light a candle for them as you walk the path in their honor.

Find your own meaning this season. Allow God to heal the wounds and lessen the holes in our hearts. Cast the questions aside for just one night, and know that God is in control and that he is omnipotent all knowing! For me, that will be enough!

Please join us; you will leave with a renewed spirit having the opportunity to RELEASE your emotions and the ability to RESUME your life. God Bless you all.

12/24/14 – Constructive Act #279 – Support Your Community

Tonight there is an event scheduled from 8:30-10:00 p.m. in the Polk Street Park behind the Marietta First United Methodist Church. The park belongs to the church and they have graciously offered it for us to host the "Lighting of the Way for HOPE." This event is an opportunity to support the community in the effort to address the opiate/heroin epidemic we are experiencing. You don't have to be an addict or even know an addict to attend. But you do have to know that we have a problem in our community and that young people as well as older people are dying in record numbers from overdose of these drugs. Please come walk through the park as it will be beautifully and simply lit with the flickering lights of HOPE. You can pray as you walk and experience the presence of God. Ask Him to lead, guide and direct our efforts as we move forward to help our community address this epidemic. 2,000 teenagers try drugs for the first time on a daily basis and every 19 minutes a person in our country dies from an overdose. For the first time in our history, the number of people dying from addiction has surpassed the number of people dying in automobile accidents. We need your support and prayers. PLEASE join us.

Enjoy a cup of hot apple cider as you stroll through the park. Bring a picture of your loved one who has passed on, or who is struggling from addiction. Place their picture on the tables and light a candle in their honor. Offer the "Gift of Prayer" for this horrific disease. Enjoy the sounds of music and hear beautiful scripture of HOPE read aloud. Feel the presence of God.

**********************************TONIGHT********************************

T'was the Night Before Christmas and all through the park, the journey was prepared to begin with each spark.The luminaries were burning, sending the flare, requesting the presence of God to be there.

The children remembered, were placed on the table, saved by the one who was born in the stable.Parents, Grandparents, loved ones and more, came offering prayers to the God we adore.

Up in the sky the clouds disappeared and the stars in the heavens shone as it cleared. The journey we started, one step at a time, knowing the effort was an uphill climb.

The waxing crescent moon will be shaped like a smile, offering HOPE to those praying and walking a while. Sweet Jesus in Heaven knows of our need, He has promised to bless us and bless us indeed. Lord hear our prayers from high up above, comfort our hearts and wrap us in love.

12/25/14 – Constructive Act #280 – Plans Are Just Plans

I looked and looked for a descriptive acronym that fit this post and I could not find one. So, I made one up. A plan is just a "Preliminary List of Altered Negotiations." I've made a lot of "Plans this year, that have been altered due to negotiations, whether it was because of time, money, family or just plainly because I changed my mind. Anyone dealing with addiction in any way knows that plans can change at the drop of a hat and you have to be prepared for it. Plans can also change because you realize that what you were trying to achieve or avoid cannot be accomplished. Plans can change due to the actions of others and because your life was altered in some way beyond your control. It's okay! At some point we have to stop living according to expectations and just live for who we are and what we stand for. Sometimes that is hard to figure out. Sometimes I think I stand for others and what they expect of me and I lose sight of what is important and what is not.

It's okay to break with tradition if tradition causes unbearable pain. It's okay to change plans, when those plans were made to alleviate feelings that aren't going to be alleviated if the plans are carried out. It's okay to change plans if those plans don't cause others pain. Sometimes I think we go through the motions over and over again without meaning because that is what is expected of us. Well, if I've learned nothing else over the course of the last 9 months, it's that life is too short to live for others. Life is too short to bottle up emotion and life is too short to not please yourself when it feels good and it feels right. So many times when we are growing up, we are taught to serve others and I think that we often get that confused with living for others. If pleasing your family and serving them feels good to you, then do it. But, don't do it because you think you have to. Teach them independence instead and then you are able to serve with a joyful heart.

Everyone has choices to make and if we can just make those choices with good conscience and be straightforward about the fact that they are indeed our choices and we are accountable for them, then that should be okay. Guilt comes along with doing things for ourselves sometimes because of being taught to serve others all of our lives. Sometimes I think we so overcomplicate things. Other people don't always know what is best for someone else. You and only you know that! I remember one time a friend was in a relationship that for all practical appearances seemed not to be going so well for her. From the outside it seemed somewhat abusive and everyone that loved her was telling her what they thought she should do. I remember telling her that I loved her and that she needed to "follow her heart." I'll never forget that she looked at me and tears filled her eyes and she said "Thank you" and she gave me the biggest hug ever. At the time, I didn't really understand why that meant so much to her, but now I do. When everyone is telling you what you ought to do or what you need to do or what you should do, it's nice to hear, "follow your heart." It's rather tragic that we feel that we need permission to do that, but nonetheless, the feeling exists. Even in death, hospice often tells people you need to give them your permission to die. Think about that! That's a LOT of pressure. God is calling someone home, and they still feel like they need our permission to go! How did we get to this?

Addiction alters lifestyles! There's no explanation necessary! There are lots and lots of people out there who want to tell you how to handle your life, your addicted loved ones life and your other affected family members' lives. The truth of the matter is, if someone really had all the answers, we would not be experiencing an epidemic. We can offer support, we can share our stories, we can remind people to follow their hearts and to move forward if at all possible. BUT, beware of the people who tell you what to do. Until someone has walked a mile in your shoes and has lived through your pain, they don't have a clue as to what you should do. Make your own plans, and if you need to change them along the way, change them and make the best of your situation any way you can according to what works for you and your family. PLANS—a Preliminary List of Altered Negotiations— NOTHING MORE!

12/26/14 – Constructive Act #281 – The Day After … Now What?

Well, we made it through the Dreaded Christmas Day and the day AFTER is here. Nothing has changed—our loved ones who have passed are still gone, our addicted children, parents, siblings and friends are still addicted, and as an addict, you are either still addicted or still in active recovery! Our lives are still full of uncertainty and challenges! So, where do we go from here? We stick to our mission statement! We promote awareness, affect change and preserve life by providing Naloxone kits until there is a better solution.

Many of you write often and ask how you can help. I saw many of you at our October Symposium and again on Christmas Eve at our "Lighting of the Way". You wanted to know how you could help. You offered your services and wanted to become involved. Now is the time to become active. You can begin by inviting any political figures throughout the State of Georgia and your own personal doctors and ministers. Over the last nine months, I have come up with several conclusions based on what I have witnessed through the workings of the DDF. The most compelling ingredient for recovery in my opinion is God. We need your ministers at the January Symposium. We need the senior pastors, we need the youth ministers, we need the ministers of education, we need your church represented at the Symposium.

Another extremely compelling ingredient for recovery is the medical community: the gatekeepers of the opiate drugs. We need your doctors! We need every pediatrician, every family doctor, every orthopedic doctor, every obstetrician, every neurologist, every psychiatrist, every dentist, every doctor who has the capability and is currently prescribing opiates for any reason or ailment. Invite these doctors to our January Symposium.

We need your pharmacists! We need every Mom and Pop pharmacy, every chain, every independent or grocery store pharmacy. We need every dispensing organization in our community at our symposium. We will be rolling out an initiative at this Symposium where our pharmacists will have a choice to become involved on a whole new level!

We need our legislators, our senators, our representatives, our Lieutenant Governor and our Governor. We need our judges, our law enforcement agencies, our first responders, our lawyers, our Rehabilitation Facility directors and our addiction counselors. We need the families of addicts, the families of teens, the families of those caring for the elderly.

WE NEED EVERYONE AT OUR JANUARY SYMPOSIUM!

Change will only come about through awareness and education. We need to bring the key players to the forefront of this epidemic. They need to be educated about the drugs, the epidemic, the movement to stop it, and the efforts being made to educate the public. The right hand needs to know what the left hand is doing and we need to join forces to increase our force!

If everyone on the DDF page would come to the Symposium and bring one friend, we would have over 10,000 in attendance. Of course we could not fit them in the building, but if one tenth of them showed up, which would be 1,000 people, we could squeeze them in, educate them and get them on board with the solution!

There you have it friends – What can you do? Fill up the auditorium on January 29th at 7:00 p.m.—the Marietta First United Methodist Church on Whitlock Ave. in Marietta, Ga.,—"Laws, Limits and Loopholes" is the name of the Symposium and Attorney General Sam Olens along with the Commissioner of Behavioral Health – Frank Berry, will be our keynote speakers. We will be rolling out an initiative for pharmacies and we will have a live demonstration of how and when to use a Naloxone kit! We will also be handing out Naloxone kits to addicts, families of addicts, and those in places where overdose is likely. Join us in an effort to solve a National epidemic!

12/27/14 – Constructive Act #282 – Let The Christmas Clean-up Begin

How many of us have said, "just let me get through Christmas and I'll take care of that"? I know I did. So many times as parents of addicts, we put things off because if we didn't deal with them for one more day, maybe that would be the day that the problem would go away. Maybe if we just stayed in denial one more day, we would wake up and the world would be all right again and all our problems would be gone. Drugs don't work that way. They are addictive and they keep on keeping on even when we don't. I know this time last year, we were trying to detox Davis at home so that after the first of the year, he could enter a Rehabilitation facility and begin working on recovery. Although he did detox at home, and was able to enter the facility on January 3rd, I have to say that we waited in order to get through Christmas and do all that we needed to do without anyone in the family knowing what was going on in our confidential and solitary world. We didn't want to explain to family and friends why Davis wasn't with us during the holidays. We were trying to protect his personal pride and personal life so that he could continue to live without everyone knowing that he struggled with addiction.

Addiction waits for no one! We were lucky that it worked out for us when we waited, but then again maybe it didn't. We found out around Thanksgiving that Davis had a problem that was drug related. We didn't know exactly what that meant. One of the best-selling books on the market today tells you that detox and recovery can be accomplished on an individual basis in individual therapy. But that particular book and most others don't qualify opiate and heroin addiction separately from other forms of addiction. It is different! If you think it is not, I challenge you to support your theory. So many people out there say "addiction is addiction" Yes—if you are addicted to something, you are an addict, but there are degrees of addiction and I have stated the reasons why opiate/heroin is one of the most severe forms of addiction that we know about out there today. But, that was one of those things that "we didn't know we didn't know" when we were searching for our own answers for our own child.

If you know that your son or daughter is suffering with anxiety, depression, or even taking any of the gateway drugs to combat any of these issues, then ACT NOW – since it is the week after Christmas—you can do the "After Christmas Clean-Up." If you read this post in the future, don't wait for anything thinking that things will get better – most likely they won't. Especially if you know your child is in the throes of opiate/heroin addiction, the sooner they get help, the easier it will be to enter into recovery and stay there. The longer they take opiates and heroin, the more damage they do to their brain and their bodies and the chances for a full recovery become much more difficult. Don't Wait!

You can start with your regular doctor, but ask for a referral to see a psychiatrist who is the specialist in the field of mental illness or an addiction specialist. Please take action now and get your loved one the correct help that is needed to address addiction.

12/28/14 – Constructive Act #283 – Share Your Story

Today we hear from a young lady whom I had the pleasure of meeting on Christmas Eve night. She brought with her several pictures of the friends from her past who had lost their battle with addiction. She placed them in our memorial section and lit a candle for each friend. She has close to a year clean and she is working her recovery every day!

Here is her story:

My name is Victoria Marie. I was born and raised in East Cobb County. I am 29 years old. Today I live a happy and serene life, but it wasn't always like this. I remember trying drugs at a very young age. At about 12 years old. I smoked weed and tried acid and ecstasy. I never really had a problem until I tried opiates. I started with pills and quickly moved to heroin. I can remember doing heroin before I could even drive. I didn't think anything was wrong with what I was doing. It wasn't anything that was talked about in school or drug education classes the main focus seemed to always be weed and alcohol, so I thought I was ok.

My habit took a hold of me so fast and before I knew it I was failing out of high school and spending all my time, energy, and money on heroin. I still didn't think I had a problem. I was arrested at 17 for prescription forgery. I was sent to rehab and that still didn't make a difference. As soon as my year was up I was back at it. I have been in and out of jail more times than I can count. My addiction always won and I was doing things I told myself I would never do, but by this time I didn't care.

I'm so blessed to have God's grace and mercy because there are many things that should have taken my life but did not. I'm also so fortunate to have family and friends that have stuck by me through all the hell I put them through. Once I was so beaten and battered by my addiction and no where left to turn I asked for help. I remember being so scared, but I had gotten to the point where I hated the one thing I loved! I checked myself into a detox program and found a long term treatment center.

My clean date is April 22, 2014. I love life now and look forward to what each day has to offer. I can actually look at myself in the mirror without being disgusted and heartbroken by what I had become. This is my first sober Christmas in over 15 years! If there is anyone out there that thinks there is no way out or no options there are, just know that there is HOPE and people who care!

12/29/14 – Constructive Act #284 – Understand Emotional Guilt and Expectations

It's the 4th day after Christmas and every day I think to myself, why would I miss my son more on any given day than on another day? I know it's because of the traditions and memories associated with the day, but the truth of the matter is that everyday is associated with memories and habits, more so than traditions, that I know exactly what would have been expected or happening at any given moment. I know that on a school day that I would have gone down before I left for work to make sure that he was awake and told him that I loved him and hoped he had a good day. I know that on a Saturday, I would not have seen him or heard from him before noon. I know that on Sunday, he would have been the next to last one out the door and his hair would have still been wet but he would have smelled the best! So, like I said every day has it's own memories and habits. So I will admit I felt a little guilty that the day after Christmas I was supposed to feel relieved because I was supposed to miss him more on Christmas than any other day of the year.

Expectations and Emotional Guilt! UGH!!! Yes, Davis filled my thoughts on Christmas Day, but no more so than he does every other day of the year. Yes, it was hard opening presents around the Christmas Tree and him not being there, but it's hard around the television every Sunday night when the whole family is home and we're watching one of our favorite shows and he is not there. It's hard every time I sit through a church service and he is not in the pew with us. It's hard every time we have a philosophical discussion at my house and he is not there to bring up the latest conspiracy theory. I miss his weekly trip to Martin's biscuits and his coke and sour patch fetish. I miss the fact that every time he left the house I got a great big hug. Christmas Day was no different. I missed him just the same. So, why is no one sending me texts and private messages today telling me that they are thinking about me and praying for me? I'm still missing my precious Davis! Am I not supposed to be missing him as much because it's not Christmas Day? I'll admit there was a point in time on Christmas night that I thought to myself, well, I made it through my first Christmas Day. Looking back, that was just silly because I say that to myself every night!

Feelings and emotions are two of those things in life that you cannot control. They will take over your life in a moment when you are in the strangest places and at the most inopportune times. You can't make them go away, although you will try with everything you have, but finally you will have to succumb to them and just ride the emotional wave. Then there are other times when you actually catch yourself having fun and you are genuinely happy and you think to yourself…"if someone sees me laughing and having a good time, maybe they will think that I don't miss Davis." Then you try to calm yourself down a little bit, God forbid that someone might think you are having too much fun! Maybe the old way of "the year of mourning" was not such a bad thing after all, at least you and everyone around you knew the "rules" for mourning and you could be inside the lines!

Over the past 9 months, I've learned to hate expectations and understand emotions. Expectations are just ways to command stress and put undue pressure on people—especially emotional expectations. I understand the need for expectations in certain areas, but the expectations that most of us put upon ourselves are not always necessary. I am going to be much more analytical about the expectations that I put on myself now and there will have to be some sort of meaning just beyond "because." And as far as emotions go, understanding them simply means that they are their own entity and there is no controlling them. They come and they go and you deal with them.

I learn a little bit everyday as I forge onward through this journey. I don't owe anyone an explanation of what is in my head or my heart. I share because I want to and I hope it may help someone taking this journey with me. My emotions and my expectations are neither right or wrong, they just are! Everyone has a different grief journey and the journey that you have is completely up to you! You will know what you need and when you are ready to move on. You may need help along the way and that is okay too. It's your journey! Make the most of it and take from it what you need and want in the time it takes to complete it, if there is such a timeline. If you are the friend of someone on this journey, please don't take it personally, those of us taking the journey don't know where it will lead from one-second to the next, we are unfortunately just along for the ride. Godspeed!

12/30/14 – Constructive Act #285 – Be Your Own Advocate

It doesn't take a Rocket Scientist to figure out from the statistics in the Atlanta Journal Constitution yesterday that there is a direct correlation between the increase of Hydrocodone being dispensed in our state and the opiate/heroin epidemic that we are experiencing! The front page of the Metro section had a big bold headline: "Georgia's #1 Rx: hydrocodone" Propublica.org was the investigative website that did an analysis of the most common prescriptions and the physicians who wrote them. "The hydrocodone-acetaminophen drug was filled 200,000 more times than the #2 and #3 drugs in Georgia making it the #1 Medicare prescription by far." Dr. P. Tennent Slack, from Gainesville, Ga is a pain specialist who is leading a campaign to cut down on prescription drug use in our state. He says "I think it's fair to say that opioids have been prescribed in a less than discriminating fashion in the past 10- to 12 years." He further believes that if these opioids were doing their job that we would be seeing much greater patient satisfaction. There is no data to show that the pain relief is getting any better in these patients.

I think our whole prescribing philosophy is quite backwards! Why are we not beginning with the least abusive drug to combat the symptoms of pain? Why are we not beginning with the anti-inflammatory drugs such as Motrin and Naproxen and then moving forward if that does not work? I know that in many cases, these drugs can get people by without even using prescription drugs. Ailments such as earaches, sore throats, and even minor surgeries like trigger finger and mole removal often times can be treated successfully with over the counter drugs, but these patients are leaving the doctor's office with opioids. I know this to be true, because these are all members of my family that I am speaking of. The last time this happened, I became the family advocate (imagine that) and wrote a 4-page letter to the prescribing doctor. He was very nice and seemed to have an excellent bedside manner, but I never heard a word back from him.

Parents, especially for your minor children, I will never let a doctor prescribe opiates for my children again as a first defense against pain at home. I do understand chronic pain and I have had major surgeries that have led to opiate use, but when I left the hospital, after 5 C-sections, I left with prescription strength Motrin. I had babies to take care of and I managed just fine. Pain is bearable, but we have become a society that believes that if we can avoid pain, then at all costs avoid it. The old saying "No pain, no gain" needs to be adhered to in many situations regarding medical pain control in my humble opinion. We can stand pain! According to this article, "U.S. consumers account for nearly 100% of worldwide sales of hydrocodone and 81 percent of oxycodone, another opioid." What are people in other countries doing? We don't hear of people writhing in pain or see images of anything of the sort on world news stations. So, how are they managing their pain?

Aside from pain management, if you look at the side effects of opioids. "Death from prescribed opioids quadrupled from 1999 to 2014 according to the National Institute on Drug Abuse, which estimates that 2.1 million Americans suffer from substance-use disorders related to prescription opioids." WOW—and we continue to pop these pills like candy! WAKE UP AMERICA! BE YOUR OWN ADVOCATE! Refuse opioid prescriptions as a first line of action.

The National Institute on Drug Abuse has figures that show that opioid prescriptions in the U.S. increased from76 million in 1999 to 217 million in 2013. You no longer need to wonder why we are experiencing an opiate/heroin epidemic in our nation. The numbers tell the story! The U.S. fills prescriptions every single day for opioid pain relief. They know people are abusing these drugs and they know people are becoming addicted because these drugs are highly addictive! Yet,

317

doctors continue to prescribe them as a first line of defense. Here's something that I find very interesting though. Many of these same doctors don't know how to write the prescription for Naloxone, the life-saving drug that counteracts the overdose of an opiate, and if they do write it, good luck finding a pharmacy to fill it!!! It's just not being done although the Medical Amnesty Law passed last April in Georgia made it perfectly legal and acceptable. Why are Drugstores not carrying this prescription?

I don't have answers to that question; however, I do know of a pharmacy with two locations right here in Georgia who is carrying it and dispensing it to those who have prescriptions for it. Lacey's Drug Company does have and will dispense the Naloxone kits. Many have asked lately on websites of support and awareness. Please spread the word—these kits need to be available to those in need of them. Be your own ADVOCATE! Protect yourself and your family. Prevention is always the best solution, but it is too late for those who are already struggling with opiate/heroin addiction. We must do everything in our power to help them stay alive until better solutions are available. Having the Naloxone kit on hand is one of the ways we can help. The Davis Direction Foundation will be handing the kits out once again at our January 29th Symposium—"Laws, Limits and Loopholes" Please mark your calendars to be at Marietta First United Methodist Church in Marietta, GA at 7:00 pm. You will educate yourself and hear about the doctors and pharmacies who are on board to help us in this fight!

If you are a doctor who is prescribing opiate drugs, knowing the state of the nation is in an addiction epidemic, I personally feel that is an ethical obligation to educate yourself about the Naloxone drug and be able to write a prescription for it and know where to tell your patients to have it filled. It is the care that we entrust you with as patients.

wfsites.websitecreatorprotool.com/laceydrug/home.html

12/31/14 – Constructive Act #286 – Know Your Community

Change begins at home! National impact is obviously something that the DDF is striving for and it is even part of our Mission Statement. "To serve as a role model in our community in order to become a National Resource for Opiate/Heroin Addiction awareness and change" is part of what we strive for, but, note the nine most important words "to serve as a role model in our community," we must make a difference at home first! To know how to make a difference at home, we must know what the rules are, who the players are, what the challenges are, and what the resources to combat those challenges are.

Yesterday we found out that hydrocodone was the #1 most prescribed drug in Georgia. Today we are offered a new statistic (Atlanta Journal and Constitution), that "state overdose deaths involving prescription drugs were the lowest they've been in six years." This figure was released by the Georgia Bureau of Investigation in July—HOWEVER, its figures covered only autopsies performed by the GBI – so Cobb, Dekalb, Fulton, Gwinnett, Hall, Henry and Rockdale counties were not included. I've often heard that statistics can say anything you want them to say, so I wonder if the overdose deaths from these counties were included, how the statistic would look? I hope and pray daily that the initiatives in Georgia are making a difference in the prescription drug/opiate/heroin epidemic, but I also continue to hear daily of people who are dying of overdoses.

As part of the American Medical Association Foundation grant that the DDF received earlier this year, we received funding to prepare a packet of information to help someone in the throes of addiction find help in our community. We hope to have this packet available after the first of the year, meaning in the next couple of weeks. We are still actively adding names to the list of rehabilitation facilities and recovery resources in our area and if you would like to be added to the list, please email us at info@davisdirection.com and tell us what you have to offer. We will also have a section for "outside of community" resources for those people who feel it is best to find help farther away from home.

I have found that one of the best ways to actively keep up with the community is to READ THE NEWSPAPER! I have not been as diligent as I should in this area, but I have a couple of friends who are and they are constantly sending me articles that relate to the drug crisis we are experiencing. My intentions are to subscribe to both the Marietta Daily Journal and the Atlanta Journal and Constitution for the new year. I am going to spend part of my mornings everyday looking through the newspapers to find the rules, resources, players and challenges that I spoke about earlier. If we are to be an effective foundation, we must keep up with and know what is going on in our own community, as well as how it relates nationally.

Our community is an awesome community with more potential than most, but it is being destroyed by an opiate/heroin epidemic. We are losing beautiful and bright children to death and incarceration, and theft and burglary are rampant. According to today's paper, we still have 196 active pain clinics in our state as of the middle of December. Although, law enforcement is doing a great job of enforcing the laws and monitoring these clinics, there are still those who think they don't have to play by the rules. Cherokee County authorities searched and seized over $10,000.00 cash, a hand gun and blank, signed prescription pads in Acworth, GA earlier this week.

We have work to do in our community, and we need to keep up with the work that needs to be done and how we can become involved to help. It is not an option to stick your head in the sand and think that your family is immune to any possible effect from this epidemic. Whether it is a direct effect or a side effect, everyone in the community needs to be aware of the presence of opiates/heroin that are destroying our community. Read the newspaper, watch the news, listen to your children, and talk with each other. Make the conversation of opiates/heroin a public one and bring it to the forefront of our community so that it can be dealt with openly and without shame. Know the needs and challenges of your community!

1/1/15 – Constructive Act # 287 – Out With The Old, In With The New

I think it's safe to say that over the course of the past year, this nation has learned a lot about the devastation of opiate/heroin addiction. Because of the public conversations that are taking place, people are becoming much more educated about the disease and companies are working hard to help those suffering from addiction. The statistics that are coming to the forefront are staggering as young people and older people alike continue to die. The recognition of need to help combat this epidemic is very apparent and at the very least, most families know someone who is suffering or has suffered with this disease. Families are recognizing the need to educate their children and teach them that prevention is the only sure cure! Opiate/heroin addiction is in a league of its own, and it's a league that you don't want to be a part of. The very ones who are suffering with the addiction are the biggest advocates of "NEVER… NOT ONCE!"

Now that we understand the disease of opiate/heroin addiction more thoroughly, it is time to get down to the business of fighting back! I posted earlier in the year that I did not believe that allowing an addict to hit "Rock Bottom" was the best advice that could be offered. I even went a step further and said that if we had chosen to go that route, that I believed that Davis would have been dead even sooner than he was. Then on that same post, a superior court judge in Georgia, wrote a comment that stated "Continue to shout your message from the hilltop! The theory of waiting for your addict to hit rock bottom is very dangerous if the substance of choice is heroin. The rock bottom theory was developed when alcohol and other less dangerous substances were the focus of the addiction treatment. Heroin is unpredictable and so much more deadly." I'm sure this judge has seen many a heroin addict come through her court and knows what she is talking about.

Another item that I think we have begun to rethink is that of drug therapy. I know that many of you say that the addict is only exchanging one drug for another, but a prominent doctor in another state told me way back in April of this past year, that he believed in treating heroin addiction with drug therapy that would allow an addict to maintain his or her life while we searched for better and more acceptable solutions. I didn't know anything about drug therapy when Davis was going through rehabilitation and the rehab center didn't feel obligated to educate my family in any way, shape, form or fashion about this issue. However, after much research, if we had known what we know now, we would have definitely looked into drug therapy for Davis to prolong his life until something better came along. I know there are companies out there right now who are actively searching for better solutions. Hopefully, 2015 will be the year of the breakthrough!

It's time to put the old way of thinking to rest and understand the new and current information regarding opiate/heroin addiction. There are articles and new studies being released on a daily basis and I will be posting them as fast as I can on the DDF. If you resolve to do nothing else in 2015, RESOLVE to educate yourself and your children about the dangers of opiate/heroin addiction and to do everything in your power to raise awareness and affect change regarding this specific addiction. If we do nothing, then nothing will change! 2015 will be our YEAR of HOPE. Join with us to make a difference for 1 in every 10 people in our nation. I'll bet there are more than 10 people in your extended family! Food for thought!

1/2/15 – Constructive Act #288 – Keep Moving Forward

All I have heard about for the last couple of days is the New Year – 2015. It's January 2nd, and of course that's all I've heard about. Put the past behind you; this year is going to be great; forget the past and start fresh! Yesterday I even wrote about "out with the old and in with the new." This is the time of year when people make new plans to move on with their lives and accomplish great things. This is the time of year when things of the past seem less significant and you are allowed to put them to rest and forget about them.

My heart is hurting because a part of me feels like I am leaving Davis in a year that is gone and forgotten! There, I said it! I had no idea or fore warning that I would have this feeling and BOOM there it was and I was not prepared to deal with it!

Davis will forever remain in 2014. That's the end of his "dash." There will be no memories in 2015 that I can share with him. I will tell you that is an overwhelming feeling of sadness. Just when I think I am making progress with my grief and moving forward with my life, I have set-backs like these that come completely out of nowhere and send me spiraling into the bottomless pit of "hard to breathe" again. The tears begin to roll down my cheeks uncontrollably and I get that "numb" feeling all over my body. I was reading a passage from the Bible yesterday that said that a day in eternity could be the same as a thousand years on earth (or something to that effect); I can't even remember where I was reading it now. And then my mind started analyzing everything of course. Time has no real meaning with God, but down here on earth, it will seem like an eternity before I will ever see him again. 365 long days a year and 24 excruciating hours in some days and even 60 unbearable minutes in an hour that all I can do is think of my sweet boy. Everyone who has lost a child keeps telling me it gets easier with time, but they all say there are triggers that put you back to the very beginning of life without them as well. Expect those days and have your coping skills close at hand to make it through them.

So, my main coping skill is to write and share my feelings and my grief and to completely expose myself in hopes that others will read these words and either relate to them or use them to help a loved one take one step closer to the world of recovery. Some days I feel so close to Davis that it is like an aura that surrounds me and goes wherever I go. Then there are other days that I feel like the distance between us is so insurmountable that even Heaven is too far away. Then God sends me a gift like a fat little red bird eating from my bird feeder or a shooting star that illuminates the sky from my back deck and I know that there is a bigger plan and a greater purpose. I have to keep moving forward! It is not an option. I have other children depending on me to make this world a better place for them and their children, my grandchildren. There are already people who depend on the DDF everyday for words of support and encouragement and my purpose is to provide that and help them live to see another day—one day a world without addiction.

Yes, those are some lofty words, but words that will keep me and others like me busy, working hard to help those people struggling like Davis did to find answers and solutions for opiate/heroin addiction. God has all the answers and I know that. I also know that He loves me more than I loved Davis—although I'm not sure I can even comprehend what that means or feels like. So, I know that with that kind of love, I can do whatever He is calling me to do, because He will continue to hold me in His arms and support me while I am here on this earth. I'm sure God's purpose for me is to continue to search for answers and to rally the masses to understand the epidemic we are facing. I will continue to do this to the best of my ability until I hear differently from God or until we reach our goal and addiction is abolished from this planet forever! Godspeed on our journey!

1/3/15 – Constructive Act #289 – Know Where You Are Going and Why

Exactly one year ago this morning, on my husband's birthday, we drove Davis to his first experience with Rehab. We thought we were doing the most important thing we could do for him at the time, but time would reveal that we hadn't done our homework. After a week in rehab, we looked at him and thought that he looked amazing and better than we had seen him look in months. Over the course of 3 weeks, he gained almost 35 pounds and he was a beautiful sight to behold! His eyes were shining and his skin was glowing. His weight was unbelievably at an all time high and he was gorgeous! I will never forget visiting with him one time and he made the nurse come out and weigh him so that he could give me an update on his weight—he was so very proud. His looks were deceiving! Little did we know that opiate/heroin addiction could not even be touched within a three-week period. When the rehab told us that they had done everything they could do for him, we took that to mean that the rest was up to him, that he would be fine with out patient therapy, which had been set up before he discharged!

I do believe that the epidemic that we are experiencing in our nation took us all by surprise. We were unprepared to deal with it and very few of us understood exactly what it entailed. I know now that if a rehabilitation facility tried to tell me that my opiate/heroin addict would be treated along with alcoholics and eating disordered patients, I would tell them thank you for your time, but you don't get it! Please understand that I don't undermine any kind of addiction, but I'm not naïve enough to discount the fact that the heroin high and the addiction that follows is unlike any other in the known drug world. It is different, and that has been proven! When Davis filled out the paperwork for the rehab facility and I saw for the first time that he had done heroin, I had a terrible feeling in my stomach, but when the rehab facility did not validate the fact that it was different, I thought that perhaps I was wrong and all would be okay.

Don't be the uneducated people that we were! If you have a child that is dealing with opiate/heroin addiction, look for a specific addiction program that will address opiate/heroin addiction as an entity unto itself! It is unlike any other addiction in the United States. It puts an addict in a vice grip and refuses to let go! Any program that suggests that you can process through their program in less than six months to a years time is not being honest with you. Do your research and educate yourself if you are trying to help and support an active opiate/heroin addict.

Even the addicts themselves are so hopeful and uneducated about the rehabilitation and what it entails that they leave the facilities way too soon and think they are good to go! They try to work their programs with their "meeting a day" philosophy, but they have not been prepared for what they will be facing! I'm not sure many people know what to teach them and prepare them for if you want to know the truth.

We have got to find a way to help the general public understand what an opiate/heroin addict goes through and why they can't just walk away from their addiction.

We have got to find a way to educate the general public so they understand that no one is exempt from this addiction and no matter how hard they try, if the addiction gene is present, it will dominate their lives. Opiate/heroin addiction is an unexplainable phenomenon to the general population, but to those who have come in direct contact with it, whether through addiction or being the "addict's keeper," it is unlike anything you have ever tried to comprehend.

My husband thought that this was the greatest birthday present that he would have ever received; little did he know that it would be the beginning of the end of the demise of his son. Michael would have laid down his life for Davis if he had only known what this disease entailed, please don't make the same mistakes that we made because of the lack of education. Promoting awareness is our most prominent goal. Please make awareness one of your basic goals as a family and as a parent. If you live in the United States, you live among the 4% of people in the world who consume 100% of the hydrocodone manufactured and dispensed! This statistic came out in the AJC this past week. This means that you live alongside people everyday taking this drug. They drive on our roads, shop at our malls, attend our schools and churches, and they play in our parks. Educate yourselves and if you are one of the unfortunate ones who ends up dealing directly with the effects of opiate/heroin addiction, do the research and know where you are going and why. It will mean the difference in your life or the life of your addict.

1/4/15 – Constructive Act #290 – Share Your Story

This is one of the most incredible stories we have shared so far. I am a member of a closed group on FB called Heroin Support. It is a pretty incredible sight and I found Cody's story out there. I wrote to him and asked him if I could share his story and he quickly agreed and thanked me for allowing him to share in an effort to help others. WOW! Just WOW!

Here is his story:

Hey, Fam… I started with percs… Upgraded to Opana, and graduated to heroin in the span of about two years... In my perc era, my gf at the time became pregnant... My parents lived in Pittsburgh PA (Jefferson Hills) at the time so I decided I wanted to get straightened out and moved there from Ohio to start anew. I was introduced to AA there and began working a program. For eight months I stayed sober. When the time came to have our child, my gf wanted to come back to Ohio to have the baby near her family. Reluctantly I gave in and we came back...

I had the notion that with my new found knowledge of self and the program, I had my addiction under control… I had defeated it! Well...... Once back in town I stopped doing what I had been doing to stay sober (working a program) and began to find myself with old friends… Just one pill wouldn't hurt right?? So I took one… No problem, see? Soon it was back to everyday usage again and oh, what is this? Opana?? Hmm… Let me try… In love…

Then my son is born and I'm leaving the hospital to got get more pills… Fast forward to about a month later, her and I break up… I no longer get to see my 2 month old son (because of my own actions)… Poor me right?

Opana disappears... Enter heroin. 2 years of running the streets doing what we do to get it done... Jail for 6 months (Receiving Stolen Property) Get out and back to AA... Put together 3 months... Beat it again and had it under control lol... Relapse... Found new relationship (Hostage)... Addiction progresses and I begin to lie cheat and steal to maintain my usage, all while trying to conceal it all from her.

I was in love with a good woman and wanted to stop and be a father and a good man for her but I couldn't. She ended up leaving and I went hard out there... Robbed everyone I knew family, friends, strangers you name it... Ended up on the streets with all doors closed on me. I managed to find work out of town and stayed in the woods next to the job in a tent. All I had was the job and the tent. Eventually I ran out of dope and I couldn't work without it so I lost the job... Back to running the streets in my home town and on with robberies, burglaries ect. I was at my end... I didn't want to nor could I continue on...

One day I hustled up enough to cop enough dope to put me down for good... I copped and was about 40 yards away from my shooting range where my full intent was to sit under this bridge, shoot up and die. The cops swarmed me and hauled me into jail for a shopping list of charges... God saved me that day. 40 yards away from death, In jail a strange thing happened: I didn't get sick. On the street I would have been throwing up and crapping myself through withdrawal but for some reason I didn't. Of course I didn't feel good but it was nothing near what I went through on the street when I didn't use. I just knew it was finally over and my sickness was one of emotional and mental sickness over the realization of everything I had done and what had just happened in the past year; that was the worst part.

Anyway, when locked up I decided I was done and I truly surrendered like I never really had before. I got out on Nov,4 2014, Called my old sponsor to pick me up and we went to a meeting that night. Still faced with homelessness and love sick over the woman that I had lost, I continued on and found a hotel to let me stay in exchange for cleaning rooms there. It was so depressing. I wanted to feel sorry for myself and use but I didn't. A week later the guy tells me he don't need me there and kicks me out of the hotel. Homeless again...

That night on the way to a meeting I'm telling my sponsor that I cant do this. He says "Do the next right thing and pray about it" That pissed me off so bad I wanted to punch him. "What the crap is praying gonna do, Joe? Its cold outside and I'm homeless!!" He then said "ARE YOU GOING TO LISTEN TO ME OR NOT!??" Reluctantly I said "Alright, Joe, I'll pray and go to the meeting" And I did just that. That night after the meeting A guy in the program offered to open his home to me! Is that God or what, y'all!? I was humbled right then and there. Truly humbled...

I kept on working the program based out of this man's home and started working the steps with my sponsor, thoroughly. By step 5 my girl found out I was actually working a program and was serious and she came back into my life. Not back with me but in my life which was way more than I deserved. Then my family came back, then my son, all these things that were lost began to slowly come back. I've continued to stay focused and now have my girl back and see my son regularly. I am also now back at home. I had the first sober Christmas in years and with my family for that matter! I am now about to begin step 9 (making amends) and I'm nervous but I am prepared. Today I find myself wanting to help others fight this thing and I wish to inspire people to fight.

Thanks for being here everyone! Cody

1/5/15 – Constructive Act #291 – Map Out Your Strategy

As we move into the new year and work hard to reach our goals, it's important to remember that we need to map out our strategies. Whether you are the addict or the "addict's keeper", or a family member or a significant other, you have to know what your function is in the process and how you are going to keep things moving in the right direction. You need to know what your goals are and what your limits are. You need a vision and a purpose. HOPE—as important as it is—is NOT a strategy! Things won't happen for you just because you have HOPE! You have got to be actively working a program or a strategy in order to see progress.

Everyone's strategy will be different and made to work for them in particular. What works for someone else won't necessarily work for you. Just as we are unique and original as individuals, our strategies should be the same. Some of you may respond well to a 12 step program and others may not. Cognitive Behavioral therapy may work wonders for some of you, but others may not respond to it at all. Drug therapy may be the answer for some of you and others may not understand how to use it in your favor. As a result of your past, some of you may need individual therapy to put to rest the issues that got you started on drugs to begin with. Whatever your needs, find a strategy that works for you. You may have to try more than one and you need to understand that it may take you several tries to find the correct strategy—that is expected. Don't beat yourself up over it. Just keep working on a strategy until you find the one that works for you. Relapse is not only a possibility in the opiate/heroin world, but it is almost a given and very much expected. Don't give up if your first strategy doesn't work… you will find the answer if you keep trying.

Be open-minded and don't close the door on any strategy. A lot of people have a lot of opinions when it comes to the world of drug abuse. Many people talk very loudly and very opinionatedly about something that they know very little about.

Don't let those people sway you from your goals. I get so upset reading comments on the news media sites where people put their 2 cents in without investing in the knowledge that they need to understand the epidemic that we are experiencing. They put people down and tell them what they should or shouldn't do all the while being completely ignorant about the situation. Ignore those people and consider the source of their comments.

Sometimes you just have to trust your gut! As an addict or as an "addict's keeper,undoubtedly you will get lots of advice. Some of it will be from those who have gone before you and their knowledge will be based on their own experience. Others will just decide that they need to tell you how to live your life and how you should treat your addicted loved one. Listen to your own instinct. No one knows your child or your loved one better than you do. If you are very honest with yourself, you will know whether or not it is time to make drastic changes. Don't let an outsider make those decisions for you. Remain an active player in the addiction process if you are the "addict's keeper." Decide up front what your limitations are and then develop a strategy to stick to your guns. You too might need to change strategies in midstream. Remember, the definition of insanity is continuing to do the same thing and expecting different results. If you are not strong enough to deal with your addicted loved one, choose someone that you trust who is. Let that person help you with your strategy and you can continue to make the decisions while they enforce them.

Addiction is not "one-size-fits-all" it never has been and it never will be. As long as the addicts are individuals, the addiction will be an individual disease. Become familiar with as many strategies as you can. Remain open-minded and when something is not working, move on to something new after you have given it a fair try. MAP OUT YOUR STRATEGIES, and don't be afraid to try new ones. Keep trying until you find the strategy that works for you!

1/6/15 – Constructive Act #292 – It's Never Too Late to Follow Your Dreams

Today should have been Davis' first last day of college for his Bachelor's Degree in Business. Yes, it's another sad day for us as parents, but it's also another reminder of how very awful the disease of addiction is. I say it should have been his "first-last day," because it wouldn't have been if he were still here. He withdrew in the fall of the year before he died and we didn't know it. He took the refund money and used it for his addiction. Then, when we thought he was going to skip a semester due to rehab, we only thought he would be one semester behind. In all reality he would have been a year behind and would have lost his HOPE scholarship, all of this for a student who started out on the Dean's list and who had a full-paid tuition scholarship. WOW—how could this have happened? It's called heroin!

Did Davis have hopes and dreams? Of course he did! Could he have come back and made them come true? Of course he could have, but sadly he will never have that opportunity. If you are an addict please hear me now and understand what I am saying. It's NEVER too late for a fresh start to make your dreams come true. I know that life sometimes feels hopeless and you feel helpless to make changes, but it can be done. I do believe as a society we are behind in the help we should be offering and the changes that we should be making to help those in the throes of opiate/heroin addiction. But I truly feel that change is coming and that the future will be much brighter for those of you who are looking to make changes. I know there are things on the horizon that are actively being worked on and I know that legislation is also on the floor to be talked about and hopefully passed.

It's too late for my precious child. He will never have that college degree that he should have started to finish today. He will never be able to make a life for his precious daughter and the girl of his dreams. He will never have the opportunity to own his own business and drive the car of his choosing. He will never be able to travel the world and see the Seven Wonders. He is gone and will never be coming back. Heroin took his life and his dreams. PLEASE DON'T LET IT DO THAT TO YOU!

Seek the help you need and don't take "NO" for an answer. Look until you find the right help and the help that you can afford. Some places are free if you can abide by the rules and stay clean. Let others help you be accountable on your journey. Look into drug therapy to help you if you can get it. Visualize your dreams every day and motivate yourself to make them come true. Pray when it gets too hard for you and ask God to take the cravings away and replace them with a peace that only He can offer. Decide to do whatever it takes and then get others out there to help you! It's not about will power! It's about getting others on your side to help you in your quest.

Surround yourself with the right people and with people who are not active users. Talk with people in recovery on a daily basis and ask them how they achieved their goals. Find out how others made it work and then give it a try yourself.

There are so many things on the horizon and if you can hold on just a little bit longer then the help you need should be forthcoming. We are doing everything we can at the Foundation to make it happen! Everyday, behind the scenes, we are working to make others aware of the deadly statistics surrounding opiates and heroin. Everyday we are talking with those in prominent positions to see how we can help to bring solutions to the table. Everyday we are looking for fundraisers to assist others and ourselves with events, research and awareness pieces to gain the energy that we need to gain the support necessary to affect change. We are working!!!

Look for our new business card in a separate post later in the day with all of our information, our phone number, our Board members, and our contact information.

The Davis Direction Foundation is ready to make a difference moving forward into 2015. THIS IS OUR YEAR TO HELP YOU!

1/7/15 – Constructive Act #293 – We Need The Men To Step It Up

It's been known throughout the nation and down through the years that whenever there are problems within families and communities, it's the women who talk about it and share about it. We are verbal creatures and we are not denying it! But, I'm sure there are plenty of young men out there, one of whom would have been my son, that would like to hear reassurance and support from the men in the community and within the families. There is an organization called "The Addict's Mom" but, there is no organization called "The Addict's Dad." I do realize that it is harder for men to share their feelings on the whole, but I believe that these young men dealing with addiction need to hear from the men! They need your strength, they need your support, they need your wisdom and they need your gift for listening with your brain rather than your heart. Women often do not excel in the "less than emotional" arena. We tend to think with our hearts where our children are concerned.

Now, please don't take offense if you are a woman who has the gift of separating your heart. I know you are out there; however, I am not one of them. It often takes me quite some time and many battles with denial before I can come to terms with some of the things that Michael tells me in dealing with any of the children. And YES—there are a lot of "told you so's" that are spoken in both directions between us. But in the end, each one of us understands that we are different, and that we can both be right just thinking about situations differently. Sometimes we even agree to disagree after I have exhausted every possible situation, multiple times, and he's still not buying it! The bottom line is that he thinks like a man and I think like a woman. God made us different for a reason, but He also made it impossible for us to procreate without the other. We both agree that God in his infinite wisdom knew this was in the best interest of the children.

I would venture to say that 95% of the comments that are made on the DDF are from women. We need the men to speak up! Your boys and young men need to hear from you! Many times when a certain percentage of the population does not involve themselves in the conversation, it is interpreted as disinterest or worse yet, shame and embarrassment. I know for a fact that Michael was NEVER any less interested in Davis' situation than I was. We just internalized things in different ways and we hurt in different ways. You know that old saying, "A son is a son until he takes a wife, but a daughter is a daughter the rest of her life." There is just something about a man's ability to remove himself from the dialogue. I don't really believe that they think about it any less or ever remove any pieces of the past from their hearts, they just have an uncanny ability to pick and choose their emotions at any given time.

The bottom line is that boys and girls, young men and young women need ALL of our support. It's not enough to just have the women weigh in on the conversation; we need the men as well. According to Live Science, 2014, "by 2010, nearly equal numbers of male and female heroin users were seeking treatment." So, with both genders using and seeking treatment for this horrific disease, we need both genders to offer comments and support. Live Science, 2014 also writes that the age of first use of heroin or any opioid has gradually increased, from age 16 in the 1960s to 23 in 2010. With this being said, many of these heroin users have moved out of their homes and are out on their own. In other words they are not in a position to have a Dad around to talk with or get support from. So, hearing from our DDF male readers would be support that some of the users reading our site are not getting from anywhere else.

I feel very strongly that active users need comments from men and women alike. So, let's hear it for our DDF men. Please join the conversation and help all of us women work toward saving lives in a more verbal way. I know from personal experience that Michael may not join the conversation as much as I would like, but when he does, it is always something of value in my opinion. Don't allow the youth of our country to misinterpret your lack of comments as disinterest, shame or embarrassment, JOIN THE CONVERSATION! PLEASE. It's necessary!

1/8/15 – Constructive Act #294 – Hold Your College Students Accountable For Their Spending

Many studies have begun to show that the age of heroin addicts seeking first time treatment are in their early twenties. Many of them are also college students and began their experience with drugs while they were in college. Now, with that being said, how many of you have college students out there that you set up a bank account for and continue to deposit funds into? I know that Davis had an account and we were actively depositing money into the account for college expenses. Because he had a job of his own and was contributing to the same account with his own money, we allowed a level of privacy for that account that could have held lots of answers for us. Once again, we didn't know what we didn't know! After Davis died, we had access to his bank account and it was very obvious that he was making large withdrawals after every paycheck. He also had his tuition for the fall semester deposited back into his bank account which would have let us know that he had withdrawn from school if we had been diligent in holding him accountable for his spending.

He was very adamant about his privacy, which should have been a red flag in and of itself. When you have nothing to hide, you usually don't mind sharing your bank account with your parents – especially when they are the ones supporting you. On the other hand, as parents, we have chosen to raise our children to be independent and we try hard to allow them any level of independence that we can. I know as parents, we try to back off as our children get older and we try to let them make their own decisions and live their own lives, but when Ebola entered into the states, our Nation went into overdrive trying to protect everyone. We took extreme precautions to protect the people of this nation. Well, we are in the midst of an opiate/heroin EPIDEMIC! Many states have declared emergency situations due to this crisis. Knowing this, why is every parent in the country not taking extra precautions to determine whether or not their kids are at risk for the disease of addiction. Yes, your child might be 30 miles away or 30 states away, in either case, you need to hold them accountable for their spending if you are their financial support system. Opiate/heroin addiction comes with a high price tag and the bank account could well be your first clue.

Drugs become such a part of the college scene due to the studying and the tests that have to be taken on a weekly basis. Most colleges are a step up from the high schools that the kids have attended and the parents aren't around to help with the other things in life while the kids devote their whole attention to their studies. At college, the kids must do it all. They must wash their clothes, prepare their own meals or go out to get them, deal with every other aspect of their lives and then get their studying done on top of it. Kids begin to share their ADHD meds to help their friends and then one thing leads to another and before you know it, they are doing uppers and downers just trying to exist. They become overwhelmed and begin to self-medicate in an effort of relief.

They may begin with opiates found at home in the family medicine cabinet on a visit home, or be the recipient of a friend who found a bottle of old opiates in their home medicine cabinet. Then they begin to look for them back at school and find a source – it's not hard! One thing leads to another yet again and they find out that heroin is way cheaper than the pills they were buying. The high they experience is completely different and amazing and they go from heroin pills to snorting to shooting intramuscularly and then end up shooting up in their veins. It doesn't take long to complete the cycle and be completely addicted.

Watch the bank accounts! You will learn a lot. The sooner you realize that your child is experimenting with or taking drugs, the easier it is to get them off and rehabilitated. Please hold your child accountable for their college spending. If I had it to do over again, it would be a joint account and I would have the same access that my kids have to their accounts. My money—my accountability. Please don't think that your kids are completely capable of deciding things in their best interest when they go off to school. As a matter of fact, their brain is not even completely developed. There are still parts of it that are a work in progress. Continue to talk, ask the hard questions, and check on the things that you contribute to – meaning the bank accounts. HOLD THEM ACCOUNTABLE!

1/9/15 – Constructive Act #295 – Think Big and Be Confident

I had a conversation with a mom the other day and she was telling me her story. She too has lost a son to this horrific epidemic, and she continues, as I do, to go over things in her head and wonder "what if" she had done things differently. We shared parts of our stories with each other and we came to a conclusion that we both felt needed to be shared. Have confidence in your gut. I know I have said before to "trust your gut" but trusting your gut and acting on your gut are 2 very different things.

As parents, our first instinct is to protect our children. When they are actively using drugs, this presents a two-fold problem. You need to protect them from harm due to the drugs, but you also feel a need to protect them from societal ridicule, and jail! Because many people in our society don't recognize drug addiction as a "DISEASE," calling your child out as a drug-addicted individual creates a whole new set of problems that could cause potential harm as well. So, it feels like a "Catch-22!" If you call the police for help, you run the risk of your child ending up in jail. We all know that a convicted felon has a hard life ahead of him or her, not to mention the abuse that goes on behind prison walls. Who would want to do that to their child? On the other hand, if you leave them out there doing drugs, you run the risk of them overdosing or worse still—dying! I believe in my heart that God was merciful to Davis in calling him home. His heart was too big to endure the hurt and pain that would have come with the road he was traveling.

I don't think there is a parent out there who would hesitate to call law enforcement to help locate their child if they knew the "consequences" or better still the "outcome" would be mandated rehab or mandated medical assistance for a disease! Now I'm not talking about dealers or those who have physically harmed others through their addiction. But to file a missing persons report because you think your child is lying in an alley somewhere with a needle in his or her arm possibly overdosing and needing help, shouldn't be a "two-fold problem!" For Michael and I, we filed the report and decided to let the chips fall where they may. As you all know, it was too late for Davis, he was already gone by the time we called to make the report.

I am very confused about some things that have gone on legislatively in our state, so I won't begin to try and talk about them intelligently, but it does seem to me that at times the drug dealers are getting off easier than the "kids" who are using when it comes to the legal system. Too many of our children are behind bars when they need to be in a rehabilitation program getting help for a disease. I am going to meet with a prominent judge in the coming days who has offered to sit down with me and help me understand the plight of drug addiction and how our court system is dealing with it. Hopefully this meeting will give me some idea of the "Direction" that we need to focus our efforts on to affect change in our community.

We need to begin thinking BIG! I shared a post yesterday about the state of Arizona and how they are forcing the citizens of the state to come face to face with this epidemic. The president of the Arizona State Broadcasting agency has not only agreed to, but he initiated the 30 minute uninterrupted time slot to air an educational segment regarding the heroin epidemic and the need to promote awareness. I have already reached out to the President of the Georgia Broadcasting Association to share the link with him that I posted on the DDF. We will see what happens. Think BIG and Trust your gut with confidence! We need to make changes! Changes are never made by sitting back and waiting on others to begin the process.

All anyone can say is "NO!" I've been told "NO" before, and I lived to tell about it!

1/10/15 – Constructive Act #296 – Challenge and Support

Michael is my "early to rise" husband for those of you who don't know much about my family. That's why he is so wise . Anyway, he goes out very early on most mornings and has breakfast and reads articles related to heroin for research. Along with his position as CFO of the Foundation, he is also the #1 Researcher for the DDF and he sends me most articles that are posted on the site. This morning he sends me an article about laws being passed in KY and he prefaces his chosen quote with these words, "I COMPLETELY DISAGREE!" I knew this was going to be a doozie! So then he copies and pastes the quote that he disagrees with and here it is: "In most cases heroin addicts do not desire to be rehabilitated, but rather are only looking for their next fix." Said McDaniel, R-Taylor Mill. "However we did identify a common unifying experience wherein users are encountering government, and that is when they are arrested and booked into a county jail."

Now if you are going to make a statement like that, you better be ready to back it up! I would like to know where Mr. McDaniel got his statistics and what research he did in order to make a statement like that? I would imagine that he just made it based upon his own judgmental beliefs! If that is the case, he needs to make an apology to every heroin addict that is still alive and suffering in the throes of addiction, as well as every family that tries everyday to do whatever it takes to keep them alive! If he feels like he can back it up, I would challenge him to provide the research that he did in order to make the statement!

Now many of you are probably thinking that I might be overstepping my bounds just a little here challenging a person of "power" in the Senate of Kentucky. Let me tell you a little about Mr. McDaniel. Christian (Chris) McDaniel, 37, is a first-term Republican from Taylor Mill in Northern Kentucky's Kenton County. He is a graduate of The Citadel, a decorated U.S. Army infantry veteran, the holder of a master's degree in business administration from Northern Kentucky University, and the owner of a concrete company. It seems like he is an educated man who has had a great deal of experience in life; however, he puts his pants on one leg at a time—as my Daddy would say—and in this case, I say he's got it wrong! Speaking out on a subject that you obviously no very little about is like giving a kid a loaded gun. I'm confident that Mr. McDaniel has never looked in to the eyes of a crying heroin addict down on his knees with his head in his hands begging for help. I have! It's statements like these that will hinder progress and take us years to overcome!

I don't know how many heroin addicts Mr. McDaniel knows or how many families of heroin addicts he has sat down with and actually had a conversation with in order to understand the disease. I don't know how many neurosurgeons or psychiatrists he has asked about addiction, or how many Rehabilitation Facilities he has visited. But, I would venture to say NONE!

I only write this post and challenge this Senator of Kentucky to make a VERY PRESSING POINT. Educated people in positions or power are UNAWARE of the DISEASE of ADDICTION. They don't know what they don't know! This is the biggest challenge in the fight against opiate/heroin addiction. People make judgments and decisions based on their own beliefs and not the facts! That's why the Davis Direction Foundation's mission statement to PROMOTE AWARENESS is so very important. Education is KEY! People will not invest in what they do not understand! If Mr. McDaniel had ever spoken with Davis, he would know in no uncertain terms that he would have given anything to become Rehabilitated! He even thought he had done just that after 3 weeks in a rehabilitation facility. He was clean, detoxed, healthier than he had been in months, feeling good about himself and moving in the right direction. Then, as in most cases, the triggers, the memories and the cravings begin to creep back into the body and the fight becomes unbearable. IT IS A DISEASE!

If you are one of the DDF readers in the great state of Kentucky, PLEASE feel free to share my thoughts and "Constructive Act" with Mr. McDaniel. I have the utmost respect for public officials who give of their time to invest in public service, but I am intelligent enough to realize that they are human. Maybe, Mr. McDaniel would even like to make a donation or a public speaking appearance at our next Symposium! Perhaps he will let us know.

1/11/15 – Constructive Act #297 – Share Your Story

This may well be the best advice we have ever had on a "Share Your Story Sunday!" Talk about a Success Story! WOW! All of us who have been directly involved with opiate/heroin addiction whether we were the addict or we were the "addict's keeper," know how very true this story is. I wish I had heard it before Davis died.

Thank you for sharing your story!!

I remember the very first time I took an opiate based pain pill. The doctor had only given me Tylenol after a minor, outpatient surgery and it wasn't even taking the edge off. I was used to toughing pain out at the time, rarely so much as took an aspirin. But my grandfather walked up and said, "Here, take this." And with that a new world opened up. Not only did my physical pain vanish remarkably fast, but the depression, anxiety, stress, sadness, and grief I had been overwhelmed by in recent years, for the next hour or so it vanished as well. I wasn't high. Hell I don't even know if it was a Lortab 7.5 or a generic 10.0. It didn't seem like my state of mind was altered. I just felt NORMAL!

I was relaxed, I actually dozed off and on over the next couple hours and not once, not once did I think about the fact that my parents and I had barely spoken since I was 16 and when we did it was very strained and difficult. It didn't even enter my mind that evening that just a few months earlier my whole world had shattered as I discovered the "borderline cult" church I had been devoted to for a decade was actually a life-destroying joke and the people I had come to consider my family had "shunned" me (in the Amish sense of the word). For that one evening I was actually HAPPY. Or at least the absence of stress over being broke, where I would live, what I would drive, how I would make it out in this world alone, sure did feel like a dang good substitute for happy.

I didn't take another pain pill until a doctor prescribed me what appeared to be hundreds after a dual procedure- repairing a deviated septum and removing my tonsils at the same time. If you're ever offered that lovely little deal "And Mr. Patient it'll mean only being put to sleep one time and only one," do yourself a favor and PASS! What it means is the only place all that drainage can go from repairing the deviated septum is right down to that raw, freshly cut throat, which on its own, for an adult, would've been painful.

But, Dr. Pancake (his real name) has a great solution. These incredibly fat, reasonably tall bottles of pain pills! He wrote me a script for what looked like well over 100 when I went home. On my follow up visit, 100 more. When I went to my PCP thinking something was wrong because the pain had skipped the 1-10 chart altogether, they called Dr. Pancake who suggested they write me more pain meds. When I went to the ER (when you're nose is packed with gauze and your throat is swelling rapidly—you get the picture), you guessed it, shots of morphine and more pain pills.

When this whole ordeal was over I wound up with bottles and bottles of unused pain meds with doctors prescriptions on them. I was naive, only 23 years old, and had suffered a complete emotional break from the accumulative stress of being broke, on my own, having suffered the loss of family relationships as well as those of the cult-like groups I had been with. (I say cult-like. To call them cults would be dishonest. But there's only ten cents and a case of Kool-Aid difference between them). One thing I had determined was that I would never again allow my stress and anxiety to reach the point of cracking up again. Never again would I allow depression to take me all the way down to contemplating suicide. Not when there were some little pills in a bottle that would make ALL the pain go away almost instantly.

Well if you're reading this you probably already know the next chapter of this story. My new best friend, my favorite lover who helped me sleep, helped me relax, took my pain and depression away if only for a minute, became the worst enemy I would ever have to fight. This evil little bottle of pills would eventually turn me into somebody I hated worse than my worst enemy. Would wreck my health. Destroy my hormone levels. And worse than anything, these evil pills converted my brain into a machine that would attack me for failing to feed it more pain pills. By this time I had to take 40-80mg at a time just to take the edge off. I lived in constant fear of death. That beautiful little blissful absence of pain and stress, those days were GONE FOREVER! Now those pills were nothing more nor less than a means to survival. My brain was now completely rewired to make me puke, sweat, tremble, shake uncontrollably, and if all that didn't work and I continued to refuse to feed it any more pain pills, my own brain would begin inflicting pain throughout my body! My jaws, my low back, my shoulders, basically any place that ever felt pain in my life would now experience surges of the worst pain you can imagine. Within a couple years, here I was, an honest businessman by day, but had to sit in dark parking lots like some kind of thug with a stack of cash that would choke a mule, along with tools for my protection should someone decide they just wanted to take my cash or kill me. This is who I had become. These are the people I was dealing with. People who gave me legitimate reason to believe I would be robbed or killed. But what was the f-ing difference between them and Dr Pancake. Part of me wanted to go back and confront Dr. Pancake and just ask him if he realized the path he was laying out in front of me. But he killed himself before I got the chance. Apparently lots of agencies were after him for medical malpractice.

Here's the kicker. I came to a point where I knew I had a problem. I knew this was no way to live. After trying to quit and making it for a week at times until the withdrawals and physical agony would overtake me, I KNEW I needed help and couldn't do this on my own. But I had no idea where to turn. I was so freaking naive. For all I knew if I showed up at a doctors office and admitted I needed help, someone would smile, take down my info, slip out to call the police, and I would go straight from the doctor's office to the police station to jail where I would suffer through god awful withdrawal. I didn't know there were doctors out there who could help. I had never heard of Suboxone for sure.

I had to ask the lady to repeat herself six times. "Subursrin", "Sobotstan", I wasn't walking away without the exact name and spelling. Apparently there was a doctor right here in my city who had battled addiction himself and was committed to helping other addicts as part of his recovery. He would talk to you without treating you like you're less than human. And apparently he has a medication that will block the effects of opiates should you relapse and will stop withdrawals.

The first thought that hit my mind was "how can there be any addicts in the world?" If this kind of help exists why doesn't everyone take advantage of it? I would've stopped months and maybe years earlier if I had known there was help available without being shipped off to jail first and then to a month of inpatient rehab. But if you can avoid jail, go see a doctor on an outpatient basis, take a medication that'll stop withdrawal, why would anyone live like I'm living. I watched a few episodes of Dr. Phil where they were talking about suboxone. Back then they were speaking of it in a very positive light. Like it was no different than taking insulin for diabetes or blood pressure meds. If you're an opiate addict, take Suboxone.

Insert: I feel obligated to share right upfront that had I known then what I know now about Suboxone I would've handled things differently. If you've tried everything else and failed and you have the opportunity to get on a Suboxone program there's no reason not to go for it. It's not perfect but for gods sake look at the alternatives. Possible death by OD, death by other addicts on the street, possible incarceration, a record, (or a worse record), the self esteem issues knowing you're living the life of a criminal. A lot of people criticize Suboxone programs for its obvious flaws but only an idiot would refuse to see its better than not getting help or getting help that doesn't work. The main thing I would say is to tell your doctor right up front you want to be on Suboxone no longer than 3-6 months and you want to begin an aggressive taper off Suboxone as soon as you're stable. The problem is Suboxone can cause worse health problems and is worse for long term addiction and can be more difficult to get off of than regular pain pills.

So, naturally if you can use the program to stop opiate abuse and break the addiction cycle and then taper off Suboxone under medical supervision you're on the right track. Unfortunately, I didn't know all of this back then. I've been on Suboxone for several years and I've done a tremendous amount of damage to my health. I wish I had done things differently. But to criticize Suboxone, I won't go that far. The life of highs and lows, of sitting in dark parking lots at 1am with a stack of cash, of going days in between getting "re stocked" suffering debilitating withdrawals just to get that huge sigh of relief when I finally "scored". Those days are long over. I was able to go on with my life free from legal problems, free from the worry of being shot by a thug who didn't have the pills but still needed or wanted my cash. Though I know I won't be truly healthy until I am completely free of all substances for at least a year or longer, at least I can honestly say I don't take anything my doctor isn't prescribing and what he's prescribing doesn't create tolerance and lead me down a path of having to take more and more.

I haven't had a pain pill or anything else that wasn't something I was supposed to be taking in several years now. There is no doubt whatsoever if I had stayed on that path I would've either been arrested, shot, overdosed, etc. That lifestyle can only end one way if you don't break out of it. I will be the first to warn you or anyone of the dangers of Suboxone but sometimes you have to choose the least of two evils and make a desperate leap out of the deadly current you're caught in. Besides, nobody ever said we could get out of this thing unscathed.

But I was able to grab hold of the Suboxone program, get off the illegal unprescribed pain pills, go on with my life relatively drama free, police free, had a beautiful baby girl, bought a beautiful house, managed to build a business from scratch with only $1,500 originally, then $10,000 when we incorporated, and grow it into a million dollar company that will be able to sustain my family and take care of my daughter long after I'm gone. Best of all I spend evenings, almost every evening, playing with my daughter, reading to her, teaching her to count, singing, making sure she knows she is loved and special and that we are proud of her, as opposed to being out there every other evening trying to find six more OCs! That alone is worth it. You have to try something. Anything. Had I not found this solution when I did it is extremely doubtful I would be alive and definitely not free to write these words today. At the time of this writing, it's been over 6 years with no significant cravings and absolutely no desire to go back to that life.

I cannot begin to imagine where I would be today if I hadn't found my doctor and gotten off the dead end path I was on. The wads of cash to support the addiction would no doubt have ensured there would never be enough to keep the business going. There's no circumstance or scenario whereby I could see my marriage surviving. Without my business I don't want to think about what I would have to do to support my habit. We all think we are above robbing liquor stores but I'd dare say most everyone in prison once felt the same way. I most likely wouldn't have the most wonderful gift life has given me, my daughter, but even if I did I wouldn't be the same daddy I am today and I wouldn't be worthy to be her dad. Our lives aren't perfect but for the past 6 years, we've lived a peaceful, drama free life. I create jobs instead of desperately trying to find one hoping I pass the drug screen. As far as relapse, I don't think I'm above it and I'm no longer naive. But those pills became my worst enemy. What was once my best friend, removed my pain, alleviated my depression and sadness, became the thug with a knife to my throat, the chains that had me locked down with no visible way out. I hate them. I hate them as much as anyone could hate any enemy. These pain pills want to destroy me, kill me if they can. It is NOT a moral issue. Addicts are not inferior to non addicts. The enemy is the drug and the circumstances that lead one to try the drug. Celebrities, CEOs of Fortune 500 Companies, the homeless man or woman in the streets, no one is immune. I'm not a doctor but I understand enough to know if you're wired a certain way and if ever once one drop of opiate reaches your brain, your brain will crave more and more until it self destructs or you get help, and take specific steps to fight this enemy.

I have a habit of coming up with ridiculous analogies but this truly speaks to the situation. If you're on a runaway train headed 90 mph toward the end of the tracks where there's a giant cliff and at the bottom of that cliff is almost certain death. If by a miracle you survive the crash without dying you're guaranteed a life of prison sentences, ruined relationships, and misery. Sure, jumping off a moving train isn't a great option either. You're bound to have broken ribs, head injuries, possible internal bleeding, and might never recover 100%. But it sure beats the hell out of going off the cliff.

So I encourage you to do whatever you have to. Take whatever lifeline you can find. Call a doctor. Go online and find a support group. Call that toll free number you've noticed on flyers. Talk to someone else you know who has been where you have been. But whatever you do take the first step and get off this train. Whether you can see it or not, it is headed toward a cliff.

And whether you can believe it right now or not, there is hope. If I could go back and change things I would. But all things considered I cannot complain. There are several different ways to get help. Choose one and run with it. It's hard to believe it has been six years. What a different story would have been written if I hadn't been lucky enough to find help when I did.

For whatever excuses you may give yourself and for all the problems associated with the different recovery options, I can attest, they beat the alternative. To be able to live a life without risks of overdosing, getting arrested, constant extremes between highs and crashes, it is worth the effort to change your life. The odds are against you if you try to go it alone. So reach out and ask for help.

1/12/15 – Constructive Act #298 – Be a Sponge

As with most things, when there are not clear cut answers, a person should try to invest in the cause and be a sponge to all the education and research they can soak up. Each day I try to read articles and find out what others are doing in this country to try and combat this evil epidemic of opiate and heroin addiction. I read every comment and look up every person who likes our Davis Direction Facebook page. Knowledge is power and it is going to take a lot of power for us to figure out how to deal with this disease and turn things around in our country. I have learned so much from people who write comments or post things on the DDF. Many times other websites are shared or other organizations are mentioned who have a vested interest in the opiate/heroin crisis that we are experiencing. I look into all of them, and sometimes I even reach out to specific people for further explanation or education.

Throughout our country, different states are putting a variety of strategies into place that are showing promising results. I have learned that in many states while you are appealing an insurance denial for services, you are able to continue your stay in Rehab. You don't have to leave. In other states, Doctors are getting to decide whether or not to continue services for Rehabilitation. Drug courts are mandating requirements and trying to offer alternatives to incarceration. Safe needle exchanges are being implemented in order to combat Hepatitis C and keep law enforcement officers safe from being stuck during a search. Many states have already passed a Medical Amnesty Law allowing friends to call 911 for help without the fear of being locked up themselves and allowing families to carry Naloxone. I've heard that some judges are giving options such as Vivitrol shots as opposed to a jail sentences.

I've also seen some things that I can't even imagine are still happening. In some states law enforcement agencies are actually resisting the ability to carry the Naloxone kits because they feel that it encourages addicts to continue to use. They also feel that administering the Naloxone kits is a liability that they don't want to assume. I always want to ask the people making those decisions, "But what if it were your child?" We still have doctors who have no idea how to write a prescription for Naloxone or Vivitrol and pharmacies that either don't carry the drugs or don't know how to fill the prescriptions. Yet, the fact remains, that we are losing more people to opiate/heroin addiction, and other addictions in our country, than we are to automobile accidents.

In order to Be a Sponge, I have begun reading the newspaper. I am learning to use Twitter and other news media. I am researching websites that are sent to me and I am reaching out to those who are in charge of specific programs in my own community trying to educate myself as to how the programs already in place are working. I am reaching out to legislators, drug companies and doctors to try and understand their perspectives and how changes can be made in order to promote awareness and affect change. You need to do the same. If we all piggy back on the research and ideas of others, we will have the ability to do greater things toward changing the way addiction is perceived in our country and even in finding a cure for the disease of addiction. So, talk with your doctors and your pharmacists. Ask them if they prescribe or carry Naloxone and Vivitrol. Ask if they prescribe or carry Suboxone and Bunavail. If they don't, ask them why they don't, and if they could look into it for you. Until we all start asking the hard questions and forcing others to do their due diligence in their field, nothing is going to change.

Be a SPONGE. Learn everything that you can in order to be able to carry on an intelligent conversation with someone else regarding the opiate/heroin epidemic that we are in the midst of in our community and our country. Be able to ask the hard questions and be able to give the right answers if you are asked the hard questions. Read every article that you see, and send them to us in private messages on the DDF, so that we can post what we feel fits in with our Mission Statement and furthers the Foundation. Never stop learning, because KNOWLEDGE IS POWER!

1/13/15 – Constructive Act #299 – Don't Just Talk About It, Be About It

I was watching television the other day and there was this man who had been incarcerated for 18 years for a crime he didn't commit. He now goes around the Country telling his story and he has started a Foundation of his own. When the news anchor asked him if he had any advice for others, he said, "DON'T JUST TALK ABOUT IT; BE ABOUT IT." In other words, he was saying to get involved. There are so many people who are deep in the throes of the epidemic of opiate/heroin addiction, whether they are the addict or the "addict's keeper," and all of us want to see change in the way things are handled legally. We have a golden opportunity to show up and talk with the elected officials in our community and our state. So, Don't Just Talk About It; Be About It! Mark your calendars now for January 29th at 7:00 pm and come to the Family Life Hall of Marietta First United Methodist Church for our 3rd Symposium. This one is entitled "Laws, Limits, and Loopholes." We will hear from Attorney General Sam Olens, and the Commissioner of Behavioral Health and Developmental Disabilities Frank Berry. You don't want to miss this!

Here is a list of 12 ways that you can "BE ABOUT IT"…

- Show up to the Symposium
- Bring a friend with you
- Invite your Doctor
- Invite any local elected officials
- Invite your child's principal

- Invite your Ministers
- Submit a question that you would like answered. (via FB)
- Print our flyer and hang it in a public place (It's on Facebook)
- Make phone calls or email your state officials
- Share our flyer or make your own post on your personal FB page
- Clean out your medicine cabinets
- Educate yourself by "liking" our FB page

Pick one, several or all of the suggestions above and "BE ABOUT IT" in order to make a difference in our community. As I've said before, everyone is involved and no one is immune. You may not have a family member who is taking opiates, but if any of your family members drive on the public roads in our community, they are at risk of an accident from an opiate/heroin addict driving while under the influence of their drugs. Your family could be the victim of theft because of an addict stealing in order to support a very expensive opiate habit.

I mentioned in the above list to submit a question for the Atty. Gen. and the Commissioner to respond to. There will be no question and answer session at the Symposium. All questions must be submitted before the Symposium if you would like a response. Please either ask them in the comment section of this post or submit them in a private message through Facebook. You can also email all questions to info@davisdirection.com. Ask the hard questions; don't be ashamed to find answers for your loved ones and help them find their way into recovery. All questions submitted will be sent to the Atty. Gen. and the Commissioner before the Symposium.

Mr. Olens and Mr. Berry want the same things that we want! They want to help our loved ones find a way into recovery. They want to educate the public about the dangers of opiate/heroin addiction in our community. They want to see prevention programs address the dangers of addiction in our schools and communities. They want to promote awareness and affect change while keeping the addicts alive as we search for better solutions. Join us as we meet on January 29th to unite in the search for answers to this horrific disease. "DON'T JUST TALK ABOUT IT; BE ABOUT IT."

1/14/15 – Constructive Act #300 – Look At The Numbers

Today is a significant number because it is the 300th Constructive Act that I have written. When I started, I'm not sure what I had in mind, but I can honestly say that the writing has been overwhelmingly healing. It's been healing because there is a hole in my heart, and even though I know it will never go away, some days it feels more full than others. 2015 is also a significant number, because we just started a brand new year and in the world of statistics, some things are measured by the years. Here are 2 other significant numbers that I know of from reliable sources.

There have already been 6 opiate/heroin deaths in Cherokee County this year and 5 in Fayette County. We are only 13 days into this year as of today. There are countless other opiate/heroin addicts in our community that continue to be deep in the throes of addiction who are putting their lives at risk on a daily basis. As you can see by looking at the numbers, things are not getting any better yet. As a matter of fact, I am suspecting that they will get worse before they will get better. How long it will take before we begin to see some improvement is anybody's guess and depends greatly on the advancements that are being made in the treatment of the disease.

We are 1 Foundation with 5,145 members (I call "likes" members) in the past 10 months. We have collected just over $50,000.00 and have purchased over 300 Naloxone kits. Each kit cost $45.00 and is given for free to those in need. 300 Naloxone kits at a cost of $45.00 equals $13,500.00. So – 27% of all of our funds raised are going directly to save the lives of the loved ones living with the disease of addiction. We are in the process of printing 750 packets of information to be handed out to at-risk people or the families of those who are at risk. We are preparing for our 3rd Symposium and we are mailing out 347 letters to the 2014 Health Issue of Atlanta Magazine doctors who were named the "Top" in their field. At the DDF, we are making a 100% effort to promote awareness, affect change and save lives.

If each of our 5,145 members would invite one person to "like" our page, we could increase our membership to 10,290 members overnight. If each member donated $1.00, we could purchase 228 additional Naloxone kits that have the potential to save a life. If we all stand together our strength and our voice is multiplied 10 fold and people begin to listen. I was told today by a very informed source that until someone hears or reads your name 7 times, they don't really take notice. It's time to continue to get our name out there over and over again until people take notice.

Statistics are just numbers until you begin to put a name and a face on them. Those statistics mean everything in the world to me because one of the deceased statistics is named Davis Henry Owen. He was 20 years old when he died. He had 1 mother and 1 father and 4 siblings. He was the oldest son of 5 children. He had 1 daughter and he is gone forever. He died in 2014 after 13 years of grade school and 2 years of college. He touched countless lives and his story continues to make a difference to others.

There is however one statistic that we cannot put a value on and it belongs solely to 2 of the precious people that received a life saving kit from the Davis Direction Foundation. Their lives were spared because of the Naloxone kit they received at the last Symposium. They were given a 2nd chance at life, and that number my friends is a gift that is PRICELESS!

Please consider our Foundation for your next charitable donation. You can go to our website at www.davisdirection.com and click on the "donate now" link to help save a life. People have made donations in honor of loved ones, in memory of loved ones and in tribute to those who are trying to make a difference. Please search your heart and think of your children, your grandchildren, and your loved ones and friends. Putting a Naloxone kit in the hands of an "addict's keeper" is potentially saving a life. Funding awareness materials and prevention efforts help to ensure that your loved ones will never take opiates/heroin. What do the numbers mean to you?

1/15/15 – Constructive Act #301 – Don't Forget to Create Plan B

Failure is a given in this world of ours! It always has been and it always will be. Failure has been the creator of many inventions and the incentive for deeper thinking and moving outside the normal parameters. Failure is not a bad thing; it is an opportunity to back up and evaluate what may have gone wrong and why. It is also an opportunity to regroup and try again. Sometimes failure can even tell us that we need to choose another life path, that maybe we weren't cut out for the one that we thought we were. As a Counselor in the school system teaching Career Awareness, countless times I have asked the kids what they want to be when they grow up. Inevitably I have those who want to be professional athletes, professional models, movie stars, and the like. You get the picture. I never squashed their dreams and ambitions, but I did encourage them to pick more than one path, or in other words to choose Plan B.

This morning on Good Morning America, I heard the awful story of Renee Alway. She was a contestant on "America's Next Top Model" who placed 3rd in the reality show. She was devastated and could not find a job modeling after the show, so she turned to drugs – eventually using heroin. Long story short, she was just convicted and sentenced to 12 years in prison. She is now speaking out about her story. I realize that everyone who fails to reach his or her goals in life doesn't necessarily turn to drugs, but I also know that not everyone has the addiction gene either. I wonder if this young lady never thought about having a back-up plan for her life. She was only striving for one of the hardest and coveted positions in the world. Did she not realize that hundreds and probably thousands of young ladies were after the same shot in life? Did she not have family members or mentors who were encouraging her to look into other areas of interest? Maybe she did, but the bottom line here is that she couldn't handle the failure and didn't pursue a backup plan.

I do believe in dreams and goals and tons of ambition, but I am also grounded in reality and I think that our kids should be as well. There have been so many articles written about the Baby Boomers raising their children under an umbrella of protection that never allows for failure. We have given trophy after trophy and come up with awards for everyone in the class based upon their strengths and weaknesses. In fact, what we have done is taught our children that there is no such thing as failure! Then they grow up and enter the adult world, and BOOM... they are devastated because someone is "better" than they are. The average young business person stays in a job for less than five years now simply because they have not been promoted up through the ranks fast enough to equal success in their eyes. I fear that we have taught our children that failure is devastating!

I could sit here and write a million cliché's right now about failure. "If at first you don't succeed"... "When you fall off of the horse"... "Mistakes are opportunities"...the list goes on and on and I have not written anything here that you have not heard before. Why do you think there are so many cliché's regarding failure? BECAUSE EVERYONE FAILS! Failure is a given and we need to teach our children this fact. We need to be more open about our own failures in life and tell them or even model for them what we did or will do to "get back in that saddle."

Abraham Lincoln once said, "My great concern is not whether you have failed, but whether you are content with your failure." I believe that he hit the nail on the head with his greatest concern! Teach your children that failure is a part of life. Teach them that they WILL fail and how to handle it when they do. Don't praise less than adequate effort and DO ground your children in REALITY, because they will eventually live in a REAL world. WHAT IS PLAN B?

1/16/15 – Constructive Act #302 – Don't Take It Personally

Those words may well be the most insincere words ever spoken! They are often thrown out there as a callous disclaimer when someone wants to say something but not own the words they deliver. If you fall into the category that the words are spoken about, then why in the world would someone think that you wouldn't take it personally? People need to realize that opiate/heroin addicts and their family members are personally affected by a disease that people are very outspoken about – often with very little understanding and knowledge regarding the disease. So, when you speak out in a general statement or make a joke, or poke fun at those of us who have a personal connection with the disease...WE DO TAKE IT PERSONALLY! Not only do we take it personally, it's offensive!

Two days ago on ABC's World News Tonight it was reported that 259 million narcotic prescriptions were written in the United States per year. That equals to 1 bottle for every adult American (CDC 2012). The alarming part that followed stated that a company named Express Scripts looked at 36 million people who were prescribed one 30-day bottle of narcotics; 47% of them, nearly half, were still taking the opiate prescription three+ years later. This means at the very least, that

36 million families are affected by this disease today in our country and these are the ones who are obtaining the narcotics legally. So let's be conservative and say that each person has a family of four and that equals 144 million people directly affected by this disease and you tell us NOT to take it personally. Don't waste your breath! It is personal. In fact it is very personal. We spend countless hours every day worrying and wondering what we will come home to. Will our loved one still be alive; will our possessions be gone? Will we have to call an ambulance; will we even know where they are? This is how the family of an opiate addict lives their lives and YES – it is personal.

It's easy to sit back and convince yourself that it is someone else's problem when you are not directly affected. But the truth is that everyone is affected. When I first spoke out about Davis and his addiction, friends I have known for years private messaged me or wrote me cards or made personal phone calls to let me know that I was not alone. I had no idea of the silent struggles they were all suffering and it is for no other reason than the societal views and judgments of those who speak out without knowledge or concern. It is just common courtesy to respect the unfortunate plight of others whatever it may be. Disease, poverty, disabilities, disfiguration, deformity or any other kind of affliction that has affected a family should never be the butt of a joke – NEVER.

Please be respectful and responsible when you choose to speak out about issues that affect others. Those involved take it personally because it is personal. We are human and we have feelings. Those of us who have buried children to this horrific disease as well as those families who are suffering from opiate/heroin addiction know that there is nothing funny, silly or pleasant about the everlasting effects that we cannot cure. We realize that we cannot change what we cannot change, but if you think that makes it any less hurtful to hear, you are mistaken. IT IS PERSONAL!

1/17/15 – Constructive Act #303 – DON'T EVER SAY... "IT DOESN'T AFFECT ME"

One of the most difficult obstacles to overcome in the awareness arena of the opioid/heroin epidemic is that people think it doesn't affect them, so they don't need to invest in educating themselves about the crisis. This could not be farther from the truth. Statistics confirm that one in every ten people is suffering with the disease of addiction. So, I heard a doctor say that if you go into any hospital in the United States for a surgical procedure, and you deal with more than ten people in the facility, you have been treated in some capacity by an addict. This was the head of Anesthesiology in an Indiana Hospital who told me this, and the reason that he knew was because he was one of those people. He worked day in and day out while he was actively suffering with opioid addiction. He was actively taking sufentanil each and every day that he was on the job. How would you like to hand your child over to a potential opioid addict for a surgical procedure?

If you think you are pretty healthy and doing well in life, think about the possibility that one of the electricians that built your brand new home could have been suffering with the disease of addiction. Last year, right before the golf tournament, do you remember the evening that my house started shorting out and the appliances started blowing up one by one? It was because it had not been laid out properly when it was built. The wires were cut much too short to allow for normal settling of the land, and the wires snapped. Another interesting fact about my house is that when the foundation was laid, it was laid with four additional feet of frontage that had to be "built out" because it had been poured incorrectly. I'm sure that was a costly mistake in the fact that I have four additional feet of house all across the front of the lot. That's a huge difference! I wonder if it was a mistake made by a person who was on drugs at the time?

Do you or your children drive on public roads and highways? Consider that a person suffering with the disease of addiction is driving one of every ten cars you pass on the highway every day on your way to work; Or, better yet, on the way to class when your children drive themselves to school every morning. How can anyone in his or her right mind not understand that this disease affects everyone?

Consider the high taxes that we are paying to put addicts behind bars and keep them there for any given length of time. During our 4th symposium it became very apparent that unless our community is willing to invest in and support a solution, we will continue to suffer the devastating personal and economic impact of rising drug use and addiction. Simply stated in business terms, addiction costs our society over $400 billion each year and for every $1 invested in substance use disorder treatment and recovery, taxpayers save at least $7.46 in costs to society. As a matter of fact, according to the National Institute on Drug Abuse, every dollar spent on treatment can reduce future burden costs by $12 or more in reduced drug-related crime and criminal justice and health care costs. Our joint commitment to proactively assist and support those in recovery will certainly yield healthier individuals and families, but it could also save our country the billions of dollars we spend every year in reaction to substance abuse.

Please be aware of the devastating effects that drug addiction has on every single one of us. No one is immune and everyone is at risk. Ask any parent who ever buried a child who died of an overdose if they were prepared to deal with the overwhelming consequences of drug addiction. The answer would be a resounding NO! While this epidemic continues to claim more lives than automobile accidents in our country, I cannot for the life of me understand why more people are not getting involved in the solution.

Just think of the time that you put into deciding which car was the safest for your child to drive. Now wrap your head around the fact that more kids will be killed by a drug overdose than an automobile accident. And last but certainly not least, how many of you wonderful parents out there who pride yourself on getting your kids the best medical care available when they need it, have actually put your kids in the position of being "prescribed into addiction" because you didn't know enough to question the medications that your trusting doctor prescribed for them? Do you consider that a choice? Food for thought!

1/18/15 – Constructive Act #304 – Share Your Story

Today's story comes from a young lady down at Into Action Treatment Center. They were represented at our last Symposium and the Director – Mr. Andrey Rossin regularly sends me testimonials from the people who are in treatment down in Boynton Beach Florida with him. If you are in a treatment center and would like to send a story regarding your facility, we will gladly publish those as well. Listen to what this young lady, who has obviously been in some of the nation's finest treatment facilities, has to say.

Thanks for sharing:

I am truly grateful that I discovered Into Action Treatment Center because it has changed my life. I am not ashamed to say that I have suffered with the disease of addiction for many years and I have sought inpatient treatment more then once. At the time when I was researching which treatment centers to admit myself to, I looked for the world renown places, the ones most people hear about when celebrities need help. I learned a big lesson. These facilities are fine treatment centers, but I didn't receive what I received at Into Action Treatment Center...the solution. Yes, I did complete each of these other treatment center's 28 day programs. I graduated and was handed some blue book and was told to find a sponsor as I was completing my discharge papers.

When I entered Into Action I was told that there was no set time of stay for the program, it would depend on my progress. Not the progress of a group but, it was about me the individual. I got the same blue book I received at the other places but, this time it was explained to me that this is the book where the solution lies. And the most comforting news was that I didn't have to figure out where to find it. Into Action was going to be my guide from day one along with my sponsor that was strongly recommended that I find immediately. This Center is solution based and follows the recipe used by millions of people that have changed they way they live and enjoy a clean and sober life.

If one of my children ever came to me and said they needed help I would not send them to those other treatment centers I mentioned. I would ONLY send them to Into Action. I feel it would be a waste of money and a waste of precious time in the battle from drugs and alcohol.

Renee M.

1/19/15 – Constructive Act #305 – Mix Up Your Day

Holidays are especially hard for those who have lost a loved one to opioid/heroin addiction, especially to those of us who have lost our children way too young. A holiday was a sleep in day that the whole family would just be home and be together. Since none of my kids have married and really completely moved out – meaning they still have a bedroom in my house – it was a mother's dream to have them all home under one roof. We might get up and go get breakfast somewhere or I might cook a big breakfast to eat at home. Either way, we were all together and we could enjoy each other's company. With seven people in the family, those days were few and far between, so holidays were something that I looked forward to. I didn't make any plans for today so that I wouldn't be disappointed if the day didn't turn out the way I had planned. I also didn't make any plans because I never know how I will feel on a day like today. These days are just harder!

I slept in, which I never do, got up and immediately started cleaning – it's kind of a therapy to me. I didn't sit down at the computer, which is normal, instead I started the laundry, refilled all my bird feeders, took the plants outside for a breath of fresh air and watered them, lit a candle, and then I sat down to begin writing – also a therapy. Michael ran out to get errands done, and the rest of the house is silent, kids still sleeping in, and me...... just alone, quiet and spending time with God and the computer! I feel at peace.

Not knowing how I will feel or respond to things on a daily basis is hard to come to terms with when I used to be a person that felt in control most of the time. In the past I have been a rock for my children and a constant source of support for Michael as he is for me. But this past year, there are days that I am no good for anything or anyone. I am not in control of my own emotions and I can't focus or help anyone outside of my own private world of grief. I have had to learn to take one day at a time, let life happen as opposed to having a plan for every single day and hour, and to relish the things that are important and forget the trivial mess. I thought I used to be pretty good at getting it all done, but now I am consumed with other thoughts and I have trouble focusing and completing tasks. It takes a lot more energy than it used to and I have to be much more intentional. My world has forever changed.

Unexpected change in my life has put me over the edge on some days, as it has for all of us. We gently reel each other back in and understand in our hearts that the pain is there for all of us and how we respond to that change will be different for each of us, but no less real to any of us. We all kind of do our own thing in the healing process and respect each other's heart to grieve in whatever way necessary. We mix up our plans and our past traditions and do what we need to do to get through the day and onto the next. Maybe one day we will resume some of the old traditions and pick back up where we left off when we found ourselves without one of the beloved "Owen7."

You cannot tell others how death will affect them, because you don't know from day to day how you will feel. All you can do is to share your own experience and hope that on some level it will bring understanding and meaning to others who are going down the same path on the same journey. For me, I have to mix it up and change and rearrange plans, habits, traditions, and constants. For now, I live each day allowing life to happen and then dealing with my response. Things the kids used to could tease me about often lead to raw emotion and tears now. It's confusing and unnerving to them I'm sure, but they understand. We are all learning a new existence and our place in that existence. Some things are better, some things are worse, but all things are different without our Davis, our #4. We continue to "Move Onward Through Life…Looking Upward to God." He is our refuge and our strength.

Note* Sometime after the first of the year in 2015, I changed from using the word opiate to opioid. Opioid is all inclusive and is used more properly than opiate, although in the field of addiction, they are often used interchangeably.
Opiates are drugs derived from opium. At one time "opioids" referred to synthetic opiates only (drugs created to emulate opium, however different chemically). Now the term Opioid is used for the entire family of opiates including natural, synthetic and semi-synthetic. Thanks to DDF Medical Director Harold McLendon for educating me.

1/20/15 – Constructive Act #306 – Find A Great Church

Don't just go to church; find a GREAT church! I'm not just throwing this out there without really thinking about it, because I know that some people especially those who suffer with addiction have been totally turned off to churches and people who attend them. I truly believe that church can be a status symbol to some people and that they go because that's what they were raised to do and it represents a social environment and entity. To others, it is a place to go and feel close to God and share a worship experience with sincere people who are there for all the right reasons. There is nothing worse than not being able to find the right place to worship God.

There is nothing worse than going to a church and not feeling welcome and feeling like people are judging you and looking down upon you. With all of that being said, I will tell you that I don't believe that a person suffering from addiction can truly find pure recovery without God in their life. God is the missing link for many who are suffering with addiction and are unable to complete recovery. God is loving and God is kind and the church you choose to attend should have people who are loving and kind as well.

I love my church! I have not always been able to say that. I have felt "less than" in other churches and I have felt that I did not belong and that people turned their noses up and treated my family like we were not good enough to be a part of their congregation. I have felt shunned and attended week after week without receiving the spiritual gifts that I receive every Sunday at my current church. When you are in the wrong church, you are cheating yourself. You owe it to yourself to find the right church for you and one that feeds you spiritually every Sunday and one that leaves you wanting more. My family has found that church.

As I sat in the worship service this past Sunday morning, I noticed things that I have never noticed in any other church. I noticed beautiful people smiling and speaking words of welcome to my family. I received hugs from people as I entered and as I left. I watched and listened as my heart was filled in so many ways. Different things speak to different people, and one of the things that speaks to me so intently is the music. The choir sang an anthem that I felt was chosen especially for me this past week. It said "God has work for us to do." It laid out all of the problems of the world and said until those problems are taken care of, that God was still working in all of our lives. Then our outstanding organist played a piece during the offertory that just gave me chills. Come Thou Fount of Every Blessing – I have never heard a more beautiful rendition and one that took more talent to play. The staccato verses and the majestic ending made me want to jump up and shout "BRAVO." My heart was filled beyond belief. I could have left before the sermon ever started and been completely filled for the week.

During the children's sermon that we have each week, the pastor was speaking with the little ones, and at the end of the sermon, he took a handkerchief from his pocket and walked over to one of them. He commented that they must have a cold and he gently wiped their nose and put the handkerchief back into his pocket in an act of complete compassion. I don't even remember what the children's sermon was about, but I will never forget that he cared enough about that little one that he wiped that runny nose without question or cause. It needed to be done and he did it.

When it was time for the sermon, my pastor spoke about God's calling. He suggested that we all had a calling no matter how great or small it was intended to be. We were all called to do something and we needed to do it to the best of our ability. We all had a purpose and we all had an intentional meaning in the part that God had asked us to play. I know he was right, because God has called me to help those suffering with addiction and I feel it stronger than I have ever felt anything in my life. God has blessed our Foundation with people, with prayer, with money, and with gifts of time and talent. There is a purpose that we are supposed to fulfill and I will not stop until I know that God is telling me that I am done.

Find a church – Not just any church – but a GREAT church! Find the church that is right for you and your family. Find the church that you are supposed to be a part of and you will know it and you will be filled every Sunday. My church is right for my family and me, and my church is GREAT!

1/21/15 – Constructive Act #307 – Find Meaning In Your Dreams

I've said many times before on the DDF that I pray a lot and when I am afraid or I'm struggling for that next breath, or I want to find something meaningful to write, I pray and ask God to help me. This past week has been a really hard week for me reliving through some things with another family, and I have spent a great deal of time talking to God. Good feelings and sad feelings have come from this situation and I have been on the front seat of that emotional roller coaster ride once again. Even though I have never met most of the people on the DDF, I feel a bond and a close attachment to them because of the things we have been through. My heart was tremendously touched last week when a mother who found her precious son had passed, reached out to the Davis Direction Foundation four hours after she had experienced the most emotional trauma of her life. We were important to her and she knew that we would understand and grieve with her. Her words were simple and the hole in my heart grew bigger that day. "My son is gone; What do I do next?"

It's on days like this that I wonder if we are making a difference, and I have such mixed emotions. I was so glad to be emotional support for my DDF friend, but I was devastated that we lost yet another precious child to this deadly drug. A life is a life, but when it is a son, it tugs just a little deeper for me personally because of Davis. I was honored to be there for my friend and I immediately picked up the phone and called her just to be with her in voice and spirit. She was numb and I knew that she may not even remember the call, but it made me feel good to be there for her. I know through our relationship on the DDF, that she is a deeply religious mother and I knew that God would wrap his loving arms around her and help her find peace. My heart was bleeding once again and I felt defeated, like we were losing the battle. It seems to me like this disease is one step forward and three steps back right now. That needs to change, but it's hard to focus when the wind has been knocked out of your sails.

I prayed so hard last night before I went to sleep that God would give me the right words to write this morning, because my brain was completely empty and I had that numb feeling once again. Many nights, before I go to bed, I already have the CA for the next day planned, and I am excited to get up and write and share my thoughts. But not last night, I had nothing. Sometime during the night I began to dream and I had the most revealing dream. I don't really interpret my dreams all that often, but I do believe that this one had great meaning – at least for me.

My entire family was living in a village that was dirty and scary. There was really nothing right about this place and God told us to get out. There was a huge lake and it was the size of the sea. It wasn't the sea though, because it wasn't salty and there were no waves and no shoreline. God told us to get in the lake and start swimming. We would swim for two days and then on the third day, we would see a shadow on one side of the lake. We were to swim into the shadow and God would be there to rescue us. We went into the lake and we began to swim. It was all seven of us, and each person was doing his own stroke in the water. At one point, my youngest son was swimming under the water and the youngest girl cried out ,"Spencer, where are you?" As a mother, I was terrified and I worried that one of us would get too tired to go on and would drown. So all of the sudden in my dream, the Davis Direction Banner, which we bring to all of our events, was in the water with us and it became our flotation device. I told each member of the family to hold onto the banner and when one of us got tired, the others would carry them as long as they could hold onto the banner. Just before I awakened, all seven of us were working together to follow God's instructions and the plan was working.

In my humble attempt to analyze my dream, it was simply God saying…The plan is in place and if we all continue to work together, carrying others when they are too weary to carry on, He will be there to meet us in His perfect timing. God has a way of showing us what to do when we are struggling and need direction. So for today, I am encouraged and have a new determination to follow through with God's plan for the Davis Direction Foundation. Will you join me?

1/22/15 – Constructive Act #308 – Focus On The Good

Focusing on the good becomes a means of survival for those of us who lived through the hell of addiction or are currently experiencing it. Whether you are the addict or the "addict's keeper," you train yourself to focus on the good because it is the only thing that allows you to continue to put one foot in front of the other. No we are NOT Pollyannas; we are just trying to maintain some sense of sobriety or life in general. For all appearances, if you see us out and about, you will think that we are "normal." The fact is that we are far from "normal" internally. On the inside, everything has a double meaning for us, and in public, and privately, as much as possible, we try our best to focus on the good. If we did not focus on the good, we would crumble and dissolve into a state of catatonic isolation. Addiction is a nightmare that you never completely wake up from because there is no cure. Sometimes you go through good periods, but you only realize it in hindsight because you are so worried about it when it is happening.

Sure you can attend meetings of one kind or another, and you can read inspirational websites or join groups that help you to focus on the good, but the bottom line is that we – the "addict's keepers" have to work a program of psychological stability, just as our addicts work their programs of sobriety. Even after they are gone and the nightmare of daily living is over, the struggle then becomes how to choose your fate for the day. I will admit that there are days that I choose to remember my sweet boy and be sad and feel guilty and go over and over in my mind how I could have done things differently. But, for the majority of the time, I choose happiness, and I have to work at it 24/7.

Here's a good example. Last night I went to see "Newsies" with 2 of my children. As I sat and watched the most amazingly talented, young performers, I should have felt nothing but pure joy and admiration. But addiction has left me leading somewhat of a double life. Whenever I see young people who are close to Davis's age, it makes me think of all the talent he possessed, and then I begin to think of all the things that he never got to experience and I can't help it. Those thoughts just blatantly pop into my head and take over all of the enjoyment that I am trying to experience at the moment. I always see two sides of things now, one from the old enjoyable frame of reference, and the other from the point of view of the life that my sweet son will never have. As hard as I try to choose happiness, I cannot control my thoughts and what my brain wants to throw out there from my recent past. I can sit down to a beautiful dinner out with my family, and joy fills my heart and soul as I sit with four beautiful, smart and talented children and my wonderful husband. NOTHING should rob me of the joy of soaking in every moment of that experience, but my brain will send me the image of the "empty chair" and rob me momentarily of the blissful joy I feel. I cannot help it, it just happens.

In a way, I think the experiences of the past couple of years have made me a more complete person, better able to be empathetic and understanding of others. On the other hand, I know my life has forever changed. I will continue to focus on the good and the good that I can hopefully bring about for others. But I will tell you that as much as I want to choose good everyday, my past will not allow that. So, I will understand that my life is the sum total of my experiences and I will deal with that and try to focus on the good as I begin to understand my "changed forever" life.

1/23/15 – Constructive Act #309 – Don't Cry Over What Could Have Been

The alarm clock goes off at 5:00 this morning and Michael rolls out of bed. The first words out of his mouth are… "I miss my little Buddy; He was taken from us way too soon." That's pretty much the first thought each of us has every morning as we roll out of bed, although it's not always vocalized. Whenever it is spoken out loud, it just reminds both of us that we are the only two people on the face of the earth that know the pain in the other one's heart. Only the "other" parent shares the pain of losing a child. We often think of what could have been or what should have been. Then fast forward to 7:00 am when Michael is usually sitting somewhere having his breakfast researching on his iPhone, and he sends me an article that pretty much sets me back for the rest of the morning. I'll post the article at the end of the CA, but first let me say that as a society, we all hope for cures for everything that we now know of that has no cure. We hope for a cure for cancer; we hope for a cure for diabetes; we hope for a cure for MD, MS and Alzheimer's. The cure for these diseases would be amazing and would save so many people. But how would you feel about a cure that was passed over because it was possibly "bought off" by another drug company who wanted to remain the top drug for fighting one of the diseases that could have been cured? Yep – that's the article he sent to me this morning.

Of course we all want cures, but for a mother or father who just lost a child ten months ago, it's hard to hear about a cure that is now available – even if it is in another country. You are so thankful in your heart that something is available, but you mourn the fact that it was too late for your own child.

Think of a child who just lost a parent to cancer, of course their first thought is not going to be overjoyed, it is going to be a thought of great sorrow that it wasn't in time to save their parent. We are human, and as ecstatic as I would be today if they found a cure for diabetes, those who lost a loved one last week to the disease, would probably feel an even greater sense of loss. Sometimes I just think God's timing is off!

For those of you who "Don't know what you don't know"... Ibogaine – the new miracle drug for opioid/heroin addiction – is illegal in the United States because of its hallucinogenic properties. However, it is legal in Mexico, Canada, Norway and a few other countries. It does have the power to turn the pickle back into the cucumber! It works about 70% of the time according to this article. How great would it have been to know about this treatment along with all the other things that I have learned about opioid/heroin addiction in the past year? If you are the "addict's keeper" and you are still suffering daily trying to help your addict... You should really read this article and consider this treatment. My thought is ... "What have you got to lose?" If it could put an end to the addiction, think of the money, the time, the energy, and of course the LIFE you would save in the long run.

If you know someone or you are someone who has had this treatment and you can shed any light on it, PLEASE do so. Either comment below or send me a private message and give us the true story! We cannot afford to sit on this information any longer. If this is a cure, pharma's or no pharma's,... WE NEED TO KNOW!! Opioid/Heroin addiction is taking the brightest and best from us on a daily basis now at the rate of 120 people a day according to the CDC. Everyday that passes, we lose 120 more beautiful souls to this disease. Something has got to change. We have to step outside of the box and we have to demand clinical trials and provide funding. If you only knew of some of the projects that the government funded, you would lose your mind as to why they don't fund life-saving treatments like Ibogaine. Can you put a price tag on your child? Numbers speak volumes and numbers change the world.

I can't know for sure if the claims in this article are entirely true, but I know one thing for sure. It makes no difference for my sweet Davis. The timing was just off for him.

1/24/15 – Constructive Act #310 – There Is No Magic Answer

This post was inspired by one of my favorite fellas on earth who has struggled with addiction. Just like Davis, he is one of those who always thinks there is more to something than meets the eye. We had a great laugh over it yesterday and I told him - "sometimes the status quo just has to be enough." We all know if there were a magic answer to addiction, there would be no need for this page and many others like it as well as the thousands of rehab facilities, recovery residences and out-patient programs that exist today. Anyone who knew Davis knows that one of his favorite things in the world was Conspiracy Theory! He and Michael used to talk for hours about what probably really happened as opposed to what the American people were encouraged to believe! I would laugh and shake my head because to be quite honest, conspiracy theories are sort of scary to me. They're so secretive and so "out there."

Anyway, as we were talking about his situation, I began to give him some ideas to de-stress and lessen his anxiety. We began talking about Yoga and how it can be very relaxing. He started telling me that he would love to do Yoga, but he only wanted to do the Indian Yoga that had seven chakras, or "shockers" as I called them, and was so far away from just beginning to stretch and relax that it is probably the reason he has never started any Yoga in the first place. Sometimes we want things that we don't even understand completely and they get in the way of our progress because we don't know how to begin. I gave him one of my Yoga balls and told him to pull up a youtube video and get started!

I think that we spend way too much time looking for that magic answer, and making things so much harder than they are, that more often than not, we are defeated before we ever start. Life doesn't always have to be so complex. Sometimes the simple things are the most basic things. Trying to practice a scientific form of something that you have no experience with to me is like trying to perform "Swan Lake" without any ballet lessons! Working a program, any kind of program, requires you to start at the beginning and work your way into more advanced practices or techniques. When I gave my sweet fella the Yoga ball, he asked where the handle was on top! Haha – He was kidding of course, but just like all little boys, they first have to play with the equipment before they can get down to business. He wanted to bounce around like Tigger!

Now understand this bright and talented kid has ALL kinds of things going for him. Understand as well, that I am making light of the situation with the ball and the Yoga. But I told him to understand that he has all the answers, and for now, he just has to decide to work the program and stay the course. Diet, exercise, relaxation, conversations with God, and plenty of rest are the main ingredients to health and happiness. Addiction throws a monkey wrench in the entire process, but those who have come out on the other side will tell you there is no magic answer. If there were, somebody would be very rich because we would all know about it and invest in it.

There is no easy fix for addiction, short of the Ibogaine treatment that I mentioned yesterday as a possibility. That particular treatment will hopefully become reality in the coming weeks and months. For those who have the ability to travel and receive treatment in foreign countries, it will come sooner rather than later. Keep in mind, it has only been successful in 70% of the study group according to the study posted yesterday. So, it's back to the drawing board for the rest of those suffering with addiction.

I am not writing this post to be less than hopeful, because I am hopeful every day. But rest assured, when that magic answer is found, we will all know about it. Until then, you know the answers, you probably taught them your first time in Rehab. The program has not changed, when it comes right down to it, the routine is still the same. You have to invest in the program and work it 24/7. STOP looking for an easy way out! It's simply not available!

1/25/15 – Constructive Act #311 – Share Your Story

Today's story is a letter written to Heroin by the mother of a precious daughter who is now celebrating recovery. Her letter is inspiring, passionate and so very heart-felt. It chronicles a journey that is so typical of a family in the throes of opioid/heroin addiction.

Thank you Lee Ann Rose L. for allowing us to share your story today.

Here is her story…

Dear Heroin,

A little over a year ago I dropped my baby girl off to a year long rehab program because you had taken hold of her. I feared you when I first found out about you, but then you pissed me off. I watched you take the child that I bore and turn her into a liar, a thief and a criminal. I saw what you did to my grandchildren and how you tore their little lives apart. Although my daughter didn't complete the program, she spent 10 1/2 months in rehab building her life back. She rebuilt her relationship with God, her family and most importantly, herself. You are a vile, vicious, murdering bastard. I will go to my grave making sure you NEVER get a hold of her again.

Because of you, she has been beaten, raped and threatened. Because of you, her children missed out on almost a year with their mother. Because of you, I watched the news every night waiting to see if there was an unidentified body of a female, fearful it would be my daughter. Because of you, I slept with a gun by my side to protect my family. Because of you, I lost a job and plenty of so called friends. Because of you, I almost lost my home. Because of you, I held my son when he cried because he was afraid he would never see his sister again. Because of you, I put myself in harm's way when I went to the ghetto and the hood and looked for my baby girl. Because of you, I became stronger than I ever thought I could be. I will forever be your enemy. At one point, you tore my family apart. However, we were strong enough to rebuild our relationship and with God's grace, we are winning the war against you. I hope you rot in hell.

Signed,
Ashley's Mom

1/26/15 – Constructive Act #312 – Always Be Prepared To Act

Over the course of the last couple of months, I have heard twice of people who have Naloxone kits in their homes, but they were unable to use them because they just couldn't figure them out under the duress of the situation. I think that both families realize in hindsight that it was too late for using the kits unfortunately, but the fact remains, that you have to be mentally and physically prepared and ready to act if and when the time comes for using the kit. Naloxone is a miracle drug when it comes to reversing an opioid overdose. As a matter of fact, many times the addict will come back very angry and violent that the effects of the high have been reversed. They may be belligerent and ready to shoot up all over again to go back to that place that you just "saved" them from. You also have to decide at what point you are going to administer the Naloxone. There are decisions that have to be made and as the keeper of the kit, you will need to make decisions and know the protocol like the back of your hand in order for it to be effective. All of these things need to be taken into consideration when you are dealing with an opioid overdose.

The number one indicator of an opioid overdose is "unresponsiveness." That does not necessarily mean that the victim is not breathing. It just means that they are not waking up. Other indicators may include turning blue, snoring, gasping, gurgling, and a slow and faint heartbeat. You have to decide if and when to use your Naloxone kit! Have you processed this in your mind? Have you played out the scenario over and over again? If not, start today and visualize what would happen if you found your precious child or loved one unresponsive and possibly not breathing. What if he or she was snoring, but you couldn't wake them up? Is it time for Naloxone? All of these decisions are ones that you will have to potentially face if you are living with an addicted loved one and own a Naloxone kit. Please understand that. "According to Harmreduction.org, Naloxone has no effect on someone who has no opioids in their system. It will not help anyone who is not in an OD, but it will not hurt them either, unless it means wasting time or delaying getting access to emergency medical services." So – Make sure to call 911 BEFORE you administer the Naloxone! Or better yet, if you are with someone else, have them call while you administer!

Know where your kit is at all times. If you are an addict and you are using among others, always let them know if you carry a Naloxone kit. If you overdose and the kit is in your pocket, but no one knows about it, you could die with a life saving kit in your pocket or in your backpack. If you use alone, please realize that you are doing the most dangerous thing you can ever do – that is how my precious son died. Go ahead and put the parts of the kit together if you can secure it in a place that it is not in constant motion. At least go ahead and attach the Nasal aspirator. Practice putting your kit together and memorize the steps to administer the medication. Whenever the DDF hands out a kit, it will be a nasal kit and it will come with instructions. Memorize them! Be able to perform the task in your sleep! If you are unprepared to use the kit, you may not be successful if and when the time comes. BE PREPARED!

If you are lucky enough to have a doctor who will write a prescription for the kit, Lacey Drug Company Inc. with 2 locations – one in Marietta, GA and the other in Acworth, GA – will be happy to fill your prescription and will be glad to show you how the kit works. They will also hand the kit out in a zippered pouch with our website, Facebook and email information on it. That way, you will have a support system in place to walk with you along this opioid/heroin addiction journey. We understand how lonely it can be. One of our DDF readers, wrote this after searching high and low for someone to fill her prescription.

"Detox, ER VISIT, 'the prescription'...Over 20 pharmacies called and visited, crossed 1400 miles...spent hours on phone and a 40 mile trek this morning... but FINALLY...it's in my hands. Much thanks to the Davis Direction Foundation for referring me to Lacey's Pharmacy in Marietta...they are wonderful and if you have any questions call Jeff…he is so informative and understanding of this national epidemic that has now become our 'normal plight'…"

Unfortunately, this way of living and thinking has become a normal occurrence for far too many families throughout our nation. Please educate yourselves, "ALWAYS BE PREPARED AND READY TO ACT." The life you save may be that of your own precious child; And even if it's not, that precious child and life you just saved, certainly belongs to someone!

1/27/15 – Constructive Act #313 – Keep Telling Your Story, Even If It Hurts

Last night I spent the evening with parents from Marietta High School telling the story of my sweet Davis and how things escalated so quickly leading to his death. As a matter of fact, I am scheduled to tell my story six more times in the coming weeks. I have found one thing for certain, that no matter how many times I tell the story of how my baby boy died, it never gets any easier. It brings back feelings that make me search for that next breath and sends me to bed in tears. It hurts! I do realize the necessity of telling the story though, because kids are still dying in record numbers, and we are not making a lot of progress in the fight against opioid/heroin addiction! I look out into the audience as all eyes are on me waiting to hear about the demise of my beautiful, amazing first-born son. I see the fear in the eyes of parents and I know that people are beginning to realize that this epidemic is real and we need real solutions to offer our loved ones.

I heard a statistic last night at the presentation that really kind of blew me away. I heard the average life of a heroin user is nine months. Meaning that on average, after a person starts using heroin, their life span is reduced to an average of nine months. That is mind-boggling! I do believe it though. I don't even think that Davis made it that long, but then on the other hand I know of people who have been using for over ten years that are still around to tell about it. I'm not even sure that I would refer to them as the "lucky" ones. There is nothing "lucky" about using heroin.

Last night we were able to provide an education for many parents at Marietta High School. As we were walking out, people were so appreciative of the presentation that was given and kept saying that they had no idea about the depth of heroin in our community. Every time that I tag-team a presentation with others, I come away learning even more than I already knew. I think that is because the information regarding opioid/heroin addiction is growing and changing on a daily basis. Organizations are just now beginning to roll out actual statistics for the 2014 year and they are staggering. At the Symposium, we will be offering statistics and graphs from our own community for the first time, trying to paint a picture of what 2014 looked like in reality according to opioid/heroin addiction.

It is important to continue to spread awareness in regard to the epidemic that we are suffering through. There are still so very many people who have no idea of the widespread use of prescription medication leading to heroin. With every gut-wrenching slide in my presentation, I continue to spread the word in hopes that other families never have to go through what my own family experienced. It never gets any easier to tell the story of Davis because I think too many people out there are still under the impression that addiction can be controlled by the addict. Like I said last night in the presentation, "Heroin addicts are sick people trying to get well, not bad people trying to get good." Until our society begins to embrace this philosophy and truly get on board with finding solutions, the change that we can facilitate, will be slow and hard to come by.

With each click of the remote control, I see a new slide in my presentation that brings a swell of memories. With the childhood slides, my heart breaks all over again as I look at that sweet baby face and remember those little arms around my neck and realize that for that point in time, I was his world. Then as we progress through the baseball years, I remember the most fun vacations any family could have ever had. With each slide, my anxiety builds knowing that we are coming to the beginning of the end as we get to the young adult slides. The story is so personal and so completely exposed. Somewhere, at some point in time, things went drastically wrong and I couldn't fix it. Isn't that the mother's job?

At any rate, I forge on because there are lives out there hanging in the balance. They may not belong to you or your family now, but tomorrow all of that could change with one hit of heroin. Please educate yourselves. Listen to the stories of others and realize that no family is immune.

1/28/15 – Constructive Act # 314 – Realize The Potential Within

I sat in my living room floor yesterday and packaged 130 life-saving Naloxone kits to hand out at the Symposium tomorrow night! As I packaged each one, I just looked down into that little zippered pouch and realized that the contents within could have saved my sweet Davis. But because of the shame and embarrassment that he felt regarding his heroin use, he used alone and isolated from the rest of the world. It was his dirty little secret, and it cost him his life. Our Foundation has spent the majority of donations on purchasing these kits and handing them out. They are not cheap! We do this for one reason – to give those suffering with opioid/heroin addiction a second chance at life. WE DON'T WANT TO LOSE YOU! Please if you are an addict, or an "addict's keeper," come to the symposium tomorrow night and get the kit and learn how to use it. Carry it with you at all times and let your friends or family members know that you have it and that you are actively using. NEVER use alone; you run the risk of dying! You have a

DISEASE! There is nothing dirty or bad about it. Don't be ashamed or embarrassed to show up and get a kit – We do this for YOU!!!

When I talk about the "potential within," I'm not talking about the kits alone, I'm talking about those suffering with opioid/heroin addiction as well. Each and every one of them has so much potential, but because of the disease they are unable to tap into to all of that potential right now. They need help and guidance, but mostly unconditional love. I am a member of many of the closed group Facebook sites regarding heroin, and as such, I continue to learn so much about what families go through when one of their members is struggling. I also learn so much from the addicts on these sites as I see them continuously reach out to help one another and encourage one another to get into recovery and remain there. They are the most compassionate and empathetic people and they are the ones who truly understand the disease and can provide honest and sincere answers and advice.

I will be brutally honest here and say that when I first found out about Davis's drug use, I was so naïve and ignorant about it, but as I began to understand through reading and allowing him to educate me, I began to understand. Although, because of the way I had always thought about drug addiction being completely controllable by the addict, my transformation came about slowly. Only toward the end of his life, and seeing the struggles, the tears, the look in his eyes, and the complete defeat that he embodied, did I really understand the DISEASE. By then it was too late. I could not do enough research and learn enough to help him before he died. This DISEASE is so mental, emotional and physical – unlike anything else I have ever known. People just plainly don't get it and sad to say, I was one of them. I owe it to my son and to every other child who lost his or her life and to every grieving parent out there to make a difference moving forward. No parent who ever lost a child wants to see any other parent have to go through this.

That's why it breaks my heart to see and hear other parents who are fighting for their children's lives, talk about them as if they have some control or will power that they are not using to fight this addiction. The truth of the matter is that if money, time and outside responsibility and immediate availability were not factors, every opioid/heroin addict out there would head to the Rehab centers and stay there until their addiction was completely under control and manageable. A three week stay in a Rehab center isn't even enough to complete the withdrawal and detox process and that is about the average stay with insurance. The FREE facilities are full and most have an active waiting list. If they are 18 years old or older, they can leave of their own free will, but it is the disease that makes them walk – not anything else. We need good counselors at all detox facilities talking kids off the ledge – just as if they were getting ready to jump from a 100 story building. Instead, I hear and see posts from parents complaining about having to take care of their children. I've never seen this from a parent of a child suffering with any other disease!

I know we all get frustrated, but please write as if your child is reading what you are saying about him or her – because to them, it's personal. Many times they leave and don't come home or you don't hear from them because they know how you feel about their disease and they internalize it as to how you feel about them in general. I've even seen parents call their addict's degrading names and joke about how stupid they believe the addict is. I saw a post last week about how the addicts were the least deserving of prayer! PLEASE STOP! Talk to your addicts about the POTENTIAL WITHIN! If you can't be there for them and you are trying tough love – that is your choice…but remember it's tough "LOVE" – not tough times and hateful and hurtful words! There's a difference between venting and saying hurtful things that you can never take back. If you have to say things like that, please call a friend and don't put it in black and white for others to see. It hurts our cause and it doesn't help us help others understand the disease, because it sounds like you believe they are in control of themselves. THEY ARE NOT!

If you want to see the true heart of an addict, listen to one who has been through recovery, and come out on the other side, help one in active addiction. It is beyond emotional! REALIZE THE POTENTIAL WITHIN!

1/29/15 – Constructive Act #315 – Spread Awareness Whenever and Wherever You Can

Today will be an early posting because I have a lot to do today! Tonight the DDF will be hosting its 3rd Symposium regarding the opiate/heroin crisis that continues to reach epidemic proportions in our community. The only way we will ever be able to make changes in regard to this crisis is by making others aware of it and the devastation it is bringing to our community. Tonight we will have the opportunity to meet with state leaders and community leaders under one roof. We will have some of the state's brightest and best at this meeting helping us to figure out the best way to bring about change. I am excited to hear what the Attorney General, Sam Olens, and his four colleagues from the state capitol have to say to help us understand the "Laws, Limits and Loopholes" that either promote or stand in the way of us getting our loved ones help. They are definitely coming to spread awareness about what is available, what is already in the works and what needs to be in the works in order to affect change. I hope you will be there to gather information to turn around and spread throughout our community about what you hear tonight.

You have a responsibility as a community member to come and support our leaders, find out what you don't' know and how you can help. The leaders of every school in Cobb County have been invited and the TOP 347 doctors in the metro area have received personal letters. Legislators and chamber members have been invited and hopefully will show up to support our state leaders and learn what they don't know about our community epidemic. Members of our faith community are planning to show up and parents all over our county have shared our information through social media and word of mouth. It's not too late to invite others… neighbors, relatives, friends, doctors, teachers, counselors and ministers. Invite everyone. The more we have in our community who are aware of this problem, the sooner something will be done.

Tonight for the first time publicly, the 2014 Cobb County statistics regarding heroin will be shared. The Cobb County Sheriff's Dept. has gathered data and released it to us to share tonight. You will be the first to see our new awareness packet made possible from a grant through the American Medical Association Foundation. You will see and hear the most up to date information that is available regarding this epidemic. Over one hundred Naloxone kits will be available to individuals who are in need of a personal reversal kit. These kits are also made available through the grant from the AMA Foundation. They have been packaged in beautiful DDF Green zippered pouches provided to us through a grant from WellStar Foundation. We are truly blessed as a Foundation. God has placed his hand over us and has blessed our efforts and concerns.

This is truly an event that you don't want to miss. You will understand the difference between Rehabilitation Facilities and Recovery Residences and who governs who and who isn't governed at all. There will be no stones left unturned after our symposium tonight. You owe it to yourself to be present and bring your family with you.

You will see the newest Naloxone device that works much like an epi pen and have an opportunity to speak with a pharmacist and the rep from the drug company that is manufacturing it. Our own DDF Medical Director, Dr. Harold McLendon will also be available to answer questions and address any concerns. You will be among the best-educated people regarding this epidemic when you leave the symposium tonight. You have a responsibility to spread the knowledge and make others aware whenever and wherever possible. Remember the life you save may be someone that you love. DON'T MISS THIS EVENT!

1/30/15 – Constructive Act #316 – When You Hear Something Worth Repeating, Repeat It!

WOW – Last night was amazing. So many things that I heard gave me HOPE for the future of opioid/heroin addiction. I also heard some truths that created set-backs, but the good news is, people realize now that the things created – such as longer sentences for non-violent offenders, didn't work in the way that was intended. The statement was made that this epidemic happened so fast and furiously that we were unprepared for it and I know that could not be any more true! Each member of our panel added a different element to the discussion and the wealth of knowledge on that stage last night was astounding!

To begin with, Attorney General Sam Olens gave us great advice about moving forward and affecting change. He said it was absolutely our obligation to educate our community, including commissioners, councilmen and representatives, and that was how to get the funding for our Foundation. He also said that in order to affect change, we needed to get very specific and choose one thing to focus on at a time. If we took a broad approach with the legislature, nothing would ever happen. He also taught us last night that "Numbers" are key! The more people we have on board working toward the same goals, the louder our voice will be. Numbers are important at the state capitol. He used the "sex trafficking advocates" as an example of bringing the masses to make a statement. He said that their group was very effective due to the numbers they have when they come to the capitol.

Commissioner Frank Berry just reinforced what I wrote about last week, which was continue to tell your story – even if it hurts. He went on to say that the impact of individuals who have a personal connection and story with addiction are the ones who have the greatest ability to connect with those who aren't aware of the problem. He said that he could present the problem anytime, but that it would not have the same effect as someone who was telling a personal story about how it had changed their lives. He also said that we needed to focus on supporting the people suffering from addiction within our own community. As a community we need to provide the answers and solutions to help our own.

Executive Director Jay Neal addressed the revolving door of the prison system and said that it was one of the ways that we are not meeting the needs of our people. He admitted that this is one area that we needed to address, but he also stated that changes are being made in that area and that the Governor is completely on board with funding to make changes. He also stated that each person put into the system is evaluated upon entry and if it is determined that treatment for mental illness is indicated then that treatment will be provided.

Deputy Chief of the Dept. of Community Health, Gia Compton, made a statement that is so true and it was the fact that this epidemic has hit our communities throughout Georgia so fast and furiously that we were unprepared to deal with it. We are still learning what is available and how it can be funded. She spoke with compassion and it was evident that she has a heart for foundations such as ours.

Cassandra Price, who is the Division Head of Addictive Diseases for the GDBHDD, was absolutely amazing last night. She was a wealth of information and had more resources than "Carter has little liver pills" – as my Daddy used to say! She divided her presentation into 3 parts of equal importance: Prevention, Treatment and Recovery. As a division head, she is doing great things in all three of these areas and has offered to speak with me further about resources for funding, education, and recovery opportunities. She was profoundly knowledgeable about opioid/heroin addiction and it came through in her answers. She is truly a person that I want to get to know in order to "pick her brain" about the things we can do to advance our mission. Her ending statement was…"Prevention is Effective; Treatment Works; and Recovery is REAL!"

The clinical director of MARR, Jim Seckman, broke down the different treatment options for addiction and taught us how to choose one that met our individual needs. He also taught us about the different accreditations offered by different organizations.

Metro Atlanta Ambulance gave such an outstanding demonstration along with the help of a couple of our DDF Youth Ambassadors, that many people in our audience were emotionally affected. They taught us how and when to use the Naloxone kit and to ALWAYS call 911 when using a kit.

Last night had many statements that were worth repeating, so if you were one of those in attendance, or perhaps saw the story on Channel 2 news, or read the story in this mornings Marietta Daily Journal, PLEASE make it your priority to REPEAT something that you learned to someone who may need to know TODAY! It could save a life.

1/31/15 – Constructive Act #317 – Realize that Winding Down is Just Part of the Process

Yes… I had a rather "down" yesterday. I was exhausted from the events of the week, and I was really missing my sweet Davis. I was not in a rush to get a folder stuffed, or a Naloxone kit packaged, or an email answered or a phone call returned and it left a lot of time for me to think about how much I miss my precious son. It was just one of those days when it's really hard to look at a picture of him or go past his room. Every time I did, I felt that lump in my throat and I immediately turned away and tried to redirect my actions and my thoughts. Being the mother of five children is a full-time job and I'm so glad that the other four have kept me busy this past year so that I haven't had time just to dwell on the fact that Davis is gone. I can't imagine not having a beautiful and large family to take care of and I don't know what I would have done without them. I have stayed busier this past year than I have ever been in my life and it was intentional. If I "wind down," my mind begins to fixate on the "whys" and "hows" and I get really sad.

Next week will mark 11 months that he has been gone and I already dread the thought of even trying to wrap my head around the fact that he will have been gone for a year very soon. Everyday is a first, no matter what day it is, it can be the first 6,874th day and I will always have that empty feeling inside of me. So, I can't really figure out what make certain firsts harder than the others. Maybe it's because those are the days that others remember with you and even though it feels good for others to remember your sweet child, it makes it more talked about and more thought about. That's a good thing though, because I would be devastated if no one remembered those days. It's a catch 22 either way, and it doesn't even really matter because when it hits you it hits you! There's nothing that can stop your heart from having a full fledged hemorrhage if that is what is going to happen.

One of the hardest things about being in a really big family is that we don't all have our hemorrhages on the same day. It's really hard to be having a good day and see another family member having a really hard day. You always know when it's happening though because you know when something is wrong, but the other person says… "I'm fine" because nobody wants to take a good day away from another family member. So we love each other through those days silently, and try to be especially gentle with each other's hearts and feelings. We'll walk away from each other and try to get busy in another room, but everybody knows what is really going on. Respecting each other's grief is a sacred and understood process. It's just necessary.

So, when you have a down day, you just have to pray your way through it and know that it's part of the process. It will get better but you will never be the same. You learn that your aura can be contagious and that if you can't snap out of it, you will bring everyone else in the family down. On the other hand, someone who is having a really good day can bring you to a better place if you are struggling. Family is golden and nobody knows each other better than the members of an immediate family. You almost get to where you can anticipate when someone is going to have a hemorrhage and you go into rescue mode. We take care of each other and we respect each other at the same time. Grief does strange and beautiful things to people in a family. You take your journey together, but the process is individual. I've even begun to notice that when I write about especially emotional times, that I begin using the word "YOU" as opposed to "I." It separates me from all that pain and makes it easier for me to write. Like I said, grief does strange things to people.

Today will be better because I will be able to spend it with Michael and he is my rock! He knows me like no other and he always knows what I need. He sees my heart and knows my feelings sometimes even before I do because he's just that way. I know that he is the only person on this earth that shares the same hole in my heart because we both love and miss our Davis in the way that only parents can. On days like yesterday, I want time to fly, but then I would rob my other children of the lives that they are supposed to experience and that would be wrong. So, "fake it 'till you make it" as they say and find your way back into the light.

2/1/15 – Constructive Act #318 – Share Your Story Sunday

This young man is just glad to be alive and here to tell his story. It is the first time he has ever written his story and he stepped out in a leap of faith to do so. I, for one, am very proud of him and his family and for the time he has enjoyed being alive over the past nine months. Thank you Josh – Stay Strong!

I'm Josh and I'm and addict.

First and foremost, I just wanted to say that because I am used to saying that now days, meaning I go to meetings on a weekly basis. I have tools to keep me clean, but the steps are where I get my recovery from. This will be hard for me to do because I have never shared my story; actually, I have not done anything like this yet… meaning a lot of people being able to see it

The first time I ever smoked weed was when I was 14/15. Then, I ended up getting caught, and could not stop laughing (if I remember correctly). My uncle caught me. Then I started smoking on a daily basis when I was about 16. Then, once I got my license, I started to sell weed while I smoked it. Then all of a sudden my "best friend", reason why put "quotation marks" beside best friend is because he was until we started using heroin together. We met this guy that was from New York, and we asked if he smoked. He said "yes" we smoked with him and he bought weed from us. Then one day he was asking us if we knew where to get "boy" from. We were both like what the crap is that, and he said "heroin." We sat there and laughed and told him to get off our property.

Then all of a sudden he started to come back to cop more weed from us and what not. Then I tried heroin for the first time. I think I was about 19. I started on and off snorting it, then all of the sudden I started going to the needle. That was my DOC (drug of choice) the needle actually. Then I started going to the bluffs on a regular basis. All of the sudden I ended up doing this thing addicts call "speed balling" Heroin and coke (cocaine). That feeling was the best feeling I ever had felt... ever in my life. Even though that crap put me in OD's a couple of times. I've gotten 2 charges because of it, actually because of me doing it, and people not trusting me. I ended up in a coma for about 3 days, stayed at the hospital for 12 days, BUT... I am nine months and a few days CLEAN.

Honestly, there are days I'm like... "damn it"...I want to go back out and use, but that's what NA (Narcotics Anonymous) teaches me. I don't have to use. I'm grateful to be here with you all today and be able to share my story. Actually, I share the part that I can remember, because my memory is one thing that was screwed up from the coma. I also had to get hearing aids. It's all good though. Thanks to all of you, I was able to wake up today.

Thanks to my Higher Power that I am able to share my story and have another day CLEAN! "NARCOTICS ANONYMOUS" IS WHAT KEEPS ME CLEAN. JUST FOR TODAY. Thanks for letting me share, and again... "My name is Josh, and I am an addict."

2/2/15 – Constructive Act #319 – It's Okay To Say, "I Don't Know"

As a matter of fact, it's the responsible thing to do if you really don't know the answer. I have written many responses lately to people who have irresponsibly written things regarding heroin addiction. It's not that they are trying to put things out there that are completely untrue, it's just that they don't know, so they go ahead and make a statement anyway and set the "cause" back in a multitude of ways. For example, last month, a KY politician said that "heroin addicts don't really want to quit, they just want their next fix." That's completely untrue, but in the interest of "being a good and knowledgeable politician," he went ahead and made a statement anyway. I'm sure that he really believes what he said, but in all reality, I would guarantee you that he has done completely "zero" research and has no clue as to how far he set the "cause" back.

Last week, the DDF invited over 345 metro Atlanta doctors to our third Symposium, which was an effort to promote awareness and affect change. I will tell you that I know of only three doctors who were there and one of them was our very own Medical Director, Dr. Harold L. McLendon. How can that be? I find it very disturbing that the very people who are writing the prescriptions that are putting the Rx pain killers out in the playing field, aren't even attending the meetings that are trying to "fix" the problem. I can only imagine that they are unaware of the problem that it is creating. I sent 347 of the top doctors in the Metro Atlanta area (according to Atlanta magazine) a personal invitation via US mail to our Symposium, outlining the problem in our Nation regarding prescription medication and they did not find it necessary to come and find out more about the leading cause of death in our country. That is irresponsible to me.

I read an article yesterday that was in a local paper, that was actually pretty accurate, but it was only accurate in one slanted way. The last paragraph of the article said that "not only" were heroin addicts those who are imagined by many to be sickly, pale and strung out...... And then they left off the "but also"! The next line stated that Professionals, parents and young people "CAN BE" heroin users. How about saying that they "ARE" not that they can be? How about saying that they are "Mostly" according to new studies...... "young, white people from middle class suburban families who are bright and stressed out." How about saying that teachers, administrators, CEO's and business professionals ARE adding to the statistics of heroin users on a daily basis? How about saying that fully functioning individuals, with seemingly everything in the world going for them, are dropping like flies in our country due to heroin addiction?

I am truly disappointed to see that three or four people who come into our country with Ebola get headlines for an "epidemic" while our children continue to die from heroin addiction every day for over a year. I have seen more this weekend on Measles and the devastation that it can cause than I have seen on heroin addiction which is the #1 cause of accidental death in our nation today. What is wrong with this picture? Although, I have seen several communities doing great stories lately regarding heroin addiction, it seems to me to be a "did you know" story, rather than a "National Crisis" story. There is no comparison to the "scare" tactics used for Ebola and Measles as there is for heroin or prescription drug addiction and abuse. Perhaps it is because the way it is being presented, it excludes people who are innocent and ignorant. It defines the at-risk population as those "who traveled outside of the country," or "those who were not inoculated with a specific vaccine." It's hard to define the parameters of an epidemic that has no parameters!

So, a word of caution to those of you who are in positions of power and are being asked the hard questions... "If you don't know the answers to the questions regarding opioid/heroin addiction......PLEASE SAY SO!!!" Don't just irresponsibly throw an answer out there based off of your own judgmental thoughts and beliefs. Do your research and your homework. Know what is happening in your own communities and speak responsibly when addressing the issues. If you can't do that, PLEASE say "I DON'T KNOW, I HAVE NOT DONE MY RESEARCH!!!"

2/3/15 – Constructive Act #320 – Never Underestimate The Power Of One

Whether it be one small person, one small state, one small idea or even one small organization, when God is on your side, things can multiply and become massive. When 4'9" and 93 pound Mary Lou Retton took the floor at the 1984 Olympics, who ever thought that she would win the overall gold medal and become the most celebrated athlete in the World? How about the ALS Ice Challenge? Can't you just imagine whomever it was sitting around that table saying "Why don't we tell people to pour ice cold water all over their heads?" I'm sure people laughed and scoffed and said "Good Luck with that..." Did you know that the small state of Georgia has the very best Medical Amnesty Law written to date and that other states are emulating it all over the nation? Last night I spent the evening with 16 ladies from the Alpha Delta Kappa educational sorority around an oblong table sharing my story and telling them all about the Davis Direction Foundation. They were all very worried because their attendance was down last night and they were somewhat relieved when the 16th person walked through the door making a quorum. They listened to my story and asked questions and pointed out some really good things that the DDF will take into consideration.

I explained to them that one of the biggest obstacles with our organization and our cause is that people "don't know what they don't know." I told them that people don't realize that the stigma for a heroin addict has changed and the disease has changed due to the overuse of prescription medication and the fact that people don't know what they have and leave it sitting around in medicine cabinets. I explained to them that when people are given pain medication by names other than "Hydrocodone" or "Oxycontin" on the labels, that they often don't realize that what they have are actually opioids or narcotics. I will never forget the day I went with my mother to her doctor appointment and the Dr. prescribed the drug Norco for her trigger finger. I asked the nurse if Norco was an opioid and she looked at me very confused and asked... "What's that?" I knew right then that even people in the medical field are unaware of the epidemic that our nation is facing.

These wonderful ladies – many of whom probably taught either you or your children in our community — were very concerned and were ready to leave and go home and clean out their medicine cabinets. Many of these sweet ladies had grandchildren and didn't realize that prescriptions of this kind needed to be under lock and key. And Yes, some of these ladies even had relatives who were already addicted to opioids and knew the plight of the disease all too well. Some of these ladies were also still teaching in our local school systems and were going back to teach their high schoolers what they learned and even took informational materials back to share with them. Overall the evening was a great success and I walked away knowing that the education that they received last night will be shared over and over again.

Because of this very small organization, today we will have 16 more DDF Packets placed in and around our community for others to read. We have 16 more homes with medicine cabinets that are all cleaned out. We have 16 more families that know to question their doctors about opioid prescriptions and the necessity for an enormous amount of them and 16 more families that know to dispose of these leftover drugs in a Prescription dropbox located at the local police and sheriff's office. We have 16 former and current educators who can now educate their own families and friends regarding opioids and heroin and the devastation it can cause a family. We now have 16 more people that know that drug addiction is now the leading cause of accidental death in our country. It truly felt great to educate a group of teachers because you know the old saying… "Once a teacher, always a teacher."

There is no doubt in my mind that these wonderful ladies will turn around and share what they learned with others keeping a cycle of knowledge going and saving lives.

Thank you Alpha Delta Kappa for the invitation and the interest in learning about opioid/heroin addiction and the toll it is taking on our community. Thank you for the kit you decided to provide funding for after I left the meeting last night. Thank you for offering to help with service projects and offering to get involved. Thank you for the huge number of new "likes" I saw on the DDF Facebook page this morning. When you think about it, there were over 500 years of combined teaching experience in that room last night…… I can only imagine what can happen from here.

2/4/15 – Constructive Act #321 – Time Marches On, and So Should We

Today is one of those significant kind of days that is a milestone in my journey. Today is the 11th month anniversary of Davis's death. It is the last time that it will only be a number of months; next time, it will be a year. That's hard to say, it's hard to write and its even harder to comprehend. I've said it before and I'll say it again today. "It's as if time stood still as it flew by all at the same time." When 2015 rolled around and I left 2014, I felt as if I was leaving a time period that I wanted to stay in forever, because Davis had been there with me. I'm in a year now that I have only memories of him and no experiences and I have sort of the same feelings coming up on a year without him. I can no longer say, "this time last year," or "back in February" without naming the year I need to identify. It pulls at my heartstrings and it expands that hole in my heart.

When someone that you love more than life itself dies, you always hear others talk about that first year, like if you can make it through that time period, there is something magical about coming out on the other side. I really don't expect to wake up on March 5th and have any different perspective on what has happened over the past 365 days. It's more like... when it hits you – it hits you. There have been times this year, that I have truly enjoyed. There have been times this year that I have been able to talk about him and remember things with a smile. There have been times this year that I wanted to die and I didn't know where my next breath would come from. I cannot predict from day to day or even from minute to minute how I will be.

Last Saturday morning I went to a Cobb Energy master class with Shelbea to hear a Broadway director speak. During his interview with the Executive Director of the Alliance Theatre, there were singers sharing songs from different shows. One of the singers began singing "Proud of Your Boy" from Aladdin, and I thought I was literally going to throw up. One minute I was fine, and the next minute it was everything I could do to hide my feelings from everyone I was with, and continue to breathe. I was "set-back" for the rest of the day. I can't imagine if I hear that song 10 years from now, that I will have any different of a reaction than I did on Saturday morning. It was hard to hear.

There are already time periods that I am dreading to go through – one is coming up in a few short months. It will be so hard to see and hear about all of his friends graduating from college. He should have been there with him. I am so proud of each and every one of them for their accomplishments, but at the same time, it will be a truly hard time for me because it should have been his time as well. When his friends all start getting married, when he would have become an uncle for the first time, or when his daughter reaches her milestones in life, I know I will miss him and mourn for him as if it were brand new all over again. It won't matter if those things don't happen in the "first" year, and they haven't and they won't. When they do happen, it will be hard and I know that. I will always wonder "what if" and I will always be sad when I do.

I realize that time stands still for no man, and that I must continue with my journey, Michael with his and the rest of the children with theirs. We do what we have to do, and we go on with our lives. Davis would want that. We feel like he watches over us and he is our guardian angel. It works for us and it helps us to keep moving forward. You do what you have to do to put one foot in front of the other everyday. Time marches on...and so will we.

2/5/15 – Constructive Act #322 – Don't Be Afraid to Speak Your Mind

I have found that over the past year, people who are actively collecting data regarding the opioid/heroin epidemic are so afraid to speak out about their findings because they don't want to put false information out there. I do understand that and I know that when it is your organization that is on the line, you don't want to lose credibility by putting false information out there. But, what about saying what you see trending, kind of like on Twitter. I would daresay that drug overdose is the largest killer of 19 – 36 year olds in our country today. I don't have statistics to support it, but I do have a pretty good idea that if something out there was killing more people in this age group that we would all know what it is. I'm just going to stick by my statement until someone proves me wrong. I'm not afraid to say that it is my opinion, and my educated guess. It's kind of like the elephant in the living room, everyone knows the destruction that it is causing, but we have to wait on hard core numbers to make it real? WHY?

If it waddles like a duck and quacks like a duck, I'm going to call it a duck. It's not really that hard of a concept. If you don't know if you believe this or not, let me challenge you to get on a website called Heroin Support. I am a member and I go on daily. There are wonderful people on there supporting each other and encouraging each other. There are also people asking for support because they've lost a friend or a loved one. It happens almost daily. We are in the middle of an epidemic and I don't have to wait on numbers to tell me that. Just get on some of these sites and read back several days or weeks. You can do the same things on the DDF. We have asked for support for families and loved ones who have suffered loss due to opioid/heroin addiction. If you ask an addict if they have lost a friend, most of them can name several friends. I know that Davis lost at least 2 friends while he was in Intensive Outpatient Therapy.

You would think that if you lost a couple of friends doing the same thing that you were actively involved with, it would be more than enough to deter you from the behavior. Heroin is different. It just calls you back over and over. I don't have to have experience with the drug to know that. Once again, I can look at the evidence that I know to be true and know there is something different about this drug. It's like playing Russian Roulette…except that nobody really plans to die. You know that if you play with a bullet in a gun that with 7 pulls of the trigger someone is going to die. Heroin addicts expect to defy the odds. Over and over again they continue to die, but no one stops playing the game. Something is different about this drug! Why do we have to wait on stats and evidence to tell us what we already know? Is it protocol? Is it customary? Is it WASTING TIME?

Go with your GUT! Tell what you know and believe to be true. Statistics are all over the place and somehow they are never the same. Some days I hear that a fatal overdose happens every 19 minutes. Other days I hear that it is every 17 minutes. Two minutes doesn't make that much difference to me. I believe that no matter what the numbers say, that we are losing way too many people way too often. We need to act now. People need to fund solutions now – before one more precious soul dies.

Speak up and speak out about what you know. There are enough numbers out there to support the fact that opioids and heroin are killing way too many of our children and other loved ones. Speak your mind to your doctors when they try to hand you a prescription of opioids that you don't need or want. When they try to give you 30 pills and you only think you need 10. Ask your doctor to re-write the prescription and give you less. Tell them why you are making the request.

SPEAK UP and SPEAK OUT. Even if you are slightly off of a margin, you are still getting your point across and the fact remains that we are losing people to opioid/heroin addiction everyday. Someone once told me that you have to hear something seven times before it has meaning to you. KEEP TALKING. Don't be afraid to SPEAK YOUR MIND.

2/6/15 – Constructive Act #323 – Keep Advocating For What You Know Is Right

There was much hype yesterday when Dr. Oz was airing a show on the "New Face of Heroin." We posted it on the DDF and I was messaged more than several times to make sure that I knew that Dr. Oz was airing a show on Opioid/Heroin addiction. While we are all very appreciative of the exposure and awareness created by Dr. Oz yesterday, I find it very disturbing that the three points that he decided to highlight in yesterday's episode were very controversial. His three points were: 1) only allow ONE doctor to prescribe all of your pain medications (opioids). 2) stop all opioid prescriptions after ONE week of the prescription. And 3) flush leftover medications down the toilet. Each of these three points has significant problems.

To begin with, point #1, "Only allow one doctor to prescribe all of your pain medications." While in all fairness this seems like a good idea, let's think about it. Does insurance even allow this? If I go to my Ob/Gyn because I am having pain due to a cyst, can I really tell him that I need my Family Practice doctor to prescribe my pain meds because that's what I need to happen? First and foremost, what doctor in his right mind is going to sign off on a prescription for opioids that he didn't have anything to do with the evaluation or the diagnosis? Isn't that called malpractice? Why would I have my family practice doctor prescribe medication for me when she didn't have anything to do with the evaluation or the diagnosis? That's NOT going to happen. My doctors would look at me like I had three heads if I went to them and said, "I need an opioid prescription for a problem that another one of my doctors has diagnosed." Yeh right!!! Sorry Dr. Oz, – good thought – but in theory, it's impractical. At the very least I would have to pay for two services and medical services aren't cheap as it is. My family practice doctor would certainly charge for that service and quite frankly I wouldn't blame her because she would be the logical one to be that ONE doctor. And, let's face it… that means that the prescribing doctor would have to have a HUGE level of trust for ALL of her patients' other doctors. That really doesn't seem quite fair to me to ask that ONE doctor to do that. She would be putting herself out there to take the fall for all addiction. Isn't that what the PDMP's were designed to address in the first place?

Secondly, point #2 was to stop all opioid medications after one week. Well that too is good in theory, but the truth is that if you don't need pain meds for a week, then anything you take after the first couple of days that you do need them, is just a way to increase the chances that you will become an addict for opioid/heroin addiction. Opioid medication is for pain. When the pain is gone, then if you continue to take the medication, you are just increasing the chances that addiction is a possibility. When the pain is manageable, you need to make sure that you switch back over to an "over the counter" medication that has no addictive properties. You can also ask your doctor to cut your prescription in half at the inception of your prescription so that you don't have leftover medication. I had a friend who had a knee scoop and torn meniscus repaired this past week and she told them she preferred not to have any opioid pain relief prescribed. They very strongly suggested for her to take it and she felt rather pushed into taking the prescription. They scared her into not having it due to the amount of pain she would be in. She took one pill the first night and took the remainder of the prescription to a drop-box.

Finally, point #3 is unheard of. NEVER flush your medication down the toilet. There are prescription medication drop-boxes at most Sheriff Offices and many police departments. Also, many of the chain pharmacies have filed paperwork to take back opioid medications. I think that we will start to see lots more drop-boxes popping up around town for leftover prescription medication. When you flush any medication down the toilet, you risk compromising the water supply. There are certain properties in certain prescription medications that cannot be broken down and remain in the water. Find a drop-box to return your medications. Be responsible.

Just my thoughts! I'm really appreciative that Dr. OZ devoted 15 minutes of his show to address the epidemic of opioid/heroin addiction, but I don't think he really got across the enormity of the problem. I didn't like the fact that he asked "What was your rock bottom?" without pointing out that many opioid/heroin never hit rock bottom because they die en route. I also didn't like the fact that he asked his guest when she realized that she had become a "junkie?" Could he not have asked her at what point she realized she had become addicted? I like the fact that he did address the "stigma" of the disease and I also liked the fact that the mother was allowed to say "Addicts are not bad trying to get good, they are sick trying to get well."

I wish the Nation would take the kind of proactive measures taken by Arizona when the Broadcasting Association for the entire state shut down regular communication for 30 minutes on ALL airwaves statewide to warn the citizens about the perils of opioid/heroin addiction! Now that's what I call AWARENESS!

2/7/15 – Constructive Act #324 – Contribute as a Community

At the last Symposium, one thing was made perfectly clear. The one recurring theme was "community." The panelists were convinced that every community needs to come together and take care of their own citizens. The people that are deep in the throes of addiction are our children, our parents, our brothers and sisters, our friends and our colleagues. They belong to us and we need to help them. When we help them, we help ourselves as well. I've said before that everyone is involved whether you like it or not. If you drive on the streets in our community, you are at risk of being in an accident because someone on opioids/heroin will also be driving on the roads. If you live in our community, you can potentially be the victim of a theft or robbery because of an addict trying to support his or her habit. Unemployment in our community will be rampant because our loved ones who have had a "non-violent" felony charge are not able to find jobs.

These people suffering with addiction and NOT bad people, they suffer from the DISEASE of addiction and we need to pull together as a community to help them. I have lived in Cobb County since 1982, and I know without a doubt that it is one of the most giving and caring communities in the world.

In speaking with one of the other Board members of the DDF, we concluded that Georgia, on the whole, is doing a better job than most states in providing help for the citizens suffering with the disease of addiction, but we are still not doing enough. We need to be coming together to offer resources, information, awareness education, and opportunities for success for those who are trying their best to enter recovery and stay there. We need to be working with the court systems to see what we can do for the citizens when they are released to help them assimilate back into the community successfully.

This upcoming week I will be meting with a middle school, a pharmaceutical company, a Rehab facility, a local church young adult minister, the Georgia Prescription Drug Abuse Prevention Collaborative, and local Business Association members as well as other parents to brainstorm ways that we can come together and provide what is necessary to embrace our community members suffering from the disease of opioid/heroin addiction. We have already lost and we continue to lose beautiful, bright, gifted and compassionate people every single day. A study came out several weeks ago that stated that "relationships" were as vital to recovery as were the emotional, physical and mental support necessary to be successful. We need to work on community relationships and find the compassion and understanding to treat these citizens as people who want to contribute and get back on the right track. It is our responsibility.

With all of this being said, I am proud to announce that the Davis Direction Foundation will be hosting a vendor fair and JOB FAIR at our upcoming April 14th Symposium. If you or your business would be willing to make applications available and speak with former "non-violent" addicts who have taken the steps to enter recovery, please email us through the info@davisdirection.com. We are waiting to hear from you and make your business a part of our Spring symposium. Step up to the plate and make a difference for our community members who need our help. If you have a story to tell about hiring a former addict in recovery and it is a story that can offer hope and inspiration to others considering the possibility, please let us know, we will put you on the Symposium agenda. This one is going to be FANTASTIC! Please let us hear from you!

I have been offered some community resources that include all of our Georgia communities. They are listed below:

heroin.net/help/Georgia/
www.addiction-treatment.com/find/opiate/georgia/

2/8/15 – Constructive Act #325 – Share Your Story Sunday

Thank you Chelsea, Davis' older sister, for sharing some of your deepest and most personal thoughts surrounding the time that we lost our sweet Davis. Here is her story.

The day before Davis died, I attended Bible Study where we talked about who God calls us individually. I was praying that God would reveal to me whom He calls me, and I heard the name "Martha." Having always been a Type A personality, I initially saw a correlation between this Biblical woman and me. However, I was not fully convinced and decided I would continue to pray and try to listen to God to make sure that this is whom He called me.

The next day, my sweet baby brother lost his life to the disease of addiction. I can't even begin to describe the pain I felt, and for the next couple of days, everything was a blur. The only thing that became clearer to me was that God had clearly spoken to me that night. Suddenly, my life was becoming eerily similar to Martha's because in John 11, Martha's brother, Lazarus, dies. Jesus weeps and tells Lazarus' sisters that He is the resurrection and the life, and whoever believes in Him will never die. Then, Jesus performs a miracle and raises Lazarus from the dead!

Two very important lessons were forever ingrained in me from this story. First, even though Davis was not physically raised from the dead, he is able to live eternally with our Heavenly Father! Secondly, even though Jesus knew He was about to raise Lazarus from the dead, He still wept with and empathized with Martha and her sister. I knew that even though my brother was pain-free and rejoicing in Heaven, Jesus still "wept" with me and was there to comfort me. Not a day goes by that I don't think about Davis and miss his big bear hugs. I am so thankful that we have a Savior who loves us so much that He was willing to die for us so we can live eternally with Him! We will meet again one day, little brother! I love you!

2/9/15 – Constructive Act #326 – Don't Be Greedy

This weekend I watched a series of television shows about the history of our country. The series began with stories back in the 1800's and brought to life the stories of Rockefeller, Carnegie, Edison and JP Morgan. It showed how they were able to build their dynasties and how they were able to "treat" the nation with their ideas and products. I literally watched the nation go crazy over oil, electricity and steel. I watched as these great leaders, as we know them, competed against each other to see who would be the greatest, the wealthiest, the smartest and the most powerful . I watched as they literally schemed to put the others out of business and to selfishly self proclaim themselves as the greatest and the most innovative people of the world. I watched as they literally snubbed each other and each other's ideas so that no one could get ahead of them for any reason and at any cost. I saw great ideas and great minds refuse to work together for the good of the country as a result of greed. I watched as Edison refused to work with or listen to Tesla who was willing to share his ideas about the alternating electrical current with Edison. Edison could have had it all, but he refused to believe that anyone could be equal in intelligence to him and it proved to be his downfall.

I also watched a nation of free enterprise where there was no government intervention and no "hoops" to jump through to help mankind with new life saving inventions and ideas. There was only true freedom to live the American Dream and to help others do the same. There was no bureaucracy and no agencies standing in the way of life-saving technology and inventions. I watched the banks of the Mississippi River become connected with a bridge and no government or political groups stand in the way of a good idea.

Today if we have a potential life-saving treatment for addiction, it is years away pending the approval of the government agencies put in place to make sure that no law suits will be filed over it while we stand by and watch person after person die while waiting on the approval of the treatment. Are we truly the greatest nation on earth? We are a political mess standing in a dead stall while we make sure we are not offending anyone or stepping on anyone's toes with what we have in place for the good of others. I have even heard that there is a type 1 diabetes cure in Europe (discovered by an American citizen) awaiting all the bells and whistles of America just to begin clinical trials. What has our nation come to? Why is it not our choice to do what we can to save our loved ones?

I know that over and over when we were doing the research for "Laws, Limits and Loopholes" Symposium, I kept hearing the words "Affordable Care Act" and how it alone prohibits the individual states from allowing any changes in the laws to make things better for our citizens. We can't do this because of ACA we can't do that because of ACA! Can anyone tell me what good came out of the Affordable Care Act? The only thing that I can see that it did was to prohibit the states from helping their own citizens because of being "trumped" by the Federal Government. Maybe I'm wrong or maybe I'm just bitter that now we can't help our struggling citizens get the insurance changes that they need to treat their disease or we can't pass laws helping the parents with legislation to take over their adult kids' medical care. We can't do the good and right things for our loved ones because of "Laws" that are already in place. Once again, whatever happened to the American Dream?

All of these things came about because of power and greed. Someone out there wanted to be greater than someone else. Someone wanted to dominate. I watched this weekend as JP Morgan bought out Andrew Carnegie's steel industry for the equivalent of 480 billion dollars by today's standards, making Andrew Carnegie the wealthiest man in the world – even wealthier than Rockefeller. Andrew Carnegie stood out on the porch of his beautiful mansion a broken man because he had nothing to strive for, nothing to work for, and nothing to dream about because he sold out for greed! JP Morgan bought him out for power. I watched the political ploy of these three wealthy men as they strategically had McKinley name Roosevelt as his Vice President so that he would be powerless to make changes in their empires. Things like this have been going on forever, and now instead of personal power and greed, we see the pharmaceutical companies doing the same things to the people to keep their industry alive and well.

The movie made me realize the importance and the need for all the organizations formed to combat addiction to work with each other to gain significant footage to help our loved ones who are suffering. The DDF is actively setting up meetings and attending meetings to collaborate with others to learn what we don't know and to understand how we can help in the grand scheme of things. We are only one small foundation presently, but if we combine our efforts with others, we become a voice loud enough to be heard and an entity strong enough to be effective. There is no room for individual greed or power in this fight. The DDF will remain diligent in our mission… "Moving Onward Through Life……Looking Upward to God."

2/10/15 – Constructive Act #327 –Treat Your True Love

With Valentine Day approaching, it reminds me of the love that I have for my husband and all of my children. It reminds me of the last Valentine's Day that I spent with my sweet Davis. I remember driving him to his Intensive Outpatient Therapy and dropping him off and coming home and making chocolate covered strawberries for him. I loved that precious child with every ounce of my soul and I wanted him to beat his addiction more than life itself. Little did I know that in less than three weeks, I would never see him alive again. I would have given him the world and everything in it if I had but known what was down the road. My family – Michael, Chelsea, Davis, Connor, Spencer and Shelbea are my TRUE LOVES! They always have been and they always will be. I hope that I tell them enough and I hope they know that no one on this earth will ever love them more than I love them. They are my world.

Regardless of addiction and what it does to our loved ones, whether they be children, spouses, parents or siblings, our true loves are the ones we love unconditionally. I read the posts on the Heroin websites and no matter what the events are that have happened, or the tragedies that have been lived through, the posts from the "true loves" continue to be posted because we love these people more than life itself. We can't help it, they are a part of who we are and who we will forever be. They are FAMILY! So, this week, let's reach out to them and show them through a week of significant meaning, how very much they mean to us and how very much we love them. WE may not be able to allow them into our lives without conditions right now, but that doesn't change the fact that they are loved unconditionally and without reservation. This is the week to focus on that love and to share it with our "addiction suffering" true loves.

I love significance in my life and I love for everything to have meaning. I learned that from a very dear friend of mine who has been a wonderful mentor in my life since I began my career in Cobb County. She was the one who came over to my home the first day that I lost Davis, and when I wasn't there to see her, she came back and this time had her bag of significance with her. She gave me a journal, an oil lamp to light for when I was journaling and several books – including the poem about the "dash" so that I could get in touch with my feelings and be close to God throughout my journey of grief. She taught me how to find meaning in all things in life and I love her dearly for everything that she taught me.

So, with all of that said, let's begin this week with the goals in place to make our addicted loved ones remember that no matter how sick they are, we love them unconditionally and we are there for them when they are ready to lean upon us. This could be the last Valentine's Day you ever spend with your loved one; don't have any regrets.

On the first day of Valentine's my true love gave to me......a light so that I could always see. Whether you find a flashlight, a lamp, a tiny keychain light or a candle, give your loved one a light to remind them that there is light at the end of the tunnel and it is there for them, if they can make their way through the tunnel and endure the pain of coming out on the other side. On the second day of Valentines, my true love gave to me, two boxes of conversation hearts and a light so that I could always see. The two boxes of conversation hearts are so that there are multiple ways to begin the conversations that open doors and allow the hard conversations to take place that provide understanding and knowledge of the disease.

On the third day of Valentines, my true love gave to me three simple scriptures, two boxes of conversation hearts and a light so that I could always see. The three simple scriptures are easy to remember and so very important to allow the addict to know that no matter where they are in the journey, God is there with them. 1) "God is love." 1 John 4:8; I can do all things through Christ who strengthens me." Philippians 4:13; and of course… "For all have sinned and fallen short of the glory of God." Romans 3:23.

On the fourth day of Valentines, my true love gave to me four beautiful memories, three simple scriptures, two boxes of conversation hearts and a light so that I could always see. Find four very significant pictures and have them printed to give to your loved one this week. Make them pictures of your family, a time in the past that was meaningful and fun, memories of better times and pictures that instill a sense of longing for the past.

On the fifth day of Valentines, my true love gave to me five chocolate covered candies, four beautiful memories, three simple scriptures, two boxes of conversation hearts, and a light so that I could always see. Give your true love a small box of chocolates with five different chocolate covered candies. Remind them that inside each chocolate is a surprise just waiting to be discovered and enjoyed just as life in recovery can be. It can be delicious, exciting, surprising and sometimes not as great as the chocolate before, but still better than any day that they lived previously in active addiction.

Do something special for your addicted loved ones this week. Everyone deserves to be loved and cherished no matter what his or her disease may be. It may well be the last Valentine's Day you ever share with them. Be able to look back upon it with fond memories of how you reminded your addicted loved one that they are special, and they are loved! Everyone is worthy and God created each of us in His image. He is not giving up on them, and neither should we. Happy Valentines WEEK! Make someone feel special.

2/11/15 – Constructive Act #328 – Never Give Up

Sometimes I know it seems like we are moving two steps BACKWARD and half a step FORWARD, but nevertheless, we are in constant motion trying to promote awareness, affect change and save lives. We are listening to the needs of our community and meeting with leaders and families who have been touched by the disease of addiction. We were given some great advice by State leaders last month at the Symposium and now we are moving forward trying to incorporate that advice into action! We are busy planning our 4th Symposium, "Creating Community" which will take place at Kennesaw Mountain High School on April 14th at 7:00 p.m. Mark your calendars now for this spectacular event! We are pulling out all the stops and involving as many members of the community as we can. We will not only have a "Vendor Fair" but we will also have "Job Fair."

When we listen to our community, this is one of the most common obstacles that "Non-violent" offenders face as they begin searching for a job with a felony record. They make it all the way to the final interview and background search and then they are promptly kicked to the curb as the potential employer sees the "felony offender."

Some of the people are highly educated with Master's Degrees and even Doctorate Degrees. They lost everything they had worked so hard for at the hands of addiction. They are trying to rebuild families, homes, relationships, and community standing. They have worked harder than they have ever worked in their lives to enter recovery and stay there. They are ready to re-enter society and work for the things they lost the first time. They have great incentive because they have been on the other side of success and it was not a pretty place to be.

So the way I see it, is that the community needs to work hard to help the recovering addicts to reclaim their spot. It is beneficial to the community as a whole. It keeps them off of the opioids and heroin and makes our community a safer place to live and raise a family. It keeps our roads safer and our homes safer. It keeps our costs down and our jails free of overcrowding. It keeps our court system from bogging down with non-violent cases of possession and trafficking. It is just a good thing for us to reach out to help these people who are truly trying to turn their lives around.

In my daily devotional today, Galatians 6:9 was the verse: "Let us not become weary in doing good, for at the proper time we will reap a harvest if we do not give up." I've heard more times than I wish to remember that we are going to see this epidemic get worse before it gets better. That makes me sick to my stomach and it makes that hole in my heart grow bigger with every breath I take. I know too well what that means to other families, young children, brothers and sisters, Mom and Dads. It is HELL on earth. The fact that even one more family will have to go down that road is heartbreaking. Every step we take as a community now puts us one step closer to a solution and a community that is once again living in harmony.

If you are a business owner or in a hiring position in our community and you are willing to come out and take a stand to help those people in our community who are willing to work hard to make a place in this town for themselves, PLEASE let me know so that we can reserve a spot for you and your business at our first ever Job Fair to help those suffering from the disease of opioid/heroin addiction. Our community has always been one of the most giving and loving communities I have ever known. Let's reach out in faith and love to help our own.

2/12/15 – Constructive Act #329 – Sink Or Swim. It's Your Choice.

Two frogs fell into a deep cream bowl;
The one was wise, and a cheery soul.
The other one took a gloomy view
And bade his friend a sad adieu.
Said the other frog with a merry grin,
"I can't get out, but I won't give in;
I'll swim around
till my strength is spent,
Then I will die the more content.
And as he swam,
Forever it seemed,
His struggling began to churn the cream
Until on top of pure butter he stopped,
And out of the bowl he quickly hopped.
The moral you ask?
Oh, it's easily found!
If you can't get out, keep swimming around!

I know this is how many of us have felt or are feeling… a life with a heroin addict or the life of a heroin addict is like drowning. Every now and then we get to come up for air and then we go back down under and hold our breath for as long as we can. Then, there are those of us whose loved ones never resurface and we know they couldn't fight the fight any longer. Heroin pulled them under and took them from us. If you are one of the ones (and I won't say lucky ones – because there is nothing lucky about this) who is still coming up for air from time to time, I will tell you that I truly believe that HOPE is out there. I believe that more and more people are getting on board everyday with the effort to find a solution. Hang in there and continue to come up for air. Keep swimming around and eventually, there will be a place to hop off.

Looking back there was so much that "I didn't know that I didn't know" when Michael and I were trying to help Davis find his way. Every time that we thought we had the disease under control, something else would happen and the nightmare would continue. In less then three weeks from now, it will be a year – March 4th – when the nightmare took a tragic ending. My family is already suffering from the anticipation of the anniversary. My oldest daughter called me last night and said she had a really rough day and she couldn't put her finger on it. She didn't cry all day, and she wasn't depressed, but there was something different and she felt that it had to do with Davis. Those two were very close; they had lived with each other longer than the rest, and they had just finished high school "together" meaning that Chelsea was headed off to college and Davis would be going back with his little brother, but not Chelsea. He truly hated to see her go, but he was so proud of her.

For me, the tears have returned every night, and the late nights are becoming later with each passing day. I will no longer be able to say... "This time last year," because there will be no "this time last year with Davis." Time marches on, and with each passing step, there are happy things and sad things that march along beside us. I kept telling myself and I know that I have even written about the fact that each day is just another day without him, but the anticipation of the anniversary is becoming an entity within itself. It is beginning to consume our thoughts and our days. We have not talked about plans for the day and I don't even know that we will make any, but one thing I do know is that we will all know that the day is here when it arrives. There will be no forgetting this "anniversary."

Anniversary seems like such a celebratory term, and it seems wrong to use it in this context. I know that an anniversary commemorates or celebrates, but I've just never experienced the commemorating end of an anniversary in such a way. When my Dad had his first anniversary of death, even though I missed him terribly, he had lived a good and long life and I did feel like it was a celebration of sorts. With Davis, he was robbed of his life and was taken from us way too soon. Even though he lived a great life for the time we had him, there was so much more life for him to live that he will never know and it is heartbreaking.

If he could have "struggled" just a little longer, maybe he would have been around to see the "cure," but that option is gone forever for him. For those of you who still have options... PLEASE KEEP SWIMMING! Do everything you can to keep yourselves alive until we can figure this terrible epidemic out. Don't use alone and carry a Naloxone kit with you. Parents and the rest of the "addict's keepers," keep coming up for air and go back down and work hard for your addicts on the "affecting change" end of things. Don't take "NO" for an answer with your insurance companies, advocate for opioid/heroin addiction any way you can, show up with your addicts to courts and visit them behind bars. Openly discuss the disease and educate those around you! There is nothing shameful about having this disease – it is only by the grace of God that others don't share the addiction gene. Above all…PRAY… Ask God to deliver us from this horrific epidemic and protect your loved ones and yourselves as we continue to search for answers. God speed.

2/13/15 – Constructive Act #330 – Try A Little Emotional Honesty

Earlier this week I wrote a "CA" about the five days of Valentines. I made suggestions of ways you could "treat" your addicts for Valentines week and the significance of each item. That post was primarily for the "addict's keepers," and so I chose to write a "CA" today for the addicts themselves. There is a strategy that we use in the world of counseling, called "emotional honesty." I have used this strategy all throughout this past year as I have allowed my heart to hemorrhage all over this Facebook page as I write my posts each day. My goal has been to help others understand the disease of addiction and the raw emotional pain, love and HOPE that comes with this illness. I have done everything that I can to help others understand that addicts are not "dirty people trying to get clean," "bad people trying to get good," but in fact they are "sick people trying to get well." I hear back from lots of addicts, but usually the comments come through in private messages because they choose to be personal about their disease. My greatest fear is that it is because they don't feel that the outside world is ready to hear their comments on a page that is not specifically for addicts.

I do want addicts to feel comfortable to write in the comments section of the DDF Facebook page. I have said more than once, they are the experts in this disease and it will be through their understanding and knowledge that we find solutions. They are some of the brightest, most compassionate, outside the box thinkers that you will ever know. They care deeply for their families and it is my opinion that they have more "conscience" than we know about their situations and their actions and that is what keeps them from seeking help far too often. They don't feel worthy to receive the help. This is a direct result of the misunderstanding that prevails throughout our society regarding the disease of addiction.

If you are an addict, and you are reading this, I want to give you a suggestion for a Valentine to your families. Write them a letter. You can hand deliver it, send it through the US mail, have a friend deliver it or send it through a text or email. It doesn't matter how you get it to them, just make sure it gets there. The letters that Davis wrote to us are some of the things that we treasure most in this world now that he is gone. Each of us have something that he wrote to us – a handwritten note or letter – and we cherish it with every ounce of our beings.

The day that Davis entered his first and only Rehab facility was his Dad's 46th birthday. Michael and I had spent the entire day with Davis the day before getting him entered into the facility and getting him ready to leave us for what we knew could be a long period of time. The following morning that Davis entered Rehab, he handed me a letter to give to his Dad. He had written a letter to him for his birthday. He wrote if the night before, because he knew he had to be at the facility very early in the morning and that I was going to drive him down.

Hey Dad,

Happy Birthday tomorrow! I wish I could be there to celebrate it with you. If the weather was nice we could've gone golfing or driving. That sounds pretty dang awesome right about now. Thank you for all the love and support you and Mom have given me; I don't know how I would have managed without you guys. It's gonna be a while before I'm back home, but it will most certainly be worth it. I Love you Dad, you're a hero to me.

Love Your Son,
Davis Henry Owen

I cannot tell you what this letter means to Michael and me as well. He didn't have to write it, but he did. We loved this little guy unconditionally and people have often told us that love was evident in our actions. Davis was a big hugger and a very secure person when it came to sharing his emotions. He was quick to say "I love you" and mean it! I miss those big Bear hugs, and so does Michael!

So – you may think that no one wants to hear you say "I'm sorry for the pain that families are involved in due to this disease," or "I love you with all my heart and I want to be well again," or "I am trying with every ounce of my soul" ... But... as a parent of an addict that has left this world, I will tell you... YES THEY DO! They will treasure every note, every thought you put on paper and every ounce of effort that shows you still have HOPE! That is just what parents who love unconditionally do. It does not mean that anything will change physically, or that you will be allowed privileges that have been revoked due to the disease. But emotionally, it will mean the world to them. I know, because I have a box full of them, and it's so much better than chocolate.

2/14/15 – Constructive Act #331 – When In Doubt, Turn To The Good Book

Happy Valentine's Day to all of you! On this day of love, I'm having lots of mixed emotions as you can imagine, but I have it on my heart to talk about the treatment of those suffering with opioid/heroin addiction. I hear a lot about love and how the addicts can be "loved to death" due to enabling. I hear a lot about "tough love" and how the "addict's keepers" have resorted to using it. I hear about "unconditional love" – the kind of love that God has for each one of us. I hear about "love not being enough" to keep an opioid/heroin addict from using. I think about all the ways these types of love can manifest in our hearts and what they look like to others. There are rarely definitions accompanying these types of love and exactly how they can be applied and used in our daily walk with our addicts, while staying true to our Christian beliefs. In thinking about these things, I have always tried to ask myself two questions… 1) What would Jesus do? and 2) What does the Bible say?

Love is patient, love is kind. It does not envy, it does not boast, it is not proud. It does not dishonor others, it is not self-seeking, it is not easily angered, it keeps no record of wrongs. Love does not delight in evil but rejoices with the truth. It always protects, always trusts, always hopes, always perseveres. Love never fails. To me, the Bible defines everything we need to know about love in the Love chapter, 1 Corinthians 13: 4-8. All you need to do is ask yourself, "Am I following the directions of the Good Book?" Am I patient and kind? Am I doing this for all the right reasons and am I honoring others in the process? Am I protecting, trusting and persevering as I provide HOPE for all? Am I paving the way for success? If the answer to all of these questions is YES…then you are doing the things that God is asking of you.

On the other hand, if you are talking dishonorably about your addicted son or daughter or not showing patience or kindness, then you need to stop and ask yourself, "Am I doing what God requires of me?" This is no way goes against tough love, or unconditional love. It does not conflict with loving an addict with the disease of addiction, or with the heartbreak of all that comes with loving an opioid/heroin addict. There is a line drawn regarding helping addicted individuals, but it does not cross the line of enabling them just because one decides to live by Biblical principles. The two are not conflicting.

The instructions of the Bible are very clear. Love is patient and kind, It does not envy or boast and it does NOT dishonor others… No matter how mad the disease makes you or how frustrated you become!!! It keeps NO records of wrongs and it ALWAYS rejoices with the TRUTH! LOVE NEVER FAILS!!! It may not be enough to keep them from using or even dying for that matter, but they will know they were loved and that love will reign supreme. Love your addicted loved one today…It could be your last opportunity.

2/15/15 – Constructive Act #332 – Share Your Story Sunday

This week we will hear from a guy from my hometown. Although I do not know him, his story is one that is not uncommon, beginning with abuse. Dan has turned his life around and is embarking on a very exciting journey. We wish him luck. Thanks for sharing Dan.

Here is his story:

My name is Dan D... I am from the small town of Carrollton, GA...I have spent the majority of my life running from all my problems, guilt and shame. I was sexually abused at age eight by an older woman that was close to the family and after that I was so covered in the shame of that situation that I hid it from my whole family for years. At 16 I began drinking and doing drugs. By 21, I was a full-blown opioid addict. At 25, I landed in my first rehab and chose to fake it 'til I made it and left without any change and with zero will to get off painkillers.

I then made it worse by moving up to heroin and had my first and only overdose on the streets of Atlanta. When I got home, I told my mom and dad, with tears in my eyes, that I needed some help and fast. When we found No Longer Bound I thought it would be a waste because of it being faith based. But, in the confines of that place I found a perfect daddy in God and watched him as he took away all my sexual shame. I had been healed and reconciled to all my family and I had also been given the courage to forgive the lady that had sexually abused me all those years ago.

After being there for 18 months, I found my calling to be a pastor and to help anybody and everybody I could, not only to be drug free but also to find the love and peace in Christ.

Three weeks ago I was accepted to an internship in Ventura, CA for 12 months to further my walk and education and life towards being a pastor. It's the Generation internship at the City Church... I will be raising money by sharing my testimony around my home town. Thank you and God Bless......DAN

2/16/15 – Constructive Act #333 – Realize Addiction Is Not a Moral Issue

I guess this Constructive Act would be better entitled "Realize that addiction SHOULD not be a moral issue." For so long drunkenness and drug addiction have been such an embarrassment to families and such a shameful issue for children and loved ones who are suffering with the disease, that until you have an up close and personal encounter with it, and truly try to understand the disease, it's just the norm to become morally judgmental regarding those who suffer from it. I know that before Davis became addicted to drugs, that's exactly what I did. I'm not proud of the fact, but it all goes back to awareness and the fact that people "don't know what they don't know." How many times have I said that? Awareness is key in this fight, and until we educate people about the neuroscience of the disease, we will never make any real progress. People have got to realize the potential for the disease to reach their personal families and loved ones before it actually does and it is too late. In this fast paced world that we live in, it's hard to make it a priority to educate yourself about something that you don't have to deal with at the time.

I remember one day driving down the street by the hospital with Chelsea when she was probably around six years old. It was early one morning and an sloppily, dressed elderly person, at the time we couldn't really tell that she was a lady, stumbled across the street in front of us and fell to the ground. It appeared that she was extremely drunk and I was the next car in line in front of her. I quickly positioned my car in front of her so that no one would run over her, but I hesitated to get out of the car to run and help her. The person who had pulled past her and apparently seen the incident in her rear-view mirror immediately jumped out of the car and began running over to the lady. At first, I was scared and worried about Chelsea's safety and of course all the things running through my mind were about drunk people and was it a scam and would Chelsea get car-jacked if I jumped out… Was this a set- up? As it turned out, the elderly lady who probably was not really that elderly, had just come from an early morning chemo treatment at the cancer treatment and she had passed out as she was walking back to her car across the street. Another person had been watching from the cancer center as well and by the time I had gotten out to help – reluctantly – because I still was somewhat afraid thinking I was dealing with a drunken person, there was a nurse on the way with a wheelchair from the cancer center. I remember feeling so ashamed of myself for not putting my judgmental thoughts aside and immediately jumping out of my car and going over to this person to help first and ask questions later. The thought that somebody was drunk immediately made me think that nothing but trouble would ensue. It still haunts me to this day that I did not react differently. I will say that I have always been somewhat of a scaredy-cat, but when another human being is in obvious need, I should have jumped into high gear to help.

If I had known that this person suffered from a disease and was physically ill, I would have jumped into action without question, but I did not because I made a moral judgment based on addiction! That was really hard and shameful to admit. But I did it, because I was ignorant! Well I'm not ignorant anymore and it has become my life's goal to educate others. How many times have we turned our heads or walked away from people who we knew were either drunk or high? How many times should we have taken keys away from others or served people in our own homes more than we knew they should have consumed and then allowed them to drive away? We never would have sent an asthmatic away struggling to breathe. We would have never allowed a diabetic to leave who was struggling to hold their head up and wobbling due to low blood sugar. Why do we treat addiction differently? It's so simple; it's because we see it as a choice and a moral issue.

This is the hardest part of what we have before us…explaining to people why addiction is a brain disease. I have found a model from Kevin McCauly – "Pleasure

Unwoven" who explains why we have such a hard time convincing others why addiction is a disease.

Exploring how we can address the problem of a dysfunctional (addicted) brain, from all possible angles… neurological, psychologically, sociologically should be a matter of urgency! When will this change?

The National Institute of Drug Abuse states… "Nearly all addictive drugs directly or indirectly target the brain's reward system by flooding the circuit with dopamine. Dopamine is a neurotransmitter present in regions of the brain that regulate movement, emotion, cognition, motivation, and feelings of pleasure. The overstimulation of this system, which rewards our natural behaviors, produces the euphoric effects sought by people who use drugs and teaches them to repeat the behavior. However, when addiction takes over, a person's ability to exert self-control can become seriously impaired. Brain-imaging studies from people addicted to drugs show physical changes in areas of the brain that are critical for judgment, decision-making, learning, memory, and behavior control. Scientists believe that these changes alter the way the brain works and may help explain the compulsive and destructive behaviors of an addicted person."

I often wonder how many people may have driven past Davis, walked past Davis or even wondered if he was okay the night he lay dying in his car. I wonder how many people may have considered him a "Moral Issue" and turned away. Maybe no one, but I know that I have changed the way I approach people who seem to be sleeping in parking lots, or those whom I know suffer with the disease of addiction.
Therefore by the grace of God… go I.

2/17/15 – Constructive Act #334 – Never Doubt Your Relationship With God

I feel that I should preface this "CA" by saying that yesterday someone made a comment on "CA #333" that stated and I quote… "An abuser will NOT enter into the Kingdom of God. PERIOD" Although I realize that when you open a site to comments, sometimes you will receive comments that you disagree with and I have left all but 2 of those comments up over the course of the past 11 and 1/2 months. However, there is nothing in my soul that would even remotely let me allow that kind of comment to remain on our site without addressing it! I removed it, and I will continue to remove any comments of that sort in the future. This is not a "Christian Only" page, however, it is part of who we are and we don't deny that. It is a page for anyone and everyone who wants to learn or receive support from others regarding opioid/heroin addiction. God did not instruct Christians to only love each other, He instructed us to love, encourage, be kind to, care for, and pray for everyone. I'm sorry for posting so late today, but this situation has been heavy on my heart and I wanted to get it right. Please join me in praying for the individual who made this comment.

Nothing makes me angrier than a Judgmental Christian! There…I said it! I fretted and fretted over whether or not to say it, but I have to think about the big picture and the young kids in their late teens and twenties who are searching for answers and are impressionable all at the same time. I get irate when someone – some totally "human" being – we're not talking super powers here, tries to become judge and jury and begins to announce publicly who can get into heaven and who can not. There is not one sin on earth that will keep you from entering heaven's gates except for not believing in and accepting the love of God and his son Jesus Christ! When people try to qualify sin and decide themselves what God will and will not tolerate, young people, especially, become turned off to Christianity and begin to doubt their relationship with God because some older and "more experienced" person begins to confuse them. All I can say to that is that there are a lot of people out there who profess things in the name of God, who have nothing to do with the God I love and serve and who loves me in return. They are NOT a part of my religion!!! Your relationship with God is yours and yours alone! It is personal and it is individual. It is between you and God and no one else! If you don't believe that then read the Bible…IN CONTEXT!

Shortly before Davis died, he came to me because somewhere down the line, someone had confused him and caused him to doubt his salvation because he had not had a "Come to Jesus"… "Holy Rolling" … "Road to Damascus" experience in his lifetime! I explained to him that people who grow up in the Faith rarely have those moments because there is no need for them. When you grow up and always know that God is your Heavenly Father and know that He loves you unconditionally, there is no need for you to have that "Out of Body" experience. People who grow up with God feel God in everyday things like music, the beauty of the earth, the stars at night, and holding a baby right after it is born. God is always with people like us and we are truly the lucky ones. I've said before that Davis knew that what he was doing was dangerous, and I'm sure looking back that he worried that he might die if he couldn't stop using. I prayed for God to watch over him and Davis prayed for God to take care of him. We prayed together and we prayed as a family. Davis is now safe in God's loving arms, and no one can tell me or anyone else who believes in God any differently.

I become totally offended by people who portray God as less than a loving and understanding God who loves us, his children, way more than we love our own children if you can even imagine that! I believe that God is such a necessary part of entering recovery from opioid/heroin addiction and I personally believe that it would be very hard without Him. I also know that God helps those who help themselves and that an addict has to work "all" the factors of recovery together to ensure success – and I include drug therapy, if one so chooses, in that "all."

I get angry at people who sit on the outside of opoid/heroin addiction and make judgmental remarks and tell others what they should or should not be doing when they have not invested in the research or the solutions or have never struggled with that particular addiction. A dysfunction of the Opioid system is NOT a choice. It is backed up and explained by SCIENCE!

The Davis Direction Foundation maintains this site as a support for families and addicts suffering from addiction as well as those who wish to educate themselves about the epidemic we are currently experiencing as it relates to opioid/heroin. We use this site to promote awareness to everyone, affect change (including the stigma of addicts, rehabilitation for opioid/heroin addiction, and laws that get in the way) and to save lives. If you cannot support these goals, then perhaps you should look for a different site on which to publish your comments. God is LOVE…and there is no way that He would not allow one of HIS proclaimed children into the Kingdom of Heaven because he or she fell victim to opioid/heroin addiction.

Romans 8:38-39 King James Version (KJV)38 For I am persuaded, that neither death, nor life, nor angels, nor principalities, nor powers, nor things present, nor things to come, 39 Nor height, nor depth, nor any other creature, shall be able to separate us from the love of God, which is in Christ Jesus our Lord.

www.faithalone.org/magazine/y1989/89april2.html
www.faithalone.org/magazine/y1989/89march2.html

2/18/15 – Constructive Act #335- Realize Time Stands Still For No One

The countdown has arrived. Two weeks from today will be the 1st anniversary of Davis's death. Michael has awakened me twice this past week from my nightmares and the rest of the family is having emotional days and nights as well. The subconscious is an entity that I really don't understand, but I do realize that it is powerful. Letting go of that first year is very emotional for no other reason than the fact that I will no longer be able to say "This time last year" and include Davis in the rest of the sentence. Death of a child is a very complex situation. With the passing of time, I feel like I am letting the memory of Davis fade and that feels like a betrayal of love. With keeping his memory alive and not letting go, that feels like a sick person who cannot deal in reality and has emotional issues. How does one do death of a child properly? And who cares? I'm so tired of what I am supposed to do and what looks and feels right and what is socially acceptable. On a night like tonight I get really sick of social acceptance and social expectations. The fact of the matter is that I lost my precious child and I will deal with it however, whenever, wherever, and with whomever I darn well please!

When Davis lost his battle to heroin addiction, I vowed that I would not let his death be in vain. At the time, I think that statement was more necessary for me and the fact that I didn't want him to be forgotten and become just another lost memory. As time has passed and I have seen the destructive results of this terrible epidemic of addiction, I know that I want his legacy to live on as a remembrance that it didn't have to be this way and we have to band together to find HOPE for those who have lost their way. Keeping the children alive to live another day until a solution is found has become paramount to me just because of the destruction opioid/heroin addiction has caused so far. Now, sharing my story and Davis's story has become a means to educate and empower others to save their loved ones and help them learn to live in recovery.

Learning to live again has become a journey. It is a journey of grief, of new surroundings, of new skills and expertise, of education and psychological evaluation. It has become a soul-searching struggle everyday because of the pain that is caused by the loss of a child. It's a 24/7 battle within, never knowing at what moment my heart will begin to hemorrhage and the main goal will be to stop the flow of emotion. There have been times that I wanted to feel the full force of the emotion that comes from losing a child and then there are other times that I think the pain is unbearable and I only want it to go away. I never know from moment to moment which mood I will be in and what course I will be willing to take. Life has become so uncertain for me.

Sometimes I want to sit in complete darkness and feel the emptiness of missing someone so intensely that my whole world is black, and then other times I can't get the lights on fast enough to brighten up the darkness of depression and sadness. Then there are the times that I have no idea what I want, what I'm doing or what I need at any given moment. I have not felt one time since Davis died that my whole family is with me; something is not right and something is missing. I begin to wonder if I will ever feel complete again...ever. As the entire family sat in church last Sunday, there was just not the feeling of balance. Something was off; we were incomplete. I knew that we were all there, but it just was not right.

I know everyone in the family feels the same way, Davis is gone and "The Owen7" is forever skewed. We will work toward balance, healing, and finding our new complete as time marches on, but Davis will be forever a missing link and a piece of the puzzle that was lost far too early. There are no words to explain how it feels, and I hope if you are reading this, you never understand what I am talking about. The vocabulary to describe this experience has not yet been unveiled.

2/19/15 – Constructive Act #336 – Know That They Know That You Don't Know

When our kids were born and we became parents for the first time, I remember being told that our babies didn't know that we didn't know how to be parents and that whatever we did, would just become the norm for them. Just because we didn't have experience, didn't mean that we were not going to take care of our children, it just meant that our sweet babies didn't have anyone to compare us to. Thank goodness for that! In other words, they didn't know that we didn't know what we were doing. With addiction, it is very different, our kids know, that unless we were opioid/heroin addicts ourselves, that we don't know what they are experiencing or what they are going through and they know that no matter how hard they try, they will never be able to explain it to us.

As an elementary school teacher beginning my career in a first grade classroom, I remember how extremely frustrated I would become when I was trying with every ounce of my being to teach a concept to a child, but no matter how hard I tried, I couldn't get them to understand the concept. I knew that there had to be a way to get through to the child, but I didn't have enough tricks in my bag to make it happen. I would become angry and more angry – with myself of course – for not being a good enough teacher to find a way to help my students learn what they needed to know. I wanted them to understand so badly, but I could not figure out for the life of me, how to explain it so that they would understand. I think that opioid/heroin addiction is a lot like that, except for the fact that instead of it being only one or maybe two students who could not comprehend the concept, for the opioid/heroin addict, it's hard for them to help anyone understand unless the other people are actively involved in it.

Can you even imagine how frustrating that must be? You want help so badly with the addiction, but you can't explain the problem to anyone and you sure can't come up with a solution for a problem that you can't even explain – or you can't expect others to offer a solution for what they don't understand either. How do you explain something to a person who has no point of reference? It kind of goes back to the age old example of... "How do you know you are in love?" and the age old answer is... "Well, you just know." That really tells me a lot – NOT!

Davis tried so hard to help me understand what addiction felt like and why he couldn't kick it. He compared it to me wanting to lose weight for so long, but having failed so many times. The difference was that if I broke a diet by eating something off of my diet, I wasn't in danger of dying. They know that we don't understand what they are feeling and why they can't stop, but what we do know is that every time they use, they are putting their lives on the line by using something that they are unsure of what the contents may be – especially if they are using heroin. Even some of the heroin now is being disguised as prescription drugs such as oxycontin to get it over the border of Mexico and in to the States. Opioid/ heroin addicts are living a dangerous life of addiction, but they are risking the behaviors because of the overwhelming power of the disease. It is a vicious cycle with a deadly drug.

Our only hope as the "addict's keeper" is to LISTEN and try our best to UNDERSTAND their plight without judgment and/or preconceived ideas of what addiction is and how it works. It is our responsibility to support, encourage, care for and search for answers alongside our loved ones suffering from the disease of addiction. This in no way conflicts with the act of enabling, it only means that you are there for your loved one in the most supportive capacity that you can afford to be there in, and that your love for them will always be first and foremost. Relationships are KEY for RECOVERY!

2/20/15 – Constructive Act #337 – Open Your Heart

This past week I was honored to be asked to visit the Georgia Council on Drug Abuse, and spend time with them understanding what their organization is about and how they work to support people working to stay strong in recovery. Over the past year I have opened my heart to a world of ideas and people that I had no prior experience with and I have met some of the most beautiful, non-judgmental people God ever created. I had the distinct pleasure of dining in with the Empress, the Queen, the Princess and the man who was hired because of his inability to get pregnant, the beautiful, youthful latino, and several others who were amazing... among others! What a delightful crowd of people who were the most welcoming, the most genuine, the most passionate people experiencing recovery in the most glorious way.

I learned that everyone who works for the Council, is in recovery and is working everyday to stay there. They are proud to tell their stories and share their past with anyone who needs to hear it. They are eager to put a beautiful face with an horrific past and a successful present looking forward to a happy future ending. They were some of the most open, honest and willing recovering addicts that I have ever had the pleasure of spending time with. They had amazing insight into the recovery stigmas, as well as the future of recovery and how it needs to change in order to have meaning. Not one of them considered themselves more important than the other and their ability to work together as a team was so evident. Each one of them brought a solid discipline to the table and the respect with which they treated one another was a beautiful thing to witness.

They believe whole-heartedly in what they are doing and it drives the integrity of their program. Instead of telling me all about what they were about, I got to sit around the table with them as they asked each other questions and then intently listened to the answers given by their colleagues. What I experienced with these people confirmed the fact that recovering addicts are not egotistical people. They are individuals who understand the concept of teamwork and are willing to work to help others achieve the freedom that they have found in order to live life to the fullest as a recovering addict. Spending time with these new friends gave me HOPE for the future of addiction. These were some of the brightest minds and forward thinkers that I have been around collectively in a very long time. This was definitely a group of change makers.

They believe in public exposure regarding their recovery and they have agreed to keep us in SUNDAY STORIES for a very long time beginning the second Sunday of March. Please look for the wonderful stories of these very successful individuals and look for them to be an integral part of the Davis Direction Foundation, Inc. Meeting with these people was uplifting, inspiring and eye-opening for me. I am looking forward to working with them to sponge up the knowledge and the experience that they have to offer. They have one goal and that is to SUPPORT RECOVERY. What a blessing I received through spending time with them. I even got to wish Joyce a very Happy Birthday and eat Neil's delicious cheesecake. They are truly a family of love and inspiration! Oh the gifts you can receive by opening your heart! Thank you to the wonderful employees of the GA Council on Drug Abuse! You made my day!

2/21/15 – Constructive Act #338 – Learn To Deal With Unwanted Memories

When I say unwanted memories, I don't necessarily mean bad memories, I just mean that everywhere I go, there seems to be a memory. It would just be nice to take a drive down Hwy 41 and not be consumed with memories of Davis, but instead be focused on the reason I'm traveling down the highway in the first place. Every neighborhood sparks a memory; every building sparks a memory; every restaurant, every storefront and even signposts spark a memory that is completely subconscious and I can't make the memories stop. Before Davis died, I could drive down 41 and not have a care in the world about what I was seeing on the way to the destination. Now, every time I travel down the highway, the landmarks along the way trigger memories of a time that Davis and I had a conversation, shared an experience or stopped along the way to go inside of a building and I can't make them stop. Sometimes driving down the road is such a painful experience that all I want to do is turn around and go home!

I can have a trip planned for another one of my children or a meeting to plan an event, or just the need to travel downtown to go shopping and I am totally focused on the event of the day until I turn the corner off of the street I live on and turn on to the familiar stomping ground of my precious son. Before I ever get to the main road, I have passed his elementary school, his middle school and his High school. I never once can pass these buildings without thinking of him. Then I turn the corner and find myself on the main road that leads straight into Atlanta…Hwy 41. As soon as I see a certain digital billboard, it becomes the time that I first saw the Heroin billboard with Davis's picture on it. Then I go a little further down the road and there is a Martin's restaurant. Every time I see that place, I think of Davis and Bobby heading that way on a Saturday morning to get their biscuits and enjoy breakfast together – one of their very favorite things to do. I keep driving and I pass Davis's favorite automotive shop where his beloved car was painted and made so beautiful while we spent a week together as a family in Florida. Right past that, I get to the QT which was our first stop after we left Davis's memorial service where we treated a homeless man to a drink and a biscuit – because that's what Davis would have done.

As I continue down the Highway, I chuckle as I pass Krispy Kreme and remember the time that Davis was with his Friend 'Zimm" who got an alert on his phone telling him that they had "Hot Doughnuts Now." They promptly got in "Zimm's" car and picked up a dozen doughnuts and consumed them on the spot. Soon enough I find my self passing Pep Boys – his favorite car parts shop and right past that is the Audi shop where he loved to go and check out all the new cars and marketing pieces. Then there is the side street that we turned down to go and test drive a Q7 SUV that Davis had his heart set on before we found his Audi. As I continue down the road, I pass the computer shop where we purchased his Mac for college and then come up on the Sheraton where he picked up his Daddy after the big snowstorm of 2014. Then right up the hill from that, where I take my daughter frequently for musical theatre master classes, I see the dreaded Hooter's restaurant parking lot where my precious Davis was found dead.

That is how I drive down highway 41 now. I don't plan to think about all these things, it just happens. I can't stop it and I can't control it. It just is what it is!

I've tried to start thinking of all these things as good memories and happy times, but the fact remains that I only think about them because he is gone and I miss him. Grief is a continual learning experience…it is something that you don't know how to deal with until you are dealing with it. There are times that you may deal with it one way on one day, but the next day you may choose a completely different plan. Grief is a process. It's not a "set in stone" process, but nevertheless, it is a process. Learn to embrace it, learn to accept it and learn to let it go! Don't ask me how, I don't have the answers yet. I'm still learning.

2/22/15 – Constructive Act #339 – Share Your Story Sunday

This week's story is kind of unique. Our writer actually reached out to me on the DDF and began a conversation. She was a delight to talk with and her insight into her recovery is refreshing and inspiring. She has chosen to lead by example and she is doing a fabulous job of doing just that! Her story is actually bits and pieces of our conversations online that she gave me permission to post ending with an

article written about her early on in her recovery. Stay strong Laura, my friend…
We are all praying for you and celebrating your recovery!

Here is her story:

I am a heroin addict named Laura. I introduce this way because this is how I introduce myself at 12 step meetings. I am also the mother and wife of heroin addicts. My son and husband are currently in active heroin addiction. I live with the fear of losing my son everyday.

I am currently 14 months clean from heroin and that is a miracle. I am writing to share my experience, strength and hope as I have learned in the rooms. The rooms being AA, NA, CMA, and HA. There is a solution to addiction and it is in the big book of alcoholics anonymous.

See I am the heroin addict who didn't have a problem with alcohol, that loved opiates of any kind. I would be clean if only I could physically kick the heroin cause I was just physically addicted. I wasn't that alcoholic addict. When I got out of jail, into treatment and got honest I needed treatment. I still wasn't honest enough and being on felony drug court probation at the age of 50 wasn't enough, to keep this junkie clean, I had to get a sponsor, admit I was an addict alcoholic, and start working the steps of alcoholics anonymous. By getting honest I had to admit I was that addict and it didn't matter what 12 step meeting I went to I identified with the other addict alcoholics that I am just like them. I am the mother of a heroin addict. My own son (or his dad my legal husband) won't get help. Whenever I talk to him (I can't see him in person because of safeguarding my own recovery)

I recommended he go to detox and then try to get into treatment and attend meetings. It breaks my heart daily. The struggle is real! The problem is real! There is a solution and it can be found in the rooms of all 12 step meetings. I encourage all addicts to find a fellowship they are comfortable in and work the steps with a sponsor. I know I cannot get my son clean on love cause he'd be clean and working a program. All I can do is lead by example, stay clean and show him it works if you work it. I thought I was unique being a heroin addict until I broke out in handcuffs and went to jail.

So many heroin addicts there and all so young! Breaks my heart seeing these beautiful young girls dealing with this disease. It is an epidemic!

In Arizona I participated with some journalists who did a documentary on the epidemic here. A documentary entitled "Hooked" shown on all our TV channels a month or so ago. It's heartbreaking!

A few years ago a documentary was done on the methamphetamine crisis and the same journalists decided to do a similar piece on heroin. One of my girls from treatment was actually in the show. I was interviewed and my story was in the newspaper kind of promoting the show. It was very surreal to have my picture on the front page of the Tucson newspaper and my story out their like that. Its very humbling to think I could inspire or encourage anyone.

Wow, that is an honor for you to ask me to write for "Share Your Story Sunday!" My bottom was very deep but there are so many deeper ones than mine! I really don't mind if you share my story!. I mean the jig is up with my extended family over my felony charges and probation. The jig is also up with my 37 year old boyfriend how old I really am! Again thank you for your encouragement!

XOXO Laura J

2/23/15 – Constructive Act #340 – Spot Clean Your Recovery

"TINKLE' HAPPENS"

In this post I'm going to tell you a story about cleaning my carpets a couple of weeks ago and what happened right after I finished. But first I want to clarify one thing, I do not consider anyone struggling with addiction "DIRTY" – It just works for the analogy that I will be using. I know that even on the heroin group pages that I read, posts from those struggling with addiction often refer to themselves as "clean" and of course the opposite and often unspoken word that people think about in relationship to clean, is "dirty." I don't like those terms – either one of them actually – I like to use words like "sick" or "struggling" and I use them when I can.

Sometimes I do slip up and use the words that I write about, but it just goes to prove that as a society we have a long way to go and lots of habits to break to get rid of the common way of thinking about the disease of addiction. Maybe one of these days I will come up with a "NEW" vocabulary list for addiction, We'll see.

So here is my story about cleaning the carpets. My family has a little Papillon named Bear. Bear is getting up there in years, and has succumbed to arthritis. He struggles on the wood floors and we have laid as many rugs for him to use as pathways as is possible without looking ridiculous. Bear likes to stay on the carpeted areas and he has started having accidents as he adjusts to the new medication that he has been prescribed. He is taking steroids and it makes him thirsty and he goes "tinkle" a lot more frequently. Even though we clean it up every time it happens, I just wanted to go over the entire area with a power shampooer. So, with all of that knowledge in place, haha, my rugs definitely needed cleaning. I went to the grocery store and picked up one of those "Rug Doctor" machines and the pet treated shampoo that goes in it and came home ready to get started with the carpets. I worked for several hours cleaning every inch of my living room carpet and I will tell you it looked amazing when I was done. Apparently, with all of my hard work going on, I had forgotten to take Bear out to let him go "potty." YEP – you guessed it! No sooner had my beautiful carpet dried, that I turned around and he had "tinkled" on it again.

I had become so wrapped up in what I was doing, and so happy with the result I was seeing, that I forgot to take care of Bear. He depended on me for "potty" support and I didn't do my part. Those relationships are important; Never underestimate them. Bear didn't want to mess up my carpet, but he just couldn't hold it any longer. Needless to say, my carpet had a very small, yet easy to reverse spot on it and I knew right where it was and what to do about it! So, I still had the tools, I knew how to restore my carpet back to its original beauty, and I didn't have to start from the beginning this time, I just had a little spot to repair. It took only a few minutes to get back to where I was with my beautifully clean carpet. All was not lost, and no one knew but Bear and me!

I tell you this analogy, because I think this is how it goes with long-term recovery. There will be accidents. I haven't heard from anyone – and I don't deny that they may be out there – but I haven't heard from anyone who didn't lapse and then relapse again while trying to maintain recovery from opioid/heroin addiction. Don't be so hard on yourselves. You are human and "tinkle happens." You have the knowledge, you have the tools and I hope you have the support in place to "spot clean" your recovery. If you don't, please let the Davis Direction Foundation help you by reading our daily posts and writing to us through private messaging and letting us connect you with resources and supports in our area – or your area. If we don't have the answers, we will ask on our page and our readers will come through with the support that you need. At least, they have up to this point.

All is not lost when accidents occur. Anywhere you read, when you are in the throes of opioid/heroin addiction, the average times to enter recovery include multiple attempts. The problem with this fact is that far too many of our loved ones are dying in the process of recovery. I'm by no means supporting "relapse" by writing this post, but I am being realistic and I do understand that recovery is a journey. "TINKLE HAPPENS." Learn to restore your recovery and have the tools in place to make it happen. Godspeed.

2/24/15 – Constructive Act #341 – Educate The Whole Family About Recovery

Too many times, IF (big if) the addicts get information on "what to expect" in recovery – the rest of the family does not. I have read too many times where people who have just recently entered recovery are asking questions about what to expect and asking others if they are crazy or if something is terribly wrong with them or will they ever be "normal" again. We need to begin to educate the "young recoverers" on what to expect in recovery. I had never heard of a term called "PAWS" Post Acute Withdrawal Syndrome – until Michael was doing research after Davis died. It is out there, it is real, and it explains a lot about the journey of recovery and why the death of so many opioid/heroin users follows this timeline. The common assumption is that the longer you are in recovery the easier it becomes to maintain it. According to PAWS, about 2 – 6 months down the line, you will hit a bump in the road and you need to hold on tight through the white water rapids. So many times knowing what to expect and how to get through is MORE than half the battle. Learning to recognize the symptoms and knowing that it will go away and that it does not last forever can also be a huge incentive to stay the course.

The longer that Davis was out of Rehab, the better I felt about his addiction. I felt that every minute he was one minute closer to being as good as new again. I had NO idea that there would be a massive bump in the road as early as 6 weeks out and if I had known, I could have watched for the signs and symptoms and reminded him of what to expect and how to cope with it. We could have had conversations about it and what it might look like and devised a plan to combat it. No one ever told us coming out of Rehab, that this time would be a dangerous time and that his chances of dying because of relapse during this period were much more of a threat than at other times. The education that we did NOT receive still blows my mind and I can't stop putting it out there for others so that they don't make the same mistakes that we did. PAWS is real and documented scientifically! Please do the research if you or a loved one is in the early stages of recovery.

Learning how to get through the first year of recovery is key to remaining there. We all know it's not a matter of "will power." It takes a complete bag of tools, relationships, plans, education, physical care, spirituality, and lots of HOPE! So – I do have a couple of stats that provide lots of HOPE in my opinion. The Georgia Council on Substance Abuse advocates that 67% of people who make it in recovery for 1 – 3 years can expect to remain in recovery for another year. Even better than that… 86% of people who make it in recovery for five years can expect to remain in recovery for another year. The longer you can make it the better the odds become after that first critical year! Forewarned is Forearmed! If you know what you are up against, you can prepare to come out on the side of SUCCESS!!!

It breaks my heart to see people struggling early on in their addiction because they believe that for the rest of their lives they will have to struggle with the cravings and feelings they are struggling with when they continue to reappear over a period of time. Up to a point, they confess that each craving is stronger than the last and this concept has taken them completely by surprise. As I understand it through PAWS, it peaks after several months and then begins to diminish and that is when recovery becomes much more easily manageable and it also explains why the odds go up percentage wise as explained in the above paragraph. Just prepare yourself and find your "safe haven" of support whether it be a meeting, time spent with a friend, exercise, time spent alone with God or whatever gets you through the craving period – to each his own, whatever it takes. Then celebrate yourself for another craving denied and add another tally mark for you against the cravings of withdrawal. Hopefully this post gives you a sneak preview into the light at the end of the tunnel of Recovery if you are in recovery or the necessity for the long-term relationships of support and unconditional love if you have a loved one in recovery.

2/25/15 – Constructive Act # 342 – Create Community to Rebuild In Recovery

So many times I have been asked questions regarding recovery issues concerning our very own community. Then I have also been asked questions of other people in other communities. My question is, "Why is it so hard to find help if you are deep in the throes of addiction?" No one knows where to turn for detox, addiction counseling, suboxone, vivitrol, the list goes on and on. Only recently has the life-saving Naloxone become available to the public in our area, and it has been around for years! Does anyone know where to get it? Do you even know what it is? It's an opioid antagonist... in other words, it brings an addict back from an overdose by reversing the opioid receptors. Who knew? Think about it – If you are going to have a baby, everyone knows about everyone else's hospital experience, who their baby doctor was, what hospital has the best "spousal" arrangements, and who gives the best diaper bag! We need to start talking publicly about addiction so that we can begin to save our children and our loved ones. I always say children because everybody is somebody's child! We don't need to have to be scrounging around on the internet or social media sites when an emergency occurs and we need immediate help for an addict. I had no idea when the Davis Direction Foundation went public on the social media site – Facebook that the majority of my time would be spent helping families in the throes of addiction find resources for their addicted loved one and the family members. I'm happy to do this and I feel so happy when I can help others, but I guess I never knew what a necessary site we would become and that breaks my heart! What were people doing before we began reaching out?

At our last symposium, Attorney General Olens and his staff made it quite clear that the community had a responsibility to create an environment that reached out to families – including those in the throes of addiction as well as those succeeding in long term recovery. It will be beneficial to our community and it will also bring members back into the fold and help them become productive members of society. With that being said, we will spend less money in the court systems and the jails. We will have less people depending on social welfare systems, on food stamps, depending on the government for their well being and draining our pools of federal as well as state money for purposes of reaction rather than proaction. These people in many circumstances are bright people, with bright futures – if someone will allow them a chance. Did they make a mistake? Well that's a hard question. Many of the ones that I speak with began opioid addiction when their wisdom teeth were pulled or they were recovering from surgery and they were given an exorbitant amount of pain pills. Is that really a mistake? Many people were only doing what they had been told to do in order to recover. In the world I raised my kids in, the Doctors were looked up to as some of the most brilliant individuals in the community. For goodness sakes, they even took an oath to save lives and to help people who came to them seeking medical advice.

So I look into our community and although I have been a school counselor for 26 years and a teacher for an additional 7 years, when Davis fell victim to opioid/heroin addiction, I had no idea where to turn. I was too embarrassed to start asking questions publicly, and you don't want to call your child out and label them as an addict because of social ridicule, so you search in silence and do everything you can to make your child feel better while praying hard all the time that this evil plight will go away! The young people are asking over and over again for options other than a 12-step approach. Although 12-step has worked well for many people down through the years, and continues to work, some young people of today seem to be looking for alternative groups. We need to provide them!

We need to provide skills groups — groups where people are learning necessary skills to become valuable in the workplace. Skills like working on cars, cooking, floral arranging, plumbing, painting and construction, gardening, yard work, data management systems, computer skills. The list goes on and on.

It is our responsibility to embrace our own and not only make it possible, but also make it probable that they will succeed after entering long term recovery from opioid/heroin addiction. It benefits all of us. Ask yourself, "What can I do to help my community be receptive and nurturing to 1 out of every 10 people who are members of my community and also suffering from the disease of addiction?" They are not necessarily suffering from the disease because they are actively using, they are suffering because they are not able to assimilate back into an unforgiving community. Life is about second chances! What if your child needed a second chance? "Verily I say unto you, Inasmuch as ye have done it unto one of the least of these my brethren, ye have done it unto me." Matthew 25:40 Food for thought...

2/26/15 – Constructive Act #343 – Create Your Own C.H.A.T. Group

Have you ever had those conversations with someone and you talk about the future or the past because that person knows you so much better than any others? You can talk about the past without having to explain everything that happened, or you can talk about how you can make things different for the future. Those people that you know will always be there for you and help you through your weak moments and of course help you to dream big dreams for the future. Sometimes they don't necessarily even need to be your best friends, but people that you have things in common with or people who are going through the same struggles or even people that you look up to and admire that you know are never going to judge you or put you down. Everyone NEEDS a C.H.A.T. group like that. I would say no more than four – six people in it.

The huge Facebook pages are terrific for everyone and give lots of people encouragement and even insight for the struggles that they are facing. But it seems to never be the same people, and when new people do come on, they don't know how far you have come or what you have been through. I suppose that is sometimes a blessing, but with a new study that has come out in the past few months, reporting how very significant relationships are for long-term recovery, I want to suggest that everybody have your very own "off-line" private C.H.A.T. group. It will allow you to "C"reate "H"ope "A"nd "T"alk. There don't have to be any "group rules" and no one gets to decide whether or not what you say gets to remain in print or gets removed! Everyone needs at least two – four friends like that. For some of you, it may be the people that you have gone through Rehab with, for others like me, it may be other women my age who want so badly for their loved ones to get help, or those who have lost a loved one. Sometimes I need to tell someone else, or show someone else a picture of something that may break a "group" rule or it may just plainly be something that I don't want everyone else to know. Maybe I'm having a selfish feeling, or maybe I want to scream at the top of my "FONT" that things need to be different! I don't want to do that for the masses, but it would make me feel better to have my C.H.A.T. group. Sometimes, everybody needs validation!

I visited with one of my favorite friends in recovery not too long ago, and he was telling me about his experience in a CHAT room. Of course there were strangers in there with him – It was kind of like a "Help Line" phone in – except in the form of a chat. He said it was so much easier to C.H.A.T. for his generation (26 yo) because you don't feel pressured to respond orally and immediately like you would if you were on the phone. You can honestly process what you just read, and even re-read it, if necessary. There is no mistaking what you heard because you have the printed version. It made a lot of sense! You could even use a group text on your phone and remain completely off-line. I think the groups online and even many of the Rehab facilities have made groups that are too large. I think that more than four-six people would defeat the purpose of what I am talking about. Six people may even be a stretch!

It has to be a small core group and it has to be people that you are so comfortable with, that you don't mind bearing your heart and soul, as well as asking for help from time to time. It has to be people that you know are either frequently online, or who carry their cell phones with them all the time in case you are ever in need of an emergency situation. It needs to be people who are expecting to at least have a group C.H.A.T. arranged at a specific time once a week if not twice a week, and people who are committed to their long-term recovery, but are not judgmental if another member of the group gets into trouble with a relapse. We all know it happens! In other words, you would have to pick the group carefully and be willing to change if some of the group didn't meet the needs of the rest of the group.

Face to face is good, but it's not always possible. So – a C.H.A.T. group is just another alternative to staying focused in recovery and nurturing relationships that are so vital in recovery! There must be a reason that only one out of 10 people even seek Rehab – besides the money. There are free places out there, and still only 1 in 10 are going. I wonder why? Create your own C.H.A.T. group and your support will be Free and Available on your terms. I have always advocated that the experts are those in recovery. Just think of it as your own group of experts!

2/27/15 – Constructive Act #344 – Unleash The Emotion

For the last several days I have been trying like everything to suppress any kind of emotion that I feel creeping into my mind. I know where it will lead and I just don't want to go there right now. My best friend from high school came down to support me through this week and we have been working so hard at getting things for the Foundation organized and in place to move forward in our second year. She is an expert in non-profit organizations and is giving me way more help than I ever imagined. There are no questions that she doesn't have the answers to or at least know where the answer is, and she is a genius at helping me organize things so that I will be able to move forward so much more efficiently. We have been working in my new at home office and last night I just kind of had a panic attack as all of the pictures started staring back at me and I couldn't hold it in any longer. I had to leave the room and I couldn't go back in the rest of the night.

Sometimes you have to give in to the emotion and just release the pressure of your hemorrhaging heart. There's just something about coming up on that "one year" mark that makes things very clear and very real. It's like for the past 365 days you have been waiting to find out that the ending of the story was not as tragic as you had first thought. One year makes it real. You realize that he's never coming home, he will never sleep in his bed, or wear those clothes; he'll never come through the door whistling and swinging his keychain lanyard around his finger. He'll never come up the stairs shaking his freshly washed hair or asking if his clothes look alright; he'll never sit on the couch with his back against the side and his long legs thrown up stretching all the way across. He'll never tell me about another conspiracy theory or a funny story about the kids he used to work with; he'll never sit beside me and show me pictures of his precious daughter and tell me how she wraps her arms around his neck and says "I love you Daddy." It's real and he's never coming home. That's so cold and hard.

I have always been OCD with numbers and patterns and schedules and plans. Yesterday was the first day of the last week and today is the last Friday of the first year. Tomorrow will be the last Saturday and you can imagine the rest of the "last week" until we come up on Wednesday, next week. I'm already beginning to feel a little numb – even more so than throughout the entire past year – and that surprises me because all along I thought it would just be another day without my baby, but it's different. I don't really know why, except that, like I said before, I'll never be able to say "this time last year" again. I think back to this time last year and I go over and over in my mind what was happening and should I have known, could I have known, and if I had known, could I have done anything about it – could I have prevented it? I don't have the chance for a do-over, none of us do when it comes to death. I do regret that I did not take the family leave act and stay home with him trying to help him through the days. He was in intensive outpatient therapy and I assumed it was enough. I guess like any mother going through this, I wish he would have or could have told me what was going on in his head. I wish I had understood the world he was living in and how to help him come back to the world he wanted to live in again.

Not being able to help your child is the most unforgiving feeling in the entire world. It haunts you and never escapes the thoughts of your mind. Parents are supposed to care for and protect their children and heroin robs you of that responsibility. It strips you down to the core and pushes you into the deep dark corner of "no-control." It's like brainwashing your child and you can't get through to them no matter what you do. You watch movies all of your life and you see the power of love overcome the most daunting obstacles, and you have this secret feeling that "love will prevail" and when it doesn't, your first instinct is to doubt the love that you were sure was going to turn everything around. Heroin changes that whole philosophy and re-writes the ending. Then you realize that love has nothing to do with it. Davis loved unconditionally and was loved unconditionally in return. I know he died knowing that.

There are answers that I know I will never have until I reach the other side, and at that point, I don't believe they will really matter anyway. Davis was always there to help whoever was in need and he died making sure that I would carry out his legacy because he knew my heart probably better than anyone! I'm not doing this for him; he is safe and at peace in the arms of God. I'm doing this for the ones who are still struggling and want to change and don't know how. For the last 30+ years I have helped children – it's the profession that I chose because it felt right. Now the children need help more than ever before, and I'll keep helping because that's just what I know to do. It feels right and I feel led to do it, and I know it makes Davis happy! That's just who he was!

2/28/15 – Constructive Act #345 – Don't Try To Boil The Ocean

For those of you who know me well, you know that I have very little patience when there is an overwhelming need and I want an overwhelming fix! I want it NOW and I will work tirelessly and almost obsessively to make sure that it happens. This week has been a very necessary and eye opening experience as I have worked alongside my friend, Kim, in writing a business plan and trying to make the Foundation function as efficiently as possible and as quickly as possible. Finally, she looked at me and said, "Missy, you can't boil the ocean in a day." I knew immediately what she meant and I knew I had to begin to focus on patience and logic. That's hard for me! When people are hurting, I just feel such a need for urgency and doing everything at once. I realize that's what has caused some of this crisis in the first place. I think that too often people don't think things through and one thing leads to another, which makes opioid addicts turn to heroin in the first place. Changing the coating on the Rx meds and then the re-classification of Hydrocodone are two examples.

I know I need time to think things through specifically and thoroughly, and then time to bounce them off of the other directors in the Foundation. I also need time to network with other organizations in the same field to make sure that what we are doing is truly moving in the right "Direction." The "Davis Direction!" It's so tempting to jump the gun and just skip right to the "helping" part without really looking to see the long-term effects and how it will manifest itself in the future. Those things are important and I have witnessed the long-term effects of things that were not well thought through. "Slow and Steady wins the race" is one of the old clichés of my childhood thinking back to the turtle and the hare. One thing for sure is that when it comes to Rehab and long-tern recovery, this old cliché is certainly holding true. Staying in Rehab for at least a year gives you a head start in your next year of recovery. According to the GA Council on Substance Abuse, after just 1 year of abstinence, your chances of another year in recovery jump from 36% – to 67%. That's HUGE! That means that two of every three people will stay in long-term recovery. Those odds still need work…but it's a researched strategy that has people moving in the right direction.

Considering that it takes the addicted brain an average of six months to begin to heal, you are really only talking about six additional months to complete rehabilitation where your brain actually has the capacity to understand and comprehend what you are being told to apply into your daily life. The first six months of Rehab should be spent on healing and the last 6 months on helping. The helping months are vital to long-term recovery because those months are the ones where you are collecting the tools for your recovery toolbox and collecting strategies to use in different situations. You are learning the vocabulary and verbiage to communicate your desires or lack thereof when you are in a social situation that dictates that you will have to make a decision.

The triggers won't go away, I have found out how very powerful the brain can be with memories and the past having lost Davis. Everything triggers something and I haven't found a way to stop the grief triggers from popping up in my brain. I imagine that it is much the same for someone in long-term recovery. You just learn to handle the situation and get through it with as much grace as possible. Yes – it hurts, but as your heart begins to change, you begin to look at those memories (triggers) differently. Time doesn't heal the broken heart, it just teaches you how to care for it differently.

So, I will stop (or at least try to stop) feeling that it is necessary to "boil the ocean" and realize that a well laid out plan will do more in the long run to change the course of opioid/heroin addiction than a "quick fix." I'm not saying that a "quick fix" won't sometimes get you through to the next level of recovery, meaning drug therapy, or in-patient rehabilitation, but ultimately, long-term recovery is for a lifetime. It becomes a new way and a better way of life. It allows you to become who you were truly meant to be. As for the Foundation, we will continue to focus on awareness and education, change, and handing out the Naloxone kits, until our community has a better understanding of how, why, where and when addiction happens and why it will truly take a community to change this epidemic. We will continue to "Move Onward through Life…Looking Upward to God." We'll let HIM be in charge of boiling the ocean! Godspeed!

3/1/15 – Constructive Act #346 – Share Your Story Sunday

This week I am posting parts of a conversation that I had with one of the most intelligent opiate addicts I have ever had the pleasure of getting to know. He is trying so hard to understand and help others with the disease of addiction. He has explained many things to me that I had questions about and we kept our conversations going for quite some time. This story isn't really going to connect like most of the ones so far, because I took my part of the conversation out and just shared his feelings and knowledge regarding opioids. He has helped me more than he will ever know by allowing me an inside look into the soul of an opiaoid user. He has been in recovery for some time, but he shares that it is a process and it is not easy. Please keep this young man in your prayers as he struggles to maintain his recovery.

Here is his story:

I am an opiate addict. I am currently in recovery, but my struggles are far from over. I have been a chronic opiate user for my entire adult life. I read your posts almost every day. The recent posts on Suboxone made me feel the need to write you this message. PLEASE UNDERSTAND THAT I AM BY NO MEANS A DOCTOR. This information is just little bits of information I have gathered from my own experience and from speaking with other addicts about their experiences. I have been using opiates/heroin for quite a long time. I was prescribed Suboxone© a few different times during the course of my active addiction / recovery attempts. I have been on Suboxone for long periods of time where I did very well. I abstained from using drugs (for the most part), I was able to hold a job and perform very well at work, I saved a lot of money, and basically felt like I had finally beaten my addiction. Unfortunately, as soon as I was unable to continue taking Suboxone because of how expensive the drug was, I went on a downward spiral that ended with me using heroin heavily and being the same unemployed dysfunctional addict as before the Suboxone. Suboxone was never meant for long-term maintenance. It is wonderful to aid in detoxification, but should really be stopped after a few weeks.

You become dependent on Suboxone just as much as any other opiate/opioid. The worst part is, because of the ridiculous strength of the medication vs. conventional opiates, along with the extremely long half-life of the drug (Buprenorphine), the withdrawal from Suboxone was so terrible. It lasted over a month. There have also been people who have told me that there is an increased chance of long lasting PAWS (Post Acute Withdrawal Syndrome) after stopping Suboxone. Suboxone is a great tool, and much better than illegal street drugs or medications. I just wanted to give you my personal experience on the negative aspects as well. Again, this is all just my own thoughts and gathered information. I am by no means a doctor trying to give medical advice. I hope that you find this information interesting and decide to research Suboxone (especially long term affects) yourself. I have much more I could say on the subject, but I think this is enough for now. Feel free to message me with any questions about this or anything else related to opiate dependency/ recovery. Keep up the amazing work of the DDF. You are doing a wonderful thing.

Missy, I am currently in recovery, but one could say just barely. I have done everything I could think of to try and quit using heroin. I went to rehab(multiple times), halfway houses (what a joke), and even went to NA/AA meetings all the time hoping that maybe through osmosis I might finally have that "click" inside of myself and the desire to use drugs would just magically disappear. As much as I wish there was a one-time fix for this disease, yet sadly there is not. The fact of the matter is that most treatment doesn't work. The treatment facilities are not to blame, it is just that science has yet to provide any kind of answers, the answers which many of us seek so desperately. Ibogaine sounds wonderful, but what heroin addict do you know with the money to travel out of state to receive this treatment. To my understanding, Ibogaine has a way of re-wiring the brain in an addict so that the typical things that contribute to failure in early recovery are minimal if not completely absent. This is short term though. It is in these crucial months following treatment that one must work on recovering both spiritually and emotionally. This leads to my next point. (Again, I am no doctor. These are my personal thoughts and beliefs acquired from a life of active addiction and extensive reading on the subject.) Myself and many other addicts (I would venture to say all addicts who use their drug of choice recreationally and on a daily basis) are very sick in a way that is hard to understand. I am a very firm believer in drug abuse being a symptom of this disease and not the actual disease itself. Most addicts have a hole in their soul that yearns to be filled. For me personally, as a child I started to look for love and attention at school and from my peers.

I hated who I was and truly believed happiness came from the approval and acceptance of my peers. Well, eventually I found acceptance from my classmates… the ones who used drugs. It would take me quite a long time to explain my life leading up to drug abuse and the complete chaos and destruction that followed. If you wanted to hear it, just let me know and I will write the story for you. The point that I wanted to try and get across is that I was insecure and unhappy with myself, and I eventually used drugs as a way to escape and/or cope with this defect in my character. I finally realized that in order to put the drug abuse behind me for good, I must fix the underlying problems I had with myself that drove me to escape my life through drugs. Fast-forward to present day, and although I am clean from drugs I still feel so lost in this world. I started using at such a young age (Marijuana in my early teens, harder drugs soon after, IV heroin use at 17) that I have come to realize I simply do not know how to live and function as an adult! I look back at my life and am disgusted with my actions and the consequences that I must now face as a result. My only saving grace has been my family. Luckily, I have a father who seems unable to give up on me, no matter how many times I let him down.

Please understand, I come from a very "normal" and successful family. I have two brothers and sisters and a large extended family. There are nine of us in my generation and they have all graduated college or are about to. They are all well on the road to success and a fulfilling life. I am a high school drop out with a GED and barely a year of community college completed. Believe it or not, growing up I was the one that everyone assumed would go on to accomplish the most, and was always regarded as the "brain" in the family (ha ha!). I live in a constant state of misery and pain, knowing that I could feel healthy and feel like one of the normal people just from simply using heroin. The relief using heroin brings to me is indescribable. I very, very rarely would get "high" when I used. Instead, I would suddenly feel like a healthy and happy individual. I would feel like how I assumed all the normal people in this world felt like naturally every day. Yet, this feeling would quickly fade and I would be back to my miserable self. Still, it got so bad that I was doing anything I could to get back to that place where I felt normal regardless of who I harmed in the process.

This kind of selfish and self-destructive life is unnatural, and eventually I was unable to live with myself. This led me to recovery, and although there have been countless relapses and times in which I disagree with views and approaches of treatment professionals, I now know that I can live the rest of my life without drugs and find the true kind of happiness that God meant for us all to experience. I could go on for hours and hours, although I am sure by this point you are thinking " Good God wrap it up!". I am very thankful for the Davis Direction Foundation, and I am happy to be able to talk with you about the struggles I am facing in this journey. Until it has closely affected an individual, they have no way of relating or understanding the disease of addiction. I never had the pleasure of meeting your son Davis, but from what I have heard about him he was a truly remarkable young man. I look forward to any comments, criticism, or just your thoughts on this letter. I would also enjoy answering any questions you have regarding opiate addiction if it is within my power to do so.

Long story short, I ran from my problems but of course they ran right along with me. I am in the process of trying to get back to GA, where my loving wife and children are. I have done some shameful things and as you know, the majority of the public still perceives addiction as a lack of moral fiber. Hearing government officials say that heroin addicts have no desire to stop using drugs saddens me. It is equivalent to believing a manic-depressive, or a person with schizophrenia, has no desire to get better and live a healthy happy life.

I want to be able to one day help those suffering the misery of addiction, if only I can truly overcome my own. I find that there is no reason to be secretive or fearful of letting others know that I am a heroin addict. Anybody who knows my family or me knows already. Why try and deny or hide it?

I also want you to know that you are DEAD accurate in describing Davis and the pain he went through before his passing. Davis did NOT want to feel the way that he did. He did NOT want to leave his family or let them down. Heroin addiction robs a person of a part of their soul, and makes living life an exercise in constant pain and misery. I know because I have been there / am there myself. Life becomes a chore. You still love your family and you still love all the good in the world, but all of this does little to stifle the crushing depression that is a daily presence in the life of an addict attempting to recover. Please research Post Acute Withdrawal Syndrome (PAWS). PAWS is the leading cause of relapse among opiate addicts. There is very little understanding of it in the medical community, and it has been known to last anywhere from 3 months to many, many years after complete abstinence of opiates/drugs. One major symptom of PAWS is

412

anhedonia.: a psychological condition characterized by inability to experience pleasure in normally pleasurable acts.

Ahhh Vivitrol a.k.a Naltrexone. I have mixed feelings on this drug. Naltrexone is an opiate receptor antagonist, meaning it forms a complete attachment to the bodies many opiate receptors present in the central nervous system (as apposed to an opiate receptor agonist such as morphine/heroin/oxycodone/etc.) which attaches to these same receptors briefly while activating them, and then releases and reattaches in a continuing cycle. This produces the "high" and analgesia, or pain killing effect. Because when taking Naltrexone, your opiate receptors are blocked and unable to be activated. This leads to reduction in cravings. It also will "block" a full opiate agonist from attaching to the receptor because it already has the Naltrexone attached to it. Be aware, with the introduction of enough opiate agonists into the CNS, the blocking effects can be overcome.

This takes an unreal amount of opiates and the results of this have been known to lead to overdose. Every chemical that acts on opiate receptors has a certain "binding affinity". When one chemical has a higher binding affinity than another chemical, it will stay bound to the receptor even in the presence of the other chemical (except in certain circumstances, i.e. HUGE amounts of the weaker binding chemical). My fear with Naltrexone is that we have yet to fully understand the effects our bodies own endorphins (short for endogenous morphine) and other similar chemical peptides created naturally in our body have on mood, physical comfort, feelings of well being, etc. The question I have is, if my receptors are blocked by Naltrexone, how are my endorphins going to be able to help produce feelings of pleasure and well being like they do in healthy individuals? I am not a doctor. This is just my two cents. :)

P.S. – Beware of Big Pharma!!! They were fully aware of how addictive their opiate meds were, yet released them for public use and prescription anyways. Money is the motivating factor for pharmaceutical companies. Is it a coincidence that after the DEA cracked down on over-prescription of schedule 2 narcotics the rise of the heroin epidemic began?

3/2/15 – Constructive Act #347 – Make It Real and Make It Accurate

As most of you have probably gathered, what is recorded in the books as what is real and what is really real are two different accounts. When your precious child is dead and gone I guess the fine details don't really matter much anymore, but to a mother's heart, they matter. When the detectives arrived at the door on March the 4th, last year, they told us that our son had been found dead that day. The fact of the matter is that I know he was dead on the day before, because he left our house shortly after seven o'clock and he never came home again. The pictures of him getting his heroin on the video inside of Hooter's, show him getting it around 7:30.

So, he went back out to his car, shot up his heroin and I'm sure in a matter of an hour or so he was probably gone. He died on March the 3rd, but his death certificate says he died on March 4th, which is wrong.

Michael and I also made a phone call early on the morning of March 4th, filing a missing person's report and asking the police to please look for his car and for him. The problem with that was that whoever took the call, forgot to log the information into the system and the APB on our child NEVER went out. So, the books went down as saying that Davis was found by the police and the truth of the matter is that the guy who sold Davis his heroin went back to find him. Michael went online to search phone records for calls that Davis had made the night he left and one number appeared three times. Michael called the number and asked the guy on the other end of the phone if he had seen Davis. The guy told him he must have the wrong number. It was not until Michael told the guy that he was giving his number to the police because he was turning the information over to them did the guy all the sudden remember meeting with Davis. When the guy found out that Davis had not come home and that he was missing, he began calling Michael back every 15 minutes to see if Davis had come home yet. At around 4:30, when Davis had still not been found, the guy – yes his drug dealer, went back to Hooter's where Davis was still sitting in his car and found him.

This is where it gets really interesting. Instead of calling Michael, the drug dealer goes into Hooter's at Cumberland and asks to use the phone where he calls 911 and reports Davis in his car, dead. Then the dealer stays with Davis until the police arrive and he's interviewed, his phone is searched, information was incriminating from the phone, the videos are watched, there is passing of a piece of paper that goes into Davis's pocket, all the time while they sit at Hooter's and Davis has only a glass of water. The dealer then is allowed to walk away, and is never charged, never booked, and never had one consequence. When I asked the detectives why this guy would have gone back to look for Davis knowing the facts of what had happened, all they could figure out was that the dealer really liked Davis and that Davis had somehow touched his life and heart somewhere along the way. That part of course did not surprise me. What did surprise me was this guy had already served prison time twice and been released for drug dealing.

Then, Davis's car was impounded after having been searched by no less than 3 people. When Michael and I picked up the car three days later, unlocked in the impound yard, Michael took it home to clean it out and wash it. When he was cleaning it out, he reached down underneath the passenger's seat and he found the paper with the heroin in it that the guy had passed to Davis. So, now Missy and Michael are the proud owners of a gram of heroin that should have been taken from the scene. We had to call and have someone come back out to the house to take the heroin.

Now mind you, these are the only mess ups that I know of and it makes me wonder, what else really happened that I will never know anything about. And like I said, it only matters to a mother's heart, and I'm sure a father's heart as well. It only matters because as a parent you want to know EVERY detail so that you can make some kind of sense out of all of it. You keep hoping to find that one clue that ties everything up and makes the story complete.

When he left our house that night, he had every intention of going to a meeting, he had even looked the meeting up on his way down to Cumberland. He was having a conflict in his heart and sadly, heroin won. I will never be able to change the outcome of that horrible night that began a year ago tomorrow, but if I knew all of the details, maybe I could help someone else from having to go through what we went through and maybe just maybe, things would end up differently for someone else. I know that I will forever look back and try to figure out how it could have ended differently, but I also know it will never change what happened.

3/3/15 – Constructive Act #348 – Saying Goodbye Never Gets Any Easier

Say it ANYWAY… coupled with a BIG HUG! So, yesterday afternoon I put my Best Friend Forever on a plane back to the other end of the earth!!! Really it was just the nation, but what's the difference? Goodbyes never get any easier. As I watch my older kids pull out of the driveway on Sunday nights, my heart hurts and I thank God for every minute that He allows me to spend with them. As they get older and their lives become their own and they pull further away from the fold, I do my best to adjust to the changes, but my heart grows heavier with each child. This month, not only do we endure the first anniversary of Davis's death, but we also have to accompany Spencer to FLORIDA for a scholarship interview at FSU. Life goes on and we must learn to adjust and move on. Goodbyes are just part of the process and it brings a whole new meaning to the old saying, "Better to have loved and lost, than to have never loved at all."

Everyday as I kiss and hug Michael goodbye when he walks out the door for work, I realize how completely fragile life is and that none of us have any guarantees to ever come back home when we walk out that door. Most people don't even think about their loved ones not coming home, but when that doorbell rings, and you get the call, the doorbell never sounds the same again. The Fairy Tale is over and the nightmare begins. All we can do is make the most of every goodbye. If ever a cross word is spoken, I worry that it will be the last and it haunts me until I get a chance to revisit the conversation. Things are different now and more thought is put into how you leave a friend or loved one.

Thank God that all of our "endings" with Davis were ones that we could live with without regrets, because with people suffering with addiction, often times that is not the case. Too often, those suffering leave with hurt feelings because of things that have been said out of desperation and a desire to affect change. When those hurtful things happen, people live with regret for the rest of their lives. It's not that we want to hurt those that are deep in the throes of addiction, we just want to help them change and often times we don't know how to go about it without raised voices and hurt feelings.

When Davis was a little guy, he liked to be just like his Daddy. Michael has never liked and has never even agreed to even take a "little" taste of Potato Soup, in fact, it has always been a sore spot in our marriage ;) So, Davis would not even taste potato soup when he was little. One day, I was too tired to prepare anything else for supper and I told Davis it was "Zebra" soup. He tried it and loved it! So, for tomorrow night, the last night that we spent with Davis in 2014, we will be having "Zebra" soup and remembering our awesome son and brother! Sometimes it's the little things that make you smile and remember those who've gone before us with funny memories and genuine unconditional love.

One year ago today, Davis walked out of the back door, we hugged and told each other "I love you" and I never heard from him or saw him alive again. Life can be so fragile, especially for those who are suffering in the throes of opioid/heroin addiction. Young people are dying in record numbers and we are trying so hard to figure out the best way to help stop this awful epidemic. Last night I had a call from someone who needed advice because their loved one was in an ER throwing up, with cold chills, diarrhea, and writhing around in his own skin, yet he was turned away because they found out he was in active heroin withdrawal. Have we so little compassion that we honestly can't help those who want to get well? Dehydration would have been a reason to admit this young man. Every time I hear this kind of story or see a person who is on the street holding a sign needing a bite to eat or a bottle of water, immediately I see my sweet Davis's face and I know that I am doing what I am supposed to be doing.

I have said over and over again, "Therefore, by the grace of God go I" and I mean it from the depths of my being. I can name over a dozen times that I have been put to sleep for surgery or procedures where I walked away with opioid medication in my lifetime. I'm pretty sure that if I had the genetic make-up to become an addicted person, that someone would be caring for me right now and helping me to stay in long-term recovery, or worse I could have been gone from this earth.

Stop judging and START helping. I can almost guarantee that one day addiction will hit close to home and you will need to know what you don't know. Learn now by helping others; it is in fact what God calls us all to do. We have to become comfortable talking about opioid/heroin addiction, the conversation alone will save lives.

The sweetest goodbye that we will ever say, will be the goodbye we say to drugs and addiction and the devastation it is causing in our country. It will take all of us to make that happen. Please consider how you can help and how we can say goodbye forever.

3/4/15 – Constructive Act #349 – Honor The Dead

I wrote this poem over a week ago, but I saved it to post today, since it is the anniversary of Davis's first full day with God in Heaven. There were just some things I needed for him to know...

"If I Had But Known..."

If I had but known the terror in your eyes
Was the demon of a drug that disguises as a prize...

If I had but known that the shaking of your legs
Required the sacred help for which every parent begs...

If I had but known that the nodding of your head
Was the symptom of an illness, and not sleep deprived instead...

If I had but known that the feeling of your hugs
Would be void in my tomorrows, because of fatal drugs...

If I had but known I would forever miss your laugh
I would have intervened, and died on your behalf...
If I had but known the things that you would miss
Graduations, your wedding and the little angel's kiss...

If I had but known you felt far from success
I would have reminded you of all the hearts you bless...

If I had but known that the hemorrhage of my heart
Would have a lasting impact; completely torn apart...

If I had but known the hole that you would leave
The minutes and the hours for you that I would grieve...

I would have done my research; I would have done my best
I would have laid my life down to take this off your chest...

I would have made a difference; I would have brought you back
I would have carried you my son, taking up the slack...

I would have walked to hell and back; I would have stopped for no one
I would have faced the devil himself and not turned back till I was done...

I would have prayed tenfold more prayers and fought with my last breath
It would have been my lifelong goal to prevent your needless death...

I didn't know and what's worse...I didn't know, I didn't know
So looking back, I'm sure you felt you had nowhere to go...

The past is gone forever and we must let it go
But the path that lies before us it to let the others know...

I know this would have been your wish; I know you bent God's ear
You showed Him what He knew before, a parent's greatest fear...

He took you in His loving arms and said " Your fight is done"
"You are with the chosen now...my good and faithful son."

Missy Owen
2/23/2015
Written for my Beautiful Davis

3/5/15 – Constructive Act #350 – Allow God To Use Your Empty Vessel

Yesterday as most of you know, I was numb and like an empty vessel. Don't ever let anyone tell you that it's the anticipation of an anniversary that is the worst. For me, it was the day itself. I shed more tears yesterday as I read sweet remembrances, heard from old friends with words of encouragement and watched my children suffer, some undeniably and others silently. For one of my sweet friends, who was by my side while my children were much younger, it took her a year to make the first phone call because my journey had been too painful for her approach. I understand that, and I have learned that everyone processes grief differently. It is a journey and one that each person must walk alone. It takes place inside of your head from messages that come from the very the depths of your heart. No one can process it but the person that is experiencing it. As I try to continue my journey this morning, several things have happened that I didn't realize were happening yesterday, things that God took from an empty vessel and allowed great things to happen.

To begin with, through the grief and openness of the events of the last two days, the DDF gained 80 new readers. Our posts were shared 258 times and we reached 28,398 readers with 5,366 "likes." When you consider that our number one goal is awareness and education, I think that God took our grief and used it for a beautiful purpose. Many times, only in a tragedy, do people really begin to take notice of a situation, even if it has reached epidemic proportions. As long as people continue to believe that addiction is a choice, rather than a disease, this fact will probably not change without our continued efforts of awareness, education and prevention. People continue to stick their heads in the sand because their family has not "yet" been touched personally and possibly tragically by this horrific disease of opioid/heroin addiction. Some of these people don't even stop to consider that the roads that they travel and allow their children to travel everyday are full of addicted drivers. You don't have to be an addict or even the family member of an addict to be affected by this drug in a harmful way.

Yesterday, through all of his other emotions, Michael did his research and found the article that I posted with some of the latest stats from the CDC stating that deaths from heroin addiction had not doubled…but TRIPLED as of 2013. 23 people die every day in this country from heroin addiction. That's 23 people too many. If you consider that this particular stat is now a year old, it could be even higher than 23, and my guess is that it probably is. And of course you all know, from earlier stats that have been posted, that drug addiction has now surpassed automobile accidents as the #1 leading cause of death in the United States. I pray daily that God will show us how to proceed and help promote awareness, education and prevention, all the while making the "right" changes to address this epidemic and start reversing the numbers. We will continue to give out the Naloxone kits so that while we are waiting and working on these answers, people suffering from addiction will have a second chance for a cure and/or a successful long-term recovery.

Last but not least, a dear friend reached out to me in an effort to give my brain some much needed emotional relief yesterday encouraging me to go forward with plans for a brand new fundraiser that I am very excited about. It is in the infancy stages of becoming a reality, but I have high hopes that it will bring in a lot of donations, making our foundation one step closer to some mid-range and long-range goals. You will hear more about this as it becomes a reality and we have secured dates.

Finally, as I sit here and record my thoughts for the morning, I learn of two new deaths in our community bringing this post closer to home once again. This knowledge renews my energy and my commitment to stay focused because of the need right here at home to make a difference. This epidemic is not going away. We need everyone to commit to, at the very least, making opioid/heroin addiction a part of your public conversations. High Schools need to start having a "moment of silence" specifically for graduates who have succumbed to this disease. I know that Kennesaw Mountain High School honored Davis in this way. We are planning to reach out to the High Schools through some grant opportunities to promote awareness and provide education regarding the disease of addiction. In your work circles, or social circles, please begin talking about this epidemic. It is going to take ALL of us to make a difference. Godspeed.

3/6/15 – Constructive Act #351 – Cut The Demand Rather Than The Supply

As I've jumped back into the mission of the Davis Direction Foundation after a very emotional week, I have found that people all over the country are not truly aware of the heroin problem in their own communities. I was talking with a friend from a bordering Midwestern state asking him about the heroin problem in his community. He didn't really think it was significant, so I "googled" it and found out that his town has had a growing issue with heroin since 2011. There is even a former teacher who goes around in the schools doing a program about the dangers of heroin, because like us, he lost his 20-year-old son several years ago. This particular teacher is correct in his thinking that if you can cut the demand for heroin, the supply and the suppliers will go away. The suppliers are in it for the money, so when the money dries up, they will move on. So – the mission becomes awareness, education, and prevention, sound familiar?

I saw a very sad post on one of the addiction sites that I follow today from a mom who said that one of her friends told her that she was tired of her always asking for prayers for her family and her addicted son. How very sad. It absolutely reinforces the fact that unless you are directly involved with heroin, with an addict who is a loved one, you don't truly realize the potential devastation of this drug. Let me point one thing out to everyone reading this post. If there is a "growing" number of heroin addicts and the number continues to be on the rise, where do you think these numbers are coming from? I can assure you, they don't come from fictional characters that are thought up to make this statistic a reality. They are existing members of our community; maybe your child or your niece, nephew, sibling, or spouse will be next. EDUCATE YOURSELF NOW! Start investing in organizations, such as the Davis Direction Foundation, that are actively working on awareness, education and prevention!

Talk to your family members; if they don't want to hear this conversation, start leaving articles from the newspaper or the magazines (there are plenty of them) on the kitchen table or on the pillows of the ones you want to understand. "Denial" is not a river in Egypt folks!!! It's what happening right here in our own communities with people refusing to invest in the education of the NUMBER #1 killer of children between the ages of 18 and 44. Have you ever heard of a parent who is not worried about putting their 16-year-old driver out on the road? Parents are worried sick with new drivers and even invest in "Accident Avoidance" workshops and "Driver's Education" is even the LAW in this state...BUT... automobile accidents are NOT the #1 killer! Opioids/Heroin are, and not one thing is mandatory about the education/awareness or prevention of this deadly epidemic. THIS NEEDS TO CHANGE! (YES, I AM SCREAMING THESE WORDS)

The DDF has been to several schools to speak and has even put an informational video on YOU TUBE (search Davis Direction Foundation) for the public to share. I know my own kid's high school aired the video during Red Ribbon Week for the entire student body. This is a start, but it is still a choice and that is not good. The DDF is scheduled for more speaking engagements throughout the state in the coming weeks and we're available for more! You can contact us at info@davisdirection.com to schedule a speaking engagement. If you are a parent of a high schooler and you are reading this, stop now and call or email your school administration and ask what they are doing to address this very deadly epidemic? If you don't think it is a problem in your town or community, Google it! Share the following link with them to show the need for addressing this issue. Start doing something NOW before we are talking and reading about a drug that has quintupled over time!
www.medicalnewstoday.com/articles/290421.php

Heroin deaths in the U.S. quadrupled from 2000 through 2013. A new report states that the number of heroin-related overdoses in the U.S. have almost quadrupled since 2000, with most of this increase occurring between 2010 and 2013.
MEDICALNEWSTODAY.COM

3/7/15 – Constructive Act #352 – Let Your Requests Be Made Known Unto God

Everyday as I pray about the devastation of heroin and the beautiful lives that are taken and the families that are hurting, I ask God to take what we are doing and bless it and lead, guide and direct it. Looking back, He has blessed us immensely and guided us in directions that not even I knew where they were really going until we got there. Yesterday, I received another blessing and the date was so incredibly significant that I know God's hand was all over it. I called the IRS yesterday to check on our status as a 501(c)(3), as we have been operating as a fund underneath the umbrella of the Cobb Community Foundation – which we will remain doing in addition to our own Incorporation. I was calling to check on a couple of filings that we had completed and I was informed that our case had been closed AND APPROVED! I was ecstatic of course, but what she told me next assured me that God is in control and looking over us. We were closed, approved and determined on 3/4/2015 – the first anniversary of Davis's death. WOW – the reason this is so mind-boggling to me is that the woman who was assigned to our case had been out of town and did not return to work until 3/4/2015. So, The Davis Direction Foundation, Inc., was one of her first acts of approval upon returning to work.

Everything in life has significance for me. I'm just that kind of analytical person. Everything has a reason and a purpose and I truly believe that. I received a phone call from a man yesterday in Pennsylvania and he just wanted to talk with someone from our foundation. He said that we had accomplished so much in one year and he wanted to know how we had done it. He too has a son struggling with addiction and he has been trying to get something done in his own community and he was looking to us for support and answers. It was a wonderful conversation with a person who has the same goals and objectives of helping struggling addicts to enter long-term recovery and he got me to thinking. How had we done this?

As I thought back about things during our conversation, God became such a part of what has happened with the DDF, that I know we are doing what He has called us to do and that He has designed our efforts to help the right people and the right families. I read back over a post from last June when I had a billboard designed by a wonderful designer, Jason Gribble, that God had also placed in our path, where I was letting people know that I had the artwork available if anyone had access to Billboard space. One of my oldest, sweetest friends from elementary school on down the line, Vickie Brown Crenshaw, sent me a message back and asked who was doing my Billboards. I responded and told her I didn't have any idea, and asked if she knew someone? That one text let do an in-kind donation of over $35,000.00 from Outfront Media USA, and Mr. Doug Penner. The company was known then as CBS Outdoor. WOW. Did two little girls from Carrollton, GA do all that by themselves? Of course not…God had His hand all over it.

As we tried to think of ways to raise money for our first year of operation, we of course thought of a Golf Tournament – "A Day 4 Davis" – doesn't everyone do a golf tournament? I had no idea of what I was doing or where to get started, but I put it out there on Social Media and then, you guessed it, God sent me an angel - Mrs. Beverly Kaiser. She told me we needed to meet and the rest was history as we raised $15,000.00 for our first year with our tournament and silent auction. She and her husband, Roger, and her son, Chip, have been doing golf tournaments for years for their own foundation, "Lexi's Foundation", and I had the best advisory board imaginable. Did our little foursome do things all by ourselves? No – God had His hand all over our efforts once again.

I could tell you story after story of how God has intervened and placed His loving hands all over our efforts for the first year of our Foundation. We have touched lives and even literally saved a couple with the handing out of our life-saving Naloxone kits.

God has placed people in our path over and over again. I can't even begin to tell you how many times someone has written to me and told me how they just "stumbled" upon our Facebook page. I don't believe in "stumbling."

God has blessed our Foundation with the most incredible Board on the planet. I am amazed to this day when I look at our business card and read the names. Thank you God for these wonderful leaders that you brought together to help fight this cause. Each one of them brings a special talent or purpose to the table. Our Advisory Board is growing and we are being blessed with talented people from the far corners of the nation who are on board for ALL the RIGHT reasons. Each one involved wants to save lives and eradicate this horrible epidemic from the planet.

I won't lie and tell you that I don't continue to ask "Why my child?" But, I can tell you that because of the happenings over the last year, my faith has grown stronger and I have seen the Lord work in the most mysterious ways imaginable. I will continue to make my requests known unto the Lord, because I have found that NOTHING is IMPOSSIBLE with God and I know that He will continue to bless our Foundation and direct the path that He knows we should continue to pursue. Please join us in praying for our Foundation and expect GREAT things! Davis and God have become quite the team in Heaven; I'm glad they are watching over us! Godspeed!

3/8/15 – Constructive Act #353 – Share Your Story Sunday

My youngest daughter has struggled over the past year in ways that most of us will never know. She and Davis were my "night owls" and spent lots of time together. Davis would pick her up from late night rehearsals and they would sing all the way home – they shared a love for singing. She has written her story in a creative and symbolic way. She was 14 when Davis died. Sibling love is a powerful love, and I know there are siblings all over the nation who are struggling just as she and the rest of Davis's four siblings are. Their pain is real and the holes in their hearts will never be healed.

Here is her story.

A glass of milk, Just a tiny glass of milk. A glass of milk poured by a four year old that she got for her brother because she wanted to sleep in his bed. "You can only sleep here if you get me a glass of milk." She knew if she didn't get that glass of milk, she would have to sleep in her own bed. She knew if she slept in her own bed, monsters would come out of her closet and there would be no one there to save her from them. This four-year-old girl went racing up the stairs to the kitchen and had to jump up on top of the counter to reach a glass. She retrieved the glass and jumped off of the counter, reached inside the fridge to get the milk and poured it inside the glass. She held the glass with both hands as if her life depended on it. She carefully walked down the stairs and inside her brother's bedroom.

This girl didn't just hand a typical glass of milk to her brother. This girl handed her brother a glass of milk that represented her pride. She had done something with a purpose. She knew that when she handed him that glass of milk, she would be snuggled up to her big brother and protected from the world. A tiny glass of milk held the key to safety and protection from the scarier things of the world.

As this same girl grew up and watched her brother turn into a young man, she watched him struggle. She watched him go through hardships she hoped she would never have to face. She cried and cried because she knew there was nothing she could do. When this girl was four years old, she knew that if she got her big brother a glass of milk, she could sleep in his bed and her brother would PROTECT her from the darkness that she was afraid of.

When this girl was fourteen, she discovered a new type of darkness. It was a kind of darkness she had never seen before and one that she didn't understand. At fourteen, this glass of milk didn't exist anymore. There was no glass of milk that she could give her brother to protect her from this darkness, because this darkness had her brother wrapped around it's finger. The same monsters she was afraid of when she was four years old looked like stuffed teddy bears compared to the monsters she was seeing in her brother's eyes.

She knew she had to repay him for protecting her all those years from the nasty monsters, so she tried protecting him. She kept reminding him that she loved him and that these monsters were something he needed to break free of. The young man knew they were harmful, but the glass of milk the girl handed him only allowed him to protect her, and it lasted up until the moment he died. He had shielded her from this terrible demon, and made sure he never handed his sister a glass of milk to protect him, because he wanted to make sure that this evil monster would never touch his baby sister.

Instead of protecting himself, he protected her. The only trouble is, the girl wished he could have handed her the glass of milk so that she could have protected him from his monsters, because that girl was me. I let my brother protect me all these years from a monster as terrible as heroin, and I never realized that I should have been the one protecting him. I should have made sure that I was the type of person that someone could hand that glass of milk too. But heroin ruined that. Heroin stole my brother's pride and safety. Heroin killed him. And I'm left alone pouring myself a glass of milk.

3/9/15 – Constructive Act #354 – Break The Cycle, Whatever It Takes

Every cycle has its origin. We can preach all day long, and have people all over America clean out their medicine cabinets, but when you can return to your doctor the very next week and replenish your supply; it doesn't really make much difference. Let's focus on the elderly for a moment. How many of you are in the part of your life where you possibly have to care for your parents, aunt, uncles or even grandparents? If you are, for the most part, I would venture to say that most elderly people have some sort of pain issues. When they talk to their doctors they tell them of their aches and pains and I feel like mostly out of compassion and not wanting them to be in pain in their remaining years, the doctors give them pain pills. Then as caring children and caretakers, we continue to monitor their medications and medical conditions, but have to continually be on the lookout for their doctors as well, because they continue to prescribe opioid medication. As our loved ones get older, and especially if they live alone, they often will self-medicate with drugs they have used before or have leftover, even if they belonged to someone else in the first place. It keeps them from having to go back to the doctor, and it saves them money.

Often times, the elderly don't even know what kind of medication they are getting. The doctor just tells them to take the prescription and "it should help." So, they don't bother to tell the doctor that they have leftover meds at home that still aren't expired. What happens is that even though they didn't finish the first bottle of pain pills, now they have another one and they don't know to clean out their own medicine cabinets. So, next thing you know, the family goes for a visit to the elderly person's home and takes the younger kids, maybe late teens or early twenties. JACKPOT! Now unless the elderly person is actively taking the prescription, he or she won't even notice that the pills are gone! I had one friend tell me that her Mom had an old washtub of medications just sitting under the carport because she was meaning to get rid of them, but hadn't had time yet.

I can't tell you the times that my friends have told me that they have gone to their parents' homes to clean out the medicine cabinet, since Davis died, and they've pulled out prescription after prescription of old opioid medication. The elderly are clueless as to what an opioid is, for the most part, and if they knew the harm that was coming to the younger generation because of it, they would burn the medicine cabinet down!!! Even the people of my generation (mid 50's) are amazed at what they find in their medicine cabinets. Many of my own friends tell me that they are pretty sure their medicine cabinets are free of dangerous stuff and come to find out, they had opiates from years ago still in there. Many bottles are marked now with just dosage information as opposed to "as needed for" I guess because of HIPPA. That causes a new problem in and of itself. Sometimes the elderly get confused and think that they took a certain prescription for one thing and they take it again and it's the wrong thing. They even give their medications to each other because if they were prescribed by the doctor, "they must be okay."

So – the questions remains, "How do we break this cycle of prescribing?" It seems to me like everyone is too intimidated to bring this information up with his or her doctors. I have the utmost respect for every doctor that I call my own, but I can assure you that they all put their pants on one leg at a time, as my Daddy used to say. Sure, some of them will think that you are questioning their integrity, but something has to give! Any good doctor will certainly understand and be concerned about the current opioid/heroin epidemic in our nation. We have a program in place called a PDMP – Prescription Drug Monitoring Program. According to the National Alliance for Model State Drug Laws (NAMSDL), a PDMP is a statewide electronic database which collects designated data on substances dispensed in the state. The PDMP is housed by a specified statewide regulatory, administrative or law enforcement agency. The housing agency distributes data from the database to individuals who are authorized under state law to receive the information for purposes of their profession...DOCTORS.

Ask your Doctor how fully operational the GA PDMP is the next time you are in for a visit. Then ask your doctor if his or her practice reports to the GA PDMP on a regular basis. GA was one of the very last states to put a PDMP in place and it is not quite 2 years old yet. However, Georgia is already seeing a decrease in doctor shoppers, people who go from doctor to doctor seeking the same narcotic prescription. The less prescriptions of opioids that are available needlessly, the more preventative we can be moving forward. What are you doing to help BREAK THE CYCLE?

3/10/15 – Constructive Act #355 – Realize That Labels Are Powerful

I feel like I have lived in a world of labels all of my life and I can tell you that people react to them on either end of the spectrum. Whether it is a positive label or a negative label, people treat people according to their labels. It is a fact of life and until we change the labels that we "stigmatize" people with, we will NEVER change the way people treat those with the labels! Some labels are awesome to put at the beginning of your name or at the end of your name... "DR.", "Judge", "General", "Professor", "Coach" ... and then other labels are not something that you want attached anywhere close to your name... "addict", "special ed." "Diabetic" "fat" "retarded" because the indication is "damaged merchandise." So, I try to think of things in both directions when I speak TO people or speak OF people.

My Dad was not only a Captain in the US Army, he was also a lawyer and baseball coach when I was growing up. It was nothing to meet one of his friends on the street and hear them say "Hello Counselor", or "Hey Coach!" It made him feel good and gave him a great sense of pride and accomplishment. He liked to hear it! My husband was also a baseball coach when Davis was growing up, and to this day, his heart swells when one of his players refers to him as "Coach." It is a label of honor!

On the other hand, I have never heard anyone say "Hey Diabetic" because my husband also suffer with Type 1 diabetes. He would be offended and would feel like "damaged goods" if people treated him that way. I worked in the educational setting for 26 years as a Counselor. I dealt with children who had learning, behavioral and emotional issues all of my life and it broke my heart the things they had to deal with because of their labels. I watched parents walk away from services because they knew what the label could cause. I had children in my office crying because they didn't want to walk out of that classroom one more day to go to their Special Education classroom because it was not something that made them feel good, honorable, or even accepted. It was NOT a label they wanted in any way, shape, form or fashion. I've never heard people say to someone's face..."Hey Addict" or "Hey Sped" or "Hey Retard." Why do people not do that? One reason - it's disrespectful! We teach our kids to act compassionately and respectfully. Labeling in a derogative manner is DISRESPECTFUL! That is a fact, and what every mother I know has taught their children!

Today I've been following a very long and troublesome feed on one of the sites that I follow. I understand what an addict is and I know what the term means. What I don't understand is why people feel the need to identify their loved ones with the label of "addict." My loved ones are my loved ones. I don't refer to my husband as my "diabetic husband" when I talk to him or refer to him; he's just my husband or Michael. By the same token, I would never refer to my precious child as my "Addicted son" or call him "Addict Davis" It's Defining! Yes, he suffered with the disease of addiction, but that did not define who he was. He was a beautifully and wonderfully-made child of God, an awesome brother, a senior class president, a funny and compassionate friend, a giving grandson, a beloved after school program teacher, a nursing home ministry leader, and above all, the most amazing and lovable son two parent's could ever hope for, so why in the world would I label him with the one "damaged" and "diseased" part of his being?

I once wrote a post and asked... "If you knew your children would be reading what you wrote about them, would you reword or change things?" I have seen posts where parents have called their children "the dumb a$$", "the fool" and one woman even posted that addicts "deserved prayers least of all." How in the world do you think that is helping them? When the very people on these sites are making derogatory comments, like the ones described above, about their own children, and then try to go back and justify it because "it is what it is", it sounds like talking out of both sides of your mouth.

The Davis Direction Foundation feels so strongly about the "stigma" of addiction that we even made it a part of our mission statement. It's all about awareness, education, and changing the stigma to help others understand the DISEASE! A HUGE part of recovery is feeling worthy and accepted. It would be very hard to feel worthy and accepted while those around you were referring to you as "addict."

The worst part of recovery groups to me is the part where every time before you say something, you have to say your name and identify yourself as an "addict." Why can't you state that you are in recovery? Doesn't that make more sense? It's no wonder to me that the young people are turning away from the 12-step process in droves. They are trying their best to get better and every time they open their mouths in a group, they have to go back to their past and call themselves an "addict!" What other support group for a disease begins with "hey, my name is so and so and I'm a 'name your disease.' "

Advocating for yourselves and your children has to be the first step. If we don't understand and advocate for ourselves, how can we expect others to understand the perils of this epidemic? Charity begins at home! Teach your children respect and compassion and their hearts will be prepared to understand addiction and the fact that it is a disease. Derogatory labels, insinuations, or assumptions are not helpful regardless of the platform. They're just NOT!

3/11/15 – Constructive Act #356 – Man Up

What do you think about the fact that 81% of our DDF readers are women? Only 18% of our readers are men. But, according to the latest Cobb County statistics for 2014, 67% of the heroin deaths were white males. We need their fathers, grandfathers, brothers and uncles to step up to the plate and speak out. As I read the sites that I try and keep up with regarding heroin addiction, I often hear that the Dad's have a different view from the Mom's. I know that to be true with Michael and myself before we understood the disease of addiction. After we truly researched and understood the disease of opioid/heroin addiction, then we both knew that it was not a moral failing or something that will-power could have fixed. I know that Michael has said over and over again that the thing about all of this that he hates the most is that Davis didn't feel like he could talk about it and reach out to him for help.

I think about that a lot and I also look at it as a "learned behavior" on Davis's part. As parents, we are always teaching our young men to take responsibility for their own actions. We teach them to do this especially when they are getting ready to graduate from high school and enter the workforce or begin college. We say things like "Be a man", "make your own decisions", "stand up for yourself", "Mom and Dad won't always be around", "it's up to you", the list goes on and on. Then after we say these kinds of things we turn and walk away expecting them to handle the given situation. We try to step back from their independence and let them handle life as it comes at them. Maybe we do this because that's how we were raised.
Well, once again times have changed and maybe we, as parents, didn't make arrangements to account for those changes. Life is so much more complicated now, and I refer back to the "Generation Y" post that I wrote early on in the CA's. We've taught our young men that there in no room for emotion in the workforce

and that you need to "suck it up" and "move on." Could that be bad advice? Should we be talking more and working our problems out together? Have we role-modeled how to handle situations with our younger generation? I know that I see so many times with addiction that there are underlying problems, mental illness, and undue stress, and I totally believe that. I also believe that addiction can happen accidentally and has happened accidentally with the amount of prescription pills that have been prescribed to the last generation. We have learned to self-medicate. Even our elders are self-medicating mainly due to the high price of medical care and the trouble it takes to get themselves to the doctors. They just keep and use their left-over medications. They are role-modeling that to their grandchildren for sure.

To all the Dad's out there, when was the last time you sat down with your sons and just asked them how their lives were going? Do you spend quality time with them in conversation? Do you ask them if there is anything that you can help them with? Are our young men harboring emotion, embarrassment over something they feel they should know how to do, but don't, and even secrets because they feel like we are not ready to hear or deal with the things in their lives? Have you walked them through a situation they are dealing with and seen it through to the end? Are we helping our young men in the way that they need help?

Everyday in the United States 23 people are dying from opiate/heroin addiction and the statistics are pointing to the fact that our young men ages 18 – 36 are the fasting growing death stats out there. What are we going to do about this? I'm asking the men out there to PLEASE weigh in on this conversation. We need to see our male faith community leaders, our teachers, our coaches, our corporate businessmen, our politicians reading our posts and commenting. Opening doors for our young men in order to create an avenue for emotional health and well being is crucial. Perhaps if our Dad's aren't ready to internalize the fact that their beloved sons are dying in record numbers, then we need to find a group or faction of men who can lead the way for them until the Dads can wrap their heads around it.

Please understand that I am not being sarcastic or degrading in any way. I watched my own husband crumble inside trying to wrap his head around the fact that his oldest son was suffering with the disease of addiction. Part of him wanted to turn and run to the far corners of the earth and he buried himself in his work and keeping the household running and in order. The other part fought like hell to do what he could to save his son. It's the hardest thing a parent will ever do. Watching your child suffer with the disease of addiction is excruciating and men seldom show the pain of emotion outwardly. They have been taught to handle it within. Not too long ago, I had an elderly man apologize to me for becoming emotional in front of me. He said he was sorry and told me how embarrassed he was. I thought it was such a show of humility and emotional honesty, that I was tearing up just witnessing it. Our boys need to see this kind of thing and know that it is okay! No apology necessary! We need to teach them to talk about the things that cause them pain and share their emotions.

Today if you are one of the 81% of women who will read this post, please do me, and your sons, a favor. Print it out or take your laptop over to your husband, or boyfriend, or whomever the significant man in your son's or daughter's life is and ask them to read it and make a comment. Ask them to show support for what is happening to our young men, ask them to become part of the SOLUTION! Do it for all of our wonderful, bright and beautiful sons. THEY DESERVE THE SUPPORT!

3/12/15 – Constructive Act #357 – When All Else Fails… Ask Questions

I suppose that one of the things that I do more than anything else that drives people crazy is ask questions! I'm one of those people that has never been afraid to ask a question. One thing that I have found over the years is that people are either secure enough to understand that's how some people learn and they try very hard to help others understand, or they take it offensively as if you are questioning their knowledge or expertise. I've met both along my journey. I've also found out that people answer questions in two ways as well. There are those people who go above and beyond to share their knowledge and help people find answers, and then there are those who tend to think it's better to make up something than to say "I don't know." They don't want to risk out right exposure of not knowing information. So, I guess the moral to this preface paragraph is to say that when you get answers, you need to take them for what they are worth - someone else's experience.

Every time I ask questions on the DDF, we get a wealth of information helping others find their way through some of the experiences that others have already been through. The answers come in all shapes and sizes and sometimes you even get a completely different answer about the same facility or service. That's because every person's experience is individual. When information is shared on our site, it is just another piece of the puzzle to add to the big picture. Those kinds of questions are pretty straightforward and often times offer opinions of others. Some of the information stated is factual regarding location, services offered, and pricing. That doesn't always mean that the information will be the same though. Under certain circumstances, even the factual information may change. The questions that haunt me though, are the philosophical ones, the ones that no one has the answers to, at least not here on earth. They are the ones that people become judgmental about and try to push their views on everyone else without anything to back their answers up. There are so many times that people want to become religious experts and quote scripture, out of context I might add. They want to make their opinion factual, and actually argue with science – trying to make people believe that addiction is a choice. There will always be people like that in the world, and try as I might, those are the people who still get under my skin. I know the reason they bother me though is because when you are going through the journey of addiction, either as an addict or the "addict's keeper", you become so confused along the way that you don't know what to believe anymore. Some questions absolutely and unequivocally don't have an answer. As for now, the journey seems to be trial and error. That's okay! Some of the best solutions in the world have become solutions because of accidents that happened in the process.

Some of the questions that obsess my brain the most I know would be, "How do you find hope in a journey that seems so hopeless?" "Why was my family chosen to bear this burden?" "Am I being punished for things I did or failed to do?" "Does this nightmare ever end?" "Why isn't love enough?" "Why do the stars align for some people in recovery and not for others?" "How do I move forward?"

Dale Carnegie once said, "Most of the important things in the world have been accomplished by people who have kept on trying when there seemed to be no hope at all." I'm assuming that every opioid/heroin person in long-term recovery could attest to that. So, let's keep on trying, whether we are trying to enter recovery or we are trying to find solutions to help those who are trying to enter recovery. We only fail when we stop trying. I know how defeating it is to try and try and try again and then have life take a turn that you prayed would never happen. But, life goes on and so must we. Some days are better than others, and I've always heard that every cloud has a silver lining...I'm still looking.

3/13/15 – Constructive Act #358 – Live Life According To Your Own Expectations

Stress is one of the major causes of anxiety and depression in my opinion. Too many people of all ages are trying to live up to the expectations of other people in their circles of influence. I also believe that for the first time in our history, that the divide between generations is greater than we have ever known. Social media has caused everyone in the world to live his or her life publicly. Even though you may not participate in social media, I guarantee you that if you are friends or family with someone who is involved with it, that you have either been mentioned in a thread or your picture is out there somewhere. For the first time in history, our lives are out there for public scrutiny. Our successes, our failures, our celebrations and our defeats are in written format, sometimes accompanied by pictures. Birth announcements and death announcements are first found on social media websites. Our lives are open books! Every time I take a picture of my kids now, they say, "Are you going to post that?" or "Please don't post that." Parents post only the good things about their kids for the most part, making the identity of his or her character one that they have a hard time living up to at times. It becomes a job of "keeping up appearances."

I have often seen on Facebook, the post that expresses how very fortunate the older generation is that Facebook was not around when we were growing up. Unfortunately for the younger generation, you cannot escape your past and move on gracefully having learned from your mistakes. Now, everyone knows what you did, when you did it, who you did it with, and what the consequences of your actions were. Perhaps, in a positive light, this has caused them to be more accepting of each other and the differences of others. Sometimes the messages are "cryptic" because some people at least try to be politically correct by telling those who question their post to check their private messages. I suppose that makes them feel better about "publicly gossiping in a private forum." Is that an oxymoron?

The above paragraphs possibly explain the divide between generations. The older generation was more sheltered publicly and possibly less tolerant of the abnormal. The younger generation has read account after account of the different kinds of "normal" and are possibly more accepting of change and difference. The problem with all of this is the older generation doesn't understand this acceptance and we continue to impress our morals and social standards on a generation that has been subjectively (thanks to social media) brought up completely different from the generation trying to dictate their existence.

The younger generation is ultimately living in two generations. I have always tried to tell my kids, that one day their Dad and I will be long gone and they will still have to live in a world of their creation. NOT ours! As protective and sheltering as I tried to be in raising my own children, I'm sure to them it often times came across as controlling and I'm sure there is an element of truth to that as well. The parameters of freedom within limits are always tried and tested; that's not a new concept. The problem with limits is they continue to expand personally, socially, and even legally. We are legalizing things that were once illegal and making the statement that if you stick around long enough, everything will be justified and legal. In other words, What's real and what's not? Who made the rules in the first place? We live reactively as opposed to proactively. So who do you turn to for the answers? Kids have to decide for themselves. Even religion is changing. There are churches out there that are rearranging God's word to make it applicable for modern times. God's word is unchanging, but the fact that He sent his Son to die for our sins makes it unnecessary to change it. He laid down the laws, and then knew we would sin, so He asked His Son to make the ultimate sacrifice for us. No sin is worse than another to Him. We are forgiven for the price of sincerely asking.

Stress is the root of so many problems. We live too hard, fast and furiously to stop and relax long enough to enjoy the subtleties of life. We are always too worried about the next day, the next bill to pay, the next meal on the table and the next form to be filled out and sent in to the government. Taxes, fafsa, census, licenses,

432

the lists and deadlines that accompany them go on and on. At some point, you have to stop and ask yourself, "What stressful things can I do without?" "How much do I truly need in order to just be happy?" Lately we've seen families moving out of the suburbs and downsizing homes with larger tracts of land; they are learning to live off of the land. We've seen houses go from multiple room mansions back to a one room, one size fits all "tiny house." In the end, you have to answer to yourself and to God. I guess if we could all understand how to accomplish learning to live according to our own expectations that we would all be a lot happier and a lot less stressed out. Then, just maybe, there would be no need for "mental and emotional" drugs.

3/14/15 – Constructive Act #359 – Life Goes On And So Must We...

This past week has made it more apparent than ever that life goes on and there are things that are happening right here within our family that need our attention. Davis, and all of the precious saved souls that have lost their battle with addiction, are in the best place possible, so our focus needs to be on those we can help and care for here on earth. Sometimes the realities of life jolt us back into the present and prevent us from staying in the past for too long trying to change things that have already happened. The only place that we can be helpful and make a difference is in the present. Although the future depends on it, what we do in the present will absolutely dictate the future. As sad and harsh as it may sound, the past is now history, and try as we may, it cannot be changed. Our focus needs to be on the things that we do have control over and that is the present.

I've said to many people that I'm not fighting for my child anymore, I'm fighting for his friends and kindred spirits that are still here on this earth chasing dragons. As for the rest of my children, Davis sealed their fate as they lived through the most excruciating years of their lives trying desperately to save their brother. The irony is that while they were trying to save him, he was saving them by allowing them to see his journey up close and personal. Our goal as a family is to protect the struggling souls who are still out there looking for and hoping for help as we educate others to never ever go down that road. We understand how heroin affects the entire family. We can speak from experience and bare our souls in an effort to save others, but ultimately their journey is theirs and theirs alone.

This past month in our family, we have lived through our loved ones with open-heart surgery, stroke, and life altering decisions. In each circumstance, as a family, we were needed to come together and do what we could to help. Family is necessary. The degree to which we are necessary varies in every circumstance, but nevertheless, we are necessary. As our other children continue to grow and experience new things, move away to college, travel the world, and join the adult work force, we are still necessary, just in different ways. Sometimes we have to let go of our plans and play the hand that life deals us. At times it will be exhausting and at times it will seem overwhelming, but life is too short not to find happiness in some way. For me personally, I have always found happiness in helping others. I made a career out of it and the Foundation just seemed like a logical next step. It is necessary and I feel called to be doing what I am doing.

The Musical "WICKED" has a song entitled "For Good" and the lyrics seem to speak to me about where I am in my life with the Foundation and honoring my awesome son, Davis.

I've heard it said
That people come into our lives for a reason
Bringing something we must learn
And we are led
To those who help us most, to grow
If we let them
And we help them in return
Well, I don't know if I believe that's true
But I know I'm who I am today
Because I knew you...

It well may be
That we will never meet again
In this lifetime
So let me say before we part
So much of me
Is made of what I learned from you
You'll be with me
Like a handprint on my heart
And now whatever way our stories end
I know you have re-written mine
By being my friend...
Like a ship blown from its mooring
By a wind off the sea
Like a seed dropped by a skybird
In a distant wood
Who can say if I've been changed for the better?
But because I knew you
Because I knew you
I have been changed for good

I know I believe that's true! Thank you Davis for the life lessons you have taught me and for making my life worthwhile. I will never be the same, hopefully I will become better because of you! Hopefully I can help others to become better because I knew you. And hopefully, the world will become a better place because we all knew you. I love you son…Xxooo.

3/15/15 – Constructive Act #360 – Share Your Story Sunday

Most often when we think of those struggling with addiction, we feel so bad for their parents or their siblings or even grandparents, but the "best friends" in life are often passed over when thinking of the effect that a death might have had. Davis had ONE and only ONE "BEST" friend and it was Robert W. Novak – or to us, "Bobby." Bobby continues to be a part of our family. He comes by every time he is home and he texts or messages us often. His life has forever changed since the passing of his best friend.

Here is his story.

In sharing a single story about a life, we want to choose the best, most thought-provoking, humorous, or exciting one we can think of. There are thousands to choose from, the next always trumping the previous choice in some regard and to pick just one can be extraordinarily difficult. I faced this dilemma for a year as friends and acquaintances would ask about my best friend and the times that we shared. I would need years to tell all the best ones, there are too many to count. And yet, the possibilities for more halted a year ago.

I was studying abroad in England when I received the news. His family had been calling me throughout the night, unaware that I had left my phone stateside. After checking my Facebook later that morning, I felt as if I had be punched in the gut. The few brief sentences explaining that my best friend was dead had stopped my own heart. At first, I didn't know how to react. Hyperventilation set in and the tears began to fall, soon turning into sobs, and finally the uncontrollable mess that lasted well over an hour. Questions of how and why went streaming through my head, regret filled my heart for not being there, and my limbs were paralyzed. Car crash? Suicide? Murder? God knows what all the other possibilities were and for the rest of the day I wondered and thought. That afternoon, I called the Owen household and learned the true story of how my best friend died.

Overdose and Addiction.

I had only recently learned of this development although it had gone on right under my nose for a couple of years. I had gone north for college and left my best friend at home. We grew further apart as the months dragged on and, much to my dismay, were virtually without communication for months at a time. I received cryptic calls from friends and mentors asking me to call him and to help but when I would ask my best friend what was going on, he would respond with the same tropes of either his mother or his girlfriend – one or the other acting up and causing trouble. I would always respond by telling him that I was a phone call or text away but they never came. Requests to play video games or to hang out were left unread and unanswered.

Our last meeting was at the funeral of a mentor and friend who had committed suicide. We walked together through a loud and crowded room to the closed casket and, standing side by side, exchanged memories. I looked over my shoulder to see many of our classmates in tears and apologizing for our loss, because they knew how close we were. My best friend and I walked out of the room together, shook hands and spent the next few minutes talking about what was going on in our lives – myself writing papers and he working through his addiction at a rehab facility. I turned to leave and he stopped me, held out his hand to shake and told me that he would miss me. I told him that I had every confidence in his success and that I would see him again soon......I didn't.

I miss my best friend more than words will allow. I cannot shake the regret I feel for not sending one more text or calling one more time, or spending just one more minute with him. I knew bad things were happening and yet I did nothing. I search for more stories, more memories but very often they fade away. And so, in my attempts to find the one story that would encapsulate his life, I find one that encapsulates my story of his death. It is a tragic tale – one in which the main character is lost and confused while the antagonist is invisible, but its effects are very clear. Questions will always linger and my training as an historian urges me to find the answers. Yet, they will all be answered someday, the day that I finally see my best friend again.

3/16/15 – Constructive Act #361 – Decide What's Most Important

Four has always been a lucky number in the Owen Family. Four or a multiple of four has always been the number that we try to get when we have an audition, or a tryout. We schedule things on the 4th, the 14th, the 24th... or we try to work in multiples of four whenever possible. I decided several months ago that I would write for 365 days – one year. That would complete my journey of public grief and be a logical stopping point for a book that I have been asked to write several times by readers on the DDF.

So, I am down to four days to finish my book, and I am way over thinking the entries that will make up the last four days of my feelings, thoughts, beliefs and soul-bearing journaling. I've asked myself over and over again, "What is the most important thing for anyone who reads this book to know?" I've decided that the last 10 entries are like the last 10 pounds, they are the hardest!

My education as a teacher/Counselor has taught me that summarizing is a very important aspect and objective in any lesson. It drives the lesson home and leaves a lasting impression. It restates the most important facts and building blocks of the lesson and allows the learner to see the broader picture and divide it into the intimate details that make a difference. If you have followed my journey of grief over the course of the past year, you will know that one thing stands out above all else. Addiction is NOT a CHOICE! Those who suffer with addiction have a disease and they are first and foremost people worthy of our love, care and consideration.

You may not have been personally affected by this epidemic, and for that I am thankful and you should thank God Almighty daily that you are in this group. But I can assure you that you are not unaffected because you don't have an addict in your circle. If you drive on the public roads, or walk into public buildings, you are at risk for coming into contact with the one in ten people who are suffering with the disease of addiction. 23 people everyday in our country die from an overdose of opioid/heroin addiction (this is a 2013 stat from the CDC and I would venture to say that it is higher than this now). People suffering with addiction are overdosing in our schools, our corporate offices, our public buildings and our private homes. We need to come together and educate others and make the public aware of what the DISEASE of opioid/heroin looks like and what can be done about it.

My family made the mistake of trusting the "so called experts" of a rehabilitation facility when we were trying our best to help our son in the beginning. The truth is that the epidemic of opioid/heroin addiction hit so fast and furiously that I don't believe the community, including the Rehab facilities, had time to do enough research to find the answers for individuals in lots of situations. Many of the facilities that are out there have struggled to deal with and appropriately treat opioid/heroin addiction. There ARE degrees of addiction, some more severe than others, and please don't let anyone tell you that there are not.

Addiction is NOT addiction! Opiate/heroin addiction is more severe than other addictions out there. Please don't take offense to this statement if your loved one suffers with another type of addiction, but it is a proven fact based on scientific evidence that opioid/heroin addiction can happen faster, get you high quicker, and have double the effect based on receptors in the brain than other addictions. It's just different. More people are dying of this addiction than any other addiction in this country. It doesn't lessen the loss of other addictions, opioid/heroin addiction is just killing people in epidemic proportions and there is no end in sight. All of the predictions suggest that it will get worse before it begins to get better.

Most important is EDUCATION and keeping up to date with the latest information and treatments. If you are in the throes of addiction, new information is being published daily with new drug therapies, new life-saving Naloxone devices, new theories regarding successful long-term recovery and new programs to assist with re-entry and assimilation back into mainstream society as a productive and contributing citizen. If you have young children or teenagers, you should be educating yourself about the disease and the fact that it is not a choice. You should be very proactive in post surgery procedures for wisdom teeth, sports injuries and accidental injuries that involve pain and pain medication. You should ask your doctors always what is being prescribed for your minor children and if the medication has addictive properties. CLEAN OUT your medicine cabinets quarterly. I just assisted an elderly relative cleaning out the medicine cabinet and threw away hundreds of opiate pills from as far back as ten years ago. It is frightening what our elderly friends and relatives have accumulated over the years and have left in their cabinets because they don't know the dangers and repercussions of prescription medications.

Just knowing that huge numbers of people die on a daily basis due to automobile accidents causes people to do intense safety research before they purchase cars for their young drivers or even for themselves. We want to make sure that we have air bags, side bags and of course a sturdy frame that will withstand great pressure. We do periodic checks to keep it working properly and in optimal condition. Yet, often times, we do nothing to safeguard against the NUMBER ONE KILLER in our nation, which is ACCIDENTAL DRUG OVERDOSE. Get involved, get educated and do your research. Like our Facebook page and stay up to date on this very deadly disease and what can be done to prevent it and the latest and most successful ways to treat it. Decide for yourself what is most important.

3/17/15 – Constructive Act #362 – Don't Neglect Yourself

This "CA" will be very hard to write because it deals with lots of emotion that every mother feels who has ever lost a child. As far as this post goes, I cannot speak for anyone but myself and perhaps other mothers because it comes straight from a mother's heart. I know that Dads process things differently and less openly, but I know that Michael is the only person on this earth who has experienced the same loss as I have, over the death of Davis. I know his broken heart and his wounded soul are no greater or less that my own. I think men just have the ability to focus on what needs to happen as far as the rest of the family and day-to-day happenings that must continue and the Moms seem to dwell longer on the death and the way their children will be remembered.

Back in the 1890's, during the Victorian era, it was considered necessary to remain in mourning for an entire year. During that year, the veil remained over the face for at least three months and the black mourning garb was worn. After having lost a child, I now wonder which came first, the "rules of mourning" or the "acts of mourning." Maybe the rules were written as a way to give the parents an excuse for the way they were acting already. As I look back over the last year, I have not specifically stuck to any "rules of mourning" per se, and I don't even know if any exist any longer – perhaps in certain religions, but I do know that the way I have lived my life over the past year has probably been very similar to many mothers who have lost their precious children. Probably the most significant change is that I just plainly don't care about things I used to care about. My hair hasn't been cut, or styled in over a year, I haven't bought more than two or three new pieces of clothing. I haven't bought any new shoes, I don't think I have been to a single doctor appointment-wellness or otherwise! I skipped "Tradition" entirely; Michael and I even ate alone at Joe's Crab Shack for Christmas dinner – the kids decided to attend the extended family dinner. I could not face the "empty chair" and Michael allowed me that feeling. I can count on one hand the social events I have attended and as far as caring what happens to me – I plainly don't!

After having lost a child, I kind of have this mindset that whatever happens happens and I will deal with whatever is thrown my way. Nobody or no circumstance can possibly do more to hurt me physically, mentally or emotionally than the pain I have already endured. The way I look at death is that I now have family on both sides. I have Davis in the afterlife and I have the rest of the family here with me on earth. It adds a whole new dimension of "carefree" living. I would be happy in both places – but either way, I will miss the ones I am without. I have basically become non-existent in my own mind. This in no way means that I am suicidal or even that I want to die - I don't! It just means that I see life differently now. Nothing is about me.

When all of my children were alive and much younger, I remember getting appendicitis. I had no idea why in the world I was so very sick, but I remember sitting on the examining table waiting for the doctor to come in and check on me and thinking, "what if I die?" It literally made me nauseous to think that I would have to leave my family and go on to eternity without them. That changes when you have a baby on the other side. There are just things you don't care about any more. I have had no ambition to do the things that "at least in my mind" a mother should do as far as cleaning and cooking. I have not cared whether the kids leave their rooms in disarray or worse (at least for the most part) unless we are having company, and I have done nothing to work on a healthier lifestyle. I have projects in my house that came to a dead standstill the day Davis died and they are still in the same condition. I don't care!

BUT… I have thrown my heart and soul into making sure that what happened to our family never needs to happen to another family moving forward. Prevention is the absolute answer, but the challenges come from those who are already deep in the throes of opioid/heroin addiction. I will be no good for anything or anyone if I continue to neglect myself. So, I have begun to envision Davis as my Partner in all of this as opposed to my deceased child. I know how badly he wanted to live and beat his addiction. I know that the look into his inner soul that I was allowed to see, had to have some kind of meaning, and that meaning was so that I would know the heart of an addicted child. Their hearts continue to love but one day they just quit beating!

I will never understand why God put such a beautiful, yet deadly natural plant on the earth; It just makes no sense to me at all. For all of you mothers out there who have loved and lost, find a reason to move forward. Your children would not have wanted to rob you of the life you were given to live. Find a way to make a difference and stop neglecting yourselves. Do it for the one you loved.

3/18/15 – Constructive Act #363 – Understand The Difference Between Reality and Ideality

I was having a conversation with my 15-year-old daughter last week and she said to me, "the difference between what I thought would happen in my life and what has really happened in my life is so different." I remember when I married Michael; I thought I was the Cinderella to his Prince Charming. My wedding was a Fairy Tale in every sense of the word. All the stops were pulled out and I was allowed every indulgence that I could have ever imagined. Nine months after we were married, we gave birth to the most amazing daughter ever imaginable. She was perfect in every way and has grown up to be an amazing young woman. Eighteen months after her birth, we welcomed the most gorgeous and firstborn grandson on my side after four beautiful granddaughters. He was amazing and was the apple of his Daddy's eye. He was the one who would carry on the family name and continue the legacy of the Owen family. Eighteen months after that, the second son was born and we were thrilled again to have a happy and healthy addition to our family. He has grown into an outstanding individual who has the world at his fingertips. This was our reality and we were on cloud nine! Two and a half years later, the third son was welcomed into the world and we were done with our family! Spencer completed us and he was our ever-loving comedian and kept us in stitches. WRONG! God had other plans and blessed us with a gorgeous green-eyed blonde and our family was perfect and our ideality was perfection!

We lived in a bubble of security and no one could touch our family or our legacy. We were The Owen7! The family that every teacher wanted to teach and every friend wanted to be the best friend. We were humble, or at least that's what we taught in our family, and we thought we were no better or no worse than any other family in our community. I once had a middle school teacher write me an email telling me that she was going to write to Oprah and tell her to ask me on the show to tell her how I had raised my children so that other families could learn by our example. Of course she was one of my all-time favorite teachers, and I wish she had not retired and could have taught all of my children. I still have her email in my "kudos" box. My Daddy had taught all of his kids that everyone put their pants on one leg at a time and I never thought, nor taught my kids to believe, that we were superior to any other human beings or families. We lived a Christian lifestyle and tried to live according to Christian principles. So, when the fairy tale started to fall apart, we were dumbfounded and had to come together quickly and completely in order to maintain our relationships.

What in the world was a "drug addict" and how did one of them become a part of our family? We didn't teach those principles. We raised our kids in the "way that they should go" and now they were departing from it? What in the heck was this about? Didn't God promise that if we raised them properly that they would stick to it? All of the sudden I felt betrayed and I was very confused. What happened to my ideal world that I thought I had done all the right things to ensure it would come to pass? Where were the promises of God that I had stood upon for as long as I could remember? I wanted to hit something and/or someone. I wanted to hit them hard and challenge everything that I knew about ideality that had turned into reality. How did I answer my child? My innocent 15-year-old child had asked a perfectly legitimate question and was waiting for an answer?

Well, I didn't answer her and I still have not answered her, because I don't have the answers. I don't know what went wrong and why the promises that I thought were there for me and my family were suddenly non-existent. All I could tell her was that I continue to pray for wisdom and so should she.

For a while I asked every minister that I knew, the answer to the question, but then I decided that the answers that I received were only opinions of other human beings just like you and me. I guess ultimately I figured out that an individual has to come up with and accept their own answers dependent upon their faith and relationship with Jesus. As a matter of fact, for the most part, the parents that I know of that struggle with the disease of addiction, because of their children, are of the Christian faith and are struggling with the same questions.

I remain true to my faith because I know the love of Jesus has brought me to a place that my ideality has reunited with my reality, and I am still standing on the promises of God. My faith helps me to wake up each morning and get out of bed and carry on with my life. I don't have all the answers but I have decided that I can go on without all of the answers. God and my faith keep me grounded and help me realize that just like the characters of the Bible, ideality is what we all hope for, but reality is what we all live. Godspeed!

3/19/15 – Constructive Act #364 – Evaluate And Re-evaluate And Never Stop

The data that we have collected over the past year and the decisions that we have made based on what works and what doesn't is what drives our DDF mission moving forward. The last year has been a definite learning experience for our family and if we had been as knowledgeable about opioids and heroin as we are now, there is no doubt in my mind that we could have saved Davis. The problem is that no one studies or invests in diseases or situations that doesn't involve them, because people have enough to do without preparing themselves about every potential and deadly problem that comes down the pipes as they are raising their children. For instance, I know very little about Ebola, and I have not researched it at all over the past year as it has come into this country and threatened the lives of anyone who comes into contact with it. I heard of a handful of people who were affected by it and then the problem, as well as the threat, seemed to go away as far as I know. The difference between opioids/heroin and Ebola is that more than one person EVERY HOUR in the United States is dying because of prescription drug or heroin addiction, and that scares the living fire out of me, and it should you too!

So knowing that is what the data is saying and looking back over what we have done, we need to see if we are making a difference. If we are not making a big enough difference, how can we alter our plan to have a greater impact? Since the DDF has been established, the opioid/heroin epidemic has gotten worse. This was predicted at every level. Because of governmental and pharmaceutical changes that have been made to proactively help the situation in the future, we all knew that it would probably get worse before it got better. That is exactly what is happening. I have reliable reports that 22 young adults have died in Cherokee County since January 1st 2015. That's almost half of what happened in Cherokee last year in 1/3 of the time. This is just another piece of data that says what we are doing is not enough and more needs to be done! As much as my family has been through over the past year, I was helping to clean out one of my own relatives homes over the past month, and we carried out over 250 opiate pills that had been collecting in her medicine cabinet for over a decade. It's like people know what is happening, but they are still in the mindset of "Not Me or Mine."

People suffering with opioid/heroin addiction continue to go to rehabilitation facilities and detox and begin the journey of recovery, and when they leave, they find themselves right back in the throes of addiction searching again for the magic "cure." Parents who are parenting these children who are suffering continue to cry out for answers and change and it's as if people hear and acknowledge their cries, but change is not happening fast enough to keep up with the epidemic. Our cause is in SLOW-MOTION, and we need to find a way to bump it into FAST-FORWARD. WE NEED an Ice-Bucket Challenge!

The evaluations that I have completed regarding our response to the epidemic leave me with a few ideas for change. First and foremost, I believe that every rehabilitation center needs a parent advocate as a paid position to be available to talk with parents and ensure that their children are receiving the services that are provided in the paperwork they are given. I've said before that Davis should have had three family meetings scheduled and we never had one. A parent advocate could have handled that with a couple of phone calls and it would have been taken care of. I also know that Davis signed a waiver regarding the HIPPA laws that allowed the staff of his Rehab facility to speak with us. They did speak with us, but waiting for their phone calls to be returned was not happening in a timely manner in my opinion and rightly so, because they were there to take care of my son. A parent advocate could have handled this situation as well. A parent advocate could have prepped us for aftercare and the availability of different programs and resources in our area as well as the most recent and promising information regarding opioid/heroin addiction and long-term recovery. They could have also made us aware of drug therapy and the fact that it IS an option. In fact, it is an option that is keeping people alive and functioning in high capacity on a daily basis. If I had but known...

As far as prevention is concerned, we have written another grant to get into the school systems not only with the Naloxone kits in every high school clinic in our area, but also in the hands of every sports trainer who is always at sporting events where the masses of people are. We have written for materials to go into every Middle and High School Media Center in our area in order to educate the kids who have not yet been introduced to the dangers of prescription medicine, opioids and heroin. We have written for DVD's and accompanying study guides. Education and Awareness are key and we MUST find a way to get our message into the school systems across the country. This is simply NOT AN OPTION! I am available to speak and have spoken to many middle and high school students and parents to educate them and make them aware of the dangers. We have a You Tube video that is available on the internet with the click of a mouse to show to entire student populations and civic organizations. SHOW IT!

As always, when an epidemic is in progress, there is a segment of the population that is already involved, and it is our responsibility as a community to support those people through the epidemic and see them out on the other side. As we all know, those suffering with opioid/heroin addiction are in and out of Rehab like a revolving door because what gets them into recovery is definitely not keeping them there in the majority of cases. One of our goals needs to be to strengthen long-term recovery efforts. We are currently working with the GA Council on Substance Abuse to learn the best way to make this happen and how the DDF can get on board to support these efforts. We are looking at models across the United States to educate ourselves on best practices and success rates. I am currently visiting Rehab facilities/treatment centers/sober living homes/recovery residences and advocacy organizations each week so that I can be knowledgeable enough to speak with confidence about what is going on in our community and across the country regarding this epidemic.

3/20/15 – Constructive Act #365-Tie a Knot and Hang On

"When you reach the end of your rope, tie a knot and hang on," – Abraham Lincoln

The first thing I thought about when I read this quote was desperation. When a person feels like there is no way out and nowhere left to turn, sometimes the only alternative it to just maintain! I consider drug therapy to be the knot that is allowing many opioid/heroin users to "hang on" until either better solutions come along or until they can find their way into long-term recovery through some existing pathway. I get very frustrated when I hear people discount drug therapy as a means to recovery just because it involves medical help. For some people, this may be an avenue that will eventually lead to complete abstinence and long-term recovery. For others, it may be the only thing that stands between them and death.

I think that it is so ironic that doctors have prescribed the pills that lead to most opioid/heroin abuse. They are quick to write prescriptions for pain medication to alleviate pain for their patients, but when it comes to treating their patients for addiction, most doctors refer out to Rehab facilities and most of those don't even allow drug therapy at all. It is time for the doctors to learn to treat addiction. They need to learn what is available and be able to talk with their patients specifically about what each drug therapy entails. More doctors need to offer Vivitrol in their offices and maintain the health of their patients who suffer with addiction. If statistics hold true, one-tenth of all their patients suffer with addiction anyway, whether or not they know it.

When a person becomes an opioid/heroin abuser, they reach the end of their rope quickly. They tie that knot and hang on for dear life for what seems like an eternity to them and their families. If drug therapy helps them to function and maintain quality of life that allows them to hold a job, be a part of a family and stay away from illegal drugs, then I believe that they are entitled to that therapy and I applaud them for making the effort to make it work. Recovery is individual and every one has choices to make. Judge not, lest ye be judged.

Bonus Act – Understand the Semi-Colon

"AT ANY GIVEN MOMENT YOU HAVE THE POWER TO SAY… THIS IS NOT HOW THE STORY IS GOING TO END."

Free will is sometimes a difficult concept for people. As a matter of fact, it is never truly defined in the Bible. There are many examples of predetermination and truly, free will does not contradict that idea. God, and God alone, knows the past, present and future; He alone knows what we will choose. Sometimes I think that it would just be so much easier if God would tell us how everything is going to play out. As my daughter and I were talking yesterday, we were discussing how drastically our paths had changed over the past year. Our lives went from a fairy tale to a tragedy in the matter of one day. Death changes everything!

At this time of year, and especially on Good Friday, Christians all over the world realize that death changes everything! This day is the day that Jesus's death changed everything in the most amazing way. Jesus's death made it so that we all have the power to say…" THIS IS NOT HOW THE STORY IS GOING TO END!"

Maybe it would be so much less stressful – especially for the families of those suffering with the disease of addiction, as well as the sufferers themselves – to know who will live, who will die, who will conquer their addiction and who will suffer for the rest of their lives. Then on the other hand, I think of how we might have changed if we had known that Davis would have died regardless of all of our efforts. Would we have tried harder; would we have given up; would we have completely stopped living and waited for it to happen; Would we have never left his side? I have no idea, but I do know that it would have changed everything. God in His infinite wisdom designed the perfect plan and I accept that because I choose to. Free will is a gift from God Almighty, and you can choose Him or you can reject Him. It's all up to you. If you want you story to end differently, then you have choices to make. NO! I do not believe it is about will power, but I do believe that there are resources, therapies, relationships, and the power of GOD out there to support different endings. Is it time to re-write your story? Let us know how we can help… Godspeed!

"SAYING THE LAST GOODBYE"

Davis died on a Monday night or maybe a Tuesday morning; His death certificate said it was a Tuesday, but I believe that is only the day they found him. In my heart, I believe when he hugged me and said, "I love you" on that Monday night when he left to attend a meeting, that the meeting he attended, was with Jesus and the purpose was to be welcomed into his eternal home. On Tuesday evening around 8:30, we found out that he would never be coming home again and we had to prepare ourselves to say the "last goodbye."

We were told by the officers that came to the door that we would have to wait to "claim" his body until after the autopsy was performed and he was released to the funeral home. We then had to choose the funeral home and have his body "routed" there after the medical examiner was done with the investigation. We were told to call the Medical examiner the next morning to find out when we could finally see him. Michael called, as instructed, on Wednesday morning and got the details of when, where, and how and then was told his body would be at the funeral home on the following day.

Thursday morning I would finally get to see and hold my baby one more time. At that point it had been almost 64 hours since I had hugged him, told him I loved him, and instructed him to be careful. My family was finally on the way to the funeral home to see our precious Davis one last time. At all the funerals I had ever attended throughout my life, closing the casket was always the part that choked me up because it would be the last time that the earthly body would ever be seen. I was getting ready to "close the casket" on my baby boy and my heart was breaking.

We were greeted by the funeral director at the funeral home, and we walked up a flight of stairs and prepared ourselves to enter the viewing room. He opened the door and there, across the room, on a cold steel gurney covered in white sheets laid my baby. As I walked closer to his body I could see that he was still my beautiful, perfect, gorgeous adored and compassionate baby boy. He was laying there helpless, still and cold. His body was wet with moisture from being kept in the refrigerated morgue. His eyes were closed and his lips were chapped. His body was lifeless and the white sheet was pulled up around his neck exposing only his beautifully familiar face.

I immediately bent over to kiss him and tell him that I loved him and that I was sorry that I could not protect him from the evils of this world. I looked to my other children worrying as a mother that each of them would be forever changed from the experience. I had prepared them, but this was different. They each said their goodbyes and then they turned away and let the mother and grandmother of his child enter and say goodbye. I could not leave; I was not leaving his side until everyone else was gone. They said their peace and then my children and husband came back into the room.

I wanted to touch every part of him. I remember wanting to hold his hand and I began pulling the sheets back and as I began pulling them back I felt a dampness on my fingers. It was blood. I had touched where they had made the incision for the autopsy and I remember thinking they had wrecked his body. For some reason I wanted to see his hands and hold them. I wanted to see his chewed fingernails for further proof that he was my child. I wanted something to say that he was not Davis. I felt the leather of the body bag that he was in and I gave up the idea of trying to hold his hand.

I cupped his head in my hands to kiss his face and I got more blood on my hands from where they had cut his head. I remember thinking that his body was so mutilated because of his disease. I remember thinking that I didn't care that his blood was on my hands, because it was his blood and it was all I had left. I didn't know what to do, I was going to have to walk out of that room and leave him there. I was going to have to say goodbye and never be able to look at him again. I was panicking and I was so lost.

I remember that Michael had his arms around me and I remember thinking that he was hurting too and I should be comforting him, but I had nothing left to give. My soul was empty and I couldn't leave my baby there. He was supposed to leave with me. I was his mommy and I couldn't leave him!

I told Michael I needed a pair of scissors and he went and found some for me. I did the only thing that I knew to do and I took his hair in my hands and cut the locks just like his first haircut. I couldn't leave without a piece of him to take with me. I kissed him all over his face so many times and I kept telling him that I loved him and that I would see him again. I was talking to him as if he was hearing every word I said. But then I had to say the last goodbye…that was the hardest thing I have ever done in my entire life. I had to let go and look at his face for the last time, and walk out of the door. I would have rather gone to Hell!

I remember walking backwards out of the room because I couldn't take my eyes off of him. I stopped at the door and I just stood there not knowing what to do. Closing the door was the same as closing the casket…I would never be able to look at him again. He would be forever gone.

I did finally walk away only to collect his belongings and have a bag of everything he had with him when he died. His clothes smelled of Polo Blue and I remember just putting his undershirt up to my face and breathing in his scent for hours. I wrapped his undershirt over my pillow and it's still there to this day. He also had his wallet with one dollar and a picture of him and his precious daughter. I have saved it for her so that one day she will know how much he loved her.

Every time I pass that funeral home, I have to breathe deeply and look away because I don't want to remember that day. I cannot imagine a harder day than that day. I left with instructions to come back the next day to collect his ashes that would be placed in the beautiful green urn that we picked to match the color of his eyes. He sits on my mantle, and he will stay with me until the day I die.

No parent should ever have to endure the pain that I have described in this writing, but parents all over this nation are experiencing it at the rate of once every 12 minutes at this time. Their pain is no less real than mine and their stories are equally as heartbreaking. Saying goodbye to a child is unnatural. It is not the way life is expected or intended to be. There is no way to prepare yourself for the pain of losing a precious son or daughter. Loss is excruciating, but preventable loss is beyond description. Sometimes, there are just no words.

Rest in Peace… my precious child.
Davis Henry Owen 3-4-2014

DAVIS DIRECTION
FOUNDATION

An Open Message from Davis' Father

Davis and I loved working on our cars together when we could. And honestly that was few and far between because of work and time. But we did manage to spend this time together three weeks ago as we pulled his Audi apart to replace all the turbo hoses and the radiator. I wanted to get a pic of him when he finally got the radiator and he was smiling from ear to ear. Those are the father-son kind of moments that will never ever be replaced. This is the way I want to remember him. Full of hope, love and excitement about the future.

I love you with all my heart best buddy and will see you again soon one day. I promise to carry on your spirit and love.

And the song I played the most during all our last times together will Forever be with me to the end...Come Sail Away! And yes indeed you were the captain!!!

Davis' Eulogy delivered by his Mom, Missy, at his Memorial Service

Davis's first complete sentence in life was a very profound "I don't know." Standing here before you today I can tell you that there are a few things that, "I don't know." But there are a lot of things that, "I do know." And one of them is…. if you are sitting here today, it is because in some way Davis Henry Owen touched your life,

Countless stories and memories have flooded our Facebook pages in the past three weeks and all of them without fail have brought a smile to my face and some have even made me laugh out loud.

Growing up, Davis was full of laughter, love and mischief… Everyone that knew Davis has at least two stories to tell. One would be about how funny and mischievous he was and the other would be about how awesomely big his heart was.

Davis was our wide-open, fast and furious, boy-boy. He loved cars, trucks, big wheels, green machines, bicycles and Audis. He took great pride in watching the 24-hour LeMans every year with his Dad as the Audi outran the BMW. For those of you who know my family, you can only imagine that race in my house!

Davis kept the whole family on our toes! Whether it was baseball, motorcycles, skateboards, dancing with Cinderella (aka Chelsea) or being dumped (again by Chelsea) from the Little Tikes Grocery Cart onto the garage floor, we never knew when we might end up in an emergency room somewhere stitching him back together again just like an old familiar and much loved Teddy Bear.

Through the years, he chose the most amazing friends and he even made up some of his own. Scrolling through his Facebook, you can see just how many people tried to perfect "The Weesie Face" – which was ironically the biggest frown you could muster! Then there were those of you who rode the Middle school bus every morning with "Bernard!" I never realized the extent of that character until the day I received a phone call from Miss Elaine – the beloved bus driver – asking me to please speak with "Bernard" about being too loud on the bus. To the baseball team he was #4 and to his X-Box friends he was "Big Daddy dho." But to his family, he was always our little "Boogie Man" the one with the biggest heart in the whole family.

Davis was a magnet for fun and people flocked to him because of it. He could turn your darkest day into something good and find the sunlight behind every cloud! He was the most flexible kid you could ever imagine. One day in his yearbook class, he decided that the job of the editor would be to climb onto the eight-foot tall cabinet and position himself behind the banner and shoot people with rubber-bands. The principal walked in and Davis, thank goodness, had the good sense to freeze and go unnoticed for once. Actually, he miraculously was only suspended once in his entire educational career. That was the day in four-year old Montessori school when after numerous requests to stop…his body just refused to cooperate as he continued to perfect his Power Ranger air-kick!

Davis had people laughing at a steady clip throughout elementary school and in 3rd grade, he was awarded the Overall Best Sense of Humor for the entire grade level. What a proud day – but not as proud as the day I saw his picture for Freshman Orientation in the Dress-Code skit as he sported the "Booty – shorts" as unacceptable. He drew no lines when it came to making people laugh and feel good.

The truly proud moments were the ones where he invested his time and energy into making a difference for others…such as delivering the graduation speech as Senior Class President and dancing with Special Needs students year after year at the Special Needs Dance. He completed enough community service hours, kept his grades high enough and provided unselfish servant leadership earning himself a spot in the KMHS Hall of Fame.

As he entered college in his Daddy's footsteps of business at KSU, he began working at the After School Program at my school. For 18 years, I had worked there before he did, and everyone knew I was Mrs. Owen, the counselor. Shortly after Davis began working there, I became Mrs. Davis, Mr. Davis's Mom, and it made me smile.

Davis made great friends wherever he went as there was not a judgmental bone in his body. His best friend made a 3,000 mile journey home to speak on his behalf today. Because Davis was who he was, his life is already helping to make a difference.

In closing, I want to share a story. During the Holocaust as Hitler's troops marched into Vienna, Reinhold Niebuhr offered a response by introducing a program called the "Volunteer Christian Committee" to boycott Nazi, Germany. Neibuhr had the courage to support the rebirth of a Jewish homeland – a safe haven for God's chosen people. In 1934, he was credited with praying a prayer that Davis repeated often toward the end of his life, which only goes to prove that wonderful things are often born out of tragic events.

God, give us grace to accept with serenity the things that cannot be changed. Courage to change the things which should be changed,And the wisdom to distinguish the one from the other.Living one day at a time, enjoying one moment at a time, Accepting hardship as a pathway to peace.

Taking, as Jesus did, this sinful world as it is, not as I would have it.Trusting that You will make all things right if I surrender to Your will.So that I may be reasonably happy in this life, and supremely happy with You forever in the next.

Thank you for 20 years of entertainment, fun, challenges and lessons learned, but mostly pure and simple love. You were the best big brother three kids could have had and the best little brother and friend Chelsea could have ever hoped for. You were an amazing father to Emma and to your Dad and I….you were our hero.

I know that our son, your brother, Emma's Daddy, and your friend is supremely happy today and for that we can all Praise God.

Bobby Novak's Eulogy to Davis – best friends

My dearest Mama, Owen Family, and anyone else, who will read or hear this:
It has been 19 days since my best friend departed this earth. I have immersed myself in study to aid in dulling the pain that permeates my very soul, though the prospects of such a miracle are ever more bleak. Though I write from 3,000 miles away, I like to think that I am not alone in my grief. However, I do not wish to reflect upon suffering, of mine, yours, or anyone else's, but instead wish to speak on the life that has impacted us all.

The French philosopher Jean-Paul Sartre has a quote which reads:"Everything has been figured out except how to live. Thus the better question is not, "What are we to do with death?" but, "What are we to do with life?" Life exists in individual moments and it is up to us to make sure that those moments are vast, interconnected, and grand. To make a MASTERPIECE out of life, one we would live again, and again, and again for all eternity. This is what we should strive for.

My best friend was the strongest man I knew. He could command a room with a single breath and could make the crowd hang on every word and once that was over, he became instant and fast friends with every one of them. It is safe to say that I looked up to him in many regards, his presence and friendliness among them.

Thus it is not hard to see the masterpiece of a life that my best friend led, and the individual strands of memory that he created with all of us. And undoubtedly, we are all asking ourselves the very same question, "What are we to do with this death?" "How are we going to move on?" But as Sartre suggests, the better question is "What are we to do with life?" and with his life, my best friend touched everyone he was around all the time and in every way, enhancing all of our lives in ways left to us only through memory. Davis lived a masterpiece of a life and I know that all the time I spent with him, the jokes, antics, and adventures that we shared, I would live that life over and over and over again. And my earnest hope is that my best friend feels the same.

The morning of March 5th was the hardest I've ever known. I wept for hours remembering my best friend. It is strange how the memories come flooding back where before there were none: yearbook antics, Europe trip, late night video games and junk food until I couldn't move, all of these are my fondest memories. These are the memories I will hold for the rest of my life. My children will hear these stories and wish they knew him, just as we all did.

To this end, we remember Davis. He sits with our forefathers and all the others gone before us, smiling down onto those he loved just as we smile with the memories we will forever cherish. Tragically, he was taken from us too soon, but my best friend couldn't stand that genre. He preferred comedy, the thing that makes us laugh and smile, and the very things my best friend brought to all of us. I love you Davis, my best friend. Until we meet again.

I am, and will always remain, affectionately yours,
Bobby N'OWEN'vak.

MICHAEL, MISSY, CHELSEA, DAVIS, CONNOR,
SPENCER, AND SHELBEA OWEN 3/24/13

Made in the USA
Middletown, DE
29 March 2016